The Principles
of Bond Investment

The Principles
of Bond
Investment

By

LAWRENCE CHAMBERLAIN

AND

GEORGE W. EDWARDS

Dean, School of Busness and Civic Administration
College of the City of New York

BeardBooks
Washington, DC

PREFACE TO THE REVISED AND ENLARGED EDITION

A preface is, or should be, the last chapter of the book. It is the mellow place for rest and reminiscence, and "quiet breathing," after the burden and heat of the day. It is the nineteenth hole of the literary game. The place of knickerbockers, demi-tasse and cigarette. Perhaps the principal advantage of the preface over the grillroom is that in the former one suffers no particular temptation to mendacity. At any rate, in the preface all rules for polite writing are off, and the author (or authors) may be human.

It is sixteen years since the publication of the first edition of *The Principles of Bond Investment.* As the title implies, it was planned to retard obsolescence by a grounding in fundamentals. It still serves a purpose if one may judge by continued general distribution and by comments from those who read it. The most pleasing testimony to usefulness has been an increasing call for its revision. However basic a treatise may be, it is founded on science, and the scope of every science grows.

Even Euclidean concepts become modified. What is a straight line? How many dimensions are there? Is it true that two bodies cannot occupy the same space at the same time? The atom is now known to be divisible and penetrable, and therefore bodies, which are composed of atoms, are interpenetrable, and of the infinitesimal granular particles which compose atoms even two protons and one electron may have a combined size that is smaller than the one electron alone. But the planetary electrons pursuing their orbital courses around the shell of the atom are not penetrable by the electrons of other atoms. Who shall say when another Einstein will push Euclid back still further with the discovery of a new planetary system in each electron? So it goes. One has good company in becoming obsolete.

However, we do not have to fall back on Euclid for the justification of a "completely revised and enlarged edition" as the wrappers say. Between the first edition and this have come the most epochal war, a new banking system, and a virtually new system

iii

of taxation. Certain kinds of industry have atrophied; others have been created. Old types of securities have disappeared; others have assumed greater importance; new types have sprung into being. The old order changeth.

The principal and only change of importance in the first part of the book has been the addition of a chapter on "Diversification." In the first edition the author was so intent on letting no element of a standard investment escape him that he quite overlooked the importance of this investment element that is achieved by a multiplicity of investments. His attention was called to this glaring omission by a request from the *New York Evening Post* for some articles on the subject. The new chapter is an adaptation of those articles. One of the valuable fiscal ideas we have recently borrowed from abroad (although we are making shabby use of it) is that of the investment trust, which when properly managed depends largely on diversification for its efficacy.

In Part II, "Civil Loans," there are two entirely new chapters: "The Nature of Civil Loans" and "Foreign Civil Loans," and one entirely rewritten: "United States Bonds." The reasons for these differences are obvious, but they are expressed in the chapters. There is much new matter in the other chapters.

Friends of the text will not feel at home in Part III, "Corporation Loans," for only seven of the fourteen original chapters have any semblance of their old selves. There are seven completely rewritten studies: "Public Utility Securities," "Street Railway Bonds," "Hydro-Electric Power Company Bonds," "Real Estate Bonds" and three of Railroad Bonds. There are also three chapters on new topics: "Telegraph and Telephone Bonds," "Bonds of the Federal Farm Loan System," and "Industrial Bonds." The history of Equipment Trust Obligations has been brought to date.

The fourth and final part of the old editions was broadly divided into "the mathematics and accounting of bond investments" on the one hand and "bond prices in relation to business trends" on the other. Reference above to Euclid to the contrary notwithstanding, the reader will expect and find almost no changes in the earlier half; but the latter half, devoted to bond prices and the business cycle, is new material in line with the radical advance in thought on business barometers.

There is much new matter in an additional Part V devoted to "Classes of Investors" and "The Bond Houses."

Among the changes in public conditions that have affected investment during the past fifteen years, few equal in importance those relating to taxation. In reviewing the contributions to this subject that have been made by other writers on investment in the interim, the lack of effective presentation of this profound and intricate subject impressed itself. Not only have the presentations been more or less inchoate, but much that is pertinent has not been reviewed. Therefore, a Part VI is offered as a " Classification and Description of American Taxes," which in form if not in substance may supply a general need. Again it is a pleasure to acknowledge the assistance of Mr. W. H. Lyon, now better known to readers as Hastings Lyon. Mr. Lyon, who is familiar with tax matters (and who incidentally is himself the author of a most *thoughtful* book on investments, has read this tax study, but not in its final form, and therefore he is not responsible for its mishaps. Thanks also are due Mr. Roy Osgood, Mr. Samuel O. Rice, the Bureau of Municipal Research and Prentice-Hall, Inc. for help in matters of taxation.

We take this opportunity to air our vexation at index-makers. In the attempt to purloin ideas or citations for this new edition we have consumed, it seems, more time in trying to find the items than would have been spent in doing our own thinking and writing. We have never resented that *esprit de corps* which makes literary plagiarism not an offense but rather a virtue: a tribute to excellence in the author and a testimony to learning in the borrower. We have been glad to stand with Shakespeare —a merry stealer and an honored stealee. But we do believe in *quid pro quo;* we believe that honor among thieves should give us as easy access to the riches of others as they have to our own modest store. And the key that unlocks those riches is a complete index. *Verbum sap.*, etc.

This edition, which is so largely a new book, would not have been possible except for a year's devoted service to it by our friend and collaborator Dr. George W. Edwards. Words cannot put too strongly the preponderant share for which he is responsible in any new values that attach to it. Our inclination is to give him all the credit, but that word " responsible " stays our hand. It would not be fair to him to make him assume all the responsibility. Nor all the credit, for he in turn must share it with his pupils and associates, in the University and without, who have contributed material and read the text. Acknowledgment is due to Professor Thatcher Jones for the various chapters on public utilities, and to Doctor Jules I. Bogen for the chapters on railroads and transportation. The contributions of Professor Jones were based on painstaking original research in the several public utility fields. Doctor Bogen was able to draw his data from a number of thoroughly scientific studies, undertaken in the railroad field in which he has already become recognized as an authority. The assistance of Mr. Sanders Shanks of the Bond Buyer of New York was most valuable in revising the chapters on municipal indebtedness.

The proceedings and reports of the Investment Bankers Association of America, with which we have been identified in committee work since its foundation in 1912, have been of great help to us in this undertaking.

LAWRENCE CHAMBERLAIN.

GREENWICH, CONN., *May* 1, 1927.

PREFACE TO EARLIER EDITIONS

There is so much miscellaneous matter in this book that the reader who is seeking some specific detail is advised to consult freely the Table of Contents, and above all the Index. The Table of Contents is arranged to show at a glance the argument of the work; the line of thought can readily be traced there, and it will serve those who wish a bird's-eye view of the field of bond investment, and those who wish to refresh their memories as to the subject matter of this book. The Index is exceedingly full and should enable one to find any detail he seeks.

It has seemed impracticable to write the book, throughout, to scale. Certain topics have been treated briefly because they form the subject matter of books that are already in print or that friends now have in preparation. Part II, devoted to *Civil Loans* (i.e., government and municipal loans), is the most detailed. This is because so little, comparatively speaking, has been written hitherto about these securities. Railroad finance has received, and is now receiving, careful and elaborate study. Municipal finance has been strangely neglected and the practice of it is at sixes and sevens. It is hoped that law makers and municipal officers may find suggestions here, from illustrations of the bond practice of others, by which they may standardize and improve the laws of this country pertaining to municipal debt.

There is another sound reason for elaborating the chapters on *Civil Loans*. The conditions which occasion municipal borrowing are sufficiently uniform to make correct generalization possible. No generalizations, equally broad, are safe for the bonds of most private corporations, especially of railroads, for private corporations are so sensitive to changes in industrial conditions, in management, and in policies, and the bonds of private corporations are so diverse in nature, especially the bonds of railroads, that principles which will apply at one time may not at another.

When, however, the nature of the business is such that basic industrial conditions bear an intimate relation to investment principles, as in the gas business, one can form a clear and reasonably adequate idea of what to choose and what to avoid when buying the bonds. But for the securities of manufacturing and industrial companies generally, investment principles degenerate into a series of .caveats, until it seems as if the only dictum of common application is the caution *caveat emptor*, " let the buyer beware."

It is no reflection on the class of securities called Industrial Bonds that they do not receive treatment in these pages. The inference is merely as implied above, that the conditions governing their issuance are not sufficiently uniform for safe generalization.

Whatever has been accomplished in this book is due in large measure to the unstinted coöperation of many people, both friends and strangers. But no one except the writer, and no firm, is responsible for any expression of opinion or statement which is open to dispute. Mr. Walter H. Lyon has generously fulfilled the offices of long friendship by reading much of the manuscript. In certain textual matters Mr. Thomas L. Cole has lent his ripe scholarship and critical taste. In matters of law Mr. Lyon and Mr. Alfred D. Chandler have given invaluable aid by criticisms and suggestions, and by the loan of published and unpublished material. Mr. Montgomery Rollins' veteran experience in bond mathematics, literature, and practice and his kindly interest have been freely drawn upon. Mr. Charles A. Hobbs has also materially improved the chapters on mathematics, particularly the work in logarithms.

Mr. Floyd Mundy and Mr. John Moody have gone over what has been said about the railroads, and Mr. Joseph Talbot, Vice President of the National City Bank, has been of assistance in the preparation of the comments on bond prices in relation to credit, etc.

It is a matter of regret that ethics does not permit mention of those banking houses which have been called on to judge the correctness of the comments on the types of bonds in which they specialize.

Acknowledgment is due for permission to print the substance of a few of the writer's past and forthcoming contributions to *Moody's Magazine*, the *Rollins Magazine*, the *Banker's Magazine*, *Investments*, and the *Journal of Accountancy*.

The list of willing helpers might be indefinitely prolonged by mention of aid received from officials at Washington and in many other cities. Perhaps it will enliven this preface to say that in no case has an official of a community which shows a tendency to evade its just engagements made reply to letters of inquiry.

It has seemed best to keep the book as free as possible from footnotes; therefore a detailed acknowledgment of sources has not been possible. All the well-known financial periodicals have been drawn on, especially the *Commercial and Financial Chronicle*, without which much valuable matter would have remained inaccessible.

Errors undoubtedly will be found in this book, which has been produced in the scant leisure and amid the many distractions of an active business life. Criticisms and suggestions will be welcomed by the author and will be of value to him in a future revision of the text. At the same time he asks lenient judgment upon the faults of a pioneer work, in an extended field, by one whose daily occupation is to buy and sell rather than to expound investment securities.

LAWRENCE CHAMBERLAIN.

MONTCLAIR, N. J., *June* 1, 1911.

It has seemed best to keep the book as free as possible from footnotes; therefore a detailed acknowledgment of sources has not been possible. All the well-known financial periodicals have been drawn on, especially the *Commercial and Financial Chronicle*, without which much valuable matter would have remained inaccessible.

Errors undoubtedly will be found in this book, which has been produced in the scant leisure and amid the many distractions of an active business life. Criticisms and suggestions will be welcomed by the author and will be of value to him in a future revision of the text. At the same time he asks lenient judgment upon the faults of a pioneer work, in an extended field, by one whose daily occupation is to buy and sell rather than to expound investment securities.

LAWRENCE CHAMBERLAIN.

MONTCLAIR, N. J., *June* 1, 1911.

CONTENTS

PART ONE: CHANNELS OF INVESTMENT

PART TWO: CIVIL LOANS

PART THREE: CORPORATION LOANS

PART FOUR: THE MATHEMATICS AND MOVEMENT OF BOND PRICES

PART FIVE: INVESTMENT ORGANIZATION

PART SIX: TAXATION OF BONDS

PART I

THE CHANNELS OF INVESTMENT

CHAPTER I

INTRODUCTORY

Property, as the possession of civilized men, is fundamentally divided into two kinds: land, with whatever is permanently attached to it, and movable goods and chattels. The relative importance which these two kinds of property have held in the estimation of men has varied from age to age and has differed among communities according to the degree of civilization each has attained.

As man cultivates the handicrafts and arts, develops a commerce in movable possessions, and as the ultimate dependence upon the soil becomes less obvious, the second form of property increases in relative importance, and "personalty," to use the more modern and comprehensive term, ranks with "realty."

Moreover there has been an important and interesting development of "personalty" itself. Rights and franchises and other immaterial forms of property have obtained recognition and confidence as stable and permanent possessions in modern systems of law and order built on governmental and public faith.

With man's growth of faith in man, and with the necessity for increased facilities of exchange, has arisen the use of symbols and certificates of possession for the material and the intangible things possessed.

This development in the forms of personal property used as media of exchange is historically recorded in the etymology of the English language.

Pecuniary and *peculation* (Latin *pecus*, cattle) carry us back to the agrarian age, when beasts of the field were the media of exchange. *Expense* (Latin *expendere*, to weigh out) suggests a more settled period when currency, like commodities, was measured with scales rather than accepted at face value, or denomination. Another advance brings us to *money* (Latin *moneta*, a mint) which suggests intrinsic value reinforced by civil guaranty. A higher form of commercial development is reached when not the

3

material thing itself, but its paper certificate of ownership, of no intrinsic value, passes without question from hand to hand as an accepted symbol of the wealth it represents. Security in this stage is no longer physical possession of wealth, but the faith of the community in its system of political and commercial credit. A typical form of this representative personal property is the *bond* (cf. Old French *bonde*, and Middle English *band*, a bond, a tie).

The bond seems to violate the rule of historical inheritance. Many if not most of the elements of modern civilization are traceable to Greek and Roman antecedents, or at least to origins antedating the Christian era. Reference to mortgages on ships and landed property may be found in Demosthenes' Orations. However, bonds for investment, as we understand them, do not seem to be derived from antiquity. In fact it is not until the latter part of the Twelfth Century that we meet with them. The Venetians, at that time bankers to the world, used bonds that were in every essential analogous to our civil loans. They were direct obligations of the state, interest-bearing, redeemable and negotiable. Venice's system of certificated loans gradually spread over France and the Low Countries; and from the Fifteenth Century onward, instruments somewhat analogous to our corporation and real estate bonds appeared in other parts of Western Continental Europe.

We should take some pride, however, in the fact that it was reserved for us of the New World to develop, to the full, the latent capabilities of the sealed instrument. A security still virtually unknown to English common law, the modern negotiable bond, was conceived in the peculiar necessities of early American finance and bravely and wisely nurtured by the federal courts. To what stature it has already attained will be seen from the observations of the first few chapters of this book. Therein an effort has been made to seize the fundamental principles of investment and to show how aptly bonds conform to them. The importance of bonds as a channel of investment is also illustrated by the extension within the past half-century, of jurisprudence such as municipal bond law, to cover the exigencies arising from this new mode of financing.

From a strictly academic standpoint the development of bond investment as a science offers exceptional attractions. Unexamined material of all kinds is to be had in plenty. Of necessity, the method must be strictly inductive, for the projection of enterprise by funded debt is still largely experimental, and our habits of thought upon it have not yet become fully formulated and regulated by authority. Moreover, the scientific study of bond investment implicates a sufficient number of corollary disciplines such as banking, finance, statistics, accounting, civil government, and law, to allow association in studies with courses offered not only in the specialized school of business but also in the colleges and universities devoted to general education.

A stronger appeal than that to our American universities may be made to those who, next to the investing public, have most at stake,—the American investment bankers themselves. The most important single force in placing bond investment on a scientific basis and elevating security dealing to a professional standard has been the Investment Bankers Association of America. This organization was founded in 1912 and now includes a membership of about 600 houses and 300 additional branch offices. The Association operates through committees concerned with maintaining the standards for the various types of securities, recommending legislation and other ways of protecting the interests of investors at large.

Bond selling is too largely undertaken in a haphazard manner. It is true that there are good salesmen who have little knowledge of bonds; but it is also true that, other things being equal, the well-informed and trained bond man makes a more effective and successful salesman than one who lacks understanding of the securities he offers. The responsibility for the lack of preparedness rests less with the salesman than with the bond house which sends him out without furnishing him with means to a proper understanding of the business committed to him.

Salesmanship, however, is only one-half of the battle. What a house sells it first must buy. There is a saying that a bond well bought is already half sold. As an economic function the buying of bonds has made much greater progress toward perfection than the selling. This is particularly true of municipal issues, because in each case, the problems that confront the purchaser are, for the most part, uniform in character. The chief of these problems are those that concern legality and like questions. Every large house has one or more bond attorneys who bring professional minds to the task of investigation before them. In purchasing corporation issues the services of experts in the field of the corporation's activities are secured, and their judgments, to a degree, are the basis of the purchase. In both cases the influence of special equipment and intellectual training tends to permeate all the other elements of the functions.

But of all interested parties the investing public is most vitally concerned in the elevation of bond investment to an applied science; for the public is the ultimate repository for the issues of our corporations, both civil and private. In the past the burden of our repudiations and defaults has fallen most heavily upon Europe. In the pre-war period England, the Netherlands, and to some extent France, suffered more than we by the follies and delinquencies of our states, municipalities, and railroad and banking corporations. Since 1914 we have bought back the larger part of American securities previously held abroad. Hence if ever again over a thousand million dollars of our loans come due and remain unpaid, it will be ourselves we shall have cheated, and not our former trustful creditors of the Old World.

Therefore we must institute a sound and thoroughgoing methodology of debt-creation, bond buying, and bond selling. In the ultimate analysis the development of a bond science depends primarily upon the statistical department of the financial houses. Too much emphasis cannot be placed by a banker on his statistician or economist, who should be a well-equipped and properly compensated master-thinker. With a scientific basis in the statistician the buyer would be less the victim of the unforeseen and unexpected, and the salesman would not go on the road trained in address, primed with the latest gossip of railroad melon-cutting, and the talking points of his leading bonds, really sincere and frank in interpreting the information on his circulars, but for the most part utterly unable to explain or comprehend the essential investment qualities in the bonds he offers, —unable to tell, for instance, whether there is a difference between a bond and a note, or between a car trust certificate and an equipment bond. Think of a medical man who could not distinguish the scapula from the clavicle! Salesmanship, so represented, is not a profession but a trade. The dignity of it is barely saved by the high average of general intelligence among bond salesmen, and by the high plane of their business ethics.

What may be said of the bond investor? In absolute ignorance of the very titles of some classes of bonds, unfamiliar with bond law, bond history, and bond practice, unable generally to analyze a corporation's financial statement, and almost never the statement of a municipality, he is too often at the mercy and discretion of salesmen who are, perhaps, only slightly more conversant with bonds than he. In many instances, considering the usual difference in age, business experience, and practical wisdom, the salesman is less prepared than the client to guide investment money into proper channels. Thus a statement of the principles of bond investment is also of service to bond buyers.

CHAPTER II

GAMBLING, SPECULATION, AND INVESTMENT

"Writing a book," says somebody, "is very much like flying a kite: it is pretty plain sailing after you once get it off the ground and started." We have to do, in this work, with the principles governing bond investment in America. Granted the premises and all things follow in due course; but first it is necessary to secure acquiescence in the premises, i.e., as to the nature of investment; how investment is to be distinguished from speculation; and the position in the scheme which is occupied by bonds. From that we deal more generally with concrete and demonstrable facts, and the chances for differences of opinion are fewer.

Many would divide the efforts by which money is made to earn other money into three kinds: gambling, speculation, and investment. It would be well, if possible, to come to some general agreement as to the division lines, for then much blind legislation and several economic fallacies would be obviated.

Gambling. Simon-pure gambling, we take it, is indulged in when one risks money or any other form of wealth on any event over which he has absolutely no control nor foreknowledge. Matching coins or shaking dice fairly is pure gambling. The law of probability was well stated almost a half century ago as follows: "on the strictest mathematical principles, a man who continues to stake a constant sum in a fair wager, must expect to be ruined in the end." [1]

He is a rash man, however, who limits his definition of gambling to operations dependent on pure chance for their success. Betting on races and games is gambling, even when conditions are carefully studied,—unless we revise the dictionaries and the common language of all classes. One may use intelligence as it is ordinarily and properly understood; and if the intelligence is of a sufficiently high order of its kind, a living may be got from it, which, for all we know, may not be so precarious as some suppose.

[1] Whitworth, W. A., *Choice and Chance*, p. 208.

Speculation. To speculate, say the dictionaries, is "to make a purchase that involves a risk of loss, but also offers a chance of considerable profit: to make an outlay in the hope of probable gain." It is hard to see in what respect this definition would not do equally well for gambling as it is ordinarily conducted, except, maybe, for the word "probable." Strictly according to the definition, at the race-track one purchases of a bookmaker the right to demand a certain sum of the bookmaker providing one's opinion is verified that a certain horse has at the time of the race greater speed for the given distance, in the hands of the given jockey or driver, than any other horses entered in that race under their jockies or drivers, as the case may be.

The dictionary definition of speculation does not define, to the exclusion of gambling; but it is not sufficiently inclusive if it did. A novelist contracts with a periodical to supply it with a certain number of stories during the ensuing year; and a forfeit is stipulated if the writer defaults. These stories, we will suppose, have not yet been written. The novelist is selling something he does not possess but hopes to make. In the phrase of the market place he is selling "short," an operation peculiar to speculative dealings, but not included in the definition above. Both parties to the contract are "dealing in futures," a form of transaction native in its accepted sense to gambling and speculation, but foreign to investment. It is conceivable that if by reason of illness or prior engagements the novelist took great chances of not being able to fulfil this contract, he might justly be accused of gambling.

The distinction, therefore, between gambling and speculation is *ethical* rather than *economic*. *Both gambling and speculation are dealing in futures; and the difference between them is the difference in motive, and in the degree and character of the risk involved in pursuit of the gain.*

There are innumerable ways of saying the same thing: gambling is undertaken in the spirit of sport; speculation in the spirit of business. In gambling the attraction of the uncertainty is the leading motive; in speculation, the desire for gain.

By the usage of our English speech there is a form of business activity commonly called speculation, which, according to the distinction drawn above, should be called gambling: namely, the purchase and sale of stocks and certificates representing commodities, on a very narrow margin of equity, and without intelligent opinion as to future values. Since gambling of this sort has a kind of usefulness in "creating a market," and assuming (even though unconsciously) the risk that would otherwise be borne by producer and consumer, it is called speculation, *honoris causa*, for its economic service. The assumption of risk with benefit to the community is a speculative function, which differs further from gambling in that the latter results in no advantage to the public. Thus the gains of the speculator are not necessarily won at the expense of another party, but in every case the gambler can win only as someone else loses. Moreover, the speculator is assuming a risk which is inherent and present in modern business, while the gambler is carrying a risk which is artificially made specifically for the purpose of creating uncertainty and chance.

Investment. Just as the gradation from gambling to speculation is imperceptible, and there is no hard and fast line of demarcation, so speculation, as it avoids chance to a greater degree, in pursuit of more certain, if possibly more modest opportunities for gain, graduates imperceptibly into investment. Likewise if it is a fair contention that gambling is a lower order of activity than speculation, since it seeks to acquire something which has not been earned, and in the operation produces no new wealth, and does not more favorably distribute wealth which exists, then investment is a higher order of business activity than speculation; for chance is eliminated as nearly as possible, all operations are conducted in compliance with natural economic laws, there is a nicer relation between the effort and the reward, and there is less loss or waste even though there may be less gain. Furthermore, investment more surely and permanently creates new wealth.

Apropos, now, of the relative return from speculation and investment, what proof is there that the common opinion is correct, that the current rewards from speculation are greater than from investment? Are dividend returns greater than interest returns? Dividend returns are not the only profits from speculation, and par value is not market value. General business is now the commonest form of speculation. Proprietors expect and receive, to be sure, *when successful*, higher returns than lenders of money receive. But what proportion of business enterprises is successful? A financial writer and editor, whose opinions carry as much weight in Wall Street as those of any other student of finance, was once asked whether he thought in the long run speculation or investment yielded the greater returns. His reply, in part, was:

"I know of no data on the question of the comparative results of investment and speculation. The results would differ so much with different individuals that it would seem impossible to gather any statistics on the subject.

"My own belief is that there can be no doubt whatever that larger gains are to be made by investments than by speculation so far as the non-professional is concerned."

The story of the hare and the tortoise is not without point. Investment mills grind slowly, but they grind exceeding sure.

Leaving now any but business considerations,—when a man has acquired any means above his wants, unless he wrap the surplus up and bury it in a napkin, he is at the necessity of making a choice between the speculation and the investment of it. Two sets of influences will bear upon this choice: his temperament and his environment. The acquisitive man will have in mind the small but certain rental that his money can always command. He is the investor *par excellence*, and his savings, literally, control the destinies of nations. The daring and less patient man will seek a speculation with its superior opportunities for the employment of his creative powers, and for consequent greater possibility of gain.

The play of circumstances is equally effective, and will turn almost all men from the one to the other of the two modes of money-getting. If we remember that this act of choosing is generally an unconscious matter, and is going on all the time for all who labor and save, we have the best possible viewpoint for contemplating the eternal round of choices which goes to the making of business cycles. That is to say, not only may men be classified as individually and natively either speculators or investors, but collectively they are first the one, then the other. When, for a period, prices for materials and labor have risen, and credit may be had almost for the asking, the spirit of speculation becomes general and well-nigh irresistible. The storekeeper lays in a double stock, the clerk buys lucky-dime oil shares, and the banker extends credit with a liberal hand. Then when, according to the old figure, "the bubble bursts" and optimism gives way to fear, there comes the reaction: for a time people will only hoard; but when they make commitments again, the choices are largely for investment.

Fortunate, then, are the very few who are qualified to be both investors and speculators of their surplus funds. These men will liquidate their commitments at the flood tide and *invest* in loans, subject to their call, which at such times are almost as profitable as the better liquid speculative assets, such as dividend-paying stocks. Then when the collapse comes they are prepared to renew their investments in short or long time loans until conditions warrant the withdrawal of these funds for the assumption of speculative risks again.

Speculation the Art: Investment the Science. There is nothing invidious in a comparison of investment and speculation. Each is necessary to the other, and both to the conduct of general business. There is more or less speculation in every investment, and a certain amount of investment in every speculation. But in the large, investment is a science, and speculation is an art. In a sense, therefore, it is inappropriate to speak of "the art of investment," or "the science of speculation." To the extent that investment is a science it is reducible to definition, code, and law, and books may with profit be written about it; but in so far as speculation is an art and distinguishable from investment, it must remain a mystery to those who do not feel its spirit, or else be learned in the occult ways that any art is learned. Successful speculation cannot be learned from books. It is in accord with our thesis of speculation as an art and of investment as a science that successful speculation is a high order of finance, but unsuccessful speculation is gambling. This riddle is not hard to solve.

As art precedes science in the development of a race, so speculation precedes investment. Nothing venture, nothing have,— to invest. The Pharaohs dealt in grain futures, and perhaps Joseph explained to the King a phase of the business cycle theory when he interpreted the dream of the seven well-favored kine consumed by the seven ill-favored. It was well for Egypt that for the next seven years Pharaoh was bullish on all foodstuffs and bought 20 per cent. of the country's supply. It never matters what are the commodities dealt in, speculation takes the burden of risk from the shoulders of both producer and consumer of any kind of product, and, when successful in carrying the load, receives reward commensurate with the service rendered; for, to repeat, by whatever name speculation may be called, it always has had, and always will have, an indispensable function to perform in the world's economy.

Since the assumption of risk is a necessary and highly beneficial service when performed by those qualified to undertake it, the distinction between speculation and investment is *not* primarily ethical. The return derived from an investment may be regarded as income, and in speculation the derivative may be considered as profit. Speculation and investment are actuated by the same motive; desire for gain, and the difference between them is the difference in degree of risk willing to be assumed. This risk finds its most patent expression in the ratio of current return expected of the capital.

CHAPTER III

ELEMENTS OF AN IDEAL INVESTMENT

Security of Principal. It follows from the distinctions drawn in the preceding chapter that the chief requisite of a perfect investment is a maximum of security for the invested principal. If it is certain, humanly speaking, that the principal will be returned when demanded, or at a time agreed upon, or that it can be converted at will, or at a fixed time, into some equivalent form of wealth, equal in value and equally satisfactory to the lender, then the principal is secure.

Now there is one, and only one, word in the language to designate the employment of funds in accord with these requirements. It is the word *loan*. Contracts that are essentially purchases do not ordinarily assure to the buyer revenue from, or the return of his expenditure. No unguaranteed stock, for instance, however good, can assure a future realization equal, at a set time, to the purchase price. This is reasoning by the book, to be sure,—arguing in a vacuum,—but it is only by analyzing investment into its primary elements that we can attain a sound and enduring investment practice.

The moment we are confronted with the word *loan* we realize how few, in truth, are the classes of investment that fulfil requirements. The purchase of real estate is not investment in the strict sense. The purchase of bonds, on the other hand, *is* investment, for the purchase is in reality a loan and must be paid. The purchase of British consols, of irredeemable state "loans," and of the perpetual "loans" of continental governments, or of the ordinary town warrants, sometimes, is not a loan, and therefore not an investment in this sense, since there can be no loan where there is not a promise to pay the principal, and there is no true promise to pay when there is no payment time appointed. On the other hand, deposits in national, state, private, and savings banks, and in trust companies, are pure investments, when interest is allowed, since they are loans for a consideration,—loans which there is a written or implied prom-

14

ise to pay on demand or at a fixed time, and also certain forms of insurance policies which contract to return the principal cost, after a certain time and under certain conditions. The consideration for the loan in these latter cases may be taken to be, not only in interest accruing, or annual participation interest, but possibly even the fact of insurance itself.

It is not necessary to state that many instances of expenditure that theoretically come under the head of speculation are safer than some instances of investment; but nevertheless the fact remains that *every class of pure investment, such as bonds and mortgages and bank deposits, is safer than any class of speculation, such as stocks, real estate, and commodities.*

In fine, therefore, the perfect investment is a promise to pay; it is always a loan.

There are, however, investments that meet all the demands mentioned and yet fall short of being ideal for certain purposes. Some issues of bonds run well into the twenty-first century. From the standpoint of present generations they are hardly more available in theory than perpetual loans. As loans their liquidation value (security apart) is dependent upon current rates for money, rather than upon the fact that at some future time 100 per cent. of their face value must be repaid for them. The shorter the life of the loan the more surely does the face value govern the current value. This is why commercial banks, which must be prepared at all times to liquidate a large part of their investments and which have liabilities in the form of checking deposits and circulating notes largely payable on demand, prefer short-term notes and bonds.

But on the other hand, for convenience in complying with the laws, or for economic reasons, interminable, or very long loans have their place in finance, or else the school funds of some of the Western states would not be invested in them. Then too, testamentary trusts which the founders intended to continue as long as our laws of inheritance and entail will permit, are best fulfilled, ordinarily, when left in the form of investments that will not mature at an early date. In such investments a fixed and regular income is most desired. The principal will perhaps go to beneficiaries yet unborn, for whom there is less solicitude.

Stability of Income. An investment, therefore, to be ideal, must secure to the lender of capital a fixed rental or income for the use of it. This sum, as usually paid in regular serial instalments, is commonly called interest. When the loan is to be brief it may be taken at once out of the capital borrowed. It is then called discount. Since it is in hand, the rental, or discount, is absolutely safe.

Ideally, interest should be as inviolable as principal, and certain to be paid promptly, at regular intervals, and in predetermined amounts. This seems very trite, but thousands of investors have been misled by the deception of the title into buying " income bonds," simply because they did not realize that security of principal and stability of income do not imply each other.

Strange as it may seem, there is no direct relationship between these two investment qualities. Mortgages, which rank with bonds as to security of principal, give far less assurance of uniform and prompt returns. The whole matter of interest return is given fuller treatment in the chapter which compares these two channels of investment. Improved business property in American cities of size has a steady and usually increasing value in liquidation; but the returns from any one parcel, in which the risk is not divided by rentals from many tenants, are comparatively irregular and dilatory.

Uniformity and promptness of return are greatest in annuity insurance and in bonds; promptness without uniformity, in deposits with commercial banks. If stocks and unimproved property are classed with investments it must be acknowledged that the return from them is exceedingly irregular, and in the majority of cases amounts to nothing.

There is another situation in which fixity of income interests us: What remedy have we in default of the income? Obviously none except when investments are strictly loans. Default in the interest of mortgages and mortgage bonds renders the principal due, and thereby furnishes the best remedy: foreclosure of the property secured. Default of payment in annuities, in interest on corporation debentures, *ipso facto* renders the company insolvent and subject to whatever remedy may be had in bankruptcy proceedings.

It is a curious fact, not so well known as it should be, that default in the interest of municipal bonds (in most states merely debentures) does not mature the principal; and since bankruptcy proceedings may not be undertaken against municipalities, there is no action to recover except on the defaulted coupons.[1]

Guaranteed and preferred stocks (and of preferred stocks especially cumulative preferred) have better standing than other corporate shares [2] as regards fixity of income. But this superior standing is affected by, and limited to, the period for which dividends on the stock are guaranteed, in the one case, and to the duration of the stock, if it is callable, in the other. Owing to the peculiar conditions under which stocks of subsidiary corporations come to be guaranteed there is great probability that at the expiration of the guaranty a renewal of it will be brought about only by the lowering of the interest rate. Preferred stocks sometimes share with common stocks in enlarged distributions over the nominal rate. Departure in this direction from fixed income is certainly no objection. Preferred stocks, on which dividends must be paid when earned, and which may be retired after a certain period, have much the same investment position as income bonds.

For loans of long duration there is involved in this matter of fixity of interest a more profound question than mere certainty and regularity of payments,—and that is the future purchasing power of the money in which interest is usually payable. If dealing in long loans it is well to know that the certificate of indebtedness given by the borrower calls for payment of interest and principal " in gold coin of the United States of the present standard of weight and fineness " rather than in mere " lawful money of the United States," however synonymous these two terms may now seem; but it would be better if the lender could exact interest of so much per cent. " in present purchasing power of the necessities of life." By such a provision investment would rid itself of one ever-present speculative element that becomes increasingly important the longer the life of the loan.

The World War has retaught a forgetful people that money value, gold value, and income value are all relative terms; that

---

[1] No class of bonds is less understood than municipals. Granted that they are the very safest of investments, it is remarkable what solemn nonsense is written about them over the signature of some dealers who make a specialty of their sale.

[2] "Corporate stock" of municipalities (a term borrowed from England) does not differ in essentials from municipal bonds.

the twenty dollar semiannual coupon of an old 4 per cent. bond will, under the stress of certain world conditions, buy one-half the potatoes, theatre tickets, or kitchen help of twenty years ago. But the corrollary compensation is that twenty dollars, or two thousand dollars will buy nearly twice as much investment income as a generation ago. Yet this compensation is more apparent than real. The twenty dollars, or two thousand dollars will hardly buy any more income, measured in terms of purchasing power, than ten dollars or one thousand dollars a generation ago. We shall go into this profoundly grievous and important matter of the purchasing power of money, or the price level, in its proper place in pages to come.

Fair Income Return. We have implied in the preceding chapter that, all other things being equal, the income return varies inversely as the security. But all other things are not equal—particularly knowledge on the part of the investor of the relative merits of various classes of securities, and knowledge of the effect of laws governing the investment of savings and trust funds, taxation and of other similar artificial conditions affecting the market price of securities. It is therefore possible, by studies such as this undertaken for bonds, to make use of more intimate knowledge, and to gain thereby in income return.

Whatever the form of investment in which one is interested, there are certain propositions into which one's money is invited, that by almost common consent return less than even " perfect " security has a right to command. This is true of much central business property. The speculative prospect, or sentimental considerations, satisfy investors in such property. In business property particularly, presumptive future rental power is capitalized. To the policyholder, insurance yields less than pure investment. But the great majority of investment propositions have the opposite fault: they make such large returns as clearly to indicate that something has been sacrificed, generally security, to obtain the given rate.

Supposing that 5 per cent. represents the present rental value of money to be placed in bonds as a class, the same gauge may be worthless in six months, and may not apply now to other classes of investment. Although 4 per cent. is the rental value of a dollar in most savings banks at present, most people would believe this rate too low for real estate mortgages.

Nevertheless, no matter how elusive the standard of fair return upon pure investment, *it always exists,* and we buy foolishly and unscientifically when we neglect to satisfy ourselves by what right or opportunity we obtain a greater income from our investments than we have set for a standard, since generally it is by the assumption of risk.

Marketability. But let there be no misunderstanding. It *is* possible to get a greater income return than the standard without loss in security, if one will sacrifice other advantages. It is the old law of compensation at work. If, for instance, one will be satisfied with a bond less widely known, yet with equal security, there can be a gain in return. In such a case one may not be able to sell again with such facility:—marketability may be impaired for income. But most bond buyers demand a higher degree of marketability than they really need. The cause of this error is the pernicious confusion, in the minds of investors, of the speculative and investment functions of the stock exchanges. The generally ill-advised demand for " listed " bonds, from private investors with poorly digested knowledge of their own needs, is one of the most exasperating trials that investment houses have to contend with. The very phrase used betrays the difficulty. What they mean is " active " bonds; quite another thing.

And yet bonds as a class are the most readily salable of all the forms of pure investment in which the loan takes the form of a contract of sale. Mortgages are much less easily convertible. Insurance contracts are quick and certain in disposal, but always at the sacrifice of principal.

But of all sorts of investments bank deposits are the most quickly convertible, and in these is exemplified most clearly the law of compensation. For the privilege of withdrawal the lender of funds has to pay dearly: perhaps 25 to 50 per cent. of his income return. This is marketability at the expense of income. But only when the principal is payable on demand, as in bank deposits, is one fortified with funds to meet at his best unexpected calls for money. In savings banks, which have the nominal privilege of withholding depositors' money for thirty or sixty days, the compensation for this less dependable convertibility is a higher interest rate. And so the law will be found to work throughout the field of investment, quite independent of all considerations of security: *the price of convertibility is lessened income.*

However, convertibility may be attained in another way without such serious impairment of income, if one's invested capital is represented by an instrument for which there is a constant demand. Toward this end active speculation is in some respects an aid to investment. But great speculative activity means great elasticity of quotations, which may offset the good effects of a constant market by withdrawing the opportunity to sell, at all times, at or near the purchase price. This is marketability, or convertibility, at the expense of principal. An ideal market will not only be quick but steady. An ideal investment market does not necessarily offer chances for considerable gain, but it should be an influence against considerable loss.

A good market may be " wide " or " narrow." Properties or securities offered in quantity can be quickly converted in a wide market without materially lowering current quotations, providing the market is not only wide but " with a good undertone," i.e., supported by good demand at slightly lower than current quotations. A wide market may, however, be inactive and weak, and a narrow market active and strong. The ideal market is wide, active, and strong.

The regularity and uniformity of security issues gives them a marketability impossible to other kinds of property. The size of a security issue, and the character of the demand for it, have more to do with its marketability than the intrinsic worth of it.

Value as Collateral. When an unexpected need for capital loaned may prove temporary, the sale of the investment in which the capital is loaned may be avoided by obtaining a loan upon the principal,—a loan upon a loan. This is possible without trouble, expense, or loss of time, in only a very small proportion of investments, and sharply draws a line between what may properly be called " investment securities," and investments in general.

It is the peculiar distinction of insurance policies written in the better companies and having a loan value, that they are the only paper on which an investor has a reasonable likelihood of being able to borrow in the midst of a money panic. And not only may he borrow on it, but at no usurious rate of interest such as he would be charged by a bank, if he could persuade a bank to loan at such a time. The amount loaned in this way by insurance companies during the panic of 1907 totaled many millions.

conditions, they would have precedence over bonds; but changing rates of interest and the condition of the principal, unprotected against withdrawals by the beneficiary, are sources of trouble. Registered bonds ordinarily require merely the cashing of checks, of course, and coupon bonds, the guarding of the bonds against loss or theft, and the cutting and cashing of coupons. Mortgages require attention to many other details, which will be taken up in another chapter. Guaranteed stocks require no more attention than bonds, during the life of the guaranty; but unguaranteed stocks are in slightly less favorable position owing to the voting, and assessment possibilities of part ownership, and to bookkeeping and other adjustments resulting from changing income return. Real estate and other non-loan investments, all of which verge on speculations, cannot, of course, be compared with the securities mentioned.

Acceptable Duration. Closely akin to freedom from care is the matter of duration. If a loan is secure and has twenty years to run, there are twenty years of relief from attention to it. Few investors give enough consideration to their proper wants as expressed in duration. For some purposes, notably the disposal of surplus banking funds, three or four months' commitment may be desirable, but ten years' investment unwise. For testamentary objects, ten years is likely to be too short. Yet if there may be need of selling the loan before maturity, brevity of life tends to preserve the security in liquidation of the principal. Numerous types of bonds offer such uniformity of security with variety in maturity that bonds as a class may unhesitatingly be called the most convenient channel of investment as respects duration.

Acceptable Denomination. In academic discussions of investment virtues, the importance of denomination is seldom duly emphasized. It is evident that the more adjustable the denomination of the investment, the more useful the particular channel which furnishes it. Savings banks will accept deposits in almost any minute amount. It is the great service of savings banks that they will accept, and pay as high a rate of interest on small amounts as on large (and sometimes higher). Savings banks are without rival as an investment channel for those who have accumulated less than $500.

One of the chief elements of attraction about the purchase of stocks is that by means of corporate shares the most modest saver may participate in proprietorship. For about $100 one may become part owner in some of the largest corporations in the United States.

Bonds rank next to stocks in convenience of denomination. When this book was first published, municipal bonds were seldom to be had in less than $1,000 pieces, although a substantial minority of corporation bonds were in $500 pieces. Now a large number of municipal issues and possibly the majority of American corporation bonds are to be had in both $500 and $100 pieces. A number of bond houses specialize in small denominations and in the acceptance of serial partial payments. This catering to the small investor had made good headway before we entered the Great War in 1917, but the tremendous impetus to security buying by the small investor was caused by the Liberty Loans. The other side of the picture, however, should also be presented. It will take many years to make " baby bonds " in general common in this country, for the $100 par entails much more detail and labor on the issuer, and greater selling cost on the vendor, and therefore increased price to the purchaser. The security dealer can make no money selling baby bonds.

As an evidence of how inadequately recognized is the important part played by denomination, it may be said that in amortizing premiums and discounts on bond purchases it is the rule of bond mathematicians generally to assume that the premium or discount, and the maturing interest, should be credited, and the present or future worth of the investment computed, by compounding these balances and increments of interest at the same interest rate as the security returns at the price paid. This is particularly noticeable in investments of high yield. In bonds of this character, for instance, a more circumspect accounting would consider that a higher rate of interest can be obtained by a round thousand dollars, or whatever approximation of that amount the bond costs, than by a fractional amount, too small to invest in another like bond; for to obtain equal security and convertibility the fractional amount must be put into the savings bank or trust company, and obtain only bank interest for its use. It is, therefore, only as a matter of convenience or expediency that one can justify the general practice of computing, at 6 per cent., the premium or discount, and the interest upon the interest, to find the present worth of a 6 per cent. investment having a maturity date, like a bond. This matter receives more comprehensive treatment in its proper place in the chapter on *The Keeping of Investment Accounts*.

Potential Appreciation. The tenth element of a perfect investment considered worthy of separate treatment is potential appreciation. To what extent, if any, an investor has a right to expect or hope for appreciation is a highly debatable question. Is appreciation ever the result of an inherent quality, or always merely of an accident—of an unforeseeable combination of circumstances. If inherent, would it not be certain, and therefore would it not have to be paid for at the time of investment, like all other investment virtues. If paid for there would be no gain, or appreciation, at all. If an accident, then from the standpoint of the investor it is merely a speculative possibility, and not a principle to be sought, defined, and appraised. There seems to be no logical escape from the horns of this dilemma.

Appreciation, we are compelled to say, is not the manifestation of an inherent quality, on the same plane of scientific analysis and treatment as the nine foregoing qualities. But since it is properly and studiously sought for in an investment some attempt at defining it will be well worth while.

Appreciation, or increase in market value, is the result of a growth in the competitive demand for a security, property, or commodity; and this demand arises in turn from a wider *recognition* of one or more of the virtues of the investment: usually that of security. Therefore prospective or potential appreciation is the result of a temporary condition, rather than an inherent quality, but legitimately the object of search and attainment in a security since the discovery of it merely requires superior knowledge of all the investment qualities, particularly that of security, and its attainment does not involve any risk, and is not at the expense of the other desirable elements.

The possibilities of appreciation in *speculation* are without limit; in a pure investment they are curtailed by the fact that at maturity only the face value is returned. A strange misapprehension exists with regard to the relation of appreciation to discount, and of depreciation to premium, in an investment. Many people refuse to buy a bond selling at a premium because they feel that they are losing money in the long run in so doing.

And from similar reasoning they much prefer to buy a 20-year 4 per cent. bond at 93.45, rather than a 20-year 5 per cent. bond at 106.55, although the net return is the same. The illusion of the discount deceives them. And there is no gainsaying that this very general illusion causes a 4 per cent. bond to sell relatively nearer to par (i.e., at a lower net income) than the 5 per cent. bond of similar character and worth.

Now there is a valid reason why all sorts of investors may prefer discount to premium bonds: because they do not understand how to amortize the premium or discount, as the case may be. If it is a premium that is disregarded or inadequately charged off, the owner of the security is periodically drawing a portion of his principal as interest, and therefore at maturity he is left with less principal than he had in the first place; whereas, if it is a discount that is inadequately amortized, the owner will receive less income, to be sure, than he is entitled to from year to year, but at maturity he will have more principal (including undistributed interest) than at first. In brief, an unamortized premium eats into capital to the benefit of "interest," but an unamortized discount adds to capital by a saving out of interest. State laws concerning the amortization of premiums and discounts betray a woeful lack of bookkeeping knowledge.

Hence there is a legitimate disinclination on the part of an investor, particularly if he is a trustee and amenable to state laws governing fiduciary investment, toward the purchase of premium bonds, and a preference for discount bonds; but few investors distinguish between this legitimate preference, which is due to unfamiliarity with accounting, and the ill-grounded preference, which is due to a misunderstanding of the nature of appreciation and depreciation.

There is no true appreciation in the fact that a bond bought to-day at 95 will be worth 100 in ten years at maturity. Appreciation is a gain in market value; but the market value of an interest-bearing loan cannot be measured in mere dollars and cents. There may be appreciation in a premium bond, and yet a loss in the dollars and cents selling price. There has been appreciation in a 6 per cent. bond bought at 107.79 with ten years of life to run, that five years later is sold for 105, for on the same basis on which it was bought it is worth, when sold, only 104.38. Those to whom this is not clear are referred to Chapter XXXIX.

The only true basis of worth is the net return in income, as every bond man knows. All bond issues (it is particularly noticeable in municipals) are figured for purchase and sale from the income percentage basis. A 45-year New York City 4 is always worth more in dollars and cents, when New York City 4s are selling at a premium, than a 40-year New York City 4. But the real worth of the two maturities is practically the same, and is measured in terms of the percentage of return upon the investment. New York City long term 4s, whether 40 or 45 years, are worth a 3.80 basis, or a 4.10 basis, or whatever the fact may be.

Therefore, to repeat, there is no real appreciation in the mere retirement at maturity of a loan bought below par, since the monetary difference between the cost and par was reckoned in figuring the basis price upon which the security was bought. At least this is invariably the case in the purchase of bonds, all the price tables for which take the discount into accurate consideration. The cost prices of all investment securities which are scientifically bought are figured on the basis of their net return at the given price.

This chapter will have missed its aim if it does not impress the fact that there are numerous desirable qualities to be sought in an investment, but that, to a certain extent, they conflict with one another. It is for an investor to determine what are his essential needs, and then seek an investment in which the qualities are most prominent that coincide with his needs. He should then be content with whatever degrees of the other qualities he can obtain.

We may say then, in summary, that any investment which will measure up to the standard of these qualities mentioned is well-nigh ideal. If an investor has obtained (1) security for his principal, (2) a fixed or definite interest, (3) a fair return in income, (4) an investment that is salable without difficulty, (5) is acceptable as collateral, (6) is free from direct tax, (7) requires almost no care, (8) matures after a satisfactory lapse of time, (9) is in convenient units of denomination, and (10) has as good a chance of appreciating as of depreciating as its qualities become more generally recognized,—that man is to be felicitated. It will be instructing to apply these tests in any comparison of securities that we shall have occasion to make as our work progresses.

The three investment qualities that receive the most investigation are security, income, and marketability. Obviously all three cannot exist in a high degree in the same investment. If the investment is thoroughly safe it cannot return a high rate of interest, or rental, and at the same time have a broad and active market, for such a market implies competitive demand, and the competition for a security that is at once safe and of high yield would immediately bid up the price and thus lower the yield.

But if through ungrounded prejudice or lack of knowledge a security is without vogue and has to be sold by personal solicitation, it may be both safe and of high return. *It is the principal, and in every way commendable function of the better American bond houses to sell to their clients issues of bonds that have unimpeachable security and yet an income return considerably higher than would be the case were the issues well known to the investing public at large.*

CHAPTER IV

DIVERSIFICATION AS AN INVESTMENT PRINCIPLE

The greatest sin of omission, in the earlier editions of this text, seems to have been the absence of a discussion of diversification as a principle of investment. The ten cardinal elements of an ideal investment, as laid down in the first edition, have stood the test of sixteen years. No one has disputed them. No one has added any equally important elements. But although the cardinal elements of any one investment were covered, there was no treatment of the principle of diversification as applied to investments.

A simon-pure investment is always a loan. Of modern times, who are the world's great money lenders? The private investors and the banks. Investors, however, lend casually; it is an avocation with them, not a vocation. Banks lend all the time. Lending is almost their only proper source of income; it is their profession. Whether or not always realized, what is their first, basic, primary, fundamental principle of lending? Intrinsic integrity of the several borrowers and of the securities that may be collateral for the loans? We dare to doubt it. Rather, diversification in lending by a diversity of borrowers, and by diversity of collateral in any one loan, or, what is almost the same thing, by the distribution of risk.

A stockbroker comes to the bank officer in charge of collateral loans and asks for a loan on a block of high-grade bonds that are not listed and for which there is no general market. His request for accommodation is likely to be scrutinized much more critically than if he submitted as collateral a miscellaneous collection of active listed stocks of much inferior intrinsic worth. Marketability, plus diversification, does the trick. Marketability alone would not do it. Possibly the accommodation would not have been made on any one of the stocks alone. The bank officer figures that one or two of the stocks on the list might fall off in value overnight or while his back is turned, but a 20 per cent. margin and the law of average will generally save the situation.

29

Diversification, the fundamental principle of investments (plural), is also the basic principle of all insurance,—distribution of the risk. Insurance is merely a distribution to the afflicted (or sometimes the fortunate?) few, of a small part of the surplus income of the unafflicted many, by diversifying the sources of that income so that no one catastrophe, whether a typhus plague or a conflagration, can undermine the integrity of the income as a whole.

The private investor, then, may well emulate the bank and the insurance company. With his eggs in many baskets and his eye on the ten cardinal investment virtues we have already established, he can fortify himself as follows:

(1) *Security of Principal.* If he has $10,000, equally divided among ten investments that are "90 per cent. safe" and yield 6 per cent., and one of them becomes worthless, by ploughing in his income for two years he will have more than restored the principal sum. He might debate the preferability of putting the entire $10,000 into the one "perfectly safe investment": United States Government bonds. But if he had done this prior to the Great War there might have been times in 1916 and 1917 when he would not have been so sure; and suppose the Allies had lost the War!

(2) *Certainty and Regularity of Income.* The chief object of those who invest (as distinguished from those who speculate) is to obtain a continuous and even flow of income. Since continuity of income (interest, dividends, or rentals) is more or less dependent on the safety of the investment, if diversity helps to assure safety of principal it helps also to assure continuity of income. But since usually the purer forms of investments (bonds and mortgages) yield returns semiannually, an even flow of income is approximated by diversifying with investments having income periods falling due in each month of the year.

(3) *Diversity Favors a Higher Rate of Return, with Equal Security.* Assume that at the present time a $10,000 investment, "perfectly safe" and maturing in twenty-five years, would yield 4 per cent. without compounding interest. In twenty-five years the interest would equal the par value of the principal. Assume that ten "fairly safe" or "business man's" investments of $1,000 each running twenty-five years can still be had to yield 8 per cent. at the time of publication this figure should be 7 per cent. and

the argument is vitiated to that extent; but the principle remains. In twelve and one-half years by the same method of computation the interest would equal the principal. Or in twenty-five years the interest from one-half the investments would equal the entire present principal sum.

Consider then the advantages of this diversity. At the end of twenty-five years the "perfectly safe" investment plus simple interest would be worth $20,000. If nothing happened to the ten 8-per cent. investments, in twelve and one-half years this diversified investment would be worth $20,000. If thereafter two or three of these $1,000 investments went wrong and no more interest or even the principal was ever recovered from them, even then the investor would be ahead of the conservative who took the one perfectly safe lump investment. The advantage of the mixed investment would have been still greater if one had considered the interest as compounded, which is the proper way.

The point is reached at which diversification to obtain a higher yield on the total investment becomes of debatable value only when the chances are that the loss in principal of the diversified investments will be greater than the excess of income from these investments over the income from the single investment.

(4) *The marketability of investment* also is increased by diversity. At distinct periods certain types of investment are in much greater demand than others. For the most part the reasons may be sound and economic, but to some extent they may be quixotic; a matter of fashion. (This is well exemplified by real estate when real estate is truly an investment.) If one does not need to realize in cash the total amount of the investment, diversification permits the redemption of that part in greatest demand, therefore with greater celerity, as well as at better prices than the part in less demand. If, however, the whole investment must be liquidated at once, opportunities for marketing a diversified investment are no better than, if as good as, the opportunities for marketing the single investment.

(5) The *superior loan value* of a diversified investment has already been discussed; it inevitably follows from its superior marketability.

(6) Advantage rests with neither side in respect to *taxation*.

(7) We must concede without argument that the one great

advantage of unity in investment is the comparative *freedom from attention*. It is so much easier to watch the eggs when they are in one basket.

(8) As for the *duration* of the investment, or its date of maturity, there is little to be said for either side. If the lender has a definite date of desirability, it is simpler to find one rather than many investments of that date. But if the maturity is distant the chances are that no specific date has distinct advantages to him or his successors.

(9) As to the *denomination* (or units) of the investment, diversity does not hinder and it may even help. For instance, if a man wishes to give his daughter, during her lifetime, an income of $100 each month, or $1,200 a year, the simplest way to attain that result is to make six different 5 per cent. investments of $4,000 each, the first yielding $100 each January and July, the second yielding $100 each February and August, etc. Diversity makes this scheme possible.

(10) The *probability of appreciation* in value is neither hindered nor helped by diversification but in the sense that investment is not so much concerned with opportunities for gain as it is concerned with protection against loss when payments are due, different maturity dates (made possible by diversity) average away the likelihood of real loss in an investment due to depreciation in the purchasing power of the money received.

The United States passed through a phase of price inflation in the period immediately following the War that worked great injustice to those who possessed loans made at a previously lower price level but maturing at that time. In many cases the lessened purchasing power of the matured principal represented an investment loss of 30 per cent. If the amount of the matured principal was large and there was no need of having this principal all mature during the one year, a large part of this loss might have been saved by diversifying the investment so that some of it would have matured in a later period of lower prices.

The real test of an investment principle comes in times of crisis—a financial panic, or a World War. We might tell a true story of a man we know who, when the late War broke out, became distrustful of all securities and turned his modest fortune into bright gold. He was willing to sacrifice income and opportunity of profit for the world's most widely-used medium of exchange and common denominator of wealth. With what result? You will recall that the civilized world practically abandoned the gold basis—even the United States, though we did not admit it publicly. He who offered gold in payment had to explain or apologize. To no purpose were those eggs in one basket.

Conceive, instead, that this man had buried his basket of gold and gone to war and had been killed; that ten years later his heirs had reclaimed the gold; but that meanwhile synthetic gold had become common or that the world had chosen another medium of exchange. Better that he had distributed the risk.

About a generation ago a certain professional gentleman of Boston with large income used to convert his surplus into stocks. He would buy one share—and only one—of each likely corporation that came to his notice. It is probable that man ran less risk of dying poor than if he put his entire wealth into the bonds of any one national government. But our Boston friend might do better. A little bit of land here or there, some precious stones (but not all diamonds) as being portable, some foreign intangibles might, with advantage, take the place of some of those corporate shares.

Change is the one immutable law of the universe. Investment has to combat it. The best weapon is diversification.

Let not all your ventures be in one bottom trusted.

Methods of Attaining Diversification. There are a thousand ways in which diversity can be obtained in investments, and there are a thousand needs that diversity will satisfy.

A banker, in his thinking on this subject and in his advice to his clients, is naturally inclined to restrict his recommendations to intangible securities—perhaps to bonds exclusively, or to bonds and high-grade preferred stock, with possible inclusion of certain common stocks that through a long period of years have demonstrated the vitality of their dividends.[1] Quite unconsciously, because of his own limited investment operations, he may omit reference to mortgages, which make excellent investment for those who know real estate values, or even to guaranteed mortgages or real estate debentures, secured by

---

[1] A rather extreme reaction in this direction has occurred in recent years and finds expression in such studies as E. L. Smith's *Common Stocks as Long Term Investments*, and K. S. Van Strum's *Investing in Purchasing Power*. For a consideration of this subject, see Chapter XLI.

mortgages. Real estate mortgage loans, of whatever description, should be bought, like bonds and investment stocks, from banking houses of proven experience and integrity in the particular field.

The late war has broadened the horizon of the banker and the American investor in common with all other citizens. Before the war we were more or less insular in our outlook and some were proud of it. That state of mind has passed. Our international economic relations have forced us in the interest of trade, and for the distribution of investment risk, to place a glowing part of our loanable capital abroad.

But apart from the distribution of risk, income taxation will require many to seek in foreign countries a higher rate of return than can be obtained here. This is one of the active causes, if not the principal cause, of the Englishman's catholicity in investments. To a greater or lesser extent, long before the war he was pushed into foreign investment markets.

The lessons of the war, however, have taught us that diversification means more than the selection of different kinds of " paper securities " such as described, even when located in different countries. War is only one form of temporary chaos. Social evolution and social revolution may produce other forms. The landowner is an investor. What if landlordism in any one country becomes acutely unpopular? The jewels of the crown or of the landed proprietor may yield no income, but they are portable and negotiable and prove a very present help in time of trouble.

Obviously, the less a man has the less he can divide to distribute the risk. Yet the workman who saves $100 can put it at interest in the savings bank, and his security, which is the solvency of the bank, is backed by the bank's own diversification of investments. If the workman's savings increase to $700 he can in theory deposit in seven different savings banks.

Application of the Principle of Diversification. Now, to get down to cases and to cover the broadest range of experiences among those who have thousands, rather than hundreds, to invest, let us divide investors into the three popular classes:

(1) The active business man of means, with say $100,000 to set aside.

(2) The professional man of limited means, with $30,000.

(3) The widow or orphan class, with $10,000.

In the nature of things, the active business man is more likely to be compelled to draw on his reserves. At least a part of them must be mobile. He will seek, then, large issues with broad markets. He is also more or less qualified and in a position to watch his loaned capital. He is entitled to place some of his loans abroad, largely in government or government-guaranteed issues. His other investments will be mainly American railroad, public utility, and industrial bonds of relatively high yield because he can watch them. For his less mobile reserves he can buy the same types of bonds, but smaller issues of less known companies. For inactive reserve with high yield and relative safety he can buy real estate and real estate mortgages.

For the business man with $100,000, the following list may be of interest:

Amount	Kind
$5,000	U. S. Government bonds
5,000	British Government bonds
5,000	Government guaranteed bonds
15,000	Miscellaneous European Governments and cities
15,000	Miscellaneous South American Governments and cities
10,000	American cities
10,000	Speculative American railroad bonds
10,000	Medium-grade public utility bonds
5,000	Medium-grade industrial bonds
5,000	Medium-grade preferred stocks
15,000	Real estate mortgages or active high-grade stocks
$100,000	

For the professional man with $30,000 who seeks a compromise between safety and income, the following may be offered:

Amount	Kind
$5,000	Deposits in five savings banks
5,000	U. S. Government bonds
3,000	British Government bonds
2,000	Government guaranteed bonds
5,000	Medium-grade American railroad bonds
3,000	High-grade inactive public utility bonds in three separate companies
2,000	High-grade inactive industrial bonds in two companies
5,000	Real estate mortgages, high-grade preferred stocks or high-grade common stocks
$30,000	

For the " Widow or Orphan " class with $10,000 in which is included those of small means without capacity to care for investments and without right to liquidate part of the principal for emergencies: a typical list would read thus:

Amount	Kind
$3,000	Deposits in three savings banks or more
1,000	U. S. Government bonds
1,000	British Government bonds
1,000	Two $500 bonds of the better European governments—long term
1,000	Two $500 high-grade bonds of different American railroads—long term
1,000	Two $500 high-grade bonds of different American public utilities—long term
1,000	Two $500 high-grade bonds of different American industrial companies—long term
1,000	Guaranteed real estate mortgage bonds
$10,000	

The $10,000 to $100,000 for investment is presumed to be the available capital, not the available income. An American business man with $100,000 a year available for investment would be forced by the tax laws of this country to concentrate his investments for the most part in the funnel of "tax-exempt and securities" as described in the chapter on *Taxation*.

CHAPTER V

STOCKS VERSUS BONDS

Since stocks are the typical speculative paper and bonds the typical investment security, it is manifestly unfair to measure them both by the investment standard to the predetermined disparagement of stocks. But on the other hand stocks, as a class, are so generally thought of as investments, and the distinction between investment and speculation is so inadequately recognized, that a contrast of stocks with bonds as channels for pure investment may be worth while, even if the conclusion is foregone.

The comparison may well take the form of a test by the various postulates of our ideal investment, beginning with Security of Principal. This analysis should be confined to characteristics inherent in stocks and bonds, and irrespective of external influences arising out of the business cycle. These cyclical factors will be reserved for consideration in Chapter XLII.

Security of Principal. From which, stocks or bonds, is a man surer of recovering the funds he has once relinquished? This question of itself involves no matter of profit, or of income, but merely of recovery. The answer lies in the very nature of stocks and bonds. Legally, a share of stock is a certificate of ownership of a corporation. Unless otherwise stipulated, it represents a right to pro rata participation in control, in profits, and (if the corporation liquidates) in whatever assets are unattached. But although a share of stock represents part ownership in a corporation, and the right to participate in profits, it does not represent any property except this right.

Most people fail to comprehend the meagre property rights of stock, hence all the nonsense and farrago about stock watering,—as if there were or should be some inherent significance to the par value of stock; or that the par value should represent so many dollars paid in. The par value of bonds, even, does not signify any definite payment in purchase—or any definite amount received by the company in the first instance. Most people seem to think that a certificate of stock is, or should be, equivalent to a cashier's check, which certifies to a deposit of money equal in value to the face of the check, or of a warehouse receipt calling for the delivery of some commodity equal in weight or quantity to the amount of the receipt. There is nothing in the legal nature of stock to give the owner cause to look to the company's assets for the full recovery of his principal.

Except in bank stocks, recovery in liquidation seldom amounts to more than the merest fraction of the sum invested; for ordinarily corporations expire because of their very inability to do business at a profit; and the equitable interest in unprofitable property, which survives the prior demands of creditors, cannot, as a rule, amount to much, so long as corporations are financed largely by the sale of obligations, secured or unsecured. When, as nowadays, not only the rights, franchises, and physical properties, but even the very shares of the corporation, are pledged to secure borrowed money, the stockholder has little to expect under the hammer.

Security of principal in a stock investment is further lessened to the extent that the shares are subject to assessment.

The only resource for the recovery of principal in stock purchases is sale. Two questions then arise: is there a market for the stock; and will it sell for more or less than cost? Marketability of stock will be discussed in its turn. As to market prices, stocks, in keeping with their speculative character, fluctuate more widely than bonds.

If the stock is bought at an average price (assuming such a price), and its intrinsic worth remains undiminished, the investment can be recovered by sale a fair portion of the time. But if its intrinsic worth lessens or disappears, the possibility of sale at cost, or better, diminishes or vanishes, taking with it any element of security for the principal. So, in the last analysis, security of principal depends upon the permanency of equitable assets having a pro rata value equal to the cost of the stock.

Bonds, on the other hand, represent, in the majority of cases, an investment by the obligor of an amount at least equal to their cost. Not legally but in fact, they correspond with reasonable accuracy in the comparison to cashier's checks and warehouse receipts. Although the amount of debenture or unsecured obligations is growing rapidly, nevertheless it is small in comparison with the amount of bonds that have the backing of mortgage or collateral. The principal of bonds, therefore, is usually fortified by actual representative assets on which it has a prior claim, and the bondholders as a class are secured, or at least preferred creditors.

Stability of Income. Just as a knowledge of the relative legal status of stocks and of bonds makes clear the superior security for bond principal, so an understanding of the economic nature of each makes clear the necessarily inferior stability of dividends as compared with interest payments.

Economically, stocks represent shares in the corporate risk. If shareholders have contributed all the capital their dividends represent, in part, the return on *invested* capital, since a company doing business in good faith must have some assets realizable under any conditions. Even when shareholders have contributed all the capital, the returns are bound to vary from year to year and to show maxima and minima of net earnings. The difference between high and low earnings represents the reward to the *speculated* capital. The inevitableness of high and low tides of income often obtains recognition in the share capitalization, by the classifications, preferred and common stock, or "A" and "B" stock.

Whether the capitalization consists merely of the share liability, or of shares and funded debt, the twofold nature of the returns can be compared to the returns on capital invested in real property. A man may buy a piece of real estate with a mortgage for two-thirds of its value. The surplus income from the property, after payment of taxes, repairs, insurance, and interest on the mortgage, is his premium for the assumption of risk. He is entitled to greater return on his speculated capital than the mortgagee, who takes little or no risk.

In like manner it is easy to provide, in a spirit of conservatism, for the stability (i.e., not only for the security, but for the regularity and uniformity) of the interest charges of a company, when it is bonded, and when legal distinctions exist between the classes of its capitalization. But to the extent that earnings vary, the dividends may properly adjust themselves to preserve the integrity of the surplus, and for the disadvantages to which the shareholder is subjected by this adjustment, he should be recompensed by high returns upon his capital, if they are possible.

When the dividend rate is less than the interest rate of the same company, it is no sign that the shareholder is not being reimbursed as fully as the bondholder because the so-called par value of stock approximates less truly than the par value of bonds the amount of capital committed.

A table of comparisons will readily show how much more susceptible to unfavorable influences are the dividends of a corporation than the interest payments. We suppose a company capitalized with $700,000 outstanding bonds, $250,000 preferred stock, and $650,000 common. The ratios assumed in capitalization and earnings will not be thought unusual.

	Good Times		Normal Times		Hard Times	
Net Earnings		$150,000		$100,000		$60,000
Bond Interest (5%)	$35,000		$35,000		$35,000	
Pref'd Stock (6%)	15,000		15,000		(4%) 10,000	
Common Stock (8%)	52,000		(4%) 26,000		(——)	
		102,000		76,000		45,000
Balance for Surplus, etc.		$48,000		$24,000		$15,000

In good times each of the three classes of capital is paid something like a fair return upon par. If these three income accounts represent three consecutive years, it will be seen that funded debt has been paid 15 per cent., preferred stock 16 per cent., and common 12 per cent. If these three years were representative, the common might be considered unfortunately situated; but we must remember that a common stock subject to such fluctuations in return, or to such a low average of return, would probably cost less than par and would represent less than $100 per share of cash capital paid in; therefore the nominal annual return would be much less than the real.

In hard times, when earnings decline and the "margin of safety" narrows, and even bond interest is threatened, the equities in earnings, charged to dividends and balances, will be adjusted to preserve the integrity of the interest as long as possible. Interest must always be supported at the expense of dividends.

Although stability of interest has more to do with the economic than with the legal position of bonds, nevertheless the latter has its marked effect. In the trust agreement of bond issues, whether mortgage or debenture, precaution is usually taken to prevent the creation of future indebtedness that, in whole or in part, could become a lien prior to the obligations. In the nature of corporations there can be nothing to prevent the stockholders who are in control from imposing on the company obligations that shall be a charge upon revenues to be met before dividends are paid.

In considering securities by types and classes there is a natural tendency to have in mind the more prominent issues listed on the leading exchanges. Yet listed securities, but particularly listed stocks, are not thoroughly representative of their classes. Therefore if it is the common practice to lower the dividends on our best listed stocks it is a fair inference (supported by the facts) that, in general, reserves are not sufficiently strong to relieve dividends of their natural office in the income account.

During the first nine months of business depression following the panic of 1907, the dividends of 80 large railroad and industrial corporations were passed or reduced. Sixteen railroads passed their dividends; among them the Missouri Pacific, the Cleveland, Cincinnati, Chicago, and St. Louis, the Southern Railway, the Erie, and the Lake Erie and Western. Ten prominent railroads reduced their dividends; including the Pennsylvania, New York Central, Atchison, Louisville and Nashville, Norfolk and Western, and Atlantic Coast Line. Twenty-six prominent industrial corporations omitted dividends entirely and twenty-nine radically reduced them.

Frequently dividends are passed, or cut, or the proper rate is not declared, to serve the ends of an irresponsible directorate. The minority shareholders have almost no voice in the matter while the courts would speedily find relief for a minority note- or bondholder who was being deprived of his return.

Fair Income Return. Since the shareholder, not the bondholder, assumes the main hazard of corporate enterprise, his return in dividends, immediate or prospective, should, in general, exceed the interest returns by that ratio which fairly represents the relative risk to the two classes of capital. Any expression of opinion as to whether he does, in the long run, obtain this relatively fair return must, at present, be purely personal. Anyone with a taste for figures and ample leisure for investigation might ascertain the facts beyond cavil for listed securities; but to do so he must institute an elaborate system of constantly changing costs (or market prices) for stocks and bonds and corresponding net returns upon cost.

Marketability. We have just stated that the superior marketability of listed stocks over listed bonds was part cause of the low average return upon the cost price shown by the stocks in the above table. But again, let it be remembered that listed securities in general are in the minority, and are by no means representative for illustration of investment principles. The tendency to use them is natural because board transactions are recorded, and easily accessible for reference.

There is no statistical means of proving, among *unlisted* securities, the superior marketability of bonds over stocks, but it has been our experience that bonds are more easily sold than stocks. This, too, is the natural inference from the superior intrinsic worth of bonds, and from the fact that investment conditions are more uniform, and can be more easily and generally recognized than speculative conditions. The article of superior and acknowledged merit will be the more readily disposed of.

The American bond market,—that is, the bond market in Canada and the United States,—is an institution without parallel in other countries. Although the discussion of this market comes more properly under other heads, such as *The Bond Houses* and *Listed Versus Unlisted Bonds*, it is fitting to state that the American bond market is the basis of a special business that encourages professional knowledge of values and seeks selling places for the multitudinous issues. The result is a broader and quicker response to bond offerings than the unlisted stock market furnishes for stocks.

Hypothecary Value. The value of any security as collateral depends mainly on its market and its worth. In general, a listed security is more acceptable as collateral than an unlisted, because current quotations are an easily accessible index of current values and the frequency and volume of sales are an indication (although not always reliable) of the breadth and responsiveness of the market. The more actively dealt in a security is, the less necessary is a knowledge of its intrinsic worth as the basis of loan. For this reason listed bonds have no advantage over listed stocks. If, in general, the security and marketability of bonds are superior to that of stocks, it is the natural and correct inference that bonds, in general, are the more acceptable collateral.

Tax Exemption. As regards the burden of taxation very few people realize the great disadvantage under which bonds labor; for, although in no state are all bonds unequivocally free of tax, in 39 states and territories shares of stock may not be assessed against shareholders when the issuing corporation or its property is directly taxed.

Only Delaware, Georgia, Louisiana, and Washington assess shareholders quite irrespective of the corporation tax; but Maryland, the District of Columbia (in a measure), Alabama, and Iowa assess shareholders on that part of the value of their stock which represents the excess of its market value over the assessed value of the properties. The legal theory is that this excess represents otherwise untaxed good-will and other intangible property.

The fact that government bonds are free from tax to individuals within the country is of little avail because of their prohibitive price. However, the insular issues, the Philippines, Hawaiians, and Porto Ricans, are tax exempt and sell on approximately an investment basis. The bonds of states are now very commonly exempt to holders within the given state, and the proportion of municipal bonds exempt under the same conditions is steadily growing. In fact the tendency to exempt both bonds and stocks seems as inevitable as it is welcome.

But as conditions now are, personal property taxes work greater hardship to bondholders than to stockholders, for the demand for tax-free bonds is greater than for tax-free stocks, since bonds are the staple investment of institutions and trustees whose holdings come under the cognizance of courts and state officials.

Freedom from Care. So far as the mere instruments are concerned, stocks and bonds are about on parity in regard to care. Loss of either security is, at the most, a matter of mere inconvenience. But a coupon bond is negotiable and passes by delivery. Therefore it should be guarded as carefully as currency.

As to freedom from care in the larger sense, ownership carries with it the major responsibility, and the degree of individual thought or anxiety should conform to a degree of investment risk.

Acceptable Duration. The test of acceptability in the duration, or life, of the investment, cannot be applied in this comparison, since stocks, ordinarily, have no maturity. A discussion of duration must resolve itself into a question of marketability, on which we have already commented.

Acceptable Denomination. To the large majority, the possibility of having funds invested in small denominations is a great advantage. Occasionally a big investor or corporation objects to $500 pieces and eagerly seizes upon $5,000 bonds like the old Pennsylvania notes of 1910, so as " not to clutter up the safe deposit box." But registered bonds and stock certificates have another advantage in common, in that one certificate may serve for any denomination. Although whatever advantage there is lies with stocks, inelasticity of denomination is not so marked as in the case of mortgages, which, as channels of investment, suffer severely from this limitation.

Appreciation. The economic and legal positions of bonds and stocks, which throw the onus of risk on stocks and lessens their security of both principal and interest, will bring commensurate possibilities of appreciation. The very nature of a loan precludes great possibilities of advance in price, as we have noted and shall note elsewhere. An exception may be taken for loans which are convertible into stocks.

CHAPTER VI

THE CHANNELS OF INVESTMENT

We have commented in a general way on the merits of speculation and investment as methods of gain. We have studied stocks and bonds as most typical, in this day, of the respective methods. We have concluded that more satisfactory gains are derived from investments than from speculations. To disarm criticism, let it be said that some properties and securities, nominally speculations, are really investments. Pennsylvania Railroad stock, with a record of uninterrupted dividend for 50 years, and with relatively slight variations in the dividend rate, is almost a pure investment when bought at a low price so that it is convertible without loss most of the time, and will return 6 per cent. or better even when dividends are at the minimum.

With the understanding, then, of what is meant by investment in distinction from speculation, the discussion is hereafter confined to bonds; except that a preliminary word is in order, outlining the principal channels of pure investment, of which the main is bonds.

Starting with the premise that all pure investments are loans, then all investment securities are credit instruments, or contracts for the future delivery of money.

Investments Classified by the Nature of the Interest. Since there can be no contract without consideration, loans may be divided according to the nature of this consideration into (a) those with no *monetary* rental value, (b) those with fixed, periodic rental or interest, and (c) those with indeterminate time or rate of interest payment.

(a) Credit balances in open accounts are a form of commercial credit that may be transferred by what amounts to purchase and sale, but formal interest rarely attaches to it. We are unaccustomed to consider such a form an investment where there is no written contract and transfers of the credit are seldom made. Since 1879 United States greenbacks have been a form of public credit bearing no interest. They are callable credit contracts. Illustrations might be multiplied. It is the purpose, however, merely to indicate the breadth of the investment field and to outline its main channels.

(b) Loans with fixed interest are those, of course, with which we are most familiar, and require no comment to obtain recognition.

(c) Loans with indeterminate interest rate are, fortunately, in great minority, but by no means unknown. Income bonds are typical of the class.

Investments Classified by the Contract of Redemption. A more instructive classification of pure investments, to determine the place and importance of bonds among them, is that according to the contract for redemption. Loans may be payable as to principal (1) at the will of the lender, or (2) at the will of the borrower, or (3) at a prearranged time. As the result we have demand, optional, and time loans, respectively. Each is worth comment.

Demand Loans. Since the one essential of a loan is its ultimate return, an obligation is in its most effective state when the privilege of recall may be exercised by the *lender* at any time. Measured by this standard demand loans are the purest of simon-pure investments. Unfortunately for the lender (who buys the loan), the corresponding right to make payment is usually accorded the borrower. If there is more than a possibility that this right will be exercised by the borrower (who sells the loan), then the investment quality called " duration," is weakened. In actual practice such demand loans are not really payable on immediate notice. Banks grant extensive credit in the form of demand notes which would rarely be called, and only after the borrower has been given notice well in advance of payment. Even call and street loans are actually renewed from day to day, and so are practically continuous borrowings.

Credit balances in current accounts, which have just been mentioned, are informal demand loans. Greenbacks are really demand loans, by virtue of their formal promise of payment; but since they bear no interest, they, too, are not investment instruments.

A pass-book is a certificate of a bank's indebtedness to a depositor, and if interest is paid on the deposit, represents an investment of the demand-loan type, for, although the bank may have the right to close the account, it is usually the depositor who recalls the loan.

By power of immediate conversion a lender can protect his investment against depreciation in security, and against reduction or cessation of interest, and he is in position to take advantage of low prices in other forms of security investment. This last is no mean advantage if he is competent to avail himself of it, for interest on demand loans is highest at or near the times of periodic convulsions in security prices. The chief evil that conversion cannot directly anticipate is the decreasing value of the monetary units. But indirectly conversion may forfend loss by transfer of funds from investment to deposit or speculative account until such time as may be propitious for reinvestment. But he is a shrewd, foreseeing man who can successfully avail himself of this possibility.

The trouble with demand loans is the unreliability of this power of conversion, when it is most desirable. A bank account is a call loan; an interest-bearing bank account is an investment; but if the majority of depositors call their loans in concert, the bank must close its doors. The majority will act in concert only at the time it is most desirable to convert, namely, when the bank is weakest, whether from internal or general financial troubles. Against concerted action the laws of many states grant savings banks the privilege of requiring thirty to sixty days' notice; and conversely, again, this privilege is naturally exercised at the very time that it is most worth while to investors to have the money for more profitable use. This privilege was exercised by many savings banks in August, 1914, but since then it has rarely been invoked. As a result savings bank deposits are actually payable on demand even in periods of serious financial crisis.

The call loan secured by highly negotiable collateral is a better type of investment, technically, than bank deposit, but respecting the collateral it requires a superior knowledge of intrinsic values, and an eternal vigilance against collapse in prices. Hence such collateral loans are granted only by banks, and in fact this type of lending is confined to a small group of New York City institutions which place not only their own funds but also those of their interior correspondents with surplus money to invest.

Sometimes overdue notes, and often matured bonds, remain

uncollected for a time. If payment has not been demanded the cause may have been inertia on the part of the owner, or ignorance or forgetfulness of the due date; but probably more often than not (particularly in the case of government bonds) the reason is that the owner is more concerned in having a safe depository for his money than in getting any present return on it. Although these overdue loans are demand loans, they are not investments when they make no return.

Optional Loans. The adjective "optional," as applied to loans, usually has reference to the *borrower:* it is optional with the borrower to return the funds. We have noted that call loans, which are demand loans, are also optional loans. That is to say, if the privilege of recall is granted the lender it is also granted the borrower. Under which heading a call loan more properly falls, depends upon which party to the transaction is most likely to exercise the privilege of liquidation.

Bank "deposits," which are call loans, were classified as demand loans rather than as optional loans, because it is not the policy of banks to retire loans or borrowings. In the case of deposits, or optional loans made by a bank to others, if the account is undesirable, the bank usually insists on larger equities in the collateral or on higher rates of interest. Either requirement will eliminate the weaker loans or strengthen them.

There are many other forms of optional loans, the optional feature usually arising from the peculiar exigencies of the borrower. Among them are delinquent tax certificates, and city and town warrants. Of necessity loans returnable at the will of the borrower, the obligor, rather than at the will of the lender, the obligee, as a class are an inferior form of investment.

There is no conceivable advantage in having money invested in an optional loan, merely from the fact that the loan is returnable at any time. There may, however, be an advantage if the loan is returnable only at a substantial premium. This is the case in bonds which are callable, let us say, at 110. The buyer, who loans funds to the issuing corporation, is content that his money shall be returned to him, providing that he shall be paid a bonus of 10 per cent. for the trouble, and possible loss, to which he shall be put by the necessity of seeking another channel of investment before the regular date of maturity.

But it is safe to say that when an investor is forced to part with a security at par, which otherwise would not mature for some years, it is to his disadvantage. Naturally the security would not be called unless it was good, and reinforced by equities which the issuing company wished to bond, or because equities or current interest rates made refunding possible at a lower percentage of interest. In most cases it will be found that the outstanding issue is an encumbrance and that the option clause in the mortgage has been seized upon to clear away the old issue in order to give better defined and understood security to the new.

There are certain of the so-called "perpetual loans" that are really hybrid and properly classified under optional loans. They have no date of maturity and may not be redeemed by the owners; but the issuing government or corporation may redeem them at will or after a certain time. Examples are the "rentes perpetuelles" of France or the $2\frac{1}{2}$ per cent. British Consols of 1888 issued as not redeemable until 1923 after which time Parliament has had the power to order redemption.

Perpetual loans (particularly those that are irredeemable) are altogether the despair of any who try to think logically. They are the fourth dimension of security investment. In the first place a loan is a promise to pay, and an investment security is a formal written contract for the future delivery of specified funds. A contract of payment implies a stipulated time; and no time is set for the repayment of perpetual loans. Therefore they are not contracts; therefore they are not loans.

The flaw in this *reductio ad absurdum* is the assumption that the return upon the investment is necessarily *rental*, or interest, and nothing more. Since perpetual loans are bought with full knowledge that they are not to be repaid, and that conversion may be attained only by sale, as in speculations, the net yield on the purchase price must be considered as composed of the rental value money for very long time investments, and an insurance premium to cover the risk of depreciation in the security for a "loan" of the given grade, whether it be the good faith of a government or the tangible properties of a corporation.

To estimate the amount, per annum, of insurance premium, it is necessary to estimate the degree of risk. The better the security for the investment, the less the premium. But in considering the quality of the security, durableness is a virtue distinct from equities. The perpetual obligation of a highly-prosperous, but tariff-dependent industrial corporation, albeit secured by properties worth many times the authorized bond issue, would be considered by the discerning as inferior to the simple short-term debenture of the better American municipalities.

Considered in this light, perpetual loans do not offer such promising material for mental calisthenics. The " loan," then, is repaid in the form of an insurance premium; but how soon repaid depends on the quality of the security. The poorer the security the lower should be the price, in order that the net return may be sufficiently large to contain, beside the rental value of a long time loan, an insurance premium to cover the value of the principal of the loan, in a greater or less number of decades.

If the perpetual loan remains good, and pays interest after the insurance premiums have, in a sense, retired it, there has been an appreciation in the investment.

The longer the life of a loan the less valid is a projection of present factors of safety as determining the future safety. That is why a short-term unsecured note of company with steady earnings, largely in excess of fixed charges, may be safer than its first mortgage long-term bonds.

As far as security is concerned, a bond which runs for over a century is practically a perpetual loan. The maturity date of the West Shore Railroad First 4s, which is Jan. 1, 2361, is hardly of security value to the present generation. The character of the issuing company, and of the lien, and the guaranty of the New York Central, are factors making for stability in the market price for the bonds. It is in the ability to convert this bond in the open market that the investment principle of repayment resides.

Time Loans. Time loans, in the parlance of the Street, are those in which the contract sets a definite time for the future delivery of funds, and in which there exists no option of prior payment for either party. Of course by mutual consent, the loan may be paid before the due date; but this *de iure* is a new contract, making void the old. In bonds the situation is illustrated in the case of an issue which is not redeemable, but for which there is a sinking fund applicable to the purchase of the bonds, in whole or part, in the open market. Redeemable bonds are time loans until their optional date. If callable any time thereafter, they become optional loans. These loans may take the form of promissory notes or accepted drafts, which in turn may be the obligations of their customers or of outside borrowers. Thus there is an actual " commercial paper " market which deals in the promissory notes of large industrial concerns. There is also a growing acceptance market for the drafts particularly of the large banks engaged in financing foreign trade. The maturity of these loans runs from 3 to 6 months, and so forms a convenient channel for placing the short-term funds of banks. Individuals seldom invest their money in such loans.

There is justification, in theory, for classifying some forms of insurance as investments,—such a form for instance as endowment insurance in which the principal with interest is returned at some future time. These forms are virtually loans in the nature of contracts to deliver, for consideration, certain funds under certain conditions. Their security ranks very high. Some forms are convertible, i.e., have a " cash surrender value " and have excellent hypothecary value. But insurance policies fail as investments, because such income as may be attached to them is small and incidental. The placement of funds in insurance has protection, not income, as the primary motive. The return yielded even by annuities proves this.

The two leading investment channels, the bond and the mortgage, are worth a careful comparison, such as we essay in the next chapter,—not with the thought of extolling one at the expense of the other, but rather for the sake of employing the investment tests we have set up, and to come to a satisfactory understanding of both classes of investment.

However, this much should first be said, that a cursory glance over the loan field reveals the domination of bonds and mortgages among the various kinds of investment. Bonds indeed are closely associated with mortgages. Mortgage bonds, which form the bulk of our corporation funded issues, are merely fractional parts of ownership in a mortgage. There is very little difference, again, between a bond and a promissory note. The bond is usually one of a series and, by common law, more necessarily formal in its make-up. Promissory notes, in turn, are a form of commercial paper, and so also are drafts. A survey of the channels of investment, then, leads to the conclusion that bonds and mortgages dominate all other classes of pure investment.

CHAPTER VII

BONDS VERSUS MORTGAGES

In the financial forum no topic furnishes material of livelier interest for debate than the time-honored question: " Which are the better investment, bonds or mortgages? " The contest is fought over and over again without casualties to either side, and each time, when the tumult and the shouting dies, advantage never seems to rest convincingly with either side. An attempt will be made in this discussion to avoid the usual *parti pris* if even at the expense of the interest engendered by partizanship. There can, however, be no question that, between them, bonds and mortgages nearly monopolize the disposition of funds destined by private persons for permanent investment, if one disregards savings bank deposits. Bonds and mortgages are the principal channels of investment.[1] This being the case, it is not a matter of surprise that the discussion of their respective merits should recur perennially.

Perhaps a satisfactory way to present the pros and cons is to apply the requirements of our ideal investment. In the following comparisons it is most necessary to remember that we are dealing with bonds as a class and mortgages as a class, and that each class has within it loans good, bad, and indifferent. Comparison remains fair and profitable only by steadfastly adhering to the general types.

Security of Principal. It is unfortunate that no reliance can be placed upon statistical material in considering the relative security of funds invested in bonds and mortgages. Only by visiting every office of record could one ascertain the number and value of mortgages that go wrong from year to year. A census of bond defaults would be an almost equally Herculean labor. It is not, however, beyond possibility that municipal defaults, and the causes therefor, will be accurately recorded in the future. Henceforth all necessary facts for the appraisement of railroad bonds may be had from the Interstate Commerce

[1] A consideration of mortgage or real estate bonds will be deferred until Chapter XXXIV.

Commission. Private enterprise may, in time, collate data already extant, relating to failures of public service corporations. Indeed beginnings have already been made by the bond houses; but their investigations are for business purposes and not universally for publication. The obligations of industrial corporations will give meagre statistical returns for years to come.

Statistics aside, no one conversant with bonds and mortgages will deny that American municipal and utility bonds have been a safer investment than American real estate mortgages; or that American "industrial, mining, and miscellaneous" bonds—if they may so be classed—are somewhat more unsafe than real estate mortgages. The debatable ground respects the relative security of railroad and public service bonds and real estate mortgages; and therefore of bonds as a class, and real estate mortgages.

Overlooking the broader comparison, attempts have been made to draw conclusions particularly from railroad bonds and real-estate mortgages because both are, in the main, directly secured by material property. The line of attack by the partizan of bonds is this: About 60 per cent. (let us say) of the railroad capitalization in the United States is in bonds. The other 40 per cent., which is stock capitalization, is an equity upon the face of which about 8 per cent. is being earned. Assuming that stock should earn 7 per cent. upon its market value, the stock equity is worth 76 per cent. of the face value of the bonds. Putting the fact conversely, American railroads are bonded for four-sevenths or 57 per cent. of their value.

This statement of railway capitalization is unquestionably conservative, and the argument well enough as far as it goes; but of course we have no figures to prove that mortgaged real estate, the country over, has or has not a clear equity of two-fifths. One might find the amount of real-estate mortgages recorded within a municipal district and lay it over against the assessed valuation of the real property in that district and come to some valid conclusion as to the equity in that district; but until the time that all real property in the United States is assessed at actual value, and until the census special reports give us the total amount of recorded mortgages, one man's guess is as good as another's regarding average equity for these mortgages.

As a matter of equities, then, the comparison elicits small

satisfaction.   The *stability* of these equities is next in question; and again trustworthy figures are wanting.   If an expression of opinion is acceptable, the writer believes that in this respect there is little to choose between realty values and corporate property values as a whole.   But a decided exception must be taken in regard to railroad and industrial equities,—to railroad because the extreme marketability of railroad stocks makes them susceptible to more acute variations in market value; and to industrial because the nature of industrial business implies extreme fluctuations in earnings.   On the other hand, the equity in municipal bonds is so tremendous (usually from 90 to 95 per cent. if we may speak of the equity as the difference between the net debt and the real or even the assessed valuation) that the stability of this equity is of the highest.

Since the equities in railroad and industrial bonds are distinctly variable,—these securities' require a greater "margin of safety" than mortgages or than most other bonds.   Years ago St. Louis and San Francisco General (now First) 5s, Wheeling and Lake Erie First 5s, St. Louis, Iron Mountain, and Southern General Consolidated, and Land Grant 5s, and Minneapolis and St. Louis First Consolidated 5s, were advertised as selling on a 5 per cent. basis, with equities of from 200 to 1000 per cent., estimated by the market value of the junior securities.   At that time good Eastern real estate mortgages were paying 5 per cent. and the equity at going prices may have been 40 per cent.   These facts were stated in a circular bond offering, and put these railroad bonds in a strikingly favorable light.   The comparison was not just, however, for no allowance was made for the greater stability of Eastern realty values.   All of the companies mentioned have since been in receivership.

Perhaps it was about this time that an industrial bond gave an excellent illustration of the importance of stability in equities. Columbus and Hocking Coal and Iron First 5s were quoted at 91, bid in January, 1910, just before the collapse of the Keene pool in the common stock; but immediately afterward they could be bought anywhere from 25 to 40.   There had been no change in the material properties of the Columbus and Hocking Company.   The equity in stock value had merely collapsed,—in this case because artificially inflated.

After all has been said, probably the equities in public corporations are generally underestimated, for it is easier to remember that new enterprises are "built on bonds" than it is to realize the amount of surplus earnings that have been put back into the properties, or to recall the amount of subsequent issues of stock and junior liens, the proceeds from which improve and enlarge the plant and equipment.

The Hocking Coal and Iron incidents are by no means confined to bonds. Mortgages have their striking vicissitudes showing the mutable nature of equities. A 7 per cent. first mortgage on central business property at 60 per cent. of the assessed value was no uncommon thing in Seattle or Tacoma in 1890. By Eastern standards such a mortgage was a good investment, and the return was no more than capital in the West at the time demanded. But in 1895 that margin of safety was wiped out, and many an Eastern inventor found himself in possession of unproductive Tacoma real estate. Yet the same sort of mortgages (with lower interest rate of course), placed in New York or Philadelphia, would have remained intact and the margin of safety would not have been even threatened.

Security as Affected by Guaranty. The guaranty is a much more dependable source of security to mortgages than to bonds. Although there are many exceptions, particularly among divisional railroad issues, the fact of bond guaranty is in itself an inference of inferior security. The guaranty for mortgages as given by a mortgage guaranty company, however, is more truly an insurance against individual misjudgment of investment or individual property hazard, by distribution of the risk among many investors, and has no natural implication of intrinsic inferiority in the mortgage guaranteed. Of the hundreds of millions of dollars in mortgages thus *insured* by the New York mortgage companies, there has been very little monetary loss to the companies, and probably none to investors.

The guaranty might prove of little value as insurance against a widespread calamity, such as a long and extreme financial depression, or a flood, or conflagration—against anything, in fact, that could wipe out real estate equities generally in the territory in which the guaranty company operates. In crises of this kind the capital and surplus of the guaranty companies might be no more than a drop in the bucket, since their contingent liabilities very greatly exceed their free assets.

Unfortunately, more often than not it will be found that this capital and surplus are invested in the very class of properties and mortgages, and in the very localities that have obtained the mortgage companies' guaranties. If this were not the case, but if these funds were widely distributed in marketable obligations such as bonds and other securities that are legal for insurance company investment, the guaranty would be worth more if ever put to the test of some extraordinary catastrophe. As conditions now are, it has been estimated that under such a stress the value of the guaranty would be worth about 5 per cent. of the face of the mortgages. On a piece of property worth $100,000 upon which a guaranteed mortgage of $60,000 exists, the guaranty would be worth $3,000, and would margin the property down to $57,000.·

There is quite another point of view from which investment security may be conceived. Assuming that there is no choice between bonds and mortgages *per se* as safe channels of investment, the possible long duration of bonds can protect women and minors, and all legatees under wills from the spoliation of funds left in trust. Perhaps more money is lost to beneficiaries through unjust fees, and the like, than by unwise investment. It is not possible to protect trust funds from fees and commissions that are little short of robbery, if the funds are placed in channels that make reinvestment necessary every three or five years. Of all the uses to which bonds lend themselves, this is most distinguished and satisfying: of permitting the disposal of trust funds over a long period of years, where the funds cannot be converted at any one's pleasure and cannot even be tampered with.

Fees and other costs attendant upon the foreclosures of a real estate mortgage, eat more deeply into the principal than the same charges that are likely to be prorated among the depositors of defaulted bonds by a bondholders' protective committee, on the principle that the larger the undertaking, the less the unit of cost.

Security of Interest. When we were canvassing the elements of a perfect investment, we laid stress on the thought that there was no necessary direct relation between security of principal and security of interest. Although it is true, broadly speaking, that, within a given class of loans, the stronger the security the more certain the interest payment during the life of the loan, nevertheless, as between classes, a much inferior grade of security as respects the principal may present a much superior grade of interest. The point has its most apt illustration in the relative security for bond interest and mortgage interest.

In our conception of what constitutes security of interest it is not necessary, nor indeed advisable, to confine ourselves to the mere duration of the loan instrument. Necessity of frequent reinvestment may be considered in its relation to interest. To satisfy ourselves on this point let us submit to analysis this investment element called security of interest.

If we loan money, over a period of years, we expect a rental, called interest, for its use. We desire, first of all, to be sure of getting it; secondly, to get it at certain regular intervals; and, thirdly, to get at least as much in the future as at present. If we are not afraid of being pedantic we can classify these qualities of the interest charge as (1) *Certainty of payment;* (2) *Regularity of payment;* and (3) *Perpetuity of rate.*

In respect to (1) Certainty of payment (certainty being used in a comparative sense), bonds and mortgages are most nearly on equal terms. This is because forfeiture of property is the penalty for non-payment of interest on mortgages and *corporation* bonds. Although there is no property security for the great majority of civil loans, and the principal does not mature on default of the interest, still the high standing of civil credit, from the Federal Government to the assessment district, prevents unsecured civil obligations from lowering the *Certainty of Interest* maintained by bonds as a class.

If interest defaults on any collateral obligation it is recoverable at law out of the collateral. It follows, therefore, as a corollary to the equally good security for the principal of bonds and mortgages, that there is equal certainty of *ultimate* interest payment.

(2) *Regularity of payment* is quite another matter, and hardly less important, considering the uses to which investments are put. The payment of interest on corporate obligations is a matter of routine business and is in preparation, by the very method of keeping accounts, from the day that interest begins to accrue. The prompt payment of interest on real estate mortgages, which generally represent personal obligations, is dependent on life, health, and even memory. If payment of mort-

gage interest is not delayed by some accident of nature, the chances are much greater that a temporary embarrassment will suspend payment by an individual than by a corporation. Surpluses invested in quick assets, and systematic cash reserves, are protections of corporate accounting rarely employed by an individual. When, in a business crisis, a railroad or a public service corporation has to suspend dividends, or even to pay them in scrip, for want of ready cash, it is a matter of public comment.

Sometimes a corporation is obliged to default interest on its bonds for a time, although fundamental conditions warrant belief that a resumption can be made in the future. If its obligations were floated by a bond house of standing, the house might, although usually it does not advance the interest to those who bought the bonds of it. For the possibility of this protection of interest payments, if for no other, it is highly desirable that investors should deal with responsible principals, not with brokers, when purchasing bonds. There is no similar sponsor for the payment of unguaranteed mortgage interest.

(3) *Perpetuity of the interest rate* is a phase of interest that receives much less attention than it merits. We have said that, in our conception of what constitutes security of interest, it is not necessary, nor indeed advisable, to confine ourselves to the mere duration of the loan instrument. Credits, in the commercial world, are seldom really amortized; they are extended at maturity, or converted into other forms more suitable to changed conditions. Most short-term loans are contracted by both parties with the purpose of refunding at expiration, either with each other or with third parties. In this continuous metabolism of credits, security of interest has to suffer, especially as regards perpetuation of the rate. In a true sense then, quite apart from the security of the respective principals, a five-year railroad note offers more security of interest than a three-year note. Extending this principle to bonds and real estate mortgages as classes of investments, bonds can assure the lender a more uniform rate because of a longer possible duration.

In summary, although the " certainty " of recovering defaulted income is about equal as between bonds and mortgages, security of interest, as a whole, is greater in bonds because there is greater likelihood of regularity in payment and less likelihood of change in the rate on refunding.

The guaranty of established and conservative mortgage companies is a great assurance that mortgage interest will be paid promptly. In fact, it is the policy of these companies to contract to pay interest on the due date, with their own checks, irrespective of whether they have been paid by the mortgagor, or not. Guaranteed mortgages therefore have but one element of weakness in security of interest:—that resulting from change in interest rates due to comparatively frequent reinvestment.

Fair Income Return. It is generally conceded, even by those who are interested in making out the best case possible for bonds, that mortgages make the better return. People who stop to think do not mean by this that the average interest rate on mortgage paper exceeds the average interest rate on bonds; but rather, that with the same degree of security for the invested principal, mortgages yield the larger return.

Waiving this important point for the moment, the writer raises a question equally important but generally overlooked: suppose that a bond and a mortgage each possess the same degree of excellence in *all other* investment elements; which will yield the most? The bond, unquestionably.

To answer the question thus categorically is to anticipate comparisons yet to come.

To return to the matter of yield, relative to security. The rate for gilt-edged real estate loans varies of course with time and place. Sound loans on central business property in New York City are made at 5 and $5\frac{1}{2}$ per cent. The security for these loans is about on a par with that of the average municipal bonds, which have, however, the advantage of tax exemption. Mortgage loans average about 6 per cent. in the East and 7 per cent. in the West and South.

The return from mortgages, however, is reduced by certain costs, the extent of which will vary according to the amount of attention to the investment that the lender is able and willing to give. He may, to be sure, act for himself. He may be capable of searching the county records to see that the abstract of title has been properly drawn, and that the borrower is the actual owner of the property and that the borrower is legally competent to execute a valid mortgage, and that the instrument is binding and the lien of the character described. He may be competent to appraise the property, both as to present and future value, and to look after taxes, assessments, and insurance. But, *to make fair the comparison with bonds, the lender must be presumed to delegate to agents all attention to investment details,* since the trustee for the bonds and the vending bond house exercise all supervising functions over the bond investment. The chapter on *The Bond Houses* will develop this thought more completely.

For guaranteed mortgages the guaranty company exercises the sort of supervision referred to, and its usual charge for the services rendered is $\frac{1}{2}$ of 1 per cent. of the income. This is the price of the insurance, and for that freedom from care which is a great virtue of bond investment. But it is a high price to pay.

If one glances at the quotation sheets of the New York Stock Exchange he will find even among the quickly convertible railroad bonds many issues of very high grade, such as can conscientiously be recommended to persons dependent upon the income, that will net, in normal times, from about 4.40 to more than $4\frac{3}{4}$ per cent.: such great issues as the Atchison, Topeka & Santa Fe General 4s, the New York Central Refunding and Improvement $4\frac{1}{2}$s, the Reading General $4\frac{1}{2}$s and the Union Pacific First 4s. During the war, these bonds sold down to yield from 6 to $6\frac{1}{2}$ per cent., but they quickly recovered their old position in the years after the conflict. Numerous large issues of generally known but less active bonds, both listed and unlisted, might be mentioned, which have security at least equal to that for the above bonds, but which are not of the railroad class, and therefore do not enjoy a correspondingly wide repute and confidence, and consequently are not subject to such competitive demand. These may generally be had at a price to net from about $4\frac{3}{4}$ to 5 per cent. Among them are the Brooklyn Edison General 5s, United States Steel Sinking Fund 5s, Union Electric Light and Power Co. (St. Louis) First 5s, issues of equipment bonds on the standard railways, and many underlying mortgage obligations of various corporations.

There is still a third class of bonds, great in numbers, but smaller in size of issue, and of much narrower and less responsive market, which rank in security with those of the other two classes, but which may be bought at a price to net from 5 to 6 per cent. and even more, for they are harder to sell, both at the time of flotation and afterward, since they required detailed investigation like good mortgages of the same yield.

In view, therefore, of the necessary miscellaneous costs attending safe mortgage investment, or of the equivalent cost of insurance and delegated supervision by guaranty companies, which reduces the average net return to 5 or $5\frac{1}{2}$ per cent. or less, the writer is unconvinced that mortgages net substantially more upon the investment than bonds of equal security, irrespective of any other elements of investment superiority that bonds may possess.

The shorter *duration* of mortgage loans was seen to have a possibly unfavorable effect upon the security of both principal and interest (p. 58), and it may likewise lessen the net return, providing, as before, we desire a *continuous* investment and have our thoughts upon that rather than upon the particular mortgage instrument. Upon the expiration of a mortgage loan it may not be possible for the lender to renew the mortgage on as favorable terms, if at all, so that he must seek another mortgage. When found, title-search and " the law's delay " mean a further loss of a month's interest to detract from the net return.

The effect of taxation on net return is a topic for separate treatment.

Marketability. As relating to this comparison the other investment elements may be dealt with more summarily. Bonds are the most merchantable of all long-term investment or speculative securities, because they combine the virtues of negotiable instruments with the investment virtues. Broadly speaking, mortgages are unmarketable, except by chance, because they are not negotiable instruments, and have as security property units so different from one another as not to admit of classification and appraisal. The scale of bond issues, implying scattered and diversified ownership, creates competitive investment demand. There is an investment demand for mortgages as such, but respecting a single mortgage, no competitive demand. For this reason national banks, which are obliged to maintain liquid reserves, are limited by law in holding mortgages. On the other hand, a large part of the reserves of Eastern banks is kept in bonds. Savings banks, which are not under the same necessity to meet demands requiring sudden liquidation of their assets, invest in both bonds and mortgages.

The briefer average duration of mortgages is a partial offset to their lack of marketability; but short-term notes and early-maturing bonds are as convertible as the longer bond issues, and sometimes more convertible.

Hypothecary Value. Always closely associated with the quality of convertibility is the possibility of hypothecating the investment. This is because quick convertibility implies a consensus of opinion as to market price, and therefore a common knowledge of the equity over and above the temporary loan requested. Needless to say that it is comparatively difficult to borrow on a mortgage. Many a business man, who has dealt in real estate for years, does not know whether his bank would, or could loan in this way. The hypothecation of first mortgages is possible, even by savings banks in some states, but it is generally costly, since the bank will ordinarily require a new title search and other formalities. Moreover savings bank accommodations are not always, by strict interpretation, *collateral* loans. For instance, a savings bank in New York or Massachusetts may take as security for a loan a real estate mortgage assigned to itself; but this is a *direct* not collateral security, for in becoming the assignee, the bank becomes the mortgagee. It may not take a mortgage as pure collateral.

Mortgage hypothecation, then, will usually be undertaken only because money is needed and the mortgage cannot be sold. It will be possible to borrow on a mortgage, as well as to sell it, only in the locality in which the pledged property is situated, unless the sale or loan is negotiated through a land title company or some other kind of mortgage brokers who have moral or legal responsibility of sufficient weight to inspire confidence.

Bonds of comparatively obscure corporations, however meritorious, have a restricted market also, but not so restricted as the mortgage market. A bank will loan to a customer on a bond unknown to it except in a general way, providing the borrower is in good standing and there is a satisfactory financial statement by this issuing company. A perusal of the trust deed will satisfy any reasonable curiosity with regard to legal details. If the institution where the bond owner banks is not capable of loaning discreetly on the paper, the banking house of which he bought the bond will either loan him on the bond directly, or else refer him to one of the national banks or trust companies with which they are affiliated and to which the issue is acceptable as collateral. A loan thus negotiated will cost the borrower nothing except customary interest and the nominal cost attending the transfer of funds. The bond house will ask nothing for its services and there will be none of the vexatious fees attending almost any transaction in mortgages.

Tax Exemption. Taxation, in reference to security investments, is a subject of vital importance, because, where operative, it cuts so deeply into the return as to be a hardship.

Legislators should remember this: *Bonds and mortgages are the only two common forms of pure long-term investment. Very high-grade bonds of the kind in which trustees are sanctioned by law to invest, and mortgages of equal grade, net only about 5 per cent. A tax of $15 a thousand leaves a dependent widow or child with a $3\frac{1}{2}$ per cent. income. It is equivalent to an income tax of $37\frac{1}{2}$ per cent.* Which, then, is more iniquitous, the imposition of this tax or its evasion? For, let it be remembered that the tax on bonds is seldom paid except by those who can least afford to pay: the beneficiaries from invested funds. The evasion or oversight of a mortgage tax is difficult because of the general practice of recording real estate mortgages.

Investors, particularly those subject to the higher brackets, have available in municipal issues generally a recourse against primitive federal income taxes, but no similar recourse in mortgages; and to the more limited extent of municipal loans of the state of their domicile, this may hold true of state income taxes. But it is perilous to generalize on state fiscal policies. There are too many states, and too many inventive state legislators.

Freedom from Care. One of the advantages of investments over speculations is the comparative freedom from attention which investments enjoy. But there is great latitude within the investment class in respect to this quality. Mortgages involve no little trouble. Besides the pains of original research at the time of purchase and the trouble of renewal or reinvestment every few years, there are quite a number of petty details that require almost constant attention. It must be seen that the tax bills and water bills are paid; that insurance is kept up and assessments not allowed to run too long. It must be seen that the property, if improved, is not liable for a building contract, and that the buildings are kept in repair, and that no mechanics' liens are attached for services rendered. If the mortgage interest is delayed, there must be what is fair to call " an exchange of personalities " and possibly foreclosure with resort to one's attorneys. Relief from all these petty details is to be had by investment in guaranteed mortgages; but then the net return is brought down to the level of the high-grade railroad bonds and the Western and Southern municipals, and the comparison is no longer general.

Bonds on the other hand possess, almost in perfection, this highly desirable investment quality called *freedom from care.* The trustee for the bondholders, nowadays almost invariably a trust company, is invested with adequate authority and responsibility to conserve the interest of the bondholders in all those particulars. Failure to fulfil these duties imposed by the trust agreement renders the trust company liable.

Because of the long life possessed by many bond issues, and because bonds are subject to responsible trust company supervision, the investor may lay aside money in funded obligations where the principal may remain untouched and almost unthought of through the lifetimes of his children's children, and the interest be collected with no more pains than required to cash the semi-annual coupons or the interest check.

In bond default, there is a similar, if less gratifying, freedom from necessity to act. According to the racy saying, it is not always preferable to be an honorary rather than an active pall-bearer; but in the main more is gained than lost by committing the conduct of bond affairs to the trustee or to a bona-fide bond-holders' protective committee.

Very few corporations which have sufficient importance and dignity to accomplish the distribution of their obligations by good banking houses, will ever be wound up. Therefore a prudent bond buyer will almost never come into the possession of real property as the result of foreclosure proceedings. In the read-justment of affairs he will receive new securities,—probably bonds for the most part. He will still remain a creditor of the company, and an *investor.* But when mortgages default in interest the mortgagee must be prepared to protect the property at foreclosure sale, and if necessary, to buy it in. In this event he has the care of it, and the responsibility as a *speculator* in real estate. In general the mortgagee must expect that his dealings as creditor and litigant cannot be kept on the impersonal plane that is such a desirable aspect of bond investment.

Acceptable Duration. In the third section preceding we spoke of the freedom from care made possible by the varying duration of bond issues. In general the unlimited choice,—from presently-maturing paper to perpetual loans,—is no mean advantage and weighs heavily in favor of this type of investment.

Acceptable Denomination. In convenience of denomination, also, mortgages suffer by comparison. A man who owns a house worth $10,000 wants to mortgage it for $6,000 at 5 per cent. This might be a good loan, but he cannot " get together " with an investor who has only $5,000. We will say that the investor with $5,000 is unable to find a desirable $5,000 mortgage and has to be content with a $4,000 mortgage. He is then in the market for a $1,000 mortgage; but a first mortgage of this size is not likely to be had on such good property, relatively, as the larger mortgage. And the division of the investment means additional incidental costs and additional care and attention. In these two illustrations both borrower and lender are inconvenienced by mortgage denomination. As to the small investor,—of the type France knows well, but America has yet to recognize: the man with $100 to $500 to lay aside each year in securities, rather than in the bank,—real estate mortgages do not often meet his needs; and unfortunately bonds do not, either, as well as they will years from now. But a number of good bonds: government, municipal, and corporation, may always be had in denominations of $100 and up; $500 bonds are becoming quite common, especially among the loans of public service corporations. A $10, or $100, or $500 bond is as safe as one of larger par value; each is merely a smaller share in the same large mortgage.

One great disadvantage of the inadjustable denomination of mortgages is quite generally overlooked in discussions of investment theory. The mortgage does not admit the nice distribution of investment risk which is possible in smaller units of value. If a man has only $5,000 upon which he or his family may be dependent it may be advisable to make five separate investments of $1,000. In this way he may protect himself by distribution of risk against a total loss of principal through his own misjudgment or through unforeseeable misfortune.

Inadjustable denomination also reduces the probability of quick conversion, for it may be easier to find two buyers with $2,500 each than one buyer with $5,000.

Potential Appreciation. There is a good deal of misapprehension as to the possibility and desirability of value-changes for investments. The topic is discussed in its general phases, elsewhere. We are concerned here with the relation of Appreciation and its necessary correlate, Depreciation, to bonds and mortgages. The gist of the matter is well put in a circular issued by a New York banking house:

"The statement has been made that real estate mortgages are always worth par because the principal will be paid promptly at maturity; but it is obvious that the same can be said of long-time or short-time bonds, regardless of the price at which they are selling. The fluctuation in price is due either to the exigencies of others, or to temporary changes in interest rates, and need not disturb the investor, who has bought for income. We would emphasize that the investor receives the same income annually, regardless of the price at which his security is selling.

"Fluctuations in real estate mortgages are probably neither greater nor less than those of other short-time securities. But while it is doubtless true that a real estate mortgage cannot decline to the same extent as a long-time bond, neither can it appreciate. An investor in a real estate mortgage having a few years to run might find his security maturing at a period when interest rates were very low, and he could only extend or invest at a rate materially below that which he had formerly received. On the other hand, an investor in long-term bonds, if he makes his purchase at a time when bonds are selling below their normal quotations, has the benefit of the high yield until the maturity of the security. Or, if he has funds to invest when interest rates are low and long-time bonds are high, he can easily obtain short-time securities, such as well-secured notes or equipment obligations, and replace these when the long-time securities can be obtained on satisfactory terms."

But appreciation, or depreciation,—to a greater extent in bonds and to a less extent in mortgages because of their respective average denominations,—may be the result of something more substantial than mere price fluctuations due to market conditions and changes in the rates for money. It may be due to changes in the value of the pledged property. From the investment point of view,—always looking first to recovery of the principal,—no matter when conversion may be necessary,—mortgages appear to have the advantage in their apparently restricted possibility for price change; but if forced to sudden liquidation, the mortgage investment is liable to severe loss because there is no demand for the paper. From the speculative point of view the owner of the mortgage is at a disadvantage, for if the value of the property increases the investment enhances the security for the loan, but through this very inconvertibility it cannot add to the principal of the investment; but if the value diminishes the security is lessened, with possible diminishment of the principal from realization under foreclosure.

The bond owner, however, although receiving only the fixed income, not only benefits from the enhancement in equities by increased security for his bonds, but he enjoys the possibility of realizing on his investment before maturity more than he put into it. The tendency of well chosen, long-term investments is to increase in value with time and the advantages of such an increase accrue to the bondholder, but not to the mortgage holder, except in increased security.

Conclusion. A summary of investment characteristics suggests that both bonds and mortgages satisfactorily fill the essential requirements of time loans as to safety of principal and interest, and as to fair net return. However, though there is little to choose between them in the investment essentials, only bonds have the highly-desirable qualities of convertibility, freedom from care, convenience of denomination, and possibility of substantial appreciation. Each of these accessory advantages has been shown to contribute to investment security in its broader interpretation, and to the total, if not to the fixed, net return. Therefore it is a defensible position that bonds are a better channel of investment for those who will acquaint themselves with the essential principles of bond investment.

CHAPTER VIII

LISTED VERSUS UNLISTED BONDS

One of the stock opinions arising from half-truths in financial matters, which bond salesmen are obliged to combat, is this, that " listed bonds are the only kind to buy." Let us then apply our touchstone of investment virtues to bonds listed and unlisted, to see where the truth lies.

Of the various desirable elements in an ideal investment, only three can be advanced seriously as being affected by listing on the stock exchanges: the security of the investment, the negotiability of it, and the rate of income it yields.

Security. As to security, it is true that the listing committees of some of the exchanges require certain definite, informing statements concerning the companies whose obligations and paper they pass upon; and it is also true that the New York Stock Exchange requires that all bonds dealt in there should be certified to as regards genuineness by a trust company, and that the institution of this requirement was the cause of trust company certification; but the information necessarily possessed by any listing committee concerning the worth of its listed securities is limited compared with the intimate knowledge any bond house must have of the condition of a company whose obligations it floats. The listing committee is handed a financial statement and brief answers to set questions. If the loan was previously underwritten by a banking house that wishes the issue listed, further information may be gratuitously forthcoming; but the committee, unlike the house, is not obligated to employ engineers, auditors, and attorneys in the interest of all concerned.

Bankers in investment securities are principals: as a rule they own the bonds they sell; stock exchanges are merely associations of agents which sell for the account of others; so it is natural that real critical scrutiny should come only from the bond houses.

Thus far, then, we may decide that stock exchanges sometimes afford assurance of authenticity and validity (which are real problems only in civil loans), but not of the safety of an investment, as such. We have, however, considered security in a broader, but no less real sense. No matter how active may be the market for an issue, the more haste in selling the less the price obtained. The cost of speed may be from one-eighth to several per cent. But to a greater or less extent the markets of the larger exchanges are " free markets," and, barring manipulation, prices move in response to supply and demand. But the market created by responsible bond houses for their " specialties " is artificial, and governed more by considerations of policy. It is likely to be unnaturally favorable to those who have bought the bonds of the house that has fathered them, but very unfavorable to all others. Although unprovable, it is probably true that the average margin between " bid " and " asked " of listed bonds is much less than half that of unlisted bonds, and the loss due to the " higgling of the market " correspondingly less.

Negotiability. Negotiability, in its two aspects of marketability and hypothecary value, has much more of a bearing on the subject. It is unquestionably true that the average listed bond can be more readily sold or hypothecated than the average unlisted. An examination of the reasons may assist some in the choice of their purchases.

In the first place listing does not create a market. A whole year may pass in which there is not a single transaction in many of the bonds listed on the New York Stock Exchange. In a great many other issues there are sales of only one, two, or three bonds during the year. Surely a bond cannot be said to be fairly active, with probabilities of a ready market at close to "going " quotations, unless the sales per week average at least 10 railroad bonds of thousand dollar denomination. Probably in the average year there are not over 15 per cent. of the listed issues thus active.

It is only fair to say that the market for many inactive issues is stronger than indicated by the volume of transactions. Some divisional railroad issues of highest merit are not dealt in because they are laid away in strong boxes as investments to be held till maturity. On the other hand, some issues are not sold on the exchange because nobody will buy them.

Although listing does not create a market it facilitates transactions and thereby encourages marketability. People are now familiar with the mechanics of exchange transactions; they know to whom to apply when they wish to buy or sell exchange bonds; they know what the brokerage costs of all dealings will be, and they know they can ascertain at any time the price realized by the latest exchange sale, and the highest or lowest prices over a period. These are genuine advantages not to be ignored.

Because there are genuine advantages enjoyed by listed bonds one should not overlook the fact that listing and marketability do not stand in relation of cause and effect, but rather that both are the effects of a common cause, namely the size and reputation of issues. Mere bulk in an issue implies the economic importance of the obligor company; it implies comparatively wide distribution among investors, and a general knowledge of the issue and a growing demand for it if the security warrants. It may be worth while to list such bonds simply because they are likely to be dealt in extensively. Exchanges exist primarily for the purpose of making commissions. A study of listed bond sales will show an intimate relation between the size of the issue and the volume of sales. The underlying railroad divisional bonds are now comparatively inactive. The great blanket railroad refunding mortgages, practically all of which are listed at New York, show comparatively heavy transactions. The relation, then, that exists between size and volume of transactions is the relation that exists between size and listing.

Current Versus Uncurrent Bonds. Therefore, so far as a ready market is concerned, the question should not be that of listed versus unlisted bonds, nor quite even of active versus inactive, but rather of *current* versus *uncurrent*, i.e., the question as to whether or not on short notice one can purchase or sell a security at somewhere near the same price. In other words, whether or not transactions are numerous, the bid and asked price of current bonds must be close together *and hold good for the amount of bonds one has to buy or sell*. It is merely circumstantial that a majority of such issues are listed.

Then the buyer who throws up his hands at unlisted bonds usually makes one of two errors: Either he calls what he wants by the wrong name, or else he buys what he doesn't need. If current bonds are what he wishes he may get them on the curb, or at the bond counter, as well as on the board. But if he buys for investment (the purpose for which funded loans exist) may he not ask himself whether for his needs currency is worth what it costs? He is much more likely to say, " If I buy this inactive bond for 95, I may have to sell it for 90 to get rid of it,"—than, " If I buy this active bond for 95 which I could turn around now and sell again for $94\frac{1}{4}$, including commissions both ways, I shall be paying 5 for activity and 90 for investment value."

This is no plea for unlisted, or even for uncurrent, bonds. It is merely an appeal for the application of sound investment principles to all bond buying and selling. The fact that there are several thousand financial houses doing a general bond business in the United States and Canada is sufficient evidence of the demand for unlisted securities. The commissions on all exchange transactions would barely pay the postage and stationery of these houses, if it would do that. It is fitting that the fallacy of listed bonds, as such, be exposed in order to emphasize the desirability of analyzing one's investment needs before buying, since every investment merit has to be paid for, and lessens the net return that is the primary object of investment as distinguished from safe deposit.

Hypothecary Value. In making loans upon collateral, other conditions enter in, which give listed bonds a decided advantage. A bank has not the time or personal interest to investigate, as a purchaser should, the character of collateral security. From the nature of commercial banking, personal credit is the specialty; collateral credit or credit instruments are secondary. The national bank and the trust company look upon listed securities as authentic; reference is easy to current quotations as the basis for appraisal and loan. Therefore listed securities are, in general, more acceptable. In taking them the bank moves along the line of least resistance; the loan clerk has less thinking to do.

It is of little purport to our argument, but the fact remains that the highly sensitive and elastic condition of the New York loan market is due to this general subservience to the quotations of the hour. Investment value does not receive due consideration. The holder of uncurrent bonds must expect to be at the pains of laying the merits of the loan he desires before the investment board, as he would have to lay the merits of a real estate mortgage before the board of a savings bank. Relief from personal pains has to be paid for in investments as in transportation.

Net Income. The bulk of bonds purchased by national banks and insurance companies should be current,—perhaps listed. Instant marketability may mean much to them. But why should the treasurer of a university, or the trustee, or the private investor who is debating whether he shall buy bonds or real estate, pay the price of convertibility. He has no grievance if it takes him six months to find a buyer for his business block at a fair price. Simply because bonds are paper and represent no tangible property he should not confuse slow convertibility with investment merit.

The greatest need of most people and institutions *which buy for pure investment* is the highest return compatible with good security. Few listed bonds meet this requirement.

The System of Bond Houses as an Investment Exchange. Probably the error at the bottom of the listed-bond fallacy is this: the difference between stock-market and bond-market conditions is not generally appreciated. In several respects stocks, unlisted and uncurrent, are not so desirable as listed. Stocks as a class sadly need even the slight oversight that listing achieves; and as for salability, even high-grade shares suffer badly, at times, in liquidation, for lack of a broader market. Too generally are unlisted and uncurrent stocks interchangeable terms. But not to such an extent, bonds. The great system of American bond houses, which has no like in any European country, is really an immense exchange in itself, reaching out with its branch offices and travelling representatives over the more developed parts of the United States and Canada. This system, with the aid of telegraph and telephone, fulfils for most purposes the legitimate functions of an *investment* exchange. There is of course no similar system for stocks—no federation of houses, handling uncurrent and unlisted, *as well as* listed stocks, that through the medium of an extended clientèle and a highly developed street brokerage business puts buyer and seller in reasonably quick communication. Unlisted stocks, therefore, are not on the same plane of convertibility as unlisted bonds. So satisfactory is this system of bond interchange that over 90 per cent. of transactions in *listed bonds* (it is estimated) take place outside of the exchanges.

Another source of misunderstanding is the fact that all exchange business is done at the uniform commission of $\frac{1}{8}$ per cent., whereas a seller of bonds in the open market believes, with good reason, that his house sometimes makes several times this amount in brokerage. Consciously or not the larger commission is begrudged. The very much greater effort and expense necessary to market inactive unlisted issues are not appreciated. In a real-estate transaction it would readily be perceived and acknowledged that it is better to pay an agent 5 per cent. to sell a house worth $20,000 at its value, rather than to pay another agent 1 per cent. to make a quick sale of the same property for $18,000.

The Unreliability of Some Listed Quotations. Although exchange quotations, especially at New York, are a very convenient reference for purposes of appraisal, hypothecation, and sale, they are not always to be trusted, especially as the basis of value for large amounts of bonds. Suppose that an institution held $500,-000 of a certain railway loan which was $93\frac{1}{4}$ bid $95\frac{5}{8}$ asked. The inexperienced inference might be that these bonds would sell for 94 or thereabouts. It might well be, however, that $100,000 bonds were offered at $95\frac{5}{8}$ and only three bonds were wanted at $93\frac{1}{4}$ and that only a handful were wanted between $93\frac{1}{8}$ and $91\frac{1}{2}$. As a true basis for valuation or sale how does listing help these bonds? They might as well be part of a big municipal issue, that offered for sale will seek its investment price level with facility if offered direct to bond houses that do an institutional business.

Manipulation of one sort or another occasionally has its bearing on quotations. Some years ago Lake Street Elevated 5s were 87 bid on the Chicago Exchange. On the appearance of two bonds for sale at that price the quotation vanished in thin air and no demand materialized until the bonds were offered down 10 or 12 points. A sale was finally effected off the board, presumably in order not to hurt the feelings of banks that may have been loaning 75 cents to the dollar on them.

Conclusion. The not uncommon preference for listed bonds, therefore, is often founded on misconceptions. Listing would always be desirable if it did not cost; but except in an indirect sense there is no added security from it. For hypothecation fairly marketable bonds of quality, whether on the board or not, will serve. If an instantaneous market is the prime consideration, choose an active listed bond; but be sure it is active. For ordinary investment purposes, however, whether buying or selling, the quotation sheet may be ignored; the real market is among the bond houses. Listed bonds are not necessarily current; current bonds are not necessarily listed. And neither current nor listed bonds are necessarily the most desirable—at the price.

CHAPTER IX

THE CLASSIFICATION AND DESCRIPTION OF BONDS: ACCORDING TO THE CHARACTER OF THE OBLIGOR

One who seeks, in a scholarly temper, to classify and describe the phenomena of funded debt, is met with the obstacles and perplexities that beset the course of any scientific investigation of scope. For merely practical purposes, the possible divisions of material are limited only by the concepts and terminology already established by business uses. For instance, as bonds are bought above or below par they are *Premium* or *Discount Bonds;* as government issues sold at home or abroad they are *Internal* or *External Loans.*

The Four Schemes of Classification. But apart from these accidental and occasional divisions there are four schemes of classification of sufficient importance and extent to warrant development; for the full title of almost every bond is derived from some or all of these four; and the possible number of classes and titles of bonds is limited only by the possible combinations of names from those four schemes of classification. Bonds are divided, therefore:

I. According to the character of the issuing corporation.

II. According to the character of the security for the bonds.

III. According to the purpose or function of the issue.

IV. According to the conditions attending payment of principal and interest.

I. Classification According to the Character of the Obligor.

The most thorough-going classification—that which divides the subject best for study from the legal, economic, and financial standpoints—is according to the character of the issuing corporation, or obligor.[1] Therefore the second and third parts of this book are devoted to *Civil Loans* and *Corporation Loans,* respec-

[1] In one class of bonds described in these pages (Residuary Estate Bonds) the obligor is not a corporation but an individual.

tively, and the succeeding chapters deal, for the most part, with the types of bonds as derived from this scheme of classification.

- **Civil Loans**
  - **Government Loans**
    - Foreign Government Bonds
    - National Bonds
    - Bonds of Dependencies
    - Territorial Bonds
    - State Bonds
  - **Municipal Loans**
    - Municipals Proper
      - City Bonds
      - Bonds of Incorporated Towns
      - Bonds of Incorporated Villages
    - Quasi-Municipals
      - County Bonds
      - Parish Bonds
      - Township Bonds
      - Borough Bonds
      - Precinct Bonds
      - Assessment Bonds, i.e., Bonds of Taxing Districts
- **Corporation Loans**
  - **Transportation Bonds**
    - Railroad Bonds
    - Steamship Bonds
    - Ferry Bonds
    - Express Company Bonds
    - Interurban Railway Bonds
  - **Public Service Bonds**
    - Street Railway Bonds
    - Gas Bonds
    - Electric Light Bonds
    - Water Company Bonds
    - Water Power Bonds
    - Telephone and Telegraph Bonds
  - **Industrial and Miscellaneous Bonds**
    - Manufacturing Company Bonds
    - Real Estate Bonds
    - Reclamation Issues
      - Irrigation Bonds
      - Levee Bonds
      - Drainage Bonds
    - Timber Land Bonds
    - Mining Company Bonds

Some words in explanation of this partition will not be amiss. Of course the nomenclature is open to dispute,—as always. The authors have never seen the exact classification here presented. The bi-partite division into *Civil* and *Corporation Loans* cannot be successfully attacked. *Civil Loans* are supported and acquitted by taxation; good faith is a very necessary factor of safety. *Corporation Loans* are maintained and discharged by earnings from operation; the security *generally* is a mortgage upon property or collateral. Civil loans are generally debentures; corporation loans generally liens. *Municipal Loans* are also corporation loans,—public corporation loans; but in this country the word corporation, when unqualified, denotes the company, rather than the municipality.[1]

As each species of bond is taken up in the proper place, its order and relation to its fellows will be fully disclosed. There is no subsequent reference, however, to *Transportation Bonds* as a subdivision. The characteristics are few that bind transporta-

---

[1] The English apply the word corporation to the municipality, and use the word company for private corporation.

tion companies and their obligations, as a whole. *Interurbans,* to be sure, have been uniting *Railroads* and *Street Railways* in a common service; but the security characteristics of *Steamboat, Ferry,* and *Express Companies* are not so unified. Under the Railroad Rate Law, however, even the Express Companies are classed as common carriers and are subject to the Interstate Commerce Commission. Otherwise their obligations might be more properly classified under 'Industrials and Miscellaneous." It will be understood, then, that *Transportation Bonds* constitute a loosely united group, and the line of demarcation between it and *Street Railway Bonds* of the Public Utilities group is merely the distinction between companies that are federally supervised and those that are regulated by franchise and ordinance.

Railroad Bonds are usually given the position in the scheme here occupied by *Transportation Bonds,* and they well deserve the prominence. But since there is a perceptible tendency to recognize the more logical classification, it should receive encouragement. *Interurban Bonds,* in these pages, are treated with *Street Railway Bonds,* since they are not sufficiently distinctive to warrant a separate chapter. *Express Company Bonds* are not discussed at all, since they are not of sufficient number or importance in the investment field. Other omissions have been mentioned in the Preface.

The bonds of many kinds of companies are not included within the list; but the groups are sufficiently comprehensive as they stand, to make easy further classification with reference to the obligor.

CHAPTER X

THE CLASSIFICATION AND DESCRIPTION OF BONDS: ACCORDING TO THE SECURITY FOR THE BONDS

The second scheme of classification is less conclusive because exceptions to the divisions are very numerous, and it is often hard to decide whether the title of a bond (viz. Improvement Mortgage Bond) is more significant of security or purpose.

Simple Obligations.—It will be observed that in this second classification, also, the main division is twofold: into *Simple Obligations* and *Reinforced Obligations*. The commoner appellations *"Unsecured"* and *"Secured Obligations"* seem hardly suitable to express the division. On their face they seem to imply less security for the first division. But the contrary is the case: it is because of the superiority of the first class *as a class* that its obligations can be floated without guaranty or pledge of specific property; for in this class of Simple Obligations *Civil Loans* (both government and municipal debentures) greatly preponderate in amount and importance over *Corporate Debentures*. Ordinarily it is when a municipality or its obligation is weak, that it offers lien security. Special Assessment Bonds and Irrigation District Bonds usually pledge the property benefited. The principle applies, in a measure, to corporation issues also. A mortgage bond is almost always better than a corporate debenture of the same company; few weak companies can successfully float debentures.

Corporate Debentures. In this country, although not necessarily abroad, the word *Debenture* is the generic term for all forms of unsecured corporate obligations. Formerly debentures, with us, were sometimes secured by property; and the term *Mortgage Debentures*, was commonly used for funded loans collaterally secured. But the growing recognition of a discriminating terminology is limiting the use of *debenture* as aforesaid, in spite of the fact that there is no ground in etymology for the restriction.

Simple Obligations
- Civil Loans
  - Certificates of Indebtedness
  - Plain Bonds
  - Notes
- Corporate Debentures
  - Debenture Income Bonds
  - Preference Income Bonds
  - Receiver's Certificates

Reinforced Obligations
- Guaranty Security
  - Assumed Bonds
  - Guaranteed Bonds
  - Indorsed Bonds
  - Stamped Bonds
  - Joint Bonds
- Lien Security
  - Lien on Personalty
    - Paper Collateral
      - Collateral Trust Bonds
      - Railway Trust Bonds
      - Collateral Notes
      - Collateral Mortgage Bonds, or Mortgage-Collateral Trust Bonds
      - First Mortgage Trust Bonds
      - Collateral Income Bonds
      - Certificates of Beneficial Interest
      - Stock Trust Certificates, or Trust Certificates, or Stock Interest Certificates
      - Residuary Estate Bonds
    - Rolling Stock
      - Car Trust Certificates
      - Car Trust Bonds
      - Equipment Bonds
    - Funds
      - Sinking Fund Bonds
  - Lien on Realty
    - Property
      - Municipal Mortgage Bonds
      - Real Estate "   "
      - (Railroad) Real Estate Bonds
      - Land Grant Bonds
      - Farm Mortgage Bonds
    - Mortgage Incidence
      - Divisional Bonds
      - Extension "
      - Refunding and Extension Bonds
      - Purchased Line "   "
      - Bridge "   "
      - Ferry "   "
      - Dock "   "
      - Wharf "   "
      - Terminal "   "
    - Mortgage Priority
      - Prior Lien Bonds
      - Underlying Bonds
      - Overlying Bonds
      - Senior Issues
      - Junior Issues
      - First Mortgage Bonds
      - Refunding First Mortgage Bonds
      - First Refunding "   "
      - First and Refunding Mortgage Bonds
      - Consolidated Mortgage Bonds
      - Consolidated and Refunding Mtg. Bonds
      - Consolidated First Mortgage Bonds
      - First and Consolidated Mortgage Bonds
      - First Consolidated Mortgage Bonds
      - General Mortgage Bonds
      - General First Mortgage Bonds
      - General and First Mortgage Bonds
      - First Lien and General Mortgage Bonds
      - First General Mortgage Bonds
      - Unifying Mortgage Bonds
      - Mortgage Income Bonds
      - Second and Third Mortgage Bonds
      - Second Ref'd'g, Consol., & Gen. Mtg. Bonds
      - Improvement Mortgage Bonds
      - Debenture Mortgage Bonds
      - Mortgage Debentures

To the word Bond, custom has given the prerogative of representing all subdivided interest-bearing contracts for the future payment of money that are drawn with formality, whether they are secured or unsecured, whether the interest is imperative under all conditions, or not, as in the case of Income Bonds.

The technical strength of almost all corporation debentures, except Receivers' Certificates, depends on the duration of the loan and on the amount and stability of equities in assets and earning power over and above prior liens and charges. If these equities are sufficient during the continuance of the loan, interest charges will be met, and if they are sufficient at maturity, the company will have a basis of credit for refunding that part of the issue which has not previously been amortized.

In want of lien security or a trust agreement, there is no recourse to foreclosure proceedings. The bondholder is merely a preferred creditor. He may resort to proceedings under the contract, either to have a receiver appointed or to obtain a judgment and to levy execution; but this is all he can do.

Certificates of Indebtedness are the simplest of the several varieties of debentures. When issued by municipal or private corporations, on the other hand, they are likely to be *temporary* in nature, and of special denominations to suit predestined uses, such as the deferred payment of road and building contracts. Among municipal debentures Town Warrants, and their kin, are somewhat analogous Certificates of Indebtedness. The English call their *interminable* municipal loans "Corporation Stock," and their interminable company loans "Debenture Stock."

During the war certificates of indebtedness were issued by the United States Government to anticipate tax returns or bond flotations. These certificates were similar in nature to the British Treasury bills.

Plain Bonds is a homely term, fallen somewhat into disuse, for debentures of the pure type: i.e., those without reinforcement of lien, or even sinking fund. The Boston and Maine has adopted this term for its debentures. Plain Bonds would differ, if at all, from Certificates of Indebtedness, only in stricter conformity with bond usage respecting denomination, etc.

Corporation Notes, in bond parlance, are to be distinguished from ordinary commercial notes only in respect to formality in the drawing. The title is reserved particularly for debentures of short duration, and for those that have dispensed with the formality of an indenture under seal. The New York, New Haven, and Hartford Debenture 4s of 1956 could, with propriety, hardly be termed Notes; but the Debenture 5s of 1909–1912 were properly so called. It is an undue extension of the word Note, that the 10-year secured obligations of the Deepwater Tidewater Railway Company were called Notes. The Tidewater notes in turn suggest another fact, that secured notes more often have, as pledge, collateral securities than direct mortgage.

Short-term notes have been the resort of companies wishing to obtain funds at times, such as the period after the close of the War, when money rates would not permit the economical issuance of long term, low interest bearing securities. It is usually the intention to provide for the payment of these notes at maturity with Refunding Bonds. If the money market has not improved sufficiently to warrant this, the notes may be extended, or new notes issued to take their place.

Other things being equal, a company's short-term notes are a safer investment than its long-term debentures, for the equities in assets and earnings can be predicted with greater sureness for a short than for a long period.

Debenture Income Bonds is the full title for a class of obligations commonly called *Income Bonds*, but it cannot be conveniently dropped because not a few income bonds have some sort of mortgage security for the principal—generally a junior mortgage, although, as the very name implies, debenture income bonds have no lien security for the principal, yet the interest— up to a maximum rate of, say, 5 per cent.—may be a lien on the net earnings and probably on the net income, if earned. Income bonds are cumulative or non-cumulative, like preferred stock (which they resemble), depending upon whether a default on all or any part of the interest one year shall or shall not be made up another year when the interest has been earned. Income Bonds take precedence over all classes of stocks, for although both are "liabilities," only the bonds are obligations.

Sometimes Debentures or Junior Mortgage Bonds are payable, as to interest, during the first few years of life only when the income has been sufficient to earn the interest. During these years they are Debenture Income or Mortgage Income Bonds, although it is quite likely that they will be called by other names.

Preference Income Bonds, or briefly, *Preference Bonds*, is sometimes used as synonymous with Income Bonds, but more descriptively, when there are two or more series, like First, Second, and Third Preferred Stocks. The interest on Preference Income Bonds is paid on each series as earned, in the order of the series. Perhaps the best illustration among American railroad bonds were the First, Second, and Third Preference Incomes of the Central of Georgia Railway.

Receivers' Certificates bring us to the opposite extreme of safety. If Debenture Incomes are the weakest possible form of corporation bond, Receivers' Certificates are perhaps, as a class, the strongest, although " unsecured." These are not the obligations of the company which is in actual or threatened default, but they are issued by the receiver, at the order of the court, in order to raise money necessary to the continuance of some form of public service, the cessation of which would be contrary to public interest and policy.

If for no other reason, to make them successful instruments for raising money under the necessarily unfavorable circumstances, they have precedence in payment over all other funded obligations; but they rank second to wages and supplies, to all necessary current expenses, and to mechanics' liens. The reorganized corporation cannot regain management of the property until the receivers' certificates have been paid off. However, in quite a number of cases such certificates since 1910 have been paid only after their maturity or have even defaulted.[1]

Reinforced Obligations. There are two ways by which the original simple obligation of a bond may be modified or reinforced: by additional pledge of word, or by pledge of property. An additional pledge of word is a guaranty and a pledge of property is a lien. Let us deal first with the guaranty.

Guaranty Security. There is very general confusion as to *Assumed* and *Guaranteed* Bonds. In the acquisition of one company by another, very probably it will be found that the purchased company had bonds outstanding on its property. This is most commonly the case in railway consolidations or reorganizations, but assumed bonds may also be found in the case of traction and industrial concerns. If the purchased company loses its corporate identity,—*"non est,"* as the law says,—then the bonds become the *direct* obligation of the purchasing com-

[1] See Hale, E. P., *Receivers' Certificates*, Harvard School of Business Administration, 1926.

pany. They are assumed precisely as the mortgage on a house is assumed by the man who buys the house. If the assumed bonds were mortgage bonds, the *collateral* credit, the mortgaged property, remains the same. It is the *personal* credit that has changed.

If the consolidation is merely partial, and the purchased company still maintains a separate corporate existence, then the personal credit may remain unchanged, but the bonds may be strengthened by the guaranty of the holding company. In this case they are not assumed. The terms of the guaranty may be on the bonds themselves or in a separate document. Sometimes, after issuance, the bonds will have placed upon them the name of the holding, or some other interested company. A guaranty is implied thereby and is enforceable at law, just like an ordinary indorsed note. These are called *Indorsed Bonds*.

The term Indorsed Bonds is extended to include another class. Any writing foreign to the text (whether or not in the nature of a guaranty) which is found upon credit instruments that are formally drawn, may be a hindrance to their hypothecation and sale. Such writing brings the paper within the category of *Indorsed Bonds* by the rule of the New York Stock Exchange that "Coupon Bonds" issued to bearer, having an indorsement upon them not properly pertaining to them as a security, must be sold specifically as "Indorsed Bonds" and are not a delivery except as "Indorsed Bonds."

Bonds, for instance, secured by mortgage on real property within New York State, on which the mortgage-recording tax of $\frac{1}{2}$ of one per cent. was paid under the old law would have that fact *indorsed* or *stamped* upon them.

Very suggestive of indorsed securities, but with wider sphere of application, are *Stamped Bonds*. Stamped across the face of the instrument may be the following: "Subject to provisions set forth on back thereof." The provisions mentioned may be a digest of the agreement and supplemental mortgage (if any), that become effective on acceptance of the bond by the purchaser. The agreement may relate to the establishment of a sinking fund, to the disposal of unissued numbers, or to any other change in plan to benefit the loan. Ordinarily the trust company that acts as trustee will certify to the authenticity of the indorsement.

But paper may be stamped for other purposes than reinforcement of security. Of itself the stamping merely implies an addendum. The temporary receipts for the New York Telephone Co. $4\frac{1}{2}$s of '39 were stamped with late but necessary information regarding coupons and accrued interest. Naturally Extended Bonds are very often stamped bonds.

There is still another sense in which we may speak of stamped bonds. Bonds that may be subject to a stamp tax or a tax the payment of which is indicated when a stamp like that for postage is affixed, are Stamped Bonds when the tax is paid.

In purchasing any form of *Guaranteed Bonds* the two main considerations are (1) that the pledged property is sufficient security in itself, for the payment of the bonds, with interest, and (2) that the form of the guaranty is such as to compel the guaranteeing company to meet any deficiencies on the part of the primary obligor by payment of the amount of these deficiencies to the trustee for the bondholder.

In the upbuilding of the great American railroad systems the status of the bonds of merged and subsidiary companies has had a thorough trying out. Experience has proven that guaranties have not always been enforceable against the makers, because the guaranties stipulate no definite remedy in case of default. If all goes well the guaranteeing corporation will never be directly liable. But suppose that a corporation which has guaranteed bonds bearing interest January and July should go into the hands of a receiver in February. The issuing corporation fails then also. The *direct* obligor cannot default till July. The guaranty cannot be a *fixed* liability till July. It is merely a *contingent* liability: a contract. The receiver has a right to affirm or disaffirm contracts. He can disaffirm this guaranty. If, however, the bonds had been assumed, the liability would have been fixed, and the receiver could discharge it only by paying. The bondholders would then have the actual mortgaged property and be entitled to rank pro rata with the general creditors of the assuming corporation. We need not go into the question as to whether the receiver ever could be held to the guaranty if it had been given expressly in part payment for a lease. Our purpose is merely to show the inferiority of Guaranteed to Assumed Bonds.

Guaranties are by no means confined to railroad companies, or even to private corporations; municipalities sometimes, though not frequently, guarantee or assume the bonds of corporations like water companies, which they take over for municipal operation or ownership, or the securities of which they wish to strengthen for market purposes.

Guaranties of bonds are sometimes assumed. If through physical merger Railroad A absorbs Railroad B, which has guaranteed bonds of Railroad C, then Railroad A assumes the guaranties of the bonds of Railroad C.

Guaranty, like registration, may apply to the principal of bonds, or to the interest, or to both. Columbia, South Carolina, guarantees the interest of $200,000 Canal bonds, but the Columbia Water Power Co. is responsible for the principal.

An interesting illustration of the fact that security of principal, and security of interest are not the same, may be cited in connection with the guaranty. Some years ago one of the strongest national banks in New England guaranteed by indorsement on each bond the payment of the *principal sum, at maturity,* of an issue of about a quarter of a million dollars of bonds of a promotion company. The unsophisticated investor would naturally suppose that if the strong national bank thought well enough of the issue to guarantee the payment of the principal at the maturity date, there certainly would be no question about the interest. But the terms of the guaranty failed to state that the bank received from the proceeds of the sale of each bond a sum sufficient, when compounded at $3\frac{1}{2}$ per cent., to equal the principal at the distant maturity date.

Guaranty, therefore, as a dependable addition to lien security, should be such that on default, payment of both principal and interest become an immediate and direct obligation of the sponsor.

But it so happens that default by the subsidiary company is most likely at the very time that the major company itself is in trouble; for the same general business conditions probably affect them both. What, then, is the relative standing of various claimants if the system is reorganized or goes into receivership? Even holders of debentures fare better than holders of guaranteed securities as far as the parent company is concerned, for the former are preferred and the latter are general creditors.

Assumed bonds, on the other hand, take their place with the other bonds of the system according to priority of lien, etc.; and even though certain issues may have been guaranteed prior to the assumption of the new bonds, those assumed have the preference as obligations.

A community of interest such as exists where two or more railroads desire to use the same bridge or terminal station gives rise to bonds jointly guaranteed. Thus the Kansas City Terminal Railway Company's bonds are guaranteed by twelve railway corporations, each of which is responsible for one-twelfth of the indebtedness. A stronger assurance is had when the guaranty is both "joint and several," i.e., when each guaranteeing company is held contingently liable for the whole amount.

Joint Bonds, in the field of funded debt, correspond to the joint promissory notes of the commercial world. These bonds received greater prominence, as a class, on the issuance by the Great Northern Railway and the Northern Pacific Railway, of their joint Collateral Trust 4s, secured by the stock of the Chicago, Burlington, and Quincy at a valuation of $200 per share. In this instance the security was triple: the entire loan was the direct obligation of each railroad, and there was the pledge of the collateral contract. They were refunded in 1921 with a new $6\frac{1}{2}$ per cent. joint issue, since converted, however, into bonds of the two individual railroad companies.

Joint Bonds usually are the " joint and several " direct obligations of two or more companies. They may be simple debentures, or collateral trust loans or mortgage loans. They may be issued by any types of private corporation. A mining issue to be noted is the Norfolk and Western-Pocahontas Coal Co. Joint 4s of 1941. They are the direct obligation of the Norfolk and Western Railway Company and the Pocahontas Coal and Coke Co., but as between the two, the liability is in the Pocahontas Company. The lien security is a mortgage on coal lands.

Lien Security. In contrast with the additional security furnished by guaranty, which rests on personal credit, is the form of security furnished by lien, which rests on the segregation of specific assets, against which the creditor can satisfy his demands in case the personal credit of the obligor is not sufficient.

But since in business practice default in any sort of corporation loan, whether guaranteed or not, will in all probability have to be satisfied, ultimately, out of the pledged property, the first step in investigating a valid lien is to appraise the property. Even if, as a measure of expediency, the obligor company which defaults on its mortgage obligation is reorganized, without fore-closure proceedings, the readjustment of its obligations will be on the basis of property value and priority of claim thereto.

Bonds with lien security are divided, according to the nature of the property mortgaged, into bonds secured on *personalty* and on *realty*. The personalty, in turn, that commonly offers as security for bonds, is *paper collateral rolling stock*, and *sinking funds*.

Lien on Personalty. All funded issues that have as their principal reinforcement, not a direct mortgage on real property, but the deposit in trust of paper security, are properly called *Collateral Trust Bonds*.[1]

They come into being in this way. A corporation, owning or in control of subsidiary companies or properties, may for reasons innumerable, not wish to dispose of either the shares or bonds of these subsidiaries. For instance, the short-term note of a big railroad system of the Middle West, secured by the first mortgage bond of a new division in Louisiana, may sell for a better price than the divisional bond itself, as the direct obligation of the unknown subsidiary company, even if guaranteed by the parent company. Therefore railroad companies make loans in their own name, and in lieu of a direct mortgage pledge the securities of their subsidiaries.

The investment worth of *Collateral Trust Bonds* varies (1) according to the credit of the issuing corporation, (2) according to the value of the securities hypothecated, and (3) according to the degree of protection afforded by the deed of trust. What may be said to constitute the credit of a corporation is too large a subject to be treated here. It is developed in the chapters on *Railroad Bonds*.

A tendency to wide fluctuations is undesirable in collateral, for an increase in its market value is ultimately the avail of the owners of the collateral, but a decrease in market value undermines the security of the bonds. Therefore stock, with its comparatively unstable worth, is not so desirable as bonds. The Atlantic Coast Line, Louisville and Nashville Collateral Trust

---

[1] For legal aspects of collateral trust bonds, see L. A. Jones, *Treatise on the Law of Pledges*(1901); F. L. Stetson, *Some Legal Phases of Corporate Financing, Reorganization and Regulation* (1917). For use in the railroad field, see T. W. Mitchell, "Collateral Trust Mortgage in Railway Finance," *Quarterly Journal of Economics*, 1906, p. 443.

4s of 1952 are secured by deposit of Louisville and Nashville stock. In the early years of the life of that loan a severe financial crisis might have found the value of the collateral shrunk considerably below the par of the bonds.

It is desirable that the collateral should be the securities of a corporation disassociated as to the nature and sources of its revenues, so that a set of conditions that will unfavorably affect the credit of the issuing company, will not necessarily work to the detriment of the collateral.

But the most conspicuous failure of collateral trust bonds has lain in the weakness of the trust agreement as a protection to the bondholders. A notable case was the Detroit, Toledo, and Ironton, Ann Arbor Collateral Trust Notes. Although the Notes were due Dec. 1, 1908, and were in default some time previously, the owners were not able for two years to come into possession of their Ann Arbor Stock. Collateral should be deposited with the trustee for the bondholders on terms that would render it to the holders upon default that they might immediately enter upon the physical property represented by their securities. Against partial dismantlement of the property that is directly or indirectly pledged, the collateral trust mortgage may well incorporate provisions clothing the bondholders with sufficient proprietary rights to prevent, without their consent, the sale of parts of this property, or the consolidation of it with other properties, or the issuance of other securities on the property.

Substitution of collateral should not be permitted except on definite prearranged terms. The shifting of collateral is an unsatisfactory feature of Real Estate Mortgage Bonds. Issues that permit substitution of the collateral are called Convertible Collateral Trust Bonds. Strictly, any Collateral Trust issue that is convertible may be so called. Presumably in proportion as the bonds are converted the collateral will be released. Sometimes, the bonds are even made convertible into their own collateral.

Railway Trust Bonds is merely a title for collateral trust bonds issued by railroads.

Collateral Notes do not differ from collateral bonds except in the temporal and formal characteristics that may distinguish bonds from notes, in general.

Collateral Mortgage Bonds are Collateral Trusts that by reason of the securities pledged are indirectly secured by mortgage upon property. Real Estate Mortgage Bonds are of this class. (See Chapter XXXIV.) It is not necessary even that the immediate paper of deposit be of the realty mortgage class, provided that the ultimate reinforcement of the obligation is a lien.

Mortgage-Collateral Trust Bonds is a title synonymous with Collateral Mortgage Bonds.

First Mortgage Trust Bonds are Collateral Mortgage Bonds, the collateral for which, immediately, or at some remove, is a first mortgage upon real property. An illustration of the type with immediate mortgage collateral are the Louisville and Nashville First Collateral Trust 5s of 1931. The St. Louis and San Francisco Notes mentioned above were of the indirect mortgage collateral type.

Collateral Income Bonds may be noted as a class which has arisen, under an unnecessarily complicated system of railway finance, combining the characteristics of two classes, collateral bonds and incomes, which we have treated separately. The collateral reinforces the payment of the principal, but has no bearing on the payment of interest, which is dependent on earnings.

Certificates of Beneficial Interest is an abortive " security " of the Collateral Income type. It does not merit a separate paragraph except to call attention to the extremes to which the English language on the one hand and the inspiring faith of the investor on the other, can be drawn on by ingenious efforts to raise funds without offering adequate recompense.

The design of the issuing company may be to retain control of a subsidiary through the voting power without tying up the capital necessary to own a majority of the stock. The stock is deposited in a voting trust, and against it are issued Certificates of Beneficial Interest, i.e., interest in the earnings, and in the equitable assets if the company liquidates. To attain somewhat different ends the plan may be applied to any sort of paper for collateral, as well as stock.

If the collateral is non-maturing the certificates may be of indeterminate duration. At maturity they may be payable in money or in the securities that they represent. The basis of conversion and the scope and force of any guaranty will have to be interpreted from the trust deed. Each issue will be a law unto itself; generalization is unprofitable.

Since the informing principle of these Certificates of Beneficial Interest is the voting trust agreement made effective by the pooling of securities, we may place in the same category *Trust Certificates*, a generic term like the preceding, and *Stock Trust Certificates*, and *Stock Interest Certificates*, titles of like signification, but always referring to corporate shares. All these Certificates are properly classified among bonds when there is an obligation to pay principal, interest, or both. Most of them, also, by nature, are collateral trust bonds; and when this is the case they are classified as such by the Interstate Commerce Commission.

Residuary Estate Bonds are a collateral type which have the distinction of being the only bonds mentioned in these pages that are not public or private corporation securities. They are issued by persons who have legal rights to moneys or merchantable effects, fees, or entail, receivable at a future time under the terms of wills. The rights may be to the principal or to the interest in the property bequeathed. They are secured by a collateral instrument which transfers this right to the purchaser of the instrument. The right should be made absolute by previous admission to probate without contest.

The banking house gives to the beneficiary who decides to bond his prospects the amount of the bond, less the brokerage and the cost of an annuity (purchased of some insurance company), which will probably have the same duration as the testator's " expectation of life," and bear the same rate of interest as the bond. The annuity, made payable to the buyer of the bond if the beneficiary dies before the bond matures, protects the interest, but not the principal, during the expectation of life. If the testator dies within this period the bond owner obtains the principal of his loan so much the sooner, and thus increases that part of the net yield on his investment represented by the difference between the discount cost of the bond and par. Since the testator may live beyond this period there should be an equity in the value of the collateral sufficient to pay for the greatest possible amount of interest due during the extended term of life. In other words, the selling price of the bond should be sufficiently low to cover unexpectedly long interest payments. Obviously the net return on such a bond cannot be figured from the bond tables. It is the province of the actuary to determine the cost to return a given approximate yield, or the approximate yield at a given cost.

Car Trust Certificates, or *Notes*, on the one hand, and *Equipment Bonds*, or *Notes*, on the other, are the two common forms of securities by which railroads obtain rolling and floating stock on collateral credit.

The older form, Car Trust Notes, are usually certificates issued by Car Trusts, or Equipment associations (that built or purchased equipment to sell to railroads) to the effect that a certain sum is due the holder when certain rentals are paid by the railroad. Formerly the lease warrants covering the rentals were the collateral security for the certificates. In recent years individual warrants for the instalments of rent have been deemed superfluous, since specific references to the disposition of the rentals are in the contract of lease.

Equipment Bonds are to be broadly distinguished from Car Trust Certificates first in the maker, which is not an equipment association, but the railroad itself, and secondly in the security, which is not the lease, but a regular contract of conditional sale. In either type of security title remains in the trustee to the benefit of the security holders until the railroad has made all lease or instalment payments.

Further comments are reserved for Chapter XXVI on *Equipment Trust Obligations*.

Sinking Fund Bonds are those for which the mortgage deed requires that a stated sum shall be set aside, periodically, out of earnings in order to retire the bonds from year to year, as they mature.

The propriety of sinking funds for state and municipal loans is fully discussed in the proper chapters. From the days of Albert Gallatin there have not been wanting men of sufficient clarity of vision in financial matters to realize the unnecessary complexity and waste in sinking fund accounts and the simplicity and economy of applying a surplusage directly to the cancellation of debt. But it is only in recent times that the same principle has obtained recognition for corporation bonds.

In former years sinking funds were considered a usual and proper safeguard of railway loans, but the experience of the lean years following the panic of 1893 weakened the faith in their efficacy, for about 25 per cent. of all railway obligations so secured, defaulted. It came to be realized that sinking fund accounts could be subject to manipulative tactics which would render them a source of expense and loss of credit, rather than of income and confidence. For instance, where earnings did not admit payments to the sinking funds (which in accounting are a charge prior to interest payments) new bonds were issued to raise the money necessary for sinking fund payments, so the total debt was increased rather than decreased, with consequent loss of net earning power and credit. Thus it was realized that the best reinforcement of an obligation was obtained by putting the surplusage back into the property, and by refunding bond issues as they matured, on the strength of an increased credit, and therefore at a lower rate of interest.

It is evident, however, that this fiscal policy will not always be best for small companies, or for companies owning properties which must be depleted to produce revenue. It is imperative, for instance, that the outstanding obligations of a coal company should lessen, as the supply of its marketable product lessens. Strongly safeguarded sinking funds, therefore, should accumulate to discharge the bonded debt when due.

With the exception of telephones, perhaps, of all kinds of property commonly bonded, rolling stock depreciates with greatest certainty and rapidity. After fifteen or twenty years there is very little life left in it. Yet equipment bonds are one of our strongest securities. Most equipment issues, and the best of them, have no sinking funds. Their *principal* safety lies in the fact that the debt is paid off more rapidly than the cars and engines wear out. Here is the best exemplar of reinforced security: Serial Repayment.

But in small companies, and in those subject to the depletion of their material assets, if there is not serial repayment, then, by all means, there should be sinking fund accumulation.

The premature payment of funded debt may be schematized as follows:

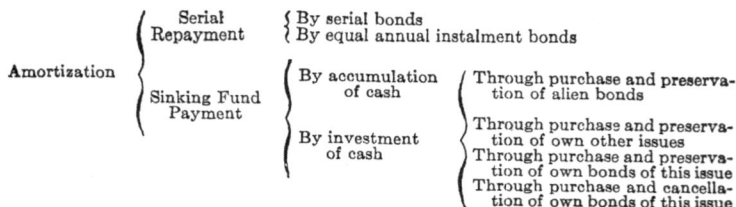

Amortization	Serial Repayment	By serial bonds	
		By equal annual instalment bonds	
	Sinking Fund Payment	By accumulation of cash	Through purchase and preservation of alien bonds
		By investment of cash	Through purchase and preservation of own other issues
			Through purchase and preservation of own bonds of this issue
			Through purchase and cancellation of own bonds of this issue

There are advantages and disadvantages in each of these dispositions of the sinking fund. Cash accumulations, even when restricted to special uses, are a help to the company's credit and banking accommodations. But cash on deposit, is at best accumulative at the rate of only 3 per cent. whereas cash converted into investment will yield at least 4 per cent., and perhaps more. This disadvantage in interest rate is felt by the company more than by the bondholder, but in a very true sense that which is detrimental to the one is detrimental to the other.

Cash funds are not only liable to ultimate misappropriation, but to temporary and expensive misuse. A railroad company, once in bankruptcy, is understood to have loaned interested bankers just before bankruptcy several hundred thousand dollars that belonged to a subsidiary, and then, for lack of cash, to have been obliged to hire equipment. By withdrawing this sum and using it as the nucleus for equipment purchase, the new management saved this some fifty thousand dollars a year.

Even though the disposition of sinking funds by investment yields a higher return, it makes, of the company, a financial and investment institution, unless the terms of the deed of trust require of the trustee a supervision more than usually close. The company, as such, is not fitted to make investments; if it purchases for sinking funds the bonds of other companies, its natural disability is increased by its possible efforts to obtain a rate of return equal to that it would have obtained if it purchased its own bonds. The company is more conversant with the investment value of its own obligations than it can possibly be with that of the obligations of other companies, but if various alien securities are purchased solely on the basis of their investment worth, then the sinking fund has distributed its investment risk. Since these purchases, and their changing value, are not ordinarily matters of public knowledge, the bondholder has no means of knowing to what extent the security for his bond is increasing in this amortization of the debt by proxy, as it were.

There are three ways in which a company may invest its sinking funds in its own bonds. It may purchase and keep alive parts of its other issues, or parts of the issue being amortized, or it may purchase and cancel parts of the issue being amortized.

To purchase parts of its other issues will increase the general equity of the company since it cannot very well owe itself, and investment in its own bonds supposes a knowledge of the securities purchased. Otherwise the plan has little to recommend it.

To purchase and keep alive in the sinking fund bonds of the issue being amortized is a truer reduction of the loan, for these bonds may not again be reissued.

To purchase bonds of the issue and cancel them, lessens, as the previous plan does not, the fixed charges of the company, but since it does not compound the moneys applied to the sinking fund, less bonds will be thus amortized for each thousand dollars of appropriation.

Appropriations to the sinking fund, like the serial repayment scheme above, may be in equal annual payments of principal amounts, or the payments may be graduated so that the heaviest charge for payment of principal may not come at the beginning when, theoretically, the company is not so well situated to meet them out of the increased earnings due to the expenditure of capital raised by the bond issue.   In common practice this difficulty is met by increasing gradually the percentage of net earnings that apply to the fund; or, with less reference to earnings and more to mathematics, the company may cumulate predetermined sums so that as the bonds bought for the fund increase the interest, payments on account of the principal may grow smaller.

From the investor's point of view it is objectionable that bonds should be callable for the sinking fund unless at a considerable premium over the investment value, for otherwise the fact tends to retard the natural appreciation of the security. Sometimes the trust deed stipulates that the bonds shall be bought in the open market when tenders are made at some reasonable price.   This helps to maintain the price and the market. If bonds may not be had at the upset price, then the trustee may be empowered to invest the fund as he sees fit, within certain restrictions.

Lien on Realty.   That reinforcement of a promise to pay which is a pledge of real property is the most easily understood and enforced, and, all things considered, is the most satisfactory.

Although Civil Loans are very largely Debentures, and in Great Britain and Canada it is customary to call municipal loans Debentures, nevertheless, as has been intimated, *Municipal Mortgage Bonds* are by no means uncommon, and occasionally are classed together and so entitled. The classification, however, may be thought rather academic, for the bonds spring from no common cause and have few common characteristics except the mortgage feature. Municipal water bonds are often secured by a mortgage on the plant. In giving the mortgage perhaps municipalities are influenced by the fact that private water companies are bonded, and in taking over such companies it is natural that the old bonds should either be guaranteed or assumed, or be refunded with a new issue of municipal origin, backed by pledge of the plant. It will be found that most kinds of municipal mortgage bonds are secured upon property which is revenue-producing.

Real Estate Mortgage Bonds, as a title, is applicable to several distinct bond classes. In the first place it is sometimes used to denote all issues having as security a lien on real estate. In this broad extension of the phrase all railroad mortgage bonds, for instance, come under the classification except, perhaps, a few that are primarily secured by a lien on leaseholds. Secondly, it is commonly used, as in this book, of that class of bonds issued by real estate companies which is secured by mortgages on real estate. Or again, it may be used of the issues of any corporation that are secured, in whole or in part, by liens on the company's real estate, rather than on its plant and equipment as a whole. The classic illustration of Corporation Real Estate Mortgage Bonds is the Western Union Telegraph Co.'s Funding and Real Estate $4\frac{1}{2}$s of 1950.

Real Estate Bonds is a common title for Real Estate Mortgage Bonds issued by railroads on property not directly used in the operation of the road. The Terminal, Dock, and Wharf Bonds, etc., which are mentioned presently, may be looked upon as subdivisions of the class. The Charleston Real Estate 4 per cent. Land Mortgages of the Boston and Maine were an excellent example. Real Estate Bonds is also an abbreviation for Real Estate Company Bonds.

Land Grant Bonds are a species of railroad Real Estate Bonds. They are secured by liens on lands granted by a government. The proceeds from the sale of the lands to settlers establishes a sinking fund from which to retire the bonds. The *Canadian Pacific* Land Grant Gold $3\frac{1}{2}$s are the leading issue of this class now outstanding in America.

Farm Mortgage Bonds were a type in great vogue in the trans-Mississippi plains, two or three generations ago. Themselves a refinement on the farm mortgage, they later became commonly used as collateral for the obligations of real estate brokers and promoters. A few successive seasons of drought and hot winds in the eighties drove the farmers further west. Western real estate companies were driven to the wall; their guaranties were worthless, and unsecured bonds were unsatisfied. Eastern holders of mortgages found themselves owners of unproductive property. The savings banks of a New England state were crippled.

The collapse of Western plains land values was a blow to the popularity of farm mortgages and farm mortgage bonds from which recovery was slow. Yet there is no inherent weakness in farm mortgages as security for bonds. When investments in either are made at first hand by competent buyers, such as insurance companies, farm mortgages are excellent security. But so little technical training and experience is required to do a farm or general real estate mortgage bond business, that many may be trusted to be in the field who are without scruple and experience. Like irrigation bonds, these securities should be bought only of houses with acknowledged standing in the special field. In latter years, the Federal Land Banks, with government support, have issued a very high type of bond based on farm values. See Chapter XXXVI.

Mortgage Incidence. The titles to several kinds of bonds arise from the fact that issues may be secured by mortgages on only a part of the company's property. They are entitled according to the character of the property mortgaged.

It is natural that most of these titles concern railroad bonds since railroads usually embrace, in one system, property spread over several states.

Divisional Bonds are secured by mortgage on railroad divisions. The division originally may have been an independent company, and as such may have issued the bonds. In case of merger, the issue is both Assumed and Divisional. The purer type is that issued by the system itself and secured on a section of the road which the railroad, as an operating company, calls a division.

It will be well to limit the term Divisional to these two forms. However, if the division maintains a separate corporate existence, but is controlled by the system, and its issue or issues are guaranteed by the system, the bonds may be called loosely Divisional Bonds. If the division has two issues, whether they are guaranteed or not, the prior Divisional Bonds may even be underlying the system's consolidated issue, for although the parent corporation cannot give a mortgage on real property that does not belong to it as a corporation, yet it may place the junior Divisional Bonds as collateral behind its consolidated issue.

Extension Bonds are, in essence, divisional bonds of the pure type, but the mortgage incidence may be such as not to coincide with operating divisions. Loosely, Extension Bonds is simply the more descriptive term when the line pledged is a continuation or extension of the system into new territory. That is, the bonds are secured by mortgage on the extension. They may be additionally secured by a junior lien on the older properties of the company. If a portion of the issue is held in escrow to retire the mortgage bonds of the old divisions the new issue is of *Refunding and Extension Bonds*.

Divisional and Extension Bonds that are not direct obligations of the system, are safe investments only when the mortgaged line is essential to the operation of through traffic, as in the case of a Main Line issue, or else when it originates an assured amount of traffic the net earnings from which will always exceed the requirements of the divisional or extension bond issue.

Extension Bonds should not be confused with Extended Bonds.

Kindred to Extension Bonds, and of the Divisional type, are *Purchased Line Bonds*, although in this case the implication is that the division or road acquired has been constructed and previously operated as an independent company. The bonds will be secured by mortgage on the line or lines purchased.

Purchased Line Bonds, in turn, must be distinguished from Purchase Money Bonds.

The following five kinds of mortgage issues differ only in the character of the property for which the money was raised, directly or indirectly. Separate companies may have been incorporated for the purpose of holding title and of issuing the securities. One or the other of two causes are generally at work when these subsidiary companies are formed:

I. It may be desired that the property come into the hands of the railroad *already mortgaged*, so that the cost of the property may be defrayed by a bond issue which can be sold on the advantageous terms that a straight, closed first mortgage will bring. If there is a blanket mortgage of the railroad outstanding which becomes a lien on " all property subsequently acquired " the funds raised to acquire this property will, perhaps, be obtained on less favorable terms, under the blanket mortgage, or perhaps that issue is all outstanding so that no funds can be raised from it.

II.   The property acquired and the works constructed may be for the joint use and advantage of several railroads.   That all may have an evident *pari passu* interest and proprietorship in the property, part ownership and control of it is best obtained by the ownership of part of the stock of the new company formed to own the property.   The bonds of this new company will be its direct obligation, further secured by mortgage on the property, and possibly also by joint or joint and several guaranty as well.

Bridge Bonds are not likely to be issued for construction purposes unless the engineering is on a scale to require separate financing.   The Kansas City, Fort Scott, and Memphis Railroad has guaranteed the $3,000,000 first mortgage issue of its subsidiary, the Kansas City and Memphis Railway and Bridge Company for the bridge thrown across the Mississippi River at Memphis.   To save the expense of several structures railroads often unite in the use of a single bridge, which may best be financed by a separate company with bridge bonds.

Ferry Bonds are seldom the result of community of interest; but rather of the first cause mentioned above: namely, a desire to bring the property into the control of the railroad with as small an equity as possible for the benefit of the blanket mortgage bondholders.   For the bonds to be safe, apart from the guaranty of a trustworthy company, it must be established that the need of a ferry will outlast the life of the bonds.

Dock and *Wharf Bonds* share the investment characteristics of both Ferry and Terminal Bonds, with distinction only as to the nature of the property pledged.   Incorporation of a separate dock or wharf company may be the result of a community of railroad interests, or may be an evasion of the "after acquired property clause."

Terminal Bonds, also, are usually the result of a community of railroad interests.   One of the most difficult problems in railway transportation is to obtain adequate terminal facilities in proper situations at a cost commensurate with the traffic return. In many of the large cities "Union Depots" solve this problem. The expense incurred and the benefits accruing are shared by the railroads that are parties to the undertaking. A common arrangement is the formation of a terminal company to be owned solely by the interested railroads. The terminal bonds of this company will be secured on the real estate, trackage, and other property of the company and will be jointly guaranteed by the railroads. Illustrations are the Boston Terminal Company $3\frac{1}{2}$s already mentioned, and the Terminal Railroad Association of St. Louis 4s. The Washington Terminal Company $3\frac{1}{2}$s and 4s are guaranteed jointly and severally by the two railroads that own the company.

A weaker form of Terminal Company bond is that secured on terminal property not owned or controlled by the lessee railroads. A bond issued under such circumstances is not likely to be guaranteed. The Chicago Terminal Transfer 4s issued in 1897 are of this kind.

Terminal bonds may be the obligation of a single railroad, and secured by mortgage on one or more terminals, as the Chicago, Milwaukee, and St. Paul Terminal 5s of 1914, or on terminals and trackage, but if the trackage is of considerable value in relation to the whole, the word Terminal may not appear in the title.

Terminal bonds that are the direct obligations of one or more interested railroads are a good class of investment paper, for they are really underlying liens. But the default on the Chicago Terminal Transfer 4s called attention to the fact that terminals, in themselves, rarely pay the cost of construction, and the investment value of their securities depends on their relation to an entire system. So considered, terminal improvements pay, but only when the expenditure is not a capital burden out of proportion to the size of the road or roads that undertake them.

Mortgage Priority. Many bond titles have their origin in the standing of the mortgage that reinforces the obligation. At times these titles are misleading. For instance, the Chicago and Alton Refunding $3\frac{1}{2}$s of 1949 are a first mortgage on 596 miles of track. The Chicago and Alton First Lien $3\frac{1}{2}$s of 1950 are a second mortgage on this same track and a first mortgage on less than 54 miles.

Mortgage priority is a matter of gravest importance, even if a property is not subjected to foreclosure, because reorganizations, to gain acceptance by the creditors, must recognize the relative strength of the several liens and make readjustment of the capitalization and the debt, on that basis.

Priority is entirely a relative matter and there are several terms which properly convey the idea of the relative strength or weakness of the lien.

Prior Lien Bonds are simply bonds which are "closer to the ground," i.e., mortgage obligations with rights on the property held in trust that are prior to some other rights. It is not unusual to hear the custom deprecated, as wilfully misleading, of calling loans Prior Lien that are not a first mortgage. This criticism is hardly defensible. Priority does not suggest primacy, but merely precedence; it is not an absolute but a relative term. However, the use of the term may be overdone, as in case of the Erie First Consolidated Prior Lien 4s, which are a sixth mortgage on the line.

Underlying Bonds is a term that should be practically synonymous with Prior Lien Bonds, for it merely implies that there are *Overlying Bonds*. But perhaps in practice Underlying Bonds are more generally secured by first mortgage or its equivalent. Just as Junior Lien is the antonym of Prior Lien, Overlying is an antonym for Underlying.

Senior Issues and *Junior Issues* make another set of complementary terms; but these differ from the foregoing since they extend over not only the mortgage obligations, but the debentures. Of the two expressions "Junior Issues" is the more common. The adjective "Junior" reverts to the security also and we have "Junior Liens." Of course the Senior are the Prior Issues and among mortgages the Junior are Overlying Issues.

First Mortgage Bonds speak for themselves. They are secured by a first mortgage on all or part of a property. In railroad companies that part of its entire property which yields a first lien to any one issue is likely to be very small, for divisional, extension, and subsidiary company liens are usually attached to most of the line. However, the tendency in corporate finance is to reduce the number and simplify the character of funded obligations. Therefore many issues that are not now very "close to the ground" will become absolute First Mortgages in future years, when divisional mortgages mature.

The term first mortgage may be used (and sometimes is) of a lien on personal property: on chattels and rights of one kind or another. First Mortgages recorded on leaseholds of realty and rolling stock are not at all uncommon. Investors have difficulty in appreciating that there is no innate legal superiority in a realty mortgage. A recorded mortgage secured by the leasehold rights on a piece of property is prior to a subsequently recorded mortgage on the fee.

Refunding First Mortgage Bonds is given separate mention that a careful distinction will be made between these and *First Refunding Mortgage Bonds*. The former is what the words imply: an issue refunding a First Mortgage Bond. The latter is the first issue (in point of time) which the company has floated to refund old bonds. Obviously, the title is misleading and unnecessary. One is justified in believing it is sometimes used to give the impression that the bonds referred to are secured in part by a first mortgage.

First and Refunding Mortgage Bonds admits of no such equivocation. What assurance of security the title gives is in the *First* which declares the bonds are secured by a first mortgage. The *First* element in the Missouri Pacific First and Refunding 5s is a first lien on 165 miles. The *Refunding* element represents a prospective betterment of the present position of the obligation as secured by second, third, fourth, and fifth mortgages in 3,616 miles.

First and Refunding Bonds are the most important class of railroad issues with which bankers now have to deal. They are the soundest means of financing, and the commonest expression in securities, of the present tendency to gather up in one general mortgage all the miscellaneous debts of the corporation.

Let us suppose a railroad has a closed Consolidated Lien of $25,000,000 covering 500 miles of track, and has just built 100 miles of track for which it must now be reimbursed by a bond issue mortgaging this new track. If the road purposes to issue a new first mortgage bond in the sum of $5,000,000 to cover the 100 miles of new construction the bankers may advise, instead, an issue of $40,000,000 authorized, First and Refunding Bonds, of which $25,000,000 will be reserved to retire the Consolidated Lien, $5,000,000 to pay for and be a first lien on the new 100 miles and $10,000,000 will be reserved for extensions and improvements under such restrictions as will protect the issue.

Open First and Refunding issues along lines similar to these are financing the needs of the Rock Island, the Delaware and Hudson, the Denver and Rio Grande, the Missouri, Kansas, and Texas, the Missouri Pacific, the Wisconsin Central, and about three dozen more of our larger railroad systems. It will be seen, therefore, that fifty years hence American railways ought to be benefiting by a much simpler scheme of funded debts.

A confusion of bond terms similar to that mentioned above, exists regarding other issues.

Consolidated Mortgage Bonds, properly, are bonds secured by a mortgage on properties that have been consolidated. There may be underlying issues on any of the properties. Another less exact and legitimate use of the title is for issues that ultimately consolidate, by refunding, several prior mortgage issues on one property.

Consolidated First Mortgage Bonds should signify an issue secured by a first mortgage on consolidated properties.

First and Consolidated Mortgage Bonds should signify a consolidated issue secured by a first mortgage on part of the consolidated properties. It is inexactly used as synonymous with First and Refunding, First and General, and First and Unified issues.

First Consolidated Mortgage Bonds should signify the first consolidated issue that the company has floated.

General Mortgage Bonds is the most honest expression for what most recent railroad issues are: viz., loans secured by a general or blanket mortgage on most, if not all, the railroad property, but subject to the prior liens which they ultimately refund.

General First Mortgage Bonds as a title is a misnomer. If it is a general mortgage it is not a first mortgage. The title is sometimes used when the amount of the underlying bonds is small and bonds of the general issue have been reserved in the hands of the trustee to retire them. But the proper title for this class is *General and First Mortgage Bonds*, or *First Lien and General Mortgage Bonds*.

First General Mortgage Bonds is, by interpretation, the first issue of General Mortgage Bonds. Since a second general issue is not likely, this is another of the equivocal titles.

Unifying Mortgage Bonds, as a title, with the usual derivatives, is virtually synonymous with *Consolidated*, or with *General Mort-*

gage Bonds. All three classes serve, in process of time, to simplify, in one general obligation and under one blanket mortgage, the miscellaneous lien-secured obligations of the company. That there may be no necessity in the near future of repeating the generalization of funded debt, bonds are usually reserved to pay for all improvements, extensions, etc., which are likely to be made for years to come. The issue, therefore, consolidates, unifies, or generalizes not only past, but also future capital requirements.

Although Income Bonds, by nature, are usually without lien security and interest is dependent entirely upon earnings, nevertheless some issues have property claim, in default of principal at maturity. Hence arise *Mortgage Income Bonds*.

Mortgage priority is clearly defined in *Second* and *Third Mortgage Bonds*. Although the second or third mortgage issue of one company may be superior to the first mortgage issue of another, and although the second or third divisional mortgage of one company may be superior to the first mortgage on another division of the same company, nevertheless the general order of preference on a given property, in default or liquidation, is the numerical order indicated in the title.

But the prospective purchaser of a bond to be bought on the basis of its closeness to the ground should remember two things: a general claim on the entire assets of a company will sometimes obtain readier recognition than a first claim on minor assets which are of themselves insufficient to satisfy that claim; and secondly, it is seldom good business to satisfy entirely the owners of the first mortgage bonds at the expense of the owners of the junior issues.

The extent to which the theoretical and legal priority will be satisfied depends very largely on the nature of the property. If it is convertible without too great sacrifice of its intrinsic value, —if for instance it is marketable real estate,—then the only hope for holders of junior mortgage bonds is that the property will realize a sum sufficiently in excess of the senior claim to satisfy them.

But it is usually the case that the property has value chiefly in connection with the purposes and business of the company pledging it. A railroad right of way is of little value except for transportation service; rails as scrap iron, and ties as lumber are almost worthless. Old freight cars are burned up. It doesn't pay to dismantle them for kindling wood. At foreclosure sale a railroad property must go to those who can run railroads. Investors cannot run railroads. Hence the necessity for comity among creditors and a reasonable compromise, even with stockholders.

The Refunding, General, and Consolidation Mortgage Bonds just discussed, are, when issued, usually Second or Third Mortgage Bonds on the major part of the property.

Second Refunding, Second Consolidated, and *Second General Mortgage Bonds,* each refer to the second issue of their kind by the one company. The need for these Seconds arises when ample provisions for extensions and betterments were not made in the provisions of the First Trust deed, and the Seconds will probably bear the same refunding relation of successorship and perform the same function as reserve funds, that the First Refunding, Consolidated, or General Bond bore to the underlying divisional liens. As yet this class is very rare.

Improvement Mortgage Bonds are of the same general nature as the bonds mentioned immediately above: they are both refunding and extension bonds. An issue is more likely to be entitled Extension than Improvement, when the chief reinforcement of the obligation is a mortgage on the newly-constructed or acquired property.

Improvement Mortgage Bonds should be distinguished from the municipal debentures called Improvement Bonds, issued for Public Improvement or specifically for Street Improvement.

Debenture Mortgage Bonds is a hybrid product, in essentials a mere promise to pay, but nominally secured by a junior lien on property of comparatively small value.

Mortgage Debentures as synonymous with Mortgage Bonds is a perfectly logical title in those countries which use the word debenture as practically synonymous with bonds in general, rather than with unsecured notes in particular.

CHAPTER XI

THE CLASSIFICATION AND DESCRIPTION OF BONDS: ACCORDING TO THE PURPOSE OR FUNCTION OF THE ISSUE

The third scheme of classification is according to the purpose for which the bonds were issued,—as expressed in the title of the bond. The detailed treatment accorded municipal issues and other civil loans, in Part II, makes it unnecessary to mention here more than a few issues of the municipal type. Bonds of this third class are noted most conveniently in alphabetical order.

Anticipation Tax Warrants is one of the many titles that is practically synonymous with Revenue Bonds, which see.

Bonus Bonds is a frank old-time title for securities issued by private corporations, as Land Grant Bonds frequently were, in payment for services rendered by promoters, et al., or to raise money for that payment; and by municipalities, as in the more specific case of Railroad Aid Bonds, to bring a railroad or manufacturing concern to a town. *Subsidy Bonds* is a more euphemistic expression than Bonus Bonds for the same general class of issues, when the proceeds reimburse a company for public service like the transportation of mails by steamships. Bonus Bonds of private corporations are looked upon with disapproval when they do not immediately represent a profit-bearing outlay, and may not increase the value of the property on which they are secured. Perhaps Municipal Bonus Bonds in general are more frequently open to charges of invalidity than Railroad Aid Bonds in particular. (See Founders' Bonds and Purchase Money Bonds.)

Charter Bonds are United States bonds purchased by a National Bank at the time of its incorporation, and deposited with the Treasurer of the United States that it may receive a federal charter to do business.

Construction Bonds is a term loosely applied to issues secured by property and plants in course of construction, before the company that issues them has an earning power of record. The term is applied with most force when it is the intention to refund the issue with a more permanent mortgage bond, either of new creation or of a general issue part of which is now in escrow for this purpose. Having reference to the character of the obligor, the bonds may be floated by a construction company, in anticipation of instalment payments on the plant or building. In this case they are probably serial notes, and like mechanics' liens, a charge on the plant prior to a regular first mortgage.

Continued Bonds is the variant for *Extended Bonds* and of less common use. In these the contract for payment has, by mutual agreement, been extended. The object on the part of the company may be to await a more propitious time for a new flotation. The fact of extension with any new terms, such as increased, or possibly reduced, interest, will be stamped or printed on the old bonds. The practice is steadily growing of extending rather than refunding issues, as a matter of mere financial expediency. It is thought that a larger proportion of the holders of the old bonds will take advantage of the "privilege" of extending their loan than would be the case if they were called upon to cancel their loan and reinvest on the same terms. New certificates, even, may be issued, and nothing of the old issue be left but the corpus of the old mortgage and the time-honored and familiar title.

Delinquent Tax Certificates, are of the municipal mortgage type. They are a first lien on land which has been sold in settlement of an arrearage of taxes. But since the former owner has the privilege of redeeming the property within a stated number of years, and since disputes may arise concerning the regularity of the sale, these certificates are more a speculation than an investment.

Drainage Bonds, as a distinct, quasi-municipal class, we treat in Chapter XXXVIII, under *Reclamation Issues*, but direct municipal obligations are often so entitled, when issued for drainage purposes.

Founders' Bonds (an English expression) may serve the same purpose as Bonus Bonds in corporation finance: to reimburse those who have undertaken the promotion of an enterprise. But again the purpose may be quite the other extreme: to pay the proprietor or founder for his interest in the company. The United States Steel Corporation First Collateral Trust 5s, issued in 1901, are in large part Founders' Bonds, for they were paid originally to Andrew Carnegie (cf. Purchase Money Bonds).

Funding Bonds represent the unification or consolidation of unfunded debt, of various informal notes, scrip, and other forms of floating indebtedness. Whether the obligations are of municipalities or private corporations, a floating debt has served its usefulness when it is found that the sum cannot be extinguished out of current revenues, and the bond market is favorable to flotations, for then a regular long-term funded issue can be put out at a lower rate of interest than these less permanent and perhaps less well-secured certificates of indebtedness. Funding Bonds should not be confused with Refunding Bonds.

Improvement Bonds, it has already been said, are quite distinct from Improvement Mortgage Bonds. The former are municipal debentures issued for any form of public improvement. They are sometimes special assessment bonds, and therefore may or may not be direct obligations of a municipal corporation proper.

For *Interim Certificates* see Temporary Bonds.

Judgment Bonds are another form of municipal debenture that share in the ill-favor of Special Assessment Bonds. This is because they are the product of litigation, usually respecting the validity of a debt. But if the municipality is able to pay, and the judgment has been obtained without fraud, the obligation should prove a safe investment.

For *Provisional Certificates* see Temporary Bonds.

Purchase Money Bonds perform the same function as Founders' Bonds: they are issued in full or part payment for a property or company. When for a property, it is probable they will be a lien on that property; when for a company it is probable that the stock will be pledged as security for the bonds, that in case the interest is not met, the company may revert to its former owners.

For *Railroad Aid Bonds*, see the Index.

Redemption Bonds are equivalent to Refunding Bonds; but a nice sense of word values might suggest the term *Redemption* for new issues that succeed called issues, and *Refunding* for issues that succeed matured issues. There is no connection between Redemption Bonds and Redeemable Bonds.

Renewal Bonds are virtually Extended Bonds, but the title may be used for Refunding Bonds.

Revenue Bonds, or *Notes*, provide municipalities with current funds to supply their needs until taxes or other income is collectible. *Tax Relief Bonds* is another title for the same class. Similarly *Arrearage Bonds* take care of deficits caused by tardiness in payments of taxes due.

School Bonds are usually emitted for the purchase, construction, and equipment of school property. Their standing in the investment world is somewhat better, perhaps, than any other class of municipals, except water bonds, for, although the object for which they are put forth is not revenue-producing, yet they represent, in the eyes of a community, the noblest purpose for which it can pledge its good faith.

Sewer Bonds may be cited as another class of municipals worthy of mention,—these in illustration particularly of the utter impossibility of cataloguing all bond titles. Among the subdivisions of sewer bonds one meets are *Sewer Trunk,* and *Intercepting Sewer Bonds.* There is little difference in legal standing between these many municipal issues, providing they are direct obligations of municipalities proper, and are payable out of unlimited taxes levied on all the property.

Subsidy Bonds. See Bonus Bonds.

Tax Arrearage Bonds. See Revenue Bonds.

Tax Relief Bonds. See Revenue Bonds.

Temporary Receipts, strictly speaking, are the formal acknowledgment by banking house, trust company, or issuing corporation, of the payment for a bond not yet prepared for delivery, and the promise to deliver the bond, when prepared, on surrender of the receipt at the proper offices.

Interim Certificates may signify the same thing as Temporary Receipts, or they may signify Temporary Bonds.

Temporary Bonds and *Interim Bonds* can be distinguished from Temporary Receipts in business parlance, for they are not merely acknowledgments of value received, but really substitutes for the more carefully engraved or lithographed, permanent, "definitive," instrument. The essential recitals which will appear on the face of the *Permanent Bond* will be typewritten or printed on the temporary bond. Temporary Receipts or Interim Certificates do not carry coupons, and perhaps the majority of Temporary Bonds do not; they carry merely the space to indorse interest payments in case an interest period should intervene before the definitive bonds were ready.

The issuance of Temporary Bonds (or Interim Certificates that are Temporary Bonds) is, or should be, specially authorized in the mortgage securing the regular bonds, for otherwise, when the Temporary Bonds were recalled, they, and the loan they represent, would be dead.

There is a broader application of the legal principle involved, that few Americans, even corporation lawyers, realize. Through a series of decisions the English courts have arrived at the conclusion that if a company hypothecates its own bonds to secure a loan, those bonds are issued.[1] Consequently, when the loan is paid, if the bonds come back into the possession of the company, they are redeemed. Since redemption increases the equity back of any bonds of the same issue that may be outstanding in the hands of the public, the company cannot reissue these hypothecated and redeemed bonds to make them rank *pari passu* with the previously outstanding bonds.

So far as we know the question has never been adjudicated in our courts, but the principle of law back of the English decisions seems indisputable. The holders of unhypothecated bonds could claim, in litigation, a position superior to holders of the bonds that had been hypothecated, redeemed, and reissued; and the American courts would undoubtedly follow the English decisions.

Temporary Bonds or Certificates may not have reference to or implication of a definite future issue of regular bonds. Receivers' Certificates are Temporary Certificates.

Water Bonds, and issues for many other purposes not specified here, are treated elsewhere in these pages; and to find them most readily the Index should be consulted.

[1] A bond, to be issued, must be not only signed and sealed, but delivered.

CHAPTER XII

THE CLASSIFICATION AND DESCRIPTION OF BONDS: ACCORDING TO CONDITIONS ATTENDING PAYMENT OF INTEREST OR PRINCIPAL

The fourth classification, relating to the payment of principal and interest, may be subdivided as follows:

(a) According to Payment of Interest:
Bonds of Unconditional Interest

Income Bonds $\left\{\begin{array}{l}\text{Cumulative}\\ \text{Non-Cumulative}\end{array}\right.$

Adjustment Bonds

Participating Bonds
Dividend-Sharing Bonds $\left.\right\}$ $\left\{\begin{array}{l}\text{Limited}\\ \text{Unlimited}\end{array}\right.$
Profit-Sharing Bonds

Registered Bonds
Registered Coupon Bonds
Coupon Bonds
Interchangeable Bonds
Tax-Receivable Bonds
$\left\{\begin{array}{l}\text{High-Rate Bonds}\\ \text{Low-Rate Bonds}\end{array}\right.$
$\left\{\begin{array}{l}\text{High-Yield Bonds}\\ \text{Low-Yield Bonds}\end{array}\right.$

(b) According to Payment of Principal:
Premium Bonds
Gold Bonds
Silver Bonds
Currency Bonds
Legal Tender Bonds

(c) According to Maturity of Principal:
Straight Bonds
Serial Bonds
Equal Instalment Bonds
Long-Term Bonds
Short-Term Bonds
Deferred Bonds
Extended Bonds
Perpetual Loans

(d) With Maturity at the Option of the Payor:
Redeemable Bonds
Callable Bonds
Optional Bonds
Irredeemable Bonds

(e) With Maturity at the Option of the Payee:
Optional (with the payee) Bonds or
Cash Surrender Bonds
Annuity Bonds
Endowment Bonds
Convertible Bonds

Division According to Payment of Interest. *Unconditional Interest* is hardly a title for a class of bonds; but it is a phrase descriptive of all issues the interest of which is obligatory as long as the company is solvent. Income, Adjustment Issues, and the like, are the only exceptions to bonds of unconditional interest.

Income Bonds already have been treated. Their peculiar characteristic is that the interest is dependent on the revenue of the obligor. Generally the trust deed stipulates that if the entire interest charge on the issue is not earned such portion as is earned shall be paid. Sometimes unpaid interest accumulates as a charge against future earnings. In this event the bonds are *Cumulative Income Bonds;* otherwise they are *Non-Cumulative.*

Adjustment Bonds is a title which nominally expresses a purpose and might at first seem to come under the third classification with more propriety: for they are issued to adjust a debt that has been compromised or adjudicated. The leading obligation of the kind is the Atchison Adjustment 4s of 1995. A reading of the trust deed will show that these are Mortgage Income Bonds, non-cumulative prior to July 1, 1900; but of course the mortgage could not be foreclosed until maturity. The use of the word Adjustment instead of Income is to avoid the more unpleasantly descriptive adjective.

Participating Bonds are, in a sense, the opposite of Income Bonds. In Income Bonds the interest paid may, without redress, run from a certain maximum rate down to nothing; whereas in Participating Bonds the income may run from a certain minimum to a certain maximum (in limited participation) or to whatever is earned (in unlimited participation). The participating bond has been rarely employed in this country; the only notable case has been that of the Union Pacific Railroad's Oregon Short Line Participating 4s issued in 1903 and retired in 1905, Participation bonds are very likely to be collateral trust, in the nature of the case; and the participation feature is conceded to offset possible deficiency in the collateral security, which is likely to be stock. When the dividend on this stock is more than sufficient to pay interest charges on the secured bonds, a portion of the surplus goes as a sort of dividend to the bondholders. Therefore bonds of this type are also sometimes called *Dividend Bonds* or *Profit Sharing Bonds;* but particularly when these issues are called Profit Sharing Bonds the indenture provides that a certain proportion of the company's entire net earnings shall go to the bondholders. Real Estate Debentures are often profit-sharing.

As to methods of collecting interest, and of transferring bonds, there are four classes: Registered, Registered Coupon, Coupon, and Interchangeable Bonds.

The ownership of *Registered Bonds* is evidenced by registration in the transfer office of the issuing company or government. Transfer of title is accomplished only by indorsement on the back of the instrument by the payee: i.e., the person in whose name it is registered. The bond must then be sent to the transfer office for re-registration.

For convenience in making sale, or for other reasons, it may be desirable to make a "transfer in blank:" i.e., the line destined for the name of the transferee or assignee may be left blank. The bonds then become payable to bearer. But, as in the case of stocks, the owner of the certificate, in the eyes of the company, is the person in whose name it is registered; and to this person the interest check will be mailed. Therefore it is desirable that transfers should be registered promptly.

Registered Coupon Bonds are bonds registered as to principal, but with interest coupons attached, which pass by delivery and are payable to bearer.

Coupon Bonds are negotiable instruments that ordinarily do not have on them the name of the owner. Therefore they pass from hand to hand like bank notes. Interest is paid on surrender of the coupons, clipped from the bonds—"little promissory notes," as they mature, one each interest day.

For many years it has been a common privilege to make coupon bonds convertible into registered bonds at the will of the owner. But only in recent years have registered bonds been frequently endowed with the privilege of conversion into coupon. When the bonds of an issue may be converted either way, at will, they are called *Interchangeable Bonds*. When an issue appears in both coupon and registered forms, and is actively dealt in, the results of interchangeability are attained by the sale of the one form and the purchase of the other. United States bonds, therefore, have the essential advantage of interchangeability; but since coupon bonds are in better demand than registered and sell at better prices, it is easier to convert coupon bonds into registered, without loss, than to reverse the exchange.

The distinct advantage of a registered bond is that payment of interest and principal can be stopped in the event of loss or theft. There is an increase in safety to the obligor, also. New York City lost about $200,000 a number of years ago, by making several payments for the same coupons.

The disadvantage of a registered bond to an investor is the inconvenience and expense attending its transfer. The expense, besides a possible registration fee, is the cost of shipment, including insurance and the loss of interest. Registered bonds, moreover, are more difficult to hypothecate.

Tax Receivables are civil coupon debentures, both state and municipal, the coupons of which are receivable (i.e., limited legal tender) in payment of taxes due the issuer. The legal tender provision enhances the security of interest quite independently of security of principal, for it gives the coupons a theoretically certain redemption value. Nevertheless, even tax-receivable bonds and their coupons have been repudiated. Needless to say, since the tax-receivable device is a bolster to poor credit, such municipals are seldom issued of late years.

The interest rate that issues bear gives rise to the self-explanatory designations *High Rate* and *Low Rate Bonds*. Those practiced in bond dealings can read much history into the interest rates of a state, city, or corporation. The rates prevailing on United States bonds, both long and short term, issued during our several wars, are a sufficient index of the mutable credit of the strongest governments.

In those states (and they are in the majority) that do not permit municipalities to sell their loans below par, it is possible to sense the growth in credit and the decline in interest rates for money, by noting the gradual decline in the interest rates borne by municipal loans. Much significant bond history is told in the City of Albany, N. Y., Washington Park Bonds, with gradually lowered interest rates from 7 per cent. in 1870 to 6s in 1875, to 5s in 1878, to 4s in 1880, to 2s in the money-drugged market of 1894, and up to $3\frac{1}{2}$s under the withdrawal of funds from investment channels in 1896.

High Yield and *Low Yield Bonds* do not necessarily correspond with High Rate and Low Rate. A 6 per cent. bond selling at a high premium may be of lower yield than a 3 per cent. bond selling at a discount. The whole matter of net yield is treated in Chapters XXXIX to XL, inclusive.

Division According to Payment of Principal. Several bond titles are derived from facts relating to the amount or character of the principal repaid. Frequently European government bonds and rarely American municipal and corporation issues must be retired at a premium. These are called *Premium Bonds*. New Orleans has a municipal issue of the kind. Bonds selling at a premium are also called Premium Bonds; and bonds selling at a discount are called Discount Bonds.

As to the funds acceptable in payment at maturity, *Gold Bonds* call for payment in gold "of the present standard of weight and fineness," if demanded. *Silver Bonds* are practically unknown to us, although common enough in the past in countries that had a silver standard. *Currency Bonds* are payable in currency: i.e., may be paid in anything that is a legal tender, including paper money. *Legal Tender Bonds* is a title practically synonymous with the preceding.

Currency or legal tender bonds are usually internal issues. Since the war many of them, such as German or French obligations, have depreciated sharply. International bonds are payable not in one but in several currencies. The Brazilian 5 per cent. loan of 1895 was payable in sterling, francs and marks at the current rate of exchange. Such international bonds could also be payable at a fixed rate of exchange as the Argentine 4 per cent. loan of 1908 which was payable in London, Buenos Aires, Paris and Berlin at fixed exchange of 48d per $1., 25 francs per pound, and 20 marks per pound respectively.

If there is a difference in the value of the several kinds of currency the bondholder will be given the least valuable. If it were certain that this country would always maintain a gold standard, no importance could be attached to the title *Gold Bonds*. The weaker an issue is the more emphasis laid on the word *gold*.

Division According to Maturity of Principal. Relative to the amount of an issue that matures at any one time we have Straight, Serial, Instalment, and Equal Instalment issues.

"Straight" Bonds are by far the commonest. They are issues that nominally mature all at one time, although they may be redeemable in whole or in part before the ultimate maturity date.

Serial Bonds are issues that are retired in regular instalments. If serial the presumption is a reasonable uniformity in amount retired each period and in the interval between periods. Serial retirement does away with the necessity for sinking funds, and therefore is the most economical way to attain the maximum of assurance through amortization. The serial principle is explained in the chapters on Equipment Bonds and Municipal Bonds.

Equal Instalment Bonds (generally *Equal Annual Instalment Bonds*) carry the serial retirement principle to its ultimate refinement: namely, that the amount of principal and interest to be paid each period shall be such that the periodical cost to the obligor shall not vary. Since the interest charge lessens with the decrease in principal, that part of the total periodical payment which is the repayment of principal, grows constantly larger. In order that it may not be necessary to issue bonds of odd denominations, the equal periodic instalment payment may be approximated at each interest period, to the nearest $1,000 or $500 piece, according to the denomination of the issue. If the issue is of any size this approximation will distribute the burden of repayment with sufficient uniformity for all practical purposes.

Thus far Equal Instalment bonds have had their greatest vogue among Canadian municipalities, although some American industrial obligations are of the class.

Long-Term Bonds and *Short-Term Bonds* are self-explanatory terms. The conditions governing the expediency of issuing and purchasing the one or the other are treated in various places throughout these pages as indexed. Sufficient here that most short-term loans are an emergency resource on the part of the obligor—from the short-time notes of the Federal Government issued by Secretary Chase during the Civil War, to the railroad and industrial notes that are put forth when money rates are high, pending the time that long term loans will be accepted at rates of interest advantageous to the corporation. Commercial paper is the species of short-term obligation that is founded on the best principles of credit.

As far as the expression "deferred" is applied to bonds it must signify what it does in deferred stocks—in antithesis to preferred stocks—the postponement of payments. *Deferred Bonds*, then, are such as do not receive interest, or at least the maximum interest they are to receive, until certain conditions have been fulfilled respecting earnings, or an interval of time. Income Bonds, therefore, are potentially of the Deferred class. Austin, Texas, Refunding bonds of 1931, bear 3 per cent. interest for the first five years, 4 per cent. for the next 10 years, but the maximum 5 per cent. is deferred until the last 15 years. Respecting the functions this issue performs, it is Refunding, Adjustment, and Deferred.

When the payment of the *principal* is deferred, but there is no change in the status of the mortgage or other security, the issue may be called Extended. New *Extended Bonds*, with the proper number of coupons, may be created to replace the old bonds, or the facts and terms of the extension, with the changed interest rate, if there has been a change, may be stamped or printed on the old bonds.

Perpetual, or *Indeterminate* Loans are another class with a self-explanatory title, which has been discussed elsewhere in this book. If they are coupon-bearing, the bonds will probably be replaced with new paper when the coupons on the old bonds are exhausted. The Public Service Corporation of New Jersey has outstanding Perpetual, Deferred, Interest-bearing Stock Trust Certificates.

Division According to Maturity as Affected by the Payor's Option. *Redeemable, Callable,* or *Optional Bonds* are so entitled because the maturity of the loan is affected by the payor's right to retire the obligation before the obligatory maturity date. But the privilege to retire usually can be exercised only on an interest day or after some weeks' notice. The redemption feature is considered a disadvantage to the investor, particularly in municipal loans, which are usually retirable at par;[1] but when the bonds may not be redeemed except at a premium sufficiently high so that the proceeds may be invested in another instrument

---

[1] An exception is the Cabell Co., W. Va. Court House and Bridge bonds, redeemable 6,000 yearly at 102.

of like safety but with greater returns, no real disadvantage exists.

Although the privilege of redemption may permit a company to refund its debts at a lower rate of interest when its credit becomes greater, or when it can, by so doing, avail itself of lower interest rates, it is not solely for such purposes that this right is reserved;—but rather to place the company in a position to consolidate its mortgages, reorganize its affairs, or to change its scheme of financing in any other way that may seem desirable.

Since the net return from a redeemable investment depends on the length of time the loan has to run, and the redemption value, it is desirable to establish certain rules for the guidance of those who seek this net return. The rules are given in the chapter on the *Use of the Bond Tables*.

Issues that may not be called by the payor are *Irredeemable Bonds*. To avoid confusion the denotation of Irredeemable Bonds should not be extended, as it commonly is, to cover what we entitle here Perpetual or Indeterminate Loans.

Division According to Maturity as Affected by the Payee's Option. Under certain circumstances a loan may be terminated at the option of the payee as well as of the payor. In the effort to make real estate bonds marketable, real estate companies sometimes give their bonds "cash surrender value," as it is called in insurance. That is to say, after a period, which may be two years, the purchaser may return his bond and receive the cost price plus perhaps 3 per cent. per annum after deducting what has been paid him in interest. Since the interest he has received is always more than 3 per cent. this provision is tantamount to an agreement on the part of the company to repurchase the bonds at a discount which increases as the loan grows old.

The authors know of no title by which this class has been denominated. They are *Optional* as regards the payee, but this term offers no distinguishment from bonds Optional or Redeemable by the payor. In want of a better suggestion, the authors venture to submit the title *Cash Surrender Bonds*.

Convertible Issues as a form of bonus bonds were common enough in railroad finance in the sixties and seventies, and are now revived to a greater popularity than ever, not only among the railroads, but among many other kinds of corporations. The bonds are convertible generally into other securities of the same corporation, but sometimes into the securities of another corporation. Or again, the bonds are commonly convertible into stock; but occasionally, if unsecured (i.e., notes or debentures), or if not sufficiently secured they may be convertible into secured bonds as in the case of the Hudson Companies' two issues of Convertible (Collateral) 6 per cent. Notes.

When it is the intention to convert bonds into stock it must not be forgotten that conversion is seldom possible when the transfer books are closed; also that accrued dividend, as well as accrued interest, must be reckoned, unless the dividend and interest fall on the same date, or are of the same rate; and that one selling and one purchasing commission must be paid.

To complicate matters further, different companies have different ways of figuring accrued dividend;—it may be from the payment of the last dividend, or from the declaration of the present. Furthermore, there is no general custom regarding the treatment of fractional shares, when at the conversion price the bond is not a multiple of the stock.

Fewer difficulties are met in converting bonds or stocks into other bonds, for interest dates almost invariably coincide. Therefore there is only the probability of an adjustment for difference in interest rate.[1]

The basis of the popularity of issues convertible *into stock* is the genuine alliance in them of investment and speculative virtues. It is as if for once oil and water would mix. As an investment these bonds are to be judged like any other corporate obligation,—quite irrespective of the convertible feature. It will be found that they are usually debentures, or at best, junior liens. Sometimes, however, they are the sole or major obligation of the issuer.

As a speculation, an issue convertible into stock will advance with the stock—there is no limit when the stock reaches the price at which the bonds are convertible and until and unless the company has the right to retire the issue and exercises that right. On the other hand, however low the stock may fall, the bonds will not decline below their true investment value as an obligation of the company; and they may not decline even to the investment level because of the potential speculative value of the conversion

[1] For further details and helpful tables consult the excellent work, *Convertible Securities*, Montgomery Rollins, Boston, 1909.

privilege. It is not, of course, necessary to convert the bonds to realize profits. The sale of the bonds themselves will probably suffice.

Bonds convertible into stock, but especially convertible bonds of industrial and other corporations that have for sale a commodity which is not restricted by law or custom as to price, have possibly an advantage over other bonds in case the increase in the world's supply of gold shall lessen the purchasing power of money. For, as the purchasing power of money declines, and commodities advance in price, the corporations prosper that control or manufacture commodities, and the stocks of those corporations increase in value. As the purchasing power of money declines, so also the purchasing power or value of a fixed sum like bond interest or principal. But the convertible bondholder is prepared for either event: the increase in the value of money or of commodities. Therefore, as the saying is, "heads he wins with the stock, and tails he wins with the bond."

PART II
CIVIL LOANS

CHAPTER XIII

NATURE OF CIVIL LOANS

The Tax Power. For the broad divisions of this text it is well to establish the phrase or title most aptly descriptive of the obligations issued by all forms of government,—whether sovereign powers, federated or subsidiary states, or the various political subdivisions of the state down to such unincorporated and informally administered entities as school and fire districts. There is one characteristic of all such bonds that distinguishes them from all others: they are sustained, and ultimately retired, by the exercise of the power of taxation. They may have other forms of security common to other types of bonds, such as the direct pledge of the issuer, a lien on physical property or on intangible property, and a prior claim on certain revenues, but the ultimate security, the characteristic security of this class is the tax power. These issues in the earlier editions we chose to call "Civil Loans," and the title has met with acceptance.

Sovereignty. As the tax power is the economic characteristic common to all civil loans, so the grace of sovereignty is a legal characteristic of most of these loans. This condition of the state has been defined by Story as "the supreme, absolute, uncontrollable power, the *jus summi imperii*, the absolute right to govern." To investment the significance of sovereignty, is that a sovereign state is "judge of its own competence," and "a sovereign cannot be sued in his own courts without his consent. His own dignity, as well as the dignity of the nation which he represents, usually prevents his appearance to answer a suit against him in the courts of another sovereignty, except in performance of his obligations, by treaty or otherwise voluntary assumed."[1] We shall observe hereafter that civil divisions of a state are incompletely possessed of sovereignty and are subject to the redress of suit.

External and Internal Loans. There is an informal division of all types of civil loans, whether domestic or foreign, whether international, national, state, municipal or district,—namely into external and internal loans. In the early stages of government

---

[1] United States vs. Dickelman, 92 U. S. 520.

debt history, national loans were predominently internal, issued at the instance of the sovereign ruler to fund casual and current obligations, and offered to or forced on subject institutions, companies or individuals at a stage in the country's fiscal development when international confidence would not necessarily admit of flotation abroad.   Instances are the early British, French, and Austrian national debts.   In fact all the British national debts after the seventeenth century were internal until the unprecedented credit demands of the World War led to the issuance of the Anglo-French $5\frac{1}{2}$s which were not only the first external loan but also the first joint, or international, obligation.

The youth of the United States occurred in a sophisticated stage in national credit.   Therefore we were able to obtain many of our earliest accommodations from without the national boundaries,—from France, Spain, and Holland.   Later our states, also, in certain cases of internal financial impecuniosity, were able to borrow outside of the country—in England and Holland,—when they could not borrow either at all within, or else at much less advantageous terms.

This situation raises the question as to whether an extraterritorial borrowing by a state, if a sovereign power or if not, should be considered an external loan, provided the funds emanate from within the limits of the larger national domain.   When a state within our union emits an issue that is more acceptable to markets elsewhere in the United States than within itself, we should not consider that an external loan, for usually there would be no hindrances in the terms of issue or sale to its purchase locally.   This would apply equally to the issues of any province of Canada that was to be absorbed within the Dominion of Canada.   But probably there will be general consent to the designation of "external loan" to any issue of any province or of the Dominion itself that was destined for placement in the United Kingdom or elsewhere in the British Empire.   Certainly an issue of any of the provinces, or of the Dominion, primarily destined for placement in the United States or in any other foreign country is an external loan.

The primary incentive for an external loan is the fact of a better market for its absorption without the borders of the issuer than within.   A secondary incentive may be the desire to strengthen mercantile relations between the borrower and the lender. Both of these considerations are basic in the development of England's foreign fiscal policy. The World War has occasioned the greatest upheaval of credit in history. It has caused the issuance of external loans of England to other nations, and of ourselves to England and other nations in unprecedented amount and character.

Characteristics of External Loans. 1. The chief differentiation between an external and an internal loan, other than the situs of its placement is the medium of payment. It is almost always payable in the soundest currency of the lending country. In the United States it is payable in gold dollars of the present standard of weight and fineness.

2. Principal and interest are usually payable within the creditor country.

3. The price and interest rate and terms of sale are adapted to the customs and requirements of that country.

4. Specific security is at times offered in the form of liens on property, customs duties, or other revenues of the debtor or guarantees of a debtor with better credit.

5. Historically, nations have been wont to consider their external obligations as prior to their internals, in order to maintain their international credit, and to avoid military and commercial reprisals. But exceptions to this spirit will be found in the history of some of the Balkan nations, some of the American states and Russia.

6. External loans foster commercial and political intercourse.

Characteristics of Internal Loans. Internal loans, on the other hand, particularly in the adolescent period of a nation's public financing, or in time of national crisis are often payable in irredeemable paper currency, and the currency is likely to be "uncovered," i.e., not secured in whole or in part by specie into which the currency is convertible on demand. This paper is usually subject to great depreciation in value through inflation on inflation. If these loans are issued at rates of interest advantageous to the debtor's subjects, there is temptation later on when credit is improved and interest rates decline to force a refunding operation, or a "consolidation" of several high-rate issues, into a lower interest rate issue of "consols."

Purposes of Civil Loans. Civil loans may also be grouped according to the purpose for which they are issued. They may be raised either to alleviate government deficits or to undertake public works. Deficits may be of a casual or of an emergency nature. Revenues may unexpectedly diminish or expenses may increase beyond anticipation. A resulting deficit may then be met by borrowing. Casual borrowing differs from an emergency indebtedness only in the urgency of the fiscal need. Emergency loans may be raised when a state is subjected to a calamitous flood, earthquake, war, or revolution.

Public works may be commercial or non-commercial. The erection of a power plant or the building of a railway from state funds would be the undertaking of a commercial public work. But the construction of a courthouse or a school building would not add directly to the revenues of the state, and would be regarded as non-commercial in nature.

Maturity. All classes of loans may be grouped according to their duration. Yet civil loans in this respect have peculiar features. On the one hand the state may borrow in the form of very short-term obligations, as in the case of municipal warrants, certificates of indebtedness, and treasury bills. But at the same time a state may also borrow on obligations which have no date of maturity. These so-called perpetual obligations have been quite common on the Continent where the policy of debt repayment has not been followed as in the case of England and the United States. France has outstanding her "rentes perpetuelles," Italy her five's of 1917, and Germany her various "Unkundbar" war loans. These perpetual obligations rest on the principle of a permanent debt that in turn is based on the political theory that the life of the state is eternal.

CHAPTER XIV

FOREIGN CIVIL LOANS

The subject of Civil Loans was introduced in the previous editions by stating that "the scope of this work does not bring us into the general field of government securities as investments. It is perhaps as profound a subject as any in the category of finance.—For the purpose of an elementary treatise on the principles of bond investment it is sufficient to confine the discussion to the desirability of United States government bonds for private purchase." Since the first edition, in 1911, the United States has changed from the world's greatest debtor to its leading creditor. Our foreign investments in recent years are estimated by the Government as follows:

ESTIMATED VALUE OF AMERICAN INVESTMENTS ABROAD AT END OF CALENDAR YEARS 1923, 1924, AND 1925

(Report of U. S. Dept. of Commerce on *The Balance of Payments in 1925*, p. 15)
[Millions of dollars]

Regions	Government-guaranteed Obligations	Industrial Securities and Direct Investments	Total
At end of 1923 (revised):			
Europe	950	350	1,300
Latin America	610	3,150	3,760
Canada and Newfoundland	1,050	1,400	2,450
Asia, Australia, Africa, and rest of world	360	235	595
Total	2,670	5,485	8,105
At end of 1924 (revised):			
Europe	1,500	400	1,900
Latin America	840	3,200	4,040
Canada and Newfoundland	1,100	1,500	2,600
Asia, Australia, Africa, and rest of world	440	250	690
Total	3,880	5,350	9,230
At end of 1925:			
Europe	1,825	675	2,500
Latin America	910	3,300	4,210
Canada and Newfoundland	1,175	1,650	2,825
Asia, Australia, Africa, and rest of world	520	350	870
Total	4,430	5,975	10,405

It is still not inappropriate to omit detailed treatment of the bonds of foreign corporations; but to overlook hereafter the subject of foreign Civil Loans is to neglect one of the most important financial problems that now confronts not only this republic but the world. In terms of par value the greater importance of foreign government as against corporate issues is seen in the following table:

DOMESTIC AND FOREIGN LISTINGS

As of Jan. 1st, 1926

(Report of the President of the New York Stock Exchange, 1925, p. 41.)

SECURITY	No. of Issues	% to Total Issues	Market Value	% to Value Total
U. S. Gov't........	78	3.24	$17,852,191,833	25.50
Foreign Gov't......	116	4.81	3,024,726,064	4.32
U. S. Corp'ns......	2,126	88.22	47,726,990,765	68.19
Foreign Corp'ns....	90	3.73	1,394,529,921	1.99
Total..........	2,410	100.00%	$69,998,438,583	100.00%

In appraising the value of foreign government bonds, we are moved mainly by the same considerations that control our judgment of domestic civil loans. As far as these considerations are common to all civil loans,—both domestic and foreign—it is more appropriate to canvass them in detail in connection with our own issues. Therefore they will be found elaborated in the chapters that follow, particularly those on *State Bonds* and *Municipal Bonds*.

But there are certain well-defined problems connected with wise investment of funds in foreign loans that prospective purchasers should always have before them. With these we are concerned here.

We repeat, and later shall emphasize again, that the obligations of sovereign powers are not enforceable against them in the very nature of their sovereignty. Since there can be no recourse to superior political or legal power, but merely to force of arms, the inherent business honesty of a nation is of greater relative importance than in the case of debtor political subdivisions or of private corporations.

INTANGIBLE ASSETS

The Gauge of Government Credit. This is a reminder that, for convenience of thinking, the aspects of security for government bonds have two broad divisions, first with respect to the character of the debtor nation, and second with respect to its physical and pecuniary resources. We often speak of the character of a person as his chief business asset. It is, so to speak, an immaterial or intangible asset. His material or tangible assets complete his resources. The two together comprise his credit. It is so with a nation. The credit of the nation at any time is the sum of its tangible and intangible assets.

In the case of government credit, there is little doubt of the greater importance of the intangible asset of character than of any tangible asset such as pledged collateral. This thought has been well expressed by Mr. Dwight Morrow in the following words:

"What then is the security for a foreign government loan? The answer is clear. Loans are made to foreign governments in reliance primarily upon the good faith of those governments. The intelligent investor recognizes that in the long run of government that defaults upon its obligations hurts itself even more than it hurts its creditors. Even where specific taxes or customs are allocated for the service of a loan the main reliance of the creditor must be upon the desire of the debtor government to see the particular revenues maintained and made available.

"Even where a foreign expert is placed in charge of revenues the arrangement is helpful only when made with the hearty concurrence of the debtor government, and with the belief and expectation on the part of the debtor government that the fiscal arrangement will rebound to its own advantages." [1]

Nevertheless the attitude of nations toward the payment of debts is ultimately determined by their ability to pay. That is to say the condition of their tangible assets governs almost to the point of predomination their moral condition. A review of the financial history of the two dozen more important nations fails to show many instances of default in meeting the maturity of interest or principal with payment of the promised kind, unless under the load of staggering burdens. In fact, in the 30-year period, from 1882 to 1911, of an average value of $32,500,-000,000 in foreign government bonds outstanding, only $126,-000,000 or .39 per cent. on the average were in default. Within the same period, American railroads were in default to the extent of 1.84 per cent. and American industrials 2.07 per cent. [2]

We shall presently find in surveying the debt history of our

[1] *Foreign Security Investor*, April 28, 1926, p. 13.

[2] Statement by Thomas Lamont in the *Annals of the American Academy of Political and Social Science*, Vol. 88, p. 123.

own states that a low standard of business ethics in certain sections of the country in certain periods in our history affected state credit and the realization of state debts only when the debt burden became distressing.

But this is merely stating that a morally weak character is delinquent under temptation which a morally strong character may resist. In the course of several generations (mindful of the government debts like the British Consolidated Annuities and the French rentes that are without date of maturity) the temptation to mitigate or repudiate obligations has been presented to every civilized power, and probably will be presented as long as history is made. The moral resistance may be appraised from the *racial characteristics* of the several nations, from these characteristics as expressed in the *history of the national debts*, and more broadly still from the *international repute* of each.

From the credit point of view, the intangible assets of a nation may be studied in three parts, viz: racial characteristics, debt history, and international repute.

Racial Characteristics. It would be invidious and presumably untrustworthy to specify certain nations as possessed of traits that make for fulfilment of promises. Some have pointed to the Teutonic nations, or generally to nations in the colder northern climes, as borrowers at low interest rates. In the United States this general distinction will be seen to have held good in the history of state debts in earlier days. But it is a question whether, after all, the distinction is so fundamental as to race or climate, but rather to mercantile development. In general it is good business to be honest, but it takes a good business man to see it. It would be difficult to convince Americans that the Chinese merchants or the Chinese people are less honest than the Japanese, but the latter, *as a race*, have attained a more highly developed national consciousness, national solidarity, and therefore a sense of the importance of national credit. If their chief racial characteristic is imitativeness, they have imitated the commercial development of the Occident and the establishment of national credit that is a concomitant.

The republics of Central and South America are peopled by mixed races, of course, but with predominance of Latin strains. The handling of government loans in these republics, and the national credits are affected by the commercial characteristics of the Latin races. These distinctions will become less marked in process of time, as in the Old South, by the development of the commercial and financial sense of the several nations.

Social Character. National credit is affected by social character, i.e., the general intelligence of the population and the kind of occupations in which they are engaged. Statistics on illiteracy and other data on the extent of popular education have a direct bearing on national credit. It is also well to ascertain whether a country is predominately agricultural or whether it derives the major part of its income from manufacture or commerce. One must be mindful that commerce is most productive of wealth, manufacture next, and agriculture least.

Political Character. The credit of a nation is measurably determined by its political character, that is, by the ability of its population to govern itself. In some countries the ruling power rests in the hands of a few and their removal might cause political chaos. In others, like England or Sweden, government rests on a broad basis, the instinct for self-government is general and party changes matter little in the administration of affairs.

The international political character of a state deserves careful study on the part of the prospective owner of its obligations. If the borders of the state have been won by the sword and are maintained only by means of expensive military establishments or complicated foreign alliances, its credit position suffers. It is more assuring when boundaries have been fixed for years by the force of economics or geography.

History of National Debts. The history of foreign government loans as manifestations of national good faith and indices of intangible security for bonds is not reassuring, unless studied with a proper sense of proportion. The chapter on *United States Bonds* will show that we ourselves have stumbled. The various "consolidations" of national debts in Great Britain (from which is derived the famous "British Consols") from the seventeenth century on were usually nothing more than reductions in interest rate more or less forced by the power of sovereignty from which there is no appeal, on unwilling but helpless creditors and bondholders. In the course of time not only were face interest rates reduced from 8 per cent. or more to $2\frac{1}{2}$ per cent., but other investment features were altered, irredeemable annuities were made redeemable and debts secured by specific liens were converted into unsecured obligations. All these changes were not necessarily forced. Creditors who would not accept reduced terms were generally paid off: but the same sort of pressure that is now brought to bear on recalcitrant bondholders in corporate reorganization was exerted to accomplish reduction of principal and interest. Yet for a hundred years the credit of England has led the world.

Less creditable has been the history of France. From early in the fifteenth century until the middle of the nineteenth there was a succession of forced "conversions" i.e., reductions of the principal of debts and of the rate of interest paid. Finance ministers rose and fell in accordance with their ability or willingness to repudiate the national debts.

Yet during the last century the credit of France has been second only to England.

Austria's record is worse than that of France. From the eighteenth century national bankruptcy succeeded national bankruptcy. Forced conversions of debt into bank notes and other quasi-private paper repeatedly decimated the acknowledged obligations. But for generations before the Great War, Austrian rentes sold on a basis of net return generally accorded very high grade securities.[1] How short is the public memory!

Germany, Italy, and Japan are of too recent origin as nationals for historical comparison. Russia during the nineteenth century had more or less compromise of internal debt, due to the fact that these loans were payable in fiat money that depreciated as it inflated, but the external loans (largely held in France) were met until the overthrow of the monarchy and the ascension of the Soviet Government.

Before the World War American investors were accustomed to the purchase of the bonds of the Dominion of Canada, of Mexico, and of some of the South American republics of which Brazil, Argentina, and Chile have been the principal.

In contrast to the leading countries of Europe the credit of South American states has been inferior to that warranted by the facts. Few realize that the leading states have a credit history as nationals as long and on the whole nearly as satisfactory as that of Italy, Japan, and China. Both Chile and

[1] For an excellent history of national bankruptcy, see Manes, A., *Staatsbankrotte*. (Berlin, 1922).

Brazil had made substantial loans in England decades before any of these three countries had negotiated a foreign loan. Revolutions in South America are a stock and fertile theme in our literature, holding a place out of all proportion to their political importance, especially within recent years.

If then, one will make a comparison on the basis of the investment principles established in these chapters on Civil Loans, of the debt history of Argentina, Brazil, Chile, Peru, Bolivia, Paraguay, and Uruguay with that of representative states of North America, he will be satisfied that the intangible aspects of governmental credit are fully as assuring among them as were those of our Northern states in the first half of the nineteenth century and our Southern states in the latter half; and that with the closer relationships between countries which recent inventions and closer commercial intercourse make inevitable, the stabilizing of national credits in South America will proceed very rapidly.[1]

TANGIBLE ASSETS

The tangible assets may be either general or special. General assets may be either fixed or current. Nations may possess extensive fixed assets of natural resources in the form of minerals, waterfalls, or forests. These should be lightly treated in the appraising of the national obligations except in so far as they are actually worked. They have less bearing on the security of invested principal than have undeveloped mineral assets on the mortgage bonds of a mining company. Of far greater importance are current fixed assets such as the extent of railway development, of telegraph communication or of land cultivation. A borrowing government may find its credit position so low that it cannot obtain funds on its unsupported word and must pledge particular assets. A special asset may consist of a lien on either collateral or on the revenues of the state. This collateral may be either commercial (as coffee pledged for the various Brazilian loans) or security as the stocks and bonds pledged under the French two-year $5\frac{1}{2}$ per cent. loan of 1917. Usually the lien is based on revenues derived from taxes, rates, or fees. The German 7 per cent. external loan due 1949 is secured by revenues from taxes on luxuries and duties on imports.

[1] For detailed statement of South American defaults, see the Annual Reports of the Council of the Corporation of Foreign Bondholders.

Guaranties may be given by a stronger state in order to enable a weaker to float a loan. These guaranties may be either virtual or actual. A virtual guaranty is implied and not expressed. Thus, the Kingdom of Holland is virtual guarantor of the various loans floated by the Dutch Indies in the New York market. On the other hand, actual or direct guaranties have been given, as in the case of the Austrian Government external 7 per cent. loan, endorsed by a number of signatory powers which agree to make good a portion of the issue in case of default. This loan may be regarded as an example of an actual guaranty of the single type. An illustration of a joint and several guaranty is the Greek $2\frac{1}{2}$ per cent. loan of 1898 which is guaranteed by Great Britain, France, and Russia.

Validity. Validity of foreign issues placed in this country is a matter which requires careful consideration due in part to the uncertain political conditions that have followed the War. Questions of validity are twofold: has the agent of the borrower the right to bind his principal? Agents are either special or general. Special agents are given authority to negotiate for a foreign state under strict limitations as to terms and time within which the dealings must be completed. Bankers negotiating with such agents should examine their power of attorney. General agents have more latitude, notably the large banking houses acting for the British colonies.

The more important question is the right of the principal itself to borrow. In general a sovereign state can borrow only in accordance with its constitution, or the acts of its legislature, and these should be closely scanned. The nation, in turn, usually exercises strict control over the international borrowings of its civil divisions. In this respect, foreign countries differ from the United States which exerts no restraint on the borrowing operations of its component states. A province in Austria must obtain the consent of the Federal Government, and in France cities must seek the permission of the nation. In fact, French private companies—railroads or power plants—cannot borrow abroad unless the state has granted permission.

The leading creditor nations of the pre-war period, England, France, and Germany, are no longer able to meet the demands of the world for financial assistance. The United States has passed out of the stage of greatest capital expenditure for development of its own resources and therefore the domestic demand for capital is not so insistent as in the past. Therefore it has definitely embarked on a course of foreign investments, forced by post-war economic conditions. The new policy requires careful study of foreign conditions in order to judge accurately the true credit position of alien debtors.

The large banking houses of New York City in recent years have established close connections in foreign lands and have developed extensive sources of information. The Investment Bankers Association, through its committee on Foreign Securities, has sought to advance the knowledge of foreign investments and in 1926 established the Institute of International Finance. This organization acts as a clearing house for information on foreign investments. Data are gathered from sources abroad and in New York, and the material is made available to dealers and investors interested in foreign bonds.

CHAPTER XV

UNITED STATES BONDS

The bonds of the United States Government represent the nearest approach to pure investment; the element of delay or uncertainty concerning the payment of the investment contracts respecting interest or principal seems at a minimum. The obligations of this government are therefore the standard by which all other forms of investment may be measured. Nevertheless, in the United States, there is probably greater confidence in and respect for the integrity of our federal obligations than is warranted by the lessons and perspective of history. Our government has no innate superior morality; it is notoriously lax in meeting other forms of financial obligations not represented by funded debt. But the funded debt is relatively safe. The government bonds are a relatively pure investment because we happen at this time to be a nation of sound commercial instincts with a well-grounded government, and with enormous wealth and strong international position.

The United States Bonded Debt. In general a government may adopt one of two policies regarding its public debt: to allow the debt to run even unto perpetuity or to repay it. Many European countries have throughout their history accepted the political doctrine that the state is perpetual and have had no policy of debt repayment. In many cases their loans bear no date of maturity and are so-called perpetual debts. The United States always has subscribed to the policy of redeeming its public obligations at the earliest time possible. Alexander Hamilton, in establishing the principles that have governed the debt policy of this government, said: "as the vicissitudes of nations beget a perpetual tendency to the accumulation of debt, there ought to be in every government a perpetual, anxious and increasing effort to reduce that which at any time exists as fast as shall be practical consistently with integrity and good faith." Again in the dark days of the Civil War Salmon P. Chase, then Secretary of the Treasury, laid down the following policy for regulating the public debt: " It will hardly be disputed that in every sound system of finance adequate provision by taxation for the prompt discharge of all ordinary demands, for the punctual payment of the interest on loans, and for the creation of a gradually increasing fund for the redemption of the principal, is indispensable. Public credit can only be supported by public faith and public faith can only be maintained by an economical, energetic and prudent administration of public affairs and by the prompt and punctual fulfillment of every public obligation." [1]

The same policy of debt-repayment has been closely adhered to by subsequent secretaries of the treasury, particularly Andrew Mellon in whose secretaryship the war debt was greatly reduced. Probably history will declare that one of the outstanding credits to the Coolidge administration was achievement of economy in the operation of the Federal Government when excess wealth, revenues, and prosperity and the example of the civil subdivisions of the state, and the example of the people led most naturally to profligate spending.

Funding of the Revolutionary Debt. The Revolutionary War was financed in large part through domestic and foreign loans made by the State Assemblies and the Continental Congress. Due to the political weakness of the Confederation, these debts were unpaid both as to interest and principal. When the Constitutional Government came into power these debts with arrears amounted to the following:

Foreign debt	$12,556,874
Domestic debt of the Confederation	40,256,802
Domestic debts of the states	19,962,219
	$72,775,895

As part of his financial program, Alexander Hamilton caused to be adopted by Congress, in the Funding Act of August 4, 1790, a plan for refunding these obligations. In fine, the various domestic and foreign obligations of the states and of the Confederation were taken over by the new government through the sale of stock at home and through loans placed abroad, particularly in Holland.

Finances from the Revolution to the Civil War. From this period until the Civil War, the size of the national debt alter-

---

[1] Quoted from Harvey Fisk, *Our Public Debt.*

nately rose and fell. The purchase of Louisiana added $11,250,-000 to the National Debt which in 1804 amounted to $86,427,120. However, through the operation of the sinking fund plan devised by Hamilton, the debt was reduced to $45,200,000 by 1811. The War of 1812 came upon the United States at a time when the country was financially unprepared. Little effort was made to raise money from taxes. The reliance was mainly on public credit. As a result the public debt rose to $127,334,933 in 1816. The growing revenues of the government in time reduced this amount, but the Mexican War added $50,000,000 to the national indebtedness. Again it was reduced through the application of large public returns, and by 1857 the outstanding obligations of the United States totalled only $10,000,000.

Civil War Finance. All these earlier financial operations of the United States dwarfed into insignificance with the outbreak of the Civil War. As in the War of 1812 the government obtained only a small part of the needed funds from taxation. In fact the normal revenues of the Federal Government in the pre-war period were never well developed, and in 1860 had yielded only $80,000,000. The war was therefore financed largely by the issue of legal-tender notes and bonds.

These obligations have been summarized by Professor Davis R. Dewey in his, *Financial History of the United States* (p. 316) as follows:

Long-term loans	$1,044,600,000
Interest-bearing notes	890,300,000
Non-interest-bearing notes	458,100,000
Temporary loans	207,700,000
	$2,600,700,000

Of the first group the most important were the so-called " five-twenties " which were redeemable in five, and payable in 'twenty years. These bore an interest rate of 6 per cent. and were payable in gold coin. The second group included the " seven-thirties " so named because they carried an interest of 7.30 per cent. or 2 cents a day on every $100 bond. The interest was payable in paper currency and not in gold coin. Although these notes were interest-bearing and had a definite date of maturity, the government also issued non-interest-bearing obligations in the form of the legal-tender notes mentioned above and fractional currency.

Finally a limited amount of temporary funds was raised by the issue of certificates of indebtedness.

Certain general features in the flotation of these loans may be distinguished. With the exception of the twenty-year bonds, the Civil War loans were of short maturity due to the insistence of Secretary Chase on this form of financing. It should also be observed that these obligations bore a nominal interest rate which was exceptionally low. In fact it declined from 7.3 to 6, and in the later years of the war to 5 per cent. But one should be mindful that this was only a nominal rate, for the government had suspended specie payment and the dollar had declined in gold value. For illustration, in 1864, when the dollar had a gold value of 38.7 cents, the corresponding premium on gold raised the true interest cost on the government's gold loans to 15.5 per cent. An innovation in public finance was the addition of circulating privileges to certain of the government bonds. This feature was devised in 1863 when the military reverses of the Northern armies were seriously affecting the marketing of Federal bonds. At the same time the old independent treasury system, by preventing coöperation with the banks of the nation, was grievously impeding the financial operations of the government. In order to overcome these two difficulties, Congress passed the National Bank Act of 1863, which provided for the establishment of banks under a federal charter, and at the same time conferred on them as national institutions the right to issue circulating notes provided they were secured by Federal Government bonds. Although the circulation privilege did not succeed in stimulating the sale of federal bonds to any marked degree during the war, in later years it became an important perquisite of the American Government loans and continued so until the passage of the Federal Reserve Act.

Funding the Civil War Debt. The Civil War left in its wake two serious financial problems: the restoration of specie payment, and the funding of the national debt. Since the government had suspended specie payment, its currency in the form of the " greenbacks " were irredeemable inconvertible paper money. For several years after the war there was considerable popular opposition to the redemption of the greenbacks and to the payment of the government bonds in gold coin. The controversy was settled by the Public Credit Act of 1869 which definitely gave assurance that the bonds of the government would be paid in gold. In 1875 the Resumption Act applied the same principle to the greenbacks which were ultimately made redeemable in gold.

The summation table of Civil War debt given above showed that the greater part of the debt consisted of short-term obligations. The need of converting them into long-term bonds was fully appreciated by Secretary McCulloch, who induced Congress in 1866 to pass the first refunding measure. This Refunding Act, supplemented later by similar acts in 1871 and 1875, completed the task, and fixed the nature of the national debt until almost the close of the nineteenth century.

The payment of the cost of the Spanish-American War, the settlement of the Philippine Indemnity and the construction of the Panama Canal occasioned additional issues of government bonds; but the amply precedented debt-payment policy of the government was closely followed so that in 1916 the public indebtedness of the United States amounted to only $989,200,000. Of this sum $720,000,000, about two-thirds, bore an interest rate of 2 per cent.

A new era in American public finance was ushered in by the declaration of war against Germany in April, 1917. That same month Congress authorized the first Liberty Loan and the second followed in October. The heavy expenditures of 1918 required the flotations of two additions Liberty Loans, and in 1919 a final Victory Loan was placed.

In anticipation of the proceeds of these loans and of tax payments, the government issued so-called " treasury certificates." Their general nature was very like the British exchequer bills or the French *Bons de la defense nationale*. The American certificates, however, were issued not at a discount but at par, and were interest-bearing, usually with duration of one year.[1]

War financing augmented the public debt of the United States in 1919 to a maximum of $26,596,701,648. Since then the policy of the government has reduced this amount, so that by the middle of 1926 it had declined to $19,643,216,315.

Foreign Obligations of the United States Government. Although this enormous sum represents funds applied to the conduct of the war, as offsets there are obligations of foreign gov-

---

[1] The treasury note introduced in 1921 to facilitate the refunding operations of the United States ran from three to five years.

ernments held by the United States. During the War our government, together with England and France, granted financial assistance to weaker nations associated in the struggle against the Central Powers. In fact the United States extended aid to England and France themselves. Not even these countries of stronger credit could have floated loans in the American market except on almost ruinous terms. So instead the United States borrowed from its own citizens by means of the Liberty and Victory Loans, and credited the proceeds to its war-associates. These also purchased war materials from our government and received assistance from the American Relief Administration and the United States Grain Corporation. The various operations are summarized in the following account:

Proceeds of the Liberty and Victory Loans.......	$10,904,137,661
Credits from sale of surplus war materials........	592,917,941
American Relief Administration................	96,286,331
United States Grain Corporation..............	63,590,800
	$11,656,932,733

Since the close of the war there has been an active controversy concerning the desirability of cancelling these claims against the former associates in arms. In order to settle the financial arrangements between the United States and the foreign governments, Congress in 1922 passed the Foreign Debt Funding Act which provided for a commission composed of members of Congress and of the Presidential Cabinet. The Commission was not given power to settle the foreign debts but to make recommendations to Congress which retained full authority. Actually, however, Congress has accepted the terms arranged by the Commission.

Although the Commission nominally accepted the principle of non-cancellation, in its final adjustments it has really been forced to adopt a policy of partial remission by reducing the rate of interest and by extending the time for the payment of the debt. In the case of the British Debt Settlement of January, 1923, the interest was reduced to 3 and to $3\frac{1}{2}$ per cent. and the time of payment extended to 62 years, thereby bringing actual payment down to about 80 per cent. of the amount calculated on a $4\frac{1}{4}$ per cent. basis. Similarly, the French and the Belgian debts have been pared to about 50 per cent., and the Italian to approximately 25 per cent. These varying proportions are indicated in the following chart showing the funding schedules of the foreign debts to the United States.[1]

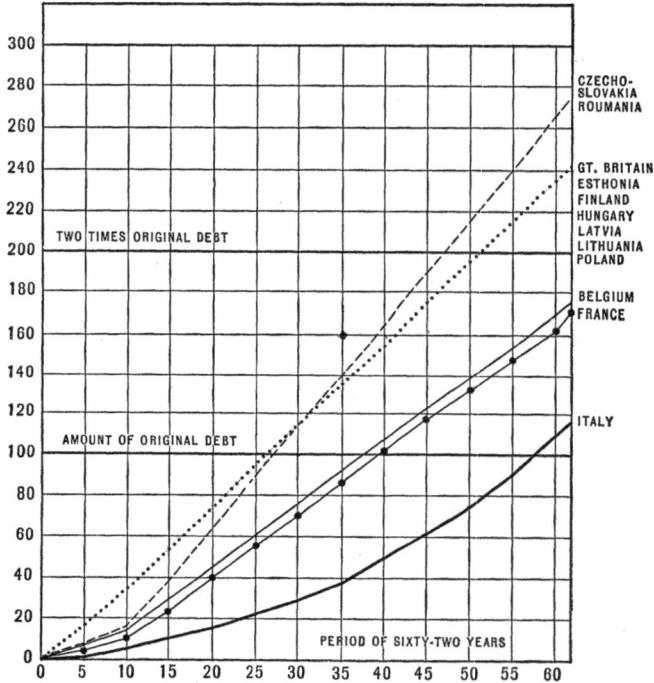

FUNDING SCHEDULES OF FOREIGN DEBTS TO U. S.

Nevertheless the payments actually made have already been substantial as indicated in the following table showing the principal and interest received in 1925.[2]

---

[1] *Bulletin of the Cleveland Trust Company*, June 15, 1926.

[2] Bulletin issued by the United States Department of Commerce on the Balance of Payments for 1925, p. 12.

PAYMENTS RECEIVED IN CALENDAR YEAR 1925 FROM FOREIGN
GOVERNMENTS ON ACCOUNT OF PRINCIPAL AND
INTEREST DUE ON OBLIGATIONS

Government	Principal	Interest	Government	Principal	Interest
Belgium........	$875,839.30	$1,575,599.91	Lithuania....	$30,000.00	$90,903.38
Czechoslovakia .	1,500,000.00	....	Nicaragua....	49,513.86	10,189.92
Esthonia........	....	1,441.88	Poland........	....	864,534.32
Finland........	47,000.00	267,300.00	Rumania.....	4,451.54	....
France.........	....	20,367,057.25	Russia........	....	[1] 275.94
Great Britain...	24,000,000.00	136,620,000.00			
Hungary.......	10,018.00	44,498.94	Total....	26,516,822.70	159,846,364.30
Latvia.........	....	4,562.76			

[1] Paid in sterling.

Obligations Outstanding. As a result of the various financial operations thus outlined, the United States Government has now outstanding the bonds and notes described in the table prepared by C. F. Childs and Company and reproduced on pages 144 and 145.

Price Fluctuations; Past and Future. The price of government bonds, of course, like that of all other commodities, is subject to economic law. The floating supply and the demand vary from year to year and even from day to day. The fluctuations are not so rapid nor sharp as in most other issues, and are the result of somewhat different influences, but in the course of years they are much greater than most people suppose. In 1901, for instance, the 4s of 1925 sold at about 140. The price when this chapter was originally written (in 1911) was about 114, a loss of 26 points, or 19 per cent. A brief review of past great price movements in the securities may be instructive. They will be more easily appreciated if put in terms of approximate income yield.

Fluctuation in Time of Panic. In time of panic experience has shown that no other security will so nearly hold its own. When almost all industrial and commercial enterprises are under suspicion, government securities, by force of contrast, seem all the stronger. It is well known to bond dealers that the first securities to enhance after business depression are the highest grade bonds, especially municipals. The principle that begins to work in this case is the one that is operative in government bonds at the worst of times. Furthermore there is usually less pressure to liquidate among the classes of institutions and investors that hold government bonds, and for the bonds that are offered a ready market may be had among the stronger national

United States Bonds and Notes

(Not including Consol 2s, Panama 2s, Postal Savings 2½s)

Issue	Rate	Maturity	† Redeemable	Interest Dates	Issue Date	Amount Issued	Outstanding Dec. 31, 1925	Notations
Treasury Note	4¼%	Sept. 15, 1926	No option	Mar.–Sept. 15th	Aug. 1, 1922	$ 486,940,100	$ 414,922,300	(2) (3)
Treasury Note	4¾%	Mar. 15, 1927	No option	Mar.–Sept. 15th	May 15, 1923	668,201,400	668,201,400	(2) (3)
Treasury Note	4½%	Dec. 15, 1927	No option	June–Dec. 15th	Jan. 15, 1923	366,981,500	355,779,900	(2) (3)
Third Liberty	4¼%	Sept. 15, 1928	No option	Mar.–Sept. 15th	May 9, 1918	4,175,650,050	2,724,413,600	(1) (2)
Fourth Liberty	4¼%	Oct. 15, 1938	1933	April–Oct. 15th	Oct. 24, 1918	6,964,581,100	6,324,478,250	(1) (2)
Second Liberty	4% and 4¼%	Nov. 15, 1942	1927	May–Nov. 15th	4s Nov. 15, 1917	3,807,865,000	3,104,541,900	(1) (2)
First Liberty	4% and 4¼%	June 15, 1947	1932	June–Dec. 15th	4¼s May 9, 1918	575,889,000	538,031,050	(1) (2)
First–Second Liberty	4¼%	June 15, 1947	1932	June–Dec. 15th	Oct. 24, 1918	3,492,150	3,492,150	(1) (2)
First Liberty	3½%	June 15, 1947	1932	June–Dec. 15th	June 15, 1917	1,989,455,550	1,402,143,100	Tax Exempt
Treasury	4¼%	Oct. 15, 1952	1947	April–Oct. 15th	Oct. 16, 1922	763,962,300	763,948,300	(1) (2)
Treasury	4%	Dec. 15, 1954	1944	June–Dec. 15th	Dec. 15, 1924 Mar. 15, 1925	1,047,088,500	1,047,088,500	(1) (2)
Treasury	3¾%	Mar. 15, 1956	1946	Mar.–Sept. 15th	Mar. 15, 1926	494,898,100	....	(1) (2)
Conversion	3%	Jan. 1, 1946 Jan. 1, 1947	No option	Jan.–Apr. 1st July–Oct. 1st	Jan. 1, 1916 Jan. 1, 1917	15,761,000 13,133,500	15,761,000 13,133,500	Tax Exempt
Panama	3%	June 1, 1961	No option	Mar.–June 1st Sept.–Dec. 1st	June 1, 1911	50,000,000	49,800,000	Tax Exempt

TAX EXEMPTIONS UNDER PRESENT LAW (REVENUE ACT OF 1926):

Corporations:

Since corporations only pay a 13½ per cent. normal tax on their total net earnings, the interest from all issues is non-taxable.

Individuals:

No issue is exempt from estate and inheritance taxes.

All issues are exempt from other state and local taxation and from normal Federal income tax.

(1)—$5,000 in the aggregate, Liberty 4s or 4¼s, Treasury 3¾s, 4s or 4¼s, Treasury Certificates of Indebtedness, War Savings Certificates and Treasury Savings Certificates are wholly exempt for the life of the issue.

ACCEPTABLE FOR TAXES:

(2)—All Liberty 4¼s, Treasury Notes, Treasury 3¾s, 4s, and 4¼s, if owned continuously for at least six months prior to death are acceptable at par and accrued interest in payment of any estate and inheritance taxes imposed by the United States under any present or future law.

(3)—Treasury Notes are acceptable at par and interest in payment of Federal taxes payable at or within six months of maturity.

SINKING FUND:

Beginning July 1st, 1920, and for each fiscal year thereafter until all Liberty and Treasury Bonds and Notes are retired, there is appropriated out of any money in the Treasury not otherwise appropriated, an amount equal to the sum of (1) 2½ per cent. of the aggregate amount of such bonds and notes outstanding on July 1, 1920, less an amount equal to the par amount of any obligations of foreign Governments held by the United States on July 1, 1920, and (2) the interest which would have been payable during the fiscal year for which the appropriation is made on the bonds and notes purchased, redeemed, or paid out of the sinking fund during such year or in previous years; to be applied to retirement at maturity, redemption or purchase at an average cost not to exceed par and accrued interest.

DENOMINATIONS, FORMS, ETC:

Coupon 3½s are not issued in larger denominations than $1,000.
Treasury Notes, Treasury 3¾s, 4s and 4¼s, and Registered 3½s are not issued in denominations of $50.
Treasury Notes are not issued in Registered form; are issued in coupon form in denominations of $100,000.
Treasury 3¾s and 4s are issued in coupon form in denominations of $100,000.
Otherwise all Liberty and Treasury Bonds and Notes are issued in denominations—
  Coupon—$50, $100, $500, $1,000, $5,000, $10,000.
  Registered—$50, $100, $500, $1,000, $5,000, $10,000, $50,000, $100,000,
and are interchangeable, registered for coupon or vice versa.
Conversion 3s are issued in denominations—
  Coupon—$100, $1,000.
  Registered—$100, $1,000, $5,000, $10,000.
Panama 3s are issued in denominations—
  Coupon—$100, $500, $1,000.
  Registered—$100, $500, $1,000, $10,000.
Conversions and Panamas in registered form cannot be converted into coupon form.

BOOKS CLOSE in Washington for transfer of Registered bonds one month prior to interest date, except for Panama 3s, which close the fifteenth of month prior to interest date.

† Redeemable at the Government's option in the year indicated on the same day and month as maturity date; or on any interest date thereafter. When bonds are "called" for redemption, advance notice must be given of 3 months for 3¼s 1st 4s and 4¼s; 6 months for 2nd 4s and 4¼s, also 4th 4¼s; 4 months for Treasury 3¾s, 4s and 4¼s.

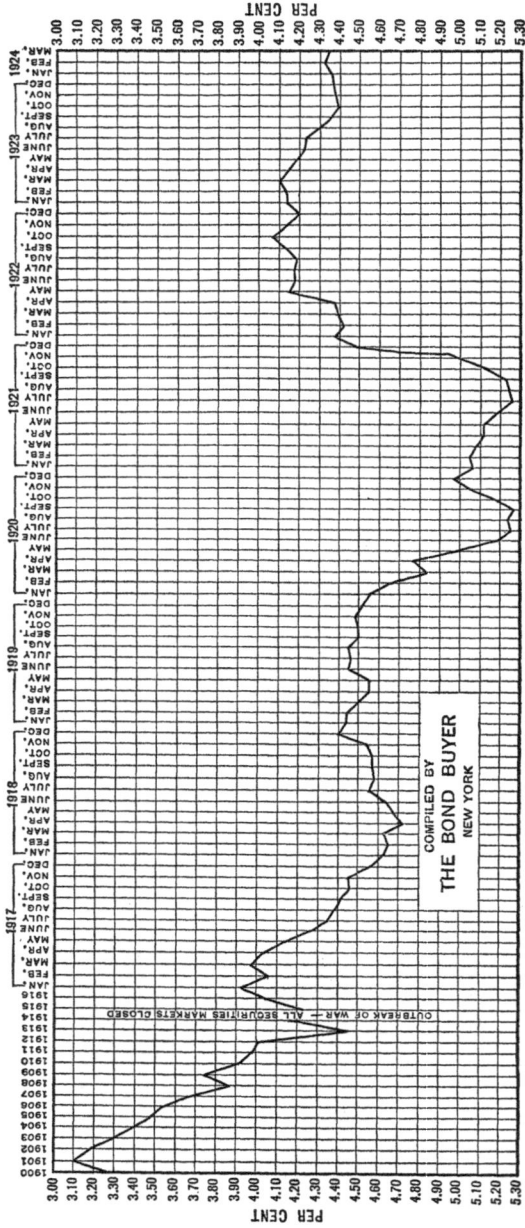

COMPILED BY
THE BOND BUYER
NEW YORK

OUTBREAK OF WAR — ALL SECURITIES MARKETS CLOSED

institutions. In the panic of 1893 the average extreme variation of governments was about 5 points, and in 1907 5.7 points; [1] for even the better class of municipals and railroads during these years the variation was from twice to four times as much.

Fluctuation in Time of War. It is in time of war, naturally, that government credit is most impaired. In the earlier periods of our history when the central government existed by mere sufferance and the primacy of statehood and the right of state secession were not yet treasonable doctrines, armed conflict was even a more serious thing to investors than it would be under present conditions. The War of 1812 caused the issuance of loans upon a basis of from 7 to $8\frac{1}{2}$ per cent., and the War of Secession upon a basis of 12 per cent., maximum. No bond value tables at our command are extensive enough to record the price of the old 2s of 1930 on a 12 per cent. basis.

In this chapter in the earlier editions appeared the following prediction (§ 364):

" Although a future war of magnitude would not threaten the disintegration of the country, yet it might have sufficient train of evil consequences to work temporary havoc to our credit; for a great conflict, with or without blockade, seriously curtails income from customs duties, and almost over night empties an unprepared treasury. The relief invoked through war-taxes is unwelcome and tardy. Then recourse must be had to large and numerous loans when people are least desirous of taking them up. At such a time, if ever it comes again, there will be great shrinkage in the value of our public funds."

The World War soon brought verification of this principle which is pictured in the accompanying chart showing the market for the principal U. S. Government World War loans from date of issuance.

These comments on United States government bonds have failed in their purpose if they have not impressed the fact that recent as well as early American history warrants the use of our national loans as a standard for the study of funded debt as an investment, but that one may not take counsel of them as of perfection, nor believe that they are not subject to the vicissitudes of time, accident, and error.

[1] The extreme variation of the 2s and 3s was only 3.05 points, but the average was raised by the greater variation of the less active 4s.

CHAPTER XVI

STATE BONDS: THE HISTORY OF STATE DEBT[1]

State Bonds in the Scheme of Classification. Although, as we said in discussing the various kinds of bonds, there are some technical grounds for classifying what are commonly called Municipal Issues as Government Bonds, still the more reasonable line of severance is between Federal and State Government Bonds on the one hand, and Municipal Bonds on the other. Not all civil and political divisions, by the way, are strictly governmental divisions; many are created by legislative enactment for the sole purpose of internal betterment by means of funds raised from the creation of debt, and have no administrative functions apart from the creation and discharge of the debt and the distribution of its proceeds. Therefore it is best to consider United States Government and State Bonds as the upper division of Tax Bonds or Civil Loans, and County, City, Village, District Bonds, etc., as the lower.

The logic of this bipartite division will be clearer when we have considered the nature of state and municipal debt.

State Debt and Constitutional Law. One of the fundamental tenets of our constitutional law relates to the so-called sovereignty of the several states. Not the general nature or scope of this familiar principle, but only its reference to financial matters concerns us.

Among the many privileges reserved by the individual states at the birth of the Republic was a large measure of autonomy in their fiscal relations. To be sure the states could not coin money,[2] emit bills of credit, make anything but gold and silver a tender in payment of debts, lay any duties on imports or exports or tonnage, and could not impair the obligation of con-

---

[1] Because of the intimate relation between state and municipal credit, the two chapters on State Bonds should be read not only by those interested in state bonds, but by all to whom American government or municipal issues of any sort are of interest.

[2] A right still retained by them under the Articles of Confederation.

tracts, (Constitution, Article I, Section 10), but they secured, within four years from the adoption of the Constitution, the specific concession that such powers as were " not delegated to the United States by the Constitution, nor prohibited by it to the States," were " reserved to the States respectively, or to the people " (Amendments, Article X). This and one or two other of the ten amendments that were adopted before the close of 1791 were a direct result of the still growing tendency toward what was called " state sovereignty." If not mentioned in the Constitution itself, the right of the states to create debt in the manner of the National Government, and upon the basis of state credit, as in the days of the Confederation, is certainly implied in the Tenth Amendment.

Therefore we derive the basis of our division particularly from this residual sovereignty of the states,—from their ability to contract debt without the let or hindrance of a superior power, as distinguished from the dependence of the civil divisions of the states upon statute and state constitution.

There is, however, another feature of American constitutional law that associates bonds of the commonwealths still more closely with those of the nation, and draws us further into a study of their character and history. There was nothing of especial moment to state credit about the Tenth Amendment or any of the other provisions that had gone before. In fact the ordination of finance, important as it was in the years of depleted resources following the drain of the War for Independence, took a place, in the minds of the people and of the framers of the Constitution, quite secondary to the development of a political system which was to be the wonder and study of continental Europe. Nevertheless this instrument itself contained the assurance that " all debts contracted, and engagements entered into, before the adoption of this Constitution, shall be as valid against the United States under this Constitution as under the Confederation " (Article VI, First Clause). That no mention is made of state debts is not to be wondered at; it was hardly a subject for treatment in such a brief document as the National Code.[1] And

---

[1] State debt was indeed touched upon nearly a century later, in the Fourteenth Amendment, Section 4, inhibiting the states from assuming or paying obligations incurred in aid of rebellion against the United States; but this was passed in that reactionary period when the cry of "States Rights" was

besides, the bulk of the Revolutionary War debt of the states had been assumed by the Federal Government. However, from the tenor of the whole Constitution, particularly from that clause of the First Article prohibiting the states from the impairment of the obligation of contracts, one would be led to expect an integrity in financial affairs on the part of the states, safeguarded by law and by constitution, similar to that national integrity which was soon achieved and has since been preserved almost without interruption. But this was not to be the case.

In 1792 a citizen of North Carolina[1] brought suit in the Supreme Court of the United States against the state of Georgia, and thus raised the important question,—again involving the limits of state sovereignty,—as to whether a state could be sued by an individual. The majority of the Court decided in the affirmative, Mr. Justice Wilson giving the opinion and Chief Justice Jay supporting. This of course aroused the Anti-Federalists and resulted four years later in the ratification of the Eleventh Amendment, by the terms of which:

" *The judicial power of the United States shall not be construed to extend to any suit in law or equity, commenced or prosecuted against any of the United States by citizens of another state, or by citizens or subjects of any foreign state.*"[2]

It is possible that when the amendment was submitted to the legislatures of the states for ratification, although the idea of state repudiation was wholly foreign to the spirit of the times, some pressure was brought to bear in the interest of the already harassed taxpayers who feared the increased burden that a final settlement of the many unassumed outstanding war-claims would involve; but,—to repeat,—political considerations all over

anything but a popular slogan, yet was inspired not so much by opposition to state independence in fiscal matters as by desire to make impossible the financing of future uprisings.

[1] Chisholm vs. Georgia, reported in 2 Dallas.

[2] See Bank of Washington vs. Arkansas (1857), 20 How. 530; Hagood vs. Southern (1886), 117 U. S. 52. Although a state cannot thus be sued without its own consent, nevertheless it can be sued by another state of the Union. See U. S. Constitution, Art. III, sec. 2; accordingly a holder of North Carolina bonds donated $10,000 of them to South Dakota, which carried the case to the United States Supreme Court and received in settlement $27,410. Based on this success, attempts made to persuade New York, Michigan, Rhode Island, and Nevada to sue. See also the West Virginia-Virginia case, p. 154.

the Union were paramount at the time, and the issue was the logical result, rather of hostility toward further centralization of government than of local resistance to the tax-burden.[1]

Georgia, naturally, was the vortex of this embroilment. Upon the decision of the Supreme Court in the case of Chisholm vs. Georgia, the legislature prohibited, on pain of death, any attempt on the part of United States marshals to collect the judgment. No state would then have proceeded to such extremes in language and measures merely in the interest of a depleted exchequer. Nothing could condone such a course except encroachment upon a cherished prerogative. The spirit of repudiation, then, does not date back to the youth of the Republic.

It is true that even prior to the agitation in 1793 for this amendment, Delaware had declared in her second constitution that suits might be brought against her. It is true also that in 1796, before the adoption of the article, Tennessee had granted her own citizens the same right, and that in after years, as the feeling in regard to state sovereignty became less tense, seventeen other states incorporated this provision in their revised constitutions. But some of the seventeen have since stricken it out, only five[2] have passed supplemental statutes making it possible to enforce the provision, and in most, if not all cases the wronged bondholders have been brought to realize that it is one thing to sue an unreceptive state, under its own laws, before its own judges, and another thing to seek redress before disinterested courts deriving their authority from the National Government and presided over by officers with life tenure.

Except for that clause of the Fourteenth Amendment disavowing all obligations incurred in aid of secession, the bearing of constitutional law upon the subject of state debt ends with the Eleventh Amendment. The misuse that has subsequently

[1] To this origin Mr. John Hume, in his well-known articles on repudiation in the *North American Review* (1884,Vol. 139, p. 564, and elsewhere), attributes the Eleventh Amendment, and by manifest implication traces the subsequent evils of "state roguery." Probably he got his suggestion from *The Nation* for January 31, 1878, which says, "The reason for engrafting such an inconsistency upon a code that professes 'to establish justice' among men and communities was the embarrassed condition of the states at the time the Federal Union was formed." This traditional view, widely held and important if true, is controverted by the facts.

[2] Indiana, Wisconsin, Nebraska, Nevada, and Mississippi.

been made of the Amendment is a matter for further study. But before continuing let us revert once more to our classification. We now know only too well that State Bonds are analogous to Governments proper and in contrast to Municipals in this further respect that there is no practical remedy at law against their default. Since both are the obligations of sovereign powers, we must turn to history for an adjustment of their valuation upon a basis of credit.

Debts of the Commonwealths: Default and Repudiation. In the early years of the Republic the American people were exceedingly careful of their financial standing. As we have said, at the close of the War for Independence the Federal Government assumed, for a time, the larger part of the debts of the thirteen states. It was no part of the doctrine of Hamilton and his Federalist successors that a large national debt was a public blessing; and later, under the peace administration of the Republicans, aided by the wise operations of Gallatin, Hamilton's policy became traditional in the Treasury Department, to the material reduction of the national debt (see pp. 356, 357). The War of 1812 of course postponed for years any idea of its immediate extinction, and movements toward that end were again retarded by the financial depression of 1819-22, particularly because the fiscal policy of the Government made the treasury largely dependent for revenues on import duties. But without further serious setbacks the national debt gradually dwindled away and was finally paid off in 1835.

Up to this time a conservatism had been displayed by the commonwealths also. In 1825 the aggregate outstanding loans of the states amounted to $13,000,000,[1] or $5,000,000 less than at the time of national assumption in 1790. By 1830 they had increased to $26,000,000, and by 1835, the year of the extinction of the national debt, to $46,000,000; but although the increase was in greater ratio by far than the increase in population, and somewhat more than the increase in wealth,—all three being assisted by great industrial development and the accession of new states,—still it could not be called excessive or alarming.

But the next five years entirely changed the status of things. The results of a general Continental peace were reflected in the

---

[1] Round amounts are sufficient for the purpose in hand. The exact figures are in doubt.

demand for our manufactures and in the growth of our export trade; the seasons had been favorable to crops; virgin territory had been opend up to agriculture and mining; foreign commerce had been stimulated by the use of bills of exchange; for various causes connected with national banking and currency laws, state and local banks had rapidly augmented their capitalization and deposits and consequently their notes; on the basis of this inflated currency and the resultant inflation of prices, credit became unduly extended, and, to use the familiar but appropriate figure, nothing was lacking but a first occasion to puncture the financial bubble.

It is not surprising, however, to one at all conversant with the history of the times, that these same conditions which made possible the extinction of the national debt should effect an opposite result upon state debt. These causes are both general and particular. The national moral consciousness has always been more sensitive and more sober than that of the constituencies. There seems to be a close connection between magnitude and integrity in American political units. This truth has been plainly evident in our history from the first deliberations of the Continental Congress to the present hour. It is undoubtedly inherent in the peculiar composition of our body politic, but accentuated by local causes, geographical, ethnological, and historical, which will in time disappear, and are even now disappearing under the influence of assimilative processes. This national moral consciousness, particularly well represented for the most part by the early Presidents and by the Secretaries of the Treasury, seized upon these seven fat years beginning before 1830 to discharge the national obligations and even to distribute surplus revenues to the states. But the states for their part saw in their own swelling revenues only the opportunity to embark in speculative enterprises of internal improvement upon such a vast scale, and by means of such enormous bond issues, that in some cases a tax of hundreds of dollars per capita would have been necessary to liquidate them.

Widespread antagonism toward further extension of the federal functions undoubtedly helped preserve the Government from the same temptation. Undoubtedly too these public undertakings by many of the commonwealths originated in perfectly good faith; not honor, but sound business sense, was lacking.

Nowhere is the naïve speculative-patriotic spirit of the times, as it affected state debts, more aptly illustrated than in the first Constitution of the state of Michigan, which came into the Union in 1837, at the culmination of the period of prosperity. This instrument made it " the duty of the legislature, as soon as may be, to make provision by law for ascertaining the proper objects for improvement in relation to roads, canals, and navigable waters." And the lesson of the seven succeeding lean years was so poorly learned and quickly forgotten that Florida entered the Union in 1845 handicapped by its constitution with directions to its General Assembly of the same purport and couched in almost the same words.

Yet when all allowances are made with understanding and sympathy, the fact remains that in 1836 the United States had paid off its funded debt, and for some years, in face of the times, strove to keep free from foreign obligations; whereas the aggregate debt of the states, which in 1835 we found to be $46,000,000, grew in the next three years to $175,000,000!

There was no one section of the country conspicuously infected by this debt-making fever, although, in the light of subsequent events we are accustomed to refer vaguely to " the West and South." New England to be sure, the most mature large sectional division of the country, always conservative, and in less need of material exploitation and social advancement, at this time withheld itself for the most part from bond issues. Maine, parted from Massachusetts in 1820, assumed without question one-third of the Massachusetts debt, though by no means possessing one-third of the territorial resources of the original undivided unit.[1] Maine's debt thereafter was slowly reduced, partly with the help of indemnity money from Great Britain, and has never since been an object of serious concern to her people. New Hampshire, with credit as solid and enduring as her rock-bound hills, always was, and now is, loath to incur debt. The difficulties of the late thirties were scarcely felt by New Hampshire and no bonds or stock were outstanding from

[1] In contrast was the policy of West Virginia which for over a half century refused to assume its share of the pre-war Virginia debt. After lengthy litigation the matter was finally settled in 1919 when the West Virginia legislature made payment to the Virginia Debt Commission. See 220 U. S. 1; 231 U. S. 89; 234 U. S. 117; 238 U. S. 202; 241 U. S. 531; 246 U. S. 565.

that time till the War of '61. Vermont had no debt till 1859; Connecticut and Rhode Island, no debt from the Revolution till the Civil War. Of all the New England states, Massachusetts, aware of her own resources and power, was the only commonwealth somewhat profuse in creation of indebtedness.

The Middle Atlantic states had no such reticence. New Jersey indeed did not bond herself before 1838, and in her constitution of 1842 set an early and desirable example by limiting the debt to $100,000, with the now common exception for purposes of war, etc., as the result of which her conservative fiscal policy has been more in alignment with that of the New England states than with that of her neighbors; and Delaware, too, with no debt at all prior to the war and none since worth considering, should be favorably mentioned. But New York, Pennsylvania, and Maryland, although acquitted on the score of honor, acted in those troublesome, debt-incurring times with an unwisdom forgotten only because retrieved. The causes for all three were about the same: the financing of needed canal construction and improvement, and the aiding of the railroads. A beginning was made in moderation, and then, when enthusiasm had been aroused and discretion thrown to the winds, a riot of contractual obligations was entered into with much anticipation of what the money raised was to be spent for, and little of how it was to be repaid.

The history of New York's state debt is too well known to require much comment. Although the burden in the early forties was critically large, the Empire State always managed to take care of principal and interest when due. It is not so well known, if indeed it has not generally been forgotten, that both Pennsylvania and Maryland had to suffer the shame of temporary default. Both were compelled to stop the payment of interest in 1842, owing particularly to state construction of canals, and to the abolition of direct taxation during the hard times preceding. Pennsylvania resumed payments in 1845 in " relief notes," which then were the state currency; they were speedily retired. Maryland had made up all delinquent interest by 1848. The majority of her citizens acted during these years in good faith, although the body of those dishonorably inclined rose to the dignity or indignity of a Repudiation Party. In 1837 Maryland had paid her debt interest in gold, as did Massachusetts during the Civil War,—and both at times when the banks had suspended specie payment.

Although debt history in the depression of 1837–45 cannot be geographically divided, it was inevitable that the less developed West and South should suffer more than the East, and that the result should be written in financial history. It is for us to consider, however, whether the West and South, in whole or in part, both in this depression and in those subsequent to it, maintained that sort of financial integrity which, in spite of temporary reverses of fortune, gives to a nation, a municipality, a firm or an individual, a credit that is worth as much to the holders of the debtor's paper as the realizable assets itemized upon the treasurer's books.

The First Repudiation Period. It is hardly necessary to say that Pennsylvania and Maryland were not the only states to default for a time in the seven lean years following 1837. Indiana, in 1840, Illinois, in 1841, Michigan, Florida, and Mississippi, in 1842, did likewise. This is not only the ordinary geographical order, and the temporal as well, but it marks perfectly the degree of obliquity involved. Of the four Northern states, only the last, Michigan, did not reimburse all creditors to the full. Michigan acknowledged and acquitted her obligations on all bonds for which she had obtained payment, irrespective of any benefits received from the money; but on such as she had obtained only part payment she acquitted the debt only in that part, even though title had passed to innocent holders. Of this entire list of seven defaulting states only the last two, Mississippi and Florida, were of the South, and only the last two, Mississippi and Florida, were guilty of deliberate repudiation, and of these two, Mississippi repudiated twice before the Civil War, and Florida once in each repudiation period.

We are concerned in this recital only with the history of state debts as it has a bearing upon state credit. It is to be hoped that in the study of history we may reach some broad and justifiable conclusions pertinent to the purchase of state bonds. We shall show that on these grounds it is legitimate to pass lightly over the defaults of the Northern states. To be sure almost every default, irrespective of time or locality, arose out of conditions that will never be met again in this country. Default was the result of an unwise zeal to hasten by arbitrary legislation, and, for the most part, in undeveloped territory, the spread of material progress and the slow growth of institutions. And so, successively in the East, the South, and the West, it was the same story: state ownership of, or aid for canals, railroads, turnpikes, banks, and eleemosynary and educational institutions. But there is this all-important difference to the ending of the tale: barring Minnesota in war time, the North paid its debts and the South shirked them.

These states we have mentioned were not the only commonwealths in serious difficulties. Ohio, in the North, was one of the earliest to contract debts for extensive internal improvements, placing a foreign loan for canal and railroad purposes as early as 1825. The maximum amount of her debt, reached in 1845 (a total of over $19,000,000), was a very heavy load to carry in those days; but before it was too late the state came to her senses, and in the new constitution of 1851, prohibited further aid for public improvements.

At about the same period Alabama, in the South, laid herself open to financial ills by subscribing to the stock of the state bank and its branches to the extent of some $8,000,000. Relying on the income of this stock, like Pennsylvania she abolished direct taxation,—in 1836. When as the result of the suspension of specie payment the bank became insolvent in 1842, the state avoided default during the ante-bellum period only by resort to now doubly burdensome taxation. Since the intent of these two states at that time was honorable, but their financing only a little less hazardous than that of the defaulting but non-repudiating Northern states, there is no reason for discriminating against the former or in favor of the latter because of a brief and unavoidable suspension of interest payments.

On the other hand, it is but just to mention the two other Northern states, Wisconsin and Iowa, which, organized as territories and admitted into the Union during the times of which we write, had to look as far as the Atlantic seaboard, either before or after the Civil War, to find their fellows in reluctance to incur indebtedness or in preparedness to discharge it. All other states of the Union which we have not mentioned or shall not mention in this connection are clear of the charge of fiscal folly or dishonor, but all such states came into the Union after the War.

If the conduct of the five Northern states which defaulted in the forties, and of other non-defaulting states in both North and South, was indiscreet to the point of foolhardiness, it was not dishonorable. Undoubtedly even Michigan felt she was discharging her full moral obligation in refunding only that part of the issues for which she had been paid. But the conduct of the two Southern states that repudiated had no justification in ethics, if it had in law. The Governor of Mississippi, replying in July, 1841, to a letter from Hope and Co., of Amsterdam, who represented a large number of holders of the Union Bank bonds, made a brave show of five causes of unconstitutionality in the issue,[1] and Jefferson Davis, in the following month, with less logic and more Southron eloquence, abetted the course,[2] and the people by their subsequent elections to the legislature approved of the repudiation of the Union Bank bonds. In 1852 Mississippi made perfectly plain whether invalidity was the ultimate cause by repudiating by popular vote the Planters' Bank bonds on which there was not the slightest shadow of invalidity.[3]

Florida raised the excuse of invalidity on both occasions when it became convenient to withhold moneys due. The state had better grounds for default than Mississippi in actual inability to meet her obligations in full; but her two expedients to escape payment were much more pernicious as precedents, for the first was based upon the principle that a state on being admitted into the Union might be absolved under certain circumstances from financial covenants entered into by Congressional enactment when a territory, and the second upon the tacit understanding that the state courts were justified in returning interpretations and decisions biased to the popular will. Even Mississippi had not gone so far; repudiation there had met some opposition in the courts.

Before coming to the later repudiation period certain war-time cases are to be noted.

War-Time Repudiation and Default. In 1860 the legislature of Minnesota, following the will of the people, adopted an amendment to the constitution, forbidding the payment of principal or interest (except after a referendum) of the bonds issued in aid of

[1] *Bankers' Magazine*, November, 1849, p. 345 et seq.
[2] Ibid., p. 363 et seq.
[3] Scott, *Repudiation of State Debts*, New York, 1893 (out of print), p. 42.

the railroads. This was popular repudiation pure and simple, and utterly inexcusable because utterly unnecessary. The people indeed suspected with reason that fraud had been perpetrated upon them, just as the people of the South did after the Civil War. In Minnesota's case, however, the proved instances were not flagrant enough to be submitted in extenuation. The significance in this Northern state is that the ghost of repudiation would not down. Time after time that matter was brought before the people in one form or another, by the bondholders, the legislators, and the governors, and finally after an agitation continuing off and on for twenty years the State Supreme Court decided that the Amendment of 1860 was unconstitutional, and in 1881 the legislature passed a refunding act, compromising the old bonds at fifty cents on the dollar, but *with accrued interest*. That the people of Minnesota should for so long have been morally more obtuse than their agents and representatives is best explained by recalling the primitive condition of the state and its inhabitants at that time.

There is little more of vital interest to state debt to chronicle till 1870. It seems, however, to have escaped general notice by historians of American finance that as the immediate result of the war, Missouri was at one time heavily in arrears in interest on her debt, and that therefore it is with questionable legal right that the bonds of Missouri cities have been owned by savings banks in certain states. In 1865 the amount was $5,000,000, but thereafter was rapidly reduced. During the war Alabama paid the interest upon that portion of the debt we have mentioned which was held in London. This was possible and politic as her ports were open. Of course interest was defaulted on the portion held in the North. In 1865 all interest ceased. Alabama's subsequent troubles were due to the enactment of laws authorizing what may be called blanket endorsement, by the state, of railroad bonds upon a mileage basis. The amount of business folly concentrated in these acts is probably greater than in any hitherto perpetrated by a state legislature, yet the default and repudiation which followed as a matter of course were the most excusable of any because the state was sincere in its endeavor to meet its obligations. The Funding Act of 1876 by which it scaled its obligations about 50 per cent. closed this unfortunate period of its career.

The Second Repudiation Period. The second or reconstruction period of repudiation which we have now entered lasted from 1870 to 1884. During it nine states, all in the South, sought relief from their debts by repudiation:—Virginia, North Carolina, South Carolina, Georgia, Florida, Alabama, Louisiana, Arkansas, and Tennessee. No satisfactory dates can be furnished as in the first period because in most cases defaults were so frequent. In some of the states, e.g., North Carolina, defaults around 1870 on some fresh portion of interest or principal were almost annual occurrences.

It is hardly necessary to say that the hardships of the war were reflected in the state debts. Of course the bonds of the Confederate States and the bonds of the seceding states issued for the purposes of the war were void.[1] Therefore the new debt burden of the South was not a direct, but an indirect result of the war. It was due particularly to the incompetence, extravagance, and rascality of the Northern war-governors and the black-Republican legislatures of their creating, and generally to the fact that the South had committed itself, even more deeply than the North, to the policy of railroad aid, both before and after the war. The accumulation of interest unpaid during and after the war was also a very heavy charge. From these various causes and some others, the debt of the repudiating Southern states, which in 1860 was $87,767,690, had reached in 1870 the total of $170,025,340, an increase of $82,257,650, or 94 per cent.

While the funded obligations and in turn the annual tax burdens were thus increasing, the ability of the states to meet them grew correspondingly less; for the assessors' value of taxable property (both real and personal, including slaves in the first period), which in 1860 was $4,065,965,607, had declined in 1870 to $2,014,614,448, a loss of $2,951,351,159, or 52 per cent. Furthermore, in the prostration of the decade following the war the railroads, upon which the people had fondly relied to take care of such a large portion of the interest, were unable to meet their

---

[1] "Neither the United States, nor any state shall assume or pay any debts or obligations incurred in aid of insurrection or rebellion against the United states, or any claim for the loss or emancipation of any slave; but all such debts or obligations shall be held illegal and void."—Amendment XIV, sec. 4, U. S. Constitution.

charges, and this source of anticipated revenue for railroad aid and state guaranteed bonds was almost entirely cut off.

The Ultimate Cause of Repudiation. If now, with the two periods of default and repudiation, thus roughly sketched, before us, we seek the main underlying weakness in state credit, we have not far to look. In the first place a careful distinction should be made between unavoidable default and general repudiation. The former evil was more prevalent in the first period and the latter during the second. In so far as default by a state was unavoidable, and subsequently redeemed, it has no bearing upon future state credit because it was the outcome of transitory financial conditions. As to wilful repudiation it is a curious fact that, with the exception noted in the case of Mississippi, and in one or two others, all efforts on the part of states to avoid payment of outstanding bonds has been on the score of illegality of some sort or other. In connection with this fact and in significant commentary on it, two others should be noted: first, that the dates of issue of the three hundred and odd millions of repudiated bonds do not fall in definite periods; but, second, that the dates of the acts of repudiation fall for the most part within the two periods outlined. Illegality, or invalidity, therefore is a pretext, or rather a convenient refuge, which ordinarily will not be resorted to, but only under the urgency of extreme material or moral impoverishment, or both.

This brief explanation leaves two facts unaccounted for: that the South did not default to the extent that the North did in the first period; and, that in both periods repudiation was the characteristic source of relief in the South.

Although the liabilities of the repudiating Southern states were doubled and the resources were halved in the decade 1860-1870, it would be difficult to prove that the South had retrogressed during this period in purely material well-being any more than the North and Middle West in the seven lean years following 1836. During that earlier period of distress the South had been engrossed in agricultural pursuits, had lived very close to the soil, and had given less political attention to those public works of improvement that benefited the people at large rather than the dominant classes. Therefore the South had not felt the earlier trial in its full severity. But when after the war and with the passing of the old plantation life the South sought to stimulate mercantile and manufacturing interests by those very artificial devices of railroad—and banking—aid which had previously proved the source of such disaster in the North, she laid herself open to the full effects of the more insidious temptations which the politics of the Reconstruction Period offered. And when, in addition to this, she came to realize in defeat the loss she had suffered by those dearly cherished attributes of state sovereignty that were particularly Southern, it is not surprising that moral disintegration followed. It would be hard to find in history a stronger combination of circumstances at work undermining a state's financial integrity.

But even this explanation is not sufficient to account for the conduct of Mississippi and Florida in the ante-bellum period, and for the very low order of business ethics revealed in the speeches and correspondence of leading Southerners and in the minutes of Southern state conventions both before and after the war. In this connection Mr. Justice Curtis has been aptly quoted,[1] and the passage warrants repeating. Speaking of the repudiation of Mississippi he says:

"An intelligent foreigner, who feels a just indignation when he hears of repudiation, probably knows the difference between a Highland Chieftain and a London Merchant, but is profoundly ignorant that differences quite as great exist between the people of Mississippi and the people of Massachusetts. Probably there are few points in which these differences would be so likely to be exhibited as upon the matter of paying debts. To pay debts punctually is *the* point of honor among all commercial peoples. But the planters of Mississippi do not so esteem it. They do not feel the importance of an exact conformity to contracts. It has not been their habit to meet their engagements on the very day if not quite convenient. Certainly they attach no idea of dishonesty to such a course of dealing. They mean to pay, but they did not expect when they contracted the debt to distress themselves about the payment. If a friend wants a thousand dollars for a loan or a gift, he can have it, though perhaps a creditor wants it also. We do not mean to intimate that there are no high qualities in such a character, but they are different from those which make good bankers and merchants; and therefore bankers and merchants ought not to expect such men to look at a debt just as they do."

Prof. Scott, who quotes the passage in his work just mentioned in the footnote, remarks that this comment, written in 1844, should be given more weight in explanation of the repudiation

[1] Debts of the States, *North American Review*, January, 1844; p. 109-57.

acts during the first period than of those after the War when a commercial spirit had been awakened in the South; and that is true.

The ultimate cause of state repudiation, then, is a low standard of business ethics. This low standard in a broad and general way may be said to be a racial characteristic, and eradicable only as the race changes, by process of fusion with immigrant population or otherwise; but its ill effects will rise to the height of disturbing state credit only when the pressure of the debt burden becomes distressing. And it is very probable that this burden will never again be intolerable in any of our states.

CHAPTER XVII

STATE BONDS: THE ELEMENTS OF SECURITY

SECURITY: INTANGIBLE ASSETS

When considering United States Bonds in a preceding chapter the question of security was taken for granted to a large extent, —these bonds being by common consent the safest form of security investment in America. In the present chapter security is the main theme, because there can be no general reason for preferring state bonds to municipals unless they can be bought with greater safety. And since there is no practical remedy at law for their default, nor (with minor exceptions) any sort of recourse to property in satisfaction of just claims, the emphasis of this chapter is upon those intangible assets of the state that are the chief inspiration of its credit.

The Gauge of State Credit. The credit of a *municipality* in this country may be estimated with reasonable correctness, by those not in a position otherwise to know, from the market value of its bonds, expressed in income yield. The yearly flotation of municipal issues, amounting in value to hundreds of millions of dollars, is so free, and the demand from vested interests so intelligent and steady, that one cannot go far astray who uses the gauge of credit that is measured by percentage of income from the investment. Concretely, the security behind a municipal yielding $3\frac{1}{2}$ per cent. is to be presumed greater than that behind a municipal yielding 4 per cent. There is no such free market by which to judge the credit of state bonds, as we shall observe later, so that it is necessary for the investor to acquaint himself at first hand with the factors that make for state credit.

The Lesson from History. The payment of loans to the Sovereign depends on the will of the Sovereign; the will of the Sovereign is known only by past and present acts. We have examined the debt history of the states and have found it anything but reassuring. Yet, so far as history is concerned, there is justification for placing the same confidence in the bonds of certain states that we do in the federal funds.

164

In the nature of the case, however, the power of discrimination based on the teachings of history is wanting in many bond buyers who may in other respects have a nice sense of investment values. These persons through lack of that range of vision which historical training encourages, are wont to consider state credit in its present legal and material aspects only. They may make the mistake of approaching all classes of securities by the same road. But this is not best; for industrial bonds, to illustrate, should be studied intensively; but state and equipment bonds extensively.

History, measured by events, is rapid in the making, and new epochs of good and ill press hard upon one another. In times of national prosperity a people so naturally optimistic as Americans grow forgetful; they overestimate their own qualities and resources and become oblivious to former reverses. Thus are created the regularly recurring industrial cycles. In the matter of state debts, therefore, it is best to be open-minded. Who can tell what reverses in fiscal policy a generation may bring forth?

When in 1839, during that long depression of the first repudiation period, Baring Bros. of London inquired of Daniel Webster concerning " the measure of security which the purchasers of bonds issued by the states of the American Union would have for their investment," he wrote in reply:

"The states cannot rid themselves of their obligations otherwise than by the honest payment of their debts . . . they possess all adequate powers of providing for the case, by taxes and internal means of revenue. They cannot get round the duty, nor evade its force. Any failure to fulfil its undertakings would be an open violation of public faith, to be followed by the penalty of dishonor and disgrace; a penalty, it may be presumed, which no state of the American Union would be likely to incur. . . . I hope I may be justified by existing circumstances in closing this letter with the expression of an opinion of a more general nature. It is, that I believe that the citizens of the United States, like all honest men, regard debts, whether public or private, and whether existing at home or abroad, to be of moral as well as of legal obligation; and I trust that I may appeal to their history, from the moment when those states took their rank among the nations of the Earth to the present time, for proof that this belief is well founded. If it were possible that any one of the states should, at any time, so entirely lose her self-respect, and forget her duty as to violate the faith solemnly pledged for her pecuniary engagements, I believe there is no country upon Earth—not even that of the injured creditor—in which such a proceeding would meet with less countenance or indulgence than it would receive from the great mass of the American people." [1]

Yet within two years Governor McNutt of Mississippi had recommended, and within three years the legislatures of Mississippi and Florida had voted, the repudiation of nearly $9,000,000 of bonds.

In view of the fact that state indebtedness had doubled since 1835, it is not surprising that London, which had taken a large, if not the largest part of these securities, should have become anxious regarding its holdings. And it is not surprising to find that Webster should have been trustful, with the clean record of the states and the splendid example set them by the Federal Government.

Increase in State Debt Since War. In recent years there has again been a rapid increase in the debts of the American states. In 1925 the gross bonded debt of the state governments within the Union totalled $1,558,742,434. [2] Of this debt $903,000,000 or 57 per cent. was incurred since January 1, 1920. The total indebtedness of the states in 1925 was $550,000,000 greater than the entire federal debt in 1916.

The various purposes for which this state indebtedness has been incurred are indicated in the following table:

THE PURPOSES OF STATE DEBTS

(From *A National Survey of State Debts and Securities*, compiled by The Bank of America)

Purpose of Debt	Amount Outstanding 1925	Per Cent. 1925
Highways	$626,852,350.00	40.2
Waterways and Harbors	220,141,800.00	14.1
Soldiers' Bonus	287,097,600.00	18.4
Funding Operations	106,735,471.27	6.8
Other Improvements	108,130,912.00	6.9
Agricultural Aid	74,822,839.39	4.8
Public Buildings	27,599,523.26	1.8
Welfare Institutions	49,002,250.00	3.2
Miscellaneous	27,960,909.55	1.8
Other Military Purposes	13,395,787.54	.9
Education	17,002,990.67	1.1
Total	$1,558,742,433.68	100.0

[1] Text as of *Webster's Works*, Vol. XII, pp. 211–214.

[2] *National Survey of State Debts and Securities*, compiled in 1925 by The Bank of America.

It will be seen that 40 per cent. of the state debt has been raised to finance road building. The value of good roads in reducing accidents, in increasing the comfort of travel and in raising property values is unquestioned. However, the enormous sums spent for highway construction are regarded by many persons with concern. The *New York World* (October 8, 1923) made the following editorial comment on this subject:

"Building State roads is found to figure largely in this startling expansion of state expenditure. It is the newest thing in State activity and comparable with the railroad building fever of seventy years ago. States are binding themselves right and left for these improved highways and the interest cost is yet to figure in the fast-mounting construction and maintenance costs of the taxpayers. Cities, towns and counties are chipping in additional sums. The Federal Government is there as well with an actual and prospective expenditure fairly staggering. It is the day of the automobile, where private extravagances are forcing a public extravagance in due proportion.

"States as sovereign bodies have been noticeable in recent years chiefly for their shrinking place in the American scheme of government. But as free and independent debt contractors and road builders and taxbuilders they are glowing with new life."

A state may follow the policy of " pay-as-you-go " and meet current expenses out of current taxes, or it may finance certain undertakings by long-term borrowing. The former policy may well be followed by Eastern states which are more developed, adequately populated and are possessed of abundant local capital. Western states, with undeveloped resources, sparse population and insufficient capital must necessarily finance particularly their permanent constructive works by long-term borrowing especially from without.

Constitutional Debt-Restrictions. Because of the various periods of increasing state debts, restrictions on such borrowings have been placed in the constitutions of many of the states.

In the original constitutions of the older states these limitations are almost entirely absent. They usually show the working of bitter experience, as in the Ohio constitution of 1851, and are the result of amendments or of constitutional revisions. The tendency is toward greater strictness—there being an apparent rivalry in conservatism. The very wording of the limitations in many constitutions from all parts of the country is so uniform that a harmonious co-working of the commonwealths toward better conditions of state credit is manifest. There are a very few states, e.g., Massachusetts, the Carolinas, Kentucky, and Kansas, which are more or less lax (when they have any restrictions at all), as to the creation of state debt; but the spirit of the time is best illustrated in Georgia, which, by the constitution of 1877 has prohibited the creation of any further funded debt, and limits to $200,000 the floating indebtedness which may be outstanding against deficient revenue at any one time. Wisconsin's constitution of 1872 will furnish a still better model of utmost rigor in its restrictions.

In general the constitutions permit the legislatures to contract debt

1. to meet casual deficits in revenue,
2. to defray ordinary expenses not otherwise provided for,
3. to redeem existing funded indebtedness,
4. (sometimes) to pay interest on funded indebtedness,
5. to undertake public improvements,
6. to repel invasion and suppress insurrection.

The New York legislature is empowered to issue long-term bonds only " to repel invasion, suppress insurrection or defend the state in war."

But on the other hand the constitutions generally forbid the legislatures

1. to incur floating indebtedness beyond certain limits,
2. to incur ordinary expenses beyond certain limits,
3. to incur further funded indebtedness, or at least indebtedness beyond a certain sum,
4. to incur indebtedness for " internal improvements,"
5. to assume the debts of any private enterprise or political subdivision,
6. to use funds raised as above in behalf of war, insurrection, etc., or funds raised in the interests of amortization, for any other purpose.

In most states this is the tenor of the fundamental law. And it is most reassuring, especially in view of the fact that the entire West and most of the South adheres to its general terms. To be recommended for particular notice are those sections of each code forbidding the loan of the state's credit for corporate enterprise or for works of internal improvement.

To offset in slight degree this recent record of antipathy to debt-creation it must be said that Mississippi and one or two other repudiating states interdict in their revised constitutions the payment of the old defaulted bonds.

Statutory Debt-Restrictions and Corollary Acts. So much for the constitutions. As for the statutes, though there is an intimate and significant relation between them and the state's attitude toward its debt, the details are too technical for this place. To read the relation aright requires assistance from the bond attorney. An illustration will suffice. We have noticed previously that several of the commonwealths, by the terms of their revised constitutions, permit themselves to be sued. To what extent the people or their present representatives abet this provision, and therefore to what extent they are acting in good faith respecting this particular amendment, may be learned in each case by consultation of the statutes supplementary to the constitution. When none is to be found it is assumed by the legal fraternity that the provision is practically annulled by the will of the people. Webster, in that letter from which we have already quoted, seems to be more correct in his diagnosis of the security of statutory law than he was of the people's good faith. He said: " If it " (the state) " could not or would not make provision for paying the bond, it is not probable that it could or would make provision for satisfying the judgment."

Value of Debt-Restrictions. Political and financial expediency underlie the various legal restrictions of debts thus far described. During the Reconstruction Period, state credit was so misused that the public lost faith in legislatures and curbed their power. A second reason for restraint was the growing belief that a state should live within its income, that is, follow the pay-as-you-go policy. Borrowing was considered as having bad results in reducing the amount of capital available for private enterprise, and in tending to impair public credit which might therefore fail in real emergency.

In recent years many students of public finance have come to doubt the value of placing legal limits on the borrowing power of the states. It has been contended that such restrictions have proven ineffective in checking the extent of state borrowing, and the statistics presented on page 166 certainly bear out this view. It is also held that restrictions interfere with a rational administration of the state's finances and often render difficult the use of state credit at a time when economies could be made. Because of the ineffectiveness and inflexibility of debt-restriction, a wider discretion in state borrowing is often recommended.

SECURITY: TANGIBLE ASSETS

It has been made sufficiently clear that the security behind the bonds of a state rests mainly on its credit, and since the state is a quasi-sovereign, that this credit is represented mainly by the state's will toward the debts of its own creating, and that this will is to be judged in the light of the history of the state debt and of the state's present attitude, however determined, toward its debt.

These factors which make for state credit are intangible factors, or to revert to the metaphor of the preceding paragraphs, —in the inventory of a state's wealth they are not measured in dollars and cents: they are intangible assets.

The Tax Power. And yet though not measurable, and exceedingly subtle, the intangible assets of the state, on evaluation, are found very sensitive to the condition of the tangible assets, or material wealth. In tracing the history of state debts we noticed that the two chief outbreaks of default and repudiation closely attended two periods of severe business depression. The direct connection between the two kinds of assets is the tax power. There has been no case of default on state bonds, *whether valid or invalid*, when the resources of the state were sufficient to pay without hardship the annual state levy.

To him who seeks the material sources of a state's credit, the tax power is an immediate consideration. He should learn in the first place whether the state now levies a general tax. If it does without any tax, well and good; in an emergency this might prove a fresh resource. Vermont, Pennsylvania, Delaware, and Wisconsin have this distinction. In lieu of a general tax, revenue is dependent upon interest from treasury assets, and from license taxes and special taxes on corporate capital stock, stock transfer, corporate loans, collateral inheritances, charters, automobiles, etc.

Secondly, he should note the tax rate and the comparative degree of burden it imposes. In comparing the tax burdens of two states he should see that he has in hand the real, rather than the nominal tax of both as a basis. Sometimes the nominal state tax is the average of the municipal tax rates, and the tax for the immense contingent debt is annually levied directly upon the cities and towns benefited by it. Sometimes the tax is somewhat split up, and therefore deceptive. Indiana has the usual General Fund tax, but special taxes for benevolent institutions, public schools, sinking funds, and educational institutions. Vermont has no general state tax, but in the capacity of agent relieves the districts of direct taxation by raising special levies for such district purposes as school and highway-building and redistributes the proceeds to the towns, etc., by process of equalization. Connecticut in like manner remits the proceeds of its corporation taxes.

Thirdly, the investigator should particularly note that in one or two instances the commonwealths have imposed a constitutional limit to the rate of the state tax levy.[1] Georgia limits the tax to $5.00 a thousand; Alabama to $6.50 a thousand. This is not only placing the restriction where it does not belong, but, if the custom should spread, might come to have an important bearing on validity. If the tax limit in a given case had been nearly reached, such a provision might make impossible the levy of a remedial tax in time of emergency, such as arose in Nebraska in 1877. That year a pest of grasshoppers destroyed vegetation, and by means of a special levy the state was enabled to borrow funds to distribute seed grain to the farmers.

Lastly and most important, some well-grounded opinion should be arrived at on the following questions: What is the ratio of the present to the possible or practicable state tax? What is the ratio of the present state tax to the possible aggregate of municipal taxes? What is the ratio of the present state tax to the present aggregate of municipal taxes? A commonwealth may be without real public bonded debt and yet be less prepared to support one because of high internal tax rates, than another commonwealth with many and large funded obligations, which has, however, a light load of internal debt.

Taxable Wealth and Assessed Valuation. With the exception of states having a constitutional tax-limitation, and even possibly then,—ultimately, the resources of the tax power depend on the ratio of the actual total state tax to the taxable wealth. This ratio is not always the same thing as the tax rate; it depends on whether the taxable wealth and assessed valuation of a certain

[1] Not to be confused with the more common municipal tax limitation.

state are synonymous terms. In other words, it depends on whether the state assesses all property within its borders at full valuation. Since the taxable wealth of the state is known to the public at large only in terms of assessed valuation, and since assessed valuation is arrived at in various ways by the different states, and by various ways within a single state, we are confronted not by an insular but a comparative study, with statistical materials requiring careful analysis. The analysis, however, is well worth while, for assessed valuation represents the chief of the tangible assets.

Equalized Valuation. It is disconcerting to find the number and variety of means by which the figures for assessed valuation are attained. If it is the year of a state census, the results are more likely to be dependable, especially in the West, because obtained under state supervision and by more uniform methods. If not such a year the aggregate may be compiled wholly from inventories of cities and towns, or else from county totals, which in turn, to save time and labor, have been constructed by changing to scale the figures of the preceding assessment. But since in those states which do not uniformly require assessment at full value, the differences in tax rate require adjustment by a board of equalization or state tax commission, the whole subject has its full share of perplexities.

In not a few of the states there is a general assessment of real estate only once in a period of several years (Michigan every five years, Illinois every four years), although personal property may be listed every year. In the intervening annual returns, therefore, the valuation of real estate (the larger part of the whole), is arbitrary and detracts, like the process of equalization, from the accuracy of estimates and from the value of comparisons. Even in states that are presumed to revalue property annually, there is a general suspicion among officials that a thoroughgoing reassessment is occasional rather than periodic.

Relation of Assessed Valuation to Real Valuation. To be welcomed therefore as a tendency toward betterment in statistical methods is the movement to make assessed valuation, or at least appraised valuation, when the two differ as in Illinois, the same as real valuation.[1] Massachusetts, Connecticut, and Illinois

[1] See also the *Financial Statistics of States* published by the Bureau of Census, Department of Commerce, Washington, D. C.

took this step years ago; West Virginia in 1905 and New Jersey in 1906. Any tendency toward uniformity is to be welcomed as removing obstacles to comparative studies. And yet in this case the reform brings its own troubles. On comparing successive valuations in a state over a period of years to determine the rate of its growth or retrogression, the change in basis of appraisement is likely to be overlooked. In Connecticut for instance:— on the face of things Connecticut shows a remarkable growth in wealth for such a settled state, having almost doubled its assessed valuation in past years. But the cold reality is that Connecticut's basis of appraisement was not much over 50 per cent.; yet to-day, as stated, it is at actual value.

Comparison of Valuations. With these precautions in mind much light on a state's financial condition may be gained by comparison of its present with its past valuations, and of its present with the present valuations of other states. Surely no one has any but himself to blame, who in 1870 or thereafter bought the loans of Louisiana, which were subsequently repudiated, when he had before him the fact that the debt had doubled in the preceding decade and the assessed valuation of all property had declined one-third. And the same course of reasoning would have applied to the loans of any other repudiating state.

The Components of Assessed Valuation. Assuming now that the investigator appreciates the statistical difficulties of the appraisal and comparison of assets, he should analyze the assets themselves, for they vary greatly in degree of resource should need arise of sudden increase in state loans.

The large division of assessed valuation into real and personal property goes without saying. Many states separately itemize in their general reports the tax resources contained in bank and trust company stocks and deposits, in the capitalization of railroad, telegraph, telephone, and insurance companies, and generally in the chartering and capitalization of corporations. These resources are entirely at the command of the legislatures in the same sense that real property is. Here again we find no uniformity of use in regard to the tax power. In some states objects are taxed that in others are not; and the rates on the same objects vary.

Other Items of Material Wealth. There is other material wealth which, being the property of the state, as such,—proprietary assets,—is not usually a resource of the tax power, but may prove on examination to be of first importance as immediately balancing state liabilities. Some states have revenue-producing realty; South Carolina has beds of phosphate deposit which formerly were of great help in meeting the annual budget. Treasury assets pure and simple are very generally neglected in comparisons of state resources.

Of course the value of all revenue-producing loans and the justification for discarding them in arriving at a state's real net debt, depends upon the character of the enterprise they assist and the assured permanency of its income. The old canal, railroad aid, and bank bonds, of ill repute, were at one time technically in this revenue-producing class. Perhaps the line of cleavage between issues which may and which may not be discarded lies in the purpose of issue. Revenue-producing corporate aid bonds, should, from the lessons of the past, not be booked by the bond-buyer as anything but a pure liability, and revenue-producing loans issued for purposes of public improvement, like the California " Sea Wall " bonds, should be omitted as at least self-subsisting.

Population. An indirect asset, if it may so be called, that should not be neglected, is population. The poll tax of itself is no inconsiderable resource. As an index of growth or decline in material wealth statistics of population are serviceable. In Nevada, for instance, the decline in population suggests the subsidence of silver mining, its chief industry, and in California the growth of population is in keeping with the marvellous development of this state during the period. Needless to say municipalities there sell their bonds with a lower interest rate and at a higher figure than in previous years.

In comparisons of population, temporal and geographical, certain extraneous and occasional influences should be taken into account, viz., the enfranchisement of the negro after the war, and from the census of 1900 on, the inclusion of the Indian population on the Reservations.

Obviously the character of the population is of first importance, and closely second to it the character of present or expected accretions from birth and immigration. Those Northwestern states which are being settled by the virile races of Northern Europe will in all probability make impossible a repetition of

Minnesota's repudiation. In the South it is a question to what extent the growth in population of the blacks is a menace to credit. Their rate of increase per cent. is not so great in a majority of the Southern states as the rate of increase among the white population.

Bank Statements. Another index of growth in prosperity is the bank statement. It is not unusual to see on a bond circular a comparative statement of bank clearings.

Offsets of Liabilities. Just as there is reason to offset against gross bonded indebtedness such quickly convertible treasury assets and stable income-producing properties as a state may have, so again, it should be understood that these assets have their like offsets,—that state bonded indebtedness is by no means the only or chief liability of the people of the state, and therefore of the state, since the courts recognize as the ultimate obligor, not political or corporate bodies, but the very people themselves. The chief encroachment on state tax resources is the existence of municipal indebtedness. Put in other words, the security behind state bonds is partly dependent on limitations as to municipal indebtedness. Only the surplus revenues of business activity are taxable, and the interest on and redemption of municipal loans eat into this directly. It is a well-established principle of law, relating to civil governments and corporations as well as to individuals, that a debtor's right to life and liberty is prior to a creditor's claim. No court would prejudice the solvency of a state (when sued) or of its civil divisions, in the interest of any bondholder. And so it is for the bond purchaser to see that the tax burden of the lesser civil divisions is not perilous to the interests of the state debt. The principles here outlined apply in the same way with equal force to a state's contingent debt. It is to be doubted whether any state has repudiated its bonds without, as part or main cause, the failure of revenues for bonds of its guaranteeing,—in other words, for its contingent debt.

Warrants and other floating indebtedness should also be considered. The list of states without bonded debt, given previously, would have been misleading were bonded and floating debt virtually the same. There is a moral distinction of importance between the two kinds of obligations. A floating debt may be carried along from year to year, indefinitely, but the very fact that it has not been funded indicates (in lack of constitutional provisions) an unwillingness to create debt of long standing and an intention to retire it when revenues permit. However, as a pure liability, floating debt should be looked to as seriously as any other. Colorado at one time had such a debt in excess of constitutional limits.

SECURITY AS VESTED IN THE BOND ISSUE

We have considered up to this point the security for state bonds vested in a state's intangible and tangible assets,—that is, in its " sentimental " credit and in its tax resource as they are dependent on each other. There is a word to be said in closing as to the security vested in the issue itself.

Amortization: Sinking Fund and Serial Repayment. First as to sinking funds. This subject in its large aspects has been thoroughly covered already. It is necessary here only to repeat that the sinking fund principle, whether applied to government, state, municipal, or corporation issues, is wasteful, and renders a fund liable to depletion by misappropriation, embezzlement, and other fraud, and to depreciation in its investments. Of what use to Virginia was that part of her sinking funds which held the Riddleberger bonds, when the state paid interest on those in the hands of the public, but, for years, not on those in the sinking funds? Mississippi illustrates best the vicissitudes of this method of amortization. In 1830 a sinking fund of $250,000 was started for the Planters' Bank bonds from the premium secured at their sale.[1] By 1839, when the bank failed, this sum had increased to about $800,000, but *within one year*, by mismanagement and depreciation in its investments, had dwindled to $525,765, and by 1848 to about $100,000! By the constitution of Pennsylvania her sinking funds may be diverted, at the will of the legislature, from the extinguishment of the public debt, for use in war, invasion, or insurrection.

A railroad president has said: " The best way to sink a debt is to pay it; the surest sinking fund is *payment.*"[2] A few of the younger states have set a much needed example to the older by adopting the serial method of payment, or at least by making redemption possible before regular maturity. All Idaho bonds with one exception are subject to call ten years before regular

[1] "Banking and Repudiation in Mississippi," *Bankers' Magazine*, 1863.
[2] *The Sinking Fund*, G. M. Browne, 2d ed., p. 10.

maturity, and because that one exception is not now redeemable the state is obliged to pay one per cent. more interest on the face of the loan than on any of the others. By the constitution of Wisconsin a law creating a debt " shall provide for levying an annual tax sufficient to pay the annual interest of such debt and the principal within five years from the passage of such law . . . and such appropriation shall not be repealed, nor the taxes postponed until the principal and interest . . . shall have been wholly paid." The wording of Minnesota's constitution is practically the same, except that ten years, not five, is the period set.

Maine, however, has adopted the best plan of all: straight serial repayment. When Maine refunded her old debt in 1889 she caused her new loans to mature in annual instalments. West Virginia, by the constitution of 1872, requires the serial method of retiring any loan she may put forth. Massachusetts, with the most need of all, because of the immensity of her debt, has done less than she might to improve her condition by sound fiscal methods, and, in respect to the contingent debt, which is the larger part of her obligations, until 1905 even withheld from the forty and more cities and towns which must pay it, the privilege of discharging it by the serial method. It is a pleasure to record that through the public spirit of a gentleman who saved his own town of Brookline nearly a million dollars in interest during a period of twenty years by agitation and exposition of the serial method, the cities and towns in the Metropolitan District of Massachusetts were privileged to avail themselves of the serial method of financing the obligations of the Metropolitan District. Had the three principal loans of the District (running forty years) been issued in serial form, even at one-half per cent. higher rate than under the sinking fund form, the saving in interest account would have been $26,000,000, and the saving in actual cost to taxpayers about $8,360,000 on a $3\frac{1}{2}$ per cent. basis.[1]

Validity. But if there is any one thing an issue ought to bear on its face, metaphorically, and literally as far as possible in the recital of the bond, it is validity. It has been said previously that no state has repudiated its bonds, whether valid or invalid, when the tax-burden was not a hardship; but conversely, seldom

[1] Cf. *The Metropolitan Debts of Boston and Vicinity*, Alfred D. Chandler, Brookline.

(Mississippi in 1852 and one or two other instances excepted) has a state with an unbearable tax-burden repudiated its obligations without some show of invalidity. More than one volume would be needed to develop adequately this topic of validity. Bond law, however, has progressed to such a stage that opportunities for doubt seldom arise in connection with state issues. But the method of authorization and flotation, and the purpose of issue have been fruitful sources of trouble in the past.

Texas has the distinction of guaranteeing the legality of her county and municipal issues. All loans of date subsequent to 1893 must bear the certificate of the Attorney General that they are lawful obligations; and when so certificated they may not be challenged for validity. It is our recollection that one or two states do likewise for their own state loans. It is at any rate a plan worthy of advertisement and imitation, and therefore mentioned in this place.

CHAPTER XVIII

COUNTY BONDS

The Municipal Division of Tax-Secured Bonds. Upon entering the subject of County Bonds we have done with the governmental division of tax-secured issues, or Civil Loans, and have taken up the municipal division. The line of separation is very distinct. Government securities, whether federal or state, rest immediately on the good faith of the obligor. Creditors of states, other than states themselves, have almost no redress at law, and absolutely none without the virtual consent of the defendant state. This republican country did not inherit in its common law the immemorial principle of monarchy: " The King can do no wrong; " but in overriding by Constitutional amendment the ruling of the United States Supreme Court that a state *could* be sued by a citizen of another state, it surrendered this portion of its democratic birthright for what, in the light of history, many would call the pottage of state sovereignty. History has not dealt so ironically with our municipalities. Although legislatures have sometimes made the attempt, no state has openly permitted, or can permit, its municipalities to evade any part of their legal debt. To do so would be to infringe upon the Federal Constitution which prohibits the impairment of the obligation of contracts. Therefore there is no theoretical relief from unwelcome debt for the political subdivisions. An individual or a private corporation may, in certain circumstances, incur debt, and then, before the law, be released from the obligation. But not so a municipal corporation. There is no bankruptcy court nor bankruptcy law for municipal [1] debtors.

Since, now, all municipalities, in contradistinction to sovereign governments, are amenable to justice and equity vested in the law, and the law, in turn, is created and exercised by higher

[1] The several states and their legislatures are somewhat at variance upon the use of the word *municipal* and its derivatives; and in bond parlance the term is none too explicit. In this book it has been used for the most part in its broadest sense, as pertaining to all the civil divisions of a state.

authority than the municipality, or even than the state, a somewhat different set of conditions affects the security for municipal
obligations from that affecting government obligations; or at
least, if the various conditions are the same, their relative influence and importance are greatly altered.

Characteristics of the Municipal Division. In Government
Bonds, federal or state, we found, good faith was the one great
essential. Perhaps in only two instances were state loans made
in good faith which could not be repaid because of actual inability; and he would be a pessimist indeed who believed the
material resources of any state could be so depleted in the future
as to compel default on anything like present acknowledged indebtedness. In Municipal Bonds, however, good faith is not
theoretically of that supreme importance, for there is remedy at
law which usually proves adequate. The cases are innumerable
in which state courts, or on failure of these, federal courts, have
come to the relief of bondholders when municipalities have attempted to cheat. In Municipal Bonds one must *first* satisfy
himself of the financial competency of the issuing body, that the
law may not withhold relief for want of wealth to tax, for the
financial future of all municipalities, unlike that of states, is by
no means reasonably assured. And, secondly, one must seek
security in the issue itself, must make certain of a bond's validity,
that in want of good faith he may have the law at his service.
Lastly, he may weigh the evidences of good faith, by the laws
and record of the municipality, and of the state in which it is
situated, and also by the attitude of the courts of jurisdiction.
In these ways he may ascertain the degree of danger from dishonesty. This, then, is the order of investigation for municipal
issues:—financial competency, validity, and good faith,—whereas
in State Bonds it is good faith, competency, and validity. This
difference of standing in law, and diminished importance of good
faith as compared with financial competency and validity, draw
together for study in common the obligations of the lesser political divisions.

Therefore it is that the bonds of counties, parishes, townships,
cities, towns, villages, boroughs, districts, precincts, etc., etc.,
are logically grouped together and often entitled municipals,
whether the entity of the issuing authority arises from incorporation, either by general or special act of legislature, or by act of

city council. Further subdivision of Tax Bonds, or Civil Loans, is quite arbitrary, and merely a matter of convenience. It is usually based on the political nature of the issuing body, for the character and purpose of the flotation are largely determined by the character of the municipality and the purpose for which it was created. Since the city (or town) is the most important of these political units, the bonds of cities and towns are called Municipals Proper, and it is under the chapter-head of *City and Town Bonds* that the principles that govern the municipal group will receive their fullest treatment. Accordingly the other members of the group will be discussed only along their lines of divergence from the City and Town type.

The Economic Function of the County. The largest political subdivision of the state is usually the county.[1] The importance of the county as a civil division varies considerably in the several states. In Connecticut, where the town is the civil unit, from which are made the grand lists for state as well as for municipal tax, one seldom hears of county bonds, for the part of the county in the state's political organization is not important. Connecticut is one of the original states,—as a colony one of the earliest settled; its population is comparatively dense; its ten cities and many towns are well scattered, and properly act as administrative centres. In Kansas, and in other states of the high plains region, on the other hand, the county usually seems to be the major civil unit, and county loans appear to exceed for the most part, both in number and in value, the loans of the included cities and towns. In these states of enormous area and sparse population the interests of a large part of the people are agrarian interests; legislation and expenditure which have to do with the raising of cattle and crops and their transportation by road and rail to market, are of utmost moment. Counties of this sort have therefore obligated themselves for the construction of turnpikes and bridges, and above all, for railroads; and in common with counties everywhere, for those general instruments of county administration: courthouse, jail, and poor farm.

The Range of Quality in County Loans. As one travels it is a journey from Kansas to Connecticut: representative in some minds of the former distance between Kansas and Connecticut municipal credit. Between the two there is a wide range of qual-

[1] In Louisiana the county-equivalent is usually called the "parish."

ity in civil loans; and the range in county bonds is as great as that in any other kind, although the legitimate purposes of issue are few. There are counties that are merely bad lands, creations of the surveyor; counties rich in mineral wealth; counties without railroad transportation; inland counties, worthless without drainage or irrigation; counties embracing a dozen cities and towns; metropolitan counties coextensive with a great city. For the loans of all of these we must organize a criticism sufficiently catholic to appreciate justly each and every kind.

Material Assets

The County Statement. Our first business in County Bonds, as in all Municipal issues, is with the financial competency of the municipality. To that end a circular, offering County Bonds, will have upon it a statistical statement, furnishing us, probably, with the county's Real and Assessed Valuation, Gross (or Total), and Net Debt, Population, and perhaps Tax Rate. These facts are very useful in determining the value of the security, but not one bond buyer in a multitude is able to interpret them. Let us take them up in their logical order. First the tax.

The Tax Power and Its Limitation. The immediate security for all Civil Loans is the tax-power; but although the tax-power is directly dependent on the various assets, it may not be possible to exercise it to its full capacity because of artificial restrictions. We have deprecated these restrictions, in the preceding pages, for their artificiality; maintaining that restriction should be put not upon the very organ by which the amortization of debt is accomplished, but rather upon the debt itself; and the objection holds for county, as well as state tax-limitations. By her constitution Alabama in this way restricts the county tax for all purposes to $\frac{1}{2}$ of 1 per cent. of the assessed valuation, or $5.00 a thousand; and Kentucky likewise. Kentucky very naturally permits her cities and towns greater leeway. They may tax themselves from $7.50 to $15.00 a thousand of their assessed valuation, according to population. Alabama restricts all municipalities and Arkansas her counties, to $5.00. Arkansas does not restrict her other municipalities. Oklahoma restricts her counties to $8.00 and other municipalities more or less according to their importance. Apart from any legal complications which this strange sort of limitation may arouse, it will be hard to convince the skeptical layman that if calamity should overtake county or town, and the tax-burden become harassing, the assessors might not yield to the temptation to lower the assessed valuation, and thereby cut into the annual tax and prevent the satisfaction of municipal contracts; for it must not be forgotten that the current expenses of the municipality have the right of way over the discharge of municipal obligations.   This base resort of untrustworthy municipalities is made impossible by the constitutions of California, Georgia, Idaho, Illinois, Iowa, Kentucky, Michigan, Missouri, New Hampshire, North Dakota, Oklahoma, Pennsylvania, South Dakota, Texas, and Wisconsin. In Illinois the provision reads as follows: " Any county, city, school district, or other municipal corporation incurring any indebtedness as aforesaid, shall, before or at the time of doing so, provide for the collection of a direct annual tax sufficient to pay the interest on such debt as it falls due, and also to pay and discharge the principal thereof within twenty years from the time of contracting same."

Although constitutional limitation of the tax rate for counties is rare, statutory limitation is by no means uncommon.   West Virginia limits her counties to 6-10 of 1 per cent.,[1] or $6.00 a thousand; and New Jersey, on a scale down to an ultimate $5.00 a thousand.   If the statute limits the tax rate in a general municipal taxing act, i.e., if, in the limited tax rate, are included the taxes for all public purposes (and this is usually the case), it may prove dangerous, for current expenses are or can be made very elastic, and an expansion of them to defraud would be hard to prove at law.   In times past (e.g., in Missouri), taxes raised in virtue of a special bond-enabling act have come into contact with the general statutory limitation of tax rate, and the special bond-tax has been required to come within the limits of the tax rate for all municipal purposes.   But the Supreme Court of Missouri has recently relinquished this construction to the benefit of all municipal bondholders.

The Tax Rate.   To attempt to draw conclusions from the tax rate of a county is well-nigh hopeless without the possession of facts never found on a bond circular.   At the time of this

---

[1] This statutory limitation is more stringent than that of the Constitution of 1872, which set the maximum county tax rate at 95-100 of 1 per cent., or $9.50 a thousand.

comparison the tax rate of Hartford County, Connecticut, is 25 cents per $1,000, and of Adams County, Ohio, $17.35. Surely the burden borne by Adams County property holders is not seventy times as great! Such absurd discrepancies are seldom found in city and town statements. The cause must lie in the nature of the civil division. Counties and districts of all sorts will be found to make returns like these, utterly at variance with any principle of uniformity in administration.

To a large extent the lower tax may be said to obtain in counties with the higher valuation. Concentration of wealth economizes the expense of wealth's maintenance. Yet little satisfaction will be got from the principle in this form. Perhaps the only form of the principle worth application to county tax rates is this: " Municipal Counties," i.e., counties containing one or more cities like Hartford County, can maintain a tax rate justifiably lower than " Rural Counties," since in municipal counties the city or cities, by municipal tax, may carry the burden of public improvements. Therefore, although the rural Adams County, Ohio, had a tax rate of $17.35, Summit County, Ohio, at that time had a tax of only $2.35, because Akron, the county seat, came to its relief with a valuation of over $25,000,000 to tax at the rate of $32 per thousand. In such a case the rate for the county will be higher than it would otherwise be, and to all intents the county could be classified as a rural county.

Under this condition too, the assessed valuation and all other components of the county statement should be presented minus the non-participating city's share. What has just been said applies only in part to the municipal county of Suffolk, Massachusetts, which includes Boston, Chelsea, Revere, and Winthrop. By a contract between these cities and towns, dating back to 1822 (when Winthrop and Revere were a part of Chelsea), only Boston is liable to taxation for any county purposes until the legislature shall otherwise order; and in return, Boston has all interest in and jurisdiction over the real and personal estate of the county. All statistical considerations for these municipalities should be governed accordingly.

It is not always evident what is included in the tax rates as presented by county officials. One should make certain whether the state tax has been deducted and the special taxes for schools or institutions, if there are any such. When the statement is worded " Total Tax " these generally are included. On the other hand, if the county is coextensive with, or overlapping any other civil division, such as a levee district, one should make sure, in computing the annual burden, that the divisional taxes are included, for the same property must bear the two or more imposts.

Assessed Valuation. In presenting the assessed valuation the bond circular is not liable to mislead, seriously, in its statement. This valuation will be the total of the assessed valuations of the constituent civil divisions, *including cities, etc.*, irrespective of the method of appraisal. An exception should be taken when a civil division, like Lynchburg, Virginia, does not bear its share of the county tax. Any unusual situation like this at Lynchburg is to be avoided, because of the likelihood that the principles arising may not have received adjudication in the courts. No effort is made, as a rule, to indicate in the county statement whether the ratio of assessed valuation to real valuation is approximately the same for the county as the average ratio of the included towns, etc., for it must be understood that the ratios often differ, and for perfect results in comparison need adjustment such as is given by a board of equalization. In considering assessed valuation, as well as tax rate, debt, or population, we should constantly keep in view the character of the county:— whether it is " municipal " or " rural," for the amount of the assessed valuation is not the only significant feature, but the *ratio* it bears to the *real* net debt.

Other Resources: Secondary Income. Counties, and " taxing districts " such as we treat in Chapter XXII, are not so favorably situated as states and cities, in regard to secondary income. All civil divisions are on the same plan of possibility respecting revenue from sinking funds, but the nature of counties and districts precludes them from extended proprietary ownership (as distinguished from governmental ownership) of revenue-producing property. And in those states in which the public property of the municipality is seizable for public debt, the value of such county and district property, except in the case of school districts, is relatively small.

County Debt. In a large, rough way, the figures for assessed valuation, as presented, suffice for ordinary investigation. But the county debt-statement, as customarily understood, *is utterly misleading*. There is nothing else in the county statement, or in the usual statement of any other civil division, which misrepresents the facts as this. Not that the debt-statement is literally incorrect, for this is not the case, but that the ordinary inferences cannot be drawn from it. If the assessed valuation of a county is the sum of the assessed valuations of its subdivisions, then the *real* debt of the county should be the sum of the debts of the county and its subdivisions; and there is no fairness in exhibiting the ratio of county debt to county valuation, unless our methods of arriving at the totals of debt and valuation are the same. As a matter of fact, however, by county debt we do not mean the *real* debt of the county, but only the debt of the political unit called county, irrespective of the debts of the included political units. It is unlikely that this method of computing county debt arose from any nice observance of the letter of the law, but rather from the ease with which the nominal or direct county debt-statement was to be secured, as compared with the necessity of search in ascertaining the *real* debt of the county; and furthermore, because the county debt-statement is much more presentable when construed literally.

Real Debt of Municipal Counties. With the coöperation of the local officials it would not ordinarily be difficult to compute the real net debt of a county. It is a simple sum in addition; and it would have the inestimable advantage of allowing fair comparisons with the debt-statements of the other municipal division. In financial statements, as in everything else, the whole truth in the end is simpler than the half truth, and works for the best interests of every one concerned.[1] In want of the figures for real debt it is best to appraise the material credit of municipal counties at somewhat less than the credit of the leading municipality or municipalities in the county. This rule will have exceptions. Many would except Allegheny County. The bonds of Essex County, New Jersey, because of peculiar local conditions, have at times sold to slightly better advantage than the bonds of Newark, which is situated in it. Yet, in general, the principle holds good, particularly for " metropolitan counties," i.e., counties which are coextensive with, or wholly dominated by, the great cities of the country. Other influences of course are at work upon county credit beside the debt ratio, and this matter

---

[1] For the application of the "real debt" principle to city credit, see Chapter XX under the caption, "*Municipal Debt*" (pp. 225–226).

will be taken up in greater detail when we come to speak in particular of municipal and metropolitan counties.

The Real Debt of Rural Counties. Although, as we have just said, the discrepancy between real and direct county debt is greatest in municipal and metropolitan counties, it is likely to arise in rural counties as well. Rural counties, in part or in whole, may be situated in, or may include, special assessment districts for road improvement, for the installation of conduit water supply, and for the reclamation of land by drainage or irrigation. Since the taxing districts created for these purposes are usually supported by levies only on the land benefited, it often happens that rural counties have heavier tax-burdens on some parts of their territory than on others; and this fact is not likely to appear in a statement of the county debt. Still, since the financing of rural counties is so much simpler and without sophistication, their fiscal condition is generally set forth in its right light. Cass County, Indiana, for illustration, has a " general," or direct debt of $415,920; but owing to a peculiar decision of the State Supreme Court (which has analogues in one or two other states), the improvement of roads becomes a township, rather than a county, affair; and therefore townships of Cass County have issued $985,379 in bonds payable in each case by levies on the township improved. Yet since these bonds are really a contingent debt of the county, they appear, as they should, in the total debt as exhibited by the county.

Since, now, the statement of a county's net debt may be so wide of the mark, we must not permit ourselves the luxury of debt-comparisons, as between county and county, but especially as between county and city, without making due allowance for what may be called " included debts." To do so would be to indulge in the same sort of fallacy that we exposed in the comparison of assessed valuations, in the preceding chapter.

Contingent Debt: Quasi-County Bonds. The indirect sort of debt represented by the Township Bonds of Indiana counties is not the only kind of county contingent debt. Indiana will serve for example as well as any other state. Sullivan County has a direct, or " general " debt of only $5,000; but with an assessed valuation of $36,932,325, it has a contingent debt of $942,222, consisting of road, ditch (or drainage), and levee bonds. St. Joseph County, in 1910, with a direct debt of about the same

amount, had a few ditch bonds outstanding. That these indirect
or contingent obligations, with their less assured status in the
eyes of the law, were held in lower esteem, was to be seen in this
instance in the interest rate. All the other bonds of St. Joseph
County were then $3\frac{1}{2}$s, 4s, or $4\frac{1}{2}$s; but the ditch bonds were 6s.
Westchester County, New York, at about the same time issued
some $4\frac{1}{2}$s of doubtful genealogy. It was the general opinion of
banking houses that these were only quasi-county bonds,—a
sort of special assessment issue, secured by taxation against only
such portions of the county as would be benefited by the improvement; although the county itself undertook to make the collection
and father the transaction. As a result only three bids were
received for the bonds, and these only at a lower figure than
Westchester had a right to expect had they been a direct obligation.

To what degree quasi-county bonds are really a contingent
debt of the county depends, to a certain extent, on the nature of
the bond, but more, on the attitude of the courts of jurisdiction.
The federal courts, outside of the 7th Circuit, and most of the
state courts (with the particular exception of Illinois), hold the
including municipality liable for these Special Assessment bonds.
The subject will receive more extended treatment in the chapter
on *District Bonds*, under the caption Special Assessment Bonds.

Debt Limitations. A partial recognition of the fact that the
direct, or even the direct and contingent, county debt is but
part of the real debt, is seen in the stringent limitations to the
county debt, as compared, often, with the limitations to other
kinds of municipal debt. Although the other municipalities of
Indiana are permitted to incur funded obligations to the extent
of 2 per cent. of the assessed valuation, counties for the most
part are limited to not much more than 1 per cent., and certain
kinds of debt-creating activities which are permitted the other
civil divisions, are forbidden the counties. We find the same
sort of discrimination in Utah, where cities and towns are given
a nominal debt-limit of 4 per cent. In Oregon the framers of the
constitution of 1857 restricted the debt of any county in that
state to $5,000; but left the terms of restriction for the other civil
divisions to the discretion of future legislatures. Although an
inadjustable restriction such as Oregon's is highly undesirable,
and encourages resort to subterfuges to circumvent the consti-

tution, nevertheless it is a recognition of the peculiar relation which exists between a county's net debt and that of its included municipal divisions.

These that we have discussed are the leading features of the usual county statements which differ from those of city or town. For further details the investor or student is referred to the corresponding paragraphs in the chapter on *City and Town Bonds*. The second half of the chapter on *State Bonds* also may be helpful.

VALIDITY

Having disposed of financial competency,—the first consideration in ascertaining the credit of a county, in so far at least as it is to be ascertained from statistics,—we are prepared for the succeeding topic, validity.

With the gradual fixation of municipal bond law, and of bond recitals, and of methods of issue under trust company supervision and certification, the best informed of bond buyers may scarcely hope, by taking further thought, to safeguard himself to any greater extent than will a reliable banking house that serves him. If buying refunding loans he may look up the character and history of the loan refunded, and accept no bonds that refund an issue concerning which there has been trouble, as in the Muhlenberg County, Kentucky, Refunding 5s and the Hinsdale County, Colorado, Refunding 4s. Loans refunding issues validated by the United States Supreme Court might be an exception to this rule, having been approved by the court of last resort; but even then, as in Pima County, Arizona, Territorial Funding 3s, other grounds of trouble might arise.

Furthermore, he may restrict his purchases to loans created for objects properly accomplished and paid for by county organization. He will accept as proper purposes of issue when statutory authority is conferred, loans for courthouses and jails, since the county is a judicial unit; also for schoolhouses, asylums, poor farms, roads, culverts, and bridges. Irrespective of state laws he will be suspicious of loans issued in aid of state institutions or private corporations. He will refuse county bonds issued to build state normal schools, armories, sugar mills, water, gas, and electric light works, or bonds to defray any other expenditures not in strict accord with a county's functions. Above all things he will read with utmost care the statement upon the instrument he buys, remembering that in properly drawn bonds the municipality that issues them is estopped from many causes of illegality by the very recital.   Had holders of Green County, Kentucky, Railroad-Aid bonds observed this precaution before buying, they would not now be cherishing them as *priceless* mementos of the blue-grass region.

Yet it does not follow, because a bond has been issued in an irregular manner, that the courts will permit its repudiation, as Hitchcock County, Nebraska, found out in 1905 when the United States Circuit Court of Appeals decided that " although all the requirements of the law may not have been observed, that fact is not sufficient ground for the repudiation of the bonds when they come into the hands of an innocent person for value, provided there has been no legal obstacle to the county officers' complying with the requirements of the law." However, it is better to be sure than to be sorry; and the best way to avoid invalidity in municipal issues is to buy them only of the most responsible banking houses, and if the issue is new and untried, only when certified to by a responsible trust company, and when accompanied by a favorable legal opinion from responsible bond attorneys.   But, after all, this caution applies to city and district bonds as well as to county.

The Partition and Annexation of Counties.   There is one phase, however, of the legal situation in counties,—particularly large counties in the still undeveloped West and Southwest,—which sometimes causes disquiet to holders of this class of issues.   The large counties of Idaho, Arizona, New Mexico, and Montana,— counties, some of them greater in area than the smaller New England states,—which have arrived at that stage of development demanding a more intensive agriculture, often become too unwieldy for the proper exercise of county functions under the conflicting demands of diversified interests.   This is especially the case when the surface of the land in one part of the county has been retrieved by irrigation, or drainage, or otherwise, and the remainder is in pasturage.   Then the variance of two types of people may make a slight political separation advisable, as in the separation of Latah County from Nez Perces County, Idaho. The adjustment and resurvey of state and county boundary lines is another cause of the partition of counties.

Quite the opposite phenomenon, the annexation of counties,

is accomplished in the interest of various political plans, not only in the West, but in the East, also. Redistricting, as a political vote-getting device, is at least as early with us as 1812, for it was in that year, when Elbridge Gerry was Governor of Massachusetts, that the Americanism, *gerrymandering*, was coined to describe it.

The partition and annexation of counties (and the principle holds good for all municipalities) need not and usually do not cause serious disturbance of bond security. When a state legislature changes the county boundaries, it may reapportion the indebtedness in any way that seems proper, provided that in so doing it does not impair the obligation of the municipal contract, i.e., seriously impair the bond security. The difficulties arise from the fact that oftentimes the legislatures are remiss in their duties, and altogether neglect to redistribute the old debt. In lieu of specific legislative apportionment the general principle holds, that, when in the partition of a county, the original municipality is not abolished, the obligations of that county remain with it, and do not hold on the segregated territory. And in like manner, when territory has been annexed to a county, the annexed territory is relieved of its obligations under the old municipality and assumes those of the county of which it has become a part. This situation is not often met. However, in 1893 portions of Mora County, New Mexico, were reincorporated in new counties under legislative direction.

When, however, by the partition of a county, two or more counties are formed, and the old county abolished, the apportionment of the debt, in want of legislative provision, will be on the broad principles of equity established for these cases by the United States Supreme Court; the debt will be distributed pro rata, according to the relative taxable valuations of the segregated territories. For a case of extinction see the former county of Alturas, Idaho.

But by far the commonest kind of partition is that in which the remnant territory retains its municipal identity, and the fragment becomes a new county. Bond law, in this circumstance, would be more susceptible of dispute. As a rule the indebtedness has received legislative adjustment. Otherwise it generally remains the sole obligation of the parent county; and its offshoot escapes the debt. But this need not disturb the bondholder.

Under the law of contracts he has recourse upon the new county in default of the old, in so far as the new county was part of the old at the time of the contract. Those interested will find material for study of this class of indebtedness against the counties of Stevens, Washington; Spartanburg, South Carolina; Ada, Idaho; Missoula Park, and Deer Lodge, Montana; and Apache and Yavapai, Arizona.

Doubtless it would surprise many people to know with what little friction in regard to the reapportionment of indebtedness, the partition of counties has been accomplished. There is reason for this. But it is merely public good-fortune that in the partition of states or of territories to form states (Massachusetts, Virginia, Dakota, etc.) the notorious " West Virginia Certificates " represent the only embarrassment to bondholders. Theoretically the danger of loss from ownership of state bonds, in partition, is much greater, for it is not possible to compel the adjudication of disputes. But for county obligations a board of apportionment, or an arbitration committee, with legislatively derived powers, can enforce its findings, and the federal courts can give adequate relief in equity. Nowhere is that illustrated to better advantage than in Pima County, Arizona, which, with a heavy load of unsettled railroad-aid debt hanging over it, was able to accomplish the segregation of a portion of its territory to form the new county of Santa Cruz, by releasing Santa Cruz from its share of Pima County's debt on the surrender by Santa Cruz County of the equivalent in its own bonds.

Occasionally the partition of a county has weakened the standing of bondholders in case of previous default. In 1905 a writ of temporary mandamus, issued to the Commissioners of Santa Fé County, ordering them to levy a tax to amortize some defaulted bonds of 1882, was resisted by the taxpayers, partly on the ground " that considerable of the area and property of Santa Fé County at the time of the default and the first mandamus has since been annexed to Rio Arriba and Torrance Counties, and that much new property has been placed upon the assessment rolls since the default." [1]

[1] The Denver *Republican*, August 24, 1905. (Quoted in the *Commercial and Financial Chronicle*, Vol. LXXXI, p. 1059.)

Good Faith

It is to be regretted that a study of county conditions does not yield us as satisfactory assurances for the future regarding good faith as regarding validity. In relating the history of state bonds, the unpleasantness of dwelling upon past repudiation was mitigated by the unmistakably sound condition of present state credit, and by the safeguards of constitutional restriction built against future temptation and unwisdom. It is true that we have a right to believe that never again will counties of the United States be brought to face a combination of circumstances so unfavorable to civil credit as those of the forties and seventies; and we have the satisfaction of knowing that at the costly tutelage of experience, the people of this country, as a whole, have learned the simple financial lesson that it is cheaper to pay a debt than to disown it. But still, we have to face the fact that many municipalities have outstanding perfectly valid debts, obligations in ethics as well as in law, which they can pay, and won't pay, and intend never to pay. The most flagrant instances are usually in rural counties, for the reasons we shall set forth.

The Extent and Cause of County Repudiation. During the Reconstruction Period, before the vogue of reclamation and special assessment districts, and other newfangled devices for debt-making, the political unit that suffered most from war and the expansion of credit, was the county,—especially the rural county. Man for man and dollar for dollar, no other civil division at that time lay so utterly prostrate as the rural county. The typical rural county, in the nature of the case, was in the West and South. Men from Eastern cities, with a little capital, more imagination, and most shrewdness,—with well-drawn charts and easy speech,—inveigled the farmers into bonding their municipalities to help construct railroads by which their produce might reach better markets. Sometimes these roads were built; but in the flimsiest manner, and did not pay, and were discontinued. Sometimes they were built in part;—a very small part. Often they were not even surveyed. Meanwhile the bonds had been sold and somebody had pocketed the proceeds.

The extent to which practices similar to these prevailed in the less settled parts of the country, seems incredible in this day and generation. To attribute them altogether to the wiles of Eastern capitalists, or to the stupidity of the municipalities, is to see but one side of a complex situation. If the East was " criminally " sharp, the West was " criminally " dull. If loans were secured from counties, et al., for railroads it was never intended to build, loans were floated by counties which they never intended to pay. But wherever the burden of the fault lay, the results are plain enough:—from $12,000,000 to $18,000,000 of municipal bonds, it is estimated, were scaled in Nebraska, Kansas, and Eastern Dakota alone,[1] and throughout the new country repudiation and default became almost the rule, rather than the exception. The extent of this repudiation of county and municipal debts, the greater part of which occurred in the Reconstruction Period, is not known, but has been estimated to be about $1,000,000,000! " The most prolific field for municipal delinquencies has been in and near the naturally rich Mississippi valley, from Duluth to Mobile. . . . Of over three hundred municipalities in Illinois, more than one-third refused payment of bonds. Of one hundred counties, townships, and cities issuing bonds in Missouri, nine-tenths have defaulted. Kansas' record is somewhat better, but humiliating; while the bonded communities of Arkansas have been unanimous in attempting repudiation." [2]

The effect of this dispensation upon the county was most sinister. County organization and administration are very close to the people. State and city government is more complex, requires a higher order of intelligence, and is therefore at further remove from the aspiration and attainment of the average citizen. But then and now, any decent man, any respected farmer, might leave the plough like Cincinnatus, and become County Commissioner. Or more likely than not, he might be at the same time, both ploughman and Commissioner. Into such an order of things let now the leaven of corruption work,—whether it be the bedazzlement of unpaid-for improvements, or the spirit of blind retaliation aroused by contracts paid for, in a sense, but unfulfilled,—and the untutored multitude and their county administrators are aroused from the smug complacency of their foolish

[1] *Moody's Magazine*, February, 1906: "The West's Readjustment of Indebtedness," C. M. Harger.

[2] *The North American Review*, August, 1884, pp. 127–144 and 563–579. (Abstracted by A. D. Chandler.)

debt-making, and in primitive passion deny their obligations at all costs and come what will.

The soberer minds which usually prevail in city governments incline toward a wiser application of the power of creating debt, and more legal procedure in case of the violation of contracts. Then, on the part of the citizens, as the intricacies of city accounting are less in reach of average understanding, and the taxpayers are not in voting majority, as in the county, a misapplication of a municipal loan creates less turbulence, and repudiation is less often the resort. This is why the good faith of counties, especially rural counties, is not to be so implicitly relied on as that of cities and towns. Changes of county administration, too, sometimes bring more epochal results, because there is not that momentum and continuity of policy which is fostered by a partly permanent civil organization such as we find in a large city government. Hence they say it was that in Buncombe County, North Carolina (of Congressional renown), $100,000 Asheville and Spartanburg Railroad bonds were repudiated during a brief reign of the Populists in 1898. Buncombe County, of which Asheville, with a population at that time of about 12,000, is the seat, could hardly have been called a wholly rural county; but it is in North Carolina; and in a state with a record like that of North Carolina, a county would have had to contain a large population to escape in those times the thought of being rural in its credit characteristics.

The Persistence of County Repudiation. In presenting the extent and causes of county default it has not been explained why the spirit of opposition to law should persist to the present time. It is quite natural that states saddled with a tremendous and invalid debt, sometimes through no fault of the people at large, should bury it by constitutional amendment, and, being under no compulsion except that of public opinion, should be reluctant or unwilling to resurrect it.

A " modern instance " of wholly uncalled-for and unjustifiable repudiation, which arises out of those very conditions which we have described as obtaining in rural counties, is that of Henderson County, North Carolina. Henderson County had outstanding, in the eighties, some railroad bonds on which it was perfectly able to pay, and had paid, interest charges regularly. Upon the decision of the State Supreme Court invalidating the railroad-aid bonds of Wilkes and Stanley Counties, the authorities of Henderson County promptly followed suit in repudiation. Although the United States courts reversed this decision in the cases of Wilkes and Stanley Counties, and sustained the bondholders, still, it is to be seen that county credit cannot bear its own weight in the weaker states. Credit among them is not always voluntary, nor even " enlightened self-interest," but merely compulsory; credit, there, is, or was, not a matter of ethics, but of necessity and of law. The issue in these weaker states is still validity, as we saw in the chapter on *State Bonds*, in the case of Pitt County, North Carolina.

Now there is one very important aspect of county credit, brought to mind by the case of Macon, which has not been mentioned as yet, and that is the simplicity of county debenture requirements. Proper objects for public expenditure we found to be very few in the nature of county organization; and the cost of these would be comparatively small. Therefore if it ever became convenient to repudiate an issue, a county,— a rural county, particularly,—is not under the same necessity as a city to reckon the future cost of the loss of its credit. Probably we shall not see, for many a year, a public offering, successfully placed, of bonds of the defaulting counties of Macon and St. Clair, Missouri; Green and Muhlenberg, Kentucky; Lake and Hinsdale, Colorado; and Wilkes and Onslow, North Carolina.

In closing this subject of the good faith of counties it is only fair to say that the history of modern defaults is vastly more promising. Occasionally we meet with an instance like that of Jefferson County, Washington, which about twenty years ago, scaled its debt, or the interest on it, from actual inability to pay in full. No one could have analyzed the financial statement of this county and felt that the bondholders had a real grievance. They should have studied the conditions more closely before purchasing. The attitude of Lawrence County, South Dakota, is reassuring. In 1907 Lawrence County was obliged to default temporarily on an issue of $235,000 of 5s which matured during the panic. The whole amount was taken care of to the entire satisfaction of the bondholders. About $100,000 was retired, and the balance extended at 6 per cent. (with privilege of redemption) for five years. Such an exhibition of good faith should materially help the credit of that community.

Rural Versus Municipal Counties. In everything relating to the administration and credit of counties, we have had to distinguish between those which were rural and those municipal. The discrimination has been so pointed that little more need be said here. A buyer of bonds should never consider county bonds without having the distinction firmly in mind. Those features which we have observed to militate against county loans as a class are accentuated in rural county issues, and those features which prepossess in favor of city loans as a class are accentuated in municipal county issues.

Even when the county administration is entirely distinct and apart from the administration of the included city or cities, the influence of the more important city interest is bound to tell in favor of better fiscal methods, greater sobriety in debt-incurrence, less eccentricity in all relations which affect bond-holders. Particularly, having need of the good-will and confidence of investors for future issues within the corporate limits, municipal counties will see to the prompt payment of debts. Of the many counties in the United States with defaulted obligations as yet unadjusted, very few indeed can properly be called municipal, i.e., containing a city or town of 25,000 population, let us say.

Metropolitan Counties. There is little likelihood of over-estimating the influence of strong cities and towns upon the good faith of the counties in which they are situated. If the principle holds at all it can be carried to the extreme:—if there is security in a cosmopolitan population, in extensive establishments, in the presence of public institutions, and in talented civic administrations,—other things being equal,—then the larger the population, the more numerous the establishments, the greater the institutions, the more businesslike the administration,—the better shall be the security behind the loans. So bond investors are justified in their marked preference for what we here choose to call " metropolitan county loans," as distinguished even from municipal county loans. The presumption is that the metropolitan county bonds partake of the characteristics of the included great city or cities.

To ascertain in a crude way to what extent the interests of the city dominate the county, subtract the real (or in want of the real, the assessed) valuation and the population of the city

from those of the county and observe what remains. This might
be done with Seattle and King County, Washington. In this
case the ratio of assessed and real valuation being the same, there
is no need of figuring the real valuation. When there are no
constitutional or statutory limitations, note also, the ratio of
the respective tax rates, having in mind the things to consider
in tax rates,—as in Hartford County, Connecticut. When the
city tax rate is many times the county rate, very evidently the
city has assumed the major portion of civic functions which
might otherwise entail upon the county; and the county's credit
is to that extent benefited.

Other County Bond Matters. If now, when investing, he relates the principles set forth in this chapter with those relating to
credit in general, which were discussed in the preceding chapter,
and with those affecting all municipal issues, which immediately
follow in the chapter on City and Town Bonds, he will have a
good working knowledge to assist in the right choice of county
loans. Let him remember that although, *as a class*, County
Bonds are inferior to City and Town Bonds, they are superior
to District Bonds, and belong to the great division of United
States Civil Loans, the strongest kind of investment security
bought by the American people.

CHAPTER XIX

CITY AND TOWN BONDS: MUNICIPAL ASSETS

Municipal Corporations Proper. By city and town bonds are meant, generally, the funded obligations of *municipal corporations proper*, i.e., of those political subdivisions of the state which are voluntary corporations, as distinguished from the subdivisions which are created more specifically at the instance of legislatures, or of common councils, and are called *quasi-municipal corporations*, being *involuntary* in their creation. Counties, townships, and the other various taxing districts are usually involuntary corporations in the eyes of the law; but cities and incorporated villages are always, and towns are generally, voluntary bodies, or municipal corporations proper, and their funded loans may therefore be called *Municipals Proper*. More particularly, then, we deal in this and the following two chapters with the bonds of cities and of incorporated towns and villages.

This twofold distinction between municipal corporations and their securities is by no means universal. The courts, and the legislatures of the states, do not always adhere to it. But it is nevertheless a real distinction, which we have met and shall meet again, especially in discussing proper purposes of bond issue and their relation to legality. Nevertheless most of the principles which will be laid down in this discussion of City and Town Bonds are applicable to the whole division of *Civil Loans*.

Within the subdivision of *Municipal Corporations Proper*, covered by this chapter, there are no thoroughgoing distinctions. The same principles are applicable to incorporated towns and villages, as to cities. Many a town or village of this sort is larger and more important than some individual cities, especially in certain groups of states. The "city" of Williston, North Dakota, had a population in 1900, according to the federal census, of 763; and the "city" of Fort Pierre, South Dakota, of 395, and Ventnor City, New Jersey, in 1905, of 116. The "town" of Brookline, Massachusetts, had a population of 27,792 in 1910, and an assessed valuation in 1906 of over $100,000,000. The Con-

199

necticut towns outrank the cities in many respects,—quite apart from wealth or population.

Size, wealth, and prospects, then,—in other words, those conditions which make for *financial competency* are paramount; and although financial legislation often discriminates between cities, towns, and villages, as such, it is usually on the tacit assumption that this is the usual order of their size and wealth, and of their competency. So in some states the discrimination is carried further, and statutes regulating, for instance, the authority and extent of debt-incurrence classify even cities according to their population.

By the constitution of 1851 the General Assembly of Ohio organized the cities of that state into two classes of three and four grades, respectively, according to population, to " restrict their power of taxation, assessment, borrowing money, contracting debts, and loaning their credit, so as to prevent the abuse of such power." Kentucky, in the constitution of 1891, limited particularly the debt-making power of the political subdivisions by a double distinction: she recognized the kind of municipal corporation and also its number of inhabitants. *Cities* in that state with population of over 15,000 might incur debt to the extent of 10 per cent. of their assessed valuation; *cities and towns* of 3,000 and over were limited to 5 per cent., and *cities and towns* of less than 3,000, to 3 per cent.; but *counties and taxing districts and other municipalities* were limited to 2 per cent.

This recognition by constitution and statute of the importance of *financial competency*, as indirectly indicated by statistics of population, brings us again to the lines of investigation we are pursuing for municipal issues. We have already found that the three principal factors which make for the security of municipal bonds, in the order of their importance, are *financial competency*, *validity*, and *good faith*.

FINANCIAL COMPETENCY: MATERIAL ASSETS

The City Statement. The public who buy city and town bonds, as well as county and other municipal issues, depend for information as to financial competency almost entirely upon the statistical statement of the bond-house circular. Of all these municipal statements, the city statement gives the truest indication of material conditions because the records for cities are likely to be more complete and are revised at more frequent intervals, and for other reasons which we shall come to presently. Furthermore, these records are more accessible, since they are to be obtained, not only in the city's offices, but also in periodical publications, notably the *Commercial and Financial Chronicle*, *The Bond Buyer*, and *Moody's Manuals of Governments and Municipals*. The records of the smaller quasi-municipalities, and taxing districts, especially when not largely bonded, are sometimes inaccessible to any but a most persistent investigator. Apparently, in the estimation of local officers, the smaller the community, and the more dubious its standing, the more sacrosanct its books. If one wishes to go behind the most recent printed records, or if no records are to be found, his usual resource is one or another of the several municipal officers, according to the kind and size of the municipality, and to the nature of the inquiry. But it is important to remember that no municipality is in any way responsible for the correctness of the statement issued; and the truth or falsity of the statement has no bearing upon the legality of any bond issue. Not often, however, has this immunity worked detriment to the creditors of the municipality.

The Tax Rate. The circular, offering a municipal loan, will sometimes mention the tax rate of the community. Considered apart the rate means little or nothing. Of all the items on the circular this is the most difficult of interpretation. And yet it indicates to what extent the municipality is drawing annually upon its resources to sustain, protect, and improve its social and corporate life. In analyzing the rate, when this is possible, one must make sure that it does not include too much or too little. " Tax Rate " may mean the total imposition, including state and county levies; " City Tax," " Town Tax," " Village Tax," should mean the tax of only the local community, which is usually but not always, the major part of the whole. " Total Tax " is what its name signifies.

For purposes of comparison it will be desirable to separate the city tax from the county and state taxes. On the same grounds any tax rebate should be deducted. In some places this rebate is very considerable. Savannah, Georgia, is not very exceptional in allowing 10 per cent. On the other hand there will often be district and special assessment taxes of one sort or another, which are not exercised by the municipality as a corporation, and are not included even in the "Total Tax;" but which are imposts, nevertheless, upon such a large portion of the property within the corporate limits that they cannot legitimately be overlooked. It is not to be expected that those whose interest it is to make a most satisfactory exhibit will go out of their way to include indirect taxes; but since any tax is a drain on resources, and since our usual object in analyzing the tax is to discover the amount of the drain, we must include and examine any special taxes we find. Some years ago Coffeyville, Kansas, had a total tax of $70.50 on a 25 per cent. assessment. But in this tax was not included the special levy on the special debt incurred for sewers and roads, although this debt was nearly as large as the general debt. And moreover there was a Coffeyville School District which had a school tax of $24. The fact that the School District had different boundaries from Coffeyville proper did not prevent the school tax from falling on a large majority of Coffeyville taxpayers, whose real "total" tax burden was well over $100 a thousand, or 10 per cent. of the assessed valuation, or $2\frac{1}{2}$ per cent. of the real.

Assuming now that one has arrived at the real total net tax, he is justified in preferring a low to a high tax. A low tax generally implies a sound financial condition. Its natural correlate, if the city or town is economically run, is a low percentage of net debt. Conversely, a high tax seems to imply an unhealthy condition, and a high percentage of debt, as in the village of Collinwood, Ohio, with a tax in 1905 (including the school district) of $64.30, and an approximate total debt of from 20 to 25 per cent. of the assessed valuation. The real valuation was not reported.

But the exceptions to these generalizations are so numerous as to discourage any but the studious from seeking their drift. As we are led to expect from the law of averages, the extremes of high and low tax rates are to be found, generally, in small communities, which, of course, most acutely reflect in statistics any local idiosyncrasies of administration.

Under the peculiar form of civil government in Connecticut, where the unit is the town, and the town often includes a city or a borough, the city or borough tax may be returned as separate from the town, district, county, and state tax, and therefore require adjustment to the usual basis of rate.

Another difficulty one often meets in considering the tax is a variation of rate within the municipality. In cities that are not wholly built up, e.g., those which are coextensive with great counties, the tax is sometimes regulated to the locality and to the improvements installed. Pittsburgh, Pennsylvania, has a city tax of $7.50; but over 25 per cent. of the real estate is charged with only the rural tax, which is two-thirds of the city tax; and about .6 per cent. of the real estate has to pay only the agricultural tax, which is one-third the city tax. Scranton, Pennsylvania, has about the same tax plan, although there is not so much difference in the three tax rates. Greenwich and other municipalities in Connecticut, have a system of scaled tax rates, as also Seattle, Washington. In Bellingham, Washington, we find seven separate districts, each with its own tax rates. But the cause is slightly different from that in the other cities mentioned except Seattle. Bellingham is a consolidation of several towns, and the distribution of the tax burden in this way prevents an injustice to the districts which came into the consolidation. Similarly in New York, Manhattan, and the Bronx have slightly different tax rates than the other three boroughs.

We have thus far considered the tax rate in its present relation to the city in which it obtains. Such consideration begins to have value only when made the basis of comparison. Comparisons may be made with the previous annual tax rates of the same municipality, or with the present tax rates of other municipalities of the same class having other conditions as nearly analogous as possible. Better still, a comparison may be made, in settled communities, of the tax rate of a municipality, averaged over a period of years, with the tax rates of similar municipalities of the same class, averaged in the same way. But the moment we begin comparisons we must remember our principles of arithmetic; for tax rates are like fractions:—to be compared they must be reduced to a common denominator. The common denominator of tax rates is *full property valuation* (real valuation), and if for no better reason than advantages of comparison (since comparison is useful to interests unrelated to the bond business), all tax assessments throughout the country should be on the basis of full valuation. In 1907 Plattsburg, New York, had a tax of about $50; New York City, of about $15. But since Plattsburg was assessed for about one-third value and New York for full value (nominally), the burden on the citizens of the town is only a dollar or two greater. It is a pity that the tax rate does not, of itself, show this. In finance simplicity and excellence are very nearly synonymous.

This common denominator of full valuation is not necessary, of course, in comparing the tax burden of a municipality with its own past rates, providing that during the previous years the ratio of assessed to real valuation has not changed. The fixed ratio, in that case, is itself a common denominator. But in order to institute such a comparison we must know whether or not the ratio has remained unchanged. Within recent years there has been a growing tendency, especially in the East, to assess for " fair cash value." New York City made the change in 1903, and as a result the tax rate dropped from about $23 a thousand to about $14.50. Harrisburg, Pennsylvania, according to the usual financial records, had an assessed valuation in 1880 of $5,384,629, and a tax rate of $37.50. In 1889 the assessed valuation had grown to $21,396,240, and the tax rate had declined to $20.50. In want of definite knowledge one would infer that at some time between 1880 and 1889 the same sort of change had taken place in the assessment basis of Harrisburg property. But in 1890 the assessed valuation had decreased slightly (to $20,412,135), and yet the tax rate dropped to $12.25. Evidently, therefore, other influences were at work effecting these alterations.

The reasonable increase in a city's tax rate over a period of years is not necessarily an unfavorable sign, any more than is a reasonable increase in debt. Present heavy expenditures may be, and now usually are, an anticipation of increased assets and therefore of levy power. According to the Census Bureau, for the country at large the increase in rate of ad valorem taxation from 1880 to 1902 was about $2 a thousand on the estimated real value of all property, taxed or exempt. It is to be doubted if any figures are accessible to show the average increase of the tax rate for cities and towns, or for municipalities generally. The movement of population toward cities and the resulting tremendous urban development justify acquiescence in an average municipal increase far in excess of that for the country at large. Whether any city is exceeding its fair proportion of increase, whatever that may be, and whether it is justified in so doing, must be decided by the nature of its expenditures, and by the ease with which it can support its mandatory charges.

The necessity of a *sui generis* investigation of tax rates is illustrated in Pulaski County, Arkansas, which had a floating debt in 1907 of $163,011 and a bonded debt of about twice this amount. Instead of issuing long-term sinking-fund bonds with their comparatively light annual charges, the county elected (we assume, in want of knowledge to the contrary) to unburden itself of this floating obligation by heavy annual payments. The tax rate, which was about $30 a thousand on a true valuation, must have reflected this effort. We are further assured as to the motives of the county from the fact that the bonded debt is being retired in annual payments. Therefore a comparison of the county's tax rates over a series of years, or of the present rates with those of other Western semi-municipal counties, would have to take into favorable consideration this serial repayment feature of its financing. In 1925 the floating debt was only nominal and the tax rate only $17.45 on a 30 per cent. assessed valuation.

It is hardly necessary to say that most comparisons of the tax rate of one kind of political division with another are void. As a rule the state tax rate is the lowest of those of the principal civil units. Then in order come the county taxing district, and city and town rates. The principal factors which make for this order are the relative current administrative expenses, and the fixed charges on the governmental " plant " per capita of included population. Constitutions and statutes recognize this inequality in the necessary expenses of the several kinds of governments, and limit their debt-incurring power accordingly. It was only when this principle became recognized that state credit became sound.

Furthermore, interclass comparisons of tax rates are void because the different units have, in part, different sorts of wealth as taxable resources. A review of the material assets of states in the chapter on *State Bonds* will recall to mind some of these differences. Then again, in isolated instances, political units have cut themselves off from ready comparison with other units of the same class by an unusual and arbitrary method of taxation. Wilmington, Delaware, does not tax personal property. Personal property at best is an obstacle in the path of him who seeks to read the message of the tax rate. There is little uniformity in the treatment of personal property, not only among the states, but within a state.

We have already remarked upon the necessity of coming to some conclusion as to what the true tax rate really is. We are again reminded of this need in attempting to compare the rates of municipalities in different states. The difficulty is that no rule can be formulated. From the standpoint of the economist no doubt the best way to compute the total tax burden upon the property owner per thousand dollars of real valuation, rather than to accept the nominal city tax, although the bond attorney, with an eye to legality, will scan particularly the latter. The tax of Astoria, Oregon, in 1906 was only $11 on a two-fifths valuation. This, of course, was impossibly low at that time for a growing city of nearly 15,000 inhabitants. The 1924 rate was $36.50 on a 50 per cent. valuation. A little inquiry then would have revealed a small state tax, a $30 county tax, and special taxes, making a grand total of $58. In this instance, as in many others, we find a coextensive school district with its own school tax. The case is by no means extreme. The West is full of them. And yet, as often as not, these qualifying conditions are overlooked.

The Tax Power. The real municipal tax rate is the index of the extent to which the tax power is being employed to support and acquit current and fixed charges. The extent to which that tax power *must be*, and the extent to which it *may be* exercised are the most important considerations in purchasing municipal bonds. The bondholder (or other municipal creditor, such as city contractor, or water company which has rented hydrant privileges to the municipality) ordinarily has only the powers of taxation (and no lien) to fall back upon in case of breach of contract. The municipal creditor, however, has recourse to the full power of general taxation unless otherwise appropriated or limited by law.[1]

But the creditor, or for our purposes, the bondholder, must consider to what extent the statutes have conferred upon, or denied to, the municipality, the general powers of taxation; for the courts are powerless to grant a remedy when the laws fail to

---

[1] Holders of special assessment bonds are not generally so favored. See the next chapter under Special Assessment Bonds.

provide for a sufficient levy, or when they restrict it to such an extent as to make it insufficient.

Specific Bond Taxes. It is to prevent mischances of this sort, which have been too common, that at least fifteen states have constitutional clauses requiring that municipal corporations shall not incur indebtedness without passing, at the same time or previously, irrepealable laws or ordinances which create for each loan a tax levy and collection sufficient to pay the interest and retire the principal within a stated period of years. By means of this *specific bond tax* the security for municipal loans is greatly enhanced in

California,	Iowa,	New Hampshire,	South Dakota,
Georgia,	Kentucky,	North Dakota,	Texas,
Idaho,	Michigan,	Oklahoma,	Wisconsin.
Illinois,	Missouri,	Pennsylvania,	

Of these states the life of the loan is limited to 20 years in Illinois, Iowa, Missouri, New Hampshire, and Wisconsin. It is limited to 25 years in Oklahoma; to 30 years in Georgia, Kentucky, and Pennsylvania; to 40 years in California; but no definite period is set in Michigan, North Dakota, South Dakota, and Texas, although Texas achieves the discharge of the loan in much the same sort of way by requiring an annual deposit of 2 per cent. in the sinking fund.

There are not a few respects in which Canadian finance, and particularly Canadian municipal finance, is in advance of our own. This matter of special tax is an illustration. In Ontario and all of the provinces west, Manitoba, Alberta, Saskatchewan, and British Columbia,—but not in Quebec,—it is required that for each municipal bond issue there shall be a specific tax levy for its support and ultimate acquittal. In the Maritime Provinces, New Brunswick, Nova Scotia, and Prince Edward Island, a special tax levy is required, and also a special act of legislature to legalize every bond issue.

In those states which do not protect bondholders by special bond taxes a substitute for the constitutional provision is often had by the passage of a municipal ordinance of the same tenor, which recites that " there shall be and hereby is levied a direct annual tax," etc., of some specified amount or annual percentage. And even in those states which have the constitutional provision, municipalities will sometimes have their loans accepted by bond houses only on condition that a mandatory ordinance of this nature be passed; for attorneys feel that the constitutional provisions have not as yet had sufficient interpretation by the higher courts to be relied on solely.

Although a minority of the states have constitutional provisions, perhaps a majority of the bond-enabling acts passed by the various legislatures in all states have the same express authority for the levy of taxes to meet interest and maturing principal; and bonds issued under such authority offer as much remedy through the courts in case of default as if the provision was in the state constitution itself.

There is no reason why the same end may not be attained in municipal charters, and occasionally this is the case. The creditors of Vicksburg, Mississippi, have the satisfaction of knowing that the city is required by its charter to levy taxes to meet the *interest* on its bonds " and to apply any surplus of the sum so raised, after payment of interest, to the purchase of bonds at or below par."

It is not necessary, however, for the support and discharge of a debt, that specific levies be raised against it by constitution, statute, or charter. In American municipal bond law the implied power of taxation is a principle of universal application, as the federal courts have invariably held. Indeed it is only an extension of the constitutional principle that contracts may not be impaired. And even when loans have been issued, secured by pledge of certain definite collateral, such as stock, and no reference to, or provision for, the payment of the loan from general taxes has been made, the United States Supreme Court has held the tax resource valid for both principal and interest, and has issued writs of mandamus to compel levy and collection.[1]

On the other hand, the courts have not the power to levy or collect taxes, but may simply issue writs for the performance of these duties, and coerce the proper officials, when they exist and are to be found. For this purpose the political organization of the larger municipalities renders less difficult the execution of the court's order.

The Tax Limitation. But the power of taxation, general or special, implied or specific, cannot be invoked by the bond-

[1] For the application of this principle to special assessment bonds, see "The Bonds of Taxing Districts," under the caption Special Assessment Bonds.

holders when its application will conflict with ad valorem tax limitations already set by law. These limitations have already been discussed in their relation to state and county debt. Probably only three states have sweeping *constitutional limitations:* Kentucky, Alabama, and Oklahoma. Kentucky grades her tax limitations in the same general way that we have found her debt limitations graded:—by giving greater license to the larger municipalities. The maximum tax permitted cities and towns having a population of 15,000 or more is $15 a thousand; cities and towns with a population between 10,000 and 15,000, $10 a thousand; those less than 10,000, $7.50 a thousand. Counties and taxing districts are limited to $5 a thousand, except that counties may add $2 for public roads. Alabama, with certain exceptions, formerly made the flat rate of $5 a thousand for her municipalities. But of recent years repeated amendments to the constitution have tempered the restrictions materially. By the constitution of 1874 Arkansas has the $5 limit for her counties. Other municipalities in the state are not limited.

A few states have statutory tax limitations that serve the same purpose and are much more to be feared because sometimes more difficult of interpretation. Ohio, in the constitution of 1851, delegated this power to the legislature. The result attained is the same. The taxpayers are given a crude sort of protection against burdensome imports,—a protection, nevertheless, which is unnecessary with proper debt restrictions, and is prejudicial to the credit of a state and its municipalities. How tax limitations inure to the detriment of municipalities is best illustrated in the case of Alabama. Under the old constitution this $5, or $\frac{1}{2}$ per cent. tax limitation obtained; but there were no debt restrictions. The city of Birmingham, under the initial impulse of a new industrial life, which has since made it famous, felt called upon to incur debts in anticipation of an increasing power to pay, and as a result became unable to raise the annual tax for interest. To relieve the situation, an amendment to the old constitution was passed, granting Birmingham an increase of $\frac{1}{2}$ per cent. in the tax rate, that it might meet the interest charges and make some headway toward refunding. Now the amendments are becoming almost indiscriminating.

In view of this and other similar experiences, the Constitutional Convention of 1901 supplemented the tax limitation with a graded debt limitation. At this time the city of Troy, Alabama, was in default in interest and the constitution of 1901 authorized an additional $\frac{1}{2}$ per cent. to the tax limitation, *subject to the vote of the city*. " This provision, however, is not sufficient to pay the interest," said the *Commercial and Financial Chronicle*. But inasmuch as the city tax rate was and is only $5 a thousand upon an assessed valuation that has since run from $1,162,000, to $3,202,000, it is hard to see why Troy found her revenues deficient. At any rate settlement of interest was made in 1911.

In addition to the legal obstacles which a tax limitation raises against the payment of debts, it encourages a spirit of independence in the taxpayers that in the long run is bound to be reflected in the credit of the city and state. Of course this is the unfortunate fact in Alabama.[1]

It must be borne in mind that restrictions upon the tax rate usually cover, not only moneys raised to pay the interest and principal of loans, but also current expenses. In municipalities proper, expenses are comparatively heavy, and therefore the risk of the bondholder is proportionately increased; for the municipalities themselves, and not the courts, are the arbiters of their own domestic economy; and when they choose not to act in good faith it is much easier for them than for quasi-municipal corporations to swell budgetary appropriations, to the impairment of their power, within the law, to pay their debts by assessment. San Francisco, a city with splendid credit, met this phase of tax limitation in an excellent and unusual way. The city charter restricted to $10.70 the tax rate *for current expenses and maintenance*, but left unhampered the power to levy for the support and discharge of funded debts.

Assessed Valuation. A municipality acting in bad faith, especially under the temptation to default which is fostered by material calamities, may attain the same result under a law restricting the power of taxation, by reducing its assessed valuation to the point where the tax rate is little more than sufficient to care for current expenses. This is the extreme illustration of the dependence of the tax power upon wealth which it may tax.

[1] It seems incredible, but Massachusetts, by the Acts of 1910, placed a nominal city tax limitation of $10.55 a thousand. The limitation was no hardship, but it seemed a strange departure from sound fiscal policy.

Assessed valuation, or assessment, an item always on the bond circular under the city statement, is not hard to understand. It is the value put upon property by assessors as the basis for taxation. The " grand list " of certain states, e.g., Connecticut, is a synonym. But the grand list of Vermont (1 per cent. of the real value) is quite another thing. The " tax duplicate " is another synonym.

The Basis of Assessed Valuation. Assessed valuation is of importance chiefly in its relation to the tax rate and to real valuation. *Real valuation,* in its turn, is liable to different interpretations from different assessors. Even when the law stipulates the assessment shall be at full value, it is often allowed to fall far short of that. Nominal equivalents are " true valuation," " fair valuation," " market valuation," " actual valuation," " real valuation in money," " nominal real valuation," etc., etc., and in Iowa " appraised valuation " (as distinguished from " assessed valuation"). This lack of precision in terminology is itself a sign of different interpretations. But for practical purposes real valuation is an invariable *common denominator* sufficient for purposes of comparison; and assessed valuation must bear some definite ratio to it. The relation of assessed valuation to debt will be noticed in the next chapter under the topic Debt Limitations and Restrictions.

Comparison of Assessed Valuations. Since assessed valuation is such an arbitrary matter, and since there is no general fixed ratio of assessed to real valuation, those who deal with statistics should be chary of comparisons when valuations have not been reduced to the common denominator. A prominent city official of New York sought some years ago to reassure business men in regard to the tremendous increase in the metropolitan debt and the budgetary appropriations by a comparison of the assessed valuation of New York with that of other communities. " When the Commissioner presented a map showing that the assessed values in the entire United States west of the Mississippi River, including Minnesota and Louisiana, totaled $5,249,072,325 against the total assessed valuation in this city of $7,158,190,000, the business men gasped."

Whether the comparison was qualified or not, it does not gain in force when the explanation is forthcoming that New York is assessed at nominal full value, but many of the Western states at not more than one-third value at the time of the comparison. In Nebraska, under the general revenue law of 1903, property was assessed for taxation at 20 per cent. only, of actual value; In Iowa the rate was and is 25 per cent., and in Kansas, about 33 per cent. (now full value). The city of Pekin, Illinois, was exceptional, but not isolated, with its assessment at 5 per cent. of actual value.

In general it should be remembered that the North Atlantic tier of states is committed to a very high assessment ratio, and the South and West to a low ratio. Conversely, of course, the average tax rate in the North Atlantic tier is very low, and in the South and West very high. The chief cause of both facts is that the great burden of municipal debt is being borne by the North Atlantic tier. The real valuation of this North Atlantic division has been subject to less fluctuation in the past than that of the other divisions; and it has been able, with greater safety, to fix its tax rate upon full values. But later financial depressions have made us realize that land valuations in the West, under conditions made stable, agriculturally, by irrigation (which is immediately independent of rainfall), and commercially, by growth in population, are prepared for a full assessment.

If uniformity of accounting is desirable for railroad and industrial corporations, it is desirable for municipal corporations. Even now, when a city in the West is hard pressed to meet annual charges on its obligations, under customary valuations it will, at times, tax upon full valuation, the laws permitting.

Intercity comparisons of assessed valuation are not so common among the bond-buying public as comparisons of assessed valuations in the same city over a period of years. The principle need hardly be touched upon again that this sort of inquiry must be on the lookout for any influences which may have changed the basis of valuation. Such influences may be economic, as in the case of certain Nevada mining towns; but they are more likely to be bookkeeping influences. For instance, as the result of an amendment to the Connecticut statutes in 1901 the corporation stock tax was made collectable by the state, and through the state, distributable to the town treasurers. (The same thing occurred in Massachusetts in 1864.) So the assessed valuations of all the Connecticut towns are depleted to that extent, since 1901. Hartford, the home of great insurance companies, lost, in this new adjustment, two-thirds of her personal valuation. On the other hand, a comparison of New Haven's valuation at that time would show the opposite effect, since a stronger counteracting agency was at work: in 1900 New Haven changed from a 51 per cent. to a full valuation basis.

The Components of Assessed Valuation. Property, for purposes of taxation, is subject to various classifications, the main division being into realty and personalty. In some states, railroad, express, telegraph, and telephone companies make returns of city property directly to the state, to the detriment of the city statement. Stock, banks, and franchises are at times inventoried separately, and assessed and taxed on separate bases. Thus realty in Big Rapids, Michigan, used to be on a two-thirds basis, but personalty on a one-third basis. In Roanoke, Virginia, there was formerly a distinction between the real and the personal assessment basis, which was two-thirds, but the corporation assessment, a distinct inventory, is on a three-quarters basis, and bank stock, at market value. In about 21 states franchises are specifically included in the general property tax. It has been mentioned already that personal property sometimes is not taxed at all—as in Wilmington, Delaware. Figures for total valuation are rendered somewhat inaccurate when there is not an annual revaluation of real estate.

The Relation of Realty to Personalty. Just as the rule that a low tax is preferable to a high tax has so many exceptions as to discourage its application, so has also the rule that the personal component of Assessed Valuation should be a high percentage of the total. It is only by repeated application to towns of both good and poor credit that it becomes safe so to generalize. It would be invidious to call the roster of cities and towns taken as examples of poor credit; but an examination of 20 representative municipalities of each class leads to the conclusion that when personal property represents one-third or more of the real, the credit of the community is satisfactory, and its tax rate per thousand dollars of real valuation is likely to be low. In the West the personal property ratio is slightly lower for the same grade of credit.

On the other hand, it is not to be denied that personal property is getting to be less a tax resource of municipalities, with the gradual change of method in imposts. As corporation stocks, savings bank deposits, mortgages, and local municipal bonds disappear from the assessment, one may be inclined to prefer a high rate of real valuation. A large part of this personal wealth, however, disappears from the duplicate only to reappear as wealth taxable in new form. Thus the shares of public utility corporations may not be taxed in certain states, but the companies themselves may be fully taxed by the state direct, through their franchises or otherwise, even though the values do not appear on the municipal assessors' books; and the tax may be prorated among the interested municipalities. A reduction in the amount of kinds of taxable personalty has sometimes been welcomed by real estate men, e.g., in Boston, since it has been thought to attract as residents men of large affairs.

Other Resources; Secondary Income. Having disposed, now, of the wealth which is the ordinary resource of the tax power, we come to those other material assets of a municipality which, though not taxable, contribute to its financial well-being. For convenience they may be divided into assets that are, and assets that are not, revenue-producing.

A city hall, or courthouse, or library, usually brings the community no direct return on the investment; though it may be sub-let in part, and thus become productive. But in so far as municipal ownership of the structure saves rentals and other expenditures it contributes, of course, to the city's net income. This is to be remembered in connection with New York City's tax-exempt municipal property, appraised in 1926 at $2,343,-441,770.[1]

The very presence in a community of a large amount of property exempt from taxation, whether municipally owned or not, attests a civic intelligence and a regard for institutions, which inspire high public credit, even if they do not minister at first hand to the exchequer. Of such property are churches, hospitals, charitable organizations, etc. Many of these institutions are at no great remove from being real productive assets. College and university towns would be more fairly rated, commercially, at the value of all property, whether exempt or not, for the institutions bring to the towns, in yearly revenues which are converted

---

[1] Of which real estate is $1,823,796,820 and franchises $519,644,950. Tax-exempt property in private and private corporation ownership was appraised in 1926 at $895,702,700.

into taxable wealth, several times the interest on the wealth which is not taxed. In 1905, New Haven, Connecticut, estimated her tax-exempt property, including Yale University, at $22,822,-470, as compared with assessable property, $110,001,166. Cambridge, Massachusetts, has no accessible list of tax-exempt property as a whole, but the exempt real estate owned by Harvard University was appraised in 1907 at $7,378,000 on an assessed valuation for the city of somewhat less than New Haven's. " It is worth all it costs, and more," says the President of the Cambridge Taxpayers' League, " to have Harvard located in Cambridge." Ithaca, New York, because of Cornell University, had at that time an exempt valuation of $10,874,735, which is even greater than the taxable valuation, of $7,219,440.

Among possible productive assets may be mentioned treasury holdings of cash, of railroad securities, of the stocks and bonds of local water, gas, and electric companies, and the city's holdings of less readily convertible forms of wealth such as delinquent taxes, real estate, etc. The sinking funds are important assets to be considered separately in connection with net debt.

Cash assets of the larger municipalities are often of much greater value than most people realize. On January 8, 1907 Philadelphia had nearly $18,000,000 in cash in her treasury, apart from sinking funds in the sum of $1,124,000. This $18,-000,000 was equal to about 21 per cent. of the total bonded debt. The value of cash was shown by the Baltimore fire. In 1902 the City of Baltimore sold her interest in the Western Maryland Railroad for about $8,750,000, and approximately half the sum was deposited at interest subject to 30-day draft. After the fire this money was withdrawn to meet the extraordinary needs.

Another notable instance of *proprietary interest in railroads* is that of Cincinnati, Ohio. The Cincinnati Southern Railroad, owned by the city, is leased for a long period of years at an average annual rental (including obligatory charges for a sinking fund) practically sufficient to pay the interest on the city's net funded debt. Portland, Maine, in like manner, has held for years a sufficient number of shares of the Portland and Ogdensburg Railroad (under 999-year lease to the Maine Central at 2 per cent. on the stock) to pay two-fifths of its interest charges. Most of these shares have now been sold to retire the funded debt as it matured.

Sometimes municipalities acquire the *securities of public service corporations* for purposes of municipal ownership or control, or to encourage local enterprises that benefit the community at large. These acquisitions may or may not appear in the debt statement, according to circumstances; but they suggest a possible intimate relation between *secondary assets* and *municipal debt*. In the nature of the case the securities owned in this way are usually in the form of stock, though sometimes in bonds. Louisville, Kentucky, owns (through her sinking fund) all the valuable stock of the Louisville Water Company.

The *real estate* owned by a city or town may be considered of two kinds, not only in its relation to the remedies of creditors in case of default, but as affecting the financial competency of the city. It is only the real property held by the city municipality in its *proprietary*, rather than in its *administrative capacity*, that properly comes under the head of productive assets. The latter is non-revenue bearing, and is owned to carry on the non-commercial functions of the municipality, but the former may yield a net return and is a commercial undertaking. The former property may be administered on the basis of charges just sufficient to cover the cost of the service. Under the cost-plus plan the charges are established at an amount which will cover the cost of the service and still leave a net profit to the public treasury. The latter policy is usually followed by municipalities in operating public industries. Referring to them, the Census Bureau in its report on *Financial Statistics of Cities*, 1921, page 26, arrives at the following conclusion:

" The revenues derived from public service enterprises are usually sufficient to meet the interest and sinking fund requirements on account of their indebtedness in addition to the cost of their maintenance and operation."

The development of municipal ownership in the United States has not been extensive. It has been confined mainly to street railways, as in Detroit, San Francisco and Seattle, gasworks, electric plants and particularly waterworks.

In very many cities and towns the value of the municipal property is greater than the funded debt,—often several times as great. But the ratio is of less importance than the character of the assets and obligations. Colorado Springs has municipal property valued at nearly four times the bonded debt; but nearly half of the property and half of the debt is of the best kind, representing waterworks; so the city may be said to have, in a sense, no real net debt.

Waterworks. The amount and character of property owned by any municipal or quasi-municipal corporation, especially when in the less settled Southwest and West, and especially when the population is a matter of hundreds or scant thousands, have an important bearing upon the permanency of the settlement. Every statement of a town of this sort in Arizona, New Mexico, Nevada, etc., should be analyzed. Nothing else makes for stability and security like good waterworks, operated and owned by the municipal corporation. Undoubtedly the large majority of these throughout the country are self-supporting; and some of them earn a sufficient amount, not only to pay the interest and principal of the water-debt, but of all other bonded debts besides, as is evident from the following table showing the aggregate receipts, expenditures, apparent net operating revenue, outstanding debt and capital outlays in certain years within the decade 1911-1921:

SUMMARY OF THE FINANCIAL OPERATIONS OF MUNICIPAL WATERWORKS
IN CITIES OF 30,000 POPULATION AND OVER
(Thousands)
(Reproduced from Lutz, H. L., *Public Finance*, p. 202)

Year	Receipts	Expenditures	Apparent Net Operating Revenue	Outstanding Debt at End of Year [1]	Capital Outlays During Year [1]
1911....	$67,774	$27,750	$40,024	$451,543	$71,132
1915....	77,465	33,057	44,407	541,299	50,481
1919....	95,304	46,582	48,721	599,512	43,280
1921....	92,379	50,938	41,441	—	—

[1] Not given for 1921.

Municipal water bonds as a class are a premier security because of the ease and certainty of their support and ultimate payment. In municipal bankruptcy they have generally fared better than the other funded obligations (e.g., Rahway, New Jersey). By city charter or otherwise it is commonly stipulated that they are not a primary charge on taxable property, but on the use of the water itself; so it usually is given to the board of

Water Commissioners, or some similar body, to establish such water rates as will at all times insure to the city a sufficient income to pay the interest and to provide a fund to pay the principal of all bonds issued for water purposes.

It may seem at first that water loans, which do not have for maintenance and payment an express resort to the general power of taxation, must suffer in security; but this is not necessarily the case. Subject of course to tax limitations the doctrine of the implied power of taxation which is inherent in every bond enabling act that creates a direct obligation of a civil corporation, gives the holder of water bonds the same protection through the tax levy as if the bonds did not have their own special means of amortization. But when water bonds, or any other bonds, are payable from the income of designated property, and are liable, on failure of this resource, to encounter limitations of the tax power, they are better let alone. We cannot cite a failure of water bonds in illustration of this point. The interest on Selma, Alabama, Building 4s once faced this predicament. The interest is met from the rentals of the market constructed with the proceeds of the bonds; but market rentals of themselves are an insufficient security; and Alabama municipals are the worst possible paper to leave to the mercies of an abridged tax power.

Considering the absolute necessity of an adequate water supply in thickly settled communities, and the customary financial provisions, it becomes evident that water bonds are the most desirable class of municipals, and that in municipal accounting legislatures are justified in permitting water loans to be subtracted from gross debt, in computations of net debt.

The bond buyer, however, should be extremely careful in purchasing water bonds to note whether he is receiving bona fide direct municipal obligations. If memory is to be trusted, investors and even bond houses have carelessly picked up, in the course of trade, Raleigh, North Carolina, Water 6s, and Rockland, Maine, Water 5s, only to find they held public utility securities. The public attitude toward the two kinds of water loans may be shown by an instance. In 1904, Topeka, Kansas, bought the local waterworks from the Topeka Water Company for $350,000 in 4 per cent. Water Works Purchase Bonds, and at the same time assumed the $270,500 5 per cent. bonds of the Water Company. The difference in the selling price of these two issues has been equivalent to $\frac{3}{4}$ per cent. income, annually, in favor of the direct municipal obligation.

Prior Lien and Mortgage Security. Hitherto, in this chapter, we have dealt with the security for municipal bonds as dependent, directly or indirectly, upon the power of taxation and the resources of the tax power. It is the tax power, as distinguished from earning power and mortgage lien, which mainly differentiates the security of municipal bonds from corporation bonds. And yet even municipal obligations sometimes have varying degrees of priority; and not a few are secured by mortgage.

The bonds of the old city of Brooklyn, under the terms of the consolidation with New York, had to be satisfied, principal and interest, from the proceeds of taxes upon Brooklyn Borough property, before the bonds issued by the Greater New York should be provided for, from these same moneys.

Maine, Massachusetts, and Connecticut, and doubtless the other New England states, offer what is virtually mortgage security, as well as that furnished by the tax-power, for their municipal obligations.

"In the New England States judgments against municipalities are not enforced by mandamus, but in a mode peculiar to those states. By the common law of the New England States, derived from immemorial usage, the estate of an inhabitant of a county, town, territorial parish, or school district, is liable to be taken on execution on a judgment against the corporation." [1]

The importance of this resource of execution to owners of New England municipal bonds can hardly be overestimated. It puts New England obligations quite apart, in a class by themselves, distinct and superior to all other classes of corporate loans.

By the New Jersey laws of 1903, school district bonds issued under the terms of the School Act are secured by lien on all the real estate and personal estates of the district issuing them.

We know of no circumstances other than these under which any *class* of municipal bonds enjoys what is virtually mortgage security; but special assessment bonds are not uncommonly secured by lien on the improved property, notably in Illinois, and

[1] Dillon, *Municipal Corporations*, 4th ed., Note to § 849, p. 1027. See Hill vs. Boston, 122 Mass. 344, 349. There is some question whether this doctrine applies to cities. See Meriwether vs. Garrett, 102 U. S., p. 519.

in a few states the private property of municipal corporations, held for profit and charged with no public trusts, may be sold on execution.

Direct and Limited Obligations. It is well to distinguish between the direct and the limited obligations of a municipality. The former are bonds based on the full credit of the issuer and are direct obligations. The latter are only indirect obligations since they are based not on all the municipal revenues under the general taxation power, but only on specific revenues. At times the service on such bonds is met not from taxes derived from all local property but merely from property benefited by the improvements financed under the bond issue. For this reason these obligations are known as special assessment bonds in contrast to true municipal bonds. The latter, as direct obligations, and unlimited as to underlying security, possess a higher value than special assessment bonds.

The instances in which *individual* issues of municipal bonds are secured by mortgage liens are more numerous than most people suppose. They generally arise from the express sanction of legislatures, when some productive property or plant is purchased or constructed by money raised on the bonds. It may happen that the security of simple debentures is considered insufficient. This accounts in part for the fact that irrigation district bonds are so generally a lien prior to other municipal issues subsequently imposed; and this accounts in whole for the Mobile Funding bonds of 1882, the outcome of Mobile's compromise of that year. The bonds represent a purchase money mortgage given for some wharf property. The rentals from the property are of themselves insufficient for the support and early retirement of the issue, and therefore the legislature has created a special tax of $\frac{3}{4}$ per cent. of this city's taxable property toward the same end. Some of the municipalities of Tennessee, notably Memphis, have been enabled to acquire public market houses by mortgaging the market property. Memphis has mortgaged her parks also; and her School Bonds of 1937 are secured by a mortgage covering all the real estate and buildings owned by the school board.

Since waterworks offer property tangible for seizure, and the most certain, stable, and generous income to support obligations created against them, it is water bonds that are most commonly secured by mortgage liens and the pledge of revenue. Many municipalities in Georgia, Alabama, and Iowa have profited by these conditions to secure their water bonds under mortgage. North Birmingham, Alabama, has both Water and Light Bonds secured by mortgage. Columbia, South Carolina, formerly had a small issue of mortgage water bonds as well as a larger issue of plain water debentures. Duluth has a large and well known issue of Water and Light 4s which are a lien on the title of the city to the plant. And Louisville, Kentucky, in 1910 issued some second mortgage bonds on the Louisville Water Company.

The fact that these mortgage loans are municipal does not absolve them from usual foreclosure proceedings in default of interest. It will be remembered that one possible advantage in the issues of private corporations is that the principal matures on default of the interest. With unsecured municipal issues, however, action cannot be taken to secure the principal, but only the defaulted interest; and it requires the ownership of a large amount of bonds to make it worth while for any holder to proceed at law to realize upon his coupons, especially in the federal courts, which, of course, are not open to a joint action, or to an action involving less than $2,000. In the case of defaulted *mortgage* bonds, however, there is recourse upon the principal, and the ordinary procedure of equity will govern, except that in the case of mortgage water bonds, the courts, under necessity of preserving the public welfare, may be reluctant to appoint a receiver.

There is another sense in which municipal bonds are sometimes associated with prior lien security by the layman. He is, perhaps, told by the enthusiastic writers of bond circulars that since municipal bonds are "secured" by the power of taxation, and taxes come ahead of all other claims on property, therefore all the taxable property may be sold for taxes to pay the bonds,— which means that the bonds are, in effect, a first lien on all the taxable property in the community, and as such come ahead of all first mortgages on real estate, and ahead of all first mortgage bonds of any railroad or other corporation in the community.[1]

All the taxable property of a community may *not* be sold for

[1] Quoted almost verbatim from an old municipal bond circular of a then active young Western house.

the bonds. A theory is worth nothing unless it is approximated in practice. Outside of New England municipal bankruptcy and default do not even *suggest* foreclosure proceedings. Apart from the exceptions already mentioned there is nothing behind municipal bonds analogous to the real estate mortgage.

Population. In treating state credit the matter of population was touched upon in the light of an indirect material asset. The figures for population generally appear on a bond offering, and they are of no inconsiderable weight with the bond buyer. Two numbers are usually given: those of the last federal or state census, and the present estimate. Since the national census is taken only once in ten years and the majority of states do not supplement it, there is real necessity, in a growing country like ours, that more approximate returns be had. A state census helps to bridge the chasm in

Florida,	Michigan,	New York,	South Dakota,
Iowa,	Minnesota,	North Dakota,	Wisconsin,
Kansas,	New Jersey,	Rhode Island,	Wyoming.
Massachusetts,			

In addition, here and there, a local census may be authorized by the state for this or that purpose.

It is the natural tendency to be skeptical of estimates, especially when on mushroom towns of newly-developed sections in the South and West. That estimates of population are given in round numbers does not militate against their accuracy. They are usually based on school and directory returns, and assuming that they are compiled in good faith, are accurate enough for the purpose. A study of these estimates in a large number of cases leads to the conclusion that gains in population are usually computed at no greater rate than the ascertained rate of gain for the preceding census period.

The rule for population is very simple:—the larger the better. And the reasons thereof have been canvassed in the preceding chapter. In addition to what was stated there it may be remarked that 75,000 is approximately the turning point in a city's growth. At that size the town begins to take on metropolitan characteristics. Its places of amusement multiply, its mercantile life overflows the main thoroughfare; it is awake by night as well as by day; it becomes a shopping centre; traction, lighting, and other public utilities are placed on a commercial basis; its realty valuations and the growth in valuations are more secure; habits of thought and business and social proceeding lose their insularity, and tend toward cosmopolitanism. From the standpoint of the city's obligations, no one will question the desirability of all these changes.

Change in population is usually indicated on the circular by the difference between the census and the " present estimated " figures. In the United States the change is quite generally growth, irrespective of the kind of municipality, unless the municipality has lost territory by partition, or other reapportionment of boundaries. Annexation, however, has been so prevalent of recent years, that statistics of growth may at times mislead. No informed person will be misled by New York or Chicago, but one is so used to tremendous gains in the West that this explanation for part of the gains, as Los Angeles, California, is likely to be overlooked.

In this country a stationary or receding population is not to be met with favor. Except under extraordinary conditions, such as fire, flood, or earthquake, losses in population are in the smaller communities; and they are accompanied with other signs of distress, such as a high tax rate. The 75,000 mark of safety will generally exclude bonanza towns, one-industry towns, and pleasure resorts, which are more liable to vicissitudes than most municipalities.

Per capita studies in population are not very satisfactory. It has been found, strangely enough, that the strength of governments and their securities tends to vary as the per capita debt; and the same is true, for at least the larger cities of this country. Still it does not follow that strength and debt stand in any relation of cause and effect. Perhaps the relation of population to debt is best studied through the medium of wealth or real valuation. The relation of population to valuation has more significance. The real valuation per capita is greatest in wealthy residential communities,—which offer high credit. It will run from $2,000 to $4,000 per inhabitant. This is due in part to the comparatively high ratio of personal to real property valuations in these communities. In manufacturing cities it will run as low as $500. As in the matter of tax rates, villages will run to greater extremes both ways.

Population has its qualitative, as well as its quantitative, aspects. They have been referred to in previous pages. The personal equation, individually or collectively, has a great effect on credit. Since, however, there is no unanimity of opinion and no profitable appeal, except to the moral of past default and repudiation, the subject is not discussed further.

These then, in fine, are the material aspects of bond security the buyer must scan: the tax resource in its scope and limitations, and its basis in assessed and real valuations; the secondary resources of cash and collateral; priority of obligation in the bond, and mortgage lien; and lastly, population.

CHAPTER XX

CITY AND TOWN BONDS: MUNICIPAL LIABILITIES

Municipal Debt. On the other side of the balance sheet, over against valuation, is municipal debt. Municipal debt is often a very complex thing:—unnecessarily so; and there is as much difference of opinion as to what constitutes debt, and net debt, among the authorizers of municipal debts, the legislatures, as in other financial matters. There is the debt proper, the *General Debt*, more or less permanent in character, about which there is less chance of disagreement, unless the legality of some issue should be in dispute. There are also, perhaps, various forms of temporary or floating debt, which should or should not be included in the debt statement, according to the statutory or judicial interpretation of debt. They are generally issued only against perfect assets, like unmatured or unpaid taxes, unpaid assessments, etc. Of this class are *Revenue Bonds, Temporary Loan Bonds, Tax Relief Bonds*, and *Deficiency Bonds*, although all kinds are often merely notes, informally drawn, and not under seal, which, to defray current expenses, have been issued in anticipation of the year's taxes, from which they will be redeemed. These forms of short-term loans are quite generally used to equalize revenues and expenditures or to anticipate the carrying out of long-term borrowings. In the period from 1911–1920 they constituted more than forty per cent. of all municipal credit operations. (L. Lancaster, *State Supervision of Municipal Indebtedness*, 1923, p. 19.) *Warrants*, which have the main characteristics of the bonds mentioned above, may be defined as temporary certificates of debt issued in default of cash to casual creditors of a municipality or state, payable, principal and interest, like Revenue Bonds, from outstanding taxes, excess water rents, or any other surplus revenues. They are generally included in the total debt. The treasury warrant is an unsatisfactory and undignified method of financing which places an unjust burden on the creditors of the municipality. Holders of the warrants are forced either to wait until the next tax collection

225

date or to sell them to local banks often at a considerable discount. At one time warrants were quite generally used in Georgia and in North Dakota, but are now rarely employed.

Floating Debt, carried over from year to year, has no inherent advantages to recommend it. The excellent laws of California prohibit it in that state. To encourage the discharge of floating debt some states do not permit the funding of it until it reaches a certain sum, e.g., $25,000. Floating debt is almost invariably included with funded debt in debt restrictions. Whatever may be the local attitude toward the interpretation of debt limitations, and net debt, a thoroughgoing accountancy will require the amount of floating debt. When the floating debt represents merely the year's accumulations of debits, to be discharged out of the year's revenues, it may fairly be discounted; for presumably it is offset by proportionate growth in wealth, which, in turn, has not yet been tabulated in the town's assessed valuation. New York City at almost all times has outstanding in the form of revenue bonds a floating debt to the amount of many millions.

Under *General Debt* are likely to be found accidental items. Unfunded liabilities for contracts, and for land purchases, are important in large cities which are being extensively developed and improved. Less important in number and amount are judgment debts: obligations made legal by court decisions; and unretired certificates: bonds and coupons that have matured but have not been presented for payment. Occasionally, but not as often as in state debts, we find loans, generally irreducible, or perpetual, that are the result of endowments or charitable bequests, as in Lowell, Massachusetts. When they are taken into the sinking funds or otherwise absorbed, the interest becomes a bookkeeping charge, and the principal is included in the General Debt; but when the funds are set apart in trust, and there is no charge on the city for maintenance, they may properly appear, like water loans, distinct from the general debt.

Contingent Debt. Trust funds that may properly be excluded from the general debt are in the last analysis always *Contingent Debt*. Contingent Debt takes many other forms as well. Many municipal corporations, in New England and out, East and West, North and South, in an earlier era endorsed or guaranteed the bonds of local railroads. Most of these obligations, especially in the West and South, are an unfortunate heritage of the seventies and eighties, when the people of this country played fast and loose with their corporate credit. These endorsed bonds, however, are to be distinguished from railroad-aid bonds. Columbia, South Carolina, guarantees the interest, but not the principal, on $200,000 Canal bonds. Many cities guarantee the water bonds of water companies they have purchased. Austin, Minnesota, guarantees and pays the interest on moneys loaned the Southern Minnesota Normal College. As to whether special assessment bonds are a contingent obligation of a corporate body depends in part on the court having jurisdiction. If, as in Kansas, an assessment bondholder has recourse on the municipality as a whole, in default of the special tax on the property immediately benefited, then the bonds are a contingent liability. At least in cities of the first class, in Kansas, they are direct obligations. Otherwise, and more generally, as in Indiana under the Barrett Law, they are not a contingent liability.

The laws and practices of the several states vary so greatly that it is impossible to lay down any fast rule as to what forms of Contingent Debt shall be accredited to General Debt account. This much at least may be said: when the burden of the support and discharge of the debt falls directly on the municipality as a whole, a proper accounting will attribute the fund to General Debt; when it falls upon the municipality only indirectly, by default, or when it falls directly upon only a part, the item is outside of the General Debt, but embraced in the Total or Gross Debt, when the General and Total Debts are distinguished.

The Real Debt of Cities and Towns. The distinction between the nominal debt of the political division called county and the real debt which has to be borne by the county community was discussed at length in the preceding chapter. This distinction is not so important for cities, towns, and villages as a class. But nevertheless there are hundreds, if not thousands, of municipal corporations that exhibit similarly misleading debt statements.

Many municipalities have taxing districts (such as form the subject of a succeeding chapter) that are actually or practically coextensive with the cities or towns. The two commonest forms are school districts, and fire or water districts. These quasi-municipal corporations often issue their loans in such amount as to double the burden of funded debt that has to be supported by the taxpayers. The burden will appear in the two tax rates, which are based on actual property values; but it will not appear in the debt statement of the city or town alone. Therefore it behooves the bond buyer, who seeks actual conditions, to learn whether taxing districts, by a separate accounting, are concealing the liabilities that are a charge upon the community in question. Of course the bond issues of the minor quasi-corporation have no bearing upon the debt limitation of the major corporation, or upon questions of legality that issue therefrom.

Chicago furnishes the illustration *par excellence* of a city administered and financed by districts, or subsidiary corporations, each with its separate funded loans. But by constitutional amendment, the legal net debt of Chicago is interpreted as comprising, not only the present city debt proper, but the debt of all municipal corporations lying wholly in the city, and the city's portion of the debt of the county and sanitary district. This is the only important legislative recognition that comes to mind, of the true nature of municipal debt.

There is one constitutional recognition, however, that is even more satisfactory, since it applies the same principle to all municipalities in the state.[1] The debt limit in South Carolina is 8 per cent. for every political subdivision. But the debts and tax burdens are not allowed to overlap without stint, for " wherever there shall be several political divisions, or municipal corporations covering or extending over the territory or portions thereof, possessing a power to levy a tax or contract a debt, then each of such political divisions, or municipal corporations shall so exercise its power to increase its debt under the foregoing 8 per cent. limitation that the aggregate debt over and upon any territory of this state shall never exceed 15 per cent. of the value of all taxable property in such territory as valued for taxation by the state. Provided that nothing herein shall prevent the issue of bonds for the purpose of paying or refunding any valid municipal debt heretofore contracted in excess of 8 per cent."

There is adequate recognition of true debt in the admirable rules governing the investment of trust funds of Baltimore. These funds may be invested in the bonds of municipalities the

[1] The principle is recognized with less definiteness in the constitution of South Dakota.

net indebtedness of which " *together with the indebtedness of any District, or other Municipal corporation, or subdivision, except a County which is wholly or in part included within the limits of said City* does not exceed 7 per cent. of such valuation," etc. The banking law of New York state, restricting investments of savings banks and trust funds, contains a similar provision relating to bonds of cities.

New York also awakened to the danger of debt duplication and by constitutional amendment " any debt hereafter incurred by any portion or part of a city, if there shall be any such debt, shall be included in ascertaining the power of the city to become otherwise indebted."

Net Debt. The gross debt of a city, in itself considered, is of very little significance, any more than " accounts payable " in industrial corporations, irrespective of " accounts receivable." What we wish to know of a municipality is its *Real Net Debt* and its *Legal Net Debt.* The Real Net Debt is the residue of obligations which are not balanced by assets in kind,—assets that make the obligations self-sustaining and thereby prevent them from being an actual charge on the municipality. The Legal Net Debt, in many states, is that which the legislatures declare, and the courts decide, is the debt within the meaning of the provisions regulating the debts of municipalities.

The Legal Debt, in many states, is based in a crude way on the Real Net Debt. Since, however, there may be difference of opinion as to what obligations are assuredly self-supporting, we find different interpretations of Legal Net Debt, or " Debt." Thus formerly the Supreme Court of Pennsylvania held that the real debt of a municipality in that state (which was limited to 7 per cent. of the assessment) is the authorized debt less the amount of municipal certificates purchased and uncancelled in the sinking fund. But even this doctrine that municipal securities alive in the sinking fund should be subtracted is not accepted in all states.

Until a constitutional amendment in 1913 cities and towns in Pennsylvania were not permitted to recognize the self-supporting nature of water bonds, by subtracting the amount of them from the authorized debt in determining the limit of indebtedness. The same is true in Rhode Island, Montana, California, and not a few other states. Formerly the constitution of Missouri was equally conservative, but by the amendments of 1902 the two leading cities, St. Louis and Kansas City, were permitted to exempt the water debt. Furthermore, cities may by vote exceed the debt limit with issues of water and light bonds to the amount of 5 per cent. of the taxable property. This is equivalent to a restricted permission to ignore these loans in computing the net debt. The following also are among those states in which, by constitution, statute, or charter, some or all municipalities may, in computing their net debt, omit water loans, wholly or to a percentage: Alabama, Colorado, Massachusetts, Montana, Missouri, New Hampshire, New York, North and South Dakota, South Carolina, Utah, Washington, and Wyoming. New York City may except water loans incurred since January 1, 1904. The municipalities in some of these states may in like manner except sewerage and lighting obligations when incurred for plants municipally owned and operated. Municipal corporations in Illinois that have reached their debt limit may not issue water bonds to exceed that limit; but for the improvement or extension of waterworks, they may issue certificates payable out of the earnings of the plants.

The Revised Statutes of Massachusetts fairly represent these states mentioned. Net indebtedness in Massachusetts is defined as the indebtedness of a county, city, town, or district, omitting debt created for supplying the inhabitants with water, and other debts exempted from the operation of the law limiting their indebtedness, and deducting the amount of the sinking funds available for the payment of *the indebtedness included.* The phrase italicized calls attention to the fact that in subtracting the water debt, or any other legally excludable debt, it is not the gross, but the net debt which is subtracted. In other words, care should be taken that the sinking funds of the excluded debts should not be twice deducted.

As previously stated, the various debits of a transient nature are frequently excluded in ascertaining net debt. Of such, in the constitution of Alabama, are temporary loans, to be paid within one year, made in anticipation of the collection of taxes, and not exceeding one-fourth of the annual revenues. Maine and some other states do not limit the amount of temporary loans which may be excluded. In line with the common rule the Supreme Court of Georgia holds that unaccrued interest is not to be included. Almost invariably municipal corporations, as in Montana, may incur new indebtedness to refund existing indebtedness, if the total after refunding will be within the constitutional limitation, even though both taken together would exceed it.

In the rare cases in which bonded debt only is limited, and there is no restriction upon floating debt, the bondholders cannot, by mandamus or injunction, restrain the creation of floating debt, and, unless taxes have been specifically pledged for the payment of the bonds, or unless the legislature has made them a first charge, the holders of floating indebtedness have an equal right with the holders of bonds.

The holders of floating indebtedness are general creditors, who may press demands for payment with a legal suit and become judgment creditors. The bondholder in the absence of default on his paper, and prior to its maturity, has no ground for attempting the collection of his claim against the municipality. It is quite conceivable, in a school district for instance, that the claims of judgment creditors might accumulate to such an extent as to endanger the district's solvency and vitiate the interest of its bondholders. Hence the necessity, for safety, of having the floating debt construed within the debt limits.

It is patent from these judicial and legislative interpretations offered in illustration that the legal Net Debt of a municipality, upon which its debt limitation is based, is often a thing quite apart from the Real Net Debt. On the one hand the municipality may be permitted to exclude from the net debt issues that are *not* self-supporting, and, on the other hand, it may be enjoined from excluding issues that *are* self-supporting.

The Supreme Court of Illinois decided that the Chicago World's Fair bonds should not be computed as part of the net debt. The amount of these bonds in 1910 was $4,293,000 or six-sevenths of the amount of the water debt, or of the amount of the city's sinking funds. The sinking fund bonds and water debt are, of course, revenue-producing; but the World's Fair bonds were dead weight, and were not held in as high esteem and did not sell as well as Chicago's other direct obligations. Similarly the $5,000,000 San Francisco Exposition bonds are not figured in the debt limit. These were gross perversions of municipal accounting, whatever justification it may have had on grounds of expediency. St. Louis had World's Fair bonds and water bonds in practically the same amounts, respectively, as Chicago; but the Fair bonds of St. Louis were included in the net debt.

The best illustrations of self-supporting issues that may not be deducted from the gross debt in finding the net debt come from states like Pennsylvania, in which water debt may not be subtracted. It is to be observed, however, that the usual bond circular takes little heed of either the real or the legal net debt, but makes a practice of taking the general or the total debt, subtracting from it the gross water debt, and probably the sinking funds, and calling the remainder the net debt. The justification for this is that further refinement of municipal accountancy would be lost on the average bond buyer. No such liberties would be openly tolerated in presenting the financial statements of private corporations.

Portland, Maine, offers a good illustration of a businesslike system of municipal accounting, as far as it determines net debt. The total debt of Portland includes the usual city loans, bonds matured but not presented and retired, and assumed bonds of the annexed city of Deering. From this total Portland deducts, to find net debt, the conservatively estimated market value of her available assets, consisting of cash, gas company stock, and the stock of the Portland and Ogdensburg Railroad, guaranteed under lease by the Maine Central.

A form of accounting such as that in Portland, under which the legal and the real net debt approximate each other, is not possible under the laws of many states, for it is liable to abuse. And yet it makes us realize how we may mislead when we attempt to compare the debts of cities without comparing also the revenues of the properties for which the debts were incurred; or when, without making proper allowances, we attempt to compare the past debt of a city, which represents as a rule expenditures which make no direct pecuniary return, with the present debt, which in part may represent highly productive assets, as in New York.

New York City sought and obtained from the legislature an amendment to the constitution providing for the exclusion from its debt limit of obligations hereafter incurred for public improvements that yield to the city current net revenue in excess of the interest and sinking funds on such obligations; also for the exclusion from the debt limit of any obligation heretofore incurred by the city for any rapid transit or dock investments to the extent to which their net revenues shall meet the interest and sinking fund thereof. This course commends itself as more rational than that of raising the debt limit to 14 per cent., as then suggested, because, although the net result in dollars and cents may be the same, it places all kinds of " self-supporting " debt on a common basis of inventory, and is another step in the direction of more uniform municipal accounting. The danger from a spread of the custom is that cities will receive legislative permission to exclude from the net debt obligations that eventually will not prove self-sustaining.

Sinking Funds. Sinking Funds, even more commonly than water loans, are excepted from the gross debt in finding the net. To be sure it sometimes happens that the courts will hold, as in Montana, that "indebtedness" as used in the section of the state constitution limiting debts, means what a city owes, " irrespective of demands it might hold against others," but the interpretation that admits of this subtraction of sinking funds is fairly general. New York state in 1886 was the scene of the battle royal over sinking fund accounting in its relation to net debt; and the case was won in the Court of Appeals only after a year's struggle. One of the results was the creation in 1903, in New York City, of issues of General Fund bonds to absorb the surplus revenues arising from the crude sinking fund of the old city. Since these bonds, of which over $533,000,000 are now outstanding, are destined only for the sinking fund, the interest from them helps to keep down the tax rate. To include, therefore, the General Fund bonds in the city debt would be the height of absurdity.

If the sinking fund method of meeting debt is to be used at all, it is best to protect each bond issue separately, by creating a special sinking fund for it from the proceeds of a special bond tax voted before or at the time of the issue. The list of states requiring this method has been given on p. 207. If the fund is a general fund it is probably established by act of legislature " by raising annually a sum which will produce an amount equal to the sum of the principal and interest of said bonds at their maturity." As operated in Massachusetts the sinking fund is not designed to meet the interest. But since it is notorious that sinking funds, municipal and corporation, are appropriated for other than the uses for which they are instituted, the statute should explicitly state they are " to be used for no other purpose than the payment of such debt."

When a municipality has outstanding a considerable number and variety of loans, it is the custom to purchase its own securities to be kept alive in the sinking fund. Many cities invest in nothing but their own bonds. It is evident that this course does nothing more than reduce the real debt of the municipality. It is fairly comparable to the course of a man who borrows on his note and later reduces his indebtedness by buying back his note, or part of it, and owing himself the sum bought back, and paying himself interest on the sum until the maturity date.

"If the Sinking Fund is invested in the debtor's own bonds or obligations, its existence is *not of the least advantage to the creditor.* It gives him no additional security,—legal, equitable, or honorary. . . . . . It is a worthless device so far as he is concerned." [1]

Moreover a device, like that in New York, by which a city is permitted to sell its own bonds direct to the sinking fund, is not only worthless, but pernicious; for it permits " a city to market its bonds to itself, when the credit of the city or the state of the money market might be such that the bonds would not sell outside." It is understood, of course, that the plan may be pernicious, and yet the least of several possible evils under existing circumstances. This is the case in the New York General Fund bond issues. On the general grounds Minneapolis was refused permission to sell its bonds to the Board of Sinking Fund Commissioners, although no statute forbade it, the Chief Justice of Minnesota contending that " such a purpose is so radically inconsistent with a sinking fund, and so destructive of the purposes to be conserved by its maintenance, that it must be held that the prohibition is implied."

For a municipality to sell its bonds to the sinking fund is the same thing as for the municipality to borrow money from the sinking fund. It was this violation of fundamental principles that brought Pitt's famous English fund to grief.

If the object of a sinking fund is to lay aside money year by

[1] *The Metropolitan Debts of Boston and Vicinity,* Chandler. Italics ours. (Extracted from *The Sinking Fund,* Browne.) Other quoted paragraphs under the topic of "Sinking Funds" are from Chandler, unless otherwise attributed.

year toward the payment of a debt at some future time, the money in the fund is most safely disposed for accumulation until that time, and the creditors are best secured, by dispersing it in the purchase of various strong securities which to the least possible extent are subject to the control of the debtor corporation. With this in view the funds of Providence, Rhode Island, are convertible into bonds of the Federal Government, and of the state governments of New England, and of the cities of Rhode Island, and of 16 other cities of very high credit. But " the bonds of each of said cities shall be a lawful investment only so long as its indebtedness, less its water debt and sinking funds, shall not exceed 7 per cent. of its assessed valuation."

"The creditors' legal rights are very little, if at all, strengthened by a sinking fund invested in outside securities, so long as they remain under the control of the debtor himself, or within reach of his general creditors." [1]

You cannot hold a debtor to a contract made with himself.

How misplaced is public confidence in the efficacy of sinking funds (which are almost invariably in the control of the debtor), may be evinced by a survey of financial history. " The suspension of a sinking fund is at times deliberate, and is essential in sound finance if money must be borrowed to maintain it; for to borrow to keep up the Sinking Fund is a purely fictitious operation, which really adds to the debt it in no wise reduces." And so we find that England, after the War with Egypt, and after the Transvaal War, and the United States, during and for some years after the Civil War, suspended payments. Indiana, in 1905, by act of legislature, suspended taxes raised for sinking funds till 1908. Pennsylvania, by the constitution of 1873, makes explicit exception to the integrity of her sinking fund ". . . and *unless* in case of war, invasion, or insurrection, no part of the said sinking fund shall be used or applied otherwise than in the extinguishment of the public debt."

Yet, after all is said, because of the fact that sinking funds directly or indirectly reduce the amount of obligations in the hands of a city's creditors, it is right that they should ordinarily be deducted from the gross debt in computing the net.

Sinking Funds Versus Serial Payment. If not sinking funds, what then? The alternative is *Serial Repayment*.

[1] *The Sinking Fund*, Browne.

In 1872 West Virginia accepted a new constitution requiring that "the payment of any liability, other than that for the ordinary expenses of the State, shall be *equally distributed* over a period of at least twenty years." Ten years later, Massachusetts, by statute, extended to her municipalities the option of serial payment. "A city or town, instead of establishing a sinking fund, may vote to provide for the payment of any debt by such annual proportionate payments as will extinguish the same at maturity." Most of the leading cities and towns availed themselves of the privilege; and the demonstrable benefits that have accrued have been the means of influencing many municipalities in other parts of the country to adopt the same policy. A large part of the obligations of Elmira, New York, are serial in maturity, and the city is thereby enabled to do away with sinking funds. In 1913 and 1915 Massachusetts passed acts abolishing future sinking funds in cities, towns, and districts and substituted serial repayment. In 1917 New Hampshire prohibited the creation of sinking funds for new municipal issues and provided for 20-year serial amortization. The Pierson Bond Act under which all New Jersey municipal issues have been created since 1916, authorizes only serial bonds. New York state may now issue only serials and New York City is issuing serial bonds for most of its improvements.

Sinking funds do not amortize a debt; they merely convert it, or offset it. The only true amortization is extinction. The only way to sink a debt is to pay it. The simple, rational, and economic method of extinguishing a debt is to pay it in approximately equal periodic instalments. This is the serial bond method.

Sinking funds are not only liable to misappropriation, unwise investment, suspension, and the like, but *they are costly.* Their average earnings are little, if any, over 3 per cent. Serial bonds require a minimum of expense and produce a maximum of security. "When a bond issue is serial the investment grows safer as it grows older."

The following two tables, compiled by Mr. Alfred D. Chandler,[1] show the difference in actual *interest* paid out, and in *cost*, of a bond issue of $1,000,000, at different interest rates and durations.

---

[1] *The Metropolitan Debts of Boston and Vicinity. Sinking Fund and Serial Bond Methods Compared.* Printed by the Town of Brookline, Mass., 1905. Many other interesting tables are to be found there.

The first table works out the difference in *cost* of a loan of $1,000,000 for 20 years, bearing the interest rate of 4 per cent., on the assumption that the sinking fund can earn: (a) 3 per cent.; (b) $3\frac{1}{2}$ per cent.; (c) 4 per cent.

$1,000,000 AT 4% FOR 20 YEARS. COMPARISON BETWEEN SINKING FUND AND SERIAL BOND METHODS

By the Sinking Fund method the interest at 4% is........		$800,000
" Serial Bond " " "		420,000
Difference in *interest* in favor of Serial Bonds............		$380,000

(a)

$1,000,000 Sinking Fund requirements for 20 years, on a 3% basis, the decimal for $1 being .038654......................	$734,426	
$1,000,000 at 4% for 20 years, interest.....	800,000	
Cost of loan, Sinking Fund method........		$1,534,426
$1,000,000 20-year Serial Bond, 1-20, or $50,000, payable yearly.................	$1,000,000	
Interest (annually diminishing) total at 4%	420,000	
Cost of loan, Serial Bond method.........		1,420,000
Difference in *cost* in favor of Serial Bond method........		$114,426

(b)

$1,000,000 Sinking Fund requirements for 20 years, on a $3\frac{1}{2}$% basis, the decimal for $1 being .036657....................	$696,483	
$1,000,000 at 4% for 20 years, interest.....	800,000	
Cost of loan, Sinking Fund method........		$1,496,483
" " Serial Bond "		1,420,000
Difference in *cost* in favor of Serial Bond method........		$76,483

(c)

$1,000,000 Sinking Fund requirements for 20 years, on a 4% basis, the decimal for $1 being .034749......................	$660,231	
$1,000,000 at 4% for 20 years, interest.....	800,000	
Cost of loan, Sinking Fund method........		$1,460,231
" " Serial Bond "		1,420,000
Difference in *cost* in favor of Serial Bond method......		$ 40,231

The second table shows, without detail of operations, the difference in interest and cost of a $1,000,000 loan at both 3 and 4 per cent., for durations of 20, 40, and 50 years.

$1,000,000 at 3 per cent. Difference in INTEREST in Favor of Serial Bonds			$1,000,000 at 4 per cent. Difference in INTEREST in Favor of Serial Bonds		
20 Years	40 Years	50 Years	20 Years	40 Years	50 Years
$285,000	$585,000	$735,000	$380,000	$780,000	$980,000
Difference in COST in Favor of Serial Bonds			Difference in COST in Favor of Serial Bonds		
Sinking Fund	20 Years [1]	40 Years [2]	50 Years [3]	20 Years [1]	40 Years [2]	50 Years [3]
On 3 per cent. basis..	$19,426	$109,199	$173,305	$114,426	$304,199	$418,305
" 3½ " "	....	51,791	111,908	76,483	246,791	356,908
" 4 " "	....	....	58,057	40,231	194,765	303,057

[1] Decimal for 19 years, and 19 payments.   [2] Decimal for 39 years, and 39 payments.
[3] Decimal for 49 years, and 49 payments.

If the number of payments were to equal the full number of years, there would be an increase over the above in the saving in favor of Serial Bonds, the ratio of such increase being larger with the bonds of a shorter term.

If both the decimal taken and the number of payments made each equal the full number of years, there will still be a large gain in favor of the Serial Bonds.

To take the extreme case, it costs a municipality $418,305 more to issue a $1,000,000, 50-year, 4 per cent. loan, to be acquitted at the end of the period by sinking fund accumulations, provided the sinking fund earns the usual 3 per cent., than it costs to pay off one-fiftieth of the loan, with interest, each year. It should be mentioned, however, that a " straight " 50-year loan would bring a slightly higher price than a serial loan, but the difference would be only a trifling part of $418,305. Bearing this sum in mind, and remembering that New York City has very many millions of 50-year loans outstanding, one can readily appreciate the tremendous loss to the city which the sinking fund policy occasions. In 1926, New York had $270,894,605 in her various sinking funds.

The Redemption Privilege. Bonds that mature serially are almost never refunding, for the method of amortization hardly admits of it; and refunding defeats the very purpose of serial retirement. Indeed, refunding is often denied by law. But still something is gained by a municipality that does not mature its bonds serially, if the issues are made subject to call; and it is significant that very many cities which are given in part to serial amortization, have all their straight loans callable.

Bond issues may be callable either in whole or in part; at the time of issuance or at a given date; or on or after a given date; or they may be callable in a certain amount each year.

Unlike corporation bonds, municipals are usually redeemable at par, if at all. The privilege of redemption makes it possible for a city, when in funds, to cancel a portion of its debt with the surplusage, and avoid the evils of a large sinking fund. Much the same result would be attained by buying the bonds in the open market, as sinking funds often do, but since municipal bonds are seldom permitted by law to be issued at a price below par, it is not always possible for the city to buy them back below par; and the sinking fund usually has to pay slightly more than the market price if it buys openly.

Then again the privilege of recall makes it possible for a municipality to avail itself, without loss, of any general lowering of interest rates, or of any lowering in its own particular case, due to gain in its credit. One still sees many irredeemable issues of municipal 6s and 7s that were put out in the seventies and eighties. Most of these long since would have been retired or refunded, if they had been callable at par. Any experience of this sort is likely to be reflected in the policy of a community. If one issue of a city is callable we may expect to find most of them callable,—at least most recent issues. And if the practice gains any headway in one section, it is likely to become the settled policy of the state. Almost all of the municipal bonds of Wyoming have been subject to call, and the majority of the remainder have been serial.

The privilege of redemption plays no part in the net debt of municipalities, but as a topic concomitant with sinking funds and serial repayment it is logically treated here.

Debt Limitations and Restrictions. Having, now, some working information on appraised, taxable wealth, and of legally defined debt, we are prepared to consider each in its relation to the other; for their relation, expressed in percentage as a ratio, is the *usual* measure of the debt permitted by law, and introduces us presently to the study of legality.

First, however, let it be said that certain states (rapidly lessening in number) have almost no *general* limitation to the amount of debt that their municipalities may incur. They are:

Arkansas   Delaware   Florida   Maryland   Nevada   Tennessee

Florida limits her cities and towns to 10 per cent. of the assessed value. New York state puts a limitation upon the debts of counties and cities, but none upon the minor civil divisions.

The *source of the debt limitation* varies. The territories, of course, have been subject to the will of Congress. For states the constitutional limitation has been the most desirable, for that is least liable to abrogation. Also if the constitution is not sufficiently restrictive it may be supplemented by legislation. We find constitutional limitations in Kentucky, Louisiana, Montana, New York (for counties and cities), Oklahoma, Montana, South Carolina, South Dakota, Utah, Washington, West Virginia, Wisconsin, etc.

Yet more often than not the power of debt limitations and of other restrictions has been delegated, specifically or otherwise, to the legislatures. By this arrangement legislative limitation is more self-corrective and discretionary, but it is liable to abuse. Some of the New England state legislatures have been free in their employment of the discretionary power, particularly in the passage of special enabling acts. When custom sanctions this the debt limit is of very little value. North Adams, Massachusetts, has more loans outside than inside the limit, entirely apart from the water bonds. New Bedford has a debt of $3,939,000 outside. In 1903 the legislature of New Hampshire suspended the Municipal Bond Act of 1895 to permit Portsmouth to build a high school.

The debt-limiting power has been delegated in whole or in part to the legislatures of Kansas, Maryland, Massachusetts, New York, Michigan, Nebraska, New Hampshire, Ohio, Oregon, and other states. In Maryland the power has not been generally exercised.

Charter limitation, being freely amenable to legislation, is open to the same sort of objection as legislative limitation, if not to the same degree. The number of municipal corporations in which the principal limitation is by charter is not relatively large. It is the only sort of limitation, however, in North Carolina and Tennessee. When the charter antecedes the present constitution or the most recent municipal bond act, it is generally of greater latitude, as in Manchester, Virginia; but sometimes the opposite is the case, as in Danville, and Lynchburg, Virginia.

The *Basis of the Debt Limitation* is almost always a percentage of the assessed valuation of all the taxable property. In New York state and in Virginia it is the assessed valuation of real estate only. In Chicago and in all the municipalities of Iowa it is a percentage of the full or actual valuation, irrespective of the assessment. But these are the rare exceptions to the general rule.

The *Degree of Limitation* may be fixed (numerical), or, more commonly, elastic (percentile). Oregon is the only state which limits its municipalities as a whole to fixed amounts. Counties in Oregon may not contract debts in excess of $5,000; cities and towns, in excess of $2,500, without legislative sanction; school districts of over 75,000 population, in excess of $100,000. Smaller school districts have a 5 per cent. limit. Omaha, Nebraska, formerly was limited (with exceptions of certain issues) to $2,750,000, but now to 5 per cent. of the assessment. Danville, Virginia, is limited to $1,460,000.

It is obvious that the better form is the common elastic limitation by which the net debt may not be incurred,—at least without consent of the legislature,—to exceed a certain percentage of the assessment. There is one drawback, however, to the elastic form, in its relation to legality. Although in a comparatively new country like ours the tendency of the assessment (and therefore of the debt-capacity) to increase is fairly constant, yet at times, as from a local catastrophe, or in a period of serious depression, such as that of the early nineties, there may be a depletion of the taxable resources which, if not noted by the municipal creditor, may leave him with a new issue of illegal obligations on his hands. Helena, Montana, floated town warrants under these circumstances in 1893, and although the city acted in perfectly good faith, no way has yet been found to wipe out the debt incurred at that time.

In reading the subjoined list of states with their debt limitations, from whatever source, it must be remembered that exceptions to the limits are very numerous; that the limit is often raised for special issues, and special kinds of issues; that it is rated on different bases of valuation; that it is often subject to suspension at the will of the legislatures and on the vote of the people. For instance, although the debt limit in Oklahoma is 5 per cent., the constitution excepts, and does not limit at all, the amount of debt which may be created for the purchase or construction of public utilities. When two percentages are given they indicate the ordinary minimum and maximum limits for various kinds of municipalities, or perhaps for various kinds of issues, or else the first number represents the nominal limits and the second, the limit including issues authorized by popular vote. Therefore the table is almost useless for purposes of comparison.

	Per cent.		Per cent.
Alabama	$3\frac{1}{2}$–8	New Hampshire	1–6
California	15	New Jersey	4–7
Colorado (counties)	$\frac{3}{10}$	New York (cities and	
Connecticut	5	counties)	10
Georgia	7	North Carolina	8
Idaho	10	North Dakota	5–10
Illinois	5	Ohio	$2\frac{1}{2}$–5
Indiana	2	Oklahoma	5
Iowa	$1\frac{1}{4}$–5	Oregon	($2,500–6%)
Kansas	5–10	Pennsylvania	7–10
Kentucky	2–10	Rhode Island	3
Louisiana	10	South Carolina	8
Maine	5	South Dakota	5–23
Massachusetts	$2\frac{1}{2}$–5	Texas	25 [1]
Michigan	3–10	Utah	2–12
Minnesota	5–10	Vermont	5–10
Mississippi	15	Washington	$1\frac{1}{2}$–10
Missouri	5–10	West Virginia	$2\frac{1}{2}$–5
Montana	3–5	Wisconsin	5
Nebraska	5–10	Wyoming	2–10

It is curious that amid all the vagaries of municipal debt restrictions no state that we recall has recognized in the limitations it imposes, the dependence of the debt-paying ability on the margin of income over current municipal expenses. In the Province of Quebec, however, we find the principle is recognized, for municipalities there may issue bonds and provide for payment out of the general funds only until such time as the total amount required in any one year for interest and sinking fund, or interest and instalment of principal, shall exceed 50 per cent. of the total annual revenue. When this point is reached debentures may be issued only upon the authority of the Lieutenant Governor in Council.

It would not be possible to mention within reasonable limits

[1] The Texas limitation is 25 per cent. of the assessed value of real property (irrespective of personal).

of space, all the hindrances and bounds which are placed about the incurrence of debt. Most states expressly prohibit their municipalities from appropriating moneys for assuming the debts of, or becoming shareholders in, any private corporation, company, or person; although an exception often is made, especially in New England, in favor of railroad corporations, on the ground of their public nature and function. The loan of credit in any guise is also prohibited in the great majority of states.

The Referendum. A number of states require that prior to the incurrence of any new funded debt, under the general laws of the state, at least any debt in excess of the year's resources, the measure shall be submitted to the vote of the qualified electors of the issuing corporation. Among them are:

Alabama,	Idaho,	Oklahoma,	Texas,
California,	Kentucky,	South Carolina,	Utah,
Colorado,	Missouri,	South Dakota,	West Virginia.

Also a number of states require the referendum (or the petition, which is much the same thing), for debts incurred in excess of a certain percentage of the assessed valuation. Among them are:

Georgia	above $\frac{1}{5}$ per cent.	Pennsylvania above 2 per cent.	
Iowa	" $1\frac{1}{4}$ " "	N. Dakota " 5 " "	
Washington	" $1\frac{1}{2}$ " "		

In addition to these, New Hampshire requires the referendum for all political divisions except cities.

A majority vote is by no means sufficient to sanction bond issues, in some states. About as many require a two-thirds vote as require the majority vote. Oklahoma, Washington, and West Virginia, among others require a three-fifths vote. Colorado and Utah limit the voting power to those who, in the year preceding the election, paid a property tax. But Iowa requires only 200 signatures to a petition, in cities of 10,000 population or over.

The submission of every proposed bond issue to popular vote is the best warranty of good faith. By what the people themselves have willed they are more likely to abide. And there will be less unwisdom in the accumulation of debts when they are subject to the publicity of a municipal election.

Here and there we come across laws requiring certain municipalities, or loans of certain kinds, or loans issued under certain conditions, to receive special legislative sanction before flotation of obligations. In the Eastern Provinces of Canada, New Brunswick, Nova Scotia, and Prince Edward Island, a municipality must get a special act of legislature every time it makes a new bond issue. And in our own country the same thing is approximately true for all the municipalities of Maryland.

Evasion of the Debt Limit. Several devices have been employed to evade the restrictions placed about the power to contract debts. Notable among these, and usually successful (though not in Illinois or Indiana), is the plan to provide municipal waterworks by purchasing a plant privately built,—subject to the water bonds outstanding, which, as they are not a direct municipal obligation, are not a part of the municipal debt. Another plan is to issue certificates of indebtedness redeemable from the proceeds of taxes voted at the time, or prior to, the issuance of the certificates, the taxes to be collectable, annually, over a series of years. All loans which are the outcome of such dubious methods should be avoided. They form but an infinitesimal portion of all.

CHAPTER XXI

CITY AND TOWN BONDS: VALIDITY AND GOOD FAITH

Validity. With matters of validity we come to the second of the three main topics under which the security for municipal loans is treated. It may be well to recall the order: Financial Competency, Validity, and Good Faith.

It has been said, with a certain element of truth, that municipal bonds are good if legal. Whether or not this sums up the general impression of municipals, it would be hard to say. The emphasis which the statement places upon legality is not without occasion. Yet legality is not the broad term for the thing signified;—rather validity: for a bond might be issued which, though not in complete accordance with law, would still be a valid obligation.

The question of validity almost never arises for federal government or private corporation loans. But there are so many and such various circumstances under which municipal bonds are issued, the laws are so obscure, diverse, and in many cases untested, the municipal corporations so various in character, their legislative, executive, and advisory officers so often woefully inefficient, that opportunities for loss to investors would be innumerable, were the purchasing bond houses, through their experienced attorneys, not so scrupulous in all legal details.

But again let us repeat that since the usual, and generally the only, fiscal security for municipal bonds is the general power of taxation, our first duty is with this tax power, its scope and limitations, and its relation both to the wealth it levies upon, and the debts it is to sustain and discharge. Validity, in general, is secondary.

"The Supreme Court of the United States . . . has upheld the validity of bonds which have been issued in violation of all requirements of law; bonds that have been issued in excess of the constitutional limit of indebtedness; bonds that have been issued in violation of other constitutional requirements. But that court is powerless when it reaches the question of remedies, when the statutes of the state fail to provide a sufficient tax levy, or when they expressly restrict the levy to such an amount as will not be sufficient to pay the validated bonds and interest. One cannot read the municipal bond cases in the United States Supreme Court reports of the seventies and eighties without being impressed with the belief that the legality of bonds is of less importance than the power of taxation behind them."

It is fortunate indeed, not only for investors in American municipals, but for our cities, that courts, both state and federal, but particularly federal, have taken the stand that repudiation shall not be generally permissible on grounds of mere technicality; for otherwise the status of municipal credit would not be on its present high plane.

A democratic form of government must necessarily be deficient in some excellences that pertain to the rule of an aristocracy of inheritance. Among them is the peculiar training for petty government that a system of rotation in office achieves. Municipal officers, raised to position without special fitness, and with tenure subject to the vicissitudes of politics, are not the best sort of persons in whose hands to leave the power to borrow large sums of money in exact conformity with a complex body of laws.

A record of sales, during 1907, of the more important communities in the United States shows that of a total of about $200,000,000 of municipal and state bonds issued, some $4,000,-000, or 2 per cent., divided among 65 municipal issues, were finally declined by those who had bought them subject to the approval of their attorneys; and usually, but not always, declined on the ground that the issue was invalid because of some lack of compliance with minor requirements of law. This $4,-000,000, of course, does not take into account a very much larger amount of issues which the attorney of the purchaser found insufficiently protected by law, but which by further acts at his suggestion the issuing community was able completely to validate without formal resale. There is not the slightest suspicion of bad faith to be attached to these communities that had issues rejected; but there is a very significant moral to be drawn from the inference of gross carelessness.

The Causes of Illegality. The causes of illegality are legion; and it would not be practicable, nor possible, to mention them all here. In their minutiæ, they concern only the courts, the municipality, and the bond attorney. Analyzed, however, they resolve themselves into four groups: they have to do with, 1, the authority of issue; 2, the purpose of issue; 3, the process of issue; 4, the violation of debt and tax restrictions.

The ultimate *authority to issue* municipal bonds is in constitution or statutes; really it resides in the legislature. Constitutional provisions are very accessible, but the statutes have to be studied very thoroughly throughout if one seeks information as to legality at first hand, for one never can tell in what obscure place may be hidden an act that may have effect. Moreover, the statutes are sometimes susceptible of misinterpretation. So in the matter of the authority of issue, for illustration, prominent firms of bond attorneys are at variance as to the necessity of specific legislative sanction, when municipalities in Maine issue bonds.

In addition to authorization by legislature, that by popular vote is required for all issues in many states, and for certain issues or kinds of issues, and for certain kinds of municipalities (such as towns and taxing districts), in other states. Irregularities in balloting may invalidate this authorization by election, as recently in Asbury Park, New Jersey, and Dawson, Minnesota. Special legislation giving a municipality or a group of them, but not all municipalities of the class, authority to incur debts for a certain purpose, has for the past 35 years been on the decline, owing to the growth of constitutional prohibitions. The constitutions quite generally forbid legislatures to pass local laws when, in the opinion of the legislatures, general laws are adequate. One treads on dangerous ground who buys municipal bonds issued under authority of laws that are general in their form but clearly special in their application; for the courts do not agree as to the legality of such legislation.

Invalidity more often arises from minor errors connected with the *process of issue*. Advertisement may have been omitted, or may have been insufficient. Flotations of Philadelphia, New York, and Plainfield, New Jersey, have been declined on the score of insufficient advertisement; of Peru, Indiana, and Reading, Ohio, because of errors in the details. It seems hardly possible that a municipality could mistake a law so apparently simple and general as that requiring the price to be at par or above; but Matrona County, Wyoming, sold an issue of 4s at par without including accrued interest, and a resale some months later was required for validation. Oneonta, New York, committed an equally incomprehensible blunder some years ago in selling an issue bearing an interest rate in excess of what was legal. The bonds were issued as 4½s, but the village was not allowed to sell anything higher than 4s; and the bonds had to be remade and sold as 4s. A school district of North Hempstead, Long Island, had a large issue refused because the resolution failed to state the rate of interest, or the maturity of the bonds. An excellent illustration of the nice regard for detail necessary in the process of municipal bond issue, comes from Boston. Some years ago the Council of that city voted certain appropriations to be met by a bond issue. A rumor was circulated to the effect that one member of the Council had left the meeting before the vote was taken. A denial was immediately forthcoming. But since the vote had been close the mayor called for a repassage of the ordinance, in order not to prejudice the bidding for that issue.

An important detail not to be overlooked is that the special tax levy be voted if required by law, or if permissible and to be expected, although not specifically mentioned in the bond enabling act. And if there are any restrictions to the power of taxation, it is equally important that the margin between the tax rate necessary for the funded debt and the rate allowed by law be amply sufficient to allow for any reasonable charge for current expenses of the municipality, which have priority of payment.

The *purpose of issue* has played no inconsiderable part in matters of legality and therefore in the history of past default and repudiation. It is still a factor worth thought in its relation to legality. To mention railroad aid bonds is still to wave a red flag in many sections of the country, especially in the Middle West. Of the 300 municipalities in Illinois that issued railroad aid bonds in the old days, over one-third repudiated them. Yet it is statutory rather than common law (except in Michigan) that is generally hostile. There are still, however, states that specifically or inferentially permit the issuance of railroad aid bonds; for steam transportation service is commonly recognized as a public function.

But it is in furtherance only of public enterprises that municipal corporations may enter into contracts and create obligations. Even statutory authority may not transcend this limitation. And the purpose of issue must not only be public; it must also be in keeping with the political functions of the obligor corporation. Since the social and political demands of cities and towns are more varied than those of counties and taxing districts, and since their corporate existence approaches more nearly to independence, it follows that there are more legitimate purposes for which cities and towns may issue bonds.

It would be idle to attempt a list of all the purposes for which municipalities may incur debt; but it may be worth while to emphasize again the fact that, apart from all questions of legality, some purposes are more legitimate than others. No one would question the propriety of housing fire apparatus with the proceeds of a city loan, but many would deprecate the use of a city's credit to plot a cemetery or build an American Legion Hall. If rarely, yet at least sometimes, the distinction between legality and legitimacy of purpose has had a very practical bearing upon bond security. During the days of Reconstruction, while local Unionists and Northern Republicans were running the finances of Louisiana with a lavish hand, the Democrats of New Orleans, upon whom, as taxpayers, the burden principally fell, made it known through the press and by public resolves, that when they came into power again the state would repudiate such bonds as were not issued against legitimate wants of the state. And they kept their word.

The demand in some quarters for municipal ownership and operation of public utilities raises the question to what extent supplying a community with water and supplying it with light are public functions. It is a question that each state government has to answer through its legislative and judicial branches. It will pass without challenge, however, that none but municipal corporations proper,—those the subject of this chapter,—will undertake the ownership of public utilities, such as gas and electric lighting.

If the purpose of an issue, which is generally denoted by its title, is to take care of a previous flotation, a study of the antecedent issue is highly desirable. At best, "Refunding," or "Renewal Bonds," comprising not more than 10 per cent., of all permanent loans, indicate the extension of a loan that the municipality felt it could not pay conveniently. At worst they indicate a plot to float a loan under a misleading title, which might or would prove illegal if sold directly, without refunding. The legality of Refunding Bonds, then, involves its own issue, and the issue it refunds.

"Current Expense" and "Deficiency" loans betray a form of accounting improper everywhere, and illegal in some states. "Compromise" and "Adjustment Bonds" are the aftergrowth of default and litigation. Securities with titles like these indicate equivocal financing. Without investigation let no such bonds be trusted.

Validity, as affected by *debt restrictions*, gives constant concern to bond attorneys. The law is generally explicit enough, and sometimes the penalty too. The constitution of Indiana says: "all bonds or obligations in excess of such amount" (permitted by law, namely 2 per cent. of the assessment) "shall be void." The difficulty is that there may often be disagreement as to the classification of debts, especially in cities, so that the net debt, upon which the restriction is based, may be in dispute. The difficulties sometimes to be encountered in ascertaining these statistical matters, have been canvassed at length in previous pages.

Although in the United States there is little recognized relationship between the life of a loan and the purpose of its creation, there are occasional statutory limitations of life based upon the principle that a debt should be extinguished before the object for which it was incurred shall have ceased its usefulness. To this end some states do not allow street improvement or school bonds to run as long as water bonds. Again in this matter we may look for example to Canada, where bonds issued for public improvements, such as sidewalks, etc., may not exceed in term the probable life of the improvement; and they may not be refunded; and an engineer's certificate, stating this probable life, is a necessary preliminary to the passing of the debt by-law. The Pierson Bond Act in New Jersey is especially commendable in this regard. But in the good old days New York thought nothing of issuing 50-year bonds for paving Broadway, that its children might pay for work which perished before their birth. The principle of limited duration finds its most perfect expression in 10-year serial equipment bonds, but the extension of the principle to many industrial bond issues, especially those secured by mortgage on wealth like lumber and minerals which is being depleted by operation, has been very successful, and its growing vogue is one of

the most gratifying financial developments of recent years. Our
municipal lawmaking bodies might well give heed.

REMEDIES FOR INVALIDITY

Invalidity, as affected by the authority, purpose, or process
of issue, or by the violation of debt or tax restrictions, is almost
always accidental. There is seldom any deliberate irregularity on
the part of the municipality, except in the petty matter of award-
ing loans. Criminality on the part of outsiders, however, is by no
means obsolete. In one case the forgery and successful hypothecation of municipal bonds by two men, alone, amounted to
$1,600,000.

Trust Company Supervision and Certification. Therefore to
safeguard the community and the investor against forgery and
overissue there has arisen in the past two decades the custom of
placing the supervision of new municipal issues in the hands of
trust companies. Following the regulations of the leading stock
exchanges, the trust companies furnish steel engraving of highest
quality, and sometimes special paper. Upon each bond is placed
their countersignature. Often before the issue is offered to the
bankers or the public, bond attorneys acting for the trust company pass upon its legality. In these ways every precaution is
taken against invalidity; and possible loss, except through municipal bankruptcy, is reduced to a minimum.

State Certification of Validity. Another encouraging sign in
the development of bond finance is the growth of constitutional
and statutory measures to protect municipal loans from future
charges of illegal issuance. By the constitution of 1889 North
Dakota declared:

" No bond or evidence of indebtedness of the state shall be valid unless
the same shall have indorsed thereon a certificate signed by the Auditor
and Secretary of State, showing that the bond or evidence of debt is issued
pursuant to law and is within the debt limit. No bond or evidence of
debt of any county, or bond of any township or other political subdivision, shall be valid unless the same shall have indorsed thereon a certificate,
signed by the county auditor, or other officer authorized by law to sign
such certificate, stating that said bond or evidence of debt is issued pursuant to law and is within the debt limit."

In 1893 Texas passed a state law requiring the certification
and registration of all municipal loans. It will be observed that in

several respects this is an improvement on the provision of North Dakota.

"... Hereafter a county, city or town, ... before ... bonds are offered for sale, shall forward to the Attorney-General the bonds to be issued, a certified copy of the order or ordinance levying the tax to pay interest and provide a sinking fund, with a statement of the total bonded indebtedness ... including the series of bonds proposed, and the assessed value of the property for purposes of taxation ... ; ... and if the Attorney-General shall find that such bonds are issued in conformity to the Constitution and laws, and that they are valid and binding obligations ... he shall so officially certify.

"... Such bonds, after receiving the certificate of the Attorney-General, and having been registered in the Comptroller's office, as provided herein, shall thereafter be held, in every action, suit or proceeding in which their validity is or may be brought into question, prima facie valid and binding obligations ... : provided the only defense which can be offered against the validity of said bonds shall be fraud or forgery."

In 1897 Georgia passed a state law to similar effect. When a municipal loan in that state shall have been voted, the Solicitor-General, or Attorney-General, shall file a petition in the office of the clerk of the Superior Court setting forth the details of the issue. The Judge of the Court shall hear and determine all questions of law and of fact. If no bill of exceptions is filed within 20 days, or if the Supreme Court affirms the judgment of the Superior Court when contested, the judgment of the Superior Court " shall be forever conclusive upon the validity of said bonds against the said county, municipality, or division, and the validity of said bonds shall never be called in question in any court of this state." All bonds so passed upon shall have stamped or written on them, " validated and confirmed by judgment of the Superior Court."

Again turning to Canada for suggestions:—the Ontario municipal act limits the time within which action may be taken to quash by-laws purporting to authorize bond issues. But it further provides that if interest or any principal which may have become due shall have been paid *for one year* the bonds must be held valid.

Such a validating clause is not so good, however, as the North Dakota provision, which in its effect is like a mandatory Torrens Act guaranteeing title to land. Similar provisions are found also in the municipal acts of other Canadian Provinces. Alberta, and if we remember rightly, Saskatchewan, has a statutory provision with regard to school district bonds which is almost identical with the North Dakota provision.

Validation of Issues by Courts and Legislatures. Although these ounces of prevention are worth more than the proverbial pound of cure, yet there is much assurance to be got from knowing that because the legality of a loan is in question it will not necessarily be defaulted. The city of Santa Cruz, California, had outstanding water bonds which for years were considered by many to be illegal; but in 1913 the city's liability was sustained by the Circuit Court of Appeals. In 1907 Walla Walla, Washington, and Christian County, Kentucky, sold issues which were declined, and Seattle an issue which was twice declined because of questionable validity. By upholding the validity of these issues the Supreme Courts of the two states made possible the sale of the bonds. On another occasion the mayor of Atchison, Kansas, sought to refund $4\frac{1}{2}$ and 5 per cent. bonds into a new issue bearing 4 per cent. at par value. This the holders of the old bonds refused to accept and were upheld by the State Court which compelled the city to levy a tax and thereby pay off the earlier issues. (Levison vs. Finney, No. 18, 1934, Supreme Court of Kansas.) With the same object in view an issue of Custer County, Montana, declined in 1906, was subsequently validated by legislative acts.

Still another means lies open, and is getting rather common to safeguard investors from illegal issues, and that is the employment by a municipality of some authoritative firm of bond attorneys to oversee the preparation of the enabling act and the subsequent proceedings. Thus the water bonds of Tucson, Arizona, were issued pursuant to an act of Congress, and to an ordinance of the City Council; and both the act and the ordinance were drafted by one of the leading legal firms of the country.

Estoppel and the Bond Recital. Lastly, and in some respects most important of all, validity is safeguarded by the recital engraved upon the bond itself. Municipal bond recitals in the United States have conformed of late to certain patterns, all more or less closely following the phraseology held to be effective by the United States Supreme Court. The New Hampshire Municipal Bond Act of 1895 contains sets of forms acceptable to the state. The bond may or may not declare that it is one of a series of a certain number, or mention the specific purpose of issue, or the particular statute under which it is authorized. But besides promising to pay the bearer or the registered owner the principal amount at a certain time and place, it should declare in broad and general terms that it is issued under authority of law, for a corporate purpose; that all things necessary have been done to make it a legal, binding, and valid obligation of the municipality; that the indebtedness of the municipality, including the issue of which it is one, does not exceed the limit established by law; and that the tax necessary to pay it does not exceed any limitation established by law.

The courts have usually held that the *recital of regularity*, of which the above is an outline, " estops " (bars) the municipality from pleading invalidity as against an innocent holder of its bonds for value.

The Bond Attorney. Enough has been said in this and previous chapters to indicate the exceedingly important service rendered by the bond attorney. One of the strongest influences making for the present admirable credit of American municipalities has been the scrupulous care with which all questions affecting legality have been considered. To attempt an estimate of the proportion of all loans that have been put out with sufficient irregularity to cause correction by attorneys before acceptance would occasion unnecessary alarm. The bond attorney stands between the taxpayer and the investor, protecting each against the other, and working in the interest of both for a still higher development of municipal bond law and bond practice. His work is now so well done, and so systematically, that we rightly take it as a matter of course, and give ourselves, as individual buyers, in dealing with bond issues of recent years, to other considerations than those connected with validity.

In order to facilitate research regarding validity, the municipal bond committee of the Investment Bankers' Association urged all members of the Association and bond attorneys to file copies of legal opinions on outstanding issues with a central depository. The United States Mortgage and Trust Company of New York has been so designated, and now holds thousands of attorneys' opinions and legal papers relating to the validity of municipal bonds.

Good Faith. It may seem to those who are not familiar with the history of municipal credit that good faith is so bound up with the legal aspects of funded loans that it is hardly a topic for independent treatment. But this is not the case. Although prosperity is the best guaranty of debt-payment, and law an able second, and good faith easily influenced by both prosperity and legality, yet it is a thing apart, and may and does exist, and support the credit of loans which are backed by neither of the other two.

San Francisco long since recovered from a calamity that almost obliterated her. The city's extreme necessities have been the occasion of heavy bond issues. Yet the price paid for these has suffered little from the fact of the earthquake and the subsequent prostration. Of course investors are ready to buy the obligations of San Francisco because they have confidence in her material future; but this confidence is greatly strengthened by the fact that the city never repudiated any of its obligations.

On the other hand, bad faith may exist where there can be no question of either financial competency or validity. Pomeroy, Ohio, deliberately defaulted in 1910, on the interest of its largest issue of Refunding 6s. The reason ascribed was that the bonds were not callable; but the village fathers felt they would like to retire the bonds and took this means of accomplishing their purpose. Although Pomeroy may hope to lower its interest rate, the breach of faith will cost more than it comes to, for it removes the bonds of the village from the class that are legal for investment by savings banks. The matter was adjusted in 1913.

The factor of municipal credit that we entitle Good Faith has kept pace in growth with the factors Financial Competency and Validity. About 45 years ago, approximately, there was held in Missouri a general convention of representatives from various parts of the state for the purpose of seeking ways and means for municipal bond repudiation. The following extract from an address delivered there and afterwards circulated, expresses the contemporary opinion of the Middle West upon all three topics:

"Many labored efforts have been made to show that there are questions of good faith and moral obligation in reference to the payment of these bonds, wholly independent of the question of their legality. We maintain that arguments based on such considerations have no application to the payment of municipal obligations, and never had. . . . The only questions to be asked and answered in reference to a bond of that character are, Has it been issued by proper authority of law? Is the taxable property of the locality sufficient to meet the obligation, if its payment has to be enforced by law? These are the true foundations of public credit as applied to municipal corporations, and they are matters of law purely."

What are the inevitable concomitants and results of such reasoning? Repudiation. Default and repudiation. So it is that the Mississippi Valley at this period gives up a long list of defaulting cities, among which are the following: Duluth, Minnesota; Keokuk and McGregor, Iowa; Quincy and Cairo, Illinois; St. Joseph and Cape Girardeau, Missouri; Leavenworth, Lawrence, and Topeka, Kansas; Nebraska City, Nebraska; Little Rock and Helena, Arkansas; Memphis, Tennessee; Shreveport and New Orleans, Louisiana; Mobile, Alabama; and Houston, Texas. Missouri, naturally, after such an expression of sophistry, was not to be outdone. " Of one hundred counties, townships, and cities issuing bonds in Missouri, nine-tenths have defaulted." [1]

How sentiment has changed we already know from our survey of the many stringent laws regulating the amount and manner of debt-incurrence, and from the attitude of the courts towards the rights of innocent purchasers. Instead of unblushing and deliberate repudiation on the part of the municipalities that are now in difficulties of one sort or another, we find a sober acknowledgment of the moral obligation. In 1910 Helena, Montana, retired her illegal warrants of '93–'07 by the proceeds of a funding issue. Jeffersonville, Indiana, has long since refunded an illegal issue, with the permission of the legislature. Even when compromise with the bondholders shall become necessary, through visitation of catastrophe: war, pestilence, earthquake, fire, flood, or wind-storm,—*actus dei*, act of God, is the legal phrase,—we shall be led to expect hereafter that any adjustments necessary will be equitable, and that the municipality will go more than halfway in meeting its creditors to maintain its good faith. If the present is any criterion, we shall never again see a city of the size of Memphis, Tennessee, or Duluth, Minnesota, disincorporate itself with the connivance of courts or legislatures in the attempt to defraud its creditors.

[1] J. F. Hume, *North American Review*, August, 1884, p. 131.

Finally, there can be no greater assurance of good faith given investors in municipal bonds than the simple statement (for which we have authoritative support) that *no American municipality of any importance has defaulted in recent years* on the principal or interest of any of its obligations. This statement was made sixteen years ago in the first edition of this book and it still holds.

OTHER MATTERS AFFECTING MUNICIPAL CREDIT

The credit of a city or town is in no way different from that of a firm or individual. It is based on records and figures, but it is not ascertainable by means of them. Municipal credit is the composite judgment of bond buyers as to the certainty and promptness with which payments due shall be met.

Yet we have by no means canvassed all the influences that affect the security for city and town bonds. The volume of industry and commerce, as distinct from population and taxable wealth, gives up pertinent figures. They are to be found in the statement of bank deposits, capital, surplus, and clearings, and in statistics of building, employment, and wages,—some of which are, or will be, furnished by a bond house offering a municipal loan. " One-industry " towns like Marblehead and Brockton, Massachusetts, West Seneca, New York, Houghton, Michigan, and Butte, Montana, suffer in credit from the undistributed risk. The town of Gillette, Colorado, was dependent for its existence upon the life of the neighboring mines. These have failed, and Gillette, with a population reduced to about 50 souls, defaulted on its water bonds in May, 1907.

Mere age, coupled with a good record, is of great advantage. It materially assists the credit of Dubuque and Des Moines, Iowa, which are ancient burgs in comparison with most cities of their size in the West. Eastern capital will purchase their obligations at a price it will not pay for those of many younger cities growing more rapidly.

The character of the population, of course, is important. The matter is closely akin to those of sectional and race differences. Distinctly proletarian cities are not looked upon with equal favor, nor communities showing socialistic tendencies.

It will be seen that there is no limit to the number of influences affecting municipal credit, nor to the amount and range of study

that can be given it. Sciences with Greek polysyllabic titles can
lend genuine aid. The fact that the very existence of many
towns in Minnesota which are each year threatened by forest
fires, calls attention the usefulness of physiography. The experience of San Francisco, Stockton, Alameda, and Santa Bar-
bara suggests that even seismology is not without its service.
Climate, situation, and transportation facilities are matters of
commercial geography. Commercial geography speaks favorably for the future credit of Tacoma and Seattle.

Price Factors. Although we have repeatedly said that price
was more closely related to security, in municipal issues, than in
any others, and that therefore an inexperienced investor could
judge of his security by the return offered him on the investment,
the statement requires modification. There are several price
factors besides those of relative security and, of course, current
interest rate.

Of no mean effect is the *distribution* of municipal issues. Not
that it matters much whether the call for a specific loan is particularly general, but whether the city or town offering it is of
sufficient importance, and its obligations as a whole (by reason
of numbers and frequency of issue) sufficiently familiar for the
loan to be a staple of the bond market. Like equipments, loans
of towns and villages suffer in price somewhat from their comparative individual obscurity;—they lack the competitive demand;—but, like equipments, this loss is compensated by the
general excellence characteristic of the municipal bond class to
which they belong.

Local demand is a very important price factor. Naturally the
call of every section for its own municipals is strongest. The
principal sectional division is by states, for within the state laws
and regulations are fairly uniform. In those states, therefore,
where the demand is greater than the supply,—in other words, in
the older and richer states where the capital accumulated for
strictly investment uses is large as compared with local debts,—
as in New Hampshire particularly, the prices obtained discourage
alien purchase. In general few municipal bonds are listed on
an exchange and most of them are held locally.

Institutional demand is not always, but very generally, a phase
of local demand. Laws in each state regulating the investment
of state and municipal sinking funds, of trust funds, of the sur-

pluses of insurance companies, of the deposits of savings banks,—are naturally most favorable to the securities of home cities, towns, and districts; for home affairs are of immediate knowledge and subject to regulation.

Demand for Use as Collateral is another market factor. When bonds are acceptable by the Secretary of the Treasurer as security for government deposits, or when they are acceptable by state superintendents of banks in trust for trust companies, or by superintendents of insurance companies to secure policyholders, the market characteristics and prices will be governed accordingly. In March, 1909, there was an excellent instance of the effect of institutional demand on prices. It was understood that the law requiring insurance companies which do business in Oregon to deposit $50,000 of Oregon municipal bonds with the state Insurance Commissioner, had been revoked. This was expected to have such an unfavorable effect that, until prices for Oregon municipals should become adjusted to the change, the buyers of bond houses were cautioned against the purchase of Oregon bonds except at safe concessions.

Tax Exemption. *Tax Exemption*, as applied to municipal bonds, is the most important price factor apart from the character of the security and the prevailing price of money.

State and Municipal Bonds Free from Federal Taxation; Federal Bonds Free from State Taxation. In previous and in succeeding pages in these chapters on Civil Loans we mention that municipalities are creatures and therefore instrumentalities of states to perform certain functions for the states. The Federal Government is prevented from directly taxing the bonds issued by these instrumentalities, as well as the bonds of the state itself on the principle enunciated in the well-known case of McCulloch vs. Maryland that the power of taxation implicates the power of destruction, although in that particular case it was the power of the states to tax an instrumentality of the Federal Government that was at issue; and the most direct application of the principle to taxes in that case was in prohibiting the state and its agencies from taxing the bonds of the United States and of its agencies. This might be called reciprocal freedom from taxation by sovereign powers; but it does not extend to reciprocal freedom among the states themselves.

Very few give thought to the sequent question as to whether

bonds issued by municipalities in territories remained tax-exempt when the territories became states. Probably the best view is that since the imposition of a tax violates the theory that as agencies of the Federal Government these municipalities should not be hindered in the raising of funds, the tax can never be imposed, for knowledge on the part of investors that there might later be a tax, would have lessened the price the bonds would bring and thus would have hindered the debt-making power.

States and Governments Generally do not Ordinarily Tax Their Own Bonds. Since it is absurd for a sovereignty to tax the instruments by which it raises funds we find the Federal Government not taxing for the most part the income, from its own obligations and each state (when permitted by its constitution as interpreted by its courts) not taxing its own bonds, or the bonds of its subdivisions, or the income therefrom.

States can never Tax Municipals Sold as Tax-exempt. The same implication of an impairment of the obligation of a contract, in contravention of the tenth article of the Federal Constitution, which leads us to the decision that bonds issued by municipalities in territories remained tax-exempt when the territories became states, leads us to decide that municipal bonds that have been issued pursuant to a statute declaring them tax-exempt remain exempt irrespective of a repeal of the statute or of a constitutional amendment.

Otherwise States Generally Tax Bonds as Property. But there is nothing in the Federal Constitution that limits the power of a state to tax any other than federal property that is situated in that state, or that is owned, anywhere, by citizens of that state. Therefore it is general law, although not necessarily general practice, for each state that has a general property tax to tax all other bonds,—whether foreign bonds of any class, other state and municipal bonds, or corporation bonds,—that are located in the state, and therefore have a "situs" there, or that are owned by citizens of that state whether the actual bonds are in the state or not.

General Property Tax. Those states that derive their principal income from the general property tax levy the same rate of tax on taxable bonds as on real estate. We have pointed out elsewhere that a 25 mill tax on a 5 per cent. bond is the equivalent of a 50 per cent. income tax.

Since the difference in rate of yield between a tax-exempt municipal bond (which usually means a bond of a municipality of the state in which the owner is a citizen) and a corporation or taxable municipal bond of equal security is much less than the rate of the general property tax, it is obvious that tax-exempt municipals are a preferred investment for citizens of any state inflicting this tax, provided there is an intention to pay the tax.

Classified Property Tax. The rate is so punitive and so utterly at variance with most of the principles of sound taxation that some states have substituted for the general property tax the classified property tax,—which means that property in these states is commonly divided into three classes: real estate, tangible personal property, and intangible personal property, with regressive tax rates. That is, intangible personal property, of which stocks and bonds are the principal modes, are subjected to the lowest rates, which run from 1 to 5 mills.

Degree of Exemption of Federal Bond Income from Federal Tax. The Federal Government has, of course, entire control of the taxation of income from its own bonds and has exercised it from motives of expediency as follows:

All United States bonds issued prior to the World War loans are exempt. All liberty bonds and the victory notes are free from the normal income tax. The First Liberty Loan $3\frac{1}{2}$s of 1932–1947 are also free from surtax.

State and Municipal Bond Income Free from Federal Tax. There is considerable misunderstanding as to the seats of tax-authority. The constitution grants to the states all powers of taxation not specifically delegated to Congress by the constitution; and, secondly, grants to the Federal Congress the " power to levy and collect taxes, duties, imposts and excises " . . . which . . . " shall be uniform throughout the United States " . . . but . . . no capitation or other direct tax shall be laid unless in proportion to the census or enumeration."

When, therefore, the Supreme Court in another celebrated case (Pollock vs. Farmers Loan and Trust Co.) declared one of our earlier income tax laws a direct tax and therefore unconstitutional unless levied " in proportion to the census or enumeration " it became necessary to amend the constitution (Sixteenth Amendment) to realize the desired federal income tax.

It was hardly an attenuation of the principle of " reciprocal

TAX-FREE vs. TAXABLE BONDS

(Based on Revenue Act of 1926)

A Chart Showing the Effect of Federal Income Tax on Yield from Tax-Free and Taxable Bonds in 1926

Income from certain U. S. Government, state and municipal bonds is exempt from the federal income tax, rate of which, for 1926 income, ranges from $1\frac{1}{2}\%$ to 25%, according to amount of income. This table has been compiled, based on the Revenue Act of 1926, to indicate the approximate yield which taxable bonds must return to equal the return from tax-free bonds yielding $3\frac{1}{2}\%$ to 6%, when held by investors enjoying varying amounts of annual income (subject to surtax) ranging from $20,000 to $100,000 or more.

Example: Individual with income (subject to surtaxes) of about $50,000 purchases taxable bonds at price to net 4.88%. Interest derived from this investment is additional income and is subject to a normal tax of 5% and a surtax (on income between $48,000 and $52,000) of 13%, or a total tax rate of 18%. Deducting the tax computed at this rate, the actual income from these bonds is reduced to 4.00%. In other words, for an investor in this income class a tax-exempt bond yielding only 4.00% would pay an equivalent actual income yield. In the table below the yield from tax-free bonds is shown in black-face figures in extreme left-hand column, with the equivalent yields from taxable bonds indicated for each income bracket (indicated at top of columns) from $20,000 up.

This table is offered as a guide to assist the purchaser of bonds to choose intelligently between taxable and tax-free investments. It is computed on the theory that any change in an individual's taxable income resulting from a switching of investments from a taxable to a tax-free status, or vice-versa, is effective at the highest brackets or the "top" of his income and, hence, the highest surtax rate has been applied in computing these equivalent yields. Because of the change of tax rates from year to year, it is useless to attempt an exact computation of the value of tax exemption over a series of years and for this reason we believe the chart is sufficiently comprehensive to serve the purpose for which it is intended.

Local Tax Exemption: Where it is desired to make a comparison which takes into consideration exemption from a state and the federal income tax this table may also be used. The figures shown in parentheses in the column captions represent total tax rate and the figures below are computed on the basis of such rates. For example: Take case of individual with $60,000 to $64,000 income and resident of a state levying income tax of 3% on incomes of such size. Total tax rate, for purpose of comparing exempt and taxable investments, would be 24%, made up of federal normal, 5% federal surtax, 16% and state tax, 3%. Instead of using column headed "$60M to $64M (21%)," this investor would refer to column headed "$80% to $100% (24%)."

Corporation Tax Comparison: Under the 1926 law net income of corporations is taxable at the flat rate of $13\frac{1}{2}\%$. A special column headed "Corporation Tax ($13\frac{1}{2}\%$)" has been incorporated in the table below showing the yields on taxable bonds equivalent to tax-free yields shown in extreme left-hand column.

Tax-Free Yield	$20M to $22M (10%)	$22M to $24M (11%)	$24M to $28M (12%)	$28M to $32M (13%)	Corporation Tax $32M (13½%)	$32M to $36M (14%)	$36M to $40M (15%)	$40M to $44M (16%)	$44M to $48M (17%)	$48M to $52M (18%)	$52M to $56M (19%)	$56M to $60M (20%)	$60M to $64M (21%)	$64M to $70M (22%)	$70M to $80M (23%)	$80M to $100M (24%)	Over $100M (25%)
3¼	3.89	3.93	3.98	4.02	4.05	4.07	4.12	4.17	4.22	4.27	4.32	4.37	4.43	4.49	4.54	4.60	4.67
3½	4.17	4.21	4.26	4.31	4.33	4.36	4.41	4.46	4.52	4.57	4.63	4.69	4.75	4.81	4.87	4.93	5.00
3¾	4.30	4.35	4.40	4.45	4.48	4.50	4.56	4.61	4.67	4.72	4.78	4.84	4.90	4.97	5.03	5.10	5.17
4	4.44	4.49	4.54	4.60	4.62	4.65	4.70	4.76	4.82	4.88	4.94	5.00	5.06	5.13	5.19	5.26	5.33
4.05	4.50	4.55	4.60	4.65	4.68	4.71	4.76	4.82	4.88	4.94	5.00	5.06	5.13	5.19	5.26	5.33	5.40
4.10	4.55	4.61	4.66	4.71	4.74	4.77	4.82	4.88	4.94	5.00	5.06	5.12	5.19	5.26	5.32	5.39	5.47
4.15	4.61	4.66	4.71	4.77	4.80	4.82	4.88	4.94	5.00	5.06	5.12	5.19	5.25	5.32	5.39	5.46	5.53
4.20	4.67	4.72	4.77	4.83	4.85	4.88	4.94	5.00	5.06	5.12	5.18	5.25	5.32	5.38	5.45	5.53	5.60
4¼	4.72	4.77	4.83	4.88	4.91	4.94	5.00	5.06	5.12	5.18	5.25	5.31	5.38	5.45	5.52	5.59	5.67
4.30	4.78	4.83	4.89	4.94	4.97	5.00	5.06	5.12	5.18	5.24	5.31	5.37	5.44	5.51	5.58	5.66	5.73
4.35	4.83	4.89	4.94	5.00	5.03	5.06	5.12	5.18	5.24	5.30	5.37	5.44	5.51	5.58	5.65	5.72	5.80
4.40	4.89	4.94	5.00	5.06	5.09	5.12	5.18	5.24	5.30	5.36	5.43	5.50	5.57	5.64	5.71	5.79	5.87
4.45	4.94	5.00	5.06	5.11	5.14	5.17	5.23	5.30	5.36	5.43	5.49	5.56	5.63	5.70	5.78	5.85	5.93
4½	5.00	5.06	5.11	5.17	5.20	5.23	5.29	5.36	5.42	5.49	5.55	5.62	5.70	5.77	5.84	5.92	6.00
4.60	5.11	5.17	5.23	5.29	5.32	5.35	5.41	5.48	5.54	5.61	5.68	5.75	5.82	5.90	5.97	6.05	6.13
4.70	5.22	5.28	5.34	5.40	5.43	5.46	5.53	5.59	5.66	5.73	5.80	5.87	5.95	6.02	6.10	6.18	6.27
4¾	5.28	5.34	5.40	5.46	5.49	5.52	5.59	5.65	5.72	5.79	5.86	5.94	6.01	6.09	6.17	6.25	6.33
4.80	5.33	5.39	5.45	5.52	5.55	5.58	5.65	5.71	5.78	5.85	5.92	6.00	6.07	6.15	6.23	6.31	6.40
4.90	5.44	5.50	5.57	5.63	5.66	5.70	5.76	5.83	5.90	5.97	6.05	6.12	6.20	6.28	6.36	6.45	6.53
5	5.55	5.62	5.68	5.75	5.78	5.81	5.88	5.95	6.02	6.10	6.17	6.25	6.33	6.41	6.49	6.58	6.67
5¼	5.83	5.90	5.96	6.03	6.07	6.10	6.18	6.25	6.32	6.40	6.48	6.56	6.64	6.73	6.82	6.91	7.00
5½	6.11	6.18	6.25	6.32	6.36	6.39	6.47	6.55	6.63	6.71	6.79	6.87	6.96	7.05	7.14	7.24	7.33
5¾	6.39	6.46	6.53	6.61	6.65	6.69	6.76	6.84	6.93	7.01	7.10	7.19	7.28	7.37	7.47	7.56	7.67
6	6.67	6.74	6.82	6.90	6.94	6.98	7.06	7.14	7.23	7.32	7.41	7.50	7.59	7.69	7.79	7.89	8.00

Table and notes reprinted from *The Bond Buyer of New York*

freedom from taxation " which caused the framers of the federal income tax to declare specifically the income of municipal bonds exempt from federal tax. If, leaning on etymology, one may make the distinction between freedom from tax and exemption from tax, then the income from municipal bonds is tax free by the implications of the Federal Constitution, and not tax-exempt by specific declaration of the Sixteenth Amendment.

In the chapter on the Classification of Taxes is given (p. 622) a table showing the relative importance of owning municipal bonds to obviate federal surtaxation based on the amount of one's income. As of the Act of 1926 the federal income tax rate runs from $1\frac{1}{2}$ to 4 per cent. for the normal tax and from 1 to 20 per cent. for the additional on surtaxes according to the amount of income, and is augmented by state income taxes in various states.

If investors were concerned merely with the direct burden and exemption or partial exemption of bonds from property and income taxation by the principal jurisdictions, this brief sketch might suffice. But since there are other weighty considerations such as the taxation of estates and inheritances, possibilities of much more complicated multiple taxation than implied here, and many forms of indirect taxation, there has been made, (possibly for the first time) a fairly comprehensive survey of the entire field of American taxation from the investors' standpoint,—in Chapter XLV, The Classification of Taxes.

With tax exemption we come to the end of the more important factors that enter into the intelligent purchase of city and town bonds. But the three chapters devoted to this subject will have failed of their purpose if the multiplicity of principles and illustrations they present has obscured the main idea,—that American municipal bonds are the best security for the American people to buy. That is to say, as a class, they will probably cause less regret to their purchasers than will any other class now commonly bought for investment. But their relative freedom from property and income taxation causes them to sell at prices that invite investment from persons who subject themselves to general property taxes, and those of large means rather than from those subject only to the normal taxes or the lower brackets of the surtaxes.

CHAPTER XXII

THE BONDS OF TAX DISTRICTS

In introducing the subject of *City and Town Bonds*, a distinction was made between municipal corporations proper, such as cities, towns, and villages, and involuntary, quasi-municipal corporations, such as counties. Counties, townships, and the other various taxing districts, it was said, were usually involuntary corporations in the eyes of the law.

" We have recognized," declares the Supreme Court of North Carolina, "the right of the legislature to divide counties into school districts, fence districts, road districts, etc., and to confer upon them municipal powers and duties."

As involuntary corporations, agencies merely of the state, established to minister to local needs, the character of the bonded obligations put forth is determined by the *public purpose* of the corporation, and is limited to that purpose. So, for the most part, school districts issue only school bonds; irrigation districts, irrigation bonds; and water districts, water bonds,[1] etc.

Exceptions are to be taken to the singleness of the purpose of the issue in respect to county and township bonds. We have found not a few legitimate county functions; and townships may borrow money for the construction and repair of roads, bridges, schools, town halls, poorhouses, and sometimes for railroad aid.

Origin. It follows, then, that there is no limit to the possible kinds of districts except the limit of public functions for which districts may be formed. There are fashions in these matters as in everything else. Some states affect Fire Districts; Maine, in particular, Water Districts; Pennsylvania, Poor Districts. What

---

[1] The divisions mentioned are not always strictly taxing districts. "Taxed Districts" would be a more exact title, e.g., in Michigan the county tax is divided among the towns; and the town supervisors levy the tax. Per contra, in Indiana, the township tax is levied and collected by the county; and the township bonds are issued through the county commissioners.

It is only for want of better classification that Special Assessment Bonds are noticed in this chapter.

may be the necessity for Poor Districts it is hard to see, especially when the divisions are coextensive with cities or counties. Their existence, especially when they *are* coextensive, suggests the circumvention of such laws as those limiting the amount of debt or tax that may be levied by a municipality. The town of " X " may wish to buy a poor farm, or more probably, build a school, or own waterworks. But the town does not wish to exhibit its true debt for fear of hurting its commercial rating; or it may be prohibited from further debt incurrence by having reached its debt limit. What, then, could be more beautifully simple than to incorporate the same property and population into a Poor, School, or Water District, as the case may be. Not *all* fiscal sleight-of-hand has been left for private corporations. We have noticed how opportunities for this sort of thing have been limited in South Carolina.

Districts that are corporations coextensive with municipalities proper, but distinct from them, may exist for reasons less dubious than those mentioned. Then again Water Districts are sometimes formed when more than one municipality is to receive the water. This, too, is not necessarily an attempt at debt concealment, but rather an apportionment of cost. To play on words, sometimes, in violation of the Euclidean axiom, even three or more corporate bodies occupy the same space at the same time. Council Bluffs, Iowa, the Council Bluffs School District, and Kane Township are three coextensive municipalities. Los Angeles, Los Angeles City School District, and Los Angeles High School District are, we believe, also still coextensive.

Tax Districts often have their origin in the need of improvement felt by a locality which in its entirety is not a municipal corporation. This want, in the nature of the case, is territorial in character, rather than corporate. For instance, people living in a certain locality need protection from the encroachment of the neighboring river and are willing to pay special taxes (to be levied on only the property to be benefited), which their neighbors on higher ground should not have to shoulder. The needs of these lowland people are met by municipal Levee Districts; or if it is a matter of marshland, by Drainage Districts. Thus Levee and Drainage Districts may include only parts of cities, and yet extend over the boundaries of two or more counties.

The Miami Conservancy District (Ohio) and the Pueblo

Conservancy District (Colorado) are interesting examples of huge areas, incorporated in districts, for protection from floods.

Again, a certain small town may covet the improvements enjoyed by near-by cities, especially faucet and hydrant advantages. But the town may be so laid out that it is not feasible to supply with water any but the most central section. Obviously those who are not to benefit by the proposed installation of a water supply will vote in town meeting against the measure. If the recalcitrants block its passage the inhabitants of the central portion of the town may form a Water District or a Fire District, to include only the properties to be supplied with water; but the assessable value of the district may be 95 per cent. of the town's assessable wealth.

Conversely, installation of improvements may benefit a certain section which includes not only a whole municipal corporation, but the inhabitants of a large adjacent area (e.g., in the Port of Portland, Oregon, by opening navigation to the sea). Under such circumstances it is equitable that all the benefited property bear its fair share of the cost of the improvements; and to that end this district may rightly be incorporated for purposes of taxation.

The District Statement. It is evident from the origin of taxing districts that the financial statement, upon the basis of which the bonds are usually bought, is more generally misleading than the statement of counties, cities, or towns. Cities and towns, for instance, may have and often do have no included subdivisions upon which there is a tax drain not exhibited in the regular city tax. But taxing districts, on the other hand, are quite generally subdivisions of municipalities proper; and, with few exceptions, subject to a tax drain not exhibited in their own tax rate, but indeed several times as great. Therefore it is even more desirable that the bond buyer be informed as to the relation of the district to the larger division or divisions of which it is a constituent, than in the case when he purchases bonds of cities, towns, and counties. And yet in the bond circular he may not be so informed.

The District Tax. The district tax is generally smaller than the general municipal tax because it is levied to support and acquit obligations incurred for a single object or purpose; whereas, the general tax has to care for the multifarious needs of the municipality. In fact the district tax is a " special tax " in such a true sense of the word, and subject to such special conditions, that we may find civil divisions like the Greenfield (Mass.) Fire District, with loans outstanding but no district tax at all.

Of the tax rates of the various kinds of districts themselves, that for School Districts may legitimately average higher than the other rates, unless (as by the laws of Iowa) the same result is attained by permitting a heavier debt incurrence; for the American system of public instruction is the most important and expensive special function on which it is customary and desirable to make taxing districts; and the tax has not only a funded debt to maintain and amortize, but also a heavy annual expenditure for maintenance of school, purchase of supplies, and payment of salaries. But even the school tax is usually smaller than the municipal tax proper.

Special Assessment Bonds. The tax power has an aspect of peculiar interest in Special Assessment Bonds. These securities, quite commonly issued by cities and towns, are made payable by statute out of sinking funds raised, as the name implies, by special assessments upon the property benefited. In the past assessment sinking funds frequently have been diverted from their use,—not only by arrant peculation, but by deliberate municipal misappropriation of the funds. When, because of the resulting deficit, the interest or principal of assessment bonds goes unpaid, a vital question is raised as to the bondholders' recourse to the tax power.

On default of Special Assessment Bonds the bondholders can look to the courts for a supplemental assessment to make good the deficiency. But further than this, in certain jurisdictions the implied power of taxation has been extended even to cover Special Assessment Bonds; and the bondholders have been given judgments against the offending municipalities, to be satisfied out of general taxes, the courts holding " that the grant of power to levy special assessments for the payment of bonds was not exclusive, and that although no authority was given by the act in express terms for the levy of taxes for bonds, the corporate authorities of the city might be compelled to exercise their general powers of taxation to secure their payment." [1]

This extreme extension of the doctrine of the implied power

[1] United States vs. New Orleans, 98 U. S. 381; United States vs. Fort Scott, 99 U. S. 152; United States vs. Saunders, 124 Fed. 124.

of taxation would not hold, however, in most state courts. The Supreme Court of Wisconsin, for example, has declared that improvement bonds are not general city obligations. The Kansas City (Mo.) Park District Bonds are a notable illustration of Special Assessment of the same type. Special Assessment Bonds in Iowa, Indiana, and Illinois are not a general liability; but in Michigan and Kansas they usually are.

The law in Kansas for cities of the first class runs as follows:

"Whenever the mayor and council may cause any street or alley . . . to be graded, . . . the expense of which is chargeable to the adjacent property, . . . they may, in their discretion, . . . issue internal-improvement bonds of the city, payable in ten equal installments of equal amounts each year, none of which bonds . . . shall run longer than ten years, nor bear interest exceeding 6 per centum per annum. The credit of the city issuing such bonds shall be pledged for the payment thereof."

The Kansas Digest (Dassler 96), gives this synopsis of the law for cities of the second class as interpreted in U. S. vs. Fort Scott, just mentioned:

"Where a city of the second class issues improvement bonds for improvements, for which the law provides special assessments against adjacent property, a bona-fide holder of such bonds is not bound to enforce his judgment obtained against the city on such bonds, by the special assessments provided for by law or ordinance. He is entitled to a mandamus ordering a general levy to pay his judgment, the city to reimburse itself out of the proper assessments."

The bond buyer should always require to be satisfied on this point of direct municipal obligations, since many issues reach the public with their status not yet established. The federal courts are more inclined than the state courts to view them as general obligations.

Assessed Valuation. The Assessed Valuation of the district, especially when taken in conjunction with its population, will indicate very readily whether we have to deal with a rural or an urban district. If urban, a comparison of the assessment of the district with that of the city or town with which it is connected will indicate whether the district is only a section of the municipality, whether it is coextensive with the municipality, or whether it embraces the municipality and other territory adjacent.

This comparison will be sound because the basis of the assessment—that is, the ratio of the assessed to the real valuation—

is almost always the same as that of the municipality proper, since the valuations are adjusted by the same officers. The tax district has no genuine political or social existence; it is hardly more than an abstraction, usually conceived in the interests of convenience and justice for territorial apportionment of taxes. Hence there is no reason for separate assessment.

The assessed valuation, then, which is identical with the valuation of the same area of the municipality proper in which it is situate, or which it includes, presents to the investigator no difficulties that have not already been discussed in the preceding chapters.

Secondary Resources. Since the taxing district maintains such a slight corporate existence it has not the variety and wealth of secondary resources customary with cities. It may, and usually does, establish a sinking fund for its obligations, but it seldom is the owner of treasury assets in any other form. Franchise, corporation, and other corollary taxes, needless to say, are not resources of the taxing district as such.

Mortgage Security. The resource of foreclosure proceedings, however, is not infrequently available to holders of district bonds; for such bonds offer mortgage security more generally than do any other kinds of municipals, as may be seen by reference to the preceding chapter. Mention was made there of the fact that School District Bonds in the state of New Jersey issued under the 1903 Law were secured by lien on *all* the property in the district. In Illinois there is a sort of special-assessment Drainage District bonds which " are a lien on the lots, blocks, or parts thereof which shall be designated therein; but before the issue the owner of the lots . . . to be charged must indorse upon the back of such bond his consent, under seal, in substance as follows:

"'I hereby indorse the within bond and consent that the lot, or lots, or parts thereof therein designated shall become liable for the interest and principal therein named, and the same shall be a lien upon said property from this date until paid off and discharged."

" The bond when executed by the city or village and so indorsed by the owner shall be recorded in the Recorder's office in the county, and such record shall be a notice of the lien so created to the same extent as the record of mortgages is a notice."[1]

---

[1] See Hurd's *Revised Statutes of Illinois*, Edit. 1908, p. 372, §§ 327, 328.

In California (and quite generally in the irrigated states) all the real property of irrigation districts is liable in default. "The Board of directors of the district may pledge, by mortgage or otherwise, all property of the district, including its rights and privileges," so that, in default, not only the possession and management of the water system comes to the bondholders, but all other property of the district may be foreclosed under the mortgage in the ordinary way "so as to convey to the purchaser the legal and equitable title to the property."

District Debt. The relation between debt and taxation is so direct and intimate that it follows from the nature of municipal taxation that the debts of taxing districts are comparatively small and simple, and that the debts of school districts bear the highest ratio to the assessment. But the nominal debt of districts is a matter quite apart from the real debt, of course. The situation has been canvassed so completely in discussing the real debts of other municipal divisions that elaboration is unnecessary.

Validity. The fact that Special Assessment Bonds may come into the hands of the investor with their status as municipal obligations undecided suggests immediately the most imminent possibility of weakness in district issues: their validity. District Bonds are the product of special conditions; and the application of general principles to special conditions is likely to be a matter of variance and dispute.

This is especially so when bonds are issued in behalf of a new kind of project, concerning which questions of law have not yet had the benefit of judicial decisions. The Wright Act in California, under which so many irrigation projects were initiated, brought many bondholders to grief. Among the irrigation districts in that state which have been declared illegally organized, or the bonds of which have been adjudged illegally issued, are the Alessandro, the Escondido, the Linda Vista, and the San Jacinto and Pleasant Valley districts; and the list might be extended.

Third only to the history of State Bonds and Railroad-Aid bonds, American bond law has no more interesting chapter than that on district obligations. Railroad aid, fortunately, is a thing of the past, for the most part; but district debt incurrence was never more common than to-day. District bond litigation, even in a city like San Francisco, with excellent municipal credit, is by no means ancient history. It never redounds to the credit of the issuing municipality.

Good Faith. Good faith, which is so closely associated with validity, is not to be expected of districts in that high degree we find it nowadays in the large cities. A taxing district has not the individuality or personality of a city or town proper. It seldom has a wide reputation to sustain. There is a prevalent opinion, not wholly without justification, that, other things being equal, school districts are most safely relied on. The attitude of the public towards the objects for which funds are raised has had much to do in the past with the fate of civil loans. Just as the hostility of the people to Louisiana State Bonds issued by a republican administration, and toward Railroad-Aid Bonds, issued in the interest of designing corporations, has brought in its train default and repudiation, so the pride of the people in their public school system. has undoubtedly upheld the credit of loans raised in behalf of schools.

Rural Versus Urban Districts. In so far as taxing districts partake of the nature and dignity of urban municipalities, their paper is to be desired as an investment. But rural districts, even to a greater extent than rural counties, are difficult of appraisal; it is hard to get satisfactory and authentic statements by which to ascertain the tax burden of the rural district, its geography, its exact status as a corporation, and its territorial relations to the parent corporation.

Butte, Montana, School District No. 1 may properly be called an urban district, since it comprehends, not only the entire city of Butte, but a larger portion of the taxable property of Silver Bow County, in which Butte is located. Therefore it is able to market its bonds as 4s and $4\frac{1}{2}$s. Any other school districts of the county, obviously rural, having but little property value and a sparse population,·and being little known, would be of small interest to the bond buyer.

Metropolitan Districts. Metropolitan districts, like metropolitan counties, borrow in some degree the credit of cities with which they are associated. The best known is the great Chicago Sanitary District, which includes not only the city of Chicago, but a large area of adjacent territory—in all about 360 square miles. The credit of the Chicago Sanitary District, although not equal to that of Chicago, is exceptionally high.

Many well-known cities of the country have independent school districts which enjoy excellent credit, as being coextensive with, or as including, their respective cities.   Of such are the School Districts of Indianapolis, Indiana, Springfield, Ohio, and Sioux City, Iowa.

Conclusion.   Since, now, the range of quality in District Bonds is greater than that in any other kind of municipal issues, more knowledge and discretion are necessary to their proper purchase; and in aid of the purchase the arbitrary rules of limitation, —geographical, statistical, and otherwise,—will be of little help unless interpreted in the light of thorough investigation of the facts, fortified by the opinion of a competent attorney.   But when intelligently bought, a higher return may be had from investment in District Bonds than from investment in other municipal issues of equal security.

PART III
CORPORATION LOANS

CHAPTER XXIII

RAILROAD BONDS: LEGAL PROTECTION. PROPERTY AND PHYSICAL CONDITION

New Position of the Railroad Industry. Under present conditions of regulation in the United States, railroad bonds as a class present the nearest analogy to government bonds. Although railroad transportation is still a business enterprise in which ability, progressive policies and foresight can yield large returns, railroad management is now carefully circumscribed by government regulation and supervision. Half a century of regulation has brought to the business a stability and relative dependability of return on capital not possessed by any other important industry in this country.

The war played havoc with established ideas concerning railroad operation and regulation. Above all government operation opened the door to an unprecedented increase in federal interference with private enterprise. As a result competition has been all but eliminated. At the same time, the virtual collapse of service during and after the great conflict centered attention upon the need of a firm financial foundation for railroading. The extensive distribution of railway security ownership, indirectly in the form of bank and insurance investment and directly in that of widely spread bond and stock holdings by small investors had made explicit stabilization of railroad finance especially urgent. The result in the rate provisions of the Transportation Act of 1920, offers virtual assurance that hereafter the public good will be sought in regulation, but not without regard to the interest of security holders.

Although railroads are declining in relative importance among American industries, if agriculture be excluded they are still the largest single business in the country. On December 31, 1924, they had outstanding $21,600,000,000 of securities, of which more than $12,000,000,000 represented bonds. Insurance companies held nearly $2,000,000,000 of these bonds, and banks, mostly mutual savings institutions, held $1,700,000,000. Thus the importance of railroad securities is demonstrated.

In the chapters on railroad bonds, we shall seek the constituents of investment values. First let us see clearly the legal protection accorded American railroad investment, for in the several years of its operation, the Transportation Act of 1920 has really sponsored a new era. To overlook the special legal protection for these bonds is to ignore their most basic peculiarity of safety. Federal law now narrowly determines the characteristics of railroading as a business, and the financial position of individual railroad companies. After a study of the legal aspects, we shall turn to individual railroad evaluations. The character of a railroad bond has become an investment matter subordinate not only to the legal protection accorded the industry but also to the character of the obligor corporation. This does not deny the priority of mortgage bonds to debentures, but it does affirm the class superiority of great trunk line debentures to first mortgage main line bonds of small rail outlets for mines or timber tracts of limited life existing in a sparsely settled country.

Legal Protection

Growth of Government Regulation. During the first half century of railroad history in the United States, little public control was exercised over the carriers except through charter provisions, and therefore many abuses of management and of financing arose. These produced a popular agitation known as the " granger movement " in the Middle West during the early seventies, culminating in a series of court decisions which held that railroads, as corporations affected with a public interest, were subject to state regulation as to rates charged the public for the services they performed.[1] During the succeeding half-century this principle merely has been confirmed and extended until by the Transportation Act of 1920, which is essentially a series of amendments to the original Interstate Commerce Commission Act of 1887, the Interstate Commerce Commission, a federal body, has been given practically exclusive power to fix railroad rates throughout the United States.

This kind of government regulation was essentially restrictive, and the carriers found that almost every step taken by vested authorities not only curtailed their freedom of action, but re-

[1] The leading case was Munn vs. Illinois, 94 U. S. 113, decided in 1876.

duced their revenues. After 1907, with the enforcement of the Hepburn and later regulative acts, destructive supervision was carried to an excess that jeopardized the credit structure of the railroad system as a whole.

Fortunately, to supplement the right of the government to regulate a business affected with a public interest, another legal principle has evolved to offset the unfavorable results of negative regulation. This principle, based on the constitutional provision that private property shall not be taken without due process of law, holds that property devoted to the public service is entitled to a fair return on " the fair value of the property being used by it for the convenience of the public."   First definitely stated in the case of Smyth vs. Ames in 1898 (169 U. S. 460), involving alleged confiscatory railroad rates established by a Nebraska statute, this protective principle has been enacted into law by the Transportation Act of 1920. This principle of a " fair return upon a fair value of the property employed in transportation " is the cornerstone of a legal protection now enjoyed by investors in railroad securities to a degree never previously known.

The Transportation Act of 1920. The Transportation Act of 1920, also known as the " Esch-Cummins Act," sets forth the novel and comprehensive legal framework within which the railroad business now operates. The heart of the law is the rate-making section—a mandate to the Interstate Commerce Commission to fix rates so that a specified fair return shall be earned by the owners of property devoted to transportation. The law also contains vital provisions on " recapture " by the government of excess earnings, on new security issues, and on consolidations, which will now be briefly discussed.

The rate-making provision which becomes section 15-A of the Interstate Commerce Act, provides that the Commission shall " establish rates so that carriers as a whole will . . . earn an aggregate annual net railway operating income equal, as nearly as may be, to a fair return upon the aggregate value of the railway property held for and used in the service of transportation." The Commission has held that $5\frac{1}{2}$ per cent. constitutes such a fair return, and now allows $.\frac{1}{4}$ per cent. as an additional return to aid the railroads in making urgently needed additions and betterments. Since the post-war adjustment, the carriers have been able to approximate this rate of return. In 1924, they earned $987,000,000 or 4.33 per cent. upon the tentative valuation of their property. In 1925, they earned $1,137,000,000 or 4.83 per cent. upon this valuation.

Beyond providing for a fair return, the law fixes a basis for determining the " fair value " of railroad property, which raises one of the most complex and vexing of modern economic problems,—that of valuation. For temporary use an adjusted book value taken from the balance sheet of the companies themselves has been used. The intention of the law, however, is to base the fair return upon the actual physical valuation of the properties, which was begun by the Interstate Commerce Commission in 1913 under the La Follette Valuation, now section 19-A of the Interstate Commerce Commission Act. This valuation is nearing completion, but the principles underlying it are yet to be tested in the courts. Reports for individual companies that have appeared suggest that the final figures will not differ much from the book values of the railroads, nor from the total par value of securities outstanding.

The law provides for the recapture by the Interstate Commerce Commission of one-half of the earnings of a railroad above 6 per cent. on its property valuation in any one year. Recaptured earnings are to go into a general railroad " contingent fund " to be used for loans to weak lines or for the purchase of needed equipment and other facilities to be leased to carriers.

A vital feature of the law is the provision for " the consolidation of the railway properties of the continental United States into a limited number of systems." This feature, which reverses the traditional anti-trust policy of the Federal Government, is made necessary by the requirement in the rate provision that the fair return is to be earned by the carriers in each group as a whole. Unless the railroads were combined into a few large systems of comparable strength, a stated rate level might benefit well-situated roads unduly, while inducing the bankruptcy of weak, or poorly-located lines.

Finally, the law provides for complete control of new security issues by the Interstate Commerce Commission (section 230-A), which is to see that the issue is " reasonably necessary and appropriate." This rigid supervision, although at times perhaps unnecessarily restricting the freedom of action of the carrier, is an added protection to the investor, for the Commission requires periodical reports from the carrier on the disposition of the proceeds. Furthermore, under this part of the Act, the Commission has set out to correct the present excessive funded debt of the carriers by ruling, in the Chesapeake and Ohio case of 1926, that, whenever feasible, new capital shall be raised by the issue of capital stock.

By giving the railroads as a whole virtual assurance of a return ample for interest charges on bonded debt, and by providing for the elimination of weak lines via consolidation, the act surrounds railroad bonds with a measure of specific legal protection without parallel for the obligations or shares of other types of corporations. As the Commission gains experience in enforcing the provisions of this comprehensive legislation (and so far only a beginning has been made), railroad securities must gain from the greater reliability of return that will result. For the law partly relieves the carriers from the vicissitudes of business enterprise and positively establishes the income of railroad property as a whole, so that railroad bonds tend to acquire the preëminent merit of governmental securities: the right to levy income adequate for contractual charges of interest and amortization.

EVALUATION OF A RAILROAD'S CREDIT

Although railroad securities as a whole thus enjoy a full amount of legal protection, the investor naturally must measure the credit of an individual company in determining the desirability and value of its bonds. If a road like the defunct Kansas City, Mexico, and Orient, serves no economic purpose, no law can save it, for no rate level can give a fair return to a road without adequate traffic.

In analyzing the investment position of a railroad, we proceed logically by studying the following factors:

(1) location,

(2) physical condition of the property,

(3) earning power of the property, and

(4) valuation and the capital account.

Although complete studies of these factors are not practical for most investors, a sound judgment can be attained only by gauging each of them from available data.

LOCATION AND PHYSICAL CONDITION

Location. A railroad's location is almost as immutable as ancestral inheritance, and it plays an equally important part in the determination of the future. Not only the physical character and location of the line must be considered, but its connections, terminals, and competitive conditions.

A poorly located line has a handicap which is difficult to overcome. The Erie, the profile of which resembles a chart of cyclical business fluctuations, has always been one of the weakest lines in the East. Again, the Denver & Rio Grande, serving a rugged and mountainous region, with numerous curves and steep grades, is a road made conspicuous by repeated defaults.

Location must also be studied in relation to territory served. The Pennsylvania Railroad, with a close network of lines over the chief manufacturing area in the country, originates a great volume of traffic on its own local lines, and supplies itself with a greater traffic density than any other road in the country. The New York Central, stretching from New York to Chicago, traverses an area largely agricultural, and so originates considerably less traffic. The group of anthracite railroads, including the Lehigh Valley and the Lackawanna, tap regions often of no great importance industrially, except for valuable deposits of hard coal which give these carriers approximately one-half of their total tonnage.

The economic status and growth of the territory at times become of great importance in determining the worth of a property. The Northwest suffered a retrograde movement for half a decade after 1920. The population was not increasing and agriculture was curtailed. This territory contrasted sharply with Florida, which was passing through a period of rapid growth and was not yet adequately supplied with transportation facilities. Roads in that state enjoyed an unprecedented traffic, at the very time the once powerful Chicago, Milwaukee, & St. Paul was surrendered to the hands of receivers.

A railroad draws its business from two main sources, its own lines and its connections. Such roads as the Union Pacific and the Nickel Plate originate only a small part of their traffic. The rest comes from numerous lines with which they have traffic connections. The Western Pacific, a relatively new line from

Ogden to San Francisco, has shown a marked improvement in earning power since it established close traffic connections with the Southern Pacific in 1924. Not only the physical contact, but a mutual willingness to exchange traffic, must exist to make such connections profitable. The Union Pacific, financially interested in many of its connections, has a great strategic position in bargaining for business.

A railroad reaching important terminals is by that fact assured of a certain amount of interchange traffic. Yet it is expensive to operate a railroad in a big terminal city. The Pennsylvania spent more than $100,000,000 to establish its New York terminal, and the Illinois Central since 1920 has been investing an amount nearly as large in modernizing and electrifying its Chicago terminal. Terminal facilities are very desirable, but at times they involve excessive expenditures yielding small return on the investment. They are most profitable when they include large tracts of strategic terminal property acquired years previously at nominal cost. This is one reason that the Jersey Central and the Reading, for their size, are two of the richest companies in the country.

Competition. Competition is no longer the dominant factor in railroading that it used to be. But when too many railroads have been built it is natural that all should be adversely affected, for there is then not enough traffic to give a fair return on the investment. The Northwest presents a conspicuous case of overbuilding. As long as the Great Northern and the Northern Pacific shared this territory between them, they both enjoyed marked prosperity. When the St. Paul completed its thousand-mile extension to the Pacific coast, all three lines showed the effects of overbuilding, although the St. Paul, as the latest arrival, suffered most. Economic depression in that region made impossible the support of its capital structure. In 1925, it went into receivership and its general mortgage bonds sold below fifty.

Competition of water routes is no longer of much importance within the United States, for the railroads have been able to compete successfully everywhere with river and canal navigation, and on the Great Lakes steamboat navigation merely supplements the railroad haul. The only serious competition of this nature is suffered by the transcontinental lines, which cannot meet the competition of the Panama Canal on low-grade, slow freight. The Northern Pacific and the St. Paul have lost a substantial traffic in lumber and miscellaneous freight to the canal steamers. Yet it is worthy of note that this competition has not affected the highly profitable traffic of the Southern Pacific in perishables from California. The canal route is too slow to bid for this business.

Although the location of a railroad can seldom be improved, its physical condition can always be bettered provided enough money is spent for the purpose. If a road has poor credit it cannot raise this money, and often a receivership is necessary to raise new capital for urgently-needed expenditures. Even a road with strong credit and large resources can jeopardize its prosperity if it sells large bond issues to build up its physical plant, for which new business fails to materialize.

In studying physical condition, attention should be directed to:

a. mileage,

b. equipment,

c. terminals,

d. improvements.

Mileage. The size of a rail system is best realized by the number of miles of line operated, excluding sidings. Single-track mileage (i.e., omitting the mileage of extra track) is for purposes of comparison the common denominator of gross tonnage, earnings, fixed charges, and the like. There were in the United States on December 31, 1924, a total of 250,156 miles of railway, of which 235,894 miles were operated by 175 Class I railway companies (i.e., railroads having gross earnings of more than $1,000,000 annually). These companies had facilities as follows:

Miles of road..	235,894
Miles of second main track...........................	34,162
Miles of third main track.............................	3,083
Miles of all other main track.........................	2,489
Miles of yard track and sidings......................	112,253
Total of all tracks.................................	387,882

Therefore about 15 per cent. of the railroad mileage of the country is double-tracked. In the case of lines situated in centres of heavy traffic, double-tracking is a virtual necessity. The great Rock Island system has a number of lines converging on Topeka and Harrington, Kansas. This stretch of mileage is the " neck of the bottle " of this system. Yet this stragetic mileage is in part owned by the Union Pacific and the Chicago, Burlington, & Quincy, and is operated under trackage rights. A limited credit has for many years prevented the road from rebuilding and double-tracking this important stretch of line. Similarly the Wabash system, operating from Kansas City to Buffalo, for want of sidetrack and yard facilities, is severely hampered in operations and earnings.

Terminals. The physical condition, also, of terminal facilities, their adequacy and modernity, is an important factor of credit. Thus although the Rock Island suffers from inadequate track facilities in certain parts of the system, nevertheless it enjoys modern terminals, fully equal to the demand, in such important centers as Chicago, St. Louis, and Omaha.

Equipment. The condition of equipment can be gauged only roughly, but this knowledge may be of great value to the investor. Lack of adequate equipment was a major cause for the breakdown of the Rock Island and the Missouri Pacific systems in 1915. The condition of equipment can be judged with a fair degree of accuracy from three sources: the number of units, the average size of each unit, and the percentage of equipment in bad order. Each of the ascertained figures must be interpreted in the light of peculiar conditions illustrated here. The number of locomotives and cars will bear a certain proportion to the mileage and traffic of the line, and should increase with both. A better indication of physical condition is the average capacity of the unit. The tractive power, in pounds per locomotive, is a good index. In 1924, the average tractive power of locomotives in the easterly district was 41,551 pounds; in the southern district 40,513 pounds and in the western district 37,674 pounds. The capacity of freight cars differs for the various types of cars, but for the country as a whole averaged as follows in 1924:

	Tons
Box cars	39.1
Flat cars	40.7
Stock cars	35.7
Coal cars	51.7
Tank cars	43.1
Refrigerator cars	31.7
Other freight cars	48.9

These are means with which reports of individual roads may be compared. A line whose equipment has a substantially smaller average capacity is presumably not keeping abreast of modern methods.

The percentage of bad-order cars and locomotives varies in different parts of the country, being especially heavy in the North during the winter. The American Railway Association has fixed 15 per cent. as a desirable maximum percentage for bad-order locomotives, and 5 per cent. for bad-order cars.

Improvements. A study of the physical condition of a railroad is incomplete without an account of the expenditure necessary for special improvements over a period of future years. In 1922, the Interstate Commerce Commission ordered the installation of an automatic electric train control on at least one division of each important railroad line, involving a cost of approximately $100,000,000 for all the carriers affected. This was a hardship to the weaker lines. It is the apparent intention of the Commission to extend this order to the whole railway system in the future.

CHAPTER XXIV

RAILROAD BONDS: EARNING POWER AND INCOME
ACCOUNT

We have considered the railroad first as an object of special legal protection, and second as affected by physical location and condition. These physical factors are important because they determine the volume of traffic and the economy of operation,— in other words the earning power. Earning power is the ultimate source from which the railroad bondholder derives his income. We shall therefore study first the measurement and analysis of the traffic of a road, which is the source of its income, and then the measure of its operating efficiency, indicating the amount of expenses incurred by the railroad in earning its income.

Traffic. The most important source of revenue is the transportation of freight, which produced 73 per cent. of the earnings of Class I railway companies during 1924. No study of the investment worth of a railroad should omit an analysis of the freight traffic. The traffic can be studied from the points of view of (1) density, (2) diversification, (3) average haul, (4) amount originated, (5) seasonal and cyclical variation, and (6) probable duration, especially in the case of mineral and oil business.

The traffic density indicates the volume of traffic carried per each mile of road. It can be computed by the following simple formula:

$$\text{Traffic Density} = \frac{\text{Tonnage Moved} \times \text{Average Distance}}{\text{Miles of Line Operated}}$$

The product of tonnage moved and average distance is called ton-mileage. For the year 1924, the traffic density of the railroads of the country averaged 1,649,318 ton-miles per mile of road. The traffic density on leading roads compares as follows:

Pennsylvania... 3,958,658
New York Central...................................... 3,079,526
Baltimore & Ohio...................................... 3,374,203
Erie... 4,033,999
Union Pacific.. 1,924,458
Atchison.. 1,102,973
Reading... 5,397,667
Pittsburgh & Lake Erie............................... 9,486,809

The relatively high traffic density of the Erie is due to the relatively few branch lines it possesses. The western lines, traversing sparsely settled territory, cannot be compared with the eastern trunk lines, though within each group comparisons of value can be made. We can say, for example, that the Pennsylvania is much nearer a traffic saturation point than the New York Central. The Pittsburgh & Lake Erie is the New York Central's sole outlet from the all-important coal and iron region about Pittsburgh, which explains its abnormally heavy traffic density.

Diversification of Traffic. The quality of traffic may be determined by studying the distribution of the freight carried among the several classes of commodities. In this way the investor learns how dependent the carrier is on one industry or one crop, and something also as to how profitable the freight business is likely to be. Coal traffic, although of low grade, yields a good profit, but the carriage of logs from timber stands to sawmills seldom proves a source of much revenue to the carrier. The railroads as a whole reported the following distribution of revenue freight tonnage in 1924:

Products of Agriculture	10.63%
Animals and Products	2.23
Products of Mines	51.33
Products of Forests	9.64
Manufactures and Miscellaneous	23.04
Merchandise-less-than-carload Freight	3.13
Total	100.00

The great trunk lines show an approximately similar distribution of freight carried. The Grangers and the western lines generally show a preponderance of agricultural and animal products, and the coal roads report most of their freight as products of mines. The New York Central and the Chesapeake & Ohio, a road serving the smokeless coal fields of West Virginia, contrast as follows for 1924:

	New York Central	Chesapeake & Ohio
Products of Agriculture	7.86%	2.79%
Animals and Products	2.18	0.26
Products of Mines	54.68	84.44
Products of Forests	4.12	4.16
Manufactures and Miscellaneous	26.67	8.92
Merchandise L. C. L. Freight	3.86	1.43
	100.00	100.00

Needless to say, the New York Central presents a far more stable investment medium.

Average Haul. A very large part of the expenses of railroad operation is incurred in handling freight through congested terminals. Rates, however, are roughly in proportion to the length of the haul. Therefore the longer the average haul the more likelihood of profit. The average haul in the densely populated East is 148 miles, but in the West 212 miles, and in the South 215 miles. The New Haven, with heavy terminal charges, gets an average haul of 109 miles from its freight business. The Union Pacific, with a greater traffic density and very small terminal costs, gets an average haul of 393 miles. This is a principal cause of the financial weakness of the former, and of the consistent prosperity of the latter. A short haul, too, subjects a railroad to the telling effect of motor-truck competition, which in recent years has become a vital influence in transportation.

Freight Originating on own Lines. Another index of the traffic position of a railroad is the extent to which the freight originates on the road's own lines. A railroad exclusively serving an important mining area has a strategic advantage over one that traverses a poor, sparsely settled country, or that is dependent on connecting railroads for its business. The Chesapeake & Ohio originates 82 per cent. of its traffic, although nearly all of it is coal; the New York Central 42 per cent. and the New Haven 33 per cent.[1]

Seasonal and Cyclical Variations. Seasonal and cyclical variations of traffic are important, both as indices of operating efficiency and of stability of earnings. A railroad with widely fluctuating volume of traffic cannot cut expenses proportionately when business declines, for a large part of operating cost belongs to the class of " fixed " or " overhead " expenses. Therefore stability of traffic is a very desirable factor. Agricultural freight shows a wide seasonal variation. The heavy movement of ore from the Minnesota iron ranges to the Lake ports over the Great Northern Railway, which gives this system one-third its freight revenues, is concentrated in the Lake navigation season; and it varies in amount with changes in the business cycle and in the activity of the steel industry. In 1921, the volume of ore carried declined to 5,000,000 tons, yet in 1923 it amounted to 17,700,000 tons.

[1] Poor's *Manual of Railroads* gives this data in convenient form for most roads.

Duration of Traffic. Finally the prospective duration of any particular type of traffic is of moment as well as its prospect of growth. The Michigan lines were hard hit by the removal of the lumber industry to the South, and then to the Far West, and only recovered real prosperity with the growth of the automobile industry in that state. The Minnesota iron ore traffic on its present scale will not last longer than twenty years, in the opinion of many mining engineers. On the other hand, the smokeless coal fields of West Virginia, served by the Chesapeake & Ohio, Norfolk & Western, and the Virginian Railway, are adequate at the present rate of extraction for centuries to come.

Passenger Traffic. Passenger business, which provided eighteen per cent. of the operating revenues of American railways during 1924, is of great importance on only a few roads. On the New Haven, it accounts for nearly half the gross earnings. Competition of automobiles and busses has affected passenger service in recent years, and dependence on this type of traffic may generally be regarded as a disadvantage.

Operating Efficiency. Equipped with an analysis of traffic, the investor next determines the efficiency with which it is moved, for in this way only can he obtain a clue to the present and future margin of profit. Several convenient indices of operating efficiency are readily available. These are (1) average freight trainload, (2) average freight carload, (3) average passenger trainload, and (4) operating efficiency.

The average freight trainload on all railroads was 647 tons in 1924. On the Chicago & North Western, with a policy of running light, frequent trains, the average trainload was 445 tons. On the Union Pacific, a road similar in many ways but noted for greater operating efficiency, the average trainload was 610 tons.

The average carload indicates the intensity to which a railroad is utilizing productively its car equipment. The average carload is in large part based on the type of business done. The average for each class of freight during 1924 was as follows:

Products of Agriculture	24	tons
Animals and Products	12	"
Products of Mines	50	"
Products of Forests	28	"
Manufactures and Misc	26	"
Merchandise L. C. L. Freight	34	"

The American Railway Association has fixed a load of 30 tons per car as a desirable average of efficiency for all American railways, but in 1924 an average of only 27 tons was attained. The New Haven operated at an average loading of only 19.5 tons; the Pennsylvania, with 28.5 tons, was near the ideal figure.

The average passenger trainload is worthy of attention only on railroads of which the passenger business is significant, like the New Haven, the Boston and Maine, the Central of New Jersey, and the Long Island. On the New Haven, the average in 1924 was 28 passengers; on the Long Island, 34.

Operating Ratio. A summary of operating efficiency is expressed by the operating ratio; the percentage of expenses to earnings, which is determined by the formula:

$$\text{Operating Ratio} = \frac{\text{Operating Expenses}}{\text{Operating Revenues}}$$

The cost of operating most roads has increased sharply since pre-war days and in 1925 averaged 76 per cent. The nine roads with the lowest operating ratio for 1925 were these:

Norfolk & Western	65%
Great Northern	66
Atchison	69
Atlantic Coast Line	69
St. Louis San Francisco	69
Southern Railway	70
Union Pacific	70
Northern Pacific	71
Chesapeake & Ohio	72

But it must not be forgotten that too much striving after present economies may cripple future efficiency. Therefore, the operating ratio should always be checked against the amount spent in maintenance as shown by the earnings accounts, to which we now turn.

Railroad Accounting. After many years of effort, the Interstate Commerce Commission has succeeded in giving a laudable degree of uniformity to railroad accounting. Since 1907, these accounts have been kept under rigid supervision by the Commission, and capital expenditures, which increase the value of the railway property, are carefully separated from those incurred in the ordinary course of operation. The old-time jugglery of railroad accounts is no longer possible.

It is necessary to appreciate the significance of the several accounts, for otherwise the annual report cannot be read with understanding. The summary report of all railroads of the country for 1924, as published by the Interstate Commerce Commission, was as follows:

Railway operating revenues	$6,147,069,411
Railway operating expenses	4,688,241,646
Net revenue from railway operations	$1,458,827,765
Railway tax accruals	361,169,715
Uncollectable railway revenues	2,463,625
Railway operating income	$1,095,194,425
Equipment and joint facility rents (net deduction)...	82,031,765
NET RAILWAY OPERATING INCOME	$1,013,162,660
Non-operating income	145,090,204
Gross income	$1,158,252,864
Deductions from gross income	609,229,833
Net income	549,023,031
Appropriations of net income	366,905,274
Remainder to profit and loss	$182,117,757

Operating Revenues. The great bulk of the operating revenues are received in the form of freight receipts paid on goods moved and of passenger fares. The relative importance of the chief sources of operating revenues in 1924 is shown in this table:

Freight	73.18%
Passenger	18.16
Express	2.42
Mail	1.65
Switching	1.00
Milk	.59
Other rail-line transportation	.68
Water-line transportation	.24
Incidental operations, etc	2.08
	100.00

Operating revenues for roads similarly situated can be studied to advantage on a per-mile basis. Another illuminating figure of relative earning power is the average rate received per ton-mile, which for all Class I roads was 1.116 cents in 1924. This number, indicating the average rate level, has been tending downward in recent years, after a sharp advance (caused by the higher general price level) culminating in 1921. Finally, operating revenues should be considered in relation to net capitalization, which will be described in the following chapter.

Operating Expenses.   Since 1914 the operating expenses of the railroads have been classified under seven general accounts. Their relative importance is indicated herewith.

	Per Cent. of Total Expense
1. Maintenance of Way and Structures...............	19.05
2. Maintenance of Equipment......................	28.48
3. Traffic Expenses...............................	2.59
4. Transportation Expenses........................	45.87
5. Miscellaneous Operations.......................	.78
6. General Expenses..............................	3.56
7. Transportation for Investment Co. (credit).........	−.33
	100.00

Maintenance Expenditures.   Maintenance expenditures, to a considerable extent subject to the whim of the management, merit careful attention.   The Interstate Commerce Commission has the power to instruct a railroad in which account a certain expenditure must be entered, but it cannot see that a property is fully maintained in every essential respect if the management wishes to make a fictitious display of earnings.

Maintenance of Way and Structures.   The adequacy of maintenance of way expenditures can be studied from two indices—the percentage of total expenses that is devoted to this purpose, and secondly, the amount actually spent per mile.   The amount of maintenance per mile needed will depend on the type of territory traversed, the previous condition of the road, and the economy of securing necessary labor and materials for maintenance work.   The Great Northern, the property of which is in good condition, spent only $1,684 per mile on maintenance in 1924; the Delaware, Lackawanna, & Western spent $7,800 per mile.   The reason in part for this discrepancy was that the Great Northern has a single line of thin traffic across half the continent, and is now exercising rigid economy because of depressed earnings, and the Lackawanna is a wholly double-track line kept up to almost a luxurious state of maintenance and enjoying very heavy earnings.   However, when maintenance of way expenditures fall below $1,500 per mile, the investor should exercise special caution towards the securities of the road economizing in that fashion.

A long period of complete or overmaintenance may be followed by a drop in this percentage. Otherwise a steady decline, especially for a road with weak credit, is a fairly sure sign of trouble.

Maintenance of Equipment. Maintenance of equipment is of even greater importance than maintenance of way, for neglect of rolling stock is followed by far swifter and more disastrous results. It was demonstrated during the shopmen's strike of 1922 that locomotive service begins to deteriorate rapidly when all repairs are halted for two weeks, and at the end of a month the service is in danger of collapse. The interpretation of maintenance of equipment account is too difficult for general analysis, but investors can check this item from the report of percentage of bad-order locomotives and cars. Inadequate allowance for equipment maintenance will quickly be reflected in the proportion of units needing repairs. We have seen that 15 per cent. of bad-order cars is not unsatisfactory. The conditions of the nine roads with best reports in this respect on January 15, 1926, are as follows:

	Unserviceable Locomotives	Unserviceable Freight Cars
Norfolk & Western	7.2%	0.8%
Atlantic Coast Line	8.8	2.7
Union Pacific	10.09	6.9
Southern Railway	13.1	3.7
St. Louis-San Francisco	13.2	3.3
Chesapeake & Ohio	13.5	2.8
Atchison	16.8	6.7
Great Northern	16.9	7.7
Northern Pacific	19.2	5.8

Traffic Expenses, a small item, cover the cost of solicitation of traffic. The traffic department makes direct contact for the railroad with shippers.

Transportation Expense, the most important group, covers the actual work of providing service, including the wages of trainmen and yardmen, fuel, etc. They vary much less than do maintenance expenditures.

General Expenses cover the cost of maintaining the general administrative offices of the railroad, insurance, etc.

Comparisons of the railroad transportation ratio $\dfrac{\text{transportation expenses}}{\text{operating revenues}}$ are perfectly valid between roads carrying the same kind of traffic. A low ratio indicates either efficiency of operation or high rates or both. In 1925 the Norfolk & Western had the lowest percentage, 26.7 per cent. The Chesapeake & Ohio, a comparable line, had a transportation ratio of 28.2 per cent.

Income. The Interstate Commerce Commission prescribes that taxes, bad debts, and rents paid out for the use of equipment or joint facilities used with other carriers, should be deducted after net revenue from railway operations is computed. From the investor's viewpoint, however, these are expenses in the same way as any other, and he is interested chiefly in *net railway operating income*, giving the actual profit made out of conducting the business of transportation. To this is added *non-operating income*, including the return received on securities of other railroads not operated by the present company's organization, and rents received for joint facilities and equipment. For example, the gross income of the Union Pacific for 1924, consisted of $27,552,006 in net railway operating income and $21,375,271 in non-operating income.

The gross income is the fund that has been earned by the railway company from every source. This fund is available for three chief purposes: the payments of fixed charges, dividends to stockholders, and balances which may be used to improve and build up the property. The fixed charges, contained in the " deductions from gross income " account, consist chiefly of interest on funded debt, but include three other substantial items: rent for leased roads, hire of equipment, including payments on equipment trust certificates, and joint facility rents paid. Dividends are the chief appropriation of net income, since the sinking fund for railway bonds has almost disappeared. In the early days of railroading it was thought that funded debt should be incurred only as a temporary expedient, and that the permanent capitalization should consist solely of capital stock. That attitude ceased several decades ago, and now sinking funds persist in a few cases only, or in response to special conditions.

The final amount, transferred to profit and loss, represents income reinvested in the property. E. H. Harriman believed that the best railway financial policy was to reinvest one dollar for every dollar paid out as income. James J. Hill, on the other hand, thought that the stockholders should get a larger part of the earnings, improvements, and extensions being made with new capital raised by security issues. The majority opinion in railway management to-day veers towards the former viewpoint. The steady improvements in standards and operating methods, and the growth in business, makes it necessary to reinvest a part of earnings in the property. One should not be satisfied with a statement in the annual report that " the property of the company is in as good condition as it was last year." One should rather seek a statement that "the property has been kept substantially abreast of its competitors " or that " the improvement programme was carried forward during the year." [1]

Margin of Safety and Factor of Safety. Earning power creates the fund from which all bond interest in the long run must be derived. A wide margin of earnings above bond interest assures the investor that interest payments will be met on his bonds. Stable earnings at a good rate maintain the general credit of the company and keep up the market quotations of its bonds. Obligations of a weak company, no matter how well secured individually, nearly always sell at a relatively lower price.

The margin of safety, to bondholders, is the balance of gross income left after the payment of fixed charges. This fund, the property of stockholders, represents the amount by which net income may decline before interest payments will be jeopardized. The factor of safety is found by the following formula:

$$\text{Factor of Safety} = \frac{\text{Net Income}}{\text{Gross Income}}$$

When the factor of safety is 50 per cent. it is an indication that charges are being covered at least twice, which is considered a good margin. The Chicago, Rock Island, & Pacific Railway Company in 1924 reported net income or margin of safety, after the payment of charges, of $6,835,221, and gross income of $18,305,157. The factor of safety was $\frac{\$6,835,221}{18,305,157}$ or 37 per cent. This is rather poor, especially in view of the fact that 1924 was generally a good railroad year; but this ratio must be appraised in the light of the known stability of the earnings of this system in recent years.

[1] Mundy, *Earning Power of Railroads*, 1925, p. 20.

MARGIN OF SAFETY FOR A SPECIFIC BOND ISSUE

An investor holding an underlying bond issue is as much interested in the factor of safety for his individual issue of bonds as in that of all the fixed charges taken together. The factor of safety for a specific bond issue is found by the formula:

$$\text{Factor of Safety (of specific issue)} = \frac{G-C}{G}$$

where G = gross income
and C = fixed charges on this specific issue of bonds and all equal and prior liens.

Thus, the specific factor of safety for Chicago, Rock Island, & Pacific Railway Company first and refunding mortgage gold 4s in 1924 equalled $\dfrac{\$18,305,157-\$7,673,320}{\$18,305,157} = 58$ per cent.

In other words, interest on this and all prior issues was earned more than twice over by the Rock Island in that year.

The elimination of grade crossings, especially in the well-settled parts of the country such as Long Island, is an expensive improvement that railroads are often compelled to undertake. These expenditures do not increase the earnings of the roads, and merely saddle them with unproductive debt carrying a fixed charge.

Electrification is another important development, but one that may be reflected in larger earnings. It is suitable for two kinds of railroads: those having great density of traffic, like the Pennsylvania and the New Haven, and those having difficult grades to overcome, like the Rocky Mountain divisions of the St. Paul. Wherever such conditions exist, prospective investors in the bonds of the road should make allowance. For although the Transportation Act calls for a rate level that will yield a fair return on this additional capital, an excess of unproductive investment may make it economically impossible to secure such a return. If a fair return must mean excessively burdensome rates, business will not suffer the present law to continue unchanged.

CHAPTER XXV

RAILROAD BONDS: VALUATION AND THE CAPITAL ACCOUNT .

Railroad income statements are now sufficiently standardized to justify a large degree of confidence in their accuracy and exactness. Balance sheets, however, showing property values resulting from years of haphazard and unsystematic accounting, are of little value as an aid in judging security worth. The chief asset item—investment in road and equipment—is now of no importance, since the Transportation Act provided there should be substituted for it an actual physical valuation of the property of the carrier made by the Interstate Commerce Commission. Accurate values for non-railroad properties are of importance in many cases, although the ascertainment of them on the same basis is not called for in the Act. On the liability side, book figures of capitalization must be revised to include all fixed charges against the company's income, including lease rentals and charges on securities of subsidiaries. In this way, the actual property security can be disclosed, and an indication obtained of the value of the mortgaged asset in the event of foreclosure and receivership. Yet it must be remembered that in the event of receivership railroad property must be operated, and that almost never is a railroad enterprise wound up as a result of failure. Therefore it is necessary to appraise the strategic position of a particular bond issue to determine its value in a reorganization.

Valuation. The Transportation Act of 1920 provides that the physical valuation of the carriers, which is now being completed under the Valuation Act of 1913 (section 19-A of the Interstate Commerce Act), should be used as the basis for rate-making, earnings, recapture, and all other purposes for which property valuation of a railroad is required. This valuation is to take account of (a) original cost to date, (b) cost of reproduction less depreciation, (c) an analysis of the methods by which these several costs were obtained, and (d) other values and elements of value. The work was substantially completed by 1925.

The actual single-sum valuations submitted by the Commission are based upon (1) cost of reproduction, less depreciation, at pre-war prices; (2) land values, based on 10-year average value of adjacent land, and (3) a relatively small working capital allowance. The railroads claim that valuation should be based on present reproduction cost, as held by the United States Supreme Court in the famous case of the Southwestern Bell Telephone Co. vs. Public Service Commission of Missouri (262 U. S. 276), and, should their contention be granted, the aggregate valuation of railroad property will be about $30,000,000,000. The tentative valuations, as handed down by the Commission, indicate a total value in excess of $20,000,000,000, which is not far from the book valuation of the carriers themselves. Certain critics of the railroads favor a much lower valuation based on the " prudent investment " at original cost figures in railroad property. The full significance of valuation figures to investors will be impossible to determine until the method of ascertainment is finally adjudicated, but it is interesting to compare completed tentative valuations of " owned carrier property " with the book account of " investment in road and equipment " as kept by the railroad companies. They compare as follows for several leading roads:

	I. C. C. Valuation	Book Valuation
Boston & Maine	$239,261,346	$202,872,676
Chesapeake & Ohio	187,140,675	221,396,181
Great Northern	396,290,320	390,578,223
Illinois Central	346,171,353	302,558,454
New York, New Haven, & Hartford	385,465,142	285,211,378
St. Louis-San Francisco	186,367,830	354,108,995

When these valuations are accepted and tested in the courts, they will have to be completed by the addition of the valuation of subsidiary and separately appraised controlled lines, as well as of other properties owned. In the case of a road such as the Union Pacific, which owns more than $150,000,000 of stocks and bonds of unaffiliated companies, this supplement is especially important.

Capitalization. Many American railroads have very complex corporate structures, but to the investor it is of vital importance to know the investment position of a system as a whole. The strength of the parent company may be sapped by weak subsidiaries. This truth has been illustrated time and again in American railway history. Therefore it is necessary to learn the total actual capitalization of a railroad before investment analysis. Once computed, the capitalization should be analyzed as to: (1) ratio of funded debt to capital stock, (2) bonds outstanding per mile of line.

The capitalization of a railroad will include the capital stock, the funded debt of the parent company and of subsidiaries and the capitalized rentals of the road. Annual rental payments are commonly capitalized at 5 per cent. Another possible method is to include the total par value of stocks and bonds of the leased company with those of the parent road. The capitalization of the New York Central as of January 1, 1926, would stand as follows:

Capital Stock	$383,258,235
Funded Debt	696,501,507
Rentals Capitalized at 5 per cent	281,589,680
	$1,361,349,422

If the method of including the par value of securities of controlled and owned companies were followed, the capitalization would have been:

Capital Stock of New York Central	$383,258,235
Funded Debt of New York Central	696,501,507
Capital Stock of Subsidiaries in Hands of Public	29,000,000
Funded Debt of Subsidiaries in Hands of Public	344,499,000
	$1,453,258,742

With the true gross capitalization once derived by either of the above methods, we are now prepared to analyze its significance. The ratio of funded debt, including capitalized rentals to stock, shows the degree to which the enterprise has depended upon borrowed capital with a fixed return which must be paid to avoid bankruptcy. For the older, stronger roads a ratio of 2:1 may be considered good, though 3:1 under present conditions of stability, is conservative if the capital stock enjoys a good rate of earnings. The New York Central, on the basis of capitalized rentals considered as funded debt, had a ratio of $3\frac{1}{2}$:1 in 1926.

Owing to an impaired credit position, the ratio of railroad bond to stock capitalization has been steadily rising. The change since 1904 has been striking as seen in the following table:

OUTSTANDING RAILROAD SECURITIES IN HANDS OF PUBLIC

(In millions of dollars)

	1904	1914	1924
Capital Stock	$4,397	$6,041	$ 6,805
Funded Debt	6,315	9,718	11,396
Total Capitalization	$10,712	$15,759	$18,201

This tendency, which threatened the integrity of railroad bonds for a time, latterly has been somewhat corrected. Many railroads are now able to finance their new capital requirements with stock issues, and the Interstate Commerce Commission has refused to sanction new bond issues for a railroad which is able to sell additional stock at par.

Bonded Debt Per Mile. A second investment factor to be studied in the capitalization of a railroad is the amount of bonds outstanding per mile of railroad. For the United States as a whole, this averaged $47,158 per mile in 1925. This figure is of value only for comparisons of properties with similar physical and traffic characteristics. The Virginian Railway, a short line carrying coal from West Virginia to Hampton Roads, and built on a very expensive scale, by the late Henry H. Rogers, the Standard Oil magnate, has bonds outstanding at the rate of $105,000 per mile, and is well able to support this debt. The Baltimore & Ohio with a substantial amount of branch mileage of light traffic naturally has a lower per-mile bonded debt, namely, $87,000 per mile.

Capitalization figures are often inaccurate because no account is taken of outside investments. The Erie, for example, has a bonded debt of $105,000 per mile of road operated. But this figure takes no account of investments in affiliated companies carried on the books at $152,000,000 and including coal properties valued at about $80,000,000. Since part of the bonded debt was incurred in obtaining these investment holdings, accuracy requires that the value of these investments be deducted from the figure of bonded debt to reach the amount of *net bonded debt per mile of railroad.*

Fixed Charges. The burden of bonded debt is not so much the total par value as the total of fixed charges. A long-term issue with a 6 per cent. interest coupon is twice as heavy a burden as that with a 3 per cent. coupon. Therefore the average interest rate is an important consideration. The fact that the bulk of the bonded debt of the New York Central carries $3\frac{1}{2}$ and 4 per cent. rates gives that road an advantage over the Pennsylvania, most of the bonds of which bear 4, $4\frac{1}{2}$ and 5 per cent. coupons.

The refunding problems of a road are important from this point of view, especially in times of high interest rates. The credit of the Great Northern and the Northern Pacific was adversely affected because they had to refund $142,000,000 of Chicago, Burlington, and Quincy Joint 4s in 1921 at an interest cost of over 7 per cent. Heavy maturities during the recent period of high rates bankrupted the St. Paul and all but wrecked the New Haven. The Baltimore & Ohio in 1925, a year of fairly high interest rates, had to handle $130,000,000 of maturities of $3\frac{1}{2}$ per cent. bonds, an operation which clouded the financial outlook of the company for several years. It was successfully accomplished, but with an increase in the fixed charges of $2,136,-000 annually because of the higher coupons on the refunding bonds.

Consolidation. Until the railroad consolidation program is completed, prospective mergers will have an important effect on the worth of securities of the weaker roads which are being absorbed by the stronger. The overburdened Erie will greatly relieve itself by absorption into a larger system with a conservative ratio of bonds to shares. First mortgage bonds of weak lines, now of doubtful investment value, may become gilt edge issues in a great system by becoming an underlying divisional lien, backed by a strong general credit.

Position in Receivership. Railroad liens become of special significance only in case of receivership and reorganization, for then the treatment of each issue depends on its strategic importance to the railway company as a whole. It is well known that foreclosure of a mortgage does not mean the liquidation of the railroad, but merely the prelude to reorganization in which fixed charges are cut down and new money raised. It is the aim of the reorganizers to lighten the load of debt and interest payments as much as possible, and holders of bonds without a prior claim on valuable property must convert at least part of their principal sum into income bonds and into stocks, on which a return is received only if earned.

Recent railroad reorganizations have tended to recognize three important groups of securities. These are (1) underlying bonds on main lines, (2) junior liens on main lines and liens on important branch lines with independent earning power, and (3) liens on unimportant branch lines. Bonds of the first type have the best strategic position, and are almost never disturbed. The second class of bonds, including the general mortgages and refunding mortgages which have been issued by most railroads, is usually affected,—often being exchanged in part at least for income bonds or preferred stock. The third group, with little strategic value, generally receives income bonds or stock, since the small earning power of the mortgaged security makes it impractical for bondholders to exercise the right of foreclosure. But if the issue is very small, or if it covers branch lines of potential value as traffic producers, probably it will not be disturbed.

Priority of Lien. To determine the specific security position of any issue of railroad bonds is very difficult. Railroad debt structure is a mysterious and wonderful thing—more wonderful than creditable. This is especially true of the great systems, built up from scores of individual companies, many with a complex bonded debt structure of their own—the whole mileage then being covered by a variety of blanket liens. Precedence of bond issues is as subtle, debatable, and involved as precedence at a state dinner. The only principles that stand out clearly are, that a secured obligation is superior to a debenture; that lien security is surer than guaranty, and that a lien on property of independent earning power is better than a lien on unprofitable assets. A first mortgage has a better claim than a second, a second than a third; primary liens anticipate secondary liens, and secondary liens anticipate junior liens.[1] These differences, no matter how fine, are usually reflected in the listed prices of the bonds.

Legal Investments. The great financial institutions of the country, the savings banks and insurance companies, are limited by law in their investments to securities of a specified kind meeting certain requirements of safety. Savings banks hold a billion dollars of these bonds, and insurance companies even more.

---

[1] Maps of individual railroad systems showing the incidence and ranking of almost all American railroad mortgages may be found in *White and Kemble's Atlas and Digest of Railroad Mortgages.*

Numerous estates, charitable institutions, and universities have placed a substantial amount of their funds in railroad securities, for they offer the most stable and certain security outside of civil loans.

The regulations governing savings banks investments in New York state are considered a model for such legislation. The essential features of the law follow:

1. *Size.*　　The company must have 500 miles of line, or gross earnings of $10,000,000.

2. *Earnings.* Gross earnings should be five times interest charges, and dividends of at least 4 per cent. must have been paid on the capital stock for a period of five years.

3. *Specific Lien.* The bonds must be secured by a mortgage satisfying one of the following descriptions:

　　(a) A first mortgage on 75 per cent. of the mileage.
　　(b) A refunding mortgage which is to retire all prior liens on 75 per cent. of the mileage and which is a direct lien on at least 25 per cent. more mileage than is covered by all prior liens and authorized at an amount less than three times the capital stock.
　　(c) Underlying mortgages of roads the refunding bonds of which are legal.
　　(d) A first mortgage of a road all the stock of which is owned by a railroad whose last issue of refunding bonds is legal, if the bonds are guaranteed and outstanding at not over $20,000 per mile.

CHAPTER XXVI

EQUIPMENT TRUST OBLIGATIONS

A decade of impaired railroad credit after 1914, during which financing by the sale of capital stock was impossible on most roads, compelled the carriers to resort to every known means of raising money at low interest rates. As a result, the issue of various special types of obligations, bringing an adequate price because of special security, has increased at even a faster rate than the indebtedness. Most important of these is the equipment obligation, secured by the indispensable rolling stock of the carrier. There were outstanding at the end of 1924 $1,056,700,000 of these obligations, nearly 10 per cent. of the total funded debt of American railroads.

Origin. After the panic of 1873, which was predominantly a railroad panic, certain lines found difficulty in securing capital to finance the acquisition of new facilities to meet the requirements of increasing traffic and territorial expansion. The original capitalizations had been converted largely into roadbed and terminal structures. But, as the more perishable rolling stock wore out and its replacement became necessary, many roads found it necessary to raise money for new purchases. The increase of mortgage debt for this purpose was imperative in many cases, either because of the low price or the heavy issue of the bonds, therefore several companies arranged with the car and locomotive builders, eager for business, to make a cash payment of from 10 to 25 per cent. on the purchase price, and the remainder in the form of serial notes. The practice was not original with the railroads, for it had been tried with success by the Schuylkill Navigation Company in 1845 and by the Lehigh Coal & Navigation Company in 1868.

This scheme permitted the road to pay both principal and interest out of current income. It distributed the maturities so that money earned by the equipment paid for it during its life, and left no increased debt after the rolling stock had been retired, so that there was no paying, as it were, for dead horses.

With the extension of this practice, the financial burden became too great for the equipment manufacturers, and the loss from defaulted notes became large during years of depression. Accordingly, a method had to be devised for passing on the securities to the public. For reasons of economy, it was desirable to give buyers of equipment obligations a first lien, or otherwise the interest rate would rise to a prohibitive level. But, since most every railroad had issued refunding and consolidated mortgages, with after-acquired property clauses giving them the first lien on new equipment, title to which was taken by the railroad, this could not be done in the ordinary manner. Furthermore, since many states require mortgages to be recorded wherever the property is situated, in order to protect the mortgages, and since rolling stock of one railroad may in its life travel over the entire country, a chattel lien was impractical. Even a conditional sale, which would avoid these pitfalls, was impracticable because of specific legal prohibition in several states, notably Pennsylvania. There was general and well-grounded prejudice against such sales of any kind of merchandise, as enabling debtors to withhold recourse to property by general creditors.

Car Trust Certificates. The solution to this vexing problem was the creation of the car trust, vesting title temporarily in a trustee for the benefit of the holders of the equipment obligations. This trustee, in turn, leased the equipment to the railroad on terms assuring funds sufficient to pay the interest on the trust certificates, and to retire the principal serially. Originally the contract of lease was supplemented by lease warrants, which represented the deferred payments and interest. The lease and the warrants, in the hands of a trustee, the lessor, represented the immediate assets against which *Car Trust Certificates*, or certificates of participation and beneficial interest in the lease, were issued. But the ultimate assets were the cars themselves, for the deed of trust authorized the sale of the cars to satisfy the certificate holders, in case the lease was broken.

It is evident that the investment principles underlying the early Car Trust Certificates did not differ in essentials from modern practice. Legal refinements, to be sure, were introduced subsequently, but they are matters of minor interest. The lease has been found sufficient without the supplemental warrants, which have been discarded. Of recent years the equipment obligation has been reinforced by the railroad's guaranty of the payments representing principal and interest, endorsed on each certificate. But there has yet to arise an instance when this guaranty has saved money for security holders.

When the Car Trust Certificates are association stock, the stock may be limited to the amount covering the lease in hand, or it may be unlimited except in the relation of the amount outstanding at any one time to the value of the equipment; but the certificates will always be in series, each series represented by its own rolling stock, as in the case of equipment bonds. In its purest form, however, the Car Trust Certificate is not stock of an organization, but a share in,—a certificate of beneficial interest in,—a fund raised to purchase the equipment.

Car Trust Bonds. Since we are using care in distinguishing types of equipment obligations,—more care than the railroads themselves use,—we reserve the term *Car Trust Bonds* for the direct *obligations* of corporations (let us say car manufacturers, or leasing associations), as distinguished from mere certificates of interest in the leases. The collateral security for these bonds is a mortgage on the lease of the rolling stock, assigned to the trustee. But since the informing principle of Car Trust Bonds is the lease rather than the conditional sale, they are of the category we have already discussed, rather than that of Equipment Bonds, to which we shall come presently. It is necessary that all leasing persons, associations, and corporations shall have identity distinct from that of the lessee railroad to make the loan valid.

The " Philadelphia Plan." Pennsylvania is about the only state that does not recognize the conditional sale as a proper principle for the issuance of equipment bonds. Hence the Car Trust plan has come to be localized in this state, especially in its investment centre, Philadelphia, and to be called the " Philadelphia Plan."

Pennsylvania is a state of unusual laws. It is the only state in which prevails the statute of mortmain. It is a state in which a conditional sale is not good against creditors of the vendee. A sale of personal property, with change of possession and control, passes a good title to the vendee, and any agreement of which the purpose is to cover up the sale and preserve a lien in the vendor for the price of the goods is void as against creditors of the vendee.

The principle at law is that a creditor presumes that the possession of personal property implies ownership, and he is likely to extend credit on the presumption. But it has been decided that where the possession of personal property has been transferred under an express contract of lease, or other bailment contract, the mere fact that there is superadded an executory agreement for the sale of the property to the transferee upon the payment of a certain price, at any time during bailment, does not convert the bailment into a sale. Therefore, until the execution of the contract by payment of the price, the title remains in the bailor, even as against the bailee's creditors.

This, then, is the method used in Pennsylvania to circumvent the law against conditional sales. The principle has been adjudicated there time after time. The legality of the lease is well established.

When the Car Trust Certificates are issued by a Pennsylvania trustee, association, or corporation, and the railroad agrees to pay such issuer money sufficient for any taxes, assessments, etc., which the issuer may be required to pay or deduct from interest or dividends on the certificates, then these certificates are free of state tax to resident owners. By this device any railroad, wherever chartered or operated, can make its car trusts free from state tax in Pennsylvania.

The agreement to pay this tax is not such a hardship to the railroad company as might appear, for although it is the duty of the trustee or the railroad company to pay this tax when the owners are known to be residents of the state, yet the trustee or company is not obligated, and it is not customary, to inquire as to the residence of the holder of a coupon presented for payment.

Equipment Bonds or Notes—The New York Plan. The other form of equipment obligation is called Equipment Bonds, or with equal propriety, because of the shortness of average standard duration, Equipment Notes. Car Trust Certificates and Car Trust Bonds are not synonymous terms; Equipment Bonds and Equipment Notes are. For comparison, this method is often called the "New York Plan."

Whereas Car Trusts are issued by persons, associations, or trustees, and are secured by deposit of the contract of lease, in trust, and are guaranteed usually by the railroad, Equipment Bonds are usually issued by the railroad, and are secured by a lien on the contract of conditional sale. The transition from a certificate of beneficial interest in a contract of lease (the Car Trust) to a direct railroad obligation secured by chattel mortgage on rolling stock (the Equipment Bond), has been gradual. The disuse of lease warrants, the supplemental railroad guaranty, the substitution of a formal obligation of the lessor for the certificate of interest in the lease,—these mark the initial stages of the change.

The incentive for this change is the fact that the lease is an obvious evasion of the law. In most states the courts have regularly held that where the plain intent and purpose is a conditional sale, one cannot avoid the sale by calling it a lease. The practical difficulties of making conditional sales are the difficulties encountered in recording chattel mortgages. To avoid multiplicity of registration most states have passed equipment statutes, like railroad mortgage statutes, permitting a single act of registration at the state capital, rather than in the many registration districts.

As conditional sales of equipment have been facilitated by legislation the indenture of lease has slowly given way to the conditional sale, although the inertia and timidity of the legal mind have not yet, in all cases, rid the trust deed of the lease idea. So the parties to the agreement still may be termed the Railroad and the *Vendors*, but the equipment may be designated as transferred to the trustee for *lease* to the Railroad.

A survey of recent issues of equipment securities shows that the equipment bond, based on a conditional sale, is now used almost exclusively on all important railroads except the Pennsylvania, New York Central, Missouri Pacific, Norfolk & Western, Southern, and Chesapeake & Ohio. It is noteworthy that the Railroad Administration used the equipment bond under the " New York Plan " financing the large purchases of new equipment during the period of federal operation.

Present Legal Status of Equipment Obligations. Enough has been said to indicate that the present legal status of Equipment Bonds is complicated and peculiar. The trust deed, covering movable property, is a chattel mortgage; and representing the transfer of property under certain provisos, it is a bill of conditional sale, so to speak. It is the chattel mortgage aspect of the trust deed that affords the material security to the bonds, just as in any mortgage bonds; it is the conditional sale aspect that prevents title from going into the hands of the railroad and the equipment from going under the railroad's blanket mortgage. Although title, as distinct from possession, does not pass to the railroad until the fulfilment of the deferred payments, yet, to all intents and purposes, the equipment does belong to the road and is the tools with which the road does its business.

In this connection it is customary to compare the legal situation of a road's mortgaged rolling stock, in foreclosure, with that of a mechanic's tools, which are exempt from seizure in bankruptcy proceedings. Possibly the comparison was suggested originally by early decisions such as that of Judge Hallett, in the United States Circuit Court, in the case of the Denver and Rio Grande in 1886, who held that " car trusts, principal and interest, are preferred securities to all mortgage claims and must be paid out of the revenue of the property the same as wages and labor." It is extremely questionable whether, even in the same jurisdiction, this legal principle would be upheld.

The analogy is somewhat hasty. The mechanic actually owns title to his tools, and their exemption from execution is a legal exception; but the railroad does not have title to the equipment, and the result that the equipment cannot be levied upon for the company's debts is an ordinary legal consequence and not any exemption or exception at all.

Yet the analogy is ordinarily valid as respects the underlying principle of business expediency. Both tools and rolling stock are personal property *usually* necessary to the conduct of business and to the ultimate satisfaction of creditors' claims. Courts, both state and federal, have passed upon this point for rolling stock, and in receivership have *usually* authorized the issuance of receiver's certificates, or otherwise have provided for the prompt payment of interest and maturing principal, on a virtual parity with the payment of wages and the purchase of necessary materials and supplies.

The trend of decisions in the past generation has been such that when, as in the case of the Detroit, Toledo, and Ironton, the equipment is not essential to the upkeep of the road, the bondholders must look for reimbursement to a real equity in the mortgaged property. They even may have to face decisions such as that given by a Missouri Court to the effect that

"a mortgage of the property acquired, and to be acquired, and of the income of a quasi-public corporation, such as a railroad company, takes a lien on the net earnings after the current expenses of operation in the ordinary course of business are paid, and impliedly agrees that the gross income shall be first applied to the payment of these expenses.

"The test of the quality which entitles a claim to a preference over the mortgage in foreclosure is whether the consideration of the claim was, or was not, a part of the current expenses of the ordinary operation of the corporation.

"Neither the fact that the consideration of the claim conserved the property and increased the security of the mortgage, *nor the fact that it was necessary to keep the mortgagor a going concern or to continue its business or operations, will raise a preferential equity in its favor,*[1] if its consideration was not a part of the ordinary operations of the mortgagor.

"*Claims for the purchase price or the rental of engines, freight and passenger cars are not entitled to preference in payment out of the income or out of the corpus of the mortgaged property over those of creditors secured by prior mortgages.*"[1]

It will be understood that under such a ruling a court might hinder a receiver in the performance of his plain duty as business manager of the railroad by withholding permission for the issuance of certificates. But it is not probable that any body of legal decisions will overlook the fact that equipment trust obligations may have a preferential claim from a business, though not from a legal point of view.

The Modern Trust Deed. In describing the development and present forms of equipment obligations we have touched upon the more important aspects, especially legal, of the modern equipment trust deed, but these further features are of moment. It is usually a three-party agreement subscribed to by the railroad, the bond house (or other company) as vendor, and the trust company as trustee for the bondholders. It provides for the conspicuous marking of each piece of rolling stock with the serial number under which it was built, and even for metal plates inscribed with " ——— and Co." (the vendors), the plates and numbers not to be changed without consent of the trustee. " The railroad will not allow the name of any person, association, or corporation to be placed on any of the said equipment as a

---

[1] The italics are ours.

designation which might be interpreted as a claim of ownership by the railroad "; provided that the railroad may letter its engines, tenders, and cars with its own name for proper identification.

The railroad shall keep the equipment in proper and complete repair and renew and replace such as may be worn out, lost, or destroyed, with other of substantially the same quality and character. The railroad shall furnish a complete statement concerning the equipment and its whereabouts, at least once a year, and allow the vendors access to the premises and facilities for the inspection of the property to which it holds title. The railroad shall insure the property in trust for the holders of bonds against loss or damage by fire and other loss that is a usual, insurable risk, to an amount equal to (say) 20 per cent. of its value and in companies approved by the vendors (20 per cent. being amply sufficient to cover all possible risk to such scattered property as rolling stock). The railroad agrees to pay all taxes, assessments, or charges against the equipment, and agrees not to permit it to be pledged for taxes or other obligations of the railroad.

Financial History of Equipment Trust Obligations. It will be observed from the abstract that the trust agreement is very exacting in its requirements for the protection of bondholders. Indeed the development in this document of legal and financial principles of safety has been remarkable. How well the trust deed has served its purpose, even in days when they were not so carefully drawn as at present, is evidenced by the history of equipment trust obligations when put to the test of railroad receiverships and reorganizations. An examination of the reorganization plans of companies having car trust or equipment bonds and being in receivership shows the following results.

Since 1885 there has been an average of approximately more than one company a year, with equipment securities outstanding, that has been in such straits as to default on its direct obligations.

In 1886 the Denver and Rio Grande Railroad, reorganized after foreclosure, owed $3,467,000 in 6 per cent. and 7 per cent. equipments. It was in adjudication of these bonds that Judge Hallett rendered the favorable, but untenable, decision quoted previously. Under an agreement with the car trust holders,

$600,000 of the bonds were paid in full and the remainder exchanged for consolidated mortgage bonds and preferred stock that later were worth about 40 per cent. more than the car trusts. During receivership no other issues received interest. This is one of the very few instances in which cash in full was not paid in receivership on maturing principal and interest of equipments, and in all cases of exception to the general rule it is to be remembered that the consent of a majority of the bondholders was, of necessity, first obtained.

In 1888 the Chesapeake and Ohio was reorganized without foreclosure, and the equipment bonds, amounting to $1,371,000, were undisturbed though all other securities were reduced in rate or refunded for a less amount

In 1892 the Central Railroad and Banking Company of Georgia, then leased to the Georgia Pacific, went into the hands of a receiver; in 1894, the Georgia Pacific, which, in turn, was leased to the Richmond and Danville, followed suit, drawing down with it the Richmond and Danville in foreclosure of the latter's consolidated mortgage. The interest and maturing principal of the equipments of all three roads, amounting to several millions, were paid in full. In several cases the mortgage and debenture bonds were unfavorably modified or temporarily reduced in amount under the Richmond Terminal Company's reorganization plan. A division of the Richmond Terminal System had outstanding Improvement and Equipment 5s which were exchanged for 4 per cent. bonds and preferred stock, ultimately worth considerably more than the replaced bonds, but the 5s were not strictly an equipment issue and should not be considered.

In 1892 the Savannah, Americus, and Montgomery, now a part of the Seaboard Air Line, suffered receivership. The equipment bonds were untouched.

In 1893 the Toledo, St. Louis, and Kansas City Railroad, now the Toledo, St. Louis, and Western, went into receivership. It defaulted upon its $9,800,000 mortgage bonds. The equipment payments were met, as usual, by the receivers.

In 1895 the Atchison, Topeka, and Santa Fé was reorganized after foreclosure. During receivership, the court authorized payment of interest and maturing principal on over $2,000,000 of equipment bonds and car trust obligations. Interest was defaulted on the mortgage bonds. At reorganization $1,200 in new general mortgage bonds was reserved to retire each $1,000 equipment bond at maturity. Practically all other securities were reduced in rate or refunded at a less amount. Of equipment bonds the reorganization plan says: " These constitute charges upon the revenues of the company prior to the General Mortgage bonds, the interest and instalments on the same " (equipments) " having been paid under the order of the court by the receivers."

In the same year the New York, Lake Erie, and Western, now the Erie, was reorganized after foreclosure. During receivership, receiver's certificates were issued to pay maturing principal and interest on the $2,000,000 of outstanding equipments, and after foreclosure securities were sold for the same purpose. First mortgage bonds were left intact, but other securities were reduced in rate or amount.

In 1895, also, the Union Pacific was reorganized after foreclosure. The equipment bonds, of which $1,149,000 were outstanding, were undisturbed and new general mortgage bonds were reserved to pay them at maturity. All other securities including the first mortgage bonds were reduced in rate or amount.

The following year the Baltimore and Ohio passed into the hands of receivers, and was reorganized without foreclosure in 1898; $300,000 in equipment obligations, maturing within these three years, were extended with the consent of the holders till 1899, at increased interest. And during the same period the United States Circuit Court authorized an issue of $3,400,000 car trust certificates and $5,000,000 receiver's certificates, part of which latter were " to pay for the restoration of the rolling stock and equipment of the railroad company." In all about $11,000,000 were applied, directly or indirectly, by the issuance of receiver's certificates, to the upkeep and improvement of the company's equipment. The charges incurred by these certificates were paid in full though almost all other securities were reduced in rate, and interest and rental obligations suffered temporary default.

In this same year, 1896, the Norfolk and Western was reorganized after foreclosure. Of the $7,239,000 equipments, $3,125,000 were paid and $4,114,000 were refunded at par in bonds with a bonus of preferred stock. The refunding bonds and preferred later became worth 140 cents on the dollar. Several issues of mortgage bonds were reduced in rate or amount. This was another instance in which cash was not paid on all maturing equipments.

In 1896 the Philadelphia and Reading was reorganized after foreclosure. The $7,300,000 of equipments were paid, partly by assessment. Junior securities were refunded for a less amount.

Regular and full payments were made on $3,000,000 equipment bonds of the Northern Pacific, reorganized after foreclosure in 1896. In this case all other securities suffered in rate or amount.

The next foreclosure (1899) on a road with equipment obligations was that of the Columbus, Hocking Valley, and Toledo Railway, now the Hocking Valley Railroad. All mortgages defaulted. Interest on the $1,000,000 equipments was paid, and 10 per cent. of the principal was retired regularly according to the provisions of the equipment sinking fund.

In 1900 the Kansas City, Pittsburg, and Gulf was succeeded in foreclosure by the Kansas City Southern. All the old securities except the equipments were reduced in rate and amount when exchanged for new first mortgage bonds on the latter company, but sufficient of the new bonds were sold to pay off the equipment charges when due ($1,900,000).

On August 1, 1905, a receiver was appointed for the Pittsburg, Shawmut, and Northern Railroad. Both mortgage issues, the $164,000 First 5s and the $14,491,600 Refunding Mortgage 4s, made their last coupon payments in the previous February. The equipment bonds were promptly paid as usual, although the road's misfortune caused an immediate decline in market value from a $4\frac{3}{4}$ to a $5\frac{1}{2}$ per cent. investment basis. Moreover, in 1907, the receiver issued $592,000 more on a $6\frac{1}{2}$ and 7 per cent. basis. The high rate was due to the very poor credit of the road. In October, 1910, $220,000 receiver's equipment trust certificates were authorized.

On December 4th of the same year (1905), the Cincinnati, Hamilton, and Dayton, and its subsidiary, the Père Marquette, went into receivership. The interest on the underlying mortgage bonds of the Cincinnati, Hamilton, and Dayton, and the interest and maturing instalments of the $2,640,000 equipments, was unaffected, but at the time of reorganization in 1909 the road was $1,046,000 in arrears of interest on its junior mortgage bonds, not including the interest on the $15,000,000 Consolidated Mortgage bonds held as collateral. Ultimately defaulted interest was made up and only the note holders suffered materially. For each note they were given $60 in cash and $1,000 New General Mortgage (Deferred Income) Bonds.

The Père Marquette, like its lessee, readjusted its finances in 1907 without foreclosure of the property. Some of its mortgage bonds were in default for about two years, but the payments on its $4,700,000 equipments were maintained.

The court authorized the receiver of the Père Marquette to issue $1,730,000 equipment obligations to purchase new equipment, and also some short time equipment 6 per cent. notes to take up the $2,600,000 5 per cent. notes, maturing March 2, 1908. Some of these refunding equipment notes were offered at par and interest. What other sort of short-time bond upon a road in such a condition as the Père Marquette could sell upon a 6 per cent. basis?

In January, 1908, the Seaboard Air Line went into receivership. On January 1st, in anticipation of default, two New York banking houses offered to purchase at full value maturing interest on all underlying bonds and car trusts, and maturing principal of the latter. Receiver's certificates were issued to reimburse the bankers.

Until the company resumed possession, without foreclosure, in November, 1909, the First Mortgage 4s and the General Mortgage 5s were in default of their interest. The plan of readjustment caused the majority of the First 4s to be stamped callable. Otherwise they were not disturbed, but the General 5s were exchanged at parity for 5 per cent. Interest Adjustment (cumulative income) bonds. The immunity of equipments had become so much a matter of course that the $6,000,000, approximately, of these bonds were barely mentioned in the plan of readjustment.

Immediately following the Seaboard Air Line (February 5th, 1908) the Detroit, Toledo, and Ironton was turned over to a receiver. This road furnished the first case of a serious, permanent equipment trust default. Until purchased by Henry Ford in 1920, this road was one of the poorest railroad properties of any size in the country. Unwise management had then brought the road to such a pass that, when it became insolvent and defaulted on all of its other notes and bonds, there was not, for a time, sufficient business to necessitate the retention of all the equipment, nor had the company sufficient credit to raise the necessary funds as rapidly as the manufacturers of this equipment (who held a large part of the bonds) desired. Therefore, about a year later, in April, 1909, the equipment covered by the $1,656,000 Equipment Trust $4\frac{1}{2}$s of 1905 was surrendered to the Trust Company of America as trustees for the American Car and Foundry Company et al. The equipment was sold at auction the following month to the St. Louis-Union Trust Company, in behalf of, and acting for the holders of the entire outstanding issue. The price of $1,200,000 was paid simply by the cancellation of the debt to that extent. Eventually, the note holders received more than the face value of their certificates. This is termed the case *célèbre* of equipment issues.

A reading of the deed of trust leaves no question about the regularity of the issue as an equipment obligation of the conditional sale type. We have emphasized the fact that so far as concerns collateral security, equipment bonds become stronger as they grow older. The $1,656,000 $4\frac{1}{2}$s of 1905 were part of an issue of $2,070,000, due $207,000 annually. Two instalments only, therefore, had been paid. The theoretical equity was not great.

The Detroit, Toledo, and Ironton, however, was also responsible in 1909 for the remaining $200,000 of an issue of $400,000 Detroit Southern car trusts, $40,000 of which were due annually. The equity in this property was greater and hence all payments were made on the Detroit Southern bonds, although there was about a two-months' delay in interest when the road first became insolvent.

On February 13, 1908, the Chicago, Cincinnati, and Louisville was turned over to a receiver after default on all its mortgage bonds. There was a floating debt of $1,750,000 and many small claims were overdue. The road was short of equipment and on May 26 the receiver was authorized to issue $1,000,000 3-year 6 per cent. certificates, part of which were used in the purchase of new cars and $100,000 for the rental of the equipment held under car trust agreements as payments matured during the succeeding six months.

No further provision of moment seems to have been made for the equipments during the receivership, for when the road was acquired at foreclosure by the Chesapeake and Ohio of Indiana, the purchase was made subject to the following unpaid equipment liens:

Hoosier Equipment Company First Mortgage 5s (with interest from January 1, 1909)........................$200,000
Car Trusts, American Loan and Trust Company 5s (with interest from December 1, 1908)....................... 150,000
Burnham Williams Equipment Agreement (with 5 per cent. interest on $50,656 thereof from March 2, 1908)........ 91,194
Haskell and Barker Car Company Equipment Agreement (with 4 per cent. from May 17, 1909)................ 177,744

Railroad receiverships, after the panic of 1907, were numerous. In the same month that the Detroit, Toledo, and Ironton and the Chicago, Cincinnati, and Louisville went under,—on the 26th,—the International and Great Northern followed, having for some time been in arrears of interest on its Third Mortgage 4s. At the next interest period the Second Mortgage 5s omitted payment, and neither issue has yielded anything since. At the time of bankruptcy, the road had about $500,000 of equipments outstanding. Care was taken of these regularly.

When the Wheeling and Lake Erie became bankrupt in June, 1908, interest was defaulted on the $8,000,000 5 per cent. notes, secured by $12,000,000 General Mortgage 4s. No interest had ever been paid on this collateral, which at no time had ever been in the hands of the public.

For a month or two there was default on the Equipment 5s of 1922, but only until the receiver obtained permission from the United States Circuit Court to pay the July coupons. On July 1, 1915, interest was defaulted again, six months after sinking fund payments had ceased. The price fell to 60. In the reorganization the following year, the equipment, now 14 years old, was found to be of doubtful value. The reorganization managers agreed, however, to pay the back interest and 35 per cent. of the out-standing certificates in cash, and to give new 4 per cent. Sinking Fund Equipment Notes for the remaining 65 per cent. secured by the old unmatured equipment bonds and payable in six annual instalments. This was the only case in the recent history of railroad finance in which equipment trust certificate holders were forced to accept a compromise.

But the Wheeling and Lake Erie equipments well illustrate the danger of departure from the ten-year serial form on which we lay so much emphasis. The original amount of the issue was

$2,500,000, and the cost was, as usual, 10 per cent. in excess, or $2,750,000. The bonds were a direct obligation of the road, but they ran for 20 years, with the annual sinking fund only 3 per cent. for the first four years, and 4, 5, 6, and 7 per cent. for the succeeding periods of 4 years each. At the time of the temporary default only $502,000 (20.1 per cent.) had been amortized, although $525,000 (25 per cent.) should have been paid according to the terms of the trust deed. This is another illustration of the inefficacy of sinking funds. If, however, the issue had been of standard form, $1,625,000 (65 per cent.) would have been amortized.

The theoretical depreciation of the rolling stock, based on a 15-year life, was about $1,200,000 (or $43\frac{1}{3}$ per cent. of the $2,750,000 cost), leaving a value of $1,550,000, against which the outstanding debt was $1,998,000 or $448,000 more than the property was worth. But by the 10-year serial method, with semiannual payment, only $875,000 of bonds would have been outstanding and the value of the property would have been $675,000 (or 77 per cent.) more than the debt.

When the Norfolk and Southern was turned over to receivers on July 1, 1908, there were outstanding $2,203,047 three-year collateral trust notes dated November 1, 1907, that had as part collateral $1,200,000 Norfolk and Southern " straight " 10-year 5 per cent. equipment bonds, the principal of which was to be paid the trustee when due. As collateral, none of these equipments were in the hands of the public, and no interest was paid on them. The collateral notes themselves were not affected, although there was default of interest on the $15,000,000 First and Refunding 5s. In the road's reorganization, May 5, 1910, as the Norfolk Southern, the equipments were cancelled with the retirements of the notes.

Still two other roads with equipment debt went wrong in 1908. On August 19th, when the Chicago Southern was turned over, a majority of the $78,121.78 equipment notes were in default. These notes were not of the formal equipment type, nor in the hands of investors. The rolling stock pledged was 235 side-dump cars for company service, which, with 10 locomotives, was all the rolling stock the company owned. On March 10, 1909, the vendor of the cars claimed the right to retake and sell them, and also claimed there was due from the receiver, for rental and destroyed cars, the further sum of $15,000. The vendor, moreover, claimed that a sale of the cars would fail to pay the amount due on the notes by $33,000, and therefore that this amount would be a further claim on the receivership estate. Against this claim the receiver had a counterclaim for repairs and transportation amounting to about $6,800. Believing that the dump cars were practically useless for the purposes of the road, the receiver made a complete settlement of the respective claims, under which the notes were discharged, the cars were returned to the vendor (as in the case of the Detroit, Toledo, and Ironton), and a cash payment of $5,000 made by the receiver.

The subsidiary Southern Indiana, which went into receivership at the same time as the parent company, had defaulted the first of the month, on its First Mortgage 4s. On November 1st the General Mortgage bonds suffered the same way.

At that time there were in the hands of the public $753,333.95 of equipment notes, including interest due. In settlement, the note holders accepted $200,000 cash, raised by receiver's certificates, and $553,333.95 payable one-fourth on November 1, 1909, and one-eighth each May and November until the final settlement, November 1, 1912.

The Chicago, Terre Haute, and Southwestern took over both the above properties on January 1, 1911, without disturbing the principal of the Southern Indiana First 4s, but holders of the other securities were given the usual cumulative income bonds, and some stock.

The record of the equipment bonds of the Atlanta, Birmingham, and Atlantic is next in order. The road went into receivership on January 2, 1909, as the result of default the day before on the First 5s of 1936.

Most of the road's equipment and cars were held under the equipment trusts, which amounted to over $2,600,000. The January, 1909, interest and the maturing instalment of the Series B Equipments was not paid until February 10th. Several other temporary defaults occurred, but although all junior securities were obliterated, and even receiver's certificates were refunded into junior lien income bonds, the equipment obligations were all paid in full in cash in 1915.

On May 1, 1910, the Buffalo and Susquehanna Railway defaulted on its $6,000,000 First Mortgage $4\frac{1}{2}$s and went into receivership. The road had for three years been operating the Buffalo and Susquehanna Railroad, and guaranteeing 4 per cent. dividends on both classes of the railroad's stock and paying the bond interest, etc. On July 23, the railroad also went into receivership. The railroad has no equipment bonds, but the railway had four series of equipments amounting to $1,606,000. The railroad assumed three of these, and paid them in full. The fourth was not assumed, but was left for the Wellsville and Buffalo Railroad, successor to the railway, which was dismantled in 1916. A syndicate of Buffalo men bought the equipment, depositing with the trustee a sum equivalent to the unpaid certificates and their interest to maturity. As in the case of the Detroit, Toledo, and Ironton, the equipment proved ample to protect holders of the obligation which it secured.

Since 1910, the position of equipment securities has further improved, and even temporary defaults have been quite exceptional, despite the large number of receiverships which followed the outbreak of the World War.

The Wabash Railroad Company went into receivership in 1911. Of the four series of certificates outstanding, default occurred on only one—the series "C" $4\frac{1}{2}$ per cent. issue. Foreclosure proceedings were begun, but the court authorized receiver's equipment notes to pay them, holders of the issue in default being offered full cash payments, or at their option, new 6 per cent. notes. Of the other issues, two were paid at reorganization and the third, a long-term issue, was taken over by the reorganized company and paid at maturity.

A receiver was appointed a second time for the Père Marquette. On April 6, 1912, there were outstanding $3,000,000 of certificates in several series. J. P. Morgan & Co. and the Guaranty Trust Company, acting on behalf of the railroad, purchased and held equipment notes and coupons as they matured. As the road showed poor earnings, the court in March, 1914, stopped all payments on funded debt. On representations from a protective committee of holders of the equipment trust certificates, however, the receivers were directed to issue new obligations to take care of equipment securities and the reorganization plan of 1917 provided for paying off the remaining outstanding certificates.

Another recent case of difficulty met by holders of equipment trust certificates occurred on the Chicago, Peoria, & St. Louis.

This road defaulted on its general and refunding $4\frac{1}{2}$ per cent. bonds on June 1, 1914, and a receiver was appointed July 31. One issue of equipment trusts was outstanding, amounting to $590,000 in 1913 at time of issue, and falling due in ten annual instalments.   This short term was the strongest factor in the position of the security.   A default occurred on November 1, 1918, but the sum due with 6 per cent. interest was remitted in July, 1919.   Payments of interest and principal for 1919 were made May 1, 1920.   Further remittances were made until November 1, 1923, when default was made on the final payment.   The road was about to be dismantled and there was a substantial equity above the sum due.   Payments were finally made out of the proceeds of a sale of the entire property in 18 parcels for the benefit of the bondholders.

The Atlanta, Birmingham, and Atlantic again defaulted on February 25, 1921. Equipment notes aggregating $982,500 had been given the Director General of Railroads in 1920 for new locomotives and cars allocated to it.   A default occurred on July 15, 1921, and payment was not pressed.   In 1926, the Atlantic Coast Line reorganized the company under a plan which gave bondholders 60 per cent. in new 5 per cent. guaranteed preferred stock, but provided for the full payment of the equipment notes in cash.

Depreciation and Serial Payment.   The fact that the prior payment of equipment bonds is not an inherent legal right, but a matter of business expediency very generally recognized by the courts, probes whatever weakness there is in equipment bonds. If, because of its special nature (as in the case of the Chicago Southern), or because there is too much of it (as in the case of the Detroit, Toledo, and Ironton), the receiver rejects the equipment and permits the mortgage to be foreclosed, then it becomes very pertinent to inquire whether the rolling stock will sell at auction for the full value of the bonds.   Let us consider, then, what material or auction values lie behind the bonds.

In the first place there is from 10 to 25 per cent. equity in the property when the bonds are issued,—that proportion of the cost, as we have stated, being paid in cash.   Since the principal usually matures in equal semiannual instalments over a period of (usually) ten years, the outstanding amount of the mortgage decreases 5 per cent. every six months.   Rolling stock, particularly engines and passenger coaches, depreciates rapidly, but not so rapidly as the mortgage decreases, and has an average life for selling purposes of from fifteen to twenty-five years. With the development of steel-frame construction and the general improvement in car-building the tendency is toward longevity. Reckoning upon fifteen years and an arbitrary uniform decrease in selling value, and assuming a 10 per cent. equity when the bonds were issued, we can readily figure what theoretical auction security is behind the bonds at any time during their life. The accompanying diagram may assist:

CHART I

Diagram showing the growth of equity in a ten-year serial equipment bond

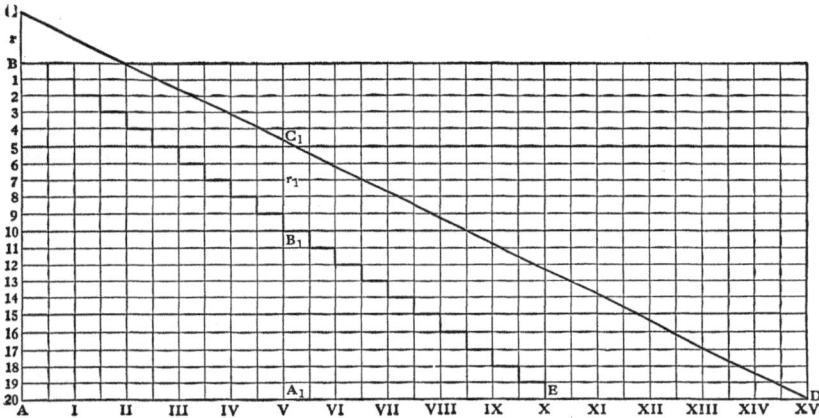

Perpendicular distance represents value.	Horizontal distance represents time.
AB = Amount of mortgage at issuance.	I, II, III, etc. = Number of years since issuance.
AC = Value of rolling stock at issuance.	
BC = Equity in rolling stock at issuance.	1, 2, 3, etc. = Serial Instalments of mortgage.
BE = Line of diminishing mortgage debt.	r = ratio of equity to value, i.e., margin of safety.
CD = Hypothetical line of diminishing value.	

Problem (the simplest case and the simplest solution).
Find the margin of safety for the bonds at the end of five years.

Let A_1B_1 = Amount of mortgage outstanding at end of 5 yrs.
      A_1C_1 = Value of rolling stock at end of 5 yrs.
      B_1C_1 = Equity of rolling stock at end of 5 yrs.
      r_1 = Margin of safety at end of 5 yrs.
Then $A_1B_1 = \frac{1}{2}$ AB (50% of mortgage having matured)
And $A_1C_1 = \frac{2}{3}$ AC (value having depreciated $\frac{1}{3}$ in 5 yrs.)

Now $r = \dfrac{BC}{AC} = \dfrac{1}{10} = 10\%$ at issuance

$r_1 = \dfrac{B_1C_1}{A_1C_1}$

But $B_1C_1 = A_1C_1 - A_1B_1$ (See Diagram)

And $\dfrac{B_1C_1}{A_1C_1} = 1 - \dfrac{A_1B_1}{A_1C_1}$ (Dividing by A_1C_1)

$= 1 - \dfrac{\frac{1}{2} AB}{\frac{2}{3} AC}$ (Substituting)

$= 1 - \dfrac{3}{4}\left(\dfrac{AB}{AC}\right)$

$= 1 - \dfrac{3}{4} \times \dfrac{9}{10}$ $\left(\dfrac{AB}{AC} = \dfrac{9}{10}\ \text{by Diagram}\right)$

$= \dfrac{13}{40} = 32\frac{1}{2}\%$

But $\dfrac{B_1C_1}{A_1C_1} = r_1$ (Above)

Therefore $r_1 = 32\frac{1}{2}\%$

The Margin of Safety. Other cases could demonstrate mathematically, as the diagram does graphically, that the hypothetical margin of safety grows from 10 per cent. at the making of the mortgage to $92\frac{17}{19}$ per cent. at the beginning of the last half year. It is a purely hypothetical margin, however, for the line of diminishing value necessarily is not straight, but composed of broken curves determined by the fluctuating supply and demand throughout the entire country for rolling stock. If this demand during a heavy crop movement in a prosperous year should become acute, it is quite possible that the value of rolling stock that had not become overworn, might approach, temporarily, even after months of use, its purchase price, or under converse conditions, might make a much poorer showing than the diagram indicates. As it is, depreciation the first year must be abnormal, for once a car is used at all it becomes secondhand and must be priced accordingly. But the diagram and figures, as a whole, are useful. They show that for a short-term investment the later maturities, bought when an issue has been long outstanding, have a greater margin of safety than the earlier maturities of a newer issue—indeed many times as great. The history of equipments in reorganization bears this out. In this diagram the minimum original cash equity and minimum of life for the rolling stock are assumed; in case of greater original cash payment and greater equipment longevity the showing would be very much better.

Variations in Form. The New York Central system floated a $30,000,000 equipment loan that varied in several respects from the normal type. The maturities, which are annual, are distributed over a period of fifteen years, with what loss to the material security of the loan a mental readjustment of the diagram will show. In this case the loss is compensated for by the guarantees of four of the Central's subsidiary companies. A more radical departure from the type is that of the Delaware and Hudson, which in 1907 issued an equipment loan maturing in 1922 that substituted a sinking fund for the usual semiannual repayments. This is to be regretted, since, apart from the dangers attendant upon sinking funds in general, it opens the way for further inroads into the integrity of the perfect form, namely, the ten-year, semiannual, serial bond, protected with at least a 10 per cent. cash equity. As it is, we are threatened with redeemable equipment issues and already have car trusts not intended for public absorption, but for use as collateral. We have also seen that junior equipment liens, trolley equipment liens and even warehouse trust certificates have been issued. These departures from the form, however, have not always turned out satisfactorily.

Equipment securities are now regarded generally by investors as of the very highest quality, and we have seen that nothing in their recent record fails to justify this view. In the case of the strongest roads, equipment securities now sell at approximately the same level as underlying mortgage bonds. On the weaker lines, the equipments give a lower yield than any other security. In 1926, the certificates of the bankrupt St. Paul sold to yield a little over 5 per cent. or only one-half per cent. more than those of the strongest roads.

Equipment bonds are necessarily of short duration. Therefore, it is to be expected that they will be preferred to underlying mortgage issues when interest rates are rising, as a fall in the value of the principal is then avoided by the near maturity. Conversely, long-term mortgage bonds will be preferred in times of falling interest rates and rising bond prices. One may, therefore, in virtue of security and yield, recommend the purchase of equipment issues of the present standard when longevity is not a requirement of the investor.

CHAPTER XXVII

STEAMSHIP BONDS

Steamship Bonds naturally find a place among the loans of transportation companies although they have no prominence as a type of security. The body of investment principles which characterize and differentiate them is small; and the application of principles peculiar to them is rendered difficult by the variety of conditions under which steamship companies operate.

Blanket Mortgage Steamship Bonds. Those issues which can be most nearly judged as we should weigh many of the other types of private corporation bonds, are blanket mortgages, the obligations of companies operating several or many vessels, and possibly operating in many waters. We should expect the mortgage to be a first lien, and the company to have a satisfactory record of earnings derived from a kind of traffic that is steady and promising. But, since the war, this industry has suffered from a large excess of available tonnage, and, as a result, only the strongest bonds of this type have retained a high investment status. Even the largest American Company, the International Mercantile Marine Company, has not been able to make its service profitable under post-war conditions. Several leading European companies have made a better showing, in part because of government aid, and they have sold mortgage securities here of considerable merit.

Equities. The valuation of the ships, docks, terminal buildings, or other property of the company under the mortgage, should be the estimate of disinterested appraisers, and should show an equity of about 100 per cent. over the authorized amount of the bonds. It is best for the maintenance of the equity that the vessels be new, or nearly so. Any bonds in escrow should be issued for additional property only to about 75 per cent. of its value.

It is very desirable that the bond issue mature serially, especially if much of the equipment is not new. The action of water, fresh or salt, is not favorable to material property, and deterioration is rapid. Changes in marine transportation,

326

both engineering and commercial, are rapid, and transfer by sea or lake is not a natural monopoly. Therefore the margin of safety should be increased, annually, by the serial retirement of the bonds. In any case, the issue should mature many years before the end of the estimated life of the boat, as an old boat has a doubtful market value in the event of foreclosure. Boats on the Great Lakes have a life of from 50 to 60 years on the average, but appraisers seldom give a rating of first class to a steel boat more than twenty years old. Good issues mature serially in ten years.

Insurance. Insurance in favor of bondholders is a factor of safety for almost any kind of funded corporation loan. It is desirable as collateral for equipment bonds. If there are insurable buildings or plants, it is essential to timber and real estate bonds. But it is the very life of the security for steamship bonds.

It is customarily provided that insurance covering all the property shall be maintained in amount 25 per cent. in excess of the mortgage. But this is not necessarily sufficient. The policies should be deposited with and made payable to the trustee for the bondholders. They should cover, not only land hazards, and the ordinary marine dangers of fire, collision, stranding, sinking, etc., but also afford protection against claims for damage done to other vessels, to docks, bridges, and any fixed or floating property. It is also necessary that the managers of the vessel obey such requirements as keeping the boat in port where only a limited sailing season is allowed. The reason is that claims could be defeated if it were shown that restrictions stated in the policy have been violated.

The mortgage should make provision for the disposition of any insurance moneys paid in:—either arranging for the replacement of the property destroyed, and requiring that the steamship company should pay the difference between the cost of the new property and the amount of insurance obtained, or else reinforcing the security for the bond issue by diverting this money to the sinking fund.

Mr. Montgomery Rollins has quoted some legal principles which apply to the mercantile marine.[1] They are as follows:

"The liability of the owner of a vessel for loss or damage to another vessel or to the cargo of either vessel, happening through errors in naviga-

[1] *Money and Investments*, Boston, 1907, pp. 375–376.

tion or management, or from perils of the sea, but without his knowledge, or privity, is limited to the value of his vessel, and the freight then earned, in the condition in which it is after the happening of the loss or accident.

"The owner is also not liable for loss or damage by fire to the cargo carried in his own vessel unless caused by his own neglect.

"If the owner exercise due diligence to make his vessel seaworthy and to see that she is properly manned and equipped, neither he nor his vessel is liable for loss or damage to the cargo carried, from errors of navigation or management, or from dangers of the sea.

"The owner may relieve himself of all liability by transferring all his interest in the vessel and the freight then pending to a trustee for all claimants.

"Insurance on the vessel, recovered by the owner, is no part of the owner's interest in the vessel, and is not liable to be taken to pay for the loss or damage.

"In case of a corporation, the 'knowledge and privity' which would make it liable must be the knowledge and privity of its officers or managers, and not of the masters of its vessels.'"

" Single Boat Bonds." When the bonds are secured by lien upon only one boat it is obvious that its physical excellence must be the object of close scrutiny. Yet it is by no means to be inferred that any inferiority attaches to the single boat type. In many, if not most cases of this sort, the obligor company is owner of only one or two boats. Although the capital of the company may have been fully paid in, and the amount may have been approximately equal to the bonded indebtedness, nevertheless, after paying necessary organization expenses (including the purchase of wharfage facilities and rights), the stock does not represent, in event of failure, much merchantable property except the equity in the boat itself.

Steamship Bonds of the Great Lakes. " Single Boat Bonds," if we may coin this expression, are studied at their best in the case of the grain and freight-forwarding companies of the Great Lakes. These loans deserve mention because of their particular excellence, and because of the amount of them that have been put on the market. These bonds are now held in sufficient esteem for the legislatures of seventeen states to make them legal for savings bank investment. These include Maine, Delaware, Maryland, and Washington, where the laws are stringent because of the existence there of mutual savings banks.

The Michigan law is given below, in full, because it is such an excellent summary of the investment principles.

Act 262, P. A., 1905, as amended by Act 480, P. A., 1907, Section 27, provides that a savings bank may invest any part of three-fifths of its total deposits in certain kinds of municipal and corporation bonds; and

(g) "in the legally authorized first mortgage bonds of steamship companies: Provided, That such mortgages shall be upon steel steamship or steamships for the carriage of freight or package freight and passengers combined, upon the Great Lakes and connecting waters, of at least five thousand tons carrying capacity each: Provided, Such bonds are issued at the time of completion and enrollment of such steamship or steamships, or within one year thereafter: and Provided further, That by the express terms of said mortgage, at least ten per cent. of the total issue of said bonds shall be retired annually, beginning within two years from the date of said bonds, and that the mortgage liability against said property shall not exceed one-half of its actual cost: and Provided further, That the trustees of such mortgage shall be required to protect the lien of said mortgage by attending to the recording thereof and by causing property covered by said mortgage to be insured against all risks on vessel property ordinarily covered by such insurance, including marine risks and disasters, general and particular average, collision liability, protection and indemnity insurance, and insurance against liability for injuries to persons, in insurance companies and under forms of policies approved by the trustees, for an amount equal to the full insurable value of such steamship, such insurance to be made with such loss payable to said trustee, and the policies deposited with it: and Provided further, That there shall be filed with the commissioner of the banking department of this state a schedule of the insurance upon such property, which schedule shall be signed by the trustee under said mortgage and shall be accompanied by the certificate of said trustee that the policies mentioned in the said schedule are held by said trustee and are payable to said trustee in case of loss for the benefit of the holders of the outstanding bonds issued under such mortgage; and further, that similar certificates be filed from time to time by said trustee with said commissioner of the banking department of this state, evidencing renewals of said insurance by proper policies or legal, insurance binders: Provided further, That by the terms of such mortgage, the mortgagor shall not suffer such steamship to become indebted in an amount exceeding five per cent. of the original amount of the principal of said mortgage at any time and that the failure of the mortgagor to forthwith secure the release of such steamship or steamships from mechanics', laborers', admiralty, statutory or other liens, claims or charges against such steamship, shall constitute a default in the provisions of such mortgage: and Provided further, That such bonds shall have been approved by the securities commission hereinafter provided for."

These bonds came into use after 1890, when steel vessels began to displace the old wooden ships on a large scale. Since then, a large and increasing volume of these bonds has been sold, without a single record of default. Of these bonds a growing proportion is given better security by a lien on a whole fleet of boats, or on terminal and other property in addition to the vessels themselves. Several issues have also appeared which were put out by a holding company, which pledges bonds and stocks of its subsidiary operating companies to secure the issue. In the latter case, the securities of the subsidiaries should be closely scrutinized for limitation on additonal loans.

There is a marked and highly desirable uniformity of conditions under which the steamship bonds of the Great Lakes are being issued. The boats pledged are steel-clad vessels, of A1 rating in the Registers, designed, say, to carry down cargoes of wheat from Duluth to Buffalo, and return between decks cargoes of package freight. They may be steel freighters built to carry ore eastward from the mines of the Messaba district. They may be coalers or other carriers of the enormous Great Lake traffic.

The classification societies will give such steamship an A1 rating for 20 years. The bonds, issued in amount to about one-half of the cost of the vessel, mature within ten years in about equal annual series. The equity, therefore, grows more rapidly than in the case of equipment bonds.

Insurance. The necessities of ample insurance protection are even more easily realized in the case of these single boat bonds. It should be imperative by the terms of the mortgage that the general insurance itself considerably exceed the bonded indebtedness and cover, not only the liabilities of collision, sinking, etc., previously mentioned, but also the breaking of machinery and bursting of boilers, and any hurt to the vessel through the negligence of master or crew.

In addition to full general insurance, the vessel will carry protection and indemnity insurance against liability for loss of life or personal injury. The bond circular should state the respective amounts of general and indemnity insurance, and the mortgage should stipulate the minimum of each permitted. It is to be doubted if the terms of the mortgage are usually strict enough or explicit enough, for frequently the interest of the owners makes them carry an insurance in excess of the requirement.

Earnings. The supervision of the trustee will extend beyond matters of insurance. The trust company will see to it that the company owning the vessel does not contract a temporary indebtedness in excess of the necessary operating expenses. As a rule the mortgage limits this amount to $1,000. The trust company will require that a statement of the earnings and expenses of the vessel be returned to it, say quarterly, in order that it may know how the vessel is being managed.

Another way in which the mortgage may require that the vessel operate on practically a cash basis is by providing that it may become indebted in an amount not more than 5 per cent. of the bonds.

The construction of new, or the extension of the present systems of transportation by rail, canal, or river, cannot, it seems, cripple the freight business of the Great Lakes for many years to come, at least, and so endanger the earning power of vessels now being built and bonded. Ore will continue to be dug, and wheat to be cut, in the Northwest, after all the outstanding loans have matured. According to engineering reports, the ore ranges have an assured life at present rates of production of 20 to 30 years.

New standards of luxury may call for the relegation of passenger boats to inferior and less profitable service, but freight carriage is independent of fashion, and governed by laws almost mathematical. Hence, it is well carefully to avoid liens on passenger vessels.

But even if it is conceivable that the Lake traffic, passenger or freight, could diminish to the extent of making certain lines unprofitable, there are other waterways adapted to the same service. Whalebacks, through prejudice or inadaptability, and other special and abortive types, might encounter greater resistance to occupancy of other waters, but the prospect is remote. Moreover, every year diminishes, by about 10 per cent., the necessary interest of the bondholders in the future of Lake transportation.

CHAPTER XXVIII

PUBLIC UTILITY SECURITIES

Definition and Classification. A public utility may be defined as an enterprise organized under special privilege to provide a service considered necessary or desirable by a community and regarded as a public function. Public utilities are affected with a public interest [1] but so also are enterprises not commonly regarded as such. The manner in which public interest is affected is the essential criterion when one has classification in mind. The usual list of public utility enterprises consists of so-called franchise corporations, such as electric light and power, hydro-electric, and electric traction corporations, gas companies, water supply companies, and telephone and telegraph companies. Technically all common carriers are included; but railroads, as observed from the previous chapters, are given separate classification because of their earlier development and greater magnitude. There are other enterprises frequently classed by the various states as public utilities, such as heating companies, warehouse and storage companies, concerns engaged in the conveyance of oil or gas by pipe line, refrigerating corporations, grain elevators, sewerage corporations, bridge, wharf, or turnpike corporations, express and sleeping-car companies, and in some southern states ice companies and even cotton gins.

Franchises. The investor is directly interested in the nature and duration of the contract between the government and the public utility, for this contract expresses the special privileges and obligations. Failure to recognize the mutuality of the undertaking, as evidenced by the terms of the franchise, has often proved disastrous to both the public and the investor. Therefore the need of satisfactory operating agreements is apparent.

There have been many attempts to arrive at a satisfactory solution of this contractual relationship, and use has been made

---

[1] See Munn vs. Illinois, 94 U. S. 113, 1877; also Charles Wolff Packing Co. vs. Court of Industrial Relations of State of Kansas, 267 U. S. 552, April 13, 1925.

of four general types of franchises: (1) long term or perpetual, (2) short term, (3) indeterminate and (4) service-at-cost. At first the public utility was not well regarded, and the only effective means of control was through either actual or potential competition. Long-term and even perpetual franchises, with their irrevocable provisions, predominated. These contracts implied a static condition. They lacked the flexibility that made the terms adaptable to changing conditions.

From the state's viewpoint, an obvious correction of the evil was time limitation of the franchise, commonly to twenty-five years. Perhaps even greater evils arose under this short-term than under the perpetual contract. The efficiency of the service invariably declined a few years before the termination of the franchise, unless there was adequate assurance of a renewal. Necessity of renewal resulted in political bickerings with their attendant evils which adversely affected the investment status of the securities concerned. The bondholder should acquire only those securities which mature several years in advance of the expiration of the franchise, for otherwise the utility is compelled to resort to costly short-term financing. This is well illustrated by the present uncertainty and the attendant low price of the Chicago Railway 5s of 1927.

Recognizing the mutual advantage of satisfactory franchise agreements, several states attempted the solution of the problem through indeterminate franchises. Massachusetts led the movement, but Wisconsin has made the greatest progress in this direction. The indeterminate or terminable permit makes possible revocation by the government whenever adequate service at just and reasonable rates is not rendered. The necessary corollary from the viewpoint of the company is flexibility of service standards and of rates in harmony with changing conditions. With the creation of public utility commissions, the essential provisions of the indeterminate franchise are rendered practicable. Economical purchasing, efficient service at reasonable rates, modern plants, cheaper financing, and more general satisfaction are some of the outgrowths. Then, too, assurance of the continuity of satisfactory working relations between the interested parties, or a fair purchase price of the company's property at its going value, materially improves the investment position of the securities.

The fourth kind of franchise, which is of recent origin and the outgrowth of the sliding-scale franchise used in a city as Boston, is known as " service-at-cost." This type is applied principally to urban railways. With this kind it is necessary that valuation of the property serve as a basis for rate making or for public purchase. A suitable rate of return is determined, and when any excess is paid to the security holders there must have been previously a reduction in the fare; or, as in Chicago, after the stipulated rate (5 per cent.) on the capital value is paid, the utilities receive a percent age of the remaining profit (in Chicago 45 per cent.), the balance accruing to the municipality. Therefore the company and the public enter into a sort of partnership arrangement designed for their mutual advantage. Opponents of this type of franchise assert that inefficiency results and investment incentive is stifled. If this be true the investor is likely to suffer a decline in the value of his securities. Experience thus far does not justify such a fear, although the tendency seems not improbable. Incentive provisions in the franchise have been designed to obviate this objection.

Financial Aspects. The investor in public utility securities should carefully consider certain financial aspects. Fixed charges should be compared with the earnings available for their payment. In general interest charges should not exceed one-half of the income available for their payment, and earnings available for dividends on preferred issues should be at least twice the requirements. It is also customary to compare the property investment in utilities with the total capitalization, and normally there is a rather close correspondence between them. Attention should also be directed to the financial policy of the companies.

Expansion, so essential to modern development in utilities, is frequently checked to the distress of all interested parties, including the old security holders. Approximately one billion dollars is required annually for the development of the power and light industry alone, and about $500,000,000 additional for the other utilities. The Commonwealth Edison Company of Chicago, for instance, spent $26,900,000 for extensions and improvements in 1923; over $30,000,000 in 1924, and about $16,500,000 in 1925, when its authorized capital stock was increased from $100,000,000 to $125,000,000. During 1926 the company spent about $33,500,000. Likewise the American

Telephone & Telegraph Company requires enormous sums to provide for its ever-increasing expansion program. In 1924 the authorized capital stock was increased $125,000,000, the amount issued and sold on instalment increased $163,843,000, but the funded debt was reduced $38,203,000, making a net capital increase of $125,639,000, while in 1925 the capital stock increase amounted to $33,119,000 and that of the funded debt to $116,-071,000, showing a total increase during 1925 of $149,190,000. Even greater capital increases in public utilities will take place in the future. In fact the capital structure of to-day may be quite different from that of tomorrow. Progressive financing is indispensable to prosperous communities, because of the many new uses to which the service is put. Although increase of population does not result in geometric increase in demand for service, it does require more than a proportionate increase. This is especially true of street railways.

The application to be made of the funds procured from the sale of securities should not be ignored by the investor. Investment funds should be used for productive purposes. So important is this principle that most states in their public service commission laws specify the purposes for which stocks, bonds, notes or other evidences of indebtedness may be issued. The New York statute[1] restricts the application of funds to uses " necessary for the acquisition of property, the construction, completion, extension or improvement of its plant or distributing system, or for the improvement or maintenance of its service or for the discharge or lawful refunding of its obligations, provided . . . [that the] indebtedness is reasonably required for the said purposes of the corporation."

Relation of Bonds to Stocks. The proportion of bonds to stocks in a typical public utility is quite different from that in an industrial. Not much over 25 per cent. of the total industrial capitalization usually consists of bonds, whereas with utilities from 50 to 60 per cent. is common occurrence, and even as high as 75 per cent. is at times reached. In fact S. Z. Mitchell, President of the Electric Bond and Share Company, favors a rather high percentage of funded debt to total capitalization.[2] There seems some justification for the large percentage in the case of

---

[1] Laws of New York, 1907, Vol. I, Art. IV, § 69, pp. 930–931.

[2] See *To-day's Problems in Public Utility Finance*, 1920.

holding companies, or for other control purposes, in order to effect control of operating subsidiaries without the necessity of large contributions by the organizers, but a more desirable capital structure would restrict the bonds to 50 per cent. or at most 60 per cent. of the total capitalization,[1] preferred and common stock each to about 20 per cent. Because of the stability of the gross revenues of utilities a larger percentage of funded to total capitalization is permissible.

Perhaps the wisest legislation regarding the relation of bonds to stocks is that which does not fix the percentage, but leaves this problem to the commission, as is true in Illinois. In Massachusetts the law restricts bonded debt to 50 per cent. of the total outstanding capitalization, California permits 75 per cent., Wisconsin 75 per cent. of the total value of or investment in the property, and the New York, Second District, to an amount not to exceed fixed charges that are reasonably sure to be earned.[2]

Many investment bankers favor a rather substantial issue of bonds provided there is adequate security. As bonds are sold on a lower basis of yield than stocks, a larger percentage of the earnings become available for dividends than could otherwise be the case, and therefore stockholders frequently assent to substantial debt. If the stock issue is relatively small its market price will be subject to a wider range of fluctuation, so tending to rise and fall with current earnings. The American Telephone & Telegraph Company has noticeably decreased its percentage of funded debt in the last few years. The fact that the company is earning rather large returns on the total capitalization, with the possibility of adverse public sentiment if the percentage of earnings were substantially to increase, together with the comparative ease with which it disposes of its stock, justify its present policy. Then, too, it is preparing splendidly for any financial distresses by its relatively low fixed charge. From this viewpoint the ideal capitalization is all common stock.

Public utilities at times use coupon notes running from two to

---

[1] But see Charles S. Morgan, *Regulation and Management of Public Utilities,* pp. 311 et seq.

[2] For authority of commission to control security issues and pronouncement regarding percentage of bonds to value of property, see Alabama Public Service Commission et al. vs. Mobile Gas Co., P. U. R. 1926, C. 266.

five or to ten years but secured only by the general credit of the company. They are intended primarily for short-term financing, and the length of time they are permitted to remain outstanding depends on the status of the money market and on the company's own condition. Short-term notes are used by street railway companies to finance the acquisition of rolling stock instead of the serial notes employed by the railroads.

Since rates are fixed by the public service commission, more or less independently of the capitalization of the utility, rates tend to control the capitalization, rather than the converse. Therefore the investor in his analysis of the capital structure should compare the rates permitted with the average of other utilities operating under similar conditions; he should learn the attitude of the public toward them; and the net returns based on the existing rates. Such a study would reveal any tendency to over- or under-capitalization.

Public Control as an Investment Factor. The idea that competition in industry is always conducive to increased efficiency at reduced costs to the consumer has gradually given way to the conception that certain activities are essentially monopolistic in nature, and therefore, should not be subjected to competitive tests but rather to regulative supervision. This conclusion is the outgrowth of years of costly experimentation by both the enterprisers and the public. In harmony with experience the public has sought other methods to secure continuous, efficient, and undiscriminating service at reasonable rates. Utilizing its police power, the state has established various means of regulation designed to achieve this service.

The history of the development of regulation is interesting but not within our province. Our concern is primarily in the present relations between the public and their utilities as established by legislative acts and judicial interpretation and in the probable future tendencies.[1] Following the early lead of New Hampshire and Rhode Island which in 1844 established railroad commissions for regulative purposes, other states have created

[1] Students interested in a comprehensive discussion of this entire subject will find enlightenment in John Bauer, *Effective Regulation of Public Utilities*, Charles S. Morgan, *Regulation and the Management of Public Utilities*, L. R. Nash, *The Economics of Public Utilities*, and Lamor Lyndon, *Rate Making for Public Utilities*.

commissions, and at present only Delaware is without some form of commission regulation.

There is substantial variation in the powers and duties of the commissions, but in general, legislation does not lose sight of the fundamental purposes of establishing reasonable rates, maintaining satisfactory service standards and assuring financial stability.

Rates. Rate regulation has been the most controversial problem before the commissions. Both the courts and the legislatures have attempted to define the " fair value " of the utility property as a basis for rate making, but as yet, no accepted meaning has been evolved. On the one hand, the Smyth vs. Ames decree (169 U. S. 466, May 7, 1898) requires a " fair return on fair value " with all its vagueness, with which later decisions have concurred without clarifying the meaning of this generalization for practical rate making. On the other hand, the legislatures with due regard to present and future values, have been slow in prescribing definite measures and in providing means of effecting a continuous and automatic control of rates. Likewise extensions, improvements and the acquisition of additional properties should be supervised to the advantage of all parties concerned.

One must not assume, however, that even though construction and improvements and the ensuing increase in capitalization are approved by a commission, there is any guarantee of satisfactory return on the additional investment. Efficient management should be expected to earn a fair return on the capital actually devoted to the service of the public, but it may not. Past performance and all the factors contributing to future operations must form the basis of judgment. Are the returns sufficient to defray all operating expenses, charges of the government, a proper return on the capital devoted to the business, and in addition a sum sufficient to provide for contingencies, also are these returns created by rates that do not appear excessive in comparison with rates charged by other companies operating under similar conditions? Public sentiment cannot be ignored, for an adequate rate of to-day may suffer reduction under public agitation to-morrow.

Valuation. Valuation may be undertaken as a basis for purchase or condemnation, taxation, capitalization or rate making. To attempt a comprehensive discussion of all these objects is beyond our purpose. Valuation as far as it affects rate making is the essential matter to an investor and therefore will engage our attention. As previously stated fair and reasonable rates cannot be ascertained without due consideration of the value of that part of the property devoted to public use and also to the nature and cost of the service rendered. In fact, so closely allied are these three factors that a discussion of any one involves the others.

A number of methods have been devised to ascertain the value of public utility properties for rate making, but as yet none has become standard. Those most frequently used are: [1]

      (a) Original or actual cost.
      (b) Reproduction cost.
      (c) Replacement cost.
      (d) Combination of all contributing factors.

Original Cost Valuation. If the investor is assured that a reasonable valuation will be placed on the physical properties now in use and that proper recognition will be given intangible values, his further concern may be respecting the efficiency of management and the suitability of the territory operated. He will not expect more than a fair return on the property devoted to public use, and will, therefore, be inclined to favor a valuation based on the actual or original cost of the property being used. Supporters of the original cost method claim that it involves less likelihood of later downward revaluations to the distress of both bondholders and stockholders. Likewise, it is contended the public will recognize the fairness of rates based on this kind of valuation and will clamor less for rate adjustments.

The many difficulties[2] involved in the determination of original cost need not occupy our attention. The commissions and courts have endeavored to use original cost with all other contributing factors, such as the capitalization of the utility, reproduction cost of the plant at present prices, market price of the securities,

---

[1] Reports of the Committee on Valuation of the American Electric Railway Association, for 1921, 1922, 1923, 1924, 1925, classify the leading cases on the various methods used to ascertain fair valuation. It will be observed that no one method prevails, but that the dicta point to a choice of the reproduction theory, whereas actual decisions are based on original cost with due consideration of reproduction cost as supplementary evidence.

[2] See W. H. Maltbie, *Theory and Practice of Public Utility Valuation*, Chap. I.

and replacement cost, in the ascertainment of a fair value for rate-making purposes. Therefore it will be observed that no single standard is adequate in most cases, especially of old properties where the cost records are either incomplete or inaccessible.

Reproduction Cost Valuation. The second method of valuation, the cost of reproduction, at best is nothing more than a check on the original cost basis.[1] Cost of reproduction involves the cost at present prices to reproduce the plant under the conditions existing at its establishment. To ascertain this basis for rates involves the ever-recurring task of new investigations with each adjustment of rates. Then, too, there will result a permanent disadvantage to the stockholder, if the valuation is made at a time when prices are below those which obtained at the time of acquisition; on the other hand, a disadvantage to the public if the converse be true. In periods of declining prices, the public will suffer if the valuation has been determined at higher price levels, but the security holder will profit as the purchasing power of his return will have increased.[2] But observe that the bondholder does not receive any material advantage from rate changes unless they affect the income of the corporation to such an extent as to render the rate confiscatory and thereby to undermine the integrity of his investment. In other words, the bondholder expects only a stipulated money return and is not primarily interested in increased income to the utility, since it all accrues to the benefit of the stockholder. The bondholder, therefore, is concerned with a valuation based on the commitment of his funds to public use, or the original actual investment, and such valuation, plus additional investments, may serve as a permanent basis for rates. In this way there is a definite basis which destroys the element of uncertainty in the valuation proceedings for rate-making purposes. Although there is some basis for the opinion that the United States Supreme Court favors cost of reproduction, yet its actual decisions incline toward the original cost basis.[3]

[1] John Bauer, *Effective Regulation of Public Utilities*, Chaps. V and VI, gives an instructive discussion of this subject.

[2] For an opposite view see L. R. Nash, *The Economics of Public Utilities*, Chap. VII. Note particularly pp. 162 et seq.

[3] Georgia Railway & Power Co. vs. Railroad Commission of Georgia, 262 U. S. 625, 1923.

Replacement Cost. The replacement method does not involve the valuation of the property now in use, but has to do primarily with the cost of plant and equipment designed to render service equally satisfactory to that already being given. Improved methods frequently require the complete abandonment of old properties to make room for more efficient plants, such as the substitution of busses for urban and interurban rail systems. Without adequate assurance the investor is likely to discover suddenly that the equity in back of his mortgage is entirely eliminated and that he is " holding the bag." It is advisable, therefore, to ascertain the attitude of the public service commission relative to the protection of the property devoted to public use, otherwise he is likely to experience a considerable diminution in the market price as well as in the actual value of his commitments. To the investor the replacement method is unsatisfactory, since no consideration is given to the original or to the present value of his investment.

Combination Valuation. Undoubtedly, original cost is the most desirable valuation method whenever applicable, as in the case of new properties constructed since the origin of modern accounting practice. But since it is often impossible to use this method in many instances, a combination of all methods should be employed in order to give the most complete information available. Frequently courts have been compelled to resort to the combination method even to approximate a fair rate basis. The necessary latitude involved creates a combination of conjecture and fact that increases the speculative aspect of the securities involved. After such a basis has been established, however, future investments may be added at cost to provide a permanent rate base.

In addition to valuation of the physical properties there are other elements of value that must not be ignored. Too frequently there is a tendency to underestimate the importance of, or to ignore entirely, working capital requirements. This error was especially true in earlier decisions. Adequate allowance for working capital is essential and is now generally reckoned.

Going concern worth, as an element in valuation, is now usually allowed both by the commissions and the court, although controversy over it still exists. That there is a legitimate cost of establishing a business and that there is frequently a loss involved during the early stages of development cannot be denied. Any other intangible values that present an actual outlay of funds or a forbearance of return on capital investment should be added to the physical value, if the rate base is to be fair and reasonable. If these items have already been included in the capital assets, further consideration of them will be unnecessary.

In spite of our firm conviction that the original cost, or investment, method is the only logical economic basis of valuation for rate-making purposes,[1] the fact cannot be ignored that the legal aspect, as evidenced by many recent decisions, is paramount, and that therefore, economic principles must necessarily be relegated by the investor to a secondary position. To be practical, therefore, the utility should offer as evidence of fair value not only the original cost, but also the present reproduction cost, the present fair value, as well as the future probable trend in prices. By this method only can the utility guard its interests against marked fluctuations in earnings. The cautious investor will analyze the basis or bases of valuation on which the rates are fixed.

Service. Undoubtedly the paramount concern of the consumer is the nature of the service rendered. Even the charge for it is secondary. In fact it is rather difficult to conceive of a satisfactory rate for service without first ascertaining the quality of the service rendered. Commissions are continually passing on the question of adequate service, and in most cases have established rather complete standards to which the utility must either conform or incur disapproval.

Recognizing the importance of fixing some standard measurement of satisfactory service, about twenty-five states have adopted state-wide gas service standards; thirty-one [2] electric service standards; and fourteen water service standards. These service-standard rulings cover the following subjects: Furnishing and discontinuing service, efficiency of service, measurement of service, payment for service, publicity required of utility, reliability of service, safety.[3]

[1] An excellent exposition of this principle is contained in "Proceedings of the American Railway Accountants' Association," 1924, pp. 98 et seq.

[2] United States Bureau of Standards, circular No. 56. "Standards for Electric Service," Sept. 26, 1923.

[3] For a comprehensive discussion of service standards as applied to various kinds of public utilities see Cooke, M. L., *Public Utility Regulation*, pp. 73–136. See pp. 75–76 for above headings.

The quality of the service required predetermines its cost, and therefore is the chief determinant of the rate charge. As previously stated, the investor must see to it that his company is permitted to establish rates sufficient to provide for all operating expenses, taxes, depreciation, a fair return on the capital devoted to public use, and to allow sufficient reserves for contingencies. The net return in back of his investment is directly affected by all requirements for improved service. There is also less likelihood of unfavorable public agitation if the service rendered is efficient even though the charges therefor seem more excessive than if the rates are low but the service poor. Experience teaches the fallacy of allowing the efficiency of the service to decline with the excuse of inadequate returns, and, by such means, of seeking higher rates. Efficient service should be maintained; then the company will be in a position to petition for rates necessary to a continuation of the service.

Capitalization. Attention has been called to the desirable proportion of bonds to total capitalization. The commissions, in their assent to increased issues, are generally conscious of the importance of an equity adequate to support the mortgages and also of the necessity of earnings sufficient to defray operating expenses, and the interest charges, and still show adequate returns on the outstanding stock. The object of a commission is not to afford protection for the bondholder as such, but primarily to safeguard the interests of the public which would likely be sacrificed if liquidation were to follow default in payments of interest and principal. To assure themselves of the proper application of the funds received from the sale of securities, the commissions usually require signed affidavits of officials attesting the use of the funds as outlined in their application for increased capitalization. As a result of commission regulation of capital structure, the investor feels that there has been a rather intensive and intelligent investigation of the purposes to which his commitments will be devoted, and the general assurance that there is reasonable probability that earnings will justify the outlay.[1]

Accounting. Intelligent regulation requires compilation of reliable data on which to base sound conclusions. Therefore virtually all states in their public utility legislation vest control

[1] A comprehensive discussion of capitalization will be found in Milton B. Ignatius, *The Financing of Public Service Corporations*, Part IV.

of accounting procedure in their commissions. The data thus gathered are of value for other purposes than rate and service regulation. Uniform information offers the investor opportunity to compare various utilities or the same utility over a period of years, and thereby assists an intelligent selection of suitable bonds. Reliable statistics also assist the management by furnishing comparative records of past performance which indicate the tendencies toward weakness as well as toward strength. Then, too, accurate data for taxation purposes are made available.

The data are summarized in the form of income statements, reflecting the operations during particular periods of time, and balance sheets showing conditions as of certain dates. The former relate to revenues and operating expenses, and the latter to capital structure. Comparative studies of these two statements indicate the trend of activities. The tendency toward uniformity in public service accounting has progressed much further than any in the industrial field, and consequently a more exhaustive analysis of utility securities is possible.

Depreciation. Depreciation includes both a loss in value of tangible property because of inadequacy, obsolescence, decrepitude, or supersession, and also a loss in value of intangible property through abandonment or time limitation. The causes of depreciation of physical assets may be physical, functional, or contingent; intangible assets may depreciate through a lapse of time or abandonment, as with patents, trade-marks, franchises, etc. That depreciation due to some cause exists with all properties is incontrovertible. A management is often judged by its treatment of depreciation.

From the accounting standpoint depreciation is a charge against past operations, and should be allocated to each unit of output, so that the consumer thereof may be charged with the actual cost of production. The duration of the usefulness of the depreciating property is being continually thereby lessened; it is rendered less valuable; ultimately it will have to be replaced. The integrity of the original investment must be maintained, or subsequently when it becomes necessary to replace the original plant there will not have been provided the necessary wherewithal. Operating costs should contain an item sufficient to provide for the constant decrease in value of all depreciating properties so that the integrity of the capital contribution may not be impaired. A depreciation charge simply withholds part of earnings from the surplus available for dividends, the amount of which may be reflected in any one or more of the assets. Failure to make such provision causes a gradual but persistent decline in the investment, the bondholders' equity is imperceptibly narrowed and the general credit of the company in the end is impaired.

In valuation proceedings the courts have usually required a deduction for depreciation from either the original or the reproduction cost. This deduction is made, whether or not the utility has been prudent enough to charge rates sufficient for it in the past. If the management has made adequate provision for depreciation, the value of the assets as a whole will be maintained, even though that of a particular asset may have declined. Therefore a deduction by a commission for depreciation in valuation cases will not impair the original investment, provided the depreciation reserve accumulated is equal to the ascertained depreciation. Depreciation then is a safeguard against substantial reduction by a commission, in book or original value, and it also provides for the complete replacement of the asset on its abandonment. The concern of the investor is not involved in the controversial methods of calculating depreciation or the technical accounting problems, but rather in the adequacy of the provision for depreciation and the application of the earnings withheld.

The plausible argument that depletion takes place but that depreciation does not exist has some merit in the case of assets that lend themselves to periodic replacement and are of comparatively small value, such as railway ties, tools, and the like, but it is not convincing with regard to large units the replacement of which would levy an excessive burden on the earnings of any single year. Also the fact must not be overlooked that the chief purpose of depreciation is to charge each unit of output with its proportionate cost of production and thereby to maintain the original investment in the property rather than the property itself. The present consumers are not required to acquire property for future users. Hence much can be said in favor of the practice of utilities of charging rates sufficient to provide for adequate depreciation and interest on the investment but not for the retirement of the debt incurred to acquire the properties. The bondholder will also be protected, for the reserved earnings will be applied to the acquisition of other assets as an offset to those depreciated.

Taxes. According to 1923 figures compiled by the Pennsylvania Public Service Information Committee,[1] the public utilities of the United States, including railroads, paid 24.3 per cent. of all the taxes collected from corporations by federal, state, and local governments. Of a total paid by all incorporated industries amounting to $2,572,000,000, the public utilities and railroads paid $625,000,000. Taxes of the utilities amounted to 33 per cent. of their net income for the year.

There can be no serious objection to this rather heavy burden provided it can be passed on by the utility to the consumer.[2] If in the establishment of the rate base, the taxes (usually excluding income tax), are included in operating expenses and a fair return on a fair value is allowed after deduction, the investor cannot take serious exception to high tax rates. But there is the possibility that rate increases to meet the high taxes will discourage the use of the service and that substitutes will be adopted. In such a case the utility would suffer decreased returns.

Though there may be no appreciable loss to the utility when disproportionate taxes are demanded, yet there will be an inequitable distribution, for the consumer will pay more than his share of general taxes to the advantage of the public not using the service. Without entering into a discussion of the incidence of taxation and the justification for methods of collection, it is sufficient that the investor becomes directly interested when the burden cannot be passed on, that is, when the tax is not included in operating expenses in computing net income, or when its imposition discourages patronage or incurs public disfavor.

Practically all forms of special taxes, as for franchises, mileage levies on railway tracks, special car taxes, maintenance of pavement, sprinkling, snow removal, free transportation of uniformed

[1] *The New York World*, May 26, 1926, p. 25.

[2] Freeport vs. Nassau & Suffolk Lighting Co., P. U. R. 1924 A., pp. 96 et seq. Public Service Commission of Montana vs. Mountain States Telephone & Telegraph Company, P. U. R. 1924 C., pp. 545 et seq. Duluth Street Railway Company vs. Minnesota Railroad & Warehouse Commission et al., P. U. R. 1925 D., pp. 226 et seq. Re Wisconsin Telephone Company, P. U. R. 1925 D., pp. 661 et seq. Public Utilities Commission vs. New England Telephone & Telegraph Company, P. U. R. 1926 C., pp. 207 et seq.

city employees, etc., are of such a nature that they frequently benefit the general public at the expense of the patrons of the utility. Franchises are given no value for rate-making purposes by commissions. Since public service corporations operating under them are so closely regulated that only a fair return is permissible, the franchises may often be valueless, and in that event not subject to taxation. Perhaps a better illustration of injustice to public service customers is the requirement that a street railway shall pave the space between the tracks and a stipulated distance on either side. The result is an improved highway for busses and other motor vehicles operating in competition with the railway but provided at the expense of the latter. The car rider provides a suitable roadway for his wealthier neighbor who uses his private car. Perhaps only through an appeal to the fairness of all tax contributions can the utilities be relieved of such unjustifiable discrimination.

Management. The establishment of public utility commissions naturally involves restriction on the management. The extent of control proper to be exercised is a matter of dispute. However, general opinion holds that commissions are not financial managers and their judgment as such may not be superimposed.[1] Yet this does not prevent commission inquiry as to efficiency of management, and where fraud or bad faith exists, the substitution of its judgment and the issue of definite orders for increased efficiency of service; but the details of effecting the changes must in the last analysis be vested in the management. Supervisory power must necessarily be retained in the commission if there is to exist a satisfactory basis for the determination of adequate service at reasonable rates. But it must be remembered that the state is not the owner of the utility and may not impose unreasonable requirements upon the management.

In determining rates the commission frequently considers efficiency of management and will not permit rate increases if there is inefficiency or lack of sufficient initiative to acquire additional available patronage. In other words, inefficiency must not be subsidized. The investor need not expect satis-

---

[1] Missouri ex rel. Southwestern Bell Telephone Company vs. Public Service Commission, P. U. R. 1923 C, 193. Re Northern States Power Company, P. U. R. 1924 A, 325. Re Union Electric Light and Power Company, P. U. R. 1924 A, 74.

factory returns by appeal to the commission if the management is inefficient.[1] Regulation does not assure reasonable returns on investment but does usually aim to make such a desirable situation possible.

The problems of public utility management are quite different from those characteristic of non-regulated competitive industries. Utility management tends toward decentralization, due to the supervisory power of the commissions and to the requirements of municipalities. While public service commissions tend to coöperate with the managements, municipalities frequently are antagonistic. Although the management is frequently confronted with serious problems arising from commissions' rulings and court decrees, as well as from municipal requirements, yet it is relieved of difficulties characteristic of competitive industry. For example, the cash basis of most utility service minimizes the problem of financing inventories, or the necessity of sound technical judgment in commodity markets. Then, too, the marketing of the product or service in a monopolistic industry is not the serious problem it is in competitive industries. It must not be implied that the management of utilities need not be progressive and seek outlets for increased product, but rather that the monopolistic nature of the service renders the task less difficult.

Bondholders are interested in the management because of their desire for a regular return on their commitment and also their concern for the safety of their principal. Immediate control is not vested in them and arises only in case of default. Hence the investor should see to it that the management has several years of successful experience and that indications point to continued efficiency. In the public utility field there have been comparatively few failures when an efficient management was in charge. The selection of a competent management affords, therefore, considerable assurance of the ultimate success of investment.[2]

The Holding Company. Because of the monopolistic nature of public utilities there developed an early tendency toward

[1] See Indiana Public Service Commission; Re Citizens Mutual Heating Company, P. U. R. 1924 A, 783; Re New Albany Waterworks, P. U. R. 1919 C, 984; and New Jersey Board of Public Utility Commission. Re Millville Electric Light Company, P. U. R. 1924 A, 318.

[2] See Charles S. Morgan, *Regulation and the Management of Public Utilities*, pp. 130 et seq., for a discussion of the motives of management.

combination. Wastes of competition demonstrated the necessity for combined efforts to eliminate duplication of plant, equipment and management. The movement toward consolidation usually had its origin within a single city, but in time there was a recognition of important advantages to be derived from the combination of interurban utilities.[1]

Among the most important reasons for the organization of holding companies have been the following: (1) Elimination of competition, (2) Economic advantages, (3) Financial advantages, (4) Application of technical skill by small subsidiaries, (5) Intelligent coöperation with the public, (6) Investment diversification, (7) Better service at reduced costs.

Ruinous competition proved unsatisfactory to public utilities, and there naturally developed an understanding between competing companies, either through a voluntary fusion or through ruthless absorption of the weaker by the stronger. Later, the feasibility of acquiring control of many independent companies without the actual investment of any considerable sum led to the use of the holding company as a means of consolidating separate organizations. It was evident that greater efficiency at reduced costs could be obtained through the unstinted application of technical skill, engineering, legal, and managerial; through economies arising from large-scale purchases and production, and cheaper financing, by a large company enjoying higher credit rating. Wide distribution of risk to investors is also made possible through the diversification of holdings by the holding company.

Although the advantages of the holding company are evident,[2] yet the investor must realize the accompanying tendency toward overcapitalization. Competition for control of public utility territory has resulted in excessive prices paid for operating companies by certain large holding organizations. There may be less of this tendency now than formerly, but the situation at present is not exactly ideal. The fact that the holding companies do not come under commission control makes possible inflated purchase prices and correspondingly inflated holding company capitalization. Many favor commission control of the holding

[1] See Cooke, M. L., *Public Utility Regulation*, Chapter 8.
[2] See Gerstenberg, Chas W., *Materials of Corporation Finance*, pp. 570 et seq., for reprint of Senate Bill 4160 on public utility holding companies.

company as well as of the operating company.[1] Pyramiding the financial structure is not only possible but probable unless the management is exceptional. Usually, therefore, the bonds of operating companies enjoying the advantages afforded by their holding company are more desirable than the collateral trust obligations of the latter. This is doubly true if the securities pledged as collateral are insufficient to give the bondholders control of the subsidiaries in the event that foreclosure becomes necessary.

It is necessary to examine the condition of the subsidiaries in order to determine the investment value of a holding company. Intelligent analysis becomes difficult, for detailed statements of the several companies are seldom available, and that of the holding company is given only in skeleton. An examination of the dividend record, both earned and paid, over a period of years, and the number of times fixed charges have been earned, offer the best index of the investment status of the bonds.

Centralized Management. A form of organization designed to retain all the advantages accruing to subsidiaries of holding companies and to eliminate the objections, is that which centralizes control in a trained staff employed to manage independent operating companies. There is no attempt under this form of supervision actually to control through stock ownership the various companies, but merely to lend financial, legal, engineering, accounting, and general managerial assistance for a stipulated compensation or as a means of providing an outlet for products of manufacture. This service is rendered by such companies as Electric Bond and Share Co., J. G. White Management Corporation, and Stone & Webster.

Thus the small company may obtain technical training of the highest order which would otherwise be prohibitive. If for any reason the utility no longer desires such service it may be eliminated, and in this respect the central management plan is in decided contrast to its permanency under the holding company.[2]

[1] But see *Proceedings of the Academy of Political Science*, Vol. XI, Number 4, pp. 147 et seq., in which Mr. John H. Pardee, President J. G. White Management Corporation, objects to commission control and Philip P. Wells, Deputy General of Pennsylvania, favors it.

[2] An enlightening address on this subject was delivered by Mr. Henry C. Bradlee of Stone & Webster entitled "Centralized Public Utility Management," 1921; published in pamphlet form by Stone & Webster, Inc.

Trend in Ownership. Services rendered by public utility corporations are indispensable. They must be furnished either by government or by privately owned utilities. There still exists some demand for municipal operation, but a better understanding of the relative advantages of public and private ownership will usually dispel public ownership movements. In fact, at considerable expense the public is more and more learning the advantage of private operation. Proof is the relative increase of private enterprise. According to the United States Census of Central Stations for 1922, private electric light and power companies in 1902 generated 92.2 per cent. of the total kilowatt-hours produced, whereas in 1922 they generated 95.3 per cent. In 1922 there were 2,581 municipal plants; in 1925 there were only 2,138.[1] Only 6.2 per cent. of the population of the United States is now served with electrical energy produced by municipal plants. Most of the municipal plants are in small towns of 1,000 population or less. Municipal gas plants serve less than 2 per cent. of the population; municipal electric railway mileage is less than 2 per cent. of the total.

Municipal Ownership. Statistics demonstrate clearly the failure of municipal ownership. According to the United States Census Report, municipal operations require 2.7 times as much fuel and labor (the chief items of expense) to generate one kilowatt-hour as private companies require. Political influence and the spoils system are causes of the general irresponsibility and inefficiency characteristic of municipal plants. Lack of incentive renders municipal employees indifferent and the system unprogressive, although the average rate is twice as high as that received by private companies. Even taxes are higher in cities municipally served.[2] There is also a noticeable tendency for municipal plants to discontinue the generation of electricity and to purchase power from private companies. In 1912 only 8.7 per cent. of the plants purchased private power; in 1925, 39 per cent. In 1925 the municipal railways purchased more than 80 per cent. of their electric power. With these handwritings on the wall prospective investors of utilities need pay little heed to politicians who advocate public ownership. Privately-owned

[1] See *Political Ownership and the Electric Light and Power Industry*, p. 14 and passim, published by the National Electric Light Association, 1926.

[2] Loc. cit., pp. 101–102.

and operated utilities under government regulation have demonstrated their desirability and will undoubtedly remain.

Customer Ownership. There is, however, another tendency in ownership which is likely to increase with time. In recent years utilities have distributed a considerable amount of their securities among customers and employees. The primary object of such a policy is the cultivation of good will, although the ostensible purpose is the lessened costs of financing. This movement is undoubtedly an effective offset to the agitation for municipal ownership, for owner-patrons become conservative and sympathetic. Good will is thereby enhanced. That the customers have appreciated the opportunity to acquire the securities of their local utilities is evidenced by the great increase in customer ownership. In 1914, the year of the introduction of the plan, 92,310 shares of stock were sold to 4,044 stockholders by seven electric light and power companies; in 1925 2,926,271 shares were sold to 236,043 stockholders, making in all 226 companies rendering service to a population of over 75,000,000.[1] In 1925 the market value of common stock sold amounted to $16,-781,000 and of preferred stock to $254,000,000, and the total of bonds and notes to $9,820,000. It will be observed that preferred issues constitute the great bulk of the securities acquired. By such means of financing, equity is provided for bond issues by patrons who are likely to assume a sympathetic attitude toward *their* company. In fact it is maintained that the effect of " customer ownership is the most powerful single factor in the events leading up to the present well-being of the electric light and power industry." [2]

Public Utility Bond Tests. In conclusion, there are stated below certain investment tests of public utility securities. Some are common to all business enterprises, but others are peculiar to the utility industry.

1. Bonds should be issued by electric light and power, gas, and telephone companies, or a combination of the first two services with traction companies, provided not more than from 25 to 30 per cent. of the net revenues are derived from the latter enterprise.
2. Interest on the entire funded debt should be earned at least twice during a period of not less than three years.

[1] Report of Customer Ownership Committee, 1925–1926, of National Electric Light Association.

[2] Ibid., p. 2.

3. Bonded debt should not exceed $1\frac{1}{2}$ times the capital stock nor 70 per cent. of the value of the property.
4. The ratio of funded debt to gross earnings should not exceed 4 to 1.
5. The franchise should exceed the life of the bonds at least five years, or it should be indeterminate.
6. Diversified types of customers should be served in a territory expanding in both population and industry.
7. The utility should operate under suitable franchise, or under a state public service commission.
8. Bonds should be protected by senior liens on property essential to the service, and if the mortgage is open it should contain satisfactory escrow provisions.
9. If marketability is required, the company should be well known, the issue should be at least $1,000,000 in amount, and the net earnings of the company available for total fixed charges at least $200,000.
10. The utility should operate under a virtual monopoly and enjoy the confidence of the public because of efficient service at reasonable rates and under competent management.[1]

[1] The bills presented in the New York legislature February 17, 1926, designed to make the securities of telephone, electric light and power, and gas companies legal investments for savings banks in the state of New York, contain even more drastic provisions than the foregoing. The bills passed the lower house, but were permitted to lapse in the Senate.

CHAPTER XXIX

STREET RAILWAY BONDS

Nothing more clearly illustrates the immature condition of the science of bond investment than lack of precision in its nomenclature. The preliminary steps in an inductive development of any science are, of course, examination, description, and division and classification. It is at the point of classification that necessity arises for an exact terminology. It matters little whether plants, minerals, or securities are under examination, the use of properly labelled inscriptions for the specimens, or the lack of use, is a matter of moment to real progress in the study.

The Title. At this point we want for a proper title to give the bonds of railway transportation concerns that are not steam railroad companies. As yet there is no uniformity of custom. " Electric Traction Bonds," " Electric Railway Bonds," and " Trolley Bonds " seem fairly inclusive and descriptive appellations, and have some vogue, but the cable is not yet obsolete. An objection of greater weight is that the distinction between electricity and steam as motive power will not serve many years longer to separate the present two great kinds of transportation.

On the whole, the most acceptable phrase, perhaps, is that in use on the exchanges: " Street Railway Bonds," meaning by this the bonds of all transportation companies (irrespective of motive power), the rails of which, whether laid on, below, or above the streets, or on private right of way in open country, bear freight and passengers as lighter local traffic, or as traffic tributary to centres of population, or tributary to long-haul steam railroad traffic.

Variety of Kinds. No other securities commonly classed together except " Industrial Bonds " represent so many and such varied activities as these. In this respect they are the opposite of gas bonds. The gas industry is old, its technical and financial problems are simple, well understood, and reasonably uniform throughout the country. The principles of gas investment, there-

354

fore, are easy to develop and apply. It is not hard to purchase gas bonds wisely. The same holds true of equipment bonds, except that these latter want the ripening of age that a century of life has given to gas securities. Street railway transportation is not only more complicated in its characteristics and problems than gas-manufacturing, or car-building, but it lacks also maturity and experience. Its future, therefore, is not definite, and it has not yet had enough in common with steam railroading to have taken over from that business, as conducted in this country, the body of financial principles learned through a half-century of vicissitude. So, at best, any generic treatment of street railway bonds will necessarily be unsatisfactory from the bond buyer's standpoint, for little can be said that will be immediately helpful to a wise choice of securities. It requires study and a nice discrimination to purchase street railway bonds without subsequent regret.

History. The Urban Road. Electric railroading in cities began in 1888 as an improvement upon horse traction. The history of its development for the next decade was that of its gradual emancipation from the function of an improved substitute for the horse-car line to its establishment, physically and financially, on the basis of its own peculiar strength and limitations as a means of urban transportation. In 1900 it might have been said to owe nothing to its predecessor but the fare register and the franchise. In recent years a new type of transportation, the motor line, has challenged the efficiency of the railways, and in some cases has justified the abandonment of the old for the new. Nevertheless the challenge has been successfully met, so that this new form may be regarded as an important auxiliary, but not as a complete substitute. The street railways, in other words, have demonstrated their necessity, especially in populous communities where mass transportation obtains.

Physical Factors Affecting Operations. Although the topographical problem is not so serious with urban railways as with interurban, and more especially with the steam roads, yet large sums have been expended for " fills " and " cuts " in order to eliminate grades. Usually the expense involved constitutes a capital charge, as it is almost entirely borne by the utility, even though the entire width of the street be graded. At times, it is difficult in cities either to eliminate or avoid grades, and therefore the costs of operation are materially increased and with greater probability of accidents if the grades are too precipitous.

Climatic conditions cannot be ignored, especially in those communities where snowfall is excessive and where the franchise requires the company to remove the snow at its own expense. The Boston Elevated Railway Co., at times, shows an operating profit or deficit depending directly upon the amount of snowfall. It is a condition over which a utility has practically no control but which materially affects its operating profits.

For the most part street railways, especially those municipally operated, find it more satisfactory to purchase power from electric light and power companies than to generate the energy themselves. Such arrangement requires a smaller investment and permits a direct focussing of attention on the problems of transportation proper. The Interborough Rapid Transit labor strike in New York in 1926, when many of the power men did not report for duty, well illustrates the advantage of purchasing power from the electric light and power companies, which are virtually free from labor disputes.

The present population, its rate of increase, the nature of the industrial activities of the community, the topographical and climatic conditions which more or less affect the riding habits of the people and the extent of local transportation must all be analyzed in evaluating the investment merits of street railway bonds. Although some of these factors affect primarily the capital stock, yet they all have a bearing on the value of the bonds. Mr. F. W. Doolittle in his *Cost of Urban Transportation Service*, Chapter XIX, quotes Dr. Mattersdorf as authority for the statement that the rate of increase in revenue passengers is as the square of the population in cities up to about 500,000 and thereafter only proportionately greater. On the other hand, another authority is cited for the conclusion that the increase cannot go on indefinitely, as a point of saturation in time is reached. Practically all authorities are agreed that progressive communities with increasing populations, create more than a proportionate demand for transportation service, provided that expansion of facilities corresponds with the growth of population. As the population becomes more widely distributed, there is more than proportionate increase in traffic. In small cities with a population less than 25,000 the annual number of rides per capita is usually less than 100, while in cities of 100,000 the number approximates 200, and in our largest cities over 300. Passenger traffic density is a test of operating revenue possibilities for urban railways just as it is for steam roads.

Difficulty arises, however, when the population of a city exceeds 1,000,000, for the surface lines then become inadequate to accommodate the demands satisfactorily. Subways and elevated lines, with enormously increased costs of construction, become necessary. In contrast to the costs per mile of road for surface lines, ranging from about $50,000 to $150,000, those for subway rapid transit lines at times exceed $5,000,000. However, the improved facilities permit greatly increased traffic which in turn affords revenue sufficient to offset the additional capital requirements. Also the many delays incident to surface transportation are thereby obviated.

Operating Statistics. The problems involved in the analytical study of street railways, require the orderly arrangement of all reliable data and the careful calculation of various ratios derived therefrom. For intelligent investigation uniform accounting procedure is essential, such as prescribed by the Interstate Commerce Commission for interstate electric railway systems and adopted by the American Street Railway Association for urban and interurban intrastate systems. In the use of such data for comparative purposes, the investor must exercise considerable caution since there are so many varying conditions affecting the operations that statistics are misleading unless interpreted in the light of the peculiar problems of each company.

Consolidated Statistics for 1925. According to the reports of 327 companies constituting approximately 90 per cent. of the earning power of the industry,[1] the total number of passengers carried by the reporting companies in 1925 was 14,511,690,825. Of this number 11,569,799,316 were revenue passengers, indicating a large number of transfers and free rides. The total operating revenue amounted to $832,506,416 and the net operating revenue to $221,753,745, with an operating ratio of 73.36

[1] The data used in this discussion are taken from Vol. XV, May 1926, No. 4, of AERA, the official publication of the American Electric Railway Association. Because of the tardiness of the reports of the U. S. Census on Electric Railways, the more recent data are used. Great care has been observed in their compilation and so they are sufficiently accurate for all practical purposes.

per cent. The miles of track operated by this group of companies were 31,189 and the revenue car miles were 1,971,496,303.

The report [1] divides the companies into various groups. In one arrangement they are classified as city, interurban, and combination companies operating both urban and interurban lines. In a comparison of results for 1924 and 1925, the city companies showed a smaller decline in the number of revenue passengers than either the interurban or the combination lines. In fact, there was an actual increase in operating revenue for the city companies as compared with decreases for the two other groups. The interurbans showed a reduction in operating expenses, due both to greater efficiency and to lower maintenance costs. The city companies showed the greatest per cent. of decline in power costs. The combination companies evidenced some improvement, but not so pronounced as that of the other groups. All three groups considerably increased their expenditures for advertising and other means for developing new business.

The operating ratio of the interurbans was 84.61 per cent. in 1925, of the urbans 73.38 per cent., and of the combined lines 76.9 per cent. In all the groups the ratio was still too high; for an operating ratio should be under 70 per cent. With further reduction of fixed charges these ratios would not be so objectionable. The interurbans reduced their interest charges 1.14 per cent. in 1925, the combination lines 7 per cent., but the urbans showed an increase of 1.7 per cent. However, the net operating results of the city lines more than offset the minor advantages possessed by the other groups. Both the interurban and the combination lines showed a deficit in 1925.

Of the city companies the greatest improvement is shown in those of medium size—with annual earnings from $250,000 to $1,000,000. A deficit of $417,000 in 1924 was converted into net income of $519,000 in 1925. The operating ratio was reduced, but the greatest improvement was the marked reduction in fixed charges by radical improvement in the financial structures. The large companies—those earning more than $1,000,000—were in the best position, with an increase over the previous year of 10.27 per cent. or $1,680,000 in net income. The small companies, earning less than $250,000, sustained a slight decrease in earnings or, rather, a slight increase in the deficit.

[1] Ibid., pp. 5–6.

The large interurban groups showed an operating ratio of 83.57 per cent. and a deficit of $2,800 in 1925. Neither the medium nor the small-sized interurbans evidenced improvements but showed deficits and also higher operating ratios. Perhaps the chief cause of their difficulty was decline in traffic.

With the combination companies the results were practically the same. The large companies reported a slight decrease in earnings of 2.77 per cent. and an increase in the operating ratio from 74.72 per cent. to 75.65 per cent. The medium-sized combination companies reduced their deficit from $1,526,000 to $1,346,000, while the small companies showed increases in both the deficit and operating ratio.

Ranking of the Three Groups. The foregoing survey of operating results shows that the city lines rank first, the combined city and interurban lines second, and the interurbans last. Again, of the city lines, the large companies with annual net earnings in excess of $1,000,000 are in the strongest position when viewed from the standpoint of operating ratios and net corporate returns. The medium-sized companies rank second, although they showed greater improvement than the large companies. The small companies rank last. Of the interurban lines, the large companies reported the most satisfactory conditions, and the medium and small-sized companies were more or less on a par. The large combination lines fared relatively better than the medium and small-sized companies.

Let us now direct our attention to the various units of measurements customarily used for analytical purposes and also examine the actual figures for the year 1925 for comparative purposes. In some cases the ratios may not be considered ideal nor even average for a period of years. They have at least the advantage of being recent and, on the whole, will be more satisfactory than average results derived from data compiled during abnormal conditions.

Consolidated Operating Statistics. The facts necessary to develop ratios for an intelligent comparative analysis of street railways may be found in the following table of statistics of 96 city, 49 interurban, and 76 combination companies for the year 1925.

OPERATING STATISTICS OF 221 STREET RAILWAY COMPANIES
DURING 1925

	96 City Companies	49 Interurban Companies	76 Companies Operating Both City and Interurban Lines	221 Companies
Railway operating revenue....	$378,513,379	$22,669,875	$145,076,575	$546,259,829
Per mile of single track......	$36,020	$7,487	$14,582	$23,260
Gross income................	$82,144,657	$4,235,308	$29,710,829	$116,090,794
Per mile of single track......	$7,817	$1,399	$2,986	$4,941
Passenger revenue...........	$369,248,085	$14,305,650	$125,329,071	$508,882,806
Per revenue passenger.......	6.8c	¹ 23.6c	² 7.8c	7.1c
Per total passenger.........	5.2c	¹ 22.5c	² 6.9c	5.7c
Per mile of single track......	$35,139	$4,725	$12,597	$21,668
Per passenger car mile......	44.4c	37.6c	40.2c	43.0c
Per car operated...........	³ $15,972	⁴ $21,165	⁵ $16,984	$16,302
Per passenger car hour......	⁶ $4.09	⁷ $6.13	⁸ $3.90	$4.07
Revenue passengers..........	5,424,784,581	¹ 54,653,444	² 1,474,106,555	6,953,544,580
Per mile of single track......	516,238	¹ 18,695	² 160,508	307,462
Per passenger car mile......	6.5	¹ 1.6	² 5.1	6.0
Per car operated...........	³ 227,662	⁴ 92,493	⁹ 229,937	226,859
Per passenger car hour......	⁶ 60	¹⁰ 37	¹¹ 56	59
Total passengers............	7,041,296,156	¹ 57,385,061	² 1,651,027,494	8,749,708,711
Per mile of single track......	670,070	¹ 19,630	² 179,768	– 386,884
Per passenger car mile......	8.5	¹ 1.7	² 5.7	7.6
Ratio:				
Transfer passengers to revenue passengers (per cent.)	29.1%	2.0%	10.0%	24.8%
Revenue car miles...........	836,591,328	47,762,458	334,882,516	1,219,236,302
Per mile of single track......	79,613	15,774	33,661	51.915
Per car operated...........	³ 36,340	⁴ 68,365	⁵ 44,863	38,91
Per car hour...............	⁶ 9.0	⁷ 14.2	⁸ 9.8	9.31
Car hours..................	⁶ 81,572,794	⁷ 1,768,776	⁸ 27,372,156	110,713,726
Per car operated...........	¹² 3,974	¹³ 9,964	¹⁴ 4,334	4,090

¹ 48 companies.	⁵ 57 companies.	⁹ 55 companies.	¹³ 29 companies.
² 74 companies.	⁶ 87 companies.	¹⁰ 34 companies.	¹⁴ 53 companies.
³ 83 companies.	⁷ 35 companies.	¹¹ 65 companies.	
⁴ 36 companies.	⁸ 67 companies.	¹² 76 companies.	

An examination of the above table shows the wide divergence of results among the three groupings. The fallacy of any attempt to set up comparative standards as between the groups is readily apparent, and if the detailed results of the various companies comprising the three groups were available the difference between each would be further apparent. Too much emphasis cannot be placed on the necessity of comparing lines which operate under similar conditions, otherwise the results are misleading.

This table indicates that the two important physical measurements are the car-mile and car-hour units. Car-mileage gives a measurement of the earnings of the cars actually used in the service; but since overhead expenses continue regardless of operations this unit can never be independently satisfactory. Nevertheless certain definite costs, such as motormen's and conductors' wages and maintenance costs can be definitely allocated, to the benefit of the analyst. Operating revenue per mile of single track is a useful unit, if compared with the per-mile capitalization, for it indicates the probable income available for capital charges. However, gross income per mile of single track should prove more instructive, for it indicates the amount actually available for interest and dividends.

Traffic Density and Diversity. The ratio of transfer passengers to revenue passengers indicates the extent of free transfers, and if the ratio is on the increase, a greater number of passengers will not necessarily increase the net returns.

Attention has previously been directed to the usual number of rides per capita in communities of various sizes. Earnings per capita, with the riding custom, will indicate the degree of saturation in the territory, and thereby assist in the determination of probable increased revenues. Such earnings range between $7.00 and $18.00.[1] Traffic density (ratio of average load to maximum load) and traffic diversity measure the effectiveness of the plant's utilization, and, if used cautiously, are essential factors in an analysis of operating costs. Taken over a period of years, the increase of total revenue passengers compared with increases in capitalization and mileage offers a good index of the growth of the entire system.

Operating Ratio. In an analysis of the income statement, the ratio generally considered is that of operating expenses to operating revenue, or known simply as the operating ratio. Many variable as well as constant factors affect this ratio. The various costs comprising overhead expenses remain fairly constant regardless of changes in volume of business, but other costs tend to fluctuate in harmony with the variations in output of either service or product. Since the ratio measures the relationship of operating expenses to operating revenue, it indicates the revenues available for taxes, fixed charges, and dividends. Therefore, consistent with efficiency, the lower the ratio the more desirable the investment results. Some utilities require a larger investment per unit of return than others, but with such larger requirements the operating ratio frequently will be lower. This fact is particularly noticeable in a comparison of the ratios of a steam-generating electric plant and of a hydro electric. The latter requires a considerably greater initial investment, but operating costs are less, and a larger net revenue remains for the more extensive claims of investors. A somewhat similar relation

[1] Nash, L. R., op. cit., p. 321.

exists between surface and rapid transit lines, but in this case traffic density is the dominant consideration.

Depreciation. The problem of proper retirement reserves, and their charge to operations is difficult of solution. However, the task of ascertaining a standard or rate is less serious with electric railways than with electric light and power and telephone companies, although the courts have usually made general rulings without specifically fixing the rate.[1] A street railway should be entitled to a depreciation allowance chargeable to operations sufficient in amount to permit each year the retirement of a number of cars or other depreciable property.

Vigorous attacks have been made on the methods of the steam and electric roads in charging to current operations not only all repairs and maintenance costs but also replacements of retired properties with no provision for depreciation. The underlying theory is that the property is being adequately kept up through maintenance costs or that there is an enhancement in value because of increased business resulting from the growth in population. In some cases legislation has been enacted requiring provision for depreciation reserves in order to offset the loss in value of the depreciable properties. The validity of the contention of the roads is questionable, especially when it is advanced to justify the issuance of new securities for replacements and renewals, as the street railways have done. Experience demonstrates the fallacy of this method as a general practice.

The establishment of a permanent rate of depreciation is particularly difficult, for costs and the various elements of depreciation are in constant process of change. The ruling that " the annual expense of depreciation should equal the original cost, less salvage, divided by the average life," [2] seems definite enough, but to ascertain the average life or depreciation rate, is no simple task with such a variety of equipment of uneven durability.

Further reference to the case cited above,[3] indicates a marked downward trend of depreciation charges in the telephone industry. The rate of depreciation depends not only on the character

---

[1] Maryland Public Service Commission, Re United Railways & Electric Company of Baltimore, P. U. R. 1924 D, 729.

[2] See Rhode Island Public Utility Commission vs. New England Telephone & Telegraph Company, P. U. R. 1926 C, p. 245.

[3] See Ibid., p. 245.

of the utility but also on the degree of standardization or development within the industry. Utilities in the development or transitional state will be compelled to scrap equipment, whose durability may be considerable but whose adequacy may be overcome by improved methods or rapid increases in demand.

Competition From Private Motor Cars. Consolidation of competing street railways, and public recognition that the industry is essentially monopolistic have resulted in the granting of more or less exclusive franchises and the development of greater confidence in the ultimate success of the industry. The advent of the automobile, however, has made serious inroads into the earnings of the street transportation companies, and has once more injected uncertainty into the system. At the close of 1925 there were about 20,000,000 motor vehicles registered in the United States, or one car to every six persons, together with a future annual factory output of something over 4,000,000 cars. The annual automobile bill for the American people is estimated to be in excess of $14,000,000,000, or $117 per capita. Naturally the existence of this great number of cars seriously affects the revenues of the electric railways. However, it seems that the competition from private automobiles is on the wane, due to the inconvenience, delay and increasing expense of personal driving in congested traffic subject to avenue stops, parking restrictions, and one-way streets. The tendency in large cities, therefore, is toward electric railways. Particularly in urban sections it seems that street railways have now passed through the period of severest competition from private cars.

Competition From the " Jitney " and Bus. The " jitney " business, however, has offered more persistent competition. It was first introduced on the Pacific Coast in 1914, but thereafter invaded almost all the larger communities throughout the country. High wages as an outgrowth of war conditions, increased regulatory measures, and the recognition that depreciation constitutes a large item of operating expense have greatly curtailed jitney competition so that it may no longer be considered a dangerous competitor, but rather a feeder to the electric railways.

A more formidable competitor to street railways is from bus service. To prevent dangerous inroads on earnings it became necessary for the railways to operate their own busses. In March

1926, there were 297 electric railway companies operating 5,455 motor busses over 12,308 miles of route.[1] Of the total companie3, 266 operated 5,329 busses over 12,073 miles of route in conjunction with railway operations. Thirty-one companies abandoned their railway property entirely and substituted 126 busses operated over 235 miles of route. On January 1, 1926, there were in service as common carriers 30,475 busses in intrastate business, 1,500 busses in interstate, 5,150 operated by electric railways, and 375 operated by the steam railroads, or a total of 37,500 busses.[2]

The following table reproduced from the report[3] of the American Electric Railway Association indicates the tremendous growth in the number of busses and miles operated by electric railways:

GROWTH OF BUS OPERATION BY ELECTRIC RAILWAY COMPANIES

	Number of Companies	Miles of Route	Number of Busses
January, 1921	16	35	73
December, 1921	27	..	131
July, 1922	38	..	174
January, 1923	56	878	355
August, 1923	99	1,043	768
January, 1924	110	1,300	1,100
August, 1924	138	2,355	1,886
January, 1925	171	4,285	2,660
September, 1925	251	12,060	4,452
March, 1926	297	12,308	5,455

On January 1, 1926, approximately 35 per cent. of the street railways operated busses, yet the number of busses operated totalled about 5,300 as compared with 82,000 electric railway cars, or only 6 per cent. of the latter. Electric railway busses, it is estimated, carried approximately 800,000,000 passengers in 1925, and the number carried by street railways was about 16,000,000,000.[4] On January 1, 1926, the electric railway mileage totalled approximately 46,000 miles of single track, and electric railway bus routes amounted to 13,000 miles.[5]

[1] For these figures and those immediately following see A. E. R. A. Bulletin No. 74, entitled *Electric Railways Operating Motor Bus Lines*, April 1, 1926.

[2] *Magazine of Wall Street*, July 17, 1926, p. 576, taken from Bus Transportation.

[3] Ibid., Foreword.

[4] *Electric Railway Journal*, January 2, 1926, p. 29.

[5] Ibid., p. 31.

The bus has proven its superiority over the electric railway in areas of light traffic density where infrequent service is required, and for auxiliary use to the railways as feeders. In the interurban sections of sparse population but with good roads the bus lines tend to supplant the interurban service. However, where there is need of mass transportation at high speed the electric lines continue to dominate. Store pick-up and delivery assists the truck service, and thus creates severe competition to interurbans for freight business. The public hearings of the Interstate Commerce Commission in 1926, will undoubtedly bring about legislative measures to regulate all trucks engaged in interstate traffic. The several states are likely to follow the lead of the government and also regulate intrastate service. Such legislation should prove beneficial to the freight traffic of the interurban lines.

In the last few years busses have been built more commodiously. In 1925 there was a weighted average seating capacity of 28.9 seats per bus for 91 large bus undertakings, operating 1,847 busses in city service, 231 in interurban service, and 974 in combined city and interurban service. The single-deck busses had seating capacity ranging from 7 to 33 seats; the capacity of the double-deck busses ranged from 55 to 67 seats.[1] Combined city and interurban lines operate the largest busses, city lines rank second and interurbans last.

Notwithstanding the coördination of service between electric and bus lines, which should assist the latter as well as the former in the transportation problems involved, it is generally recognized that bus lines continue to operate at substantial deficits. Only about 13 per cent. of the total bus lines in electric railway service operate at a profit. A great majority of the lines are unable to show profits even before the deduction of depreciation charges and taxes. Therefore as an independent business undertaking the bus line is, on the whole, uninviting, although it may result in disaster to the street railways if permitted to compete. Fortunately for the latter, busses can be subjected to the general principle of regulation as applied to other utilities. Bus transportation must be subjected to further economic tests, such as

[1] American Electric Railroad Association Bulletin No. 87, *Study of Operating Costs of Motor Bus Lines Operated by Electric Railways*, dated July 1, 1926, p. 4.

comparative convenience, costs, and general advantage. Experience thus far indicates the superiority of the street railways in congested areas requiring mass transportation and in rapid urban and interurban service demanding frequent service.

Regulatory Problems: Franchise. The first consideration in purchasing street railway securities is the nature of the franchise. A steam railroad's right of way, once obtained, is usually its possession for all time; but the electric railway by invading the principal streets and highways in most cases must accept its privileges as temporary or at least terminable, and must plan, finance, construct and operate always with the possibility of losing in time some portion of the results of its labors.[1] Sufficient pressure even may be brought to bear to curtail the charter life granted it by legislation. In any case it is highly undesirable that a bond issue should mature at or very near the expiration of the franchise, yet a very large number do. This is seen in the case of the Chicago City Railway. Its charter, granted by the legislature, was to expire in 1958, but by reason of unsettled traction conditions in Chicago, it seemed advisable for the company to waive this right and to accept the terms of a city ordinance granting a 20-year conditional franchise. At this writing (1926) the bondholders have organized a protective committee to safeguard their rights. They appealed for receivership believing their interests would best be served, as it seemed evident that satisfactory arrangements for a new franchise were unlikely. An indeterminate franchise from the legislature was sought, but since the next session convenes in January, 1927, there is little likelihood at the present writing that a satisfactory agreement will be reached before the funded debt in excess of $103,000,000 matures on January 1, 1927. There is an exceedingly thin equity consisting of $100,000 of capital stock and a surplus slightly in excess of $4,300,000. The current price of the bonds reflects the uncertainty of the final agreement.

It is, of course, even more undesirable to have the bonds mature

---

[1] This would not apply to the Tampa Electric Company with its 999-year franchise, nor to the many companies with unlimited charter life, if the validity of these franchises can be maintained successfully. But franchise terms may be the subject of bargaining when under stress of changing conditions a public utility must readjust its relations to a municipality. In the previous chapter is a discussion of the merits of the indeterminate franchise which seems to be the best solution of the franchise problem in most cases.

after the expiration of the franchise. This actually happens in some cases. A variation of this mischance, likely to be overlooked, exists when the bonds are of a holding company that is largely dependent on its subsidiaries for revenue. Sometimes the franchises of one or more of the subsidiaries will expire before the maturity of the holding company bonds. In this event the degree of loss in security sustained by the bonds can be theoretically figured by calculating the ratio of earning power lost to the company by cessation of income from this source, if the particular subsidiary franchise should not be renewed. If the date of expiration is remote, the amortization of the holding company bonds may lessen the interest charges to such degree that even with loss of subsidiary revenue the margin of safety due to income would be proportionately as great as ever. Although there still exist situations similar to that described, the practice of issuing bonds with maturity dates subsequent to the termination of the most important franchises is now less frequent.

One of the contributory causes of the receivership of the United Railways Co. of St. Louis in 1919 was the expiration of the franchises of some of its subsidiaries and also the reluctance of the city to extend them to expire simultaneously with the franchise of the parent company in 1948. The Board of Aldermen in 1918 passed a compromise ordinance validating the franchise rights of the company until 1948, but only after valuable concessions had been extracted from the company. At present the company is unable to show satisfactory returns, and the receiver is still in charge.

Interurban electric roads often run, like railroads, largely on their own right of way, except at crossings and through streets, so that the franchise matter is of less moment. Yet its provisions must not be ignored.

Character of the Franchise. Next in consideration after the life of the franchise is its character.[1] A bond circular seldom is sufficiently explicit as to the scope and import of its terms. Is it exclusive? Does it involve a tribute (e.g., an unjust excise tax, street paving, sprinkling and snow removal, etc.), which works hardship to the grantee? Does the city or the state

[1] See Clyde Lydon King, *The Regulation of Municipal Utilities*, Chapter IX, for suggestions for a model street railway franchise. Note particularly pp. 178–181.

reserve the right to amend the charter? What are its terms as to transfers and tariffs? Both the Interborough Rapid Transit Company and the Brooklyn Manhattan Transit Company are unable to earn reasonable returns on their investment with the five-cent fare which has continued notwithstanding rising costs of operation. The instability of a satisfactory tariff designed to vary with operating costs is illustrated by the reduction in 1920 of the eight-cent fare of the United Railways Co. of St. Louis in the face of low returns even under receivership.

Fixed Fares. The fixed five-cent fare, for a long time the recognized unit of price for the service performed by the street railways, is an economic error which we will do well to discard. Custom, charter restrictions, legislative enactment and the very denomination of our currency all help to maintain an unadjustable relation between cost and selling price that has worked much greater hardship for street railways than for steam roads and other utilities. A one-cent increase on a five-cent fare means a 20 per cent. increment, which in many cases would be greater than operating costs demand. Then, too, additional pennies increase the inconvenience to the customers. Many European cities, with more favorable currency denominations, and even Canadian cities, such as Toronto and Montreal, with currency like our own, preceded us in well-thought-out systems of transportation charge in which some attempt was made to regulate price exacted according to service rendered. Increases in cost of materials and supplies, and higher wages, accentuated by World War conditions caused a departure from the old five-cent fare, and the establishment of tariffs more in harmony with actual costs.

Current Rates. Gerhard M. Dahl, Chairman of the Executive Committee, Brooklyn-Manhattan Transit System,[1] has stated that the cost per passenger on his lines averaged 7.31 cents over the ten-year period from 1913. The company then actually lost 2.31 cents on every ride. As a result of increased costs, fares have been raised in most cities. The seven-cent fare is most common, the ten-cent fare ranks second,[2] and the average rate of cash fare is about 7.62 cents.[3]

[1] *"The Car-Rider, The Tax-Payer, The Investor."*
[2] See *Forbes Magazine*, October 15, 1924.
[3] See A. E. R. A. Bulletin No. 67, *Trend of Electric Railway Fares*, 1917–1925.

It is customary to consider the railway franchise as part of the security, with " property, rights, etc.," behind the first or general mortgage bonds. If this assertion is put forward of any issue it will bear looking into. Public service corporations cannot transfer their franchises by mortgage assignment without legislative authority, which, however, is quite freely given. Many cities have passed ordinances specifically forbidding the assignment of street railway franchises. This does not prevent the making of mortgages in ordinary course, under general statutory authority, secured upon trackage and equipment, but in foreclosure the new owners will have to take their chances of obtaining municipal consent to the operation of the road.

Importance of Amortization. Unless the charter life is without limit, it is extremely important that ample provision be made for the redemption of a large part of the issue by maturity, either through a sinking fund or through the annual recall of a percentage of the bonds. One is likely to overlook this matter, since it is such an unimportant aspect of steam road financing. Practically, it is of little general consequence whether a railroad bond ever matures—there are not a few that run well into the 21st century—for the corporate life of the railroad is everlasting and the demand for its activities undoubtedly permanent; but a street railway company, with an unrenewable franchise on its hands, is ever threatened with extinction.

Importance of Territory Served. Also, let the buyer of electric railway bonds investigate most carefully the territory served. Other things being equal, a growing town or city serves his purpose best. With increase of population, wealth, and traffic will come a sure increase in the value of his security. His bonds will strengthen and profit by the further development of the country just as surely as did the early railroad bonds,—the 6 and 7 per cent. railroad bonds put out in the sixties.

If the road is an interurban, let him be certain that it can offer real advantages in economy, speed, or comfort of travel as compared with competing steam roads or bus lines, if there are any, and that a prosperous rural or suburban community, with traffic possibilities, awaits proper development. This may seem trite, but there are to be found millions of dollars in street railway bonds that lack these assurances. Sectional distinctions, relative to soundness in street railway investment, cannot be drawn.

Apart from the four special considerations mentioned, the bond buyer will, of course, take into account, as in the case of any corporation security, the character of the management, the earning power, the dividend record, and the future prospects. In particular he will analyze most carefully the income account. Another extremely helpful exercise for just discrimination,— and this will apply, although in less degree, to other classes of bonds,—is to become thoroughly familiar with some one company acknowledged by common consent to be entirely sound and flourishing, and with this as a touchstone to test others.

The Interurban. In 1895 came the interurban trolley. In its decade of predominance it passed through the same set of phases: from imitation of its predecessor, the urban trolley, through rough experience, to independent self-development as a distinct class of transportation.

At first, however, the relation between street and interurban railways was much closer than between interurban and steam roads as to character of equipment and roadbed, kind of transportation service rendered, and methods of financing. So the two electric modes drew together and at the beginning of the new century their coalition was a thing generally accomplished; and the development from coalition to absolute merging with its consequent virtual loss of identity for the constituent divisions has since been going on as rapidly as ever in the preceding decades it went on among the smaller railroads toward the upbuilding of the great transcontinental systems.

Interurban Centres. Around the chief electric railway in each community as nucleus the outlying roads became grouped as feeders, and each group so formed served in turn, of course, the larger territorial scheme through its interurban connections. At present there are great interurban centres at Chicago, Indianapolis, Dayton, Detroit, Toledo, Cleveland, Columbus, Cincinnati, Boston, Los Angeles, San Francisco, Seattle, and Tacoma.

Geography has played a very important part in this development. Until recently almost all the great electric railway systems were to be found in the New England states, Pennsylvania, Ohio, Indiana, Illinois, and Wisconsin; later development extended to the Pacific Coast. The geographical situation suggests that under normal conditions well-settled districts having towns and cities scattered about with a fifty-mile radius are necessary as *nodi* to a successful interurban network, for these are the conditions that imply a high traffic density. Territory with medium-sized towns usually shows higher returns per capita than when composed of populous urban centres.

The Western Development: Competitive. The last stage in the purely interurban phase of electric transportation development was the adoption of steam railroad characteristics: level, heavily ballasted roadbed with low gradients, heavy steel rails, Pullman dining and sleeping coaches, large terminal office buildings, the upbuilding of parcel and merchandise service, the issuance of through, excursion, and commutation tickets,—all these features of mature steam transportation have been employed, and often with success, to draw on sources of revenue that otherwise would go to the railroads.

This may be called the Western interurban phase. It is more picturesque than the Eastern, and consequently, has received more attention through periodical literature. It is a question, however, if it be not the less important.

By popular diffusion of financial intelligence, perhaps by force of economic necessity, we, as a people, have become partly reconciled to the development of transportation along monopolistic lines. Regulation by commission, we have come to believe, will serve to curb the evils that a natural monopoly fosters; the Judiciary and Executive draw a fine line in the definition of railroad competition; there is now recognized the desirability of consolidation, and the railroads no longer deem it necessary to take the preliminary steps toward further grouping with the secrecy of conspirators; now organized opposition to railroad consolidation is largely to serve either political or corporative ends, but occasionally minority interests oppose proposed consolidations as against their best interests. Witness the rejection of the Nickel Plate Merger plan at the behest of the minority stockholders of the Chesapeake and Ohio Railroad. However, as the result of popular will or through economic causes, or both, natural monopolies at present tend to grow by process more of agglutination than of fusion. That is to say the constituent companies tend to preserve a larger measure of autonomy and individuality than formerly. In railroading the catchword for this recent tendency is " community of interest," by which the results without the odium of exclusive possession are achieved.

So the fact remains, and is tacitly conceded by the public, that the business of transportation properly performed is of necessity monopolistic.

Into this present order of things the Western development of interurban units actively competing with steam roads does not seem to fit. In so far as electric traction in the West, with its vastly more adjustable service, is able to fill a different order of wants: carry small merchandise and garden truck to market, search into territory not reached by railroads and gather primitive traffic—it is doing sound business. But the ultimate interests of the community are not served where steam and electricity fight side by side for intercity business, both freight and passenger.

Competition of this kind has been keenest in Ohio. On *a priori* grounds one would expect, for electric roads, at least temporary advantage. Their fares average about two-thirds those of steam roads, their through service is often as speedy and almost always more frequent, comfortable, and cleanly, and they usually discharge their passengers at more convenient points in the terminal centres.

Electrification of Steam Roads. Lastly there is the matter of the electrification of steam roads. For years small stretches of line in various parts of the country have been operated by electricity. The thought with all it implicates has been common railroad property for a greater length of time than most people imagine. By city ordinance, the New York Central and the New York, New Haven, and Hartford are not permitted to send steam locomotives for regular transportation purposes within the city limits of New York. Perhaps the Chicago, Milwaukee and St. Paul Railroad has done more toward electrification than any other system, due to rather ideal conditions for hydro development and also because of a scarcity of suitable coal.

The Investment Principle: Caveat Emptor. From what has already been said it will be readily acknowledged that generalizations are of little avail as guides to street railway bond buying. When in 1903 the Massachusetts legislature let down the bars and admitted street railway securities for savings-bank investment it was under these provisos:—that the bonds should be approved by the Board of Savings-Bank Commissioners, that the railway should be incorporated under the stringent laws of the state, that it should be located wholly, or in part, therein, and have earned and paid regular dividends on all its outstanding stock of at least 5 per cent. per annum for the five years preceding. Some may find suggestions here to guide their own purchasing. Yet such are the vicissitudes of street railroading that several bond issues, originally approved, have become illegal holdings for the Massachusetts banks during the intervening years. In the recent bills before the New York State legislature relative to legal investments for savings banks no mention whatever was made of the electric railway securities.

Each security, therefore, must be judged individually, on its own merits, and not like municipal, equipment, or water bonds, in part by the excellencies of its class. The buyer may rest mainly on the judgment of his bond house or make his own investigation. If he chooses to do the former, he is likely to find the house financially interested in the road, and although this tends to conservative financing it prejudices the source of his advice. If he chooses to do the latter, circumstances are more against him. Yet the supervision exercised over street railway companies by the public utility or railroad commissions of most states is quite stringent at present. Many states now exercise thorough-going oversight and control. Few companies, however, make monthly reports public, but the great majority of the states require detailed annual reports in harmony with prescribed accounting systems. The Commerce Commission is less exacting with interstate electric than with interstate steam roads.

Overcapitalization. There can be no question, too, concerning the gross overcapitalization of the industry. The following tables (pages 374-375) have been constructed from the report of the Census Bureau.

The street railways have increased the purchase of electric energy instead of generating it " since 1902, for which year 240, or 29.4 per cent. of the 817 operating companies, reported no power-plant equipment. This proportion increased to 39 per cent. for 1907, 49.3 per cent. for 1912, 62.4 per cent. for 1917, and 73 per cent. for 1922. . . . The proportion which such energy (purchased) formed of the total increased from 33.5 per cent. for 1912 to 40.6 per cent. for 1917 and 47.8 per cent. for 1922." [1] The capitalization per mile of road is lower than it otherwise would be because of this tendency. In spite of that fact we

[1] Census Bureau, Census of Electrical Industries, 1922, *Electric Railways*, p. 62.

COMBINED CAPITALIZATION OF OPERATING AND LESSOR COMPANIES

	1907	1912	1917	1922	Per cent.of inc. 1922 over 1917
Funded debt outstanding......	$1,677,063,240	$2,329,221,828	$3,058,377,167	$3,117,621,457	1.9%
Capital stock outstanding......	2,097,708,856	2,379,346,313	2,473,846,651	2,329,173,090	—5.8
Total capital liabilities........	3,774,772,096	4,708,568,141	5,532,223,818	5,446,794,547	—1.5
Investments in securities and nonrailway property......	374,664,197	465,250,414	642,261,722	784,870,674	22.2
Net capital liabilities including electric light plants........	3,400,107,899	4,243,317,727	4,889,962,096	4,661,923,873	—4.7
Miles of single track owned...	38,834	40,439	43,899	43,203	—1.6
Capitalization per mile of single track owned...	111,569	116,435	126,021	126,075	
Funded debt per mile of single track owned...	49,568	57,598	69,668	72,162	

observe a tendency toward increased capitalization per mile from $111,569 in 1907 to $126,075 in 1922. In the level Ohio country where conditions favor economical construction, in 1922 capitalization per mile of single track was $68,712 of which $34,032 was in bonds and $34,681 in stock. Massachusetts lines were capitalized at $68,606. The cost of construction per mile varies, perhaps, from $50,000 to $150,000 or more. In the opinion of engineers the average may be $100,000 for good properties in comparatively large cities and slightly less for high-grade interurbans. We are then face to face with the fact that the average street railway bond represents no more than the original cost of the physical property.

The funded debt per mile in 1922 amounted to $72,162 or more than 57 per cent. of the total per mile capitalization. The net operating revenue per mile of track was $5,737 in 1917 and $6,577 in 1922,[1] or 4.6 per cent. and 5.2 per cent. respectively, on the per mile capitalization. Based on earnings there can be little doubt but that the roads are overcapitalized which explains in part the reason for so many receiverships during the last decade. Previously the roads failed properly to maintain their plants and to provide for adequate depreciation which postponed the day of reckoning for overcapitalization. No doubt this skimping policy accounts, in part, for the change from the low operating ratio of

[1] Ibid., p. 156.

60.1 in 1907 to 71.6 in 1922. The great increase is due primarily to increased costs of operations as a result of post-war conditions.

The condition of street railroading in the United States in 1912, 1917, and 1922 as reflected in dividend and interest disbursements is to be seen from the following analyses: [1]

DIVIDEND AND INTEREST DISBURSEMENTS OF OPERATING AND LESSOR COMPANIES COMBINED

	1912	1917	1922
Dividend paying common stock.........	$ 997,135,284	$ 958,305,905	$ 630,449,383
Amount paid on common stock.........	58,759,715	60,772,290	37,659,323
Average rate per cent. for paying companies............................	5.9	6.3	6.0
Non-dividend paying common stock......	973,249,719	1,053,883,389	1,212,190,050
Per cent. of all common stock not paying dividends........................	49	52	66
Dividend paying preferred stock.........	270,800,705	260,055,512	292,155,441
Amount paid on preferred stock.........	12,232,503	12,490,851	16,003,671
Average rate per cent. for paying companies............................	4.5	4.8	5.5
Non-dividend paying preferred stock.....	138,160,605	201,601,845	194,378,216
Per cent. of all preferred stock not paying dividends........................	34	44	40
Funded debt outstanding..............	2,335,319,073	3,058,377,167	3,117,621,457
Interest paid upon it..................	113,259,470 [a]	126,654,357	140,356,808
Percentage of interest disbursements to total debt.......................	4.34 [a]	·4.14	4.50

[a] Includes interest on floating debt.

An industry that paid nothing on 40 per cent. of its preferred shares and on 66 per cent. of its common shares may hardly be said to have been in satisfactory condition. [2] As to the disbursements for interest it is impossible to obtain satisfactory statements from which to estimate what proportion of the funded debt was in default. Obviously 4.5 does not represent what was due on the total debt; 5.5 doubtless would be a closer approximation and perhaps even 6.5 per cent. Of 858 companies reporting in 1922, 438 had a net income available for dividends of $85,491,997, and 420 had total deficits of $28,304,385. Thus in 1922 a large per cent. of the street railway obligations in the United States were in default.

The tables below give a succinct story of the misfortunes of electric railways: [3]

[1] *Bureau of Census*, Census of Electrical Industries, 1922, *Electric Railways*, p. 115, published 1925.

[2] Only 40.62 per cent. of all interstate steam railroad capital stock was non-dividend paying in 1922, while the average rate on dividend-yielding stock was 6.37 per cent. and the ratio of dividends declared to all stock was 3.78 per cent.

[3] *Statistical Abstract of the United States*, 1923, p. 418 up to 1924, and *Electric Railway Journal*, January 2, 1926, p. 41 for 1924 and 1925.

RECEIVERSHIPS OF ELECTRIC RAILWAYS

Year	Placed under Receivership			
	Number of Companies	Miles of Track	Outstanding Securities	
			Stock	Bonds
			Dollars	Dollars
1909	22	558.00	29,962,200	22,325,000
1910	11	696.61	12,629,400	75,490,735
1911	19	518.90	29,533,450	38,973,293
1912	26	373.58	20,410,700	11,133,800
1913	18	342.84	31,006,900	87,272,200
1914	10	362.39	35,562,550	19,050,460
1915	27	1,152.10	40,298,050	39,372,375
1916	15	359.26	14,476,600	10,849,200
1917	21	1,177.32	33,918,725	33,778,400
1918	29	2,017.61	92,130,388	163,257,102
1919	48	3,781.12	221,259,354	312,915,104
1920	19	1,065.31	28,758,455	72,283,575
1921	19	986.42	32,909,525	36,177,300
1922	14	695.43	18,140,150	20,304,400
1923	12	333.63	8,332,100	14,707,066
1924	12	1,021.88	28,489,700	35,716,000
1925	14	1,260.07	51,383,195	54,696,525

Sold under Foreclosure

Year	Number of Companies	Miles of Track	Outstanding Securities		Receivers' Certificates
			Stock	Bonds	
			Dollars	Dollars	Dollars
1909	21	488.00	22,265,700	21,174,000	Data not
1910	22	724.36	19,106,613	26,374,075	available
1911	25	660.72	91,354,800	115,092,750	"
1912	18	267.18	14,197,300	10,685,250	"
1913	17	302.28	15,243,700	19,094,500	"
1914	11	181.26	26,239,700	44,094,241	"
1915	19	308.31	30,508,817	16,759,997	"
1916	19	430.14	13,895,400	22,702,300	"
1917	26	745.19	27,281,900	27,313,045	"
1918	23	524.22	37,740,325	20,149,384	"
1919	29	2,675.48	89,893,400	79,836,738	42,300
1920	13	259.90	7,782,400	11,227,328	52,000
1921	13	777.97	33,642,255	30,863,526	5,000
1922	13	322.88	7,491,500	12,640,600	114,683
1923	15	927.45	118,077,959	110,638,250	12,265,000
1924	14	869.25	21,022,800	34,845,535	3,440,388
1925	13	569.39	18,074,300	18,329,555	53,000

RECORD OF TRACK ABANDONED, TRACK EXTENSIONS AND CARS
PURCHASED BY ELECTRIC RAILWAYS [1]
1917–1925

Year	Track Abandoned	Track Extensions	Cars Purchased
1917	120.07 miles	376.70 miles	2,455
1918	531.92 "	313.82 "	2,419
1919	402.25 "	140.57 "	2,447
1920	538.12 "	176.56 "	3,598
1921	311.24 "	147.10 "	1,276
1922	540.33 "	211.38 "	3,538
1923	193.44 "	233.15 "	4,029
1924	225.52 "	312.07 "	4,092
1925	174.19 "	339.80 "	1,659
Totals	3,037.08 "	2,251.15 "	25,513

It will be observed that the years 1918, 1919, and 1920 were, on the whole, the most disastrous in the industry and of those years 1919 proved the most severe. During 1919 there were more companies forced into receivership and also more sold under foreclosure represented by a greater number of miles and also a larger capitalization than for any other single year. Less miles of extensions were made in that year than for any year during the last decade, while in only three years did the miles of abandoned track exceed that of 1919. Abandonment of track also exceeded track extensions during the last nine years, but a study of the table indicates improvement in recent years.

It has been the well-known policy of American steam railroads (as contrasted with English, for instance) to pay for even extraordinary betterments and extensions, in part at least, out of earnings. Because of this policy a great injustice has been done our railroads in charging them in this generation with stock watering. But if there is any justice in the reproach it is when applied to the trolleys. Even now this procrastinatory financing has come into its own; as observed above, street railway receiverships are common in the land, and doubtless there are, at present, more issues of street railway bonds in default than of any other class of securities dealt with in this book.

Investment Characteristics. Let the investor not turn away because of the many failings of the electric railway class; rather let him remember that there are numbers of splendidly-equipped

[1] *Electric Railway Journal.*

and well-developed companies, with records and capacity for earning beyond question. The mortgage bonds of these companies sell on a basis of about 1 per cent. higher yield than those of steam roads and other public service corporations of the same investment grade, and in common with railroad bonds, have the advantage of readier market than many other securities of the same yield. Due to the numerous receiverships and abandonment of lines, investors are naturally chary of the bonds as a class. Out of prejudice arise attractive bargains. Evidence of a revival notwithstanding the severe tests from unregulated bus competition, unsuccessful attempts by several cities to substitute the bus for the trolley, and the unwillingness of the public to advance fares in harmony with rising costs, is demonstrated by the data contained in this study.

During the last decade changes in the financial structure of electric railways, as in practically all utilities, have eliminated many undesirable features. The old closed-end mortgage with the " after acquired " clause and the rigid sinking fund provisions have in many cases been replaced by the open-end mortgage covering both present and subsequently acquired property but restricting the bond issue to from 70 per cent. to 80 per cent. of the cost of the property additions and stipulating that earnings must cover the interest on the outstanding bonds plus that on the new issue from $1\frac{1}{2}$ to 2 times. The fact that the bonds may be issued at different times, bearing various interest rates, and having different maturity dates and redemption features, but with the same security, has made the bonds more attractive and has simplified financing.

Unfortunately the security in many street railway mortgage bonds is protected by only a thin equity due to overcapitalization or questionable construction contracts. As a whole this is a heritage of previous managements, yet the fact remains that since street railway bonds have relatively poor security, the yield on the investment is usually higher and the market normally is more responsive. As a final word, only men of affairs capable of diagnosing reports, and seeking a large return from a form of investment that is fairly convertible, should seek to meet their needs with electric railway bonds.

CHAPTER XXX

GAS COMPANY BONDS

History of the Gas Industry. In the wake of the industrial revolution and of improved methods of steam transportation, by both rail and water, came the development of the gas industry. In lieu of the tallow candle, whale oil, and the " smoky " kerosene lamp there was gradually substituted in the larger centres the cleaner, more convenient and more illuminating gas lamp. The gas industry required the successive stimuli furnished about the middle of the nineteenth century by improved kerosene lamps, by better refinement of kerosene at reduced prices, by the serious competition of natural gas, and finally, after 1880, by the rapid development of electric lighting. Although, as will be observed later, gas for illumination has been virtually superseded by electricity, yet for heating purposes gas has proved its superiority to electricity, coal, or oil, so that the present greatest channel of outlet lies in the industrial rather than in the residential field.

Successive steps in the early use of gas for lighting purposes were as follows: the lighting of Westminster Bridge in 1813, the organization in Baltimore of the first gas company in 1816, the introduction of gas in Boston in 1821, New York City in 1822, Brooklyn in 1823, and Philadelphia in 1835. But many obstacles interfered with the rapid development of the industry. The early fear that the manufacture and use of gas was dangerous, as well as injurious to health, led to organized protests, and made financing of the industry all the more difficult. Then, too, in America there was urgent need of capital for canal and railroad construction, and other requirements characteristic of a country abounding in natural resources but so lacking in labor that capital substitutes were urgent necessities. Few therefore were interested in a utility that had not yet demonstrated its value, and which was likely to prove even more disappointing than the early water companies.

Out of the difficulties and uncertainties of the first sixty or seventy years of its history, there has emerged a business rivalling in magnitude our largest manufacturing industries and offering many desirable investment securities. Not unlike many other enterprises, faced with extinction by oil, natural gas, and electricity, the gas industry was forced to prove its *raison d'être*. Through improved methods in production, the utilization of by-products which formerly were wasted, and a wider range of uses, the industry has justified its existence.

Present Importance of the Gas Industry. In the last decade the production of gas has increased 100 per cent.; during the last seven years the use of gas increased more than in the previous 100 years. In 1914, less than two hundred billion, but in 1924 more than four hundred billion cubic feet of manufactured gas were consumed. At the same time there was a tendency toward consolidation as seen in the decreasing number of plants. This movement is due largely to the recent development of super-gas plants which unite the small settlements in one system by the use of high-pressure long-distance transmission. It is not generally known that there are now super-gas plants which send gas as far as sixty miles from the source of production. The great increase in the value of the products sold also indicates the rapid expansion of the industry, as also the increased miles of mains. The consumption per capita in the territory utilizing gas shows considerable growth, even though prices have tended to rise since 1917 due to increased costs of material and labor.

Natural Gas. In those sections supplied by natural gas there has not existed the same need for higher rates because of increased coal prices, but the exhaustion of supply has frequently embarrassed the producer and has made necessary the installation of artificial gas plants with resulting higher prices. Prices per thousand cubic feet of natural gas in 1924 ranged from $.45 in Cleveland and Columbus to $1.29 in Kansas City, Mo., as compared with $.79 in Detroit and $2.40 in Jacksonville, for artificial gas. These figures are not in all cases comparable, for some of the rates carry service charges ranging from 10 cents to 50 cents per month.[1]

During the last fifteen years with slight exceptions, there has been a progressive increase in the production of natural gas; in 1910 the output amounted to 509,155 million cubic feet; in 1924 to 1,095,000 million cubic feet with corresponding values

[1] See *Statistical Abstract of the United States*, 1924, p. 718.

of $70,756,000 and $254,000,000. Naturally this enormous production cannot continue indefinitely. Each company should therefore make adequate provisions for artificial gas plants to replace the depleting natural gas, for failure so to safeguard the original investment will result in disaster. At best, securities of natural gas companies can seldom be compared with those of artificial gas enterprises due to the possibilities of sudden exhaustion. Moreover, natural gas companies experience considerable difficulty because of the variable load factor, since in winter because of cheapness it is used extensively for house-heating purposes without a balancing use during the summer months. As will be observed later, this problem is being partly solved by the utilization of gas for household refrigeration and cooling.

Changed Character of the Demand. Gas is used for domestic, commercial and industrial purposes. The relative amount used for domestic purposes is on the decline, while that used for industrial purposes shows substantial increase. In fact, gas has progressed far beyond its first function as an illuminant. As late as 1910, of the total output only 5 per cent. was used in industry, whereas to-day the ratio is in excess of 25 per cent. and is rapidly increasing. In 1910 about 45 per cent. of the gas produced was used for lighting, now about 15 per cent., while about 58 per cent. is used for domestic fuel. The industrial field for fuel purposes now offers the most attractive possibilities. A few years ago engineers proudly announced that gas was being used in a thousand different heating applications, but now it is estimated that more than 21,000 trade processes are aided by it. As a result, during the last decade the consumption of manufactured gas for industrial uses has increased 1,000 per cent.

Advantages of Gas in Industrial Use. This marked increase is due to certain advantages recognized by industry. The quality and economy in the manufacture of the product is materially improved due to perfect heat control. Gas is clean and convenient, for it obviates large coal reserves, storage facilities, the smoke nuisance, ash removal, and above all the uncertainty attending protracted coal strikes.

Peak Loads. Furthermore, the gas companies gain from wider industrial use of their product due to the relatively higher load factor. The ordinary domestic customer uses gas about 16 per cent. of the time, hotels and bakeries 28 per cent., the steel, packing, and automobile industries about 60 per cent. on the average. The peak load thus is comparatively negligible with industrials. These considerations reduce the investment in gas plant and mains, making possible lower sales prices.

Gas as an Industrial Fuel. To insure the best results, many manufacturing processes require uniform heat. This control is available only with fuel oil, electricity, and gas. Fuel oil has been used extensively because of its volume and cheapness, but there are inherent disadvantages, such as transportation and storage, irregularity and ultimate exhaustion of supply. Electricity has been conceded first place as an illuminant and it is also preëminent as a producer of power, but for heating it is wasteful. Only about 15 per cent. of the heat content of coal is made available, but as much as 85 per cent. is procured by a modern gas system. The superiority of gas over electricity for fuel is indicated in the estimate that it would take seven hundred and fifty million tons of coal to produce annually enough electricity for heating and cooking in the American homes now using electricity for lighting, as compared with only eighty-two million tons of coal to serve the same requirements if coal were utilized.

Furthermore, if all heating were done with gas rather than with coal in its raw state, it is estimated that the heating efficiency would be doubled, in that the coal would last twice as long. Therefore in the interest of national economy it behooves us to utilize gas for fuel that our natural resources may be judiciously conserved.

Domestic Needs for Gas. Although the industrial requirements for fuel are important, the greatest present demand arises from domestic needs. With about 72 per cent. of the total sales for lighting and domestic fuel for stoves, incinerators, water and space heaters, and with the probability of substantial increases as a result of the development of household heating, cooling, and refrigeration, the future domestic load is fully assured. The saturation point is indeed remote. Any industry that derives over 70 per cent. of its revenues from sources which are practically unaffected by business fluctuations is in a fortunate position. Not only does the gas industry enjoy this distinction, but it is further improving its situation by balancing its load factor through the development of refrigerating and house cooling devices to offset decline in house-heating demand for fuel during the summer months. Central gas-fired, house-heating units are being installed at the annual rate of 100,000, in addition to the annual installation of 800,000 gas ranges, 450,000 water heaters, and 500,000 space heaters. Constancy of domestic demand is assured through the present use of approximately 9,800,000 gas stoves, 4,400,000 space heaters, 3,400,000 water heaters, and several hundred thousand central house-heating units.

Gas fuel has only recently established its superiority over other heating agencies. Industry and the home require a fuel which is " presentable, dependable, controllable, comfortable, and economical." [1] The first four of these desirable characteristics inhere as much in electricity as in gas, but electricity is not relatively economical. " Electricity selling at one cent per kilowatt hour and city gas of 530 B. t. u. per cubic foot selling at $1.55 per thousand cubic feet furnish an exactly equivalent amount of heat per dollar expended. In our larger cities, when electric rates of one cent per k. w. h. and gas rates of approximately sixty cents per thousand are in effect, a dollar expended for gas will purchase over two and one-half times as many heat units as a dollar expended for electricity." [2] The cost factor decides when gas and electricity compete for fuel purposes.

Manufacturing Processes and By-Products. Of the five classifications of manufactured gas—coal oil, carburetted water, mixed coal and water, oil gas, and other gas,—mixed coal and water gas ranks first in volume and value, and carburetted water gas second. The following table clearly indicates their relative importance, the quantity and value of materials used in their production, and the amount and value of the by-products. Attention is also called to the relative volume produced by commercial and municipal plants.

Manufacture of Gas. Coal gas is made by heating bituminous coal about four hours in air-tight fire clay retorts which are heated externally. The destructive distillation of coal produces the gas which passes through the hydraulic main and exhauster to the condenser where the tar and oil are condensed through a cooling process and thus separated from the gas. The gas then goes to a scrubber where the ammonia is extracted, and to the

[1] *Proceedings of the National Gas Association,* 1925, p. 622.
[2] Ibid., p. 623.

STATISTICS ON GAS, ILLUMINATING AND HEATING: MATERIALS USED AND PRODUCTS[1]

Material or product	Unit	Quantity (Thousands of units specified)			Cost or value (Thousands of dollars)		
		1914	1921	1923	1914	1921	1923
Materials used, total cost.	......				76,779	202,253	191,120
Coal for gas making.	Short ton	6,117			20,873		
Anthracite.	Long ton		1,130	974			
Bituminous.	Short ton		5,707	6,246			
Oil for gas making.	Gallon	715,419	158,365	176,764	24,721		
Oil for enriching.	"		683,406	697,470			
Gas purchased.	M feet	28,351	44,739	90,611	8,883		
Products, total value.	......				220,238	411,196	450,097
Commercial plants.	......				218,481	405,028	443,503
Municipal plants.	......				1,757	6,168	6,594
Gas, total.	M feet	203,629	306,058	356,554	175,066	372,032	394,506
Coal gas.	"	10,510	7,329	7,551	10,727	12,519	12,963
Carburetted water gas.	"	90,018	110,053	117,317	74,517	138,513	134,744
Mixed coal and water gas.	"	86,281	169,847	208,238	72,012	196,104	220,961
Oil gas.	"	16,512	17,656	19,739	15,044	23,612	22,989
Other gas.	"	318	1,172	3,709	2,766	1,284	2,849
Coke for sale.	Ton	2,282	2,031	2,175	8,720	17,503	21,533
Tar for sale:							
Coal gas.	Gallon	125,939	60,333	58,877	3,253	3,204	3,039
Water gas and oil gas.	"		53,433	49,991		2,192	2,001
All other products.					33,199	16,265	29,018

[1] *Statistical Abstract of the United States, 1924,* p. 717.

purifier where the sulphur impurities are absorbed by oxide of iron. Coal gas is enriched with oil gas to improve its illuminating power and heat value. The important by-products of coal gas are coke, tar, carbon and ammonia.

Water gas is made by forcing steam over glowing fuel, usually coke. Contact of steam with red hot carbon generates hydrogen and carbon monoxide which produce a blue gas insufficient in illumination power or heat value for commercial use. The deficiency is supplied by forming an admixture of gas oil, a distillate of petroleum, which enriches the water gas, thus producing carburetted water gas.[1] This process yields smaller quantities of by-products, but coal consumption and labor are less. In 1924 carburetted water gas was 61 per cent. of the total gas distribution, coke-oven gas (a form of coal gas) 16.4 per cent., coal gas 15.5 per cent., and oil gas 7.1 per cent. During recent years the manufacture of coal gas, particularly coke oven, has increased more rapidly than that of the others. The growth of water gas production has been relatively smaller, while the supply of gas oil and fuel oil at the refineries has increased rapidly. Oil gas has not shown a rate of increase to the degree that might be expected with a large supply of oil at favorable prices, although the trend during the last two years seems to be upward. Public utility companies in the oil regions naturally turn to oil gas. The Pacific Gas and Electric Company, for instance, has virtually doubled its oil gas capacity during the three years ended with 1925. There seems to be no immediate danger of oil exhaustion, but there is the probability that increased demands for gasoline, oil as lubricants, the oil-electric locomotive, the Diesel engine, as well as for marine service will enhance its price to such a point that eventually oil gas will not be able to compete with coal gas.

Gas Standards. Standards required of companies are designed primarily to protect the public against irregularity of service, pressure, heat value, or danger. Many early requirements, now obsolete, should be abandoned as sources of expense and considerable annoyance to the companies. The old candle-power regulation, devised when gas was used in open-flame burners to provide illumination, and also the rigid B. t. u. (British

---

[1] A most interesting description and historical sketch of carburetted gas may be found in *American Gas Journal*, Vol. 125, July, 1926, pp. 30, 49, and 72.

thermal unit or the amount of heat required to raise one pound of pure water at 39° Fahrenheit one degree) requirements are examples of the perpetuity of standards that have lost part of their usefulness.

The heating value of gas is perhaps the most desirable measure of its usefulness, and has brought about the change from candle power to heating-value standards. Heating-value standards, ranging between 600 B. t. u. and 525 B. t. u., are customary. They should give adequate protection to the public; yet a lower standard, requiring, of course, more gas, would permit the use of lower grade coal and less oil, and thereby conserve our resources and require less expensive processes. If there should be a corresponding reduction in gas prices, it would appear desirable to lower the standard, provided relative efficiency is maintained. Gas of 450 B. t. u. has been supplied in both England and Canada since 1920. In fact there is a tendency toward lower standards in the United States. Whereas in 1920 fourteen of the twenty states under regulation (70 per cent.) had standards requiring higher than 550 B. t. u. there were in 1925 only nine out of twenty-five states (36 per cent.) with such standards. In the larger cities lower standards exist. In fact, there is some justification for the gas manufacturer's contention that there should be no state-wide or general standards but that the companies should be allowed to choose the materials and processes that give a cheaper gas, provided a satisfactory commodity at a fair price is supplied.

Pressure, too, should be consistent with efficiency and convenience. Unnecessarily wide variations involve adjustment of equipment and at times considerable annoyance. Minimum pressure from $1\frac{1}{2}$ to 2 inches water column and maximum from 6 to 8 inches water column constitute the range generally permitted by public service commissions. In some states the pressure variation is restricted to 2 or 3 inches water column. If efficiency is to be maintained the above requirement must be enforced.

There are also requirements relative to meter testing, calorimeter tests, pressure surveys, flexible tubing,[1] the amount of sulphur and hydrogen sulphide that the gas may contain, and

---

[1] See *American Gas Journal*, June 26, 1926, p. 584, for recent New York regulation relative to flexible tubing.

similar measures to protect the customer. Reasonable requirements are to be expected, but when they become too drastic the burden placed on the gas manufacturer entails additional expense far in excess of the benefits derived.

Population and Service. Gas is a commodity that cannot be manufactured, distributed, and sold to advantage on a small scale. The rates charged by the companies operating in the interior towns and cities of Massachusetts[1] clearly demonstrate the difficulty involved when small enterprises attempt to manufacture and distribute gas in sparsely settled communities where the sendout is necessarily small and the number of customers per mile of main is low. Of the twenty-one companies charging $2.00 or more per thousand cubic feet, only five had populations in excess of 13,000 but in no case did the population exceed 17,000. The customers were required to pay as much as $3.36 per M. cu. ft. in Norwood with a population of 12,627 when in Boston the rate was $1.35, and in Fall River with a population of 120,485 it was only $1.25. The larger companies, too, are usually the better dividend payers. It is generally estimated that in cities of less than 65,000 or 75,000 population, the cost of production increases inversely to population.

Similar analyses indicate that in Massachusetts the consumption of gas in cities of 75,000 or less tends to vary inversely with the price, and in larger cities the consumption tends to increase in greater ratio than the population. With the expansion of industrial use this tendency will probably increase. In cities with a population of 65,000 or more, implying the presence of extensive manufacturing and contiguity of buildings, especially those having many stories, there is the economy of concentration which lessens the cost of installation and maintenance, and increases the proportion of population served and therefore the per capita consumption. Under anything like the present diversified demands for gas, we may expect that large and well-established companies in cities of 65,000 or more will increase their sales annually without interruption as long as the population they serve increases. It is as certain as the increase in freight tonnage and passenger traffic on a trunk line, over a long period of years, and it is far steadier.

Important to the purchaser of gas company securities, there-

[1] *Annual Report of Department of Public Utilities*, Massachusetts, 1921.

fore, is the size of the company, the population and nature of the territory served, rather than the competition likely to be encountered.

Rates. The rate structure of a gas company is fundamental to the success of the enterprise. Rates, as observed with reference to electricity and traction, must be just and fair to all consumers and should yield a satisfactory return to the investor. In the determination of equitable rates due consideration must be given to the cost of the service, its value to the customer, and avoidance of discrimination. Rate hearings with these fundamental principles in mind have been numerous during the last twenty years, yet there still remains a lack of agreement as to their extent and relative importance. Only recently accurate accounting produced reliable data on which to base an intelligent judgment of the cost of service. Perhaps there can never be a unanimity of opinion as to value of the service. The price at which it can be secured from other sources may serve as a basis of comparison, but cannot measure the true value. Discrimination does not necessarily arise when different rates are imposed on patrons requiring different kinds and quantities of service.

From about 1850 to 1918 gas rates were continually lowered. The process of price-scaling is an old one. In our first edition (1911) we wrote that "from a careful survey of the rates of 172 companies in the principal cities of the United States, extending back over a period of 23 years, it is possible to state, with authority, that there is no present marked acceleration to the decline in prices. Rather that the scaling has been fairly constant for the period except in such companies as had suddenly to meet the competition of natural gas. The average price for these 172 companies in 1885 was $2.01; 11 years later, 1896, it was $1.53, a loss of 48 cents; and 11 years after that, 1907, it was $1.09, a further loss of 44 cents." By 1918 it had dropped to $.95, a loss of only 14 cents. In 1916 the lowest price, $.92, was reached; in 1925 the price was $1.27 or an increase of 32 cents over the price of 1918 and 35 cents above the low point in 1916. The highest price reached, that of $1.32 in 1921, was 40 cents above the price of 1916.[1]

The factors contributing to this general decline in prices were

[1] For average gas prices since 1912 see *Statistical Abstract of the United States*, 1924, p. 717.

the more economical processes of manufacture and distribution, better business methods, the utilization of by-products formerly wasted, the excessive competition of natural gas, electricity, and oil, production on a large scale at lower costs due to the increase in per capita consumption, and the consolidation of small inefficient plants. In general the reduction of rates has been initiated voluntarily by the companies themselves to meet competition, rather than by the pressure of public demand. The increases since 1917 have been due to rising costs of material and labor, characteristic of most utilities.

Management. Another requisite for most successful operation is modern management. It is hard to overestimate the value of a policy of aggressive advertising and public education in gas matters. Many concerns circulate among their customers pamphlets of instruction regarding the proper use and economy of gas, maintain sales departments with canvassers, and stores for the demonstration and sale at or near cost of gas appliances, and a corps of inspectors whose services are offered gratuitously to those in need of any sort of help in the solution of their gas problems.

The experimental work, publicity, and organized sales campaigns supported and conducted by the American Gas Association for the purposes of testing equipment, devising more efficient appliances, acquainting the general public with the many economical and convenient uses of gas, and assisting the members in organizing their selling compaigns, are playing no small part in the recent popularization of gas.

Investment Tests. In addition to the conventional tests of investment securities, such as affect safety of principal, rate and stability of return, taxation, marketability, nature of public regulation and franchise provisions, character of territory served, public attitude, and the operating ratio, which were discussed in previous chapters, there are other measures that may be applied to gas securities. Attention again is directed to the many variable factors, such as community development, rate changes, service requirements, and inventions.

Units for making comparative analyses of different companies are the cost of the plant, or at times the investment fixed by the public service commission reduced to cost-per-mile-of-main base (preferably reduced to the equivalent of a three-inch main to provide a common base), the investment per customer, and per 1,000 cubic feet of gas sold. On this subject the American Gas Association has compiled interesting data from the reports of cost by thirty-five companies.[1] The report reads in part as follows:

". . . it will be noted that the equivalent size of main varies considerably with various companies, the largest being 9.16" in diameter and the smallest 4.32" in diameter. It will be interesting to see just how these two companies compare all the way through. On the area of comparison the company having 9.16" equivalent size of main has approximately 4.5 times as great carrying capacity as the company with the 4.32" equivalent size main. The annual sales per mile of main for these two cities are 13,452 M.C.F. [thousand cubic feet] for the first company and 2,005 M.C.F. for the second, or a ratio of 6.55 to 1. The annual sales per customer are 39.4 M.C.F. and 31.0 M.C.F. respectively. Although the average investment per mile of main for these two cities is $12,700 for the former company and $4,700 for the latter company, a ratio of 2.7 to 1, the investment per customer is in the reverse proportion, being $34 for the former and $73 for the latter. This shows that the investment cost of capacity is a great deal less in the larger sized mains than in the smaller. Likewise the investment cost per M.C.F. of gas sold is 88c for the first company and $2.35 for the second. The maximum demand per customer is 13.4 cubic feet per hour for the first company and 18.4 cubic feet per hour for the second. As would naturally be expected from these facts, the load factor for the year for the former company is 31% and for the latter only 18%.

"The first city is very densely populated, as is shown by the fact that there are 366 customers per mile of main, while the latter city is evidently very much spread out, having only 65 customers per mile of main. . . ."

The report further states that, "The yearly sales per customer is fairly consistent, averaging about 40 M.C.F. per customer per year for manufactured gas companies, and for natural gas companies shown (only two) the average sales per customer is 162 and 192 M.C.F. per year. These latter figures may be looked upon as the goal which we may ultimately reach with cheaper gas and a house heating load."[2]

It will be observed from the excerpt that in addition to the investment tests, use was made of such measures as the maximum demand per customer in cubic feet per hour, the maximum demand per mile of main in cubic feet per hour, the customers per mile of main sales in thousands of cubic feet (M. C. F.) per mile of main, and also the sales per customer in thousands of cubic

[1] *Proceedings of American Gas Association*, 1925, p. 1008.
[2] Ibid. pp. 1005 and 1006.

feet. By such comparative data the relative positions of two or more companies may be studied. The number of consumers per mile of main usually varies from 150 per mile of main to over 600 consumers per mile of main. The former indicates suburban and rural communities of sparse population, the latter such congested urban areas as in New York City. Other things being equal, the latter condition is to be desired as the investment per M. C. F. of gas sales will be much less.

All gas plants are subject to certain hourly peak load requirements occurring but once or twice a year, such as on Thanksgiving Day from 12:00 noon to 1:00 P. M., and must therefore maintain a distribution system to meet this extremely infrequent demand. Here we observe the advantage of the industrial load, for industrial requirements are reduced to a minimum on holidays, permitting the diversion of gas to domestic consumption. With the exception of holidays the greatest domestic demand occurs between the hours of 5:00 and 6:00 P. M. The industrial gas load would not impose any excess burden on the equipment if used during the off-peak and should therefore be encouraged to smooth out the sendout curve by lower rates for service during other hours.

Another test frequently made to determine the plant facilities is the number of miles of main, reduced to an equivalent of a 3-inch main, to 100 population served. A further index is the daily capacity which should normally range between 50,000 and 80,000 cubic feet per 1,000 population served.

Fixed and Working Capital.[1] Approximately 36 per cent. of the fixed capital is ordinarily invested in production assets, such as works and station structures, boiler plant equipment, relief holders, water gas sets, accessory works equipment, and land occupied by gas works. The remaining 64 per cent. is used to acquire distribution properties, such as commercial holders, service mains, house governors, consumers' meters, transmission and distribution feeders, and similar equipment. Of the distribution of fixed capital, approximately 73 per cent. is allocated to customer and 27 per cent. to distribution demand (the maximum delivery of gas in cubic feet in any period of time by the system as a whole or to any customer or class of customers).

[1] Data presented in this section are obtained mainly from *Proceedings of American Gas Association*, 1925, pp. 300 et seq.

The working capital of a gas company consists of cash, receivables and inventories of coal, coke, oil, maintenance parts, equipment for extension to new customers, appliances and office supplies. Of the total amount about 45 per cent. is devoted to customer demand, 33 per cent. to production demand, 17 per cent. to distribution demand, and 5 per cent. to commodity needs. Working capital is from 10 per cent to 15 per cent. of the total assets of a gas company.

The distribution of fixed capital among the several classes of service is as follows: 79.1 per cent. for domestic, 6.3 per cent. for commercial, 14.1 per cent. for industrial consumers, and .5 per cent. for other gas companies. The corresponding allocation of working capital is respectively: 78.9 per cent., 6.5 per cent., 14.1 per cent., and .5 per cent.

A large percentage of capital investment, both fixed and liquid, is therefore devoted to domestic needs, for the large portion of the distribution system necessarily serves the scattered domestic customers, and the inventories and supplies essential to adequate service must also be allocated to this group. The investment per M. C. F. of sales is also larger, which justifies higher rates to this class of patrons.

Operating Revenues. The revenues of gas companies range usually between $5 and $8 per annum per capita, and between $3,000 and $7,500 per annum per mile of main, depending on the customer density and on the uses. At present the annual sendout of gas per capita of territory served ranges between 3,000 and 6,000 cubic feet, but with increased industrial and household uses the output should show considerable increase within a few years. The revenues per mile of main may be compared with the per mile investment, but a more satisfactory test is the comparison of the total income (the amount available for interest and dividends) per mile of main to the investment per mile. Not unlike hydroelectric plants, gas companies are compelled to build plants in excess of present demands to anticipate future requirements.

The distribution of gas and the operating revenues derived from the various classes of services are tabulated as follows:

GAS DISTRIBUTION AND OPERATING REVENUES CLASSIFIED ACCORDING TO
SERVICE

Service	Gas Sales		Gas Sent Out		Gas Unaccounted for	Operating Revenue		
	M.C.F.	Per Cent. of Total	M.C.F.	Per Cent. of Total	Per Cent.	Amount	Rate per M.C.F. Sold	Per Cent.of Total
Domestic........	1,300,000	71.4	1,395,400	72.1	6.84	$1,400,000	$1.077	74.6
Commercial.....	175,000	9.6	180,000	9.3	2.77	166,250	.950	8.9
Industrial......	325,000	17.9	340,000	17.3	4.41	292,500	.900	15.6
Other Gas Corps.	20,000	1.1	20,900	1.1	4.31	17,000	.850	0.9
Total........	1,820,000	100.0	1,936,300	100.0	6.01	$1,875,750	$1.3306	100.0

This table shows the discrepancy between the amount of gas
sold and the volume actually sent out. This loss in unaccounted-
for gas is due to condensation or to leakage, and is highest in
domestic service. This factor in part explains the higher cost
to domestic users who consume 71.4 per cent. of the total gas
sold but contribute 74.6 per cent. of the total revenues. This
advantage is gained by the industrial users who take 17.9 per
cent. of the gas sold and pay for only 15.6 per cent. Observe
that the rate per M. C. F. for the various users shows a considerable variation.

Operating Expenses. In the accompanying table on page 394,
showing the distribution of expenses, among the various classes
of services, the more important operating rates of gas companies
have been compiled.

The Future of the Gas Industry. It is the common assertion
of the gas manufacturer that the fuel of the future will be gas.
Because of its greater heating efficiency and resultant conservation
of natural resources with accruing advantages to the public, gas,
it is claimed, will be the universal fuel. The gas industry was
driven out of the illumination field, the least profitable, and the
management was forced to search for new uses. The competition
of electricity aroused the gas industry from its lethargy. Realizing the superiority of gas for heating purposes, domestic fuel
for cooking was first developed, and later, industrial uses have
been emphasized, so that at present gas is not only considered
the ideal fuel, but the companies entertain the hope that it will
some day become the universal fuel.

The adoption of more scientific rate schedules, to encourage
industrial uses through wholesale prices will materially increase

Distribution of Operating Expenses and Operating Ratios Classified According to Service

Items of Operating Expenses	Class of Service				Total	
	Domestic	Commercial	Industrial	Other Gas Corporations	Amount	Per Cent.
1. Production Expense	$580,965	$74,629	$148,688	$8,718	$813,000	56.8
2. Distribution Expense	133,419	7,549	10,681	351	152,000	10.6
3. Commercial Expense	102,190	4,510	3,300	....	110,000	7.7
4. New Business Expense	10,000	6,000	8,000	1,000	25,000	1.7
5. General and Administrative Exp.—Direct Portion	24,684	1,670	2,540	106	29,000	2.0
6. " " " —Joint Portion	31,821	1,923	3,164	92	37,000	2.6
7. " " " —	25,974	4,218	6,401	407	37,000	2.6
8. Property Capitalization Taxes	97,836	8,060	17,484	620	124,000	8.7
9. Income Tax	10,530	1,710	2,595	165	15,000	1.0
10. Retirement Expense	71,190	5,670	12,690	450	90,000	6.3
11. Total Operating Expenses	$1,088,609	$115,939	$215,543	$11,909	$1,432,000	100.0
12. Total Operating Revenue	$1,400,000	166,250	292,500	17,000	1,875,750	
13. Income from Operations (12−11)	311,391	50,311	76,457	5,091	443,750	
14. Total Fixed Capital + Working Capital	6,055,105	495,243	1,085,026	38,626	7,674,000	
15. Return on Total Fixed Capital + Working Capital (13÷14)	5.14%	10.16%	7.05%	13.18%	5.78%	
16. Total Gas Sales—M.C.F.	1,300,000	175,000	325,000	20,000	1,820,000	
17. Total Operating Costs Per M.C.F. Gas Sold (11÷16)	83.74c.	66.25c.	66.32c.	59.55c.	78.68c.	
18. Operating Revenue per M.C.F. Gas Sold (12÷16)	107.70c.	95.00c.	90.00c.	85.00c.	103.06c.	
19. Operating Income per M.C.F. Gas Sold (13÷16)	23.96c.	28.75c.	23.68c.	25.45c.	24.38c.	

the volume of business and thereby cheapen production costs, which in turn make possible the reduction of rates to all customers. Large volume permits plant improvement primarily through extension and makes possible the installation of modern devices, which further reduce costs. The investor should not overlook the importance of the domestic load as a stabilizer of returns. Although greatest expansion is possible in the industrial field, yet the importance of increased domestic patronage cannot be overemphasized. Water and house heating are yet in the primal stage of development. Industrial volume is much less than potential requirements would justify, as evidenced by recent expansion due to the multifarious industrial uses.

The comparatively new development of operating and financial combinations of gas companies has effected many economies incident to large-scale operations and has also simplified financing. Money is now acquired at lower costs, and public confidence is increased through customer ownership of securities. Fair rates are likely to result in consequence of the greater publicity now effectively disseminated by committees on public utility information, which have been organized to convey interesting facts regarding the problems of the industry and the many uses to which its product may be put.

Bond Security. We have recently passed through a period of financial and commercial reaction. The great distress attending the set-back following the post-war inflation put all securities to the test. Gas securities during the period 1920–1921, maintained to a conspicuous degree their stability of return. As far as the effect upon earnings of general unsettled conditions is concerned, the margin of safety is as great among the sound and thoroughly established water and electric companies and gas companies as it was prior to the World War. In the case of water companies and electric light and power companies (both steam and hydro), this is due to fixed minimum revenues, theoretically insured, so to speak, by their contracts with consumers and by a kind of operating charges (having little to do with wages and materials) that hardly varies from year to year. In the case of large gas companies in the great cities it is due to the fact that gas is no longer a commodity to be classed among the luxuries, but rather among the domestic and industrial necessities, and even economies. People do not curtail their light and fuel in hard times. If gas, as a fuel, should ever become predominantly commercial rather than domestic—should be more generally employed to drive engines and serve for heating processes than to light rooms and cook food—the margin of safety for gas bonds might be affected; but even then, the improvement of the load factor would tend towards uniformity of returns. Financial panics and physical catastrophes do not usually produce declines in gross revenues, but merely a lessened rate of increase. The operating expenses are somewhat more variable than those of hydroelectric power companies (because of the item, materials purchased), and therefore exhibit less stability, but the result upon annual surplus is not very appreciable. In fact, during the recent depression gas and electric securities not only held their own, but in some instances actually improved. The stabilized condition of these industries warrants the investors' confidence.

Investment Suggestions. As regards gas securities, by implication the investor has been advised to buy only the mortgage bonds of large and thoroughly established companies in cities of 75,000 population and over; but the matter of population is relative. Cities in the South, for instance, with a large proportion of scattered poor-white or colored population should have that fact discounted and some growing cities with less than 50,000 inhabitants are perfectly safe. We have already noted that the greater the congestion the greater the per capita consumption. Often the increase in land values alone is a noteworthy reinforcement of mortgage security in growing cities. We have yet to hear of any such companies going to the wall in a business depression. As to franchises, their tenor is important in all public franchise corporations. Many companies are operating under perpetual charters; some, like the Milwaukee Gas Company, have exclusive franchises and are a pure monopoly; others, like the Laclede Gas Light Company of St. Louis, are immune by the terms of their charters from rate regulation by city or state. Of course the bonds should mature before the franchise. Many gas corporations are controlled through stock-ownership and run by large operating companies such as the American Light and Traction Company, the United Gas Improvement Company, the North American Company, the Cities Service Company, Standard Gas and Electric Company, and the Pacific

Gas and Electric Company. This should insure the economical and efficient management we have spoken of and at the same time give the investor an inkling of the true equity in the concern above the bonds that interest him, for by a little inquiry he may learn what was paid by the holding company for the capital stock. Those to whom the fear of competition with electricity looms large, may buy many good issues of consolidated companies that furnish their communities with both kinds of service.

Market and Yield. Having found the bonds that most nearly satisfy his requirements, the investor should expect to obtain them at such price as to net him from 5 to 6 per cent., according to the condition of the bond market and the excellence of the security. If he purchases for business reserves or under any conditions requiring possible quick disposal he may find prominent issues for which there is always a broad and ready market,— indeed issues listed on the principal exchanges; although the fact that they are listed will not facilitate the sale so much as it will prove a convenience in ascertaining the approximate price he can obtain. But apart from certain issues, which, whether listed or not, sell at higher prices because of their broader market, the investor buys to hold, just as he buys the bonds of street railways, and of power companies, and in so doing pays only for what he most desires: safety and high income. If he has to sell he anticipates the delay incident to the disposal of uncurrent securities, not expecting to get the selling conveniences for which he has not paid.

The additional fact that gas companies are resorting more to the sale of common stock to provide capital for expansion is an indication of the industry's more favorable investment position. The investment value of gas bonds is assured. Not only the record of safety, the increased equity being provided for the bonds, more scientific rate making and its direct effect on the value of securities, the rapid increase of send-out for industrial processes, the tendency toward consolidation through the instrumentality of the holding company, improved methods of production and distribution, but also better public relations as the outgrowth of improvement in service, and of employee and customer ownership promulgated by progressive managements.

CHAPTER XXXI

WATER COMPANY BONDS

Of all public service issues, none, perhaps, is more simple of understanding than Water Company Bonds. These are not to be confused with Water Power (frequently called Hydroelectric Power) Bonds, nor with the water bonds issued by municipalities. What is meant are bonds issued by companies that supply to municipalities, corporations, and individuals the advantages of hydrant and faucet for delivering water piped primarily as liquid rather than as power.

Conditions Affecting the Water Supply.[1] Water companies are not so dependent on steadiness of flow as power companies, because it is so much easier to store the fluid than the energy; but the ultimate source of supply must be unfailing from one year to another. Steam generators may substitute energy when waterpower fails, but there is no substitute for the supply of a water company. It ought never to fail. Therefore, the nature, extent, and permanency of the source, and the facilities for storage over a dry season require thorough investigation.

There is no uniformity of law throughout the country as to the right to draw water from rivers and other sources of supply. Priority of occupancy and appropriation is the cardinal principle of the arid states. Legislation elsewhere tends to conserve the flow and protect the quality of water for the benefit of all. A bond buyer will wish to be satisfied as to the protection offered by the state to the drawing of water for the fundamental uses of the water company. By law and natural conditions the company should be safeguarded from subsequent appropriation of the supply for irrigation, the generation of power, etc., as discussed in the chapter on Hydroelectric Bonds.

Since the use of water, even for drinking and other domestic purposes, requires a certain amount of energy of position, it is a pertinent question as affecting economy of operation how this head is obtained. The gravity system, sufficiently described

[1] See also the chapter on Hydroelectric Bonds.

in the name, is the most economical to instal and maintain. It is adapted, of course, to towns situated within reach of mountain heights.

The pumping system, common in the flat country of the Middle West, is not only more expensive to instal and maintain, since it requires machinery and some labor, but it is uneconomical in the sense that two sets of pumps are necessary for uninterrupted service, especially when the pumping is directly into the mains, rather than into standpipes. The use of both systems by one water company is not infrequent.

The Question of Quality.[1] The water supply interests an investigator in other respects than in quantity, steadiness, and permanency. Water companies sometimes face a serious difficulty that is unknown to power companies, in the quality of the water which they serve. Again the presumption is in favor of the gravity system. Water coming from the heights, removed from settlement and manufacturing, is generally of satisfactory quality; the impurities are usually mechanical and can be removed by sedimentation in reservoirs and settling basins. But water pumped from rivers is likely to contain vegetable impurities which can be eliminated only by filtration. Therefore it is usual to maintain testing laboratories at the pumping stations to make frequent if not daily examination of the supply for both chemical and bacteriological impurities.

Filtration, however, is not necessarily expensive; and the majority of modern plants are equipped with filtration systems. Consumers ordinarily do not object to paying for pure water; and a company's efforts to supply it, to the advantage of health and life, usually meet with adequate recognition and approval. Should the water contain salt, a more expensive purification process is necessary, such as is furnished by nitrate of silver.

In a considerable part of the West there is no potable water to deliver; the supply from the mains is too brackish. There may sometimes be relation between this fact and an unwillingness of the inhabitants, generally, to pipe from the new mains. In the long-settled East, rural communities, comfortably supplied with wells, may be reluctant to change because of prejudice, inertia, or frugality.

[1] For a review of service standards for water, see Delos F. Wilcox, *Public Utility Regulation,* edited by M. L. Cooke, p. 87.

The growth of a city expands the demand for water; but if by lack of proper foresight the source of supply has been located too near the city, the water may be contaminated. The well-known history of New York's public supply, costing $162,000,000 to obtain the desired increase, has analogues elsewhere.

It is of the utmost importance that the quality of water served be above suspicion. It is a most despicable trick of cutthroat finance to arouse in a community distrust of its water supply in the interest of a change of régime, as from private to municipal ownership;—or in order to depress the price of a company's securities. Whatever chances of success the scheme has are best in insular communities.

From the economic point of view, water companies are very favorably situated as to their supply. In a sense, water is their raw material, and is obtained free of cost except that of pumping and purifying. If the supply is good and permanent, earnings run no risk from price changes in the raw material. There may be transportation charges,—and right heavy,—as in the public works of Los Angeles and San Francisco, if the source is distant many miles; but the "cost of production," as distinguished from the cost of plant and properties, is low in relation to earnings. The utilization of the Los Angeles water for power purposes helps to defray the extra transportation charges.

Generally the water supply is a natural monopoly in that there is never a substitute for the raw material, and generally the company owns all the commercially practicable sources. Competition, relying on lessened costs or superior service, cannot, like Moses, strike the rock for this material. Less even than gas lighting, street railroading, and telephony, does water service lend itself to competition. In fact the writers know of no city where there is competition in the same district. Large cities may be served by two or more companies,—London has six (now municipal) water companies, each of which operates in its own section,—but it is to be doubted if any cities have companies competing in the same section.

Conditions Affecting the Water Demand. It is truly said that the demand for water is as certain and constant as the demand for food, and it is equally true that increase in demand is as certain as increase in the population of communities large enough to be served by water companies. Indeed the demand for piped water in this country is like population in this respect, that it never decreases. The question is merely as to the rate of increase. Therefore, the only instances in which we may fear that established water companies may fail for lack of demand for what they have to offer, is when the communities they serve are wiped out by some great catastrophe, or by the failure of the crops, product, or industry upon which the community thrived.

A progressive management may, however, obtain additional patronage by inducing industrial users operating their own pumping systems at heavy cost to abandon their private systems. Also the advantage of using the company's water may be demonstrated to those owning their own wells, by testing impurities in well water and by emphasizing the inconvenience of drawing water. It must be conceded, however, that the possibilities for increased use are dependent primarily on the growth of population, to a much greater degree in fact, that is true of either gas or electric service.

Even the fire and earthquake in San Francisco, and the flood in Galveston, did not cause suspension of business by the waterworks companies of these cities. Although the dividends on the Spring Valley Water Company of San Francisco were suspended from April, 1906, to December, 1908, yet, in 1907 the surplus was over 300 per cent. of the previous highest surplus. We know of no waterworks company in this country which has suspended business owing to a catastrophe.

The Plant and the Business. When a water service has been intelligently instituted and built in good faith, the elements of chance and danger are remote from the other departments of the business. The plant itself is not subject to rapid depreciation, and it is almost immune from fire. Repairs and renewals made necessary by wear, or the progress of invention, are few.[1] The mains, of cast-iron pipe, have an indeterminately long life. Cyclones, floods, and conflagration will not affect them. Hardly anything but earthquakes can.

The dependability of the water supply business is subject to the proviso that in the community there is a real need of piped water, and that the plant was honestly constructed of fair materials. Unfortunately, manufacturers of piping, pumps, or other

---

[1] For the most part, the same style of pump has been in use for the past forty years.

material, and general contractors often covenant with a small town to supply it with water protection against fire, in order to find a profitable outlet for materials and labor. The building of waterworks offers an excellent opportunity to bury the evidences of cheap material, and construction and labor. Thus in the past, the building of waterworks in this country has been overdone.

This, at least, was the situation 40 years ago. In fact, there was a circular issued in 1886 by one of the leading houses devoted to the sale of water company bonds, calling attention to the fact that many ill-advised waterworks properties were being constructed, among which some were promoted for purposes of manipulation only. Since that time, however, the inevitable weeding-out process of intelligent competition has hindered such practices and at present bond buyers are not likely to suffer from them.

The comparative simplicity of putting a water company on its feet and operating it until a customer is found for the plant and the securities has attracted many into the field who have not sufficient initiative, and capacity for organization, to undertake similar ventures into other public utilities. Here lies the danger in water bonds. The safeguard (as always) is reliance in the painstaking and intelligent examination of the property and the company's condition which any of the better bond houses will give.

In the simplicity of the business problems of the water companies one is reminded again of the hydroelectric companies. Neither have fire or labor troubles to contend with. When water pipes are metered (as they should be, especially in pumping plants) then there is something to be done, but usually the requirements on the management of a water company are less exacting than with other utilities.

Capitalization and Earnings. Without an engineer's report there is no way of ascertaining what is the fair capitalization for a water company, because the conditions under which the supply is obtained vary so widely. The necessary excess of net earnings over fixed charges can be smaller than in any other kind of private corporation because of the stability of earnings. It will be well to remember that the prime element of security is not material assets, such as those behind steamship and equipment bonds, easily convertible into money on foreclosure, but in the assurance of stable and increasing earnings, based on an inevitable demand for water. The per capita indebtedness of the company, computed on the population served, is a poor criterion of fair capitalization. An examination of 15 water companies in the United States serving communities of from 3,500 to 365,000 inhabitant shows a bonded debt per capita ranging from $12.50 to $78.88, and an average of $32.33.

With water companies there is usually a close relation between total capitalization and the book value of the physical properties. It is advisable for the investor to compare the value carried on the books with the valuation fixed by the public service commission,[1] taking into consideration the date of valuation, new additions since that date, the amount of the retirement reserve and the rate of depreciation charged against operations, the rate of return allowed by the commission on the valuation, the percentage of funded debt to valuation, the ratio of funded debt to total capitalization, and finally, to ascertain the margin of safety, the number of times interest has been earned. Commissions ordinarily allow 7 or 8 per cent. return on the value of the property; therefore with the operating ratio of, let us say, 50 per cent., the gross revenues should be at least twice 7 or 8 per cent. of the allowed value of the property. Interest charges should be earned at least two times. From 60 to 65 per cent. of the total capitalization may safely consist of bonds in a well-managed and established water company, with about 15 per cent. of the total consisting of preferred stock and the balance of common stock. Adequate equity is thus accorded the bonds, although, as previously stated, a larger percentage of funded debt is not objectionable in established communities which are expanding normally, provided always, that the utility has passed the development stage and has adequate water resources to take care of increasing requirements.

The stability of operating and selling conditions is reflected in earnings. With a virtually costless raw material, a reliable demand at a fixed rate, and freedom from competition, except from wells and similar sources of supply already established, it is not surprising that the earnings of water companies are un-

[1] See Decision on Valuation of Spring Valley Water Co., by U. S. District Court at San Francisco, July, 1918.

affected by business depression. In fact, there is no decline even in periods of depression; the earnings of water companies show a consistent upward trend. As long as the population of cities keeps increasing, so long should the earnings of established water companies grow in fair proportion. If anything further can strengthen the case, it may be recalled that water, particularly as supplied for domestic purposes, is paid for in advance, by reason of the usual initial deposit required; and all bills are paid at the offices of the company, so that it does not have even the expenses of collection. Water companies market their product also without the need or expense of a selling force, or of advertising.

Management. But the inference is not that the business of supplying water to communities runs entirely of itself. The matter of management is important; only the importance lies in the friendly relation of the management to the municipality, rather than in the necessity of technical qualifications of a high order. Hence, local management is to be desired, when, as usually, that entails favorable effect upon local sentiment.[1] If water is now supplied at a flat rate, and it becomes advisable to introduce meters, or if there is hydrant or other municipal business to be had or kept, officials skilled in diplomacy, and not antagonistic to the voters or city government, greatly aid the company's welfare.

Contracts and Franchises. In the large majority of companies the chief contract is with the city. The objects for which a municipality may need water are numerous. There are the ordinary uses to which water is put in any public building. Particularly water is needed for street hydrants: for sprinkling streets and extinguishing fires. The duration of this municipal contract, and the possibility of its abrogation if the terms are broken are matters to be considered if a large part of the company's income is derived from this source.

Not only a considerate management but reasonably favorable rates will be necessary to insure a renewal of the contract on favorable terms, at its expiration, and to discourage any thought of starting a separate plant for the public uses of the city, if this

---

[1] Local operating companies may, however, profit under the control and guidance of large holding companies, such as the American Water Works and Electric Co.

is physically possible, or the thought of buying out the existing plant for municipal ownership. It must not be assumed that rates which are apparently permanent may not be adjusted if found to be higher than the value of the service to consumers.[1]

Although naturally, and inevitably, municipal ownership and operation of industries is economically unsound, nevertheless we have lived so long with the idea, that former instinctive prejudices are dying out, and when a real, or supposedly real, advantage from such ownership appears, public service corporations may be in some danger of their existence. There is always the possibility that a city will contemplate the absorption of a public service company that controls such a natural monopoly as the supply of water; especially is this true if private companies neglect to the slightest degree sanitary precautions. Frequent testings are of paramount importance.

Theoretically, at least, municipal ownership should not prejudice the interests of bondholders. It may even strengthen the security, because the city may guarantee the bonds in assuming the indebtedness; but, practically, any change in the *status quo* of a security is liable to work injury, at least for a time.

The ideal franchise of any company is the terminable permit, when granted by cities under commission control. Communities are coming to realize the value of their gifts of public rights, and seldom will renew them on terms as satisfactory as before. If such be the case the longer the duration of the franchise the better. If limited, it should outlast the life of the bonds by a few years at least.

Another point in relation to contracts and franchises invites comment. If the company's charter requires in so many words that the water served must be pure, there opens the question of interpretation. Purity, as applied to water, the commercial product, is a relative term. It is conceivable that some ill-wisher, with ends to serve, might cause a company considerable trouble on this score, if it was worth while.

Amortization. When the franchises are perpetual there is not that great need of the gradual amortization of the debt which obtains if the privilege of doing business expires within a few

[1] See Kennebec Water District vs. City of Waterville, 97 Me. 185, Atl. 6. Me. Supreme Court, 1902.

years of the debt's maturity. Although water company property is subject to slower depreciation than steamship, timber, and equipment properties, yet amortization should not be neglected, so that each unit of output may be charged with its costs of production, but also to provide for the replacement of the depreciating asset. Sinking fund and serial bonds, so popular with public utility companies a decade ago, are now seldom issued. In lieu of sinking funds deposited with a trustee on which a low rate of interest is derived, or even the periodic redemption of outstanding issues from earnings, the modern practice is to invest the depreciation reserves, and any other sum considered necessary for the protection of the bondholder, in capital assets, thus building up the bond equity and making possible a refunding issue on favorable terms at the maturity of the outstanding bonds. Under commission regulation earnings are usually insufficient to defray necessary expenses and still pay a fair return on the investment and retire the maturing bonds. Moreover, even if the company were justified in borrowing, there should be the same justification for extending the loan. Redemption privilege is usually reserved by the company if it is compelled to finance its requirements during high money rates or when its credit is impaired, the company expecting to refund at lower rates at a more opportune time.

Water Bonds in Foreclosure. If the bondholders cannot obtain full satisfaction in foreclosure proceedings, they might do worse than run the plant themselves. What is quite impossible in railroading is very feasible in this case because of the comparative simplicity of operating the water plant.

Viewed in all its aspects the purchase of the bonds of wellestablished water companies is to be encouraged, when convertibility is not essential to the investment. And even in convertibility they are superior to irrigation, steamship, timber, real estate, and some other kinds of issues.

Some of the large holding companies not only supervise, manage, and finance many small companies, but also frequently guarantee the bonds of their subsidiaries so that next to the actual value of the lien there is the obligation of the parent company. These holding companies can seldom afford to permit their subsidiaries to default because of the general effect it would have on their own credit. At times the parent company stands ready to relieve any bondholder of his holdings which more or less assures marketability.

Bonds of established water companies operating in cities of increasing population and enjoying public confidence because of efficient service at reasonable rates are among the premier investments. Yields at present from $5\frac{1}{2}$ to $6\frac{1}{4}$ per cent. should be realized.

CHAPTER XXXII

HYDROELECTRIC POWER COMPANY BONDS

The title " Hydroelectric Power Bonds" is slightly too narrow for the subject in hand, since the sources from which companies properly associated with these securities derive their income is by no means confined to electricity generated from the fall of water. But the primary, and generally original, revenue is from hydroelectric power. As a complement to it steam-generated electric power from auxiliary stations is often produced in connection with rivers of great variability of flow, or rivers from which all possible power is immediately to be taken. These stations are usually emergency reserves, to fall back upon should the dam give way, or the water prove insufficient during a period of drought. Steam stations are not necessarily located near the water power, but rather where coal is procurable to best advantage, and this may be in the city where the power is principally marketed. A third and often important source of revenue is derived from the sale of hydraulic power to local manufactories at or near the falls. Naturally this form of power does not bring a high price,—but requiring only simple machinery and converting into profit what, at the time, would otherwise be waste water, it proves worthy of consideration. Another source of revenue, which may prove very important, though from the bondholders' standpoint highly speculative during the early stages of a company's development, is that derived from industrial operations conducted, directly or indirectly, through stock ownership by the power company itself.

Waterpower development is by no means of recent origin, for man has harnessed water to serve his purposes for many centuries. In fact, so dependent on waterpower was industry that even as recently as 1870 waterpower constituted about 48 per cent. of the total motive power. But with more powerful steam engines, more efficient electrical generation and improved transmission through the invention of alternating current and long-distance high-voltage transmission systems, the old water wheel has gradually given way until to-day it furnishes only a small percentage of total motive force. However, recent developments, primarily inventive, give new impetus to the waterpower industry through hydroelectric generation. Yet, of the water-power resources of the United States, estimated at about 55 million horsepower, less than nine millions have been developed. Approximately six millions more have been authorized.

Impracticability of Developing all Waterpowers. The estimated waterpower resources approximate the total electrical generating equipment in the United States. Yet it must not be assumed that the undeveloped water resources are immediately or perhaps even remotely available. Only 10 per cent. of the population of the United States live west of the Rocky Mountains where fully 75 per cent. of the potential waterpower exists, —i.e. 90 per cent. of our population have access to only 25 per cent. of our hydro resources.

Relative Importance of Steam and Hydroelectric Power. "When will Niagara Falls reach out here?" asked a North Dakota farmer. Little did he appreciate the problems involved in electrical transmission or the comparatively insignificant contribution of Niagara Falls. With the Falls furnishing about $4\frac{1}{2}$ per cent. of the nation's electrical energy, and Muscle Shoals' potential generating capacity less than a single steam-generating plant in Chicago, with 75 per cent. of our hydro resources west of the Mississippi River, and with 79 per cent. of the demand for electricity in the East, hydro development, though extremely important, falls far short of supplying the country's demand for electrical energy. In fact, if the total potential waterpower were now harnessed and available for use where required it would barely provide the present demand, yet every horsepower produced by water conserves so much fuel for other uses. Contrary to general opinion, hydroelectric energy is not necessarily cheap power, for, as already stated, the initial investment is so much greater than that of steam plants that satisfactory returns thereon more than offset savings in fuel, labor, and other costs more heavily incident to steam plants. Nor is the availability of waterpower the controlling factor in most industries. More important are proximity to the market of raw materials, finished products, skilled labor, suitable climate, equitable taxes, and convenient transportation. Combined costs of fuel used for heat in manufacturing processes and mechanical power, according to the United States Census Bureau, constitute, on the average, only 2.8 per cent. of the value of the product. Therefore, power costs do not determine the location or expansion of an industry.

Federal Waterpower Act. The Federal Waterpower Act of June 10, 1920, designed to promote the development of waterpower resources for the production of electrical energy, was an outgrowth of earlier regulations beginning with Colonial control and extending through state regulation after the adoption of the Federal Constitution. Precedents were established as early as 1638 for three far-reaching governmental powers: government control of waterpower resources, regulation of waterpower plants, and government ownership of waterpower industries.[1] Four definite objects sought by the states were: absolute control of streams considered non-navigable, hence not under federal control, protection from monopoly, protection of private property near power sites, and encouragement of the development of waterpower industries.[2] Many regulations obtained in the various states but those of Maine were a prototype for the Federal Act of 1920.

The Federal Waterpower Act provides for the creation of a commission comprising the Secretaries of War, of the Interior, and of Agriculture. The Commission is authorized to conduct investigations, to dispose of judicial and legal questions incident to the Act, to issue permits and licenses, to publish information, and submit copies of the commission's records. The act grew out of the demand for effective control of water resources and recognition of the fact that Congress has control of all navigable streams, government lands, and riparian rights in government lands bordering on streams.[3] It is likewise established that the

[1] Conover, Milton, *The Federal Power Commission, Its History, Activities and Organization*, p. 4.

[2] Ibid., p. 7.

[3] For federal powers in connection with control of waterpower resources and also for the unconstitutionality of the attempt of states to prevent the exportation of natural resources, or products therefrom, see "The Water Problem in the United States," Brown, Rome G., 24 *Yale Law Journal*, 12; "Federal Power of Legislation as to the Development of Water Power," Howell, Roger, 50 *American Law Review*, 883; "Limitation by a State of Exportation of its Natural Resources," 24 *Columbia Law Review*, 64.

exportation of a legitimate article of commerce cannot be prevented by a state with the exception of goods in which it has proprietary interest, such as fresh waters,[1] or even wild game. It would seem, therefore, that district development of waterpower resources without regard to state boundaries would come under the jurisdiction of the Federal Waterpower Act, but such is not the case. Only properties owned by the Federal Government or those applicable to the commerce clause relative to interstate and foreign commerce are subject to such control. However, it is estimated that about 85 per cent. of all undeveloped waterpower resources come under the provisions of the Act. The tristate negotiations between Pennsylvania, New Jersey, and New York relative to the utilization of the water resources of the Delaware River for power and municipal water systems illustrate well the difficulties involved when an attempt is made to promote the development of natural resources lying within the boundaries of several states, and not under federal control.[2]

The fear of many that all our natural resources are being appropriated to private use to the detriment of the public is to a large degree unwarranted. A private concern developing waterpower under the Federal Waterpower Act submits to regulation by three different authorities. Permission to utilize the resource is granted, under definite restrictions, by the Federal Waterpower Commission, a certificate of public convenience and necessity allowing it to do business is granted under the State Public Utility Act, and it secures franchises to use streets and highways from the municipal or county government. The federal act fully recognizes the right of the states to regulate intrastate rates and service. In fact the act is so restrictive that the Commission could not, even though it should desire, usurp the authority vested in state utility commissions. In this way adequate protection to the public through the three agencies, federal, state, and municipal, is assured.

Just what constitutes riparian rights is problematical, for there are many conflicting court decisions on the subject. Some states, notably in the East, operate under the old common-law

[1] Hudson Water Co. vs. McCarter (1908), 209 U. S. 349, 28 Sup. Ct. 529.

[2] For an interesting summary of the proposed compact, as viewed from the point of view of New Jersey, see *Report of the Water Policy Commission of New Jersey*, 1926, Parts I and II.

doctrine which requires each riparian owner to permit the unabated flow of a stream bordering on his land, but other states, mainly in the West where irrigation is prevalent, hold to the doctrine of " appropriation and use " in which all water may, under state regulation, be put to any beneficial use. The investor in hydroelectric securities should, therefore, assure himself as to the validity of water rights claimed by his company since many claims have not been adjudicated.

Coördination of Hydro and Steam Developments.[1] Steampower plants, serviceable as auxiliaries, may prove dangerous as competitors. The incentives to competition from steam-generators are the relatively low first cost, and the convenience of their nearness to demand for the energy as against the necessity of long-distance high-voltage transmission lines with attendant losses and additional expenses to the hydro plants.

The popular opinion which regards the hydro plants as more important than the steam plants is erroneous. In fact only a very small amount of steam capacity has ever been supplanted by waterpower. Of the 56,000,000 horsepower capacity of electric power plants less than nine million horsepower is hydro, and the rate of development has been continuously greater for steam plants than for hydro systems (since 1919 electricity produced by fuels has expanded almost 80 per cent., and that produced by waterpower has increased only 50 per cent.). In California, where hydro development has been extensive, it has been necessary to supplement the waterpower systems with reserve steam plants so as to assure continued uniformity of service. Since hydro service is subject to interruption from various causes, such as drought, ice, washouts or breaking of dams, steam plants as auxiliaries become necessary. Naturally the investment per kilowatt capacity rises, which further increases the burden of hydroelectric companies. In 1924 the waterpower output in California declined 29 per cent. from the preceding year due to the drought, the power produced by the hydro plants declining from 81.6 per cent. of the total power produced to 57.2 per cent. Overload operations resulted before relief was possible from increased rainfall and from additional plant construction. The Pacific Gas and Electric Company, because of

---

[1] As supplemental reading, see *Proceedings National Electric Light Association*, 1925, pp. 1704 et seq.

the drought, was compelled at considerable expense to augment its steam plant at Sacramento.

In the West, because of favorable waterpower sites and inadequate coal supplies early hydroelectric development was stimulated, whereas in the East, with fewer power sites but with an abundant supply of efficient coal procurable at reasonable prices, steam development predominates. The West depends on steam plants as auxiliaries only, but the East attempts to utilize the waterpower for the most part as a secondary source of motive power. Of course the Niagara and St. Lawrence River projects are notable exceptions. Interconnection of systems, discussed in the previous chapter, has stimulated hydro development in various sections of the East due to the practicability of power exchange without the necessity of transmitting power over prohibitive distances (usually beyond 250 miles).

Hydro development proves most effective when combined with steam stations. Plants of this character operating independently are justified only when they are more economical in comparison with cost of production by coal or other fuels. Coördination of steam and hydroelectric plants where feasible is most desirable.

The table below shows the development, actually and relatively, between hydro and fuel power plants for the years 1923, 1924, and 1925.

OPERATIONS OF HYDRO AND FUEL POWER PLANTS, FROM
1923 TO 1925 [1]

Year	Hydro Plants		Fuel Power Plants	
	Thousands of Kw.-Hr. Generated	Per Cent. of Total	Thousands of Kw.-Hr. Generated	Per Cent. of Total
1923.......	19,113,352	37.4	32,019,531	62.6
1924.......	19,646,801	36.1	34,766,602	63.9
1925.......	21,570,000	36.2	37,947,000	63.8

Conditions Affecting the Power Supply. The prime necessity, of course, is water,—for conversion into horsepower. Preliminary estimates of a stream's potential horsepower often prove wide of the mark. Engineer's optimism, as it sometimes

[1] Data compiled from the *Electrical World*. Jan. 2, 1926, p. 9.

appears on the preliminary offering, should for safety's sake be somewhat discounted. The figures may err as often by understating as by overstating the facts, but a power proposition that does not look attractive, even after reasonable deductions for the sake of conservatism, is not a desirable investment. In figuring earning capacity one should also deduct the necessary and very generous percentage of waste involved in converting the energy of falling water into electricity for distribution, and in transmitting the electricity to its markets. It should also be ascertained whether in the first place the rating was based upon the minimum flow of the river through a series of years past, for how many consecutive years readings had been taken, whether the readings were from government or private gauging, and who in general was responsible for the hydrography on which the estimates were based.

There are many conditions affecting the water supply at the point of intake by the turbines. A careful survey, an extremely difficult task, must take into consideration not only hydrographic, topographic, and geologic conditions, but also the economic benefits to be derived from proposed hydro developments. Analysis should be made of the amount of precipitation, transpiration by vegetation, evaporation from the soil, percolation of water that never enters the streams, the extent and nature of the drainage area, the feasibility of storage as affected by the topographical conditions (such as suitable sites for a plant and reservoir requirements), nature of formation, safety of reservoir, possible damage above the dam because of flooding lands or below by breakage or large overflow, and inadequate water supply in periods of drought. Also proper weight should be attributed to the economic factors affected by initial cost of installation, necessary length of transmission lines, climatic conditions affecting maintenance of equipment and transmission system as well as ditches and flumes where the water is drawn for considerable distances, and the relative advantages when compared with steam-generating plants.

Attempts to predict water supply accurately have been numerous but the results have not been entirely satisfactory. Precipitation data assist in forecasting seasonal, monthly, and daily runoffs, and enable the management to make provision for uniform flowage or adequate impounding in reservoirs. Long-time forecasts are less accurate but also less important unless considerable storage is essential. In times when flows are less than plant capacity there is urgent need for accurate data so as to utilize the water most economically and to make provision, if necessary, for steam auxiliaries or interconnection service. It is evident that accurate estimates of maximum, minimum, and average flow are important in order to ascertain the type and capacity of plant to be constructed; and after construction to regulate storage, to purchase proper quantities of coal, if steam auxiliary plants are used, and where the steam auxiliary must be used from time to time, depending on the run-off, provision should be made for dividend equalization reserves for years of drought.

Results of water-supply forecasts should be accepted only after several years' experience and when the many factors which tend to vitiate the accuracy of the results have been given due consideration.

The Drainage Area. Even if a river's flow bears a good record in the past, future conditions are quite another matter. Perhaps the source of supply is concentrated in a few springs which future deforestation may dry up, or perhaps the topography of the country is such that the headwaters may be diverted, without legal redress, for purposes of irrigation, and the like. It is well to have as many thousands of square miles of drainage area as possible. Mountain sources are excellent, for melting snows in summertime bring dependable reinforcement to an otherwise dwindling flow. In these respects nature favors the great Montana power-plants on the Missouri River, for the Missouri's headwaters are in the snows of the Rockies and its flow is greatest during the warm months when the requirements for irrigation would otherwise be embarrassing. One of the causes for the ultimate Pacific Coast supremacy of the cities of Puget Sound is the unlimited and unfailing source of electrical power in the nearby snow-capped Cascade Range. But although mountain sources are a welcome reinforcement in the dry season they do not necessarily tend to steadiness in flow, as the Missouri amply demonstrates. In this respect there is a great variability among rivers.

The Storage Reservoir. It is to the ultimate sources of water supply such as mentioned that one must look for the amount and stability of flow from month to month and season to season. The daily flow is regulated to avoid waste by creating an immediate and artificial source and storage of supply. In estimating potential horsepower engineers figure, as a rule, upon a ten-hour day, but under ordinary conditions of nature, the water during the other fourteen hours is not lost, but stored behind the dam in a reservoir which is usually an enlargement of the river and dependent for its continence on the banks of the river and the dam-wall. When water is low, the reservoir level is raised by the erection of flashboards upon the crest of the dam. The pondage, or capacity, of this reservoir is of the utmost moment in tiding the company over a period of dry weather and in determining the power-capacity of the plant. Particularly is this true of those sections of the country that have a dry season. One should be assured that all condemnation proceedings covering this area have been brought to successful conclusion and that all other necessary riparian rights, both up and down stream, have been secured without possible future liability. Some rivers, of course, have such contour that the storage of water is impossible.

The Power-Plant Construction. Then, as to the dam itself, and the power-house,—it sometimes happens that quicksand is encountered in the bed of the river, or some other deterrent to a solid foundation for the dam. Even preliminary borings do not always discover these weaknesses. It is well if the site of the dam has a rock ledge for a wall-foundation, and the rockier the natural formation of the storage basin the better. In northern waterpowers ice [1] and snow often have been serious menaces to efficiency in late winter, but these difficulties are now more easily overcome. The deposit of silt is another obstruction. Some sites are of such formation that the ice and silt factors are negligible. The power-house should be so situated that it would not be carried away if the dam should go. It seems almost as if no perfection of masonry or mathematics could achieve an absolutely sure resistance to the force of accumulated waters. Herein is the greatest element of chance concerning waterpower construction; the most approved modern work occasionally goes down before an overwhelming flood. From

[1] Note experiences of The Western States Gas & Electric Company, *Electrical World*, May 29, 1926, p. 1183.

this cause, when a series of dams is situated upon the same river, the upper ones are a menace to those downstream.

Herein lies the greatest risk in purchasing waterpower securities when the plant is in the construction stage. Although the number of physical mishaps is relatively small, sometimes they seem as unforeseeable and unpreventable as earthquakes and tidal waves.

Construction Costs. The corollary evil is that estimates of construction, figured with great care and in good faith, will sometimes fall short of the actual outlay in such an amount that when the plant is completed at the additional cost it cannot earn a fair return on the capitalization. This additional cost is particularly objectionable in the case of hydroelectric plants, for the very nature of the construction usually requires original installation in anticipation of future needs considerable in excess of immediate requirements. Unlike the steam plant, it cannot economically instal additional units as increased patronage demands. Initial investment, therefore, is frequently greater than that on which a satisfactory rate of return can be immediately realized.

The investor should study construction costs in relation to kilowatt or horsepower capacity and also in relation to gross revenues. If the construction cost per kilowatt or horsepower is compared with the gross income per kilowatt or horsepower a satisfactory basis of analysis is established to measure experience or to forecast probable results. Normally the gross income (that is, the amount available for the interest and dividends) should be relatively larger per kilowatt capacity with hydroelectrics than with steam-electrics because of the greater investment per kilowatt and even per dollar of revenue, as discussed in an earlier chapter. The bondholder is also interested to know the funded debt per kilowatt or horsepower which, when compared with the kilowatt or horsepower capacity cost, indicates the equity. For hydroelectric companies the funded debt per horsepower ranges normally between $100 and $250, and the total capitalization usually ranges between $200 and $500 but occasionally exceeds $1,000. It will be observed that definite figures are not given simply because construction costs are subject to so many variables that only general averages are of any value.

Conditions Affecting the Power Demand. Granting that the company in question makes a satisfactory showing in all respects affecting its power supply, it is equally important that it be able to meet the requirements of profitable demand, for doubtless many more companies suffer from commercial, than from engineering imperfections.

The Power Market. The broadest business consideration is the location and character of the market. The proximity of a city is desirable though not imperative, as we have seen. The delivery of power 250 miles from the source of supply is no longer an experiment. If men financially interested in the power company control neighboring industries requiring its produce, as is often the case, so much the better, for enlightened coöperation results between producers and consumers. Certain districts, by reason of their natural resources, and certain industries, are practically dependent upon electric power to do business in competition at a profit. This is particularly so in mining and smelting, and for all operations requiring portable power. The South finds it highly desirable in the cotton industry. Practically all industries, as a matter of fact, now demand electric power. The mountainous Northwest utilizes it for transportation owing to the greater tractive power of electricity. In fact, to the very minutest of domestic employments, the market for electricity is broadening to such an extent that this is truly the " Electric Age." The age of steam is surely passing. But mines are eventually worked out, and mills will shut down, so the investor will see to it that a diversity of interests is responsible for the revenues of the company to which his money is loaned. Not too great a proportion of the power should be sold for any one object or to any one organization.

In estimating the amount of power which should be taken by a certain industry or community, one cannot count on securing the custom of all those to whose profit it certainly would be to turn from steam power to electric. Small manufacturers are often inert and skeptical, and averse on general principles to capital expenditures. The process of enlightenment is slow. In some instances it may be found that for certain technical reasons the proposed change would be an advantage more apparent than real. For instance, whatever the local price of coal, oil, or electricity, woodworking plants often will find it cheaper to consume their own waste for power rather than to purchase power in the open market. Therefore, weight should be given to the estimates of none but experienced electrical engineers, in considering the market for power.

Gross Operating Revenues and Operating Costs. High load factor, provided rates are constant, increases the revenue per dollar of investment in that a larger per cent. of the plant capacity, as discussed in the previous chapter, is kept continuously in operation. The load factor is characteristically higher with hydroelectric companies than with steam. Many industrial users—usually true of hydroelectric customers—furnish considerable diversification of use, so important to uniformity of returns. An offsetting disadvantage to industrial use, however, is the fluctuation of industrial demand dependent on the prosperity of the industry. Commercial and industrial demand is usually less constant than domestic. But while the fluctuation in industrial demand is greater, as evidenced by a statistical comparison over a period of years of kilowatt-hours sold and also gross revenues, yet it helps to level down the peak load to general advantage of the company and its customers. As fuel and labor costs are negligible quantities with hydroelectric companies there accrues, with each increase of the load factor, more than a proportionate advantage to them as compared with steam companies. The hydroelectric power company must solve the problem of efficient utilization of a large capital investment per kilowatt capacity.

Unfortunately operating revenues do not rise and fall in harmony with changes in operating costs. The reluctance of public service commissions to permit increased rates in the face of rising costs causes revenues in a period of rising prices to lag behind expenses, but in a period of declining prices the advantage accrues to the company unless public agitation brings down the rates.

The Operating Ratio. With rising costs of coal and labor the hydro plant is in a much better position than the steam company as its operating ratio will not rise to the same proportions. The constancy of the ratio is determined by the character of the contracts, their duration and rates, and not by the invariables: material and labor. Such a large percentage of earnings must be devoted to a suitable return on the large investment that of necessity there must be a lower operating ratio there. In this regard fortunately the operating ratio in periods of high prices is more favorable than with perhaps any of the other public utilities. It will be observed, therefore, that with proper diversification so as to increase the load factor, and with material and labor costs less important, there will result a low operating ratio which makes possible larger fixed charges than obtains with other utilities.

Competition. Since the contracts for power are usually of shorter duration than the life of the bonds, a renewal upon favorable terms is best safeguarded by the absence of competition. Many districts are open to criticism in this respect. On the other hand, this disadvantage is often offset by the certain future growth in demand for power. Competition, again, may be mechanically possible, but commercially impracticable, or may be politically stifled by apparently exclusive franchises, only to be resuscitated under a different dispensation. Each case must be settled upon its merits.

The mere fact that electric power is cheaper than coal power is not necessarily sufficient to warrant its employment. Many industries require heat as well as power. For instance, the four-drinier machines of the paper companies are regularly run by steam power, because rolls must be heated and the steam can advantageously be used for this purpose after being passed through an engine to give the necessary power. Electric heating for industrial uses has made notable progress during recent years.

There might arise competition for waterpower which originally was considered free from competitive demand. Irrigation projects or even other waterpower companies might divert the water without infringing the existing power rights of the operating power plant. The necessity for adequate protection against such contingencies is obvious. Without assurance that no competitor may enter the territory there might develop not only competition for waterpower or water supply but also for customers if the existing company's important contracts should be of short duration.

Nature of the Contracts. In order to meet the contingencies that have been mentioned and to avoid the consequences of commercial depression, it is well for a new company to be tied up with long-time contracts which of themselves will pay a large proportion of the fixed charges. There are two sides, however, to this long-time contract matter and the layman is likely to overlook one or the other. A company in its infancy is not often in a position to dictate, and its early contracts are not usually on as good terms as its later ones. A power company does well to have some short-term contracts maturing in such way as to adjust themselves to bettering conditions on much the same principle that a trust fund distributes the maturities of its loans. There have been companies with long 10,000 h. p. contracts outstanding, which they were glad to sign years ago, but to be released from later would have been well worth $50,000 a year to them. The power company should be protected in its contracts by a clause making them temporarily voidable in case of " circumstances beyond control." The intending bond purchaser may seem hypercritical, but no harm is done, if the company is dependent upon one or two big contracts, should he require the specific terms in which they are couched. Much depends on the contract. As to actual horsepower prices, conditions vary so that no general statement avails.

The Bonds: Income Yield. But, as suggested, one of the most favorable features about investment in hydroelectric power bonds is the relative accuracy with which future results may be forecasted from given conditions, even before one stone has been laid upon another. Accountants, collaborating with engineers, can estimate with some precision, after the major power contracts have been signed, what will be the minimum income of the company after a year's operation. This is not possible, of course, in the case of many other kinds of companies that ordinarily issue bonds; few other kinds have a minimum revenue insured by contracts. Hydroelectric power bonds are therefore peculiarly adapted to purchase in the underwriting and construction stages.

Marketability and Investment Value. Bonds of hydroelectric companies are somewhat removed from speculative influences and are not subject to the extremes in price that offer opportunities for profit or loss in liquidation. Although they are classed with other high-grade securities yet the market for them is comparatively narrow. Of recent years, however, there is a marked tendency toward larger developments, several big companies rivalling the steam plants (and in one case leading them—Niagara Falls Power Company) in kilowatt-hours output, which tends to broaden the market for their securities. Waterpower company, bonds may, as a class, be considered conservative investments, because of the stability of earnings, a usually favorable relationship with public service commissions, general increase in uses to which electric energy is devoted, improved efficiency in operation and distribution, conservative managements, considerable freedom from many ills attending certain phases of the business cycle, and protective provisions in the mortgage indenture.

Several large investment bankers now specialize in electric light and power issues and so assist their marketability; other issues are listed on the various exchanges, and a number are narrowly held. They are not as a class highly marketable, but the degree of convertibility is sufficient for most investors, especially trust estates where marketability is of secondary importance.

To show moderate appreciation in value, bonds of good companies, bought with care during the period of development, need only the improved demand that comes when confidence is established by substantial earnings and a fair dividend record.

Hydroelectric bonds are a desirable investment for those who are capable of making sound, independent investigations, and who seek a fairly large return with reasonable security, rather than a high degree of convertibility.

CHAPTER XXXIII

TELEPHONE AND TELEGRAPH BONDS

Historical Development. Contrary to general belief, Alexander Graham Bell was not the first in the field of sound transmission. In 1837 Pye discovered that sound could be transmitted by the use of an iron bar which was intermittently magnetized and demagnetized. A German named Reis used electricity to assist in sound transmission for considerable distances, but he doubted the practicability of his invention. On February 14, 1876, both Elisha Gray and Alexander Graham Bell filed patents in Washington for different methods of sound transmission. Of the two Mr. Bell's method proved more practicable, yet, notwithstanding its practicability and the general interest aroused in the idea as a result of an extensive demonstration at the Centennial Exposition in Philadelphia in 1876, there were few business men who appreciated its latent possibilities from a commercial point of view and they were, therefore, reluctant to lend financial assistance to the inventor. It was not until June, 1879, that the Bell Telephone stock was actually sold to the public.

In 1876 the first complete sentence was transmitted by telephone. In 1876 also the first conversation by overhead line (between Boston and Cambridge, a distance of two miles) took place, and Mr. Bell was one of the participants. In the beginning there was a single wire connecting one's residence with one's place of business, for the idea of central stations or an independent industry had not occurred to anyone.[1] It was believed, however, that where business was insufficient to support paid telegraph operators, the telephone might supplement the telegraph system by relaying the message and thereby extending telegraphic service. During this early period of experimentation and development the telegraph wires were utilized for telephone messages. The dominating company in the telegraph industry,

[1] March 25, 1878, Mr. Bell, however, outlined to London capitalists, an elaborate system of interconnecting telephones, the lines to extend as cables underground or suspended overhead.

Western Union Telegraph Company, was incorporated in 1851 and was well established by 1876. Many telegraph companies operating in various sections of the country in time either were leased or their stock acquired.

Shortly after the first successful conversation, in 1876, the Bell Telephone Company was organized under the trusteeship of Gardiner G. Hubbard.[1] The early practice, was to lease the telephone equipment, but the lessee built his own transmission lines. The company undertook to build lines at charges ranging from $100 to $150 per mile and to lease two telephones—one for each end of the line—for $20 per annum for residence and $40 for business purposes, payable semiannually in advance. It was not until 1878 that the first telephone exchange was established, destined to promote intercommunication on a then inconceived scale. Without the development of the exchange system, with uniformity of structure and functioning, the veritable network of interconnected telephone lines which now exists obviously would not have been possible. Many companies came into existence and were given exclusive privileges and rights under Bell patents in various sections of the country. Following the organization of the New England Telephone Company in 1878 (given exclusive rights in New England), and that of the Bell Telephone Company (enjoying exclusive privileges in Canada and the United States except New England), the National Bell Telephone Company was organized in 1879 to absorb the two existing companies and to vest control of patent rights in both the United States and Canada in a single company.

Because of the financial problems involved these early companies encouraged the organization of locally owned operating companies which for a period of five or ten years were given exclusive privileges in the use of telephone instruments at stipulated rentals. The contract provided for the purchase of the operating company by the licensing company at the end of the rental period if the latter so desired. Under this arrangement installations increased rapidly. Activity was further stimulated in 1880 by the forty-five mile conversation on overhead line between Boston and Providence, followed the next year by a conversation along underground cable for a distance of one-

---

[1] July 9, 1877. The Bell Telephone Company succeeded an early organization composed of Mr. Bell and three friends.

fourth of a mile. In 1884 a conversation between New York and Boston, a distance of 235 miles, on overhead line was made possible by the use of hard-drawn copper wire. In 1892 New York and Chicago were connected by an overhead line.

Recent Improvements. Ten years later in contrast to open-line development, Newark and New York conversed by an underground long-distance cable, ten miles in length. Since 1902 considerable progress has been made in cable installation. New York and Philadelphia, a distance of 90 miles, were connected in 1906; Boston and Washington, 455 miles apart, conversed by cable in 1913; the extension of the Boston and Philadelphia cable line to Pittsburgh, a distance of 621 miles, was completed in 1921; the extension to Chicago was finished in 1925, and the cable line from Chicago to St. Louis will probably be completed in 1927. In 1921 the deep-sea cable connecting Key West, Florida, and Havana, Cuba, a distance of 115 miles, was completed. As early as 1915 speech was transmitted by radio telephone without wire from Arlington, Virginia, across the continent to San Francisco, over the Pacific to the Hawaiian Islands, and across the Atlantic to Paris. Ship-to-shore conversation was made possible in 1922, and a successful demonstration of transoceanic radio telephony between New York and New Southgate, England, occurred in 1923. Although the initial investment in cable lines is much greater than in open-wire construction, yet the expense and inconvenience caused by storms are eliminated, with assurance of uninterrupted long-distance service.

Perhaps less remarkable is the development of the long-distance open-wire construction. However, great progress has been made in this direction. New York and Chicago were connected by overhead line in 1892. The Bell management was bent on westward expansion so that by 1911 long-distance conversation between New York and Denver was possible, by 1913, between New York and Salt Lake City, a distance of 2,600 miles, and by 1915 between Boston and San Francisco,—a transcontinental overhead line covering a distance of 3,650 miles. At present there are in course of construction two more transcontinental lines, one from Los Angeles through El Paso to Dallas and New Orleans, the other from Minneapolis to Portland and Seattle.

Other developments are worthy of mention. Although one-way transoceanic telephony is successful, as evidenced by one-way talks to Paris and London, there are in progress experiments designed to develop two-way conversation.[1] The improvement in the transmission of pictures by wire makes them available commercially between New York, Chicago, and San Francisco.

Early Financing. Like most prosperous undertakings the National Bell Telephone Company was threatened by what appeared to be severe competition, for the Western Union Telegraph Company had acquired Elisha Gray's patents and the improvements thereon by Thomas A. Edison and organized the American Speaking Telephone Company which soon surpassed the Bell Company in installations. With the invention of the Blake transmitter, however, the tables were turned, but the Bell Company nevertheless deemed it advisable to acquire its competitor's property and rights.

Expansion then became so rapid that the finances of the National Bell Telephone Company were quite inadequate. Although the company was successful and its earnings were reinvested, yet growth was so fast that relief became imperative. To effect the desired results the American Bell Telephone Company with a capitalization of $7,350,000 was organized in 1880 and absorbed the National Bell Telephone Company by exchanging six shares of the new stock for each share of the old. Not only earnings but also original capital contributions and the demonstrated value of the patents justified this increase in capitalization.

During the early days of the American Bell Telephone Company the contracts made between its predecessors and the local operating companies began to expire. These short-term contracts were unsatisfactory from the viewpoint of the operating companies, and it became necessary to devise a better policy of operation. As a result there was developed a contract which made permanent the licensees' exclusive use of instruments at stipulated rentals (the average range was $5.84 in 1885 to $1.45 in 1898) but required the licensee companies to give as a bonus a part of their stock ranging between 30 and 50 per cent. Possible adverse public sentiment would be allayed since local interests, to a large degree, were to own and operate the separate companies, but nevertheless, the American Bell Telephone

[1] In 1927 radio telephonic communication was finally inaugurated.

Company, and later the American Telephone and Telegraph Company, by means of these stock holdings prepared for control of the associated companies.   The contract reserved to the licensor the exclusive privilege, at its discretion, to construct interconnecting long-distance lines which made possible the present ownership of the long-distance lines by the American Telephone and Telegraph Company.   The contract further stipulated that any continued violation of its terms gave the licensor the right to acquire at a reasonable price not in excess of actual cost the property of the violating licensee.   Control was thus made virtually absolute.

During 1893 and 1894, in anticipation of the approaching expiration of patents, the licensor reduced rates to stimulate the use of instruments and at the same time acquired larger stock holdings in the various operating companies, since prospects for larger profits increased with the decline in rental costs.   In this way the earnings of the Bell Company were stabilized, less being derived from rentals but more accruing from dividends. Stock ownership also made control more effective.

The development of long-distance service, already outlined, entailed heavy financial burdens on the licensor company, the American Bell Telephone Company, which could not be met out of current earnings.   When the Massachusetts legislature refused the petition of the company to increase its capital stock from $10,000,000 to $30,000,000[1] in order to finance long-distance construction, the American Telephone and Telegraph Company was incorporated in New York in 1885 with a capital of $100,000, as a subsidiary of the Bell Company.   The new corporation was given a contract similar to that of other licensees and was to construct and operate long-distance interconnecting lines only.   The American Bell Telephone Company from time to time acquired its stock, and the proceeds of its sale together with earnings, were used to finance construction.

Competition in the industry on the expiration of the American Bell Telephone Company's basic patents in 1893 and 1894 became intense in certain areas, especially those which had been neglected by the Bell Company.   Through the control of long-distance communication service, fairly well established by the Bell Company, private companies were unable to give satisfactory

[1] *Bell Telephone Quarterly*, July, 1923, p. 150.

intercommunity service. Competition was not so serious, therefore, as it otherwise may have been.

However, the Bell Company experienced other difficulties that were more serious. The company was a Massachusetts corporation and, after considerable difficulty, accepted the designation as a public service corporation which subjected it to special restrictions. As a public utility it was not permitted to own more than 30 per cent.[1] of the stock in other corporations which it sought to control, nor could it issue stock at par when the existing market price was actually greater.[2] Because of these two restrictions, the first defeating the company's policy of controlling operating companies, the second preventing the distribution of what might be termed stock dividends, the American Bell Telephone Company decided, in 1899, to withdraw from Massachusetts. This was accomplished by transferring its stock, most of the other assets, and also the stocks of the various licensees held by it to the American Telephone and Telegraph Company in exchange of the latter's stock on a basis of two new shares for one old. The old company then ceased to exist.

To follow the activities further would involve an historical sketch of the American Telephone and Telegraph Company. But our purpose will be served if attention is merely directed to the present state of the telephone industry as a whole, and to the condition of the dominant American Company.[3]

Present State of the Telephone Industry. It must not be assumed that the Bell interests were the sole developers of telephonic service. As previously stated, Mr. Gray and others were active factors. Following the reconciliation between those men who, under the leadership of the Western Union Telegraph Company, had organized the American Speaking Telephone Company, there developed later more serious competition by many so-called Independent Companies, especially after the expiration of the Bell patents. The following table indicates the rapid development of the industry from 1902 to 1922 and the relative impor-

[1] Ibid. p. 148.
[2] Ibid. p. 151.
[3] For the foregoing discussion the authors are indebted to *The Financial History of The American Telephone and Telegraph Company*, 1925, by Dr. J. Warren Stehman, but more especially to publications of the Bell Telephone System and to the assistance of some of its chief officers.

tance of the Bell System by 1922. It is noteworthy that the American Telephone and Telegraph Company had invested in plant and equipment 78.4 per cent. of the total of all companies, and that its revenues were 82.4 per cent. of the total. Of the net income of $96,700,000, in 1922, the Bell System received $86,-600,000.

TELEPHONE SYSTEMS IN THE UNITED STATES [1]

	Units	1902	1907	1912	1917	1922	Bell System in 1922
No. of systems and lines	One	9,136	22,971	32,233	53,234	57,253	5,795 [2]
Miles of wire	Millions	4.9	12.9	20.2	28.8	37.3	30.6
No. of telephones	Millions	2.4	6.1	8.7	11.7	14.3	9.5 [3]
No. of employees	Thousands	....	....	....	262.6	312.0	243.1
Total revenues	Million Dollars	....	....	....	389.5	684.9	564.0
Net income	" "	....	....	....	59.4	96.7	86.6
Investment in plant and equipment	" "	....	....	....	1,492.3	2,205.2	1,729.2
Dividends	" "	....	....	....	42.3	66.0	60.3

[1] *Statistical Abstract of the United States*, 1924, pp. 329 and 332.
[2] Central Offices.
[3] Bell-owned, but 4.5 millions of telephones owned by other companies are Bell-connecting. There were approximately 14.1 millions of telephones in the Bell System in 1922, and 16,-720,000 in 1925.

The rapid growth of the Bell System is clearly shown in the table below. Of the world's telephones the United States has 61 per cent. although it has only 6.2 per cent. of the world's population and only 5.29 per cent. of the total land area. The Bell System, with 16,720,000 owned and connecting telephones, makes the service accessible to practically all communities. For years there has been fear among investors not in close touch that the saturation point was in sight, yet the number of telephones per unit of population continues to increase.[4] Exchanges in the large offices and factories are still subject to considerable increase. It is the hope of the officers of the Bell System that in time at least one telephone will be placed in every home.

[4] In 1900 there was one Bell Telephone for 90 persons in U. S.
" 1905 " " " " " " 34 " " "
" 1910 " " " " " " 16 " " "
" 1915 " " " " " " 11 " " "
" 1920 " " " " " " 9 " " "
" 1925 " " " " " " 7 " " "
In 1925 813,000 telephones were added to the Bell System.

	Dec. 31, 1910	Dec. 31, 1920	Dec. 31, 1925
Number of Telephones:			
Bell Companies..............	3,933,056	8,333,979	12,035,224
Bell Connecting Companies and			
Lines.................	1,949,663	4,267,956	4,685,000
Total Telephones..........	5,882,719	12,601,935	16,720,224
Number of Connecting Companies	7,396	9,231	9,227
Number of Connecting Rural Lines	10,449	26,032	28,861
Miles of Pole Lines............	282,877	358,091	386,064
Miles of Exchange Wire:			
Wire in Underground Cable....	5,630,851	14,384,135	28,425,392
Wire in Aërial Cable..........	2,800,000	5,586,531	9,462,213
Open Wire...................	1,247,367	1,633,802	1,953,235
Total Exchange Wire........	9,678,218	21,604,468	39,840,840
Miles of Toll Wire:			
Wire in Underground Cable....	386,088	1,363,398	2,057,196
Wire in Aërial Cable..........	70,000	299,385	1,209,332
Open Wire...................	1,507,906	2,110,153	2,366,172
Total Toll Wire............	1,963,994	3,772,936	5,632,700
Total Miles of Wire............	11,642,212	25,377,404	45,473,540
Average Daily Telephone Conversations: [2]			
Exchange Conversations.......	21,681,471	31,835,353	46,702,307
Toll Conversations...........	602,539	1,327,247	2,098,163
Total Conversations.........	22,284,010	33,162,600	48,800,470
Number of Employees..........	120,311	231,316	293,095

[2] For year ending December 31.

There are throughout the United States 9,227 telephone companies and in addition 28,861 rural telephone lines operated mainly on a coöperative basis, which have arrangements with the associated Bell companies for the interchange of toll traffic. These are shown in the above table as Connecting Companies and Connecting Rural Lines, and their telephones as Bell-Connecting telephones. All other statistics are for the American Telephone and Telegraph Company and its 25 associated companies combined and do not include data for connecting companies or rural lines.

The accompanying chart[2] presents a rather clear picture of the present organization of the American Telephone and Telegraph

[1] *Annual Report of the American Telephone and Telegraph Company for the year 1925*, p. 32.   [2] Page 432.

Company. There are twenty-five companies associated with the American Company, twenty-three of which are controlled through stock ownership. These, with their subsidiaries, extend throughout the United States and form the local operating companies. The long-distance lines, entirely owned and operated by the parent company, connect the systems into a great network for inter-company communication. The Western Electric Company is the manufacturer and purchasing agent for the Bell System and this arrangement assures uniform and reliable equipment at satisfactory prices. The Graybar Company takes care of the domestic merchandise business of the Western Electric Company. The chart on page 432 makes clear the particular functions of the several other companies in the organization.

Tendency Toward Consolidation. The natural tendency in the telephone industry is to increase the scope of its operations. An increase in subscribers widens the range of communication and thereby entails additional operating expense. Because of the additional expense involved in answering calls, connecting up, and disconnecting, large-scale telephone operations, do not reduce unit costs. However, more efficient service is possible under the monopoly organization. The value of the service is measured by the number of people with whom the user can talk. Competition on the other hand reduces efficiency. The community is best served by a single company under regulation as to rates and service. Despite this fact there are many small companies serving rural sections which have proved successful because of the simplicity of the organization. There is, however, a marked tendency towards centralization of service, and the bonds of the larger companies are more desirable because of greater safety in size.

Capitalization and Earnings. Perhaps no public utility presents a more satisfactory relationship of capitalization to the value of tangible assets than does the dominating company in the telephone industry in this country, the American Telephone and Telegraph Company. For approximately $923,000,000 of stock outstanding at the end of 1925 the company received more than $966,900,000, or an excess of $43,900,000 over par. The telephone plant, general equipment, tools, and investments of the Bell System were carried at $2,757,968,000 on December 31, 1925, and the total capitalization was $2,035,627,685.

ORGANIZATION CHART OF THE AMERICAN TELEPHONE AND TELEGRAPH COMPANY

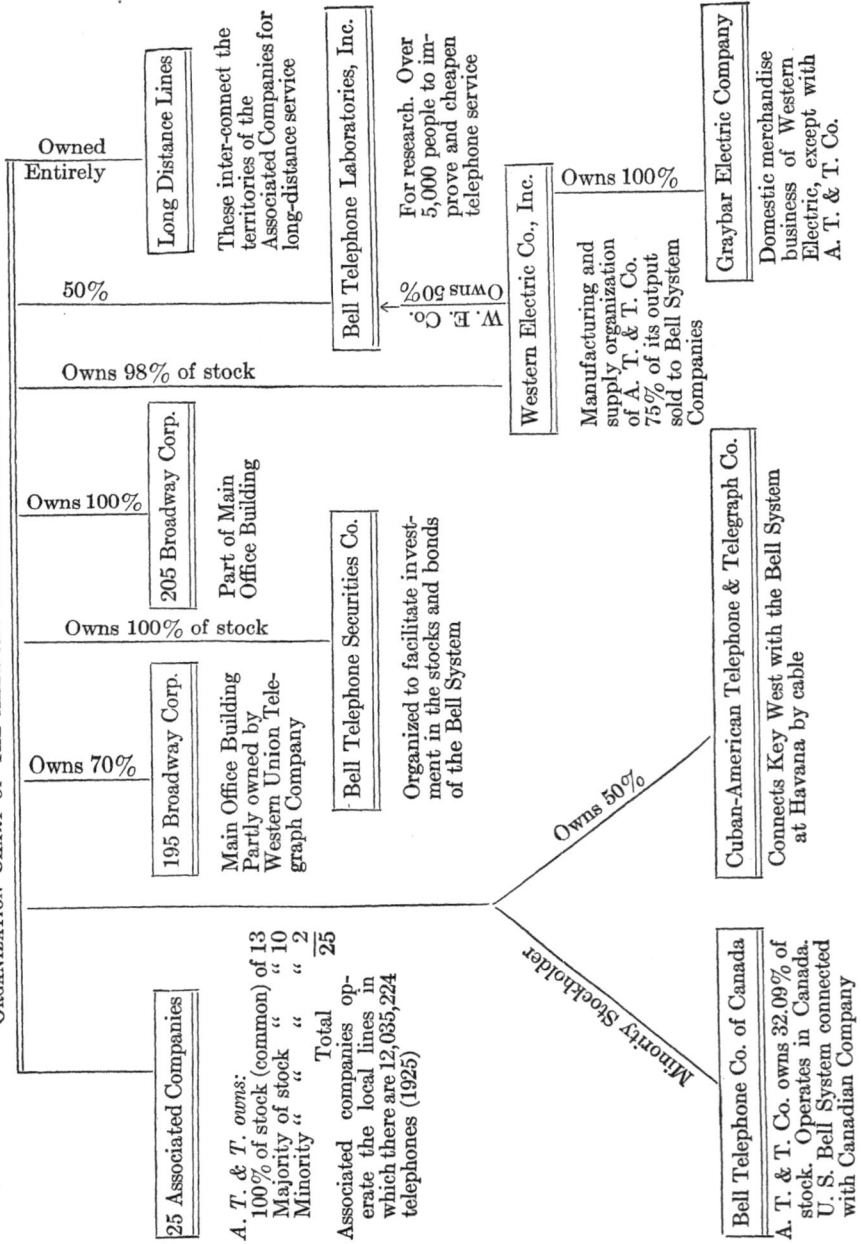

Long Distance Lines

Owned Entirely

These inter-connect the territories of the Associated Companies for long-distance service

Bell Telephone Laboratories, Inc.

For research. Over 5,000 people to improve and cheapen telephone service

50%

Owns 50%

W. E. Co.

Owns 98% of stock

Western Electric Co., Inc.

Owns 100%

Graybar Electric Company

Domestic merchandise business of Western Electric, except with A. T. & T. Co.

Manufacturing and supply organization of A. T. & T. Co. 75% of its output sold to Bell System Companies

205 Broadway Corp.

Owns 100%

Part of Main Office Building

Bell Telephone Securities Co.

Owns 100% of stock

Organized to facilitate investment in the stocks and bonds of the Bell System

195 Broadway Corp.

Owns 70%

Main Office Building Partly owned by Western Union Telegraph Company

Owns 50%

Cuban-American Telephone & Telegraph Co.

Connects Key West with the Bell System at Havana by cable

Minority Stockholder

25 Associated Companies

A. T. & T. owns:
100% of stock (common) of 13
Majority of stock   "   "   10
Minority   "   "   "   2
Total   25

Associated companies operate the local lines in which there are 12,035,224 telephones (1925)

Bell Telephone Co. of Canada

A. T. & T. Co. owns 32.09% of stock. Operates in Canada. U. S. Bell System connected with Canadian Company

The telephone properties of the Bell System cost more than $2,500,000,000. Even with generous deductions for depreciation, the ratio of debt to property and capital is favorable. The American Company prides itself in its low debt,[1] none of which is secured by a mortgage.

The present tendency towards lower debt ratios is the result of two potent factors. In the first place, the company has enjoyed a long dividend record [2] in every year of which, the income available exceeded the dividend distribution; to increase the dividend rate is to court public disfavor. In 1925 about one-third of the net earnings of the Bell System were reserved for contingencies or added to the surplus. That the reserves and surplus may continue to represent a satisfactory ratio to both the ever-increasing value of the assets and capitalization this policy of reserving a substantial portion of net earnings should be maintained. The popularity of the Bell System securities is the outgrowth of this practice. With earnings sufficient to pay reasonable returns on junior issues, it is unnecessary to sell bonds of low yield in order to finance the system cheaply.

In the second place the present debt ratio permits the reservation of high-class securities to be used in times of financial stress when junior issues are difficult to market. It is an accepted principle that companies should reserve senior securities as long as they can successfully dispose of other issues without too great sacrifice. At least, we are fully justified in concluding that the American Telephone and Telegraph Company, with less than 29 per cent. of its capitalization in funded debt and with a margin of safety approximating 83 per cent. is in a strong financial position. With the interest charges earned 6.49 times in 1924 and 5.97 times in 1925, and with earnings per share for the two years of $11.31 and $11.79 respectively, and with a long record of satisfactory earnings, a conservative percentage of which has been ploughed back into the assets, the securities are justly entitled to a high standing of credit. The bonds of the American

---

[1] In 1925 the funded debt of the Bell System was 43.9 per cent. of the total capitalization, and that of the holding company itself was 28.8 per cent.

[2] The American Company and its predecessor have paid dividends of not less than $7.50 per share per year for a period of 44 years. For approximately 15 years $8 per share annually was paid, and since 1921 the annual dividend payments amounted to $9 per share. Without an exception the earnings since 1900 have exceeded $8 per share.

Telephone and Telegraph Company and its associated companies are worthy of the investor's confidence.

The Bell System in 1925 had a capitalization of $2.74 for each dollar of revenue, and the value of the plant, equipment, supplies, tools, and investment in subsidiaries amounted to $3.72 to each dollar of revenue. In the Bell System the interest charge of 1925 was earned four times.

A source of revenue of the American Company which has been criticized is the well-known $4\frac{1}{2}$ per cent licensee payment contract between the company and the Associated Companies which in 1902 was substituted for the old rental charges on the telephones. Originally the licensees were to pay $4\frac{1}{2}$ per cent. of their gross telephone revenues to the licensor for which they were to receive the use of telephone instruments, the benefit of all new patents, and the assistance of the General Staff (with its engineering, accounting, executive, legal, and financial divisions). This contract has been assailed frequently in the courts and before commissions, especially in rate cases of the operating companies, but it has been approved by the Supreme Court. On January 1, 1926, the rate was reduced to 4 per cent.

The following comparative combined income statement of the Bell Telephone System in the United States with all inter-company duplications eliminated indicates consistent growth in total revenues, net earnings, dividend payments, and additions to surplus. Adequate maintenance and depreciation also is evident.

COMPARATIVE INCOME ACCOUNT OF THE BELL SYSTEM
(000's OMITTED)

	1925	1924	1923	1922	1921	1920
Total revenues...................	$761,219	$677,903	$623,111	$564,029	$510,709	$461,090
Operating expenses...............	$280,661	$265,324	$250,431	$228,443	$219,737	$211,379
Current maintenance..............	111,443	101,597	91,155	79,818	73,061	69,665
Depreciation.....................	115,471	99,693	87,485	80,081	70,858	65,731
Uncollectibles...................	4,652	4,130	3,436	3,082	1,844	1,209
Taxes...........................	58,187	50,498	45,649	41,215	34,512	27,841
Rents and misc. deductions........	8,362	7,884	7,579	6,897	6,498	5,756
Total expenses...............	$578,776	$529,126	$485,735	$439,537	$406,510	$381,581
Net earnings.................	$182,444	$148,777	$137,376	$124,492	$104,199	$ 79,509
Interest charges.................	45,941	41,531	37,751	37,869	36,774	31,724
Balance.....................	$136,503	$107,246	$ 99,624	$ 86,623	$ 67,425	$ 47,785
Dividends paid..................	93,243	82,603	72,429	60,305	47,848	40,000
Surplus.....................	$ 43,250	$ 24,643	$ 27,196	$ 26,318	$ 19,576	$ 7,785

Service Standards. Measurements of the usefulness and efficiency of telephone service depend on many varied factors. It is unnecessary to review the tests given at frequent intervals to determine the nature and efficiency of the service rendered. The usefulness of the service to a large degree is measured by and dependent on the number of subscribers included in the system, for potential calls are based on that number. Larger centres have a higher calling rate (originating calls) than smaller communities. It will be readily realized that the greater number of stations per hundred of population increases not only the value of the service to the subscriber but also the cost. Therefore, in striking contrast to the principle that commonly obtains in modern industry, large-scale telephone operations are more costly per unit of service than small.

In a comparison of rate charges in the United States and in European countries, the nature of the service, that is, its efficiency, the possible length of long-distance calls, the potential local calls, the duration of the " initial period," overtime charges, etc.,—all should be considered. So different are conditions and service, however, that comparison is of little value, indeed if valid at all. It is perhaps true, that telephone rates in the United States are cheaper relative to the service than those in Europe.

The average time elapsing before the originating call receives an answer from the called party should be brief, not to exceed 40 seconds for residence calls. The operator should be in a position to plug an answer, verify and plug up, ring and supervise the reply in a very brief period, ordinarily not to exceed ten seconds. The speed of the operator's answer and of ringing the called party is a criterion of the efficiency of the service. Immediate disconnection, accurate timing, and proper charges for toll calls are essential to efficiency. To offer such prompt service the company must maintain not only modern switchboard and connecting equipment but also an efficient staff of unfailing courtesy. To accommodate peak hours, an additional burden of employment and investment is placed on the company. As in other utilities, the problem of solving the peak load is of vital importance. Various rate schedules for business hours, evening calls, and night service designed to even the load for long-distance communication have been adopted by the Bell System.

Plant inspections are essential to assure the continuity and reliability of the service. Technical construction requirements to assure continuous, reliable, and efficient service are usually imposed by public service commissions. To reduce the interruptions in service and the great expense incident to storms, underground cables in large cities are almost universal, and long-distance cables, as previously stated, are being installed. Proper exchange-ringing equipment, avoidance of party line overloading, promptness of local service extensions, adequate toll facilities, tests and inspections to assure proper maintenance, time limitation of interruptions to service, and the like, are subject to regulation and to the imposition of reasonable standards. But specific standards are difficult in the telephone industry because of the variety of conditions and the multiplicity of subjects involved, for there is no simple test of service.

Maintenance and Depreciation. The straight line method of depreciation is considered the most desirable for telephone and telegraph companies. Rates allowed by state commissions show considerable variance. The United States District Court, of Indiana, in Indiana Bell Telephone Company vs. Public Service Commission, 300 Fed. 190, 1924, held that a state commission has power to fix the rate of depreciation if the Interstate Commerce Commission has not made any investigation or arrived at any rate deemed proper for rate-making purposes, and has not assumed jurisdiction or control over telephone rate-making that would deprive the state commission of this power if not thus affected. Commissions have set rates that formerly varied a great deal, but in recent cases, there has been an approach toward uniformity. Some engineers estimate the life of the telephone plant from fifteen to sixteen years. With this life expectancy the straight line method is used at a rate of 6.25 per cent. The Kansas Commission [1] allowed 6 per cent., the Missouri Commission 4.5 per cent., [2] the Tennessee Commission [3] and the Washington Department of Public Works [4] fixed the rate of depreciation allowance at 5 per cent. For special equipment or other partic-

---

[1] In Re Consolidated Telephone Co. Docket No. 5784, May 8, 1924.

[2] In Re Southwestern Bell Telephone Co. Case No. 3912, March 31, 1924.

[3] In Re Cumberland Telephone & Telegraph Co. Docket No. 534, December 22, 1923.

[4] Department of Public Works vs. Thurston County Utilities Co. No. 5649, June 9, 1924.

ularly designated properties the rate allowed may be considerably greater than that of the foregoing composite rate. Rates ranging from 10 per cent. to 20 per cent. are not unusual [1] in special cases.

It is characteristic of some of the small independent companies to neglect the factor of depreciation. Earnings are usually meagre and the management often desires to satisfy the stockholders by imprudent dividend disbursements. Investors are warned against the purchase of securities in small independent companies without first ascertaining the maintenance and depreciation policy. The rate of depreciation for the Bell System is 5 per cent., which suggests that the average life of the plant is twenty years. The foregoing income statement of the Bell System indicates a close relation between current maintenance and depreciation.

Public Relations. The management of the Bell System has cultivated public favor. Notwithstanding the dominating position of the System and its monopolistic position the public has become favorably disposed. Less agitation for lower rates or better service exists than with other utilities. This favorable situation is due partly to the efficient service. It is an accepted fact, as previously explained, that efficiency in the industry increases with the degree of monopoly. The management has promoted public favor through efficient service at reasonable rates, by intelligent publicity, and also by broad distribution of its securities among its employees and customers. The American Company in 1926 had more than 366,000 stockholders, or more than any other corporation. There were 57,000 employee stockholders in the Bell System in addition to 161,000 employees who were acquiring stock on the instalment plan.

Adverse public sentiment frequently arises against some of the associated companies or their subsidiaries, but serious agitation against the American Company is quite unusual. During the preparation of this chapter, however, there has arisen what purports to be a concerted protest by New York, Boston, Los Angeles, Indianapolis, Youngstown and other communities, as well as by the Ohio State Utilities Commission, to the Interstate Commerce Commission against the American Telephone and Telegraph Company because of recent rate increases and alleged existence of a nation-wide monopoly in violation of the Clayton Act. The allegation is not new, but the concerted action is.

[1] See *Public Utilities Digest*, 1924, pp. 92–93.

Rates. Like other utilities the telephone and telegraph companies have their rate troubles. Rate schedules, as a rule, have been more satisfactory in these industries than in most public utilities. The complexity of the large systems and failure to agree on the justice of the licensee contract, the rate of depreciation, what constitutes adequate return, the cost of service, service standards, and similar problems have usually defeated attempts to reduce rates. The dominant company, controlling its associated companies and subsidiaries (including the manufacturers of equipment), and charging a flat rate of 4 per cent. for service (the value of which is difficult to ascertain) has successfully met the complaint against excessive rates by weak companies or by communities.

There has been considerable variance in expert testimony relative to costs of installations in compliance with regulation, operating costs, rate of depreciation, and investment in plant. The system has reaped the advantage. Recent court decisions have concentrated on a reasonable rate of return to be expected on the investment [1] and have left the rate charges rather elastic. Costs and the nature of the service provide the bases for a determination of fair rates, if the management is efficient.

The following table outlines the scope of the telegraph industry in 1922:

THE TELEGRAPH INDUSTRY IN 1922

	Units	Land [2]	Ocean Cable	Wireless
Number of companies or systems..............	One	19.	5	4
Miles of single wire (land) nautical (cable)........	Thousands	1,849.3	52.4	....
Number of messages......	Millions	185.8	5.3	2.4
Income, total...........	Millions of Dollars	130.5	21.3	8.1
Net income.............	" " "	15.7	8.2	3.0
Total assets............	" " "	321.9	137.6	46.5
Capital stock...........	" " "	104.5	72.7	36.0
Funded debt............	" " "	67.4	4.0	1.2 [3]
Number of employees....	Thousands	64.9	3.7	1.3
Salaries and wages.......	Millions of Dollars	71.5	4.7	2.1

[1] The usual rate allowed is 8 per cent. on the value of the property devoted to public use.

[2] Includes Western Union cable system excepting nautical miles of ocean cable.   [3] Floating debt mortgage.

It is to be observed that there are comparatively few telegraph companies. Of necessity the miles of line and the area covered by any one must be considerable because of the inherent nature of the service. Of the land companies the Western Union Telegraph Company is the most important. The industry depends primarily for its revenue on business organizations widely separated. This condition necessitates large plant investment where duplications by competitors would be too costly for possible competition. Consolidations have been forced upon the small companies in order to render distance service. Monopoly is the necessary resolvent. Charges which have been high, have tended to discourage patronage. However, the large companies, especially the Western Union and the Mackay Company, have long records of stable earnings with satisfactory dividend records.

Possibilities of greater future revenues are implicated in the growing ticker services. Mechanical improvements, such as the substitution of copper for iron in the wire circuits and of automatic multiplex apparatus for manual operations, make for greater efficiency and patronage. Transoceanic communication has recently been facilitated by the completion in 1924 of the cable between New York and the Azores, and in 1926 by the cable between New York and London; and efficiency in transmission has been increased by loading the cable with "permalloy." The New York-London cable has a capacity of 2,600 letters a minute.

The Western Union Telegraph Company, owner of the largest telegraph system in the world, had a funded debt on December 31, 1925, of $47,559,500, slightly more than 32 per cent. of the total capital. During the ten-year period ended with 1925 the number of times the interest was earned on the bonds ranged between 6.7 and 24.57—an obviously satisfactory showing. Dividends on the common stock have been paid uninterruptedly at various rates since 1874. Operated by a conservative and efficient management, the Western Union presents an enviable record of consistent earnings, progressive development of plant and equipment in harmony with expanding demands for service.

To a considerable degree the problems of the telephone and telegraph industries are kindred. Reference to the latter, therefore, is not extended in this text. Investment principles and tests that apply to public utilities in general are applicable.

Bond Market. A study of the bonds of the more important telephone and telegraph companies shows a yield of 4.91 per cent. at the end of 1925 as compared with 4.93 per cent. for electric light and power bonds, 5.03 per cent. for gas bonds, 7.28 per cent. for electric railway bonds, and about 4.91 per cent. for railroad bonds.

The bonds of the larger telephone and telegraph companies share in common the public confidence (to which these percentages testify) for the following reasons:

The stability of the supporting earnings.

The record of prompt payment of interest and principal.

The relatively small funded debt.

Conversely the paid-in equities represented by the sales of stock.

The wide margin between the value of the service and its cost to the user.

The rates, adequate for reasonable return on the invested capital.

The nature of the two industries: indispensable to modern life; developed scientifically under efficient and economical managements with sound fiscal policies.

Although the list of telephone and telegraph companies with securities enjoying a general market is not long, yet there are many desirable issues of the American Telephone and Telegraph Company and its associates and subsidiaries and of the Western Union Telegraph Company and its subsidiaries.

The authors would not be true to their convictions if this chapter stopped at this point. There is a peculiar kind of caution to suggest that each must appraise for himself. When writing the first edition we had our doubts about the acceptance of our cautions as to the continuance of any present conditions of mechanic arts, finance, government or society. The only enduring law is the law of change. Therefore our insistence on penetrating analysis of governmental credit even though that be the most stable credit in the world. History was unkind enough in 1914 to verify most cruelly the law of change.

As a National Liberty Loan speaker in the five fiscal campaigns one of the authors had opportunity to observe the deterioration under stress of even the federal credit. He was taken to task after a mass-meeting in Cincinnati during the first loan for predicting that investors in liberty bonds would some day see them selling at a premium,—by analogy with the course of government bond prices after previous wars.

With respect to the credit of telephone and telegraph companies the law of change suggests that some day this credit may be adversely affected by the development of long-distance communication without further commercial need of wire lines of transmission.   In other words supersession (the extreme of obsolescence) is a skeleton rattling in the closet of our intelligence-communicating companies.   But historical perspective here, too, may help us maintain balance.   For three quarters of a century the same skeleton has been rattling in the closets of the Western Union Telegraph Company and in every gas company in the land.   He creates just sufficient nervous apprehension in the new business departments to keep everyone on his toes, and in the larger companies he has the inestimable value of keeping business managements abreast of competitive developments and alert to assimilate new world-wide movements.

Infant industries are not in position to do these things.   Three-quarters of a century ago the skeleton did come out of the closet and strangle the canal companies; and two decades ago, thanks to an unstabilized currency that ruined the five-cent piece, and to the invention of the pleasure car and the jitney, he came out again and strangled the majority of the street-railways.   So each must judge for himself; but *caveat emptor.*

CHAPTER XXXIV

REAL ESTATE BONDS

Although the real estate bond in its present form was originated only in the nineties, the sales of this type of investment security had grown to the second largest in volume in the United States by 1926. In that year an approximated total of $1,000,000,000 sales placed real estate bonds ahead of both railroad and industrial issues, and second only to an unprecedented volume of public utility underwritings. Inasmuch as real estate bonds have been advanced to a position of such importance only since the Great War, it seems pertinent to give some consideration to their origin and development.

Improved and income-producing real estate has been accepted as fundamental security for loan obligations in every civilization which history records. In ancient Babylonia a man pledged his fields as security for the repayment of crops or animals in kind. To-day, an individual pledges the fee, and sometimes the income as well, of a city skyscraper as security for the repayment of borrowed moneys which, added to his own available funds, made its erection possible. Time has served only to alter the form of the pledge and security offered and to add legal and insurance features for the protection both of the borrower and investor. The essential elements of safety likewise have been enhanced by reason of the fact that our civilization is more dependent than ever before on permanent dwellings and commercial and industrial buildings and plants.

Development of Real Estate Bonds. The real estate first mortgage bond represents a natural evolution out of the first mortgage on improved urban real estate. In effect, a real estate bond is simply a fractional part of such a first mortgage.

It was inevitable that real estate first mortgage bonds should have been developed to the point where they constitute one of the largest departments of our national investment program. Two underlying causes contributed to their rapid growth. First, the increasing population of our cities resulted in ever-mounting land values and forced the development of modern steel fireproof buildings, productive of proportionate increases in earnings, for both business and residential purposes. A three-story building on a certain corner in New York yielded an adequate return a half century ago when the land was worth a few thousand dollars; but, with the value of that same land increased to $2,-500,000, and taxed accordingly, the present owner has no choice but to erect a towering business or residential structure. Improvements of such scope seldom are within the financial capacity of the interested individual or corporation. They call for financing comparable to the requirements of industrial and public utility concerns and this, naturally, has fostered the growth of real estate investment banking houses capable of investigating, underwriting, and selling this specialized type of security. Secondly, the World War had delayed the normal building activities of our cities for a period of nearly five years. At the expiration of that time, the need of large sums for long-term financing of new construction far exceeded the former standard sources of supply. This gave added impetus to the real estate bond financing organizations already well past the formative stage.

Since 1919 the volume of building over the United States has been so extensive that in many sections the retarded development of the war period has been overcome. As a result there is to-day an ever-present possibility of depression in real estate values to be considered in estimating the prospective rental values which in the final analysis constitute the real basis for judging the safety of real estate securities.

Development of Underwriting Houses. The origins of many of the larger institutions now underwriting and selling real estate first mortgage securities reach back to the latter half of the previous century when their business was confined to brokering first mortgages on individual dwellings and business buildings, or conducted in conjunction with a real estate business. With the increased size of buildings and correspondingly larger amounts of first mortgage money required, it became increasingly difficult to find individual buyers for the entire mortgage. The first mortgage real estate bond enabled the brokers to break up the larger mortgage into more salable units. Prior to 1919, however, the total of such securities sold in one year had probably never exceeded $50,000,000.[1] This total was increased to approxi-

[1] *Annual Report of Investment Bankers Association of America, 1925*, page 98.

mately $500,000,000 in 1923 and to $1,000,000,000 in the next three years. As a logical reflection of this growth in volume, there is an increasing number of underwriters in the real estate first mortgage field because of the facility with which the business may be undertaken irrespective of resources, experience or salutary regulations. Many companies, which hitherto had operated primarily as real estate brokers or as agents, and who only occasionally underwrote a mortgage to facilitate a sale, entered the business claiming several decades of experience in first mortgage underwriting.

Inasmuch as general practice permitted the real estate bond houses to pool in their general assets the proceeds derived from the sale of " construction " issues until the money was needed, as well as advance payments from borrowers against principal, interest, and taxes, the investor was to that extent dependent on the financial integrity and good business judgment of the underwriting house. The failure in 1926 of a real estate bond house organized in the period of rapid growth following the war precipitated discussion and activities that clearly indicate a trend toward state regulatory measures dealing with segregation of such " construction " funds and borrowers' payments. Early in 1927, a committee composed of representatives of six large mortgage bond companies, working in conjunction with a committee of the National Association of State Securities Commissioners, formulated a code of procedure which was voluntarily adopted by the mortgage bond companies participating and which met with the approval of the committee of securities commissioners.

Two Kinds of Bonds. The older and, now, less common type of real estate first mortgage bond is that which when issued is secured by real estate improved with a completed building, generally with an established record of earnings. Twenty years ago, if it were necessary for the owners to borrow funds to construct a building, arrangement had to be made for a temporary building loan, usually from a bank, and, later, for long-term financing on the completed property. To-day, nearly all of the real estate bond houses combine these two steps in underwriting a " construction " issue of bonds, as opposed to loans on merely " completed " properties. When proper safeguards are employed, there are several points in favor of " construction " issues underwritten by experienced and conservative financing houses. In the first place, business acumen developed by experience enables the careful real estate mortgage underwriter to avoid loans that would represent " over-improvement " or " under-improvement " and to accept only those that will develop the full rental value of the land without undue risk. Again, it is evident that a new building will more nearly meet the existing demand than an old one. The experienced underwriter, too, is able to contribute sound judgment relative to location, character, and design of the building, floor plans, quality of materials, and equipment. Expert advice on these points is of great value to the builder-borrower, and besides constitutes an added safeguard for the investor in the bonds. Several of the largest underwriters of real estate bonds successfully sell bonds secured by both " construction " and " completed " properties, with little or no discrimination between the two types of security in net interest return.

Many general bond houses which formerly confined themselves to industrial, public utility, and municipal financing, have extended their activities to include real estate first mortgage securities. Their underwritings, with few exceptions, have been limited to " completed " issues. The real estate bond houses, for the protection of their investors, have developed technical staffs, composed of men experienced in building operation and management, architects, engineers, and inspectors, who are charged with the responsibility of investigating loans offered and with following through construction loans, from the time they are underwritten until the buildings are completed and producing satisfactory incomes.

Security. The common form of trust agreement underlying real estate bond issues, as developed by the older underwriters of these securities and generally copied by large and small houses now in the field, embodies two forms of security. First, it represents a direct closed first mortgage against the land, building, and equipment. Sometimes, in the case of hotels or apartment hotel buildings, the complete furnishings likewise are pledged. Secondly, there is included an adaptation of the old Saxon form of vifgage lien (i.e., a " live " lien as opposed to the mort-gage or dead lien), which is a direct first lien or a lien in effect against the net income of the property. This lien against earnings has its full effect as a security factor when employed in conjunction with monthly amortization of principal and interest as discussed in a following paragraph.

The old principle of security for mortgage loans in improved real estate was based solely on the cost and appraised value of the property, with 50 per cent. as the established maximum of conservative banking for first mortgage loans. The application of this principle to the modern developments in the real estate first mortgage field has given rise to a great deal of controversy with reference to appraisal of values and the percentages loaned. With the increased values of unimproved real estate in populous centres and the heavier investment required in the large structures that improve them, business expediency has made it necessary to scale upward the percentage to cost of the amount loaned. When sound judgment is applied to the selection of locations and expert advice dictates the decisions in regard to character of structure, degree to which site is utilized, efficiency of floor plans and soundness of construction methods, experience has shown that loans in excess of 65 or even 70 per cent. of *sound investment cost* can be made safely.[1] The 50 per cent. principle was evolved in a day of small non-fireproof buildings, dependent on rentals from a single family or a comparatively small number of business tenants, in districts subject to heavy obsolescence. When it is considered that a $5,000,000 issue of real estate bonds, representing a " two-thirds loan " on a property, has an equity of more than $2,500,000 behind it, with income risks distributed among a great number of office or apartment tenants who contribute to earnings, the soundness of the new principle becomes apparent. In the application of this principle, however, the matter of fair appraisals of value of land and of building upon completion has become increasingly important. Whereas many of the older concerns, for a long period of years, pursued the policy of making their own appraisals without giving cause for criticism,[2] the large number of new-comers in the field, lacking comparable experience and judgment,

[1] State regulations in New York and New Jersey permit building and loan associations to loan 80 per cent. on income-producing property.

[2] During a period of eight years, every property underwritten by one long-established house, which had been sold subsequent to financing and on which the exact sales price was definitely ascertainable,—38 in all—sold for more than the appraised price at the time the bonds were sold. The differences

makes it desirable to have independent appraisals by reputable and accredited appraisers.

The most acceptable practice [1] of underwriting construction loans is based on agreements between the borrowers and the real estate mortgage bankers that, before any payments are made out of the proceeds of the financing, the mortgagor should first use his own funds and proceed with the construction to such a point that the net proceeds derived from the bond issue will be sufficient to complete the entire construction and equipment free of liens.[2] In actual practice, it is impossible to determine more than an approximation of the total cost of the completed structure at the time the underwriting agreement is made. The exact amount of necessary financing can be figured only when plans have been drawn, specifications of materials determined and contracts entered into for construction. The procedure does not augur for the safety of such bonds, if underwritten by an inexperienced real estate mortgage bond house, or by one that does not have an adequate staff of technicians. Too many opportunities are offered for abuses and deceptions, private agreements for rebates on contracts and the like. The investor's protection must be found in the reputability of the mortgagors, architects, and contractors, and more particularly in the knowledge, experience, and supervision of the underwriting house. It is in these matters that a trained technical staff of competent architects, engineers, and inspectors becomes of cardinal importance to a banking house engaged in underwriting real estate first mortgage bonds.

---

ranged between $5,000 and $1,200,000. *Barron's Weekly*, June 29, 1925, "Putting Marketability into Real Estate Bonds."

[1] "The whole subject of construction payments calls for thorough experience and the careful application of sound business principles, but it involves no great mystery or undue hazard. On the contrary, the measures which feasibly may be adopted often insure greater certainty as to costs and values than can be obtained in relation to completed structures. In other words, the machinery is attainable, if properly sought and operated, to offer to the investor with precision and safety the attractive security afforded by new construction, modern in conception and execution and best adapted to supply existing needs." *Report of Committee on Real Estate Securities, Investment Bankers Assn. of America, 1925*, page 115.

[2] On all construction loans, the investor should ascertain if adequate surety bonds have been given by both the mortgagor and contractor to insure completion, if this is not guaranteed by a responsible underwriting house.

Earnings. In the final analysis, however, it is the earnings of a property rather than its cost which determine its true value and the relative safety of the bonds which it secures. After deductions for taxes, insurance, operating costs (ground rent, if a leasehold mortgage), and an allowance for vacancies, the net annual earnings of first-grade properties should be at least twice the greatest annual charge. An investor who buys real estate bonds secured entirely or for the most part by completed properties, has recourse to an established record of earnings, but in all other particulars he must give consideration to the same factors that guide the investor in bonds secured by properties under construction. The primary factors are: (1) location, (2) existing trend of city development with reference to that location, (3) existing rental demand for facilities to be provided, (4) quality and efficiency of the structure with reference to such demand, and (5) responsibility and managing ability of the borrower. Thorough investigation and consideration of these factors enable experienced underwriting houses to determine the earnings of a property upon completion with a more than fair degree of accuracy.[1]

The better the location of a building that is suited to the demands of commercial or residential tenants, the greater is the assurance of the earning capacity originally estimated by the underwriters, or even enhanced earning capacity. In other words, a good building located on or to be erected on the busiest corner of a prosperous city may be assured of adequate earnings, whereas, to insure normal safety, the keenest foresight and soundest judgment must be employed by experienced underwriters in financing a property located or to be erected in a new business centre of the same city.

Demand for the facilities which a completed building offers, whether it be for commercial manufacturing or residential

---

[1] On eight properties underwritten by one large real estate bond house, selected at random from their issues by a disinterested party, original estimates of earnings by the underwriter totaled $1,125,895. The actual net earnings for 1924 totalled $1,587,405. Five of the properties showed earnings in excess of original estimates—three slightly below original estimates. The lowest figure was equal to 14.2 per cent. of the face amount of the bond issue, leaving a substantial surplus after paying interest and principal charges for the year. *Barron's Weekly*, June 29, 1925, "Putting Marketability into Real Estate Bonds."

purposes, can be determined with a fair degree of accuracy from its record of vacancies. The underwriter and investor, however, must give thorough consideration to the character of the building which secures the bonds. If the building is filled only because more modern and satisfactory accommodations are not available, for instance, the earnings of the property may suffer appreciably from the competition of new buildings erected in the same locality. Many real estate bond houses premise their consideration of any proposed financing, whether on completed or construction issues, on a thorough survey of rental conditions in the area adjacent to the property. If there is any doubt relative to earning power of a property, the investor should call for the detailed facts disclosed by such a survey. Further, facts relative to existing rental demand should be judged in relation to other construction in progress in that locality and the likelihood of competition that might be furnished by future construction. In any case, conservative financing requires that the computation of earning capacity should be based on not more than 90 per cent. of the rental area of the building. If an appreciable part of rentable space is under long-term leases or leased to well-known individuals or corporations who will tend to lend character to the building, or both, these factors will give further assurance of permanent earning power.

It is at once apparent that the continued worth and earning capacity of a large modern building over a period of years is dependent on the quality of materials and sound engineering entering into it. Directly associated with these factors is another that inexperienced underwriters and investors do not always take into account,—namely, efficiency in design and floor plans. A building plan that does not permit of satisfactory natural lighting, or is inadequately equipped, or allows of an inordinate amount of waste space [1] utilizable as rentable area is handicapped in competition with buildings that are more efficiently designed and planned. Here again the investor is dependent to a large

[1] A study of building made by the National Association of Building Owners and Managers indicated an average plan efficiency of 68½ per cent., while many buildings are as low as 50 per cent. Some buildings have efficiencies of 80 per cent. and even 90 per cent. Obviously the higher the efficiency in plan, the lower the investment cost per rentable square foot, and consequently the greater rental return per square foot.

degree upon the knowledge, experience, and judgment of the technical staff of the underwriting house.

The responsibility of the borrower, whether an individual or corporation, is a matter of credit investigation, and these facts should be available on application to the real estate bond house. Essentially, the amount of the borrower's assets in cash or demand loans should indicate his ability to carry out the provisions of the mortgage over a period of business depression when net income might not prove adequate. The ability of the mortgagor to manage a large business or residential property, representing an investment of millions of dollars, is second only to his financial responsibility. The question of management,—of general fitness and experience to discharge attendant responsibilities efficiently and economically—varies in importance as the ratio of the mortgage debt to the total investment in the property increases.

Amortization. The principle of amortization, or the gradual retirement of a mortgage loan by partial payments each year, was introduced into real estate bond financing in the United States about 1907. Now the majority of real estate bond issues employ amortization either by retiring serial maturities of bonds each year or by requiring that stipulated amounts be set aside in a sinking fund each year. In the case of sinking funds, it is usually provided that the moneys must be used immediately to retire bonds through either purchase or call. In the first instance, a certain part of the principal amount of the bonds mature two to three years after the date of the bond issue, and each year thereafter the principal amount maturing should increase proportionate to the reduction of interest on the remainder of the mortgage obligation. It is the practice of conservative real estate bond houses to arrange serial maturities so that they will retire 35 to 50 per cent. of the principal within a period of 10 to 15 years,[1] at which time the remainder falls due.

---

[1] "In cases of exceptional merit and stability that are bound to be presented, where it is necessary or advisable to consider a term as long as 20 years, or even 15, serial maturities or rapidly operating sinking funds beginning as early as possible are most emphatically recommended. However, in thus endeavoring to safeguard the bondholder against rapid depreciation or obsolescence of his security, the underwriter should also avoid the other danger, namely, that of saddling the project with too heavy an annual fixed charge, especially in the first year or two before it has had a chance to get upon its

In order to insure the application each month of net earnings or their equivalent against principal and interest charges, before any other obligations are met or the moneys diverted to other corporate or individual uses, the majority of real estate bond houses require monthly deposits of one-twelfth of the annual total of such principal and interest. It is with respect to enforcing such payments should it become necessary that a lien against the earnings of the property is of greatest value.

Net Yield. In the beginning of the real estate bond business, it was customary for issuing houses to offer all issues of bonds at par, to yield 6 to 8 per cent. The rate was governed in part, of course, by existing interest rates, but more specifically by the interest yields offered by small first mortgages with which they competed. With their recognition as a form of bond investment, growth of competition in the field and greater discrimination on the part of investors, the offerings are made at a range of interest yields comparable to the highest and lowest yields to be found in public utility or industrial bonds, representing a spread of 2 per cent. or more between the offerings of different bond houses. It is at once apparent that bonds secured by a business building in a small or not particularly prosperous city should not sell at as high a price as bonds secured by a centrally located property in a major city where the facilities are in urgent demand. Other factors such as early serial maturities, size of the issue, exemption from state taxes, legality for trust funds and guarantee by an independent company enable real estate bonds to secure consideration at higher prices. As part of the effort to improve the marketability of the issues, the former arbitrary inflexible price of par has been discarded by the larger real estate bond houses in favor of the discount (or sometimes, premium) that can more accurately reflect the proper basis of yield.

Denomination. It is the highly useful function of the real estate first mortgage bond to give the man who has $100 or $2,500 to invest the same quality of real estate security as him who has $250,000. The denominations generally offered are $1,000, $500, and $100. When amortized through serial retirements of the principal amount, $100 pieces usually are available in only the last maturity.

<hr>

feet." *Annual Report, Committee on Real Estate Securities, Investment Bankers Assn. of America, 1924,* page 14.

Marketability. Despite the great amount of bonds underwritten, their inherent merit and enviable record of safety, real estate bonds on the whole have lacked the important factor of marketability in the degree required by many investors. In the earlier years of the business real estate bonds were more generally regarded as fractional parts of a real estate first mortgage and therefore more generally considered as investments to be held until maturity date. Serial maturities answered the question of duration for investors who anticipated a fixed time of reimbursement. In other instances the real estate bond house gradually assumed an implied obligation to maintain a market at par less a nominal discount, generally 99. Financial conditions following the war proved the impracticability of this artificial kind of market maintenance. Here again the cause was the realization that satisfactory marketability could never be built up so long as there was any arbitrary, inflexible rates and repurchase policy (par and 99 respectively). The larger houses, however, now maintain a fairly satisfactory market on their own issues, with discounts based on maturity, yield, etc., rarely exceeding 3 per cent. The increasing use of the sinking fund principle for larger issues also has tended toward more satisfactory marketability, since it provides a single maturity or an issue of comparatively large size instead of a dozen or more small issues, and also because the requirements for the sinking fund make a natural market for a portion of the bond. The trend is also toward the creation of a satisfactory secondary market for real estate bonds. The participation of dealers in syndicate offerings, beginning in 1925, has lent impetus to this trend. Several trading houses, including members of stock exchanges, now trade [1] in bonds of large outstanding issues which are underwritten by the leading real estate bond houses.

Leasehold Mortgage Bonds. Long-term leases as security for mortgage loans have been in use in Europe for a century, but the popularity of leasehold mortgage bonds has been achieved in our own country only since about 1910. The owner of valuable real estate who is unable to undertake the costly improvements necessary to bring the property to its highest efficiency, may also find that because of the high price involved there is not a ready market. Although bonds secured by a leasehold generally are

[1] Initiated the latter part of 1924 or early in 1925.

considered inferior to bonds secured by a fee, yet leasehold loans when carefully made may readily be the basis of sound investment. Moreover, they offer the advantage of investment in centrally located "downtown" property, which otherwise is increasingly difficult to obtain in some of our large cities.

There are two types of long-term leases commonly found in leasehold mortgage bonds: (1) straight lease with the same fixed rental for each year for the entire term, usually 99 years, (2) revaluation lease, with rental fixed for a given period, say 21 years, and then subject to reappraisal periodically. Obviously the former offers the best security for loans because any enhanced value accrues to the lessee. In dealing with the second form, the investor should know whether a reappraisal date is near, and, if so, the basis for determining the revised rental as provided in the lease.[1] If the fee has been mortgaged prior to the date of the leasehold, or the owner has reserved the right to mortgage the fee, the leasehold which is to be the basis of a sound investment should be protected by a separate agreement or a clause in the lease to the effect that a foreclosure of such a mortgage would not influence the rights of the lessee as long as he fulfils the covenants of the lease. If the fee is not mortgaged, and the right to mortgage is not granted in the lease, then the lease is prior in right to any future mortgage on the fee.

Adequate improvements, representing properties whose earning power constitutes a high degree of efficiency, are most necessary as security for leasehold bonds, and especially when rentals are subject to reappraisement or are progressive.

Since the mortgage on a leasehold is subject to foreclosure, if the lessee fails to pay ground rent and taxes, a right of prior action vested in the trustee of the bond issue is an important safeguard for the investor. If the lessee is in default, the lessor usually can foreclose only after having given 60 days' notice, whereas such a right of prior action enables the trustee to step in ahead of the lessor and take action to protect the bondholders, if necessary, within 15 days after default.

Guaranteed Real Estate Bonds. The high degree of safety imputed to sound real estate mortgage investments is the basis

---

[1] In New York, where the second form of lease is employed, leaseholds usually provide that the rentals shall be based on some fixed per cent. of the appraised value.

for the development of various forms of guarantees of the principal and interest amounts. Guaranteed real estate bonds usually are sold to yield about $\frac{1}{2}$ of 1 per cent. less than real estate bonds of the same grade that are not guaranteed. Many of the largest and most successful underwriters of real estate bonds do not guarantee their issues, nor will they admit the necessity for a guarantee. A guarantee that is used as a screen for " overloaning " or for careless loan methods on the part of the issuing house will not prevent it from ultimately becoming a poor investment. The investor should consider a guarantee as insurance against hazards and risks. Since the investor pays for this insurance in the form of lower interest yield, due investigation should be made as to the real reinforcement of security supplied by the guarantee.

Three different forms of guaranteed real estate bonds are currently offered to investors:

1. *Guarantees by Issuing House.* The sale of bonds guaranteed as to principal and interest by the underwriting house is from the legal standpoint a conditional sale, and, therefore, carries a contingent liability.[1] Such a guarantee should be considered only in the light of convincing proof that a definite relation between capital and guarantees is continuously maintained.

2. *Guarantees by Surety Company.* Guarantees by a surety company cannot be judged solely by a statement of the surety company's assets and liabilities. Its capital is subject to many other risks. The existence of a segregated fund for this particular risk, and the ratio between the fund and outstanding guarantees is pertinent. The surety company's experience and familiarity with real estate values and its ability to weed out inflated loans brought to it for guarantees, also are important.

3. *Guarantee by an Allied Company.* Some real estate bond houses have organized allied or subsidiary companies to guarantee

---

[1] " In 1924, four of the leading houses selling guaranteed real estate securities in New York City, with combined capital, surplus, and undivided profits of approximately $52,000,000, had outstanding guarantees of approximately $850,000,000—the ratios ranging from about six times to more than twenty-five times. In the case of two of these companies, capital was also at the risk of title guarantees or deposit liabilities as well. It is obvious that the failure of any considerable percentage of the risks outstanding would make the guarantee ineffective." *Investment Bankers Assn. of America, 1925*, page 146.

their own bond issues. If the capital of the guaranteeing company is at no other risk and maintains a reasonable ratio between outstanding guarantees and capital, surplus, and profits, this guaranty is not only sound, but the best form.

Certificates of Participation. Certificates of participation might be called Real Estate First Mortgage Collateral Trust Certificates. A fund of several hundred thousand dollars or millions of dollars is used to purchase a number of first mortgages of the quality, size, maturities, etc., permitted by the stipulations of a collateral trust deed. As mortgages mature, new mortgages are purchased and substituted. The certificates of participation, issued against this pool of mortgages, are analogous to the Investment Trust Certificates against pools of general securities which are common in England. If guaranteed real estate mortgages are deposited in such a pool, the certificates may of course carry the guarantee and be sold as guaranteed certificates of participation. Certificates sometimes are issued against a single mortgage, but usually only when a mortgage involves a large amount. Mention should also be made of " guaranteed " first mortgage certificates, which are certificates of participation in guaranteed real estate mortgages.

" Land Trust Certificates " or Certificates of Equitable Ownership. Technically this is the correct designation for certificates which represent a part ownership in land. They are commonly referred to in some cities and districts as " land trust," " ground rent," " fee " certificates or certificates of beneficial interest. When ordinary precautions are observed, this is an excellent form which embodies all of the traditional elements of safety to be found in an investment secured by improved city real estate. Representing ownership of land they are exempt from the personal property tax and consequently are particularly popular in states, as Ohio and Massachusetts, where such taxes are high.

In connection with the development of a city location, for example, the owner or owners of the land may induce a trust company to take title to the land, and issue certificates of equitable ownership, which represent divided interests in the land, in shares of $100, $1,000 or larger units, to the amount of the full appraised value of the land. The land is leased to the individual or corporation which undertakes to build improvements, assume all taxes and assessments, and pay a stipulated rental from which is paid the interest (usually from 5 to $6\frac{1}{2}$ per cent. on the certificates).

In their origins, the leases and fee certificates were perpetual.[1] The more conservative bankers and investors, however, now require that a portion of the annual rentals each year be set aside for the purchase of certificates. The original owner in this way eventually reacquires the fee.

Certificates repurchased should be held in trust for the benefit of the remaining holders of certificates until all have been repurchased, but the period should, of course, be within the duration of the lease. The city investor in " fee " certificates, moreover, should be reasonably assured relative to the earning ability of the improvement during the period the certificates are to run—not over 35 years as a maximum.

Certificates of this kind which run for too long a period may be confronted with greatly diminished earning capacity due to deterioration in values, obsolescence or change in city traffic. These hazards more than offset the chance for appreciation in value. The investor in these certificates is primarily interested in an honest appraisal of the land, but information relative to the character and earning capacity of the improvements is equally important.

[1] Ground rents on perpetual leases are more common in Baltimore, Maryland, than in any other city.

CHAPTER XXXV

INDUSTRIAL BONDS

Classification. The general term industrial securities applies to all issues not classed as government, municipal, railroad, public utility, or real estate. So varied, however, are the many industries comprehended in this designation that further classification is necessary. Industrials may be subdivided into general groups such as trading, manufacturing, extracting, and shipping. A commoner subdivision of the Street recognizes the specialties, oils, textiles, fertilizers, coppers, motors, packers, rubber, iron and steel companies, and the equipments. Only broad principles are common to each group, and so it often becomes necessary to judge each company by its own particular standards. The general term "industrials," therefore, should be used with discretion and a more penetrating understanding regarding the particular types of enterprises should be encouraged.

Risk. Risk is conceded to be greater with many industrials than with most of the other classes of securities, but the bonds of certain industrial companies contain the desirable requisites of a sound investment to a greater degree than many of the supposedly higher-grade issues in other fields of investment. The inexperienced investor would do well for the most part, however, to avoid commitments in industrials, for many factors difficult to foresee and to analyze may precipitate sudden changes in market values.

No form of business enterprise, in fact no investment, is absolutely void of risk. In all forms of business endeavor there are elements of uncertainty which make necessary the judicious selection of securities so that the risk assumed by the investor does not exceed the compensation received. In a comparative sense the element of risk is inherently great in industrials. In hazardous industries the probability of large profits must be greater than in less uncertain enterprises. The ratio of earnings to capitalization should correspond broadly with the risk involved. In the determination of the value of an industrial enter-

457

prise the rate at which the earnings should be capitalized depends on inherent risks in the particular undertaking. If the duration of the business is problematical, due to such factors as invention or change of style, the ratio of revenues to capital should be relatively high in order to provide rapid amortization of the principal.

Causes of Business Failures

The causes of business failures may be summarized as follows:

I. *External Causes.*
    1. Economic forces.
    2. Business cycle.
    3. Competition.
    4. Catastrophic changes.
    5. Inherited evils.

II. *Internal Causes.*
    1. Incompetent management.
    2. Labor difficulties.
    3. Financial maladjustment.
    4. Duration of manufacturing process.
    5. Unwise dividend policy.
    6. Insufficient earnings.

A brief discussion of these causes of failure will impress the investor with the necessity of giving due consideration to the many factors adversely affecting industrial enterprises.

In general the external causes of failure are beyond the control of the management. Measures may be adopted in anticipation of adverse influences and so may mitigate their severity, but the adjustment must come from within the organization rather than from an attempt to modify the external uncontrollable forces. Some of the causes of failure listed as external are partly subject to control, but in such cases keen foresight of management is fundamental.

Economic Forces. A shrewd management may possibly turn economic failure into success, but only with great effort. To attain economic success an enterprise must pay current wages, meet the existing rate of interest on the capital commitment, and yield profits commensurate with the risk assumed. Anything short of this is economic failure. It will be readily observed that considerable responsibility rests on the management. Yet the very nature of the undertaking may doom it to failure. Difficulties encountered by the American Hide and Leather

Company and the Central Leather Company in the leather industry were, to a degree, beyond the control of the respective managements. The industry is rendered unstable because of the long period involved in tanning hides, absence of control over sources of raw material, and inability to regulate the price of the finished product, since shoe manufacturers and other large users of leather purchase only when they see fit and at their own prices on the threat that they will establish their own tanneries if terms are unsatisfactory.

Business Cycle. Perhaps no single cause of failure approaches in importance that attached to the operation of the business cycle with its alternate periods of prosperity and depression. Industrials prove especially vulnerable to the periodic business convulsions over which the management has practically no control. The gratifying profits during prosperity often encourage unwarranted plant expansion, assumption of additional financial burdens, extravagant credit extension, and abnormal wage scales, which later serve as a boomerang when orders decline and prices fall. The downward adjustment of wages is gradual, but the decline of orders and prices is precipitous. Only the better managed companies can weather such business storms. Therefore, the investor would do well to analyze the effect of business cycles on the industry under consideration in order to ascertain its behavior in the past as a guide for future expectations.

Competition. Another potent cause of failure of industrials is the keen competition to which they are frequently subjected. In contrast to monopoly conditions characteristic of railroads with their rights of way, and public utilities with exclusive franchise privileges, and to both classes with the special supervision and protection of governmental commissions, the industrial enterprises have no safeguards other than general laws designed to prevent unfair practices. The field of industrial operations is thus virtually unrestrained. An industry operating under the protection of patents, secret processes, and the like, may suddenly experience disastrous competition as the result of new inventions, more effective advertising and selling campaigns, a more efficient delivery system, better general service, a higher grade product, or more liberal terms of credit. It should be clear to the investor, that large-scale operation is no longer considered essential to business success. In fact, well-managed plants of moderate capacity, if of sufficient size to secure the advantages of machine production, have often proved more profitable even in a well-integrated industry. Competition, therefore, may not be eliminated by the large enterprise, but is an ever-present factor encountered by practically all industrial undertakings.

Catastrophic Changes. External causes of failure classed in the foregoing scheme as " catastrophic changes," include wars, disasters, political attacks or adverse legal decisions. These need little discussion. So apparent are their evil effects on industry and so obviously beyond the control of the management that the investor need only observe the probability of such contingencies arising in the respective lines of industry and ascertain the nature and extent to which protective measures may be provided.

Inherited Evils. Although the evils inherited by the management constitute an external cause of failure when considered by the present management, yet the original cause may have been internal. Thus too costly initial promotion with consequent overcapitalization and excessive fixed charges may later result in disaster, due to no fault of the present administration. The mere fact, however, that fundamental weaknesses exist, regardless of their origin, should suggest caution.

Internal Causes—Incompetent Management. Emphasis has been placed on the external causes of failure, but of all causes the most important is the single internal cause of inefficient management. Most frequently the difference between success and failure lies in management. In no other type of enterprise is this factor so important as in industrials. Many and varied are the vicissitudes of industrial enterprises. The ease with which destructive competition, labor difficulties, the inevitable business cycle, and other distressing factors may arise, require the attention of an alert manager who is familiar not only with the problems peculiar to his own business but who has a practical knowledge of the general economic laws and business practices affecting his enterprise.

Labor Difficulties. Labor difficulties are frequently attributable to the lack of foresight by the management. Failure to recognize labor issues, such as an adequate supply, its efficiency, living and working conditions, often results in strikes, lockouts, and boycotts, which otherwise might have been prevented.

Financial Maladjustments. In not a few industries the entrepreneurs have attempted to adjust the financial requirements of the business to the capital at their command rather than to determine in advance of promotion the size of plant necessary to effect the various economies incident to unit production. Later developments indicate the need for plant expansion and additional working capital. Too frequently a financial plan has been devised that hampers the management in the quest for additional funds. At other times prosperity excites overexpansion of production and of sales without sufficient regard for financial requirements. The history of the two reorganizations of the Westinghouse Electric and Manufacturing Company lends force to this statement. Not infrequently bonds are issued without adequate provision for the payment of interest and the retirement of principal. In such cases current obligations may be neglected and financial failure results.

Duration of the Manufacturing Process. A manufacturing process requiring considerable time not only necessitates the long application of capital before a return but also increases the hazards due to future market uncertainties. Hedging, characteristic of cotton and of flour manufacturing, is not feasible in all industries. Thus the tobacco manufacturer finds it necessary to expend considerable sums for raw materials and for curing processes long in advance of any expected returns.

Unwise Dividend Policy. The desire to create a favorable impression or to realize on large common stock holdings often prompts directors to declare dividends in excess of conservative prospects. The consequent loss of working capital increases the financial difficulties and in the end often leads to default in interest payments and on the entire floating indebtedness. The astonishingly large percentage of the failures following the consolidations of about thirty years ago is attributed to the payment of dividends unwarranted by the earnings and current funds. To attract new capital or to share in large temporary returns, the managers deemed it expedient to dissipate working capital in the expectation that in some manner the treasury might be reimbursed. The investor should assure himself that dividends are paid only after earnings prove sufficient to maintain the plant, pay all fixed charges and to provide a conservative reserve for contingencies.

Insufficient Earnings. In the final analysis the outstanding cause of failure is insufficient earnings. Business failure as distinct from economic failure results when earnings are insufficient to cover the costs of raw materials and labor, exclusive of the payment of interest and dividends. For the permanence of an enterprise it is necessary, however, not only to defray the primary costs but also to pay normal interest charges and dividends. Central Leather, American Writing Paper, International Mercantile Marine, Virginia-Carolina Chemical, and the American Sugar Refining are outstanding examples of enterprises that have failed for several years either intermittently or continuously to obtain sufficient earnings from operations to meet current expenses, not including return on capital—either interest or dividends. As a result they have been forced to reorganize their financial structures and to effect economies that in some cases give greater promise for success, but almost always at great sacrifice to stockholders and even after substantial losses to mortgage bondholders.

Tangible Values.—Fixed Assets. Some students of investment stress unduly the importance of tangible values as security for bond issues. These analysts are not attracted by companies which because of the nature of the business have a comparatively small percentage of their capital in tangible assets. It is readily conceded that bonds protected by a mortgage on valuable physical property may have an advantage over bonds not so safeguarded. Yet the value of property of a going concern is frequently determined not by the original cost of producing the property, by its reproduction cost, or even by its market value, but rather by its capacity to yield income under conditions of management and operations for which it was specially designed.

An attempt to utilize the specialized property, such as machines or equipment, for purposes other than that originally intended might result in serious production difficulties and consequent decline in net earnings. The culmination of the bicycle era and the attempt to adapt the plants to automobile production brought distress to many bicycle manufacturers. The physical property, once so valuable because of large profits during the bicycle period, suddenly slumped in value. Not infrequently, therefore, bondholders who insist on physical values without due regard to the more important element of earnings suddenly realize that they have on their hands a specialized plant without a market for its proper product.

The profit curves of American companies engaged in the manufacture and sale of standard, trade-marked, proprietary foods and medicines offer truer indices of security for bond issues or stock issues than any edifices of bricks and mortar.

Depletable Assets. Bonds secured by mortgages on assets subject to depletion, such as coal and mineral deposits, oil wells and timber lands, should be protected through adequate periodic commitments to a sinking fund as the assets are extracted, so as to provide for bond retirement at maturity or for serial redemption at a rate sufficient to protect the bondholders' equity. Little value can be attached to the plant if the raw material is nearing exhaustion. Then, too, the extreme uncertainty of the continued flow of oil, the irregularity of mineral deposits, and hazards of forest fire, all increase the risk of bonds covered by mortgages on mines, oil, or timber properties.

If the physical property, which usually includes factories, is located in large cities with increasing population, the real estate alone may be valuable. As an idle factory is a dubious asset in case of liquidation, little value should be ascribed to it independent of the value placed on the plant as a going concern, and as represented partially by the market price of the stock. This price would indicate the appraisal by the stockholders of their equity in the business. The valuation by the stockholders should extend over a sufficient number of years to include all phases of the business cycle. Normally, the valuation of their equity should at least equal the funded debt.

Current Assets. In the foregoing discussion attention was directed toward fixed assets, such as land, buildings, machinery. There are other tangible assets, however, which are in a constant state of flux. They consist of raw materials, goods in process of manufacture, finished goods, and other goods in stock, all constituting a portion of current assets. Their nature and function are such that they are in the process of preparation for and finally pass to the consumer in exchange for other current assets, consisting of cash, accounts, and notes receivable, only again to repeat the process. The very nature of these current assets does not make them subject to mortgage. The condition of current assets, however, is of fundamental importance to the bondholder, for when compared with current liabilities, they measure the financial strength of the company. It is obvious that a company cannot meet its interest obligations if cash is not available. Likewise default in principal will follow if the shortage of cash becomes chronic. The Investment Bankers Association of America at the 1926 Convention stated " that the basic principle of industrial bonds and notes is that of a loan against current assets, with a secondary regard to plant and other fixed assets. . . . . . The risk inherent in fixed property used for industrial purposes properly belongs to the common stockholders." [1]

Because of the importance attached to current assets, the investor should carefully analyze their nature and their relation to current liabilities. The final test of their liquidity is the ease with which they can be converted into cash without incurring loss. Cash, therefore, is the premier current asset. The other current assets can be ranked according to the ease of conversion in the following order: securities owned, accounts receivable, notes receivable, raw materials, goods in process, and finished goods.

Liquidity of Current Assets. The degree of liquidity depends on such factors as general business conditions, the state of the receivables,—that is, whether due or past due,—and the nature of inventories. If securities owned are also included in current assets they, like inventories, should be carried at cost or market price, whichever may be the lower. Securities that are held for control purposes or not readily marketable should be included among the fixed assets as investments.

Current Ratios. There should be sufficient current assets with a high degree of liquidity to take advantage of cash discounts, pay interest, dividends, wages, and other current obligations even in periods of financial stress. Rather liberal provision should be made for these purposes. A rule-of-thumb requirement places a current ratio of two to one, that is, as a minimum requirement the industrial company should possess two dollars of current assets for each dollar of current liabilities. One should not be misled by such a generalization, however, for frequently such a low current ratio would be dangerous. Only the particular nature of the business will determine the minimum amount of net

[1] *The Commercial & Financial Chronicle*, Vol. 123, p. 2081.

working capital that can be maintained with safety. The following current ratios as of December 31, 1925, indicate a wide range at a time when business was generally prosperous:

United States Smelting Refining & Mining Co.............. 1.8
Sinclair Consolidated Oil Corporation..................... 2.2
Standard Oil Company (New Jersey)....................... 2.7
The Studebaker Corporation............................. 4.0
United States Rubber Company.......................... 5.0
Cerro de Pasco Copper Corporation....................... 6.9
American Chicle Company................................ 9.4
Allied Chemical & Dye Corporation.....................10.9
The Coco-Cola Company................................12.7
American Druggists Syndicate...........................19.1

Although these ratios do not measure the maximum range among industrial companies, yet it shows a striking variation. In periods of depression many of the companies show a less favorable condition. It must be remembered that the current ratio indicates the financial condition as of a particular time only, and this fact lessens its usefulness to the investment analyst. For instance, the United States Smelting, Refining and Mining Company had a current ratio of only 1.8 on December 31, 1925, as compared with 3.4 at end of 1924. Closer analysis discloses an item of $8,001,500 representing the 10-year 6 per cent. gold notes due February 1, 1926, and included in current liabilities. This inclusion thus presents an abnormal condition. Likewise current assets may be temporarily increased through the sale of fixed properties or due to recent financing. It becomes apparent, therefore, that the current ratios must be compared over a period of years in order to obtain a trustworthy impression.[1]

Quick Assets. In addition to a comparison of total current assets with total current liabilities (the current ratio) further analysis of the financial position could be made by comparing cash and receivables with total current liabilities. If these current assets over a period of years equal the current liabilities, the company is then said to meet the so-called "acid test." Liquidity meets its severest test in a comparison of total current assets with the total debt, including both current liabilities and funded debt. The bondholder is usually assured of immediate satisfaction of his claims in case of liquidation if the current

[1] For a discussion of business ratios, see Bliss, G. H. "*Financial Operating Ratios in Management.*"

assets exceed all obligations. Such a strong financial condition indicates conservative management and places the company in a position to meet even extraordinary contingencies.

Deferred Charges. Generally speaking, little value should be attributed to items in the balance sheet under the general caption " deferred charges." They usually consist of various expenses, such as advertising, insurance, or rent, paid in advance of the period to which they are chargeable, but in case of liquidation they would prove of little value.

Intangible Values. The average investor who insists on tangible values as security for bonds frequently fails to apply a test of security valuation which, at times, proves more important. The control of valuable patents enjoyed by such companies as General Electric Company and Eastman Kodak Company may furnish a proper basis for funded debt. Basic patents in established industries where changes are infrequent are likely to continue longer than in enterprises in the development stage, such as the radio industry at the present time. Patents, because of their limited duration, probable supersession, or the change of demand, frequently offer little security to the bonds, and in cases of forced liquidation their value may disappear entirely.

In a general way similar objections may be raised against trade-marks and copyrights as security for bonds. Time limitation always exists and any value attached to such assets should at least be written off during their lives. New processes, more vigorous advertising and selling campaigns, lower prices, more acceptable credit terms, and many other contingencies may render worthless these intangible values. The reader is well aware, however, that there are many products sold under trade-marks which enjoy a rather inflexible demand, thereby contributing great value to the trade name.

Good-will. The intangible item which has aroused the keenest controversial discussion is good-will. This intangible value manifests itself in income above that which is considered average in the particular industry and usually it is the result of superior organization or reputation. However, good-will does not generally offer desirable security for a bond issue. As already observed, earning power is a logical test of bond valuation. When average earnings over a period of years show an excess above those earned by other companies in the same industry, intangible elements of substantial value are necessarily present. How long will these excess earnings continue? This is difficult to answer, but a close estimation should be made. In the event of a forced sale the bondholder could not ordinarily realize on good-will, for its value is then negligible. In a going, prosperous concern the value of good-will is determined by the simple method of capitalizing the average net earnings over a period of years,— usually not less than five,—by a rate of return considered satisfactory in the industry as a whole and then deducting from this amount the net tangible assets. In appraising the value of assets as security for bonds, the investor should consider all intangible items with conservatism in order to ascertain the validity and basis of their valuation, and he should bear in mind that intangible items tend to vanish in the hour of need. Caution is also directed to the account " bond discount " which frequently appears in the balance sheets of industrial companies. When it is understood that bond discount is merely an adjustment of interest, its appearance among the assets will serve to inform the analyst that a certain amount of securities has been sold below par, and the difference charged to expenses during the life of the bonds. It should, therefore, be deducted from total assets in an analysis of a balance sheet.

Capitalization. Capitalization,—the par value of stocks, bonds, and long-term notes outstanding, is normally less than the value of the assets. In the case of large combinations the value of tangible assets frequently ranges from 40 per cent. to 50 per cent. of the capitalization, the balance being represented by such intangible items as patents, trade-marks, copyrights, franchises, and good-will. Economies of large-scale operations or perhaps monopolistic advantages usually afford the excuse for the wide difference. Normally, however, the property should exceed not only the capitalization but also the total of the capitalization and current liabilities.

But more important than the ratio of property to capitalization is the form of capitalization. Bonds with their accompanying fixed charges, as previously observed, should represent a smaller percentage to total capitalization in industrial enterprises because of the instability of earnings. Enterprises with fairly uniform returns may safely issue larger percentages of funded obligations than industries in which the earnings are characteristically irregular. The International Harvester Company, having no bond issues, was able without resorting to new financing to emerge from the severe depression of 1921 and 1922 when the net income in these years amounted respectively to $4,150,000 and $5,540,000 as compared with $17,155,000 in 1920 and $10,274,000 in 1923.

Classes of Capital. As stockholders derive their dividends from net returns, that is, after the deduction of all costs of conducting business, they naturally desire to distribute the amount available among as few claimants as possible. In order to reserve as large a percentage of the earnings as possible, capital may be acquired by the sale of bonds carrying lower interest rate than the return derived therefrom, the difference accruing to the stockholders. At times, therefore, it is advisable from the point of view of the stockholder, as contrasted with financial management, to trade on the equity, that is, to borrow and thus increase earnings. The lender, on the other hand, must not overlook the importance of adequate equity behind his bonds to be supplied by the stockholder.

It is difficult to fix arbitrarily the proportion of funded debt to total capitalization in industrial companies because of the great variability of earnings. The ratio ranges from zero to about 65 per cent., but the average lies between 25 per cent. and 30 per cent., preferred stock between 25 per cent. and 30 per cent., and common stock between 45 per cent. and 50 per cent.

At times, the capital set-up of an industrial company restricts the bonds to the amount of current assets, the preferred stock to the value of tangible assets, and the common stock to intangible assets based on the capacity of these assets to provide adequate earnings for dividends. If such a financial plan were adopted, current assets would be supplied by bondholders and current creditors, other tangible assets by preferred stockholders, and intangible assets by the common stockholders. A conservative management will provide in part for future expansion out of reserved earnings.

Frequently companies are condemned because of overcapitalization as reflected in " watered stock." This situation, from one point of view, arises when the tangible assets back of the stock are less than the par value, but from a better point of view overcapitalization exists only when earnings are insufficient to pay normal returns on the total capitalization. The bondholders may be affected if earnings are distributed as dividends when they should rather be retained in the business to maintain the integrity of the investment.

Mortgages. The old practice of issuing closed-end mortgages with the " after-acquired " clause has, to a large extent, given way to the issuance of bonds protected by open-end and limited open-end mortgages. Under the latter mortgage the issuance of additional bonds is limited to a certain percentage of the newly-acquired properties, and the equity in the purchased property is paid for out of earnings or through the sale of stock.

If new bond issues are restricted to 50 per cent. or at most 60 per cent. of additions and improvements, if earnings available for interest requirements must be twice the charges,[1] including the charges against the bonds presently to be issued, and if the current position is suitable—a current ratio of at least two to one—then there can be little objection to the limited open-end or even the open-end mortgage. In fact, future financing is simplified and at the same time the old bondholders will not suffer by a diminution in their equity.

Earnings and Earning Ratios. The inherent nature of industrial companies is such that changes in the business cycle are reflected in wide fluctuation of earnings; the returns for a single year, therefore, would prove an inadequate test of their sufficiency over a period of years to meet fixed charges. At least a five-year period of net earnings should be used when testing an industrial bond. The investor is interested in the variation of net earnings and should observe the high and low points. He should compare the low points with old fixed charges, and if he is considering the purchase of bonds of a new issue a comparison should be made between average net earnings and the new fixed charges. To be conservative, the investor should seek bonds in companies that show average net earnings of at least twice the fixed charges, but if the investor is ultraconservative he may require that the bonds be protected by net earnings equal even in the poorest year to the charges. In some instances investors

[1] It should be clearly understood that earnings amounting to twice the interest requirements are frequently inadequate in industrials, and that the current ratio of two-to-one is also in a great many instances too low.

demand that average net earnings shall be twice the present fixed charges, including those on the new issues. In 1921 the earnings of even strong industrial enterprises failed to meet these requirements. Expansion of the industry in general, or a more efficient management in particular, indicates the fallacy of adopting such standards without qualifications. If the company provides for lean years by adequate reserves in prosperous years, there is less need for the rigid two-to-one rule relative to net earnings available for interest charges.

When the range of net earnings is wide, the ratio of funded debt to total capitalization should be low. The capital set-up is directly affected by fluctuations in earnings. In contrast to railroad and public utility enterprises, the industrial, because of the usual wide variation in net earnings, should finance primarily through the sale of stock. There are, however, bonds of such industrials as the United States Steel 50-Year-Gold 5s of 1951, without even mortgage protection, which enjoy high investment rating regardless of wide fluctuation of earnings.

Net earnings are certainly the best criterion of investment value of industrial bonds. The value of the assets, as previously indicated, arises primarily from earnings. Assets must be profit-producing in order to attract the thoughtful investor. Notwithstanding this generalization one should not conclude that the security value of an enterprise is equal to the capitalized earnings. If the management were to remain permanent and continue efficient, and if other factors were subject to the same degree of control, there would be a closer correlation between various security values derived by the capitalization of average net earnings. But unfortunately managements change more rapidly than fixed assets, and this fact gives rise to the usual requirement that industrial bonds shall mature within twenty-five years.

Sources of Income. Inasmuch as the stability of earnings affects the investment status of the security, careful analysis of the sources of earnings is important. Sources of income are varied. The income statement if complete will indicate the various principal sources. A large part should be derived from operations. Income derived from sources other than operations such as investments, or from subsidiaries in the case of a holding company, should be subjected to careful analysis. Hazards vary in the different sources. If a large part of earnings is dependent on uncertain sources, the investor should acquaint himself with that fact. At times enterprises skimp maintenance and depreciation in order to present a favorable statement, while on other occasions capital expenditures are charged to operating expenses and excessive depreciation charges are made, thus resulting in secret reserves. Either practice is open to objection, for the former deceives the investor to his possible detriment, and the latter perhaps to his advantage.

Instead of the rigid requirement that average net earnings over at least a five-year period shall be at a minimum of twice the fixed charges and that in no year shall they be less than the charges, it is preferable to require that the ratio between both gross and net earnings to fixed charges shall show an upward trend over a period of years. A comparison of earnings with the different phases of the business cycle will reveal its effect on earnings, but will be still more apparent if a comparison with the earnings of competitors is made. If the earnings are not in line with those of other companies, it then becomes necessary to search more deeply for the reasons. A downward trend in the ratio of net earnings to fixed charges may indicate financial disaster unless corrective measures are promptly applied. Retrogression is also indicated by a decline of gross earnings at a time when competitors are enjoying prosperity. More important than gross sales, however, are net returns. Conceivably an increase in gross revenues is the result of extravagant sales practices with too liberal sales and credit terms.

Trend of Net Earnings. The table on page 472 shows the ratio of net earnings to fixed charges for several typical industrials. The figures cover a five-year period, which should be sufficient to include at least a part of the various phases of the business cycle. A weighted average is obtained by multiplying the ratio of earnings to fixed charges for the latest year, 1925, by five, that for 1924 by four, for the preceding year by three, and so on, and the sum of these products is divided by fifteen (the sum of the multiples). If the weighted average is greater than the simple average (derived by dividing the sum of the five ratios by five), there is an upward trend in earnings.

The satisfactory position of the United States Steel Corporation is seen in the actual average ratio of 4.88 and the weighted average of 5.5. The table shows that the Goodyear Tire and

RATIO OF NET EARNINGS TO FIXED CHARGES OF CERTAIN INDUSTRIAL CONCERNS (1921–1925)

Year	U. S. Steel Corp.			Goodyear Tire & Rubber			Virginia-Carolina Chemical			Baldwin Locomotive Works		
	Ratio	Times	Weighted	Ratio	Times	Weighted	Ratio	Times	Weighted	Ratio	Times	Weighted
1921	2.8	1	2.8	2.32	1	2.32	−5.30	1	−5.30	4.03	1	4.03
1922	3.0	2	6.0	1.63	2	3.26	0.37	2	.74	4.98	2	9.96
1923	6.8	3	20.4	2.14	3	6.42	0.13	3	.39	6.58	3	19.74
1924	5.7	4	22.8	3.48	4	13.92	−0.52	4	−2.08	2.35	4	9.40
1925	6.1	5	30.5	5.39	5	26.95	1.08	5	5.40	1.24	5	6.20
	5)24.4		15)82.5	5)14.96		15)52.87	5)−4.24		15)−.85	5)19.18		15)49.33
Average	4.88		5.5	2.99		3.52	−.85		−.06	3.84		3.29

Rubber Company is extricating itself from the difficulties which gave rise to its reorganization. Even the ratio of Virginia-Carolina Chemical Company shows improvement, although there still exists a deficit. The Baldwin Locomotive Works, however, showed a downward trend, although the latter part of the five-year period has been exceptionally prosperous.

Variation in Earnings. Not only do the earnings of industrials as a whole fluctuate more widely than those of railroads and public utilities, but there are marked variations among the several industries. Generally speaking, enterprises selling necessities at low prices directly to the ultimate consumer experience a narrower range of fluctuation in earnings than companies engaged in the manufacture of luxuries or of production goods. The operating ratios are high among industrials, ranging usually from 80 to 90 per cent., and so cause the net earnings to show wide fluctuations. It is apparent that a slight decline in gross earnings may entirely wipe out the profits, unless the industry is such that the expenses can be curtailed when business is slack.

Unfortunately, however, most industrials are burdened with a large percentage of fixed expenses which cannot be adjusted to the volume of gross sales. Industries which require a large capital investment in plant and equipment cannot readily reduce the costs, but in enterprises where unskilled labor is the chief item of expense costs can be reduced according as the gross volume declines. The investor would naturally expect greater fluctuations in the net earnings of companies engaged in manufacturing, transportation, and mining, where the relation among fixed assets is great, than of trading companies the investment of which consists mainly of inventories and other current assets.

Again, industries such as steel making, tanning, sugar refining, and clothing manufacture in which raw materials constitute a large percentage of the expenses are likely to show wide fluctuations in net earnings. Whenever the inventory of materials, raw, semifinished, or finished, constitutes a large percentage of the assets, net earnings will probably fluctuate considerably in sympathy with current price changes. Difficulty also arises in ascertaining costs, for the value of the inventory must be taken as of a particular time, yet such value may be only temporary in a variable market. In the oil industry the inventory is of paramount importance, for when oil prices are rising a large inventory is a good sign of large future profits, and vice versa.

The strong financial position enjoyed by such companies as the United States Steel Corporation, Allied Chemical and Dye Company, Standard Oil of New Jersey, International Harvester Company, Studebaker Corporation, and General Motors Corporation, is due to the practice of " ploughing back " into the assets a large percentage of earnings. The Standard Oil Company of New Jersey and the Studebaker Corporation have been able to finance the major part of their expansion out of reserved earnings. The surplus thus accumulated was capitalized through the declaration of large stock dividends on two occasions by each company. During the period of 1911 to 1925, the Studebaker Corporation retained 50.4 per cent. of the earnings for plant extension. The common stock of companies which follow this plan consistently and which distribute uniform dividends in time approach true investment rank.

Maintenance and Depreciation. It is evident that when the dominant cause of depreciation is wear and tear, the rate of such depreciation will be less when the company maintains its plant in a high state of efficiency. Repairs and renewals offset wear and tear directly, and consequently influence depreciation. The management has therefore the responsibility to safeguard the integrity of the original investment. Adequate repairs and renewals on the one hand, and sufficient reserves for depreciation and obsolescence on the other, offer the best assurance of sound stewardship. Operating expenses should bear this burden, and dividends must be relegated to secondary rank. Any other policy will sooner or later undermine the whole capital structure.

Depreciation arises not only because of deterioration, but also through depletion, obsolescence, and supersession. Assets subject to depletion, such as coal, ore, timber, and oil, yield suitable security for a loan only when a definite amount per unit extracted is reserved as substitute security. Such assets can neither be repaired nor replaced. Mention was made previously of the rapid depreciation of machinery and equipment in extractive industries where ultimate abandonment is inevitable. Industries in their development stage, especially if dependent on highly specialized machinery protected by inventions subject to improvement—such as the phonograph and radio industries at present—are likely to suffer heavy depreciation due to obsolescence. Such equipment should be amortized rapidly, in fact, conservatism prompts the rapid depreciation of all of the properties.

It is the policy of most industrial managements to equalize net earnings as much as possible. In lean years depreciation charges to earnings are relatively small, while in prosperous years, provision is made for the poor years. The depreciation policy of Studebaker Corporation approaches the desirable practice. A year should seldom be allowed to pass without some provision for the replacement of certain assets. In the case of mining companies, large amounts should be shown in depletion reserves, with comparatively small amounts in the depreciation account.

Industrial Bond Valuation. Since the market price of securities reflects psychological factors as well as real assets, the task of fixing a value is difficult. There are, nevertheless, certain tests that may well be applied to determine the value about which the market price is likely to fluctuate.

For an intelligent appraisal of bond values, there is need of a careful analysis of factors such as adequacy and stability of returns, efficiency of management and extent to which employees are being trained to fill more important vacancies, financial status, labor problems, market conditions, availability of raw materials, kind of product, duration of the manufacturing process, all based on the kind of manufacturing, extractive, or trading process.

The value of bonds of an investment rank is determined primarily by their yield as compared with similar bonds of like rank. The price of bonds approaches the par or the redemption price as the maturity nears. When the maturity date is remote there is less correspondence between the current price and par. The long period of amortization or accumulation is so distant as to render the annual consideration small. If, however, the bonds are callable and the company is prosperous, the market price is not likely to rise far above the redemption price. Bonds with the conversion privilege will rise in price above their investment value when the securities into which they are convertible appreciate as a result of large earnings to a point where it pays to convert. If, however, the stock should decline below conversion parity, little if any value accrues because of the conversion privilege.

Priority of claim as to interest and mortgage provisions has a direct bearing on bond values if liquidation is likely to ensue, or even if earnings are insufficient to meet interest charges on junior issues. Yield, however, will determine the value of bonds, as long as earnings are sufficient to meet fixed obligations and the value of assets sufficient to satisfy the mortgage requirements. Frequently earnings are inadequate and assets decline, thus resulting in a violation of the terms of the indenture. In that event the value of the bond will be measured by the extent of the earnings as the upper limit and by the liquidating value of available assets as the lower.

Investment bonds are purchased primarily on the yield basis. If the yield in comparison with similar issues is too low, the bond will be neglected, thus having the effect of adjusting the price. The investor is concerned with the rank and general provisions of the issue, and the financial condition of the obligor. First mortgage issues enjoy better ratings than the junior issues of the same company, yet the underlying obligations are frequently protected by adequate earnings of companies in a sound financial condition.

The value of speculative bonds cannot be determined solely on the yield basis. If net earnings fall below 200 per cent. of the fixed charges and remain so for two years or more, the bonds would then be regarded as speculative. In such event the investor would be interested in the net earnings available and also the liquidating value of the pledged assets. Only the secured issues would probably be paid in full, and that condition would probably exist when the percentage of junior issues is so comparatively large as to provide sufficient equity. It is customary to determine a suitable rate of yield for a speculative issue by determining the average yield of similar bonds, then multiplying the rate by two and capitalizing the net earnings at the derived rate. The capitalized amount would indicate the total value of the bonds. Next divide the total value by the number of bonds to determine the value per bond.

In all cases where there has been default of principal or interest, or where interest has been paid but not earned, it is necessary to study the causes of such distress. If the difficulty threatens to be permanent as a result of change in demand, a readjustment of the financial plan is inevitable. Bondholders seldom realize in full unless the liquidating value of the assets is sufficient. Not infrequently tremendous losses in value occur when the plant and equipment is highly specialized. If the concern is new no earnings record will be available, hence the best test of value is the original cost of the assets pledged which normally should be at least twice the bond issue.

It will be recalled that the efficiency of management and the adoption of methods to ensure its permanency is of paramount importance to the continued success of the company, and therefore has a direct bearing on bond values.

Industrial Bond Characteristics, Position, Market, and Yield. Previous to the consolidation movement of the later nineties when considerable impetus was given the issuance of bonds, industrial bonds were rare. Following the panic of 1903 this method of industrial bond financing increased in public favor, and with its favorable showing through the panic of 1907 it became more popular. The requirements of the World War, however, were primarily instrumental in popularizing the industrial bond. Urgent demand for both fixed and current capital, for plant expansion, and for the acquisition of large inventories at rising costs, together with higher operating expenses, all led to the emission of notes and bonds as substitutes for loans from the already overburdened banks. Since the World War, but more especially since the depression of 1920, industrial bonds have greatly increased in amount, until to-day the par value approximates $10,600,000,000, as compared with about $20,-500,000,000 market price of industrial stock.[1]

It will be readily observed that as a group industrial issues are unseasoned and should not, therefore, be regarded as high-grade investment. For this reason and for the additional fact that industrial enterprises are subject to wide fluctuations in earnings, there has developed against them a prejudice that will require a long time to overcome after their investment worth will have been established. Legislatures have been reluctant to make them legal investments for savings banks, insurance companies, and other trust funds. Only a few states have so recognized them, and then rightly under rigid restriction. There are some indus-

[1] *Moody's Industrials*, 1926, p. xxiv.

trial bonds that may be properly classed among our highest grade securities in the railroad and public utility fields, but they are few.

Unfortunately the information usually obtainable is inadequate for an intelligent analysis of industrial issues. The lack of uniformity in accounting procedure enables the managements to withhold pertinent data, and to present information in an incomplete form. Then, too, weak managements are tempted to economize on maintenance and depreciation, so that unwarranted dividends may be distributed. Managements of small companies, especially those in the extractive industries, are often inclined to pay dividends without adequate depletion reserves.

Because of the inherent risks of the industry, together with the long-standing prejudice on the part of conservative bankers and investors, industrial bonds of merit equal with railroad and public utility issues almost invariably sell on a higher yield basis. The investor who is qualified to investigate would do well, therefore, to examine the better grade of industrial issues and include some of them in his investment portfolio.

CHAPTER XXXVI

BONDS OF THE FEDERAL FARM LOAN SYSTEM

Real estate bonds assist in financing urban development. This chapter considers types of bonds created to further agricultural improvement.

The farmer requires both long and short-term capital. He must have financial aid for planting, cultivating, and marketing his crops and to satisfy these needs he looks to the country merchant, the fertilizer dealer, or the banker. The farmer must have long-term capital for such purposes as buying equipment, undertaking permanent improvements, or acquiring more land. For these purposes he may have sufficient resources of his own, but this is seldom the case, and therefore most of these funds must be borrowed. The growth of farm loans in recent years is indicated by the following table on the mortgage debt and the average farm debt in 1910 and 1920: [1]

	1910	1920
Mortgage debt	$1,726,172,851	$4,003,767,192
Average farm debt	1,715	3,356

This money has in part been obtained from individual investors who take a mortgage on the property as security. Life insurance companies also extend considerable funds to farmers on their lands. To a certain extent, banks and trust companies lend on mortgages, but such loans are restricted by the laws under which these institutions operate. Since 1916 the farmer has been obtaining a growing volume of long-term capital from the banks organized under the Federal Farm Loan System.

Passage of the Federal Farm Loan Act. Toward the end of the nineteenth century the American banking system became inadequate to meet the needs of the various economic interests of the nation. The ensuing banking reform culminated in the passage of the Federal Reserve Act. However, the Federal Reserve System is organized primarily to grant short-term rather than long-term credit, and to aid commerce rather than argiculture. Even before the passage of the Federal Reserve Act there

[1] Morman, *Farm Credit in the United States and Canada*, Ch. V.

was an insistent demand that the government should establish some mechanism to furnish long-term credit to the farmer. A number of business organizations, such as the American Bankers Association in 1911 and the Southern Commercial Congress in 1912, appointed commissions to study the agricultural credit problem. In 1912 President Taft instructed the American ambassadors abroad to make a study of European agricultural finance. The " American " Commission appointed by the Southern Commercial Congress and the " Congressional " Commission of the government submitted a joint report in 1913.[1] These various investigations led to the Moss-Fletcher Bill. This proposal recommended the German system, but this very emphasis upon foreign banking methods in the end led to its rejection. Later, the House Committee on Currency and Banking drafted a new bill more adapted to the needs of American agriculture, and in 1916 it was finally passed as the so-called Federal Farm Loan Act.

Organization of the System.[2] The organization of the Federal Farm Loan System is similar to that of the Federal Reserve System. Like the latter, the Federal Farm Loan System is headed by a Board. The Board is composed of six members appointed by the President with the consent of the Senate and the Secretary of the Treasury, who is ex-officio chairman. The function of the Board is to unify the operations of the system and to standardize the conditions for mortgage lending. To attain these ends, a system of national supervision is provided. The Farm Loan Board appoints registers, appraisers, and examiners who are public officers serving independently of the land banks.

Federal Land Banks. The Act creates two types of banks,— federal land banks and joint-stock land banks. Under the provisions of the Farm Loan Act, the Board divided the United States into twelve districts and in each established a federal land bank. Before beginning operations each institution was to have a minimum subscribed capital of $750,000 which could be held by any individual, firm, corporation, any state of the Union or the United States Government. As a matter of fact, the Federal Government, through treasury purchases, held most of the stock of the land banks at the time of their incorporation. Since then these

---

[1] Senate Document 214, Sixty-third Congress, first session.

[2] A detailed presentation of the system may be found in W. S. Holt, *The Federal Farm Loan Bureau.*

government holdings have been retired and absorbed by the national farm loan associations which now are the chief stockholders. Although the public was permitted to subscribe to the stock of the land banks, the proportion in the hands of private investors has always been small, and in 1924 amounted to only $1,585. The retirement of governmental holdings of land bank stock, and the growth of capitalization through subscription of the farm loan associations is seen in the following table: [1]

HOLDERS OF LAND BANK STOCK (1917–1924)

	Nov. 30, 1917	Nov. 30, 1919	Nov. 30, 1921	Dec. 31, 1923	Dec. 31, 1924
U. S. Government	$ 8,892,130	$ 7,693,240	$ 6,598,770	$ 2,434,385	$ 1,670,965
National farm loan associations	1,488,230	14,068,817	21,109,215	40,926,390	47,524,335
Borrowers through agents		49,215	97,395	234,505	385,160
Individual subscribers	107,870	47,230	9,720	2,040	1,585
Total capital stock	10,488,230	21,858,502	27,815,100	43,597,320	49,582,045

Land banks are required to accumulate and maintain a substantial surplus. Under section 23 of the Act, they must build up a reserve of 25 per cent. of their outstanding capital stock. In the event that this reserve becomes impaired, it must be fully restored before dividends can be paid. In addition, a suspense account must be carried to cover possible losses through defaults by mortgagors or endorsers. The development of the surplus, undivided profits, and suspense accounts of the land banks is seen in the following table: [2]

GROWTH OF RESERVE, UNDIVIDED PROFITS, AND SUSPENSE ACCOUNT

	Reserve	Undivided Profits	Suspense Account [3]
November 30, 1919	$ 350,500	$ 698,421.96	....
December 31, 1920	958,473	1,902,853.86	$ 110,389.18
November 30, 1921	1,514,800	2,355,309.78	211,986.02
December 31, 1922	3,000,500	3,616,705.53 [4]	443,664.64
December 31, 1923	4,647,700	3,294,617.47 [5]	811,113.13
December 31, 1924	6,563,500	3,868,029.37 [6]	1,125,582.38

[1] Reproduced from Willis and Steiner, *Federal Reserve Practice*, pp. 256–257.

[2] Ibid, p. 257.

[3] Amounts set aside from beginning to date specified, not held on that date.

[4] In addition to surplus of $100,000.

[5] In addition to surplus of $300,000.

[6] In addition to surplus, reserves, etc., of $104,550.

Land Bank Bonds. The land banks obtain part of their resources from their capital stock, and reserves as described above, but the most of their funds for conducting operations are derived from the issue of bonds. The essential characteristics of these issues are summarized by Willis and Steiner, ibid., pp. 258–259, as follows:

1. Security: Same amount of qualified first mortgages on real estate, or, temporarily, United States Government securities. The Board accepts Government bonds at par when accompanied by evidence that the Bank secured them at par as an original subscriber, otherwise it accepts them only at market value at time of tender. While similar to the old farm mortgage bankers' debentures, the obligations are thus really collateral trust bonds.

Every Federal land bank is primarily liable for its own bonds (section 21). It is also liable upon presentation for coupons of other Federal land banks bonds upon which the issuing bank has defaulted and is likewise liable for the portion of the principal remaining unpaid. But such losses of interest or principal are to be assessed by the Board against solvent banks in proportion to amount of bonds of each outstanding at time of assessment. As amortization payments are regularly received on the principal of mortgages deposited, the investments into which these funds are placed must be deposited, hence the equity under the bonds is continually increasing.

The liability may be traced back in last analysis to the associations, many of which are creating cash reserves against their contingent liability.

2. Maturity (section 20): Runs for specified minimum and maximum periods, but subject to payment and retirement at the option of the bank after a minimum period, (originally 5 years) from 1917 to 1920, 10–20-year bonds from 1921 to the opening of 1923, and 10–30-year bonds subsequently.

3. Denomination (section 20): In original Act $25, $50, $100, $500, and $1,000. Inasmuch as the semi-annual coupons on the small bonds technically included a fraction of a cent, the amendment approved March 4, 1921, changed the denominations to $40, $100, $500, $1,000, and such larger denominations as the Board may authorize. In actual practice the $1,000 denomination has been the standard; $5,000 and $10,000 bonds have also been issued.

4. Rate (section 20): In original Act not to exceed 5 per cent. per annum. With the post-war increase in interest rates, this was believed inadequate, and the amendment approved August 13, 1921, accordingly raised the maximum to $5\frac{1}{2}$ per cent., but provided that no bond issued or sold after June 30, 1923, should bear a rate to exceed 5 per cent. Up to November, 1919, the Federal land bank rate was $4\frac{1}{2}$ per cent.; from then until May 1, 1922, 5 per cent.; from then until July 1, 1923, again $4\frac{1}{2}$ per cent. As a leading purpose of the Act was to make rates to bor-

rowers as uniform as possible, it was essential that the bonds of the different banks be offered at a uniform rate. By the issue of consolidated bonds, it was sought to avoid possible rate differences, but to date none has been issued.

Relation of Government to Land Bank Bonds. A certain degree of confusion has arisen in the past over the interpretation of section 26 of the Act. The text states that " Farm Loan Bonds, issued under the provisions of this Act, shall be deemed and held to be instrumentalities of the Government of the United States, and as such they are and the income derived therefrom shall be exempt from all Federal, State, Municipal and Local taxation." The legality of this section and of the entire act was upheld by the United States Supreme Court (February 28, 1921) which held that the land banks were legally constituted elements of the banking system of the nation. The section cited must, however, be given a narrow interpretation. It means simply that land bank bonds are exempt from taxation with the exception of inheritance and estate taxes. The expression " instrumentalities of the Government of the United States " has frequently been taken to imply that the Government assumes responsibility for the bonds even to the extent of guaranteeing them. This is not the case, for although the federal authorities exercise a considerable amount of supervision over the operations of the banks and the issuance of their bonds, they are under no circumstances government obligations.[1]

Land Bank Bonds as Legal Investment. Land bank bonds are legal investment for all fiduciary or trust funds under the jurisdiction of the Federal Government, including Postal Savings deposits. Moreover the bonds are eligible for purchase by national banks throughout the United States. During the past few years about three-fourths of the states have amended their laws to permit savings banks to invest in these securities. At present, land bank bonds are lawful investment for savings banks in the following states:

Alabama	Colorado	Illinois
Arizona	Delaware	Indiana
Arkansas	District of Columbia	Iowa
California	Idaho	Kansas

[1] See Circular Letter No. 47 of the Investment Bankers Association of America.

Kentucky	New Hampshire	South Dakota
Louisiana	New Jersey	Tennessee
Maine	New Mexico	Texas
Maryland	North Carolina	Utah
Michigan	Ohio	Virginia
Minnesota	Oklahoma	West Virginia
Mississippi	Oregon	Wisconsin
Missouri	Pennsylvania	
Nebraska	South Carolina	

Operation of the Land Bank System. The security underlying the farm land bank bonds is the loans made by these institutions, and therefore the nature of these lending operations is of interest in judging the investment position of the securities. These operations may be summarized as follows: [1]

1. *Limits:*
    (a) Value of property—50 per cent. of value, plus 20 per cent. of value of insurable permanent improvements.
    (b) Maximum amount—$25,000 for any one loan.
2. *Location.* Anywhere within the district.
3. *Rate.* Not to exceed by more than 1 per cent. the rate established by the most recent series of Federal Land Bank Bonds. The legal maximum is 6 per cent., subject, however, to the discretionary powers of the Farm Loan Board.
4. *Purposes:*
    (a) Refund existing indebtedness.
    (b) Purchase land.
    (c) Buy equipment, live-stock or fertilizer.
    (d) Pay for farm buildings or other authorized fixed improvements.
5. *Borrowers.* Those actually operating or intending to operate their own farms.

National Farm Loan Associations. A borrower must be an owner of stock in a National Farm Loan Association in an amount equal to 5 per cent. of the face amount of his loan (section 8 of the Act). As the shares have a par value of $5, a borrower must therefore possess one share for every $100 he obtains as a loan. The Farm Loan Act in this way seeks to encourage the development of coöperative agricultural credit institutions which will enable the farmers to finance their long-term undertakings. The development of this system of farm loan associations is seen in the following table: [2]

---

[1] Adopted from data in circular of C. F. Childs, on Farm Loan Bonds, January, 1926.

[2] Willis and Steiner, op. cit. passim, p. 284.

DEVELOPMENT OF THE FEDERAL FARM LOAN SYSTEM

To	Chartered	Number of Associations Cancelled by Consolidations or Otherwise
November 30, 1917	1,839	...
November 30, 1918	3,439	74
November 30, 1919	4,018	128
December 31, 1920	4,139	173
November 30, 1921	4,316	208
December 31, 1922	4,720	233
December 31, 1923	4,831	241
December 31, 1924	4,903	250

From these figures it is evident that the total number of associations has not expanded with any rapidity. But it will be observed that the associations have grown in membership, and the tendency has been toward consolidation into larger associations.

A list of the land banks, their lending territory, rate of their bonds, and issues outstanding is given below: [1]

Name	Authorized Loaning Territory	Rate of Bonds	Bonds outstanding as of Oct. 31, 1925
Baltimore, Md.	Pa., Del., Md., Va., W.Va., D.C.	4½–4¾–5	$55,088,700.00
Berkeley, Calif.	Calif., Nev., Utah, Ariz.	4½–4¾–5	40,236,540.00
Columbia, S.C.	N.C., S.C., Ga., Fla.	4½–4¾–5	62,756,980.00
Houston, Tex.	Texas	4½–4¾–5	108,099,230.00
Louisville, Ky.	Ohio, Ind., Ky., Tenn.	4½–4¾–5	93,942,450.00
New Orleans, La.	Ala., Miss., La.	4½–4¾–5	99,816,870.00
Omaha, Nebr.	Ia., Neb., So.Dak., Wyo.	4½–4¾–5	116,285,280.00
Spokane, Wash.	Wash., Ore., Mont., Idaho	4½–4¾–5	93,149,380.00
Springfield, Mass.	Me., N.H., Vt., Mass., R.I., Conn., N.Y., N.J.	4¾–5	39,129,800.00
St. Louis, Mo.	Ill., Mo., Ark.	4½–4¾–5	69,521,240.00
St. Paul, Minn.	Mich., Wis., Minn., No. Dak.	4½–4¾–5	113,695,035.00
Wichita, Kan.	Okla., Kan., Colo., New Mex.	4½–4¾–5	85,851,495.00

Joint-Stock Land Banks. In addition to the land banks, the Farm Loan Act also provided for the establishment of the joint-stock land banks. The term "joint-stock," derived from the German "Aktiengesellschaft," "share company," has no other significance than that the organization is an incorporated body, and in no sense implies a joint responsibility of obligations assumed by the various banks in the system.

Joint-stock banks may be established anywhere, provided the organizers meet the conditions set up by the Act. A bank must possess a minimum subscribed capital of $250,000. This capital must be obtained from private investors, for the government does

[1] Reproduced from Bulletin of C. F. Child & Co.

not participate in the financing of these institutions. Most of the capital has been derived from commercial banks and trust companies which have organized joint-stock banks as subsidiaries to take over long-term loans.

The funds of the joint-stock banks come mainly from issues of bonds. These securities are essentially the same in nature as those of the farm land banks as described on page 482.

The development of the joint-stock system may be gathered from this table: [1]

GENERAL OPERATIONS OF THE JOINT-STOCK LAND BANKS [2]

Date	Numbers of Banks	Capital Stock	Surplus	Reserve	Un-divided Profit	Net Out-standing Bond Issue
November 30, 1918.	9	$2,010,850	$59,500	. . . .	. . . .	$7,725,000
November 30, 1919.	30	8,638,650	154,685	$55,232	$60,378	56,135,000
December 31, 1920.	25 [2]	7,966,000	80,750	192,550	74,358	75,282,500
November 30, 1921.	24 [3]	7,859,400	85,000	257,731	222,119	81,509,600
December 31, 1922.	61	24,570,732	1,103,767	1,276,191	919,759	212,980,100
December 31, 1923.	70	33,809,520	1,641,681	2,164,422	1,137,464	354,089,700
December 31, 1924.	64	34,487,185	1,239,29♭	2,648,535 [4]	1,257,086	435,067,400

[2] In addition, one had transacted no business, and two were in process of liquidation.
[3] In addition, two had transacted no business.
[4] Besides surplus reserves, etc., of $802,450.

The lending operations of the joint-stock banks is quite similar to those of the farm land banks as summarized on page 484; with the exception that any loan is limited to 15 per cent. of the capital stock of the joint-stock bank, and in any case may not exceed $50,000. The location of the loans is also limited to the state in which the bank is situated, and to one adjoining state, as stipulated in the charter.

A list of the joint-stock banks in operation at the close of 1925, their authorized loaning territory, the rate of their bonds, and the volume of their bonds outstanding is given on pages 488, 489.

Comparison of Land Banks and Joint-Stock Banks. From the above survey of the essential features of the land banks and the joint-stock banks a comparison may now be made from the investment viewpoint. The land banks are primarily central mortgage institutions for rediscounting the obligations of the farm loan associations. The joint stock-banks are really mortgage banks. The capital requirements of the two types of banks were given above, and it was seen that the joint-stock banks individually have a smaller capitalization. However, if the total

[1] Willis and Steiner, Ibid., 326.

capital of each group is compared with their respective bonds outstanding, the joint-stock banks present a better showing. This is indicated by the following table, stating the capital, the capital assets (surplus, reserves, and undivided profits) and the ratio of these two items to the bonds, for the land banks and the joint-stock banks as of October 31, 1925.

RELATION OF CAPITAL ASSETS TO BONDS OUTSTANDING

	Bonds Outstanding	Capital		Capital Assets	
		Amount	Per Cent.	Amount	Per Cent.
Land Banks	$977,573,000	$53,090,485	5.43	66,331,640	6.79
Joint-Stock Banks	512,621,400	41,044,918	8.01	50,863,985	9.92

There is therefore a greater margin of capital assets to protect the bonds of the joint-stock banks than to cover the obligations of the land banks.

The bonds of the two groups of banks differ in that the obligations of the joint-stock banks are claims only on the separate issuers, but the bonds of the twelve land banks are jointly guaranteed.

From the standpoint of marketability, the bonds of the land banks are also more satisfactory, since they are issued in larger amounts and have a wider market. As a result, there is a "spread" (i.e., the difference between the bid and the asked price) usually of but half a point (or per cent.) as against a variation of $1\frac{1}{2}$ in the case of joint-stock bonds.

Moreover, the Federal Government exercises closer supervision over the land banks as described above, and really has a moral responsibility over these institutions.

For these reasons the bonds of the land banks sell at a lower rate than those of the joint-stock banks. The essential difference between the two types of banks from the investment standpoint is the fact that the credit standing of the land banks, by virtue of the guaranty feature, is uniform, but the standing of the joint-stock banks varies with each institution. In considering the position of the securities of joint-stock banks such factors must be analyzed as the directorate, officers, lending operations, nature of the territory served, extent of competition, and character of the investment houses which place their securities.

Name	Authorized Loaning Territory	Rate of Bonds	Bonds Outstanding
Atlanta of Atlanta, Ga.	Ga. and Ala.	5	$ 3,960,000.00
Atlantic of Raleigh, N. C.	No. Car. and So. Car.	5	8,505,000.00
Bankers of Milwaukee, Wis.	Minn. and Wis.	$4\frac{1}{2}$-5-$5\frac{1}{2}$	15,714,600.00
Burlington of Burlington, Ia.	Iowa and Ill.	$4\frac{1}{2}$-5	2,750,000.00
California of San Francisco, Cal.	Calif. and Oregon.	5-$5\frac{1}{2}$	11,953,000.00
Central Illinois of Greenville, Ill.	Ill. and Ind.	5	8,300,000.00
Chicago of Chicago, Ill.	Ill. and Ia.	$4\frac{1}{2}$-$4\frac{3}{4}$-5-$5\frac{1}{2}$	53,250,500.00
Dallas of Dallas, Tex.	Tex. and Okla.	5-$5\frac{1}{2}$-$5\frac{1}{2}$	22,168,000.00
Denver of Denver, Colo.	Colo. and Wyo.	5-$5\frac{1}{2}$-$5\frac{1}{2}$	9,327,000.00
Des Moines of Des Moines, Ia.	Ia. and Minn.	$4\frac{1}{2}$-5-$5\frac{1}{2}$	14,990,000.00
Equitable of Macon, Mo.	Mo. and Iowa.	5	1,148,400.00
First of Ft. Wayne, Ind.	Ind. and Ohio.	$4\frac{1}{2}$-5-$5\frac{1}{2}$	7,201,500.00
First of Montgomery, Ala.	Ala. and Ga.	5	4,050,000.00
First of New Orleans, La.	Miss. and La.	5	1,990,000.00
First Carolinas of Columbia, S. Car.	N. Car. and S. Car	5	10,705,000.00
First Texas of Houston, Tex.	Tex. and Okla.	5	6,301,000.00
First Trust of Chicago, Ill.	Ill. and Iowa.	$4\frac{1}{2}$-$4\frac{3}{4}$-5	32,300,000.00
First Trust of Dallas, Tex.	Tex. and Okla.	$4\frac{1}{2}$-5-5	8,000,000.00
Fletcher of Indianapolis, Ind.	Ind. and Ill.	$4\frac{1}{2}$-5-$5\frac{1}{2}$	13,794,200.00
Fremont of Fremont, Neb.	Ia. and Neb.	$4\frac{3}{4}$-5-$5\frac{1}{2}$	11,539,500.00
Greenbrier of Covington, Va.	Va. and W. Va.	5	2,000,000.00
Greensboro of Greensboro, N. C.	N. Car. and Tenn	5	1,900,000.00
Illinois of Monticello, Ill.	Ia. and Ill.	$4\frac{1}{2}$-$4\frac{3}{4}$-5	4,700,000.00
Ill. Midwest of Edwardsville, Ill.	Ill. and Mo.	5	4,575,000.00
Iowa of Sioux City, Ia.	Ia. and So. Dak.	$4\frac{1}{2}$-5-$5\frac{1}{2}$	5,925,000.00
Kansas City of Kansas City, Mo.	Mo. and Kans.	$4\frac{1}{2}$-5-$5\frac{1}{2}$	43,021,300.00
Kentucky of Lexington, Ky.	Ohio and Ky.	5	9,900,000.00

Name	Authorized Loaning Territory	Rate of Bonds	Bonds Outstanding
LaFayette of LaFayette, Ind.	Ind. and Ill.	4½-5	$ 6,798,500.00
Lincoln of Lincoln, Nebr.	Ia. and Neb.	4½-5-5½	32,727,000.00
Louisville of Louisville, Ky.	Ind. and Ky.	5	7,000,000.00
Maryland-Virginia of Baltimore, Md.	Md. and Va.	5	1,000,000.00
Minneapolis Trust of Minneapolis, Minn.	No. Dak. and Minn.	5	5,459,000.00
Mississippi of Memphis, Tenn.	Miss. and Tenn.	5-5½	3,635,000.00
New York of New York, N. Y.	N. Y. and Pa.	5	6,369,000.00
New York and New Jersey, of Newark, N. J.	N. Y. and N. J.	5	2,500,000.00
No. Carolina of Durham, N. Car.	N. Car. and Va.	5	7,149,000.00
Ohio of Cincinnati, Ohio.	Ohio and Ind.	5	1,392,900.00
Ohio-Pennsylvania of Cleveland, Ohio.	Ohio and Pa.	5	9,000,000.00
Oregon-Washington of Portland, Ore.	Ore. and Wash.	5	3,011,000.00
Pacific Coast of Los Angeles, Calif.	Ariz. and Calif.	5	4,620,000.00
Pacific Coast of Portland, Ore.	Wash. and Ore.	5	5,500,000.00
Pacific Coast of Salt Lake City, Utah.	Idaho and Utah.	5	3,050,000.00
Pacific Coast of San Francisco, Cal.	Nev. and Calif.	5	7,825,000.00
Pennsylvania of Philadelphia, Pa.	Pa. and Md.	5	3,884,000.00
Potomac of Alexandria, Va.	Va. and Md.	4½-5	3,894,800.00
St. Louis of St. Louis, Mo.	Ark. and Mo.	5-5½	11,059,000.00
San Antonio of San Antonio, Tex.	Tex. and Okla.	5	9,283,000.00
Shenandoah Valley of Staunton, W. Va.	Va. and W. Va.	5	1,850,000.00
So. Minn. of Redwood Falls, Minn.	Minn. and So. Dak.	5-5½	27,550,000.00
Tennessee of Memphis, Tenn.	Ark. and Tenn.	5-5½	3,093,000.00
Union of Detroit, Mich.	Mich. and Ohio.	4½-5	3,800,000.00
Union of Louisville, Ky.	Ky. and Tenn.	5	3,000,000.00
Virginia-Carolina of Norfolk, Va.	Va. and No. Car.	5	3,875,000.00
Virginian of Charleston, W. Va.	Ohio and W. Va.	5	14,327,200.00

CHAPTER XXXVII

TIMBER BONDS

From official sources is derived the following summary of soft and hardwood lumber produced in the United States at certain periods within the past 44 years:

	Softwoods	Hardwoods	Total
1880			18,125,432,000 feet
1890			23,842,230,000 "
1899	26,153,063,000 feet	8,634,021,000 feet	34,787,084,000 "
1909	33,896,959,000 "	10,612,802,000 "	44,509,761,000 "
1919	27,407,130,000 "	7,144,946,000 "	34,532,076,000 "
1920	26,809,500,000 "	6,989,300,000 "	33,798,800,000 "
1921	22,185,504,000 "	4,775,360,000 "	26,960,864,000 "
1922	26,644,334,000 "	4,924,554,000 "	31,568,888,000 "
1923	Less custom mills and small mills cutting less than 5 M. feet		37,165,505,000 "
1924	Less custom mills and small mills cutting less than 5 M. feet		35,930,980,000 "

The annual growth has been estimated at 6,000,000,000 feet. The disparity largely determines the nature and the problems of American forestry and of the lumber business.

One of the chief benefits of the present aggregation of capital in constantly enlarging units, is in furnishing the sinews for a single control of a product from its primitive state, through the processes of conversion into consumptive form, and transportation to the wholesale or retail markets. In the long run, by reason of economies in operation, and standardization in service, either the product will be improved, or the price to the consumer will be less than it would be otherwise, however greater the price than in past years when consumption had not yet taxed the power of production, nor necessitated the tapping of supplies very remote from the ultimate market.

Lumber Industry a Large-Scale Enterprise. The evolution in American business methods has been operative in the lumber industry as well as in livestock, steel, milk, and oil. Whereas formerly a half-dozen companies were required to convert a

490

tree into sash, furniture, or paper,—now the lands, stumpage, logging equipment, mills and sometimes even the selling organization, are in unit ownership and direction.

There is, however, a reason for conducting the lumber business on a scale suggesting great commercial consolidations, which has no reference to monopolistic tendencies in general. It has to do with that conservation of which we hear so much nowadays. If the supply of wood should soon become exhausted, immense sums would be lost which have been necessary to the erection and equipment of modern economical milling plants with their railroad and river approaches and outlets. A way to prevent this loss is to buy tracts or " limits " of such extent and value as to permit an annual depreciation charge from earnings sufficient to wipe out the cost of the land or lease, and of the plant. But this is sometimes uneconomical as compared with the policy of replacing stripped lands with new growth. The most practical way is to acquire tracts of sufficient size, to amortize the initial purchase price and equipment cost, and at the same time obtain a perpetual supply by adopting a logging policy that will maintain an annual depletion that is less than the natural increment to the total standing timber. When such a tract is scientifically logged a perpetual supply is maintained, provided no outside influences, such as fire or insect damage, disturb this balance.

The Origin of Timber Land Bonds. Reforestation is accepted in France and Germany and other European nations as a matter of course. One can buy in New York bentwood furniture made from third, fourth, or fifth growth timber from Austrian forests. Our few forestry schools, hardly in the second generation, have taught reforestation as their first lesson; and it is now being applied particularly by the wood pulp and paper companies, which are accumulating wooded tracts on such a scale as to admit of cutting sections in rotation. In actual operation the best results are obtained by cutting only the trees over 8 to 10 inches in diameter, and yet leaving a few of the older trees in each section to act as seed trees for reforestation. In this manner on the exhaustion of virgin timber, section after section, in turn, would be in proper age for second cutting. In recent years numerous lumber companies have adopted similar forestry methods, but owing to high taxation and other high costs such measures are not generally practical.

What is a comparatively easy problem for the paper companies in America becomes more difficult for concerns that convert the better grades of stock, especially hardwood. But the principle is the same, and nothing is needed but the requisite degrees of patience, knowledge, and capital. The longer the time necessary to age the particular woods grown, the more acute the demand for those woods, and the greater the funds necessary to the undertaking.

In this way it has come about that lumber companies have been obliged to appeal for investment capital, as well as speculative, and they have turned to the bond houses.

Thirty years ago a call for investment money from the lumber interests would have met with scant response. The demand from other quarters was too great. Furthermore, investment principles had first to be worked out, by thought and experience, for the more necessary transportation problems of the railroad, the street railway, and the interurban, and for the problems of public service in lighting, heating, and power, and for problems of communication: the telegraph and the telephone. Then, again, a class of wealthy investors such as we now have in the Middle West, had to come into being, and be made acquainted with the application of investment principles to industrial enterprises of the very sort in which these investors had won competence by business speculation. Upon the fruition of these things the field was ready for timber bonds.

There are, then, several objects for the entrance of lumber companies into the field of bond finance: to enlarge mills or build new ones, to modernize old equipment, and frequently to consolidate two or more companies having established earnings with others having additional timber for future operations; to accumulate timber lands against the impending wood famine, to insure future supplies for the expensive mills and plants, and last, but unfortunately least, to reforest in the interest of a permanent wood supply.

The Requirements of Mortgage and Deed of Trust. In the evolutional stages of any business development, no funds devoted to it can be considered safe unless they are secured by a primary lien on the larger part of a company's entire assets. The value of the material property pledged should be heavily in excess of the amount of obligation, and provision should be made for the retirement of the debt in a much more rapid ratio than the depletion of the resources and the depreciation of the plant.

Most timber bonds are a lien on mill, logging equipment, logging railroads, timber lands, and standing timber. It is not customary to issue bonds unless a substantial amount of the timber is held in fee, except when the value of the plant is considerably in excess of the total amount of the issue, and when this value is independent of the value of the company's timber. Mills on the Pacific Coast at good harbors can be operated successfully by purchasing logs, and, therefore, they may be good security without ownership of standing timber.

Canadian timber limits are frequently an important element in the holdings of pulp and paper companies, and they involve ownership of the standing timber but not of the fee title to the land. If a considerable part of the assets are represented by mills, or other fee timber, these limits are placed under the mortgage.

Contracted timber from the United States Forestry Service, or from Indian reservations is not amenable to mortgage and can be only collateral security.

In addition to the lien there is sometimes guaranty by endorsement, individual, or several, or joint and several. The endorsers would naturally be men in the lumber business with commercial rating. The added security of endorsement is particularly acceptable to the class of business men who buy timber land bonds. A triple endorsement might give the bond in their eyes the advantage of being the three-name paper familiar to them.

Non-interest bearing, profit-sharing bonds in a few instances have been issued against standing timber which it was assumed had been purchased at an exceptionally low price, and in anticipation of a rapid advance in value due to the completion of some extraneous development such as the Panama Canal, a transcontinental railway, or a new seaport, as the result of which the timber was to be made accessible to markets. The issue usually has provided enough capital to pay taxes and administrative costs for a period of years, apart from the amount required to purchase the timber. Bonds of this type are highly speculative, and the only advantage they have over non-dividend paying stocks is the security of the direct lien represented by a closed mortgage on the properties and timber.

The deed of trust should designate competent parties as

trustees, whether a trust company or persons. They should be chosen with regard to their experience in this kind of industry. The lumber industry has its own rather peculiar problems connected with production, grading, and marketing, therefore the trust indenture, should be sufficiently mobile to adjust itself to changing conditions, and should not contain what might appear to be protective features that could curtail successful operations under unexpected market conditions.

The Timber Lands. Titles to the timber lands should be searched by competent counsel acting for the banking house of issue. Titles are sometimes questionable in the comparatively unsettled country that now furnishes us with most of our timber. Because that country is comparatively unsettled and less accessible, the title is usually thought of as valuable only in relation to lumber. But there are timber land bonds outstanding, notably some secured by pledge of New England land, that will probably prove far from worthless without the wood, by the time the loans mature.

The market value of standing timber depends as much on the location of the lands with reference to the market, and on the means of transportation to it, as on the lumber itself. The lands may possibly be tapped or traversed by drivable streams. Then the bondholders' money may go into the purchase of more raw material, and not be sunk into lumber railways, the earnings and usefulness of which are likely to diminish with every year of service. If these streams can also furnish power for saw, planing, pulp, or paper mills, so much the better.

If a large part of the assets is ownership merely of stumpage, and not of the land, the bearing of this fact on the future of the company may be important, as well as the terms on which the usufruct reverts to the landowners.

Other merchantable perquisites sometimes pertain to lumber companies, and are of value under the mortgage. In illustration, pine and other coniferous forests have valuable turpentine rights. The United States Forest Products Laboratory has created many by-products and also has instituted numerous economies of vast importance to the lumber industry.

The Plant. The lumber manufacturing plants may or may not be a large part of the company's pledged assets. It is evident that the mills, the kilns, the railroad, and logging equipment, and all the other property and machinery necessary for converting logs into lumber, or lumber into finished product, should bear as low as possible a ratio of cost to the value of the raw material, for the plant will depreciate. However, it must be realized that the wood will appreciate from the present level of prices, except for temporary setbacks due to artificial causes such as severe business depression.

There is greater necessity of a large factor of margin of safety in the total worth of mills, improvements, and timber over the amount of the outstanding investment securities than is exacted in other industries. There is little possibility of converting an isolated sawmill into a plant suitable for other industrial purposes, nor have the properties any appreciable realty value. Therefore the intrinsic worth depends on the integral relationship of timber and plant. Since the manufacturing units have less salvage value than is usually encountered in other industrial plants, it is well to have the sales value of the standing timber alone amply cover the bond obligations.

The Relation of Plant Cost to Timber Value. The size and cost of a plant relative to the amount and value of the tributary timber owned is of greater importance than many operators realize. The total interest, taxes and other carrying charges are diminished in proportion to the rapidity with which the latent timber resources are converted into merchantable products. On the other hand, the cost of the mill is more or less proportional to its annual capacity, therefore too large an investment in the plant involves too great a burden in amortizing its cost. Amortization will be excessive per unit of production. Yet an inadequate plant will not manufacture sufficient lumber to pay the interest and taxes on the heavy investment in standing timber.

There are two considerations regarding this relationship of mill to timber: the more important is the relationship between total interest plus taxes on timber values to the amortization of mill cost plus the total interest on unamortized mill cost. The other consideration is that the mill should not be so small as to make the early years of operation too burdensome from high interest charges on timber.

Amount of Investment. Mr. E. Maltby Shipp has derived two formulæ that now for the first time enable one to determine with precision (rather than by trial and error) the relative amounts that should be invested in plant and in standing timber, based on the considerations just given.

It is necessary to solve for the number of years that represents the least total tax and capital charges. This may be obtained in two ways, either by solving first for " N " years and then substituting " N " in two other equations, thereby giving numerical values for " N " years, cost of equipment, and productive capacity, or by combining these equations and solving for cost of mill alone.

Let S = Total stand of timber expressed in units such as M ft. or cords.
  D = Number of dollars per M. ft. or cords invested in timber.
  T = Total number of dollars invested in timber or S x D.
  P = Total number of dollars invested in plant and equipment.
  C = Cost of plant and equipment expressed in number of dollars per unit that desired equipment is capable of manufacturing per year under average working conditions.
  B = Number of units desired equipment will cost annually under average working conditions.
  I = Interest rate desired plus taxes and other fixed charges on timber expressed decimally such as 0.08 interest rate and 0.05 other expenses then I equals 0.13.
  E = Interest rate desired on equipment in investment.
  N = Number of years any equipment will require to convert "S" units into manufactured lumber or pulp.

Let $Y = \dfrac{CS}{TI}$; solve for Y and substitute the value of Y in the following equation and solve for N:

$$N = \frac{EY - 1 + \sqrt{Y(8 + 2E + E^2Y) + 1}}{2}$$

To find B solve $B = \dfrac{S}{N}$

To find P solve $P = CB$

Second Method

Let $Y = \dfrac{CS}{TI}$; solve for Y and substitute the value of Y in the following equation and solve for P:

$$P = \frac{2CS}{EY - 1 + \sqrt{Y(8 + 2E + E^2Y) + 1}}$$

$$\text{and } B = \frac{P}{C}$$

The first method is probably the most workable for it requires the person using it to obtain the period of operation, which is usually an important item in determining a bond set-up.

The foregoing, of course, only shows the theoretically ideal size or cost of plant from a financial standpoint, and the practical operative conditions will necessarily govern the actual installations desired. But one can be guided in this regard by proving the theoretical ideal, or at least not exceeding it. However, one should remember that charges during the first few years of operation should not be too excessive, therefore it is sometimes advisable to have a plant somewhat smaller than the foregoing formulæ would call for. In order to realize the conditions leading to a perpetual supply as already discussed it is necessary to purchase the standing timber at low stumpage prices, otherwise one is compelled to put too great a proportion of the investment into the operative end.

In these days when most uncut virgin timber is so far removed from centres of population, it is generally the building of the plant which gives marketability to the wood. Presumably the lands were acquired at a low figure for the very reason that there were then no facilities near for working timber. Probably it is still possible to buy timber in the Northwest Pacific Coast regions for less than $1.00 a thousand that will be worth from four to eight times as much when accessible by rail.

The Timber. Occasionally a large part of the timber assets is already in yard or mill; but generally we look to the standing timber as the principal pledge under the lien. The value of it must be appraised in accordance with the quantity, kinds, quality, and (as just stated), accessibility. Since this is a self-evident statement, little elaboration is necessary.

The method of appraisal, in its essential interest to the bondholder, is easy to understand. No guesswork is necessary as in the case of unmined coal or metals. When the tracts were bought the lumber company sent " cruisers " to ascertain, with more or less approximation, the number of thousands of feet, or cords, in the tracts. The banking house will not be satisfied with this. It will wish to learn from disinterested sources with all the exactness possible. It will, therefore, have timber estimators and compassmen sent out to reappraise, and report general conditions, viz.: as to the greenness and general thriftiness of the wood, as to whether the kinds are well-bunched or promiscuous, whether or not the plots are grouped in convenient logging distances, whether the timber has been turpentined.

The quantity of timber is not merely a matter of acreage, but a matter of growth and density. Nor is it a matter of board, but of log feet. According to the purposes to which it will be put, the stumpage included in the estimate may be, perhaps, of 8, 10, or 12-inch logs, and up.

A clear definition of what character of timber is to be estimated and entire confidence in the good faith of the estimators are essential to satisfactory returns. A gang of cruisers that once covered a certain timber property brought in an estimate five times as great as that of a second gang which worked over the property independently, and at about the same time.

Timber Values. The great and growing strength of industrial companies lies in the possession of material wealth for which the demand is bound to increase in greater ratio than the supply. Although, in a sense, the future supply of wood is not fixed as that of coal or metals, yet wood is of such slow growth as to be justly estimated on the basis of a constantly increasing demand. There are probably few materials, not including gold itself, which have future values in exchange more assured than wood. Lumber values have had no material setbacks in recent years at least; and the tendency has been upward. Lumber, therefore, looked upon as mere material, is most excellent security for bonds.

The Fire Hazard. Unfortunately, however, there is one drawback to the ideality of timber as security, and that is the fire hazard. How real the risk is in many sections, may be judged from the fact that the Lloyds of London are probably the only association known to the authors that will insure standing timber. They charge $6 a hundred on the average and require a detailed description of the property for judgment of its worth as a risk.

Admitting the danger, the case is not so bad as it looks. In the first place this danger of fire is being rapidly lessened by the organized efforts of private and government patrols. Secondly, perpetual dampness or a rainy season militates against fires during the whole or a part of the year, in some sections of the country. This is true in Canada, in certain parts of the Northwest, and in the South. In the circulars of bond houses offering timber bonds it has been asserted that standing timber located in the Southern states has never been destroyed by fire. This statement needs qualification. Nevertheless, it is true that any serious damage by fire in the Southern pine belt is very unlikely, if not impossible, because of the absence of underbrush and low-growing branches. Thirdly, even when fire kills the green stand-ing stock, that stock is not necessarily lost. Most of it may be saved by cutting within a season or two.

The trustee will at least see that every insurable risk, such as the mills and equipment, is protected by insurance.

The principle of the distribution of risk can be applied to timber tracts, and sometimes is. There are vast timber limits in the Eastern provinces of Canada, under one control, that are separated,—dovetailed as it were,—by strips in other ownership; but there are patent transportation disadvantages under this arrangement, unless the several properties are united by a drivable stream, that the logs may advantageously be sent to mill or market. Large tracts surrounded by alien property are generally operated separately.

Amortization. In common with concerns operating in any kind of fields of deposit, such as coal and metal mines, where the income is derived at the expense of the assets, lumber com-panies should arrange the maturities of their loans in regular series, preferably annual. The mortgage should contain care-fully detailed provision by which the retirement of the loan will be at a faster rate than the depletion of the assets. There can be no fixed tax for the sinking fund which should be standard; the rate will be determined by the kind and value of the timber, ranging from 50 cents a cord of pulpwood and $1 a thousand for the lower grades of spruce and balsam to $5 and even $8 a thousand for the higher grade Eastern hardwoods. Unsawed lumber, such as ties and poles, have to be specifically amortized. It may be stipulated that periodic sworn statements of the amount cut be made by the superintendent of the cutting, and verified by the principal officers of the company. It is best to have a minimum annual instalment to meet the requirements of redemp-tion, and to increase the equity annually. A wise policy is to have a minimum amortization charge during the early life of the bonds, and to increase this periodically as the interest on the unamortized investment decreases in order to create a more equalized burden.

This redemption fund will apply to the payment of the princi-pal only, and will be on the basis of about double the amount for which the timber is mortgaged, and will operate to retire all of the bonds before consuming over one-half the timber.

The sequestration, for the sinking fund, of a specified sum per annum is not as satisfactory as the scale method with a minimum attached, for if a fire should sweep through and kill a large part of the timber, it would be necessary to cut down the dead stumpage within a year or two, and the sinking fund should be protected accordingly.

If, because of the amount cut, the deposits under the redemption fund should exceed the amount of bonds maturing in any year, the trustee should be obliged to purchase, or call for redemption at some small premium, such as 3 per cent. and interest, the unmatured bonds in amount sufficient to exhaust the surplus.

Sometimes a timber land bond is the issue of a company doing business in a specialty such as cooperage. The sinking fund then may be gauged in terms of the product:—for instance, in cooperage, of perhaps $5 a cord of bolts for staves and headings. In such case the circular should translate into terms of feet, that the bond buyer may estimate the equity and the rate of redemption, or else cite from the cruise the amount of the standing timber in terms of the units manufactured. It should be provided in the mortgage that a large part of, if not all, the sums obtained by sale of timber to other companies should be applied to the redemption of bonds. Bond buyers are more likely to encounter a cord charge on pulp wood, for paper company bonds are more numerous.

Management, History, and Earnings. The personnel and financial standing of owners and managers are generally ascertainable through the commercial agencies. The lumber business in this country has credit agencies of its own. A company's stock is seldom widely distributed, and the reported standing of its principal owners, and the credit of the company itself, may be verified by application to local banks. Additional light may be thrown on these matters by testimony from banks and notebrokers as to the salability of the company's unsecured paper.

The experience and success of the company's members and also their affiliation, through stock-ownership or otherwise, in other lumber enterprises will have a necessary bearing with companies that are an outlet for their product.

The paid-up capital, the surplus, and if the company is established, the net earnings for the past five years, the relation of net earnings to gross, etc.—all will be subjects for examination.

Marketability and Income. Timber land bonds usually bear a liberal rate of interest, and are sold at par or thereabout. In spite of its excellences (providing danger from serious fire is remote), this type of loan is too new, and its acceptance as investment too limited, for the purchaser to expect a ready market. If the issue has been outstanding for some time the trustee may be interested in an offer for the sinking fund. But the buyer's main recourse is the bond house through which he bought. Hence its attitude in regard to repurchasing its specialities is of utmost interest to him.

CHAPTER XXXVIII

RECLAMATION ISSUES

One does not often meet with the expression Reclamation Issues in the nomenclature of finance. Yet there is a type of obligations, with sharply defined common characteristics, that may well bear this title, if only for convenience of designation in the discussion of fiscal theories. In its three subdivisions, Irrigation, Drainage, and Levee Bonds, it represents the financial means by which formerly unproductive territory in the United States, equal in extent to several per cent. of the total area, is working out its own salvation. This broad use of the word *reclamation* is thoroughly justified by its meaning and by its employment in Congressional acts. In Western law it is used more particularly of the work of drainage and of levee building.

Nature has dealt more kindly with us than we knew a generation or two ago. A comparatively small proportion of our immense lowland country is irredeemable desert. Latterly we have come to realize that the alchemy of modern engineering can easily convert wastes of sagebrush or marsh grass into ultimate gold. Nothing is needed but skill to lead down waters to the plains, or may be to drive them back from the soil; for all reclamation of land is concerned with water, which gives life to vegetation at one place and takes it away at another. Or rather skill is not lacking,—we have that,—but the sense of community of interest, which under government leadership and help has done so much already for lands in Western states.

Reclamation, then, is of two general kinds: irrigation and drainage. The work of irrigation is more spectacular and on a larger scale; indeed it is the more important. Up to this time it has received from the government more attention, both departmental and legislative. But in recent years considerable attention has been devoted to drainage problems these can be solved financially, as we shall see, along lines laid out in irrigation development. It seems proper, therefore, to group these kindred securities.

Irrigation Bonds

One of the several classes of securities that have only in recent years attained a general recognition if not a market in the East is the Irrigation Bond. Although irrigation itself, successful and colossal, is as old as Egypt and Babylon, and had made green the Aztec soil of America before the coming of Europeans, it is now destined to nourish the waste places of more than a dozen states. The bonds of its financing, even under present-day conditions, have been looked at askance by Eastern investors. These are prone to associate the bonds with the old Western farm mortgages to which they bear little likeness, except that they are Western and yield a high return. There has been sufficient miscarriage and undoing of irrigation projects to warrant a very critical attitude toward them.

Early Weaknesses. It will be remembered that equipment issues arose out of a need, among the weaker railroads, for rolling stock, which they were too poor to purchase out of surplus revenues, or by means of the usual funded loans. When, in the course of years, the expediency of equipment-bond financing was demonstrated, and laws were enacted in most states to protect the contracts that were the basis of the security, the custom of purchasing equipment by means of special equipment issues became quite general; and up to nearly the present time, the tendency to strengthen the security behind equipment bonds, especially by writing better and more uniform trust deeds, has been continuous. Just as, and at about the same time that, ten-year serial equipment bonds came to be issued, irrigation began to be the subject of serious study, and an outlet for speculative activity in the arid West. The growth of the West, in population, in material well-being, in engineering skill, in agricultural science, and in law,—especially in irrigation law,—has steadily raised the status of irrigation and broadened its activities. It has also greatly strengthened the security for ten-year serial irrigation bonds; although it is by no means to be implied from this, that, as a class, irrigation bonds are on anything like the same plane of security as equipment bonds.

There were three main causes of hazard in the irrigation enterprises of the early days: the immaturity of American irrigation engineering, the instability of Western business conditions, and the confusion of law as affecting land and water rights. The first two of these we may dismiss as things largely of the past and give attention to the third.

Land and Water Rights, and the Law. Irrigation, of course, as stated, has to do with the union of water and land in the interest of fertility. More difficulties of all sorts have arisen from questions concerning the supply and diversion of water than from problems concerning the allotment and ownership of land. These difficulties, now and in the past, have been accentuated on the Pacific Coast. Each of the three immense states on the Pacific slope:—California, Oregon, and Washington,—has " both a wet and a dry end "; i.e., each has a part of its territory so situated as to be rain-watered, and independent of engineering for fertility; and a part so situated that it has no rainy season, and is productive only when artificially watered. As a result, there has been a constant tendency, from the very beginning, toward a difference in judicial opinion as to the rights of the public, and of the abutters, to streams of water.

Naturally, judges of courts having jurisdiction in arid territory, have construed state law so as to favor the interests of settlers. Those in the rainy belt have taken the more usual common-law stand in regard to riparian rights, and (for illustration) have, to some extent, protected the proprietors of riparian land from upstream detention, diversion, and pollution of water. This conflict of the doctrine of appropriation with the older, world-wide doctrine of riparian rights, has unsettled the status of irrigation bonds in California, Oregon, and Washington. Under the influence of permanent geographical conditions, state law here still permits an undesirable latitude of method in the redemption of unproductive land. In the three states mentioned, and in those others in which the common-law doctrine of riparian rights obtained a foothold in the early days of their settlement, the doctrine of appropriation now prevails only where the common-law principle cannot obtain, namely, on waters belonging to the state or to the United States. This is the law established in California by the well-known case of Lux vs. Haggin (69 Cal. 255, 10 Pac. 674).

There has been no such conflict in the more generally arid states. The law has been at one with itself, and consequently favorable to general and equitable reclamation in Idaho, Wyoming, Colorado, and Nebraska. At its best it recognizes that water, when appropriated, " rises to the dignity of a distinct usufructuary estate or right of property." In some of these states there is not a vestige of riparian rights.

Federal Irrigation. Fortunately, the redemption of arid land has not been left, all this time, solely to the initiative and discretion of the commonwealths. Moved, no doubt, by the failure of irrigation enterprises in California and elsewhere, Congress in recent years has freely discussed irrigation and has enacted several laws in the interest of the reclamation of desert places in the United States. It is only natural that the line of federal action should be in evolution from past governmental policies concerning the settlement and development of public lands, since it is public lands that most need irrigation. These policies are summed up in the Homestead Law of 1872, and the Desert Land Act of 1877, amended in 1891; but the earlier law had, however, no direct connection with irrigation.

The Homestead Law gave title of public land in the extent of 160 acres to any citizen establishing and maintaining residence upon it and cultivating it for a period of five years. By amendment the lustrum was commuted to 14 months, on payment of $1.25 per acre.

The Desert Land Act differed from the Homestead Law in these respects:—it concerned the irrigation and settlement of desert land; and therefore it granted larger tracts to each settler, namely, 640 acres, and title was passed on the annual expenditure of $1.00 per acre for three consecutive years. By the amendment of 1891, 320 acres was the maximum apportionment, and the other previous requirements were made more stringent.

The National Irrigation Act. Upon these as a basis, and also upon the Carey Act, which will be taken up separately, Congress passed, in 1902, the *National Irrigation Act*, under which the government now conducts its operations.[1] A survey of this law will be helpful to a right understanding of the principles by which waste land is redeemed; but no bond issues are put forth as the result of it. It declares that the work of reclamation must be paid for by the sale of the rights on the specific lands benefited; and that when so paid for the fund shall be returned to the government, and that the purchasers of the water rights shall become

[1] For the complete text see 32 U. S. Statutes 388, ch. 1093.

the owners of the irrigation works, i.e., dams, flumes, canals, gates, ditches, etc., and all rights appertaining. The water rights may be paid for in 10, yearly instalments. It declares that all moneys received from the sale of public lands in certain (16) states and territories, shall be set aside as a special fund in the Treasury, known as the reclamation fund, to be used in the examination of, and survey for, and the construction and maintenance of irrigation works, for the reclamation of arid and semi-arid lands in the states and territories from which the funds came. It also empowers the Secretary of the Interior to withdraw from public entry the lands required.

When the Secretary determines that any irrigation project submitted to him is practicable, he may cause to be let contracts for the construction, and shall limit the area of entry to what may be reasonably required for the support of a family, also the charges that shall be made per acre (with a view of returning to the reclamation fund the cost of construction), and also the number of annual instalments, not exceeding 10, in which such charges shall be paid.

The entryman upon the irrigated lands shall reclaim at least one-half of the total irrigable area for agricultural purposes, and before receiving patent for the lands covered by his entry, shall pay the government the charges apportioned against his tract. No water right shall be sold, for land in private ownership, to a tract exceeding 160 acres, and no such sale shall be made to any landowner unless he be an actual *bona fide* resident on such land, or occupant thereof residing in the neighborhood.

When the payments required by this Act are made for the major portion of the lands irrigated, then their management and operation shall pass to the owners of the land irrigated thereby, to be maintained at their expense under such form of organization and rules and regulations as may be acceptable to the Secretary of the Interior; provided that the title to and management of reservoirs and the works necessary to their protection and operation shall remain in the government until otherwise provided by Congress.

Present-Day Irrigation Under State Law. By federal irrigation is meant the redemption of public lands of the United States, under the guidance and restriction of federal law as embodied in the National Irrigation Act, which we have just considered.

On fulfilment of the conditions, title to the reclaimed land is passed from the government to the settler, who, of course, is acting under state law as well.

In the present topic, " Irrigation under State Law," we come to those reclamation operations, in some of which the National Government does not appear at all; while in others, it appears at least at one remove from contact with the settler. Title to the land to be reclaimed, until transfer, is in individuals or private corporations, or else in the state; but not in the National Government. The operations are usually financed by the sale of bonds.

In general, state legislation in recent years has sought to overcome the defects of the older irrigation securities and has placed the modern municipal irrigation district bond on a better basis. The leadership in this movement has been taken by California where irrigation projects have been successfully undertaken for over a quarter of a century. Certain of the Western states have established state commissions which are empowered to supervise the work of irrigation and in most cases to validate irrigation district securities.

It is these projects, therefore, that interest us most; and in order to get a correct idea of the bonds they produce, it will be well to classify them. They may be " Irrigation District " projects, " Carey Act " projects, or " Private Company " projects;—each having its distinctive advantages and drawbacks as security for capital.

IRRIGATION DISTRICT BONDS

Irrigation District Bonds. In the chapter entitled *The Bonds of Tax Districts* it was explained that many municipal corporations were organized with hardly a thought for general administrative or governmental functions, but for the purpose of levying special taxes to provide funds for objects of pecuniary value to the lands thus taxed; and that since these lands were not coincident with any more strictly governmental municipal corporations, such as town or county, the bonds of these districts had come to be called " Taxing District Bonds," or for brevity, " District Bonds." Irrigation District Bonds were there cited in illustration. To these issues, the principles that govern district bonds in general are applicable; and although irrigation districts may not always be looked upon as municipal corporations, the bonds are legitimately classified under *Municipals*, and are quite distinct, as a form of security, from *Private Project* issues, which now rarely appear on bond dealers' lists.[1]

The question immediately arises, since the validity of municipal issues is so often open to question, what bearing has the doubtful standing of the irrigation district, as a municipal corporation proper, upon the validity of irrigation district bonds. Such a district is at least a public corporation, for its officials, administration, and functions are all public; and, " being a public corporation, the validity of its organization cannot be collaterally attacked, as in a suit to enjoin the sale of lands for assessments, by showing that the board of supervisors acted without their jurisdiction in effecting the organization of the district. So, also, the irrigation district cannot plead the illegality of its own organization as a defense to an action on bonds issued by it; "[2] but on the other hand it may seek confirmation of the legality of its proceedings, by submitting itself, either on petition of the board of supervisors of the district, or of an assessment payer, to the superior court of the county in which its acreage chiefly lies.

There is considerable difference of attitude in the arid and semiarid states toward the three modes of irrigation. California, Idaho, Kansas, Nebraska, Nevada, and Washington have all had considerable experience in municipal irrigation, and a more or less common body of municipal irrigation district laws. Colorado, also, is given to the prosecution of her works along strictly municipal lines. Bonds there are issued by permission of the General Assembly, and authorized by the qualified electors of the district benefited, and their legality is passed on by the district court. In many respects they are of the nature of school district loans. County commissioners fix the rate of tax levy for the district in excess of requirements for interest and maintenance charges. The County Treasurer is *ex-officio* treasurer of the irrigation district and levies taxes in the same manner and at the same time as the regular taxes on realty and personalty for county purposes; but there is this to the advantage of municipal

[1] For detailed discussion of municipal irrigation bonds, see Report of the Irrigation Securities Committee to the Investment Bankers Association, *Proceedings*, 1921, pp. 217–223.

[2] Long on *The Law of Irrigation Bonds*.

irrigation issues, that they, unlike most school district issues, are usually obligations on the district prior to any subsequently imposed.

Irrigation districts, in the nature of the case, are formed more strictly for industrial, or rather, for agricultural purposes, than are most districts. School and water districts may be part of, or include great cities; they may have corporate assets of great value, apart from any consideration of the assessable values of the property in the district; and their municipal plants may sometimes be productive of revenues even in excess of the interest and sinking-fund charges on their funded debts. But irrigation districts are not formed except when the lands that compose them are in need of greater fertility; and it is not likely that lands will be included in the district, and be subjected to its comparatively high tax, unless they are greatly to benefit by it. Irrigation districts, therefore, are usually " rural districts " and subject, as respects security, to the limitations that usually attend " rural " political divisions, as contrasted with " municipal " or " city " divisions. They suffer by comparison, as to the personnel of the administration, the providence and continuity of their fiscal policies, and the general *esprit du corps*. They are, therefore, peculiarly susceptible to the temptation to repudiate their obligations.

Irrigation districts are not only rural, rather than municipal, but they may be even arid at the time of their formation. In this event the security for the bonds would depend, as it does in Carey Act projects, almost entirely on the successful outcome of the irrigation enterprise. It is not to be expected that rightly conducted districts will suffer, in the future, through engineering miscalculation; but as rural divisions, formed for an industrial undertaking, they may be sensitive to the influence of general business conditions.

Private Irrigation Projects. Strictly speaking, all irrigation projects that are not furthered by municipal corporations, are " private projects; " but, " Carey Act projects " are so distinctly set apart from other private irrigation enterprises, in that their aim is to reclaim public land, and in that they are the result of governmental aid and direction, it is customary to exclude them from this division. Private irrigation projects, then, we shall define as those undertaken by individuals or private corporations to improve, by watering, under state law, lands in private ownership.

Factors Making for Security. The value of the bonds issued by private irrigation companies is usually determined by the following factors:

1st. The existence of an adequate and permanent water supply.

2d. The title to the water supply in the company claiming it.

3d. The character and value of the irrigated land.

4th. The title to the land.

5th. The character of the settlers.

The Water Supply. It might sometimes happen in private developments, for instance in the semihumid valley section of Eastern Washington, that irrigation bonds would have some security in the land-mortgage, even should water for irrigation utterly fail, for one cause or another; and in private projects generally, the land values, potentially greater than in Carey projects, offer some degree of security as in simple real estate mortgages. But as a broad statement, it is fair to say that the security for irrigation bonds is almost as dependent on an adequate and permanent supply of water as is the security for the bonds of hydroelectric power companies.

However, the sources of this supply for irrigation are more general than for power developments, since power itself is not requisite, but merely water. Some large irrigation undertakings are upon plateaus, and pump their water from rivers flowing at a lower level; or even, in want of watercourses, pump their water from artesian wells. Questions of minimum flow or supply, past or prospective, due to deforestation, drought, and mechanical obstruction and diversion,—all enter into the security offered by water supply.

The Water Title and the Water Rights. Questions of mechanical obstruction and diversion lead immediately to the subject of water rights, already discussed. One source of Eastern misconception of irrigation issues lies in this unfamiliarity with the " usufructuary estate " of water as developed in the laws of the arid commonwealths. Title to water supply, in these states, means title to " reasonable use," i.e., the right of a proprietor to divert his due portion of water, which shall not be diminished by any subsequent grant, to an adjacent proprietor, of right to withdraw water from the same stream.

It very occasionally happens that bonds are issued against a lien on the works and water rights alone. Unless the circumstances were unusual, these bonds are not to be commended. The better, ordinary irrigation bond represents a first mortgage on the land of the issuing company, to which land adequate water rights attach. Sometimes two companies are organized, one to build and own the water rights, and the other to own the land to be subdivided, watered, and sold to settlers. In this case the irrigation company (the company owning the works and water rights), issues to the land company certificates of water rights, legally describing the land which the water is to cover, and also guaranteeing the bonds, so that, in effect, the bonds are secured by a lien both on land and on water rights. This double security must always be looked for, since the funded credits of irrigation enterprises represent in finance what the physical elements do in irrigation: a union of water and land, so that the water becomes appurtenant and inseparable.

The Watered Land. Another source of Eastern misconception is due to ignorance of Western land qualities and land values. The arid tracts that await watering are not usually poor lands in want of enrichment, but rich lands in want of moisture. To great depths they are full of soluble salts, chemically stimulating, that have not been washed away by the rains of humid climes, and that, when wet, will draw down great deep roots of vegetation, and sustain them with vitality through a long period of drought. In such soil crop-rotation and surface-fertilization will long be unnecessary.

The values of lands like these, when irrigated, multiply by leaps and bounds beyond all precedent in other forms of stable realty. The Chief Engineer of the Government Reclamation Service says: " The open range of the arid region is capable of supporting one cow to every 20 or 30 acres; the same land watered and put to alfalfa will feed 12 cows to every 20 acres, or in orchard, in favorable altitudes, will support a family of from three to five persons. An enormous enhancement in land values, therefore, attaches to the reclamation of these arid tracts. As an open range its value may be 50 cents per acre; while under irrigation the selling price may be from $50 to $1,000 per acre."

The Land Title. It is in the matter of land values that bonds of the class described may have advantage over Carey Act bonds,

in that the lands available for private irrigation must be those
in which title has passed from the government or the state, and
is held by individuals or corporations. In the West, lands of
any considerable area, that have the title in this condition, are
almost universally in a well-established country, with established
values, and in proximity to towns and transportation. Since
the fee titles to these lands are fixed directly in the corporation,
the lands are usually sold and resold, and settled upon and
improved, from the time irrigation is started; and since the price
of these lands is being determined by a free market, not only are
the values of the lands established, but they are current also.

The Scale of Private Projects. That private irrigation projects
are usually much smaller than Carey Act projects operates
somewhat against economies of construction; but in these projects
the fact is not always to be deprecated, since the smaller the
irrigable land the briefer the period that should be necessary for
settlement, and the lighter the consequent charge against the
works for interest and maintenance during the non-productive
period. Because of their freedom from government supervision
private projects require more careful scrutiny from investors.
But if the supply of water, and the title thereto, and the quality
of the land, are satisfactory, and if the lands are salable at the
price the irrigation company ask, and if the early interest and
maintenance charges are provided for, and the construction cost
is not too greatly overbonded, and the character of the settlers
is satisfactory, private projects have conformed to the Carey
Act standard, and are worthy of study for certain kinds of
investment. But the foregoing are numerous and indispensable
provisos.

Carey Act Projects. The legislatures of some states, like
Wyoming and Idaho, especially encourage the reclamation of
segregated lands under the provisions of the Carey Act. This
bill, passed by Congress in its primitive form in 1893, was named
from the Wyoming senator who introduced it, and in his own
state first made use of it. It authorized the Secretary of the
Interior, with the approval of the President, to contract and
agree to patent to the states of Washington, Oregon, California,
Nevada, Idaho, Montana, Wyoming, Colorado, North Dakota,
South Dakota, and Utah, or any other state in which are desert
lands, an amount of these lands not to exceed one million acres

to each state, to aid them in the reclamation, settlement, cultivation, and sale, in small tracts to actual settlers of the land in question.

A supplementary act of 1896 further authorized the creation by the state of liens against the legal subdivisions of the land reclaimed " for the actual cost and necessary expenses of reclamation, and reasonable interest thereon from the date of reclamation until disposed of to actual settlers; and when an ample supply of water is actually furnished in a substantial ditch or canal, or by artesian wells or reservoirs, to reclaim a particular tract or tracts of such lands, then patents shall issue to the state without regard to settlement or cultivation."

Under the amended Carey Act the typical mode of procedure for irrigation projects is this:—A proposal, with maps, plans, estimates, etc., to withdraw certain lands from the public domain for the purpose of reclamation, is filed with the proper authorities. The proposal must obtain the recommendation of the State Engineer, the approval of the State Board of Land Commissioners, the consent of the Secretary of the Interior, and of the President. The lands are then withdrawn from the jurisdiction exercised over the public domain, and are subject to contract between the state and the construction company for irrigation purposes, according to the state law and the provisions of the Carey Act.

Under the terms of this contract the state authorizes a prior lien on the segregated lands in favor of the company, and by the provisions of the lien, the title to the mortgaged land is not released by the state to the purchaser until he has paid the company for the rights or shares in a sufficient amount of water to irrigate his land. Furthermore, title does not pass from the state until the settlement is an accomplished fact; but the settler is required to have his land under cultivation within a reasonably brief time after the introduction of water. At no time is the title vested in the construction company. Thus the security for the irrigation bonds issued against the company's prior lien is created by immediate irrigation, settlement, and cultivation, in small tracts, by home-makers, acting under an agreement which is effectual because its infringement estops ultimate transfer of title.

Irrigation bonds are almost always prior liens, and in Carey Act and private projects " first and only " liens, on waterworks and reclaimed land, or on land about to be reclaimed. Their priority as liens is a recognition of the commercial primacy of irrigation in the arid West.

In municipal, or in Carey Act projects, the bonded indebtedness represents, or should represent, the approximate cost of construction, with reasonable interest and profits, and in any case, it is secured by property usually worth several times the amount of the issue, as soon as the lands, with their inseparable water rights, are possessed and cultivated by settlers. If Irrigation District Bonds, they have the same formal characteristics as other Municipal District Bonds, and they are legitimately called Municipals. If corporation bonds, issued in accordance with the Carey Act, they have met with government sanction and with state supervision and approval. If Serial Irrigation Bonds, the equity, or margin of safety, grows from year to year, as in Serial Equipment Bonds; but unlike Equipment Bonds, the material security ordinarily does not depreciate, but rather enchances rapidly, through growth in land values. But, to repeat, it does not follow from the foregoing that the security for Irrigation Bonds is comparable with that of Equipments. History gravely disproves that.

Disadvantages. As a channel of investment Irrigation Bonds have obvious drawbacks. The legal aspect of the disadvantages has been mentioned. Furthermore, it cannot be gainsaid that, after all, Irrigation Bonds, irrespective of kind, represent at the time they are issued the funding of loans that are to pay for future developments; and these developments, in common with all construction propositions, have elements of risk. No amount of legislative direction and restriction, of itself, will assure success to an irrigation proposition. The financial record of irrigation has not been good. There are not wanting those who believe much trouble is yet to come because of overcapitalization and misguided enterprise. As distinguished from most municipal, railroad, and corporation bonds, the *immediate* security for irrigation issues is land value, rather than credit or earning power, and the value must be in the land. But the value of the land is dependent on an unfailing supply of water, on fertility of soil, a market for its products, and transportation to that market, and lastly, on the character and permanency of the settlement. To ascertain these facts at first hand and beyond peradventure is difficult.

Reliance must be placed on the bond house that sells the security. Of all classes of bonds these most particularly should be bought only of bankers who are trustworthy, and conversant with the construction and financial problems of the securities they offer.

In general, the volume of bonds of private irrigation or Carey Act projects outstanding to-day is relatively small. There is little prospect for their increase in the future, for it is the general feeling that irrigation can best be undertaken by public funds supplied either through the Reclamation Service of the Federal Government or through the district irrigation system.

The bonded indebtedness of all irrigation districts in the United States to December 31, 1921, is stated in the table on page 516.

Drainage and Levee Bonds. Drainage and levee (or river bank) bonds furnish the cure and prevention, respectively, of the opposite evil: *too much water*. Both kinds of construction are now financed in the same spirit and for the same purpose as irrigation works. The spirit, as we have said, is that fostered by a community of interest, resulting in local coöperation under government regulation and guidance; and the purpose, the furtherance of profitable agriculture in lands that hitherto have been wholly or partially unproductive.

Scope and Character. Drainage, on a large scale, has been confined thus far to states bordering on the Ohio and Mississippi Rivers, but within this field its operations have been very extensive. Particularly in Ohio, Indiana, Illinois, and Iowa, under intelligent state drainage laws the soil that formerly was waste has been brought to a condition of high culture; and on the Mississippi there is a continuous stretch of fertile land reclaimed from the river by levees.

Although much has been done, the work of drainage and levee reclamation is but well under way, and loans are constantly being made in furtherance of both. It has been found desirable to finance these improvements by municipal corporations of one sort or another. Occasionally a city will assume drainage or levee charges as direct obligations, e.g., Dayton, Ohio; but by far the larger number of drainage issues are in the form of county and district loans. In either circumstance the bonds are to be looked upon as any other municipals issued for improvement purposes and to be judged in accordance with the credit of the community, its character, population, valuation, tax-burden, debt limit, etc.

SUMMARY OF BONDED INDEBTEDNESS OF IRRIGATION DISTRICTS IN THE UNITED STATES, DECEMBER 31, 1921

(Irrigation District Operation and Finance—U. S. Department of Agriculture Bulletin No. 1177)

State	Bonds			Districts Having Voted Bonds			Districts Having Bonds Outstanding			Operating Districts Fully Financed to Date		
	Voted	Sold	Outstanding	Number	Area	Bonds Voted Average per Acre	Number	Area	Bonds Outstanding Average per Acre	Number	Area	Outstanding Bonded Debts Average per Acre
					Acres	*Average per Acre*		*Acres*	*Average per Acre*		*Acres*	*Average per Acre*
Arizona	$3,628,975	$70,500	$70,081	6	120,500	$30	2	18,040	$4	1	13,840	$4
California	110,149,011	50,654,531	45,716,061	84	3,846,682	29	48	2,327,905	20	40	1,894,216	24
Colorado	52,732,600	25,384,400	20,919,200	59	1,521,915	35	34	821,040	25	24	521,942	30
Idaho	22,976,214	6,476,500	5,494,750	44	690,620	33	31	386,351	14	28	345,851	13
Kansas												
Montana	4,405,000	2,293,500	2,211,200	34	221,244	20	20	81,999	27	20	81,999	27
Nebraska	4,596,382	4,151,682	3,346,182	29	290,169	16	18	173,729	19	18	173,729	19
Nevada	918,500	412,500	412,500	1	190,796	5	1	190,796	2			
New Mexico	1,450,000	436,000	186,000	4	74,372	19	2	23,872	8	1	14,872	11
North Dakota												
Oklahoma												
Oregon	20,961,000	7,636,800	7,437,800	28	502,086	42	21	391,360	19	17	181,080	37
South Dakota												
Texas	12,597,000	11,003,000	10,849,000	16	538,724	23	14	526,871	21	11	442,871	23
Utah	4,011,000	2,150,600	1,060,100	10	123,823	32	5	35,581	30	5	35,581	30
Washington	38,510,430	6,805,430	6,499,430	52	1,083,189	36	40	986,909	7	31	137,659	42
Wyoming	4,491,000	961,000	718,500	6	145,750	31	3	43,250	17	3	43,250	17
Total or Mean	281,427,112	118,436,443	104,921,223	373	9,349,451	30	329	6,007,703	17	199	3,886,890	25

In the nature of the case levee construction is a benefit to, and therefore a tax obligation of, cities and strips of land rather than of counties as a whole, therefore levee bonds are usually Municipal or Levee District issues.

Security. Levee District and Drainage District bonds are not dissimilar to Irrigation District bonds, or to District bonds in general. In addition to the usual considerations governing investment in district issues, one should post himself as to the laws of the several states affecting drainage districts; and he should remember that drainage districts have the same rural credit characteristics as irrigation districts.

At first drainage bonds found a market only in the Middle West where the value of drainage was fully appreciated. In time Eastern investors learned the true position of these securities; and when issued in accordance with standard practice, they may be regarded as safe forms of investment.

Duration. There is as wide a range in maturities as in security and income yield. The duration is from 15 to 30 years. The average is now slightly over eight years. Most issues are serial.

Market. The market for the city and county issues depends, of course, on the demand for the other loans of the same municipalities. Drainage and Levee District securities suffer by comparison. In general drainage bonds have found their best market in St. Louis.

Future. Future drainage projects can be undertaken with beneficial results in the Mississippi Valley and on the Atlantic seaboard. The Mississippi Valley system includes 15,000 miles of navigable waterways. Within this area lie states with millions of unreclaimed areas. The following estimates have been made:[1]

Louisiana	10,196,605	acres
Arkansas	5,912,300	"
Mississippi	5,760,200	"
Missouri	2,439,600	"
Alabama	1,479,200	"

The whole Atlantic seaboard, from Maine to Florida, is fringed with strips of salt marshland that need only the application of plant chemistry and hydraulics on the one hand and public-

[1] J. Sheppard Smith in *Annals of the American Academy of Political and Social Science*, (1920), p. 103.

spirited financial endeavor on the other to redeem them for the intensive agriculture that increasing congestion of population demands. In certain sections, private enterprise has already accomplished a great deal. Malarial tide-marshes, formerly worse than worthless, have been redeemed from rank grass and mosquitoes, and made to yield most desirable products. Good cranberry bogs made from such land on the New England coast are worth $1,000 the acre. Here, and on the south shores, small garden truck, raised from the drained marshes, has proved well worth while.

But these industries are sporadic. What is wanted for a general development of tidelands is the knowledge and confidence on the part of whole communities that their united endeavors for reclamation will be fruitful and lasting. Toward this end the United States Department of Agriculture, through its experiment stations and drainage engineers, is perfecting plans for a system of seacoast drainage and agriculture, and has submitted to the Federal Government recommendations that will help. The main contention of the Department is that each state, having within its borders considerable salt marsh, should establish simple, but equitable drainage laws that would protect those who bear the burden of development. Such laws should establish the riparian rights of the landowners and " should also make provision for doing the reclamation work as a whole and provide for the issuance of bonds to be a lien upon the lands benefited, to raise money for paying for the work as it is done. These bonds should run for a long term of years at a low rate of interest and be paid in annual instalments by a tax on the land reclaimed in the ratio that such lands are benefited by the improvement."[1]

So it seems that there is an extended future for drainage and levee issues, and in localities that will bring them more closely home to Eastern capital.

[1] See the Annual Report of the Office of Experiment Stations for the fiscal year 1906.

PART IV

THE MATHEMATICS AND MOVE-
MENT OF BOND PRICES

CHAPTER XXXIX

THE MATHEMATICS OF BOND VALUES

We have now discussed many of the important aspects of bonds as a channel for investment; but before we consider the general course and the minor movements of bond prices, it will be well to run over those practical problems of a mathematical sort that every investor has to meet when he figures the income, cost, present value, or selling price of a bond. Then, too, some defensible stand must be taken as to how an investor should keep his books to know at any time what is his capital invested in bonds, and to compare this " capital estate " with the estimated market value of his securities. Or, if he is acting in a fiduciary capacity, that he may distinguish what is legally capital in this case from what is income, in order to render the income to the life-tenants (the annuitants), and the principal to the remainderman. Bond accountancy, therefore, naturally divides itself into The Mathematics of Bond Values, with its application to the bond tables, etc., and The Basis of Bond Accounts.

Net Returns. It may be said, at the outset, that most of the difficulties met in figuring investment values arise from the fact that the net return is usually different from the periodical cash return which the investment produces. Whether the investments have a maturity or not:—whether it be stock, mortgage, or bond, —if bought at par, so that the net return and the cash return are the same, there can be no questions of moment raised concerning value.[1]

Net Dividend Yield: Perpetual Securities. Value is most significantly expressed in terms of income. Indeed we may say yield is the *only* common denominator of security values. The simplest study of values is to be found in figuring the net return of securities that have no fixed date of repayment, and are not truly

---

[1] A compounding of interest or dividends, due to conversions more frequent than once a year, will cause an almost inappreciable difference in the net rate, and therefore in the price. But the bond tables neglect this, and call the net yield of a 4 per cent. bond at par, 4 per cent., irrespective of the interest interval.

loans. Perpetual or interminable loans, such as the Republic of Cuba (Internal Debt) 5s, and the British Consols, and among American private corporation bonds, the Securities Company 4 per cent. Consols, are of this class, therefore the matter is pertinent to a bond treatise. But stocks predominate among non-maturing securities. The returns that come from stocks, therefore, may well designate what we usually seek in figuring such security values: namely, *Net Dividend Yield.*[1]

The rate of net dividend yield may be defined as the ratio of the annual cash dividend to the price paid. It is very simple. If a stock costs $116, and the dividends for the year amount to $4, the annual net dividend return will be $\frac{4}{116} = .03448 \ldots =$ 3.448 . . . . per cent. = 3.45 per cent., approximately.

It will be seen that it is not necessary to know the par value of a stock to find the net yield, if we know the cash dividend. This is convenient to remember when figuring the yield of mining and other low-priced stocks. We may have forgotten that the par value of Butte Coalition is $15, but at a cost of $20, we can easily figure that the net yield of this stock, when it is paying 25 cents in dividends quarterly each year, is 5 per cent.

The ordinary stock tables, however, are not based on cash dividends or an eclectic par value. Like New York Stock Exchange quotations, they are based on a par value of $100, and treat the dividend as percentage. A stock like Reading Common, with a par value of $50 and with $3 dividends a year, is treated like a 6 per cent. stock of $100 denomination. The result, of course, is the same, for the ratio remains the same; but having doubled par to get the interest rate in percentage, it is necessary to double the price to maintain its proportionate relation to par in finding the net yield.

To find, in the tables, the net yield of stocks that have a par value of less than $100, multiply the price in the price column by the number of times the par value is contained in the $100, and seek the corresponding decimal in the interest rate column. But,

---

[1] There is one real distinction between dividends and the revenues from perpetual loans: the dividend ordinarily is optional, therefore instantaneous; the loan-revenue is obligatory, therefore accruing. Cumulative preferred stocks, with what might be called semi-obligatory dividends, bridge the distinction. Hence the New York Stock Exchange ruling that income bonds be quoted "flat."

if the par value is more than $100, divide the price by the number of times the $100 is contained in it. But simpler by far than the use of any tables is the division of the cash dividend by the price in accordance with the definition of Net Dividend Yield.

It is the universal practice to figure net dividend returns as above. In view of what is to follow, however, attention is called to the fact that this method is open to variation; for it does not take into consideration the fact that some stocks pay dividends annually, some semiannually, and some quarterly. Obviously, the true return of a stock paying 8 per cent. annually may be considered less than that of a stock paying 2 per cent. every quarter day, for the owner of the stock paying quarterly has the opportunity to invest his dividends and get as additional compensation, whatever interest, dividends, or discount may be had on $2 for 9 months, $2 for 6 months, and $2 for 3 months. Since the reinvestment of dividends is not ordinarily pertinent to an accounting of the transaction, the stock tables do not, of course, take dividend intervals into account. If discrimination were made, as in bond tables, the current stock tables would be those to be used for stocks paying dividends annually. Dividends are usually payable quarterly. That different *interest* intervals do require different sets of bond value tables is for reasons other than the payment of semiannual coupons.

Net Interest Yield: Terminable Securities. The rate of net interest yield for bonds is not so simple. It is the ratio of the sum that the owner of the security is entitled to entertain as income, to the cost of the security (accrued interest excepted), considering the length of time before the principal is to be repaid. The trouble with this definition is that it does not define; for we do not know what sum is the owner's true income.

If the bond is bought at a premium or discount, the money value, on any basis of computation, must gradually approach par, since (with the exceptions already noted), par is the value of the invested capital at maturity. In the nature of the case the *rate* the bond yields cannot change, and therefore, as the amount (or present worth) of the capital invested in the premium bond decreases toward par, and the amount of the capital invested in the discount bond increases toward par, the *amount* of true income decreases or increases, respectively, in proportion. The net interest rate must be a constant ratio.

It is because the amount of capital invested in the bond (as distinct from the sinking fund) decreases or increases, as the case may be, that many have the entirely erroneous idea that there is a depreciation of an investment bought above par, and an appreciation of one bought below par. Let us consider a $1,000 bond bought at 90.01, having 10 years to run and bearing 4 per cent. interest. The current bond tables, hereafter fully explained, show us that the net rate of yield on a 4 per cent. bond costing $900.10 and running for 10 years, is approximately 5.30 per cent. After six months the value of this bond at the same net yield is, according to the tables, about $903.90. Since no capital has been added, why has there not been a real appreciation in the value of the instrument? Because this $3.80 of gain in the invested sum has been taken out of the earnings, or interest.

At the six months' period the owner was entitled to draw one-half of the annual 5.30 per cent. on his invested principal, but the limitations in flexibility of his instrument permit him to draw (by cashing the coupon) only one-half of the 4 per cent. of the par value. The apparent gain in the invested principal came from withholding income to which he was entitled on a 5.30 per cent. basis.

Bond value 10 yrs. prior to maturity $900.10
Bond value 9½ yrs. prior to maturity 903.90

The so-called "appreciation" . . . .$ 3.80

Semiannual Net Yield (½ of 5.30% of 900.10) = $ 23.85
Semiannual Cash Yield (½ of 4% of 1,000) =   20.00

Amount Withheld . . . .$ 3.85

(The discrepancy of five cents between the "appreciation" and the "amount withheld" is due to the fact that the shorter bond tables in common commercial use carry values to the second decimal only.)

It follows that the sum of the amounts withheld for the 20 semiannual periods will equal the discount. By similar reasoning it may be shown that the difference, in a premium bond, between the cash interest paid and the lesser interest earned is equal to the " depreciation," whether the period be full 10 years or any other duration.

A clear and incontrovertible inference from what has been said is that the one mathematical factor making for bond values is the Net Interest Rate. For this reason the bond value tables are based, not on prices, but on the somewhat arbitrary, but generally informing, rates of net income.

It is possible, however, to reverse this proposition: to consider the bond features as factors determining the net yield. So viewed, the net rate of yield is affected by the price paid, the sum to be received at maturity, the cash sum to be received periodically as interest, the length of time before the principal sum will be repaid, and the frequency of the periodic interest payments.

A summary of the whole matter of net yield reduces topical considerations to the following:

Recapitulation:

THE FACTORS OF NET RETURN

Net Dividend Yield (of stocks and other perpetual securities)	{ Price Cash Dividend	{ Par Value Nominal Dividend Rate

Net Interest Yield (of bonds and other redeemable securities)	{ Price
	Redemption Value
	Nominal Interest
	  Rate
	Duration
	Interest Interval
		{ Premium or
		  Discount
		
		{ Number of
		  Interest Periods

Ordinarily the phrase " par value " may be substituted for the more awkward " redemption value," for most bonds are redeemed at par. Then the difference between the Price and Par will be the Premium or Discount. But when an issue *must be* redeemed at a premium, or when an issue *has been* redeemed at a premium, and one desires to know what it *has netted*, the bond tables do not cope with the situation; resort must be had to formulas.

Premium. How the factors I Price and II Par, as premium or discount, work with III Nominal Interest Rate to affect the Net Interest Yield, may be seen in the following illustration: —A $1,000 bond, bearing interest at 5 per cent. payable semiannually is bought for $1,080 (" at 108 ") and accrued interest. The owner is not entitled to consider that his investment nets him $50 a year, or 5 per cent., since such part of the $25 cash interest paid each semiannual interest date must be laid aside for a sinking fund as will accumulate an amount at maturity equal to the $80 premium. Otherwise the capital of $1,080 would be impaired at maturity to the extent of $80. For the accounting of a sinking fund for a premium bond, see p. 565.

Discount. If the same bond is bought for $920 and accrued interest, the owner is entitled to consider that his investment nets him more than the $50, or 5 per cent. that he actually receives each year; for if, in addition to his coupons, at the semiannual interest dates he should withdraw from any source and unite with his coupon income sums which would amount at maturity to the $80 which the par value exceeded the buying price, then this $80 would pay for and offset the sums drawn; and the capital of $920 would remain as at the time of investment. For the accounting of an accumulating fund for a discount, see p. 566.

Nominal Interest Rate. It is the effect, upon interest rate, of premium or discount, which is wanting in stock computations. The par value of stock, therefore, is no such vital matter as the par value of bonds.

Duration. In the above illustrations we have not indicated how great should be the semiannual sums to be laid aside as a sinking fund, in the premium bond, or to be borrowed from somewhere against an accumulating fund, in the discount bond. Since the total amount to be made up is to be in hand at a definite maturity date, the sum laid aside, or borrowed, will be affected by IV the Duration of the bond. The longer the bond has to run, the smaller the compounded sum which must be set aside each time.

Interest Interval. But the sum laid aside each interest date may be looked upon as the " future amount " of the original instalment which has compounded at the net rate. It is customary to consider this interest as compounded upon the regular bond interest dates. Again, the more frequently it is compounded the smaller the sum withdrawn for premium or discount. We have, therefore, a fifth factor affecting New Interest Yield, called Interest Interval.

Dividend payments, we have said, are usually quarterly, but it is not necessary to consider the interval in finding net dividend returns. Interest payments are generally semiannual, and the ordinary bond tables are based on the six months' interval. Unless otherwise stated, this interval is to be assumed hereafter in this book. If the payments are quarterly, as in government bonds, or if annual, then tables based on periods of three months or 12 months must be consulted; or else tables furnishing multipliers by which the results obtained from the semiannual tables may be converted to conform to the new interest interval. If, however, no such tables are accessible, the results may be obtained by a simple arithmetical process which is worked out in the pages devoted to an explanation of the uses of the bond tables.

The Interest Rate on the Sinking Fund. In this illustration of the effect of premium or discount on net yield, we said that the fund set aside was compounded upon the regular bond interest dates. For the sake of clearness let us now confine the discussion of this point to the case of a premium bond. Why may the investor who is laying aside a portion of his bond interest, twice each year, to create a sinking fund, consider that the sinking fund should be figured as if compounded semiannually? Because, if he puts the fund into the savings bank it will compound semiannually.

This question is seldom raised; but another of like bearing is not so rare: Why is the interest earned by the sinking fund assumed to be the same as the net interest yield of the bond? If the 5 per cent. bond of the illustration, bought at 108, has 50 years to run, the net yield is about 4.60 per cent. But the owner cannot put out a small sum at interest, on equal security, to net 4.60 per cent., in all probability. The best he can do is the savings bank, at $3\frac{1}{2}$ or 4 per cent., compounded quarterly. The illustration would be more striking in a bond netting 6 per cent.

The answer to both questions is the same. We are dealing with mathematical tables, which should be, as far as possible, of universal application—ubiquitous and perpetual. The present principles of the bond value tables presuppose an ability on the part of the owner to do with small sums exactly what he can with $1,000. If he can compound his bond principal semiannually (is the inference), he can compound his sinking fund semiannually; it is not right to assume another kind of investment in which he can do differently. Likewise, if he can net 4.60 per cent. upon his bond principal, he can net 4.60 upon his sinking fund. In a sense, the very fact that the tables are figured upon that basis *makes* the sinking fund earn 4.60 per cent. It is fairer to assume he can earn that rate than that he can earn any other rate arbitrarily chosen.

As to the sinking fund interest rate, the advocates of a more inductive method of forming the tables say: Let the rate accord with the fact: $3\frac{1}{2}$ to 4 per cent., only, can be earned on small sums at interest. Let some such average rate be taken which will be approximately correct over a long period of years.

Granted that the matter is of sufficient importance to overcome the obstacles to change, legal and otherwise—is it possible to agree upon a rate which, in all probability, over a period of a century, and from London to Tokio, and from Seattle to Bombay, will approximate the facts more closely than the present? If so, the change would appeal to the writer. As it is, he cannot refrain from quoting against the proposal for a single fixed interest rate, for the sinking fund, the words of a friend who is one of the most prominent advocates of the principle: " Tables issued a few years ago, during the prevailing low rates of money are of little value to-day, when the rates have so largely increased." If a few years will antiquate prevailing interest rates, what may not a century do? From 1892 to 1902 there was an uninterrupted annual fall in the average rate of dividends paid by Massachusetts savings banks from 4.11 to 3.71, and from 1903 the rate has steadily risen from 3.71 to 3.95 per cent. (1908).

There is some semblance of universality, and therefore more reason, in establishing quarterly intervals for compounding sinking funds. It is quite improbable that the time will ever come when small investments cannot receive quarterly interest. The doubt in this case may well be whether quarterly interest may be had in those parts of the world which do not provide savings institutions for the public.

When the matter is thus viewed in proper perspective, one grows more content with things as they are, however crude. Further discussion of the interest rate of the sinking fund will be pertinent on deriving the bond formulas.

Inaccuracies in the Determination of the Bond Tables. Before concluding the subject of New Yield, it is desirable to call attention to the extent to which investment tables may be relied on. As far as stocks are concerned we have found no variant which undermines the mathematical accuracy of the results. The only variant discussed was that of the dividend interval, and that offered no difficulties in determining the net dividend yield.

In bonds there are several variants, two of which,—the Interest Interval, and the Interest Rate credited as earned by the fund raised to amortize the premium or discount—have already been noted. This latter variant will bear further thought. Since 4 per cent. is the present approximate average interest rate which small invested sums will return, the higher the net yield of the bonds (above 4 per cent.) the greater the discrepancy between the bond tables and the facts. Whether the bond sells at a premium or at a discount, if the net yield is greater than 4 per cent. the interest credited to the amortization fund is greater than the facts warrant. Therefore, the bond owner is not putting sufficiently large semiannual sums into the fund. Therefore, the owner of the premium bond should set aside out of his cash interest payments a larger sum semiannually, and the owner of the discount bond may borrow larger semiannual sums, in anticipation of the " discount " paid him at maturity,—than the bond tables authorize.

In other words, the present bond tables work in favor of the principal and the owner of the principal, of both premium and discount bonds, and therefore against the recipient of the interest, if another person,—always provided that the net yield is over 4 per cent. This is not a matter of importance, except when it becomes necessary to separate principal and income according to testamentary provisions.

Put in another way still, the purchaser of a premium bond which nets over 4 per cent., according to the bond tables, does not get as great a return as the tables indicate; but neither does the purchaser of a discount bond; for in the case of bonds netting over 4 per cent. the tables credit the amortization fund of the one, and the accumulation fund of the other, with an ability to earn more than they really can in the way of interest.

On the other hand, this disadvantage is somewhat offset by the fact that funds can be compounded quarterly in this part of the world, although the tables assume that they are to be compounded semiannually.

The third source of inaccuracy arises from the assumption of the tables that the semiannual instalments of the amortization fund will be instantly reinvested. Although some banks allow interest on daily balances, the savings banks, which pay interest most liberally, are accustomed to start new interest accounts only quarterly.

A fourth source is to be found whenever a bond is bought

at any other time than on dates of interest payment. Conceding the principles on which the ordinary tables are established, they are mathematically correct to two decimal places as to the percentage of net return, when no interest has accrued on the price that is the basis on which they are figured for semiannual periods. Accruing interest is an increment of the cost to which the interest yield can be adjusted.

The fifth source of inaccuracy is due to the fact that the values are ratios, and since ratios involve many decimal figures, and are seldom divisible without a remainder, the tables are correct only to a given number of decimals, usually two. For large operations a valuable set of extended bond tables has been compiled, which gives to the nearest cent the value of an investment of $1,000,000.

As a whole these five sources of inaccuracy in the derivation of the net yield are no reflection on the tables, but rather a testimony to the vicissitudes attending the strictest investment. In a measure, they counteract one another; and in transactions involving moderate amounts they are quite negligible.

The nearer to par and to an interest period a bond is bought, the less the discrepancy between the facts and the results obtained from the tables.

SUMMARY OF INACCURACIES IN THE DETERMINATION OF NET YIELD

Net Dividend Yield $\begin{cases} \text{Dividend Interval,} \\ \text{Decimal approximation, if determined by Dividend Tables.} \end{cases}$

Net Interest Yield $\begin{cases} \text{Interest interval of the amortization or accumulation fund,} \\ \text{Interest rate of the amortization or accumulation fund,} \\ \text{Implied instantaneous reinvestment of the fund,} \\ \text{Accrued interest,} \\ \text{Decimal approximation.} \end{cases}$

Those who have read the preceding pages of this chapter and realize the capabilities and limitations of the tables, but who are interested only in the superficial business use of them, may well drop the argument at this point, to pick it up conveniently in p. 538 et seq., which discuss bank discount.

The Derivation of the Bond Formulas. The explanation of how the tables are derived is somewhat complicated at best.

therefore of the several possible formulas, the two have been chosen for derivation which are easiest of understanding to those who are rusty in their mathematics. They are not, however, the shortest.

We have defined the net interest rate as the ratio of the net income to the cost. Instead of deriving our formulas from the relationship expressed in this form it will be better to start with an entirely different but equally true definition or equation.

The First Formula. A bond is a promise to pay, I, a fixed " principal sum " at maturity, and II, equal proportionate parts of the principal, called interest (usually in the form of coupons) at regular periods. The principal sum, or par, is not worth par now, since it is a future payment; but the present worth of it may be found, since we know that the entire investment, and therefore every part of it, nets a certain percentage of return. Also all the future interest payments, and their sum, may easily be computed and the present worth ascertained at the same net interest rate. Then the present worth of the bond, at the given rate,—which is the price of the bond,—is simply the sum of the present worths of the par value and of the coupons.

And so, without a book of tables, the price of a bond at any net rate may be computed by any one who has at hand tables of compound interest and of annuities, for the interest payments are nothing more or less than annuities.

This definition of the present worth of the bond furnishes us with the equation which is the basis of the formula. For convenience let us assume that the bond is of $1, instead of $1,000, denomination.

Present worth $1 bond = present worth of $1 plus present worth of coupons.

Let C = cash or coupon payment in cents (or percentage of $1) each
        semiannual interest period.
   n = number of semiannual interest periods.
   N = net interest on $1 for 6 months.

To Find the Present Worth of $1 Principal. Now we seek the *future amount* of a present sum, when compounding interest, by multiplying that sum by 1 plus the interest rate $(1+N)$ to get a new amount $1(1+N)$, and multiply this new amount by the *ratio of increase* $(1+N)$ to get a second amount $1(1+N)^2$, or $(1+N)^2$, and continue this process $(1+N)^3$, $(1+N)^4$, etc., for the number of semiannual interest periods n, until we get ulti-mate *compound amount* $(1+N)^n$.

For instance, if we are compounding at the rate of 6 per cent. per annum, the semiannual amounts of \$1 would grow as follows:

$$1 \times 1.03 = 1.03 \text{ in 6 mos., or at 1st period,}$$
$$1.03 \times 1.03 = (1.03)^2 \text{ at 2d period,}$$
$$(1.03)^2 \times 1.03 = (1.03)^3 \text{ at 3d period, and so on.}$$

In like manner at the nth period the amount will be $(1.03)^n$, and the general formula is $(1+N)^n$.

So, in seeking the reverse, namely, the *present worth* of a future amount, we discount, by merely reversing the process of accumulation, and divide the future amount (\$1) by the ratio of increase $(1+N)$, with the result $\frac{1}{1+N}$, and repeat $\frac{1}{(1+N)^2}$, $\frac{1}{(1+N)^3}$, etc., until the divisions equal the number of interest periods,—a process expressed by $\frac{1}{(1+N)^n}$, which is the formula for the present worth of \$1 principal.

Expressed in figures, if we are discounting at the rate of 6 per cent. per annum, the semiannual " present worths " of \$1 would decrease, according to the duration of the loan, as follows:

$$1 \div 1.03 = \frac{1}{1.03} \text{ in 6 mos., or at the 1st period}$$

$$\frac{1}{1.03} \div 1.03 = \frac{1}{1.03} \times \frac{1}{1.03} = \frac{1}{(1.03)^2} \text{ at the 2d period}$$

$$\frac{1}{1.03^2} \div 1.03 = \frac{1}{(1.03)^3} \text{ at the 3d period}$$

At the nth period the present worth would be $\frac{1}{(1.03)^n}$, and the general formula is $\frac{1}{(1+N)^n}$.

To Find the Present Worth of the Interest Payments or Coupons. Let us assume that this \$1, 6 per cent. bond runs 2 years and nets 4 per cent.

Then C = .03
   N = .02
   n = 4

As the future values of the coupons are each equal to C, the present worths are

$$\frac{C}{1+N}, \frac{C}{(1+N)^2}, \frac{C}{(1+N)^3} \cdots\cdots\cdots\cdots\cdots\cdots, \frac{C}{(1+N)^n}$$

These form a series known as a geometrical progression, and each term can be obtained from the preceding by multiplying it by $\frac{1}{1+N}$.

Let p denote the present worth of all the coupons.

$$p = \frac{C}{1+N} + \frac{C}{(1+N)^2} + \cdots\cdots\cdots\cdots + \frac{C}{(1+N)^{n-1}} + \frac{C}{(1+N)^n}$$

Multiplying by $\frac{1}{1+N}$

$$\frac{p}{1+N} = \frac{C}{(1+N)^2} + \frac{C}{(1+N)^3} + \cdots\cdots\cdots + \frac{C}{(1+N)^n} + \frac{C}{(1+N)^{n+1}}$$

By subtraction

$$p - \frac{p}{1+N} = \frac{C}{1+N} - \frac{C}{(1+N)^{n+1}}$$

Performing the subtraction in the first member, and taking out the factor $\frac{C}{1+N}$ in the second member,

$$\frac{p+pN-p}{1+N} = \frac{C}{1+N}\left(1 - \frac{1}{(1+N)^n}\right)$$

Multiplying by $1+N$

$$pN = C\left(1 - \frac{1}{(1+N)^n}\right)$$

Hence

$$p = \frac{C}{N}\left(1 - \frac{1}{(1+N)^n}\right)$$

Adding now the present worths of the principal and the coupons, the present worth (P) of the bond is expressed thus:

$$P = \frac{1}{(1+N)^n} + \frac{C}{N}\left(1 - \frac{1}{(1+N)^n}\right)$$

$$= \frac{1}{(1+N)^n} + \frac{C}{N}\left[\frac{(1+N)^n-1}{(1+N)^n}\right]$$

$$= \frac{N+C(1+N)^n-C}{N(1+N)^n}$$

When n is large, $(1+N)$ must be solved by logarithms.[1] If N is the unknown quantity, it must be doubled to get the yield per annum. N may be found by the method of approximations. For example, a 20-year 4 per cent. bond is bought at 95. Find the rate of income on the investment.

$$P = \text{Principal} = .95$$
$$c = .02$$
$$n = 40$$
$$.95 = \frac{N + .02\ (1 = N)^{40} - .02}{N\ (1+N)^{40}}$$
$$.95N\ (1+N)^{40} = .02\ (1+N)^{40} + N - .02$$

Since the bond is sold at a discount N is evidently greater than .02. Try $N = .021$

$\log\ .95 = 9.9777 - 10$	$\log\ .02 = 8.3010 - 10$
$\log\ .021 = 8.3222 - 10$	$\log\ (1.021)^{40} = 0.3600$
$\log\ (1.021)^{40} = 0.3600$	
	$8.6610 - 10$
$8.6599 - 10$	$.04581$
$.0457$	$.001$
	$.04681$

Try $N = .022$	$\log\ .02 = 8.3010 - 10$
$\log\ .95 = 0.9777 - 10$	$\log\ (1.022)^{40} = 0.3800$
$\log\ .022 = 8.3424 - 10$	
$\log\ (1.022)^{40} = 0.3800$	$8.6810 - 10$
$8.7001 - 10$	$.04798$
	$.002$
$.05014$	
	$.04998$

When $N = .021$ the first member is the larger; when $N = .022$, the second member is the larger. Hence the value of N is between .021 and .022. As the values of the two members are nearer when $N = .022$, work downward from that value.

Try $N = .0219$	$\log\ .02 = 8.3010 - 10$
$\log\ .95 = 9.9777 - 10$	$\log\ (1.0219)^{40} = 0.3780$
$\log\ .0219 = 8.3404 - 10$	
$\log\ (1.0219)^{40} = 0.3780$	$8.6790 - 10$
$8.6961 - 10$	$.04775$
	$.0019$
$.04967$	
	$.04965$

[1] The handiest four-place logarithmic tables that are sufficiently accurate are those by Prof. E. N. Huntington of Harvard. They are so arranged that they can be used very rapidly.

These figures are as near as could be expected. Therefore $N = .0219$, and $2N$, or the net yield per annum is 4.38 per cent.

One virtue of the first formula, especially in its earlier stages, is the clearness with which it shows the inaccuracy of valuing N in the present worth of the principal as equal to N in the present worth of the coupons. N should be, and is supposed to be, the prevailing rate of interest for securities of the kind. But the prevailing rate for $1,000 bonds is quite another thing from the prevailing rate on $30 bank deposits.

This reverts to the matter already taken up at large:—the most difficult and most controverted of all the problems of bond mathematics,—with what interest should the coupon payments be credited? It is not so advantageous, is it,—to have an investment (a real estate mortgage for instance) paid off in small instalments as in bulk? Why not? Because the instalments cannot be so advantageously reinvested; in other words, cannot be reinvested at such a high rate of interest for the same degree of security, etc. If the principal sum $\dfrac{1}{(1+N)^n}$ is invested to better advantage, how can the coupon investment be equitably credited with only the advantage which can accrue to it? By crediting the N in the coupon investment $\dfrac{C}{N}\left(1 - \dfrac{1}{(1+N)^n}\right)$ with a value that will bear the same relation to the N in the principal sum that the earning power of the coupon investment bears to the earning power of the principal sum.

In a $1, two-year bond selling to net 6 per cent., the investing public, not realizing the inaccuracy of the present method of computing the tables, and believing that this particular grade of security is worth 6 per cent. as a non-serial investment, pay the equivalent price. If, however, they realize how the bond tables were computed, and if there were a practical way of meeting their desires, they would borrow or lend at what is truly the present worth of a round sum of $1,000 (determined by what that sum could now be reinvested for), plus what is truly the present worth of an annuity of $30 (determined by what each payment could probably be reinvested for).

At a time that $1,000 sums of the given grade net 6 per cent., and savings banks, which furnish the best investment for small sums, pay 4 per cent., the N of $\dfrac{1}{(1+N)^n}$ should be .03 and the N of $\dfrac{C}{N}\left(1-\dfrac{1}{(1+N)^n}\right)$ should be .02. *If at any time the investor will make the proper substitutions in the formula to suit the circumstances of the time, he will have a more accurate idea of what his security ought to net him, than he can get from the present tables.*

A defense of the tables has been set up to the effect that an issue of serial bonds might, with equal justification, be said not to yield the given net rate, because on maturity it might not be possible to invest the proceeds of each bond at the same net rate. But the writer can see no analogy whatever between the net yield in the sinking fund and in the serial issue since it is the *denomination* of the interest sums which causes the greatest trouble, and the denomination of serial bonds is ordinarily the same as the " 1 " in the $\dfrac{1}{(1+N)^n}$ of the formula.

As already stated, practical considerations, to our mind, outweigh the theoretical advantage of trying to maintain a truer net interest rate for " N " in the coupon member of the formula. But again, although the objection, in actual practice, is acknowledged, to a differentiation of the two " Ns," there seems to be no valid defense of the common " N " of the present tables in the statement that if we figure the interest on the coupons at the same as the interest on the principal, then " it has been earned." Surely it is not a question of what *has been* earned. It is a question of what *should be* earned; what *is intended to be earned*. The whole function of the bond tables is to approximate the facts in justice to both lender and borrower. And the facts concerning the rental value of investment money do not correspond with the tables as well as one could wish.

Another virtue of this formula is the clearness with which it shows how to figure the cost or net yield of a bond which must be, or has been, redeemed at a premium. The bond tables do not, of course, show this. If a bond *must* be redeemed at 110,[1] the present worth of the principal is greater, but the present worth of the coupons is not changed. In a $1 bond the

[1] See p. 530, and note.

$$\text{Cost} = \frac{1.1}{(1+N)^n} + \frac{C}{N}\left(1 - \frac{1}{(1+N)^n}\right)$$

Likewise if a $1 bond costing 94 has been called at 102\frac{1}{2}$, what it *has netted* will be found in the same way,—C and n being given in the bond.

$$.94 = \frac{1.025}{(1+N)^n} + \frac{C}{N}\left(1 - \frac{1}{(1+N)^n}\right)$$

Based on the principles of the first formula it is possible to find the price of a bond without reference to the formula or the bond tables, providing there are at hand tables of present worth. For then it is merely necessary to find the present worth of an annuity of $1 for the given interval and duration, and at the given rate, and to multiply this by the number of dollars cash interest. To the result must be added the present worth of $1 principal, multiplied by 1,000 or whatever may be the number of dollars principal returnable at maturity.

A Second Bond Value Formula.   There are other ways of deriving bond formulas; but that which gives the simplest algebraic result is based on the fact that the cost of the bond equals the principal or par value plus the premium or minus the discount. In the case of the bond bought at a premium, how is that premium determined?

Let us again take a $1 two-year 6 per cent. bond netting 4 per cent. The amount received from the semiannual coupon is .03. But the amount entitled to be considered as income is only .02. Therefore the difference, or .01, is a semiannual annuity, the present worth of which, when compounded according to the tables at the net rate, is the same thing as the premium.

By the formula already derived, the present worth of the coupon amount is $\frac{C}{N}\left(1 - \frac{1}{(1+N)^n}\right)$; but since, in a premium bond we seek the present worth, not of C, but of $C-N$, the formula for the premium will be $\frac{C-N}{N}\left(1 - \frac{1}{(1+N)^n}\right)$. Adding par to this to get the present worth of the premium bond, we have

$$\text{Cost} = 1 + \frac{C-N}{N}\left(1 - \frac{1}{(1+N)^n}\right)$$

In the case of the discount bond the net yield is more than the coupon return. The formula for a discount bond, therefore, is

$$\text{Cost} = 1 - \frac{N-C}{N}\left(1 - \frac{1}{(1+N)^n}\right)$$

It will be seen that, even more easily than by the first formula, the cost of a bond may be found from annuity tables by the principles of this formula.[1]

The Application of the Bond Formulas.   The application of the first formula to conditions under which the tables would not apply has been illustrated in p. 531. The application to the bond tables themselves is very easily made. To avoid the use of logarithms, a brief duration is desirable. According to the tables the cost or present worth of a 5 per cent. bond running for a year and a half and netting 4 per cent. will be 101.44, or $1,014.40. This price, it will be remembered, is a decimal approximation correct to two places, or to within 10 cents on a $1,000 bond. According to the first formula in its shortest form

$$
\begin{aligned}
\text{Cost \$1 bond} &= \frac{N + C\,(1+N)^n - C}{N\,(1+N)^n} \\
&= \frac{.02 + .025\,(1.02)^3 - .025}{.02\,(1.02)^3} \\
&= \frac{.0215302}{.02122416} \\
&= 1.01442\ldots\ldots
\end{aligned}
$$

$$\text{Cost \$1,000 bond} = \quad 1014.42$$

It will be seen that the price obtained by the formula corrects a 2-cent error in the tables, due to decimal approximation.

The Application of Bank Discount to Bond Transactions.   He who buys bonds is paid interest, usually at the *end* of each six months' period. If he were paid this interest in advance it would be more profitable to lend to an issuing company by buying its bonds, because whatever interest is already returned is sure; and then again the lender (the buyer) could have this money to let out at interest, as everybody knows; but still further, the lender would not have to lose the interest on the interest accrued to the nominal buying price, as few people realize.

---

[1] For an example of a formula derived on entirely different lines, see *Investment Laws*, Albert Hale, Boston. (Out of print.)

Therefore the banks, which are constant lenders of money, and have to figure more closely than private investors, sometimes insist on buying short-term interest-bearing loans, like town notes, as they buy commercial paper; not at a " basis price," and interest, in accordance with the bond tables and formulas, but by bank discount.

Another reason why banks often prefer to purchase short loans by bank discount (hereafter called discount) is that commercial paper is their chief medium of short investment, and for purposes of comparison of rates, and pursuant to habit, they think best in terms of discount.

The mathematical gain by discount is explained as follows: (a) At a basis price the money invested earns interest on itself at the given rate; (b) but at discount the money invested earns interest on itself, plus the interest on the discount; or what is the same thing, (c) at discount the money invested earns interest on itself, plus the difference between the basis and the discount prices, plus the interest on this difference at the given rate.

Take $1,000 for two months at 6 per cent.

```
        At Basis                          At Discount
                                   1000.00  Principal
                                     10.00  Discount
                                   ───────
                                    990.00  Discount Price
(a)   990.099  Basis Price   (b)    990.00  Discount Price
        9.901  Interest               9.90  Interest
      ─────────                     ───────
    1,000.000  Principal            999.90
                                       .10  Interest gained on the dis-
                                              count
                                   ───────
                                   1,000.00  Principal
                          or (c)    990.00  Discount Price
                                      9.90  Interest
                                   ───────
                                    999.90
                                      .099  Difference bet. basis and
                                              discount prices.
                                      .001  Interest on this difference.
                                   ───────
                                   1,000.000  Principal
```

From (b), the interest gained on the discount   = .10
From (c), the difference between the two prices,   .099
   plus the interest on this difference,   .001
                                                   ────
                                                             = .10

The Difference Between Discount Price and Basis Price for Bonds Maturing Within Six Months, and the Total Ultimate Gain. It will often be of interest to know just the amount the lender gains by bank discount,—particularly on short loans falling within a six months' period. Suppose a 6 per cent. bond having six months to run, discounted at 4 per cent. in the one case, and priced to net 4 per cent. in the other:

The principal sum..................................	1,000.00
The coupon.......................................	30.00
The total principal................................	1,030.00
The discount (6 mos. at 4 per cent.)................	20.60
Discount price of the bond.........................	1,009.40
Basis price of the bond............................	1,009.80
Price gain *at the time of purchase*, by discounting	.40
Interest gained *during* 6 mos. at 4 per cent. on gain of .40	.01
Total *ultimate gain*	.41

Sometimes a quicker way to arrive at the proceeds $1,009.40 will be to take 98 per cent. of $1,030 immediately.

If the bond had been bought on basis, between interest intervals, so that interest would have accrued, the real gain by discount would have been slightly greater.

To Discount a Bond Having Two or More Coupons Attached: i.e., Running Over Six Months. In business one would never be called upon to discount a bond running longer than a year, and only rarely one running beyond six months. Suppose, however, as before a 6 per cent. bond discounted at 4 per cent., against a bond to net 4 per cent., but having nine months to run. For clearness, the purchase of the bond at discount may be looked upon as the purchase of one note (or coupon) of $30, discounted at 4 per cent. for three months, and of another note (principal sum plus the other coupon) of $1,030 discounted at 4 per cent. for nine months:

Proceeds of coupon................................	29.70
Proceeds of principal plus coupon....................	999.10
Proceeds or bank discount price of note	1,028.80

The Theoretical Gain by Buying at Discount Rather Than at Basis, on a Bond Running Over Six Months, but not Bought on an Interest Date:

Basis price of the above bond.............	1,014.60	
Interest accrued for three months..........	15.00	
Total basis cost or flat price *at purchase*...............		1,029.60
Discount price of bond as already found...............		1,028.80
Net gain by discount method *at purchase*..............		.80

Since the basis cost ($1,029.60) and the discount cost ($1,028.80) will ultimately yield the same sums, namely, $30 in three months and $1,030 in nine months, the ultimate gain by the discount method will be the 80 cents difference in cost plus whatever the 80 cents will earn at say 4 per cent. for the nine months compounded theoretically at the end of three months, when the coupon interest is paid,—or in all, 82 cents.

CHAPTER XL

THE USE OF THE BOND TABLES

The bond tables, based on the principles of the formulas, are constructed to show the cost, within at least a cent on $100, of a bond bearing interest at most of the following rates: 2, $2\frac{1}{2}$, 3, $3\frac{1}{2}$, 3.65,[1] 4, $4\frac{1}{2}$, 5, 6, and 7 per cent., and netting from 2 to 7 per cent. Since there is a much greater number of " net yields " it is desirable to know, than of interest rates that bonds ordinarily bear, the length of the page is usually given to the net yield, which is sometimes graded by eighths, such as 2, $2\frac{1}{8}$, $2\frac{1}{4}$, etc., sometimes by tenths, and even by twentieths. In the subjoined sample page of a commonly used book of bond tables,[2] one-tenth per cent. divisions have been combined with one-eighth and one-twentieth.

It will be seen that all but one of the Factors of Net Return are to be found on the page. Premium and discount are indicated in columns of value. The nominal interest rates are at the heads of the columns, and the effective interest rates or net yields, at the side. The duration (20 years) is from the day the bond is purchased until its maturity. The tables are computed usually for semiannual durations from 6 months to 25 or 30 years, and annually from then to 50 years, and, if carried further, by lustra, or five-year periods, to 100 years. The interest interval, however, is not indicated except on the title-page. In this table it is, of course, a six months' period.

Accrued Interest. The table as it stands is accurate to within 10 cents on a $1,000 bond, for a duration of exactly 20 years. For greater accuracy the extended bond tables, correct to the nearest cent on a $1,000,000 bond, should be used. No cashier should content himself with the briefer tables, even though they suffice for ordinary commercial transactions. If, as is probable, the bond was not bought on the exact interest date, to the price indicated in the table must be added " accrued interest " from the last

---

[1] As to the reason for this irregular rate, v. p. 545.

[2] *Bond Values*, Montgomery Rollins, Boston, Fourteenth Edition.

20 YEARS (Interest Payable Semiannually)

Per Cent. Per An.	3%	3½%	4%	4½%	5%	6%	7%
2.90	101.51	109.06	116.60	124.15	131.70	146.80	161.89
3.	100.00	107.48	114.96	122.44	129.92	144.87	159.83
3.10	98.52	105.93	113.34	120.75	128.16	142.98	157.81
3⅛	98.15	105.55	112.94	120.33	127.73	142.52	157.31
3.20	97.06	104.41	111.75	119.09	126.44	141.13	155.82
3¼	96.34	103.66	110.97	118.28	125.59	140.21	154.83
3.30	95.63	102.91	110.19	117.47	124.75	139.30	153.86
3.35	94.93	102.17	109.42	116.66	123.91	138.40	152.89
3⅜	94.58	101.81	109.04	116.27	123.49	137.95	152.41
3.40	94.23	101.44	108.66	115.87	123.08	137.51	151.93
3.45	93.54	100.72	107.90	115.08	122.26	136.62	150.98
3½	92.85	100.00	107.15	114.30	121.45	135.74	150.04
3.55	92.17	99.29	106.41	113.52	120.64	134.87	149.11
3.60	91.50	98.58	105.67	112.75	119.84	134.01	148.18
3⅝	91.16	98.23	105.30	112.37	119.44	133.58	147.72
3.65	90.83	97.88	104.94	111.99	119.04	133.15	147.26
3.70	90.17	97.19	104.21	111.24	118.26	132.30	146.35
3¾	89.51	96.50	103.50	110.49	117.48	131.46	145.44
3.80	88.86	95.82	102.78	109.74	116.70	130.63	144.55
3⅞	87.90	94.81	101.73	108.64	115.56	129.39	143.22
3.90	87.58	94.48	101.38	108.28	115.18	128.98	142.78
4.	86.32	93.16	100.00	106.84	113.68	127.36	141.03
4.10	85.09	91.86	98.64	105.42	112.20	125.76	139.32
4⅛	84.78	91.54	98.31	105.07	111.84	125.37	138.90
4.20	83.87	90.59	97.31	104.03	110.75	124.19	137.63
4¼	83.27	89.96	96.65	103.35	110.04	123.42	136.80
4.30	82.68	89.34	96.00	102.66	109.33	122.65	135.98
4⅜	81.80	88.42	95.04	101.65	108.27	121.51	134.75
4.40	81.51	88.11	94.72	101.32	107.93	121.14	134.35
4½	80.35	86.90	93.45	100.00	106.55	119.65	132.74
4.60	79.22	85.72	92.21	98.70	105.19	118.18	131.16
4⅝	78.94	85.42	91.90	98.38	104.86	117.82	130.77
4.70	78.11	84.55	90.99	97.43	103.86	116.74	129.61
4¾	77.57	83.98	90.39	96.80	103.20	116.02	128.84
4.80	77.02	83.40	89.79	96.17	102.55	115.32	128.08
4⅞	76.22	82.56	88.90	95.24	101.59	114.27	126.95
4.90	75.95	82.28	88.61	94.94	101.27	113.92	126.58
5.	74.90	81.17	87.45	93.72	100.00	112.55	125.10
5.10	73.86	80.09	86.31	92.53	98.76	111.20	123.65
5⅛	73.61	79.82	86.03	92.24	98.45	110.87	123.29
5.20	72.85	79.02	85.19	91.36	97.53	109.87	122.22
5¼	72.34	78.49	84.64	90.78	96.93	109.22	121.51
5.30	71.85	77.97	84.09	90.21	96.33	108.57	120.81
5⅜	71.11	77.19	83.27	89.36	95.44	107.60	119.77
5.40	70.87	76.94	83.01	89.07	95.14	107.28	119.42
5½	69.90	75.92	81.94	87.96	93.98	106.02	118.06
5⅝	68.72	74.68	80.64	86.59	92.55	104.47	116.38
5¾	67.57	73.46	79.36	85.26	91.15	102.95	114.74
5⅞	66.43	72.27	78.11	83.95	89.78	101.46	113.13
6.	65.33	71.11	76.89	82.66	88.44	100.00	111.56

interest date to the day of purchasing; and this accrued interest, figured from any book of aliquot interest tables, will be at the rate of interest the coupon bears, since " accrued interest " serves to reimburse the seller for the bond interest which he has earned up to the date payment is made, and which is paid back to the buyer in the coupon interest at the next interest date.

In accordance with resolutions recently passed by New York bankers in convention, and with the rules of the New York Stock Exchange for dealing in interest-paying bonds on their board, adopted December 23d, 1908:—contracts made after default in payment of interest, and during continuance of default, are to be " Flat " (i.e., without accrued interest). Interest at the rate specified in an interest-bearing bond must be computed on the basis of a 360-day year, i.e., every calendar month is one-twelfth of 360 days, or 30 days; every period from a date in one month to the same date in the following month is 30 days. February, therefore, is taken as a 30-day month. Income bonds must be dealt in " Flat." Except as mentioned, bonds on the New York Stock Exchange and among brokers generally, are now quoted at a price " and interest."

Suppose a 20-year 7 per cent. bond paying interest Jan. 1 and July 1, is bought April 26 for delivery April 27 at 115 and accrued interest. In addition to the $1,150 cost as of Jan. 1 there must be added $22.56, which any book of 360-day interest tables will show has accrued on $1,000 at 7 per cent. for the 3 months 26 days elapsed since Jan. 1. The total cost, therefore, as accepted by financial houses, will be $1,172.56.

The buyer sometimes objects to paying accrued interest, usually because he does not see at first how he will be reimbursed for the accrued interest outlay. We know of sales which have been lost because the prospective buyer thought the interest accumulation would alter materially the basis of net return upon the investment. He will be repaid the $22.56 on July 1, or in 64 days, when the next coupon of $35 is cashed; and the difference of $12.44 between the coupon and the accrued interest reimbursement, is, of course, the interest at 7 per cent. on $1,000 for 64 days to which he is entitled by ownership.

A more defensible objection to the arrangement of accrued interest as it is figured might be raised on the ground that the buyer loses the use of the accrued interest from the time of purchase until he regains it at the next interest period. This slight loss of interest on the accrued interest should be reckoned at the current savings bank rate, and the time should be reckoned, like bank interest time, with 365 days to the year, rather than like bond interest time, with 360 days.

The loss at 4 per cent. on 22.56 for 64 days would be approximately .16 and would probably be collectible at law from the seller. Since a variation of one point in the second decimal of the current bond tables is equivalent to a variation of 10 cents in price, the corrected cost of this bond would be 115.02 and interest. But the difference of .02 in price is too small to change the basis of net return at the second decimal, except for loans of brief duration.

Although " price and interest " is the usual way of selling bonds, sometimes the interest is added to the *basis cost* and the bond sold at a " flat price." Flat price in this case, then, means interest included. Flat price in the Stock Exchange ruling above in reference to defaulted and income bonds, means " without accrued interest,"—quite a different thing. This double use of flat price is quite confusing but general.

Bond Issues of One Fixed Duration. Having disposed of these preliminary matters, we can canvass the uses of the bond tables under all conditions, with this 20-year page for the purpose. First let us assume that the issue is not callable, or redeemable at all, prior to the date regularly set for payment.

To Find the Net Yield at a Tabulated Price is seldom the object, because such a small proportion of all possible prices can be set in the tables. Such price must be in the perpendicular column corresponding with the coupon rate of the bond. The rate per cent. per annum in the extreme left column on the same horizontal line will be the net yield at the price.

To Find the Price at a Tabulated Net Yield is a most common requirement because the ultimate determination of price is net yield, and most of the convenient and generally used decimal and fractional intervals between any per cent. and the next are to be found in the tables. Find the tabulated net yield in the extreme left column. The price along the horizontal line in the perpendicular column bearing the same coupon rate as the issue, will be the proper price. But since the shorter tables are based on bonds of $100 denomination, the price will be multiplied by

10 for a $1,100 bond. This multiplication by 10 without a third correcting decimal is the cause of a possible inaccuracy of as much as 9 cents a bond. For this reason those who deal frequently or in large amounts should be at least familiar with the extended tables.

Untabulated Figures: Interpolation. *To Find the Net Yield at an Untabulated Price.* From this point we deal with the commoner situation in which the given figures have no identical correspondent in the tables. The net yield or price sought will be found between two figures in the tables,—generally adjacent. Therefore the process of finding the untabulated figure is a process of Interpolation.

What will be the net return of a 6 per cent. 20-year bond (with 20 years to run from date of purchase) selling at 125? In the 6 per cent. column 125 lies between 125.37 and 124.19. 125.37 is a $4\frac{1}{8}$ per cent. basis and 124.19 is a 4.20 basis. The net return of 125 must be somewhere between $4\frac{1}{8}$ and 4.20 per cent., but nearer $4\frac{1}{8}$; or expressing both rates by decimals only, between 4.125 and 4.200 per cent.

There is no direct mathematical process by which this yield can be determined with exactness; but there are two methods of approximation, the first of which, called the method of proportion, can be more easily understood and applied, and suffices for most purposes. It may be expressed almost graphically:

Difference	Yield		Price	Difference
?............	$\begin{cases} 4.125 \end{cases}$	=	$125.37 \rbrace$	37
?............	x	=	$125.00 \rbrace$	
	4.200	=	$124.19 \rbrace$	81
.075........				.... 1.18

$$\frac{.37}{1.18} \times .075 = .024$$

$$4.125 + .024 = 4.149 \text{ or } 4.15$$

The simple presentation is easier of understanding than the formal statement, which is as follows: Since the lower the price the higher the net return, an intermediate rate of yield will be numerically distant from its adjacent rates in approximately the same ratio that the intermediate price is distant from its adjacent prices.

Let x = the unknown yield. The difference between x and 4.125 will bear approximately the same relation to the total income variation of .075 that the price difference of .37 bears to the total price variation of 1.18.

$$\frac{x-4.125}{.075} = \frac{.37}{1.18}$$

$$x-4.125 = \frac{.37}{1.18} \times .075 = .024$$

$$x = 4.149 \text{ or } 4.15$$

A variation of this first method shortens the computations, but inclines to be slightly less accurate, because price differences lessen as prices approach par. If instead of taking the net yield corresponding to the nearest price above, i.e., 125.00, we had taken the yield that was .10 less than 4.20, the process would have been simplified as follows:

Difference		Yield		Price		Difference
		4.10	=	125.76 ⎫		.76
		x	=	125.00 ⎬		
		4.20	=	124.19 ⎭		.81
.10						1.57

$$\frac{.76}{1.57} \times .10 = .048$$

$$4.10 + .048 = 4.148 \text{ or } 4.15$$

The second method, contrived by Mr. Charles E. Sprague, is a method of gradual approximation. The text of Mr. Sprague's explanation is as follows:

"Let us give the name of trial divisor to the difference between the values of a 4 per cent. and a 5 per cent. bond on the same basis and for the same time; or, what is the same thing, between a 5 per cent. and a 6 per cent.; always 1 per cent. difference in the nominal rates.

"Assume arbitrarily for trial any income rate; the nearer the true rate, as indicated by the tables, the less the work of approximation. Find the trial divisor at this trial rate. Divide the given premium (or discount) by this trial divisor. The quotient is to be subtracted from the nominal rate if the bond is above par, or added to it if below par; the result will be an approximate rate which will be nearer the truth than the trial rate, being too great when the trial rate is too small, and vice versa. This approximate may be used as a new trial rate, and will result in a still closer approximation."

In the 6 per cent. 20-year bond cited above as selling at 125, it is given to find the net yield. In the 20-year 6 per cent. column start with 4.20—*too large*, but the basis for a trial divisor.

A 20-year 6 per cent. bond on a 4.20 basis is worth......... 124.19
A 20-year 7 per cent. bond on a 4.20 basis is worth........ 137.63
_____
Therefore the trial divisor is.......................... 13.44

25 ÷ 13.44 = 1.86   6 — 1.86 = 4.14

4.14 is *too small*, but the basis for a new trial divisor.
The trial divisor of 4.20 = 13.44

           4.14 =   x
           4.10 = 13.56   (From the tables.)

By proportion the trial divisor of 4.14 = 13.51

25 ÷ 13.51 = 1.85   6 — 1.85 = 4.15

4.15 is *too great*, but the basis of a new trial divisor.
The trial divisor of 4.15 is 13.50.

25 ÷ 13.50 = 1.852   6 — 1.852 = 4.148

4.148 is *too small*, and 4.15 is *too great*, but the net yield is found to two decimals, and agrees with the result found from the method of approximation by proportion. 4.15 is approximately the net yield of a 20-year 6 per cent. bond at 125.

To Find the Net Yield at a Flat Price is a problem of like nature to the previous. Since flat price for undefaulted bonds means price with interest accrued, and accrued interest is never taken into consideration, commercially, in reckoning interest yield, the procedure is to subtract the interest accumulation to find the " price and interest," and continue as before.

Because bonds in default are sold flat they may reach a high premium if the prospect is bright that overdue coupons will soon be honored. Obviously the return may be no such low rate as the premium at first glance might suggest. But it cannot be computed until the time of delayed coupon payment is made known. Then it will most easily be found by substitution in the first formula.

To Find the Price at an Untabulated Net Yield calls for the interpolation by proportion of a price between two others in the tables. By the semi-graphic method employed before it is easily expressed for the 20-year 6 per cent. bond as follows: At what price (for instance) does the above bond net 4.15 per cent.?

Difference		Yield		Price		Difference
		4.10	=	125.76		
.10		4.15	=	x		1.57
		4.20	=	124.19		

Rate difference of .10 = 1.57 of price difference
Rate difference of .05 = .785 of price difference
125.76 — .785 = 124.975 = 124.98

It will occur to many that simple proportion may not always be accurate, even to the two decimal places of the tables. This conclusion will be reached on noting in the 20-year page that the difference in price of a 6 per cent. bond on a 2.90 and a 3.00 basis is not the same as the difference between the prices at a 3.00 and a 3.10 per cent. basis. The former difference is 1.93 and the latter 1.89. A careful examination of many similar cases will show, among premium bonds, that the higher the premium the greater the difference; and among discount bonds, that the greater the discount the less the difference; and since at a given yield, the longer the loan the greater the premium or discount, the greater opportunity for error lies in computing intermediate proportion in long-term loans. A means must be found for correcting these discrepancies and for ascertaining how short the maturities for which correction is needed.

Mr. Sprague has ingeniously devised a " one-eighth rule " which correctly adjusts the error; but, so far as the writer knows, no one has explained how this rule is derived.

Because the error is greater in long loans, and at high premiums, it will be most apparent and easy of correction in, say a 100-year, 5 per cent. bond. It will be greater, also, when the interpolated yield is the furthest possible (.05) from the nearest tabulated yield.

In the excerpt below, from the 100-year page of the tables, the " 2d difference " is obtained by subtraction in the column of the " 1st difference."

To correct the price of a 2.75 per cent. yield found by proportion:

	Basis		Price		1st Difference	2d Difference
(large)	2.70	=	179.36			
(small)	2.75	=	176.53	(by proportion)	5.66	
(large)	2.75	=	176.49	(by the table)		.31
(large)	2.80	=	173.70			
(large)	2.90	=	168.35		5.35	

The first column of differences shows that the *rate* of difference changes materially between each .10 per cent. of the income bases; and the second column of differences shows what the rate of change is. Since in this case we have the price at a 2.75 basis, not only by proportion, but by the tables,—it remains only to establish some approximate relation between the discrepancy 176.53 —176.49, and the rate of change in each .10 per cent. of basis (.31) to have a method for correcting the error in simple proportion.

$$176.53—176.49 = .04 = \tfrac{1}{8} \text{ of } .31, \text{ approximately.}$$

Hence the rule: Whether above par or below, subtract one-eighth of the second difference from the approximate value of the proportion to find the true value.

In order to make a correction the second difference must be more than .04, so that one-eighth of it, when "rounded off," will equal .01 or more,—to be subtracted from the price obtained by proportion. Occasional second differences of .05 will be found in the ordinary tables as early as the 22d year, and the test should therefore be applied from the 22d year on,—that is for bonds running for 22 years or more.

To Find the Net Yield at an Untabulated Coupon Rate. By the laws of some states (such as those requiring all bonds to be sold at par or above) it is sometimes necessary for the smaller municipalities to issue bonds at unusual rates of interest. On other grounds 3.65 per cent. (one cent a day on $100) is an odd coupon rate of sufficient vogue and long standing to have obtained a place in some tables. All such untabulated rates may be approximated by proportion.

To find the net yield of a 20-year 3.35 per cent. bond at 72.

Difference	Coupon Rate		Net Yield	Difference
.35	⎰ 3.00	=	5.28	
	⎱ 3.35	=	x	
.15	⎰			.62
.50	⎱ 3.50	=	5.90	

$$\frac{.35}{.50} \times .62 = .43$$
$$5.28 + .43 = 5.71$$

That results like this are only approximate is settled by reversing the process. A 20-year 3.35 per cent. bond on a 5.71 basis gives by proportion the price 72.08 instead of the price 72, with which we started.

To Find the Price at an Untabulated Coupon Rate. From the

second bond formula, we know that a premium or discount may be looked upon as a " sinking fund " to amortize, or accumulate, the difference between the coupon rate and the net rate; and that at maturity the fund so collected will equal the premium or discount.

The difference between a cash rate of 5 per cent. and a net rate of 4 per cent. is $10 per bond; and between a cash rate of 6 per cent. and a net rate of 4 per cent. is $20; and between 7 per cent. and 4 per cent. is $30, etc. Therefore the premium, or discount, or price, increases in arithmetical ratio with the increase in cash rate. Stated more generally, the price of a bond, at any net rate, and at any odd coupon or cash rate may be exactly ascertained to two decimals by proportion with the prices of larger and smaller coupon rates at the same net yield. Therefore it is very easy to find the price at a given net yield of the municipal $4\frac{1}{4}$s, like the recent New York City issues.

In proof, read the 20-year table from left to right, at any income basis. At 4.70 net, each half per cent. in cash rate increases the price by 6.44, and 1 per cent. increase in cash rate doubles the increase to 12.88; except that the increase may be .01 less, due to the rounding of the last decimal in the price.

To find the price of a 20-year 9 per cent. bond on a 4.70 basis

Coupon Rate		Price	Difference
3%	=	78.11	
6%	=	116.74	38.63
9%	=	x	38.63

By proportion a 9 per cent. bond on a 4.70 basis = 116.74 + 38.63 = 155.37. [1]

This is a more accurate ascertainment of the price than to find the price difference between 6 and 7 per cent., multiply it by 2, and add the result to the 7 per cent. price (which would give 155.35), since the loss by approximation, in rounding the second decimal in the 7 per cent. price, is doubled when multiplied by 2.

---

[1] This method is not strictly interpolation (between two given rates), but rather projection; but, as the principles are the same, we call attention to a distinction rather than a difference.

To find the price of a 20-year 3.35 per cent. bond on a 4.70 per cent. basis.

Difference	Coupon Rate		Price	Difference
	3.00	=	78.11	
.35	3.35	=	x	6.44
	3.50	=	84.55	
.15				
.50				

$$\frac{.35}{.50} \times 6.44 = 4.51 \qquad\qquad 78.11 + 4.51 = 82.62$$

To Find the Net Yield at an Untabulated Duration. Any bond not bought on an interest date may be considered as having an untabulated duration.

To find the net yield of a 7 per cent. bond maturing in 20 years, 2 months, and 15 days, the price of which is 159.83.

Duration		Net Yield
20 yrs.	=	3.00
20 yrs. $2\frac{1}{2}$ mos.	=	x
20 yrs. 6 mos.	=	3.05

$$\frac{2\frac{1}{2}}{6} \times .05 = .02$$
$$3.00 + .02 = 3.02$$

Commercial usage goes no further in correcting the net yield between interest periods; but in short-time loans the interest lost on the accrued interest may alter the yield perceptibly, as already noted.

The loss on a $1,000 bond or note-bearing interest at $3\frac{1}{2}$ per cent., bought 3 months and 27 days after the last semiannual interest date, is 8 cents, or approximately .01 in the price column. If this bond or note matured at the next interest date, and were sold at par and interest, the loss in interest on the accrued interest would bring the cost up to 101 and interest, and change the yield from 3.50 to 3.49. *Tantulum sufficit!* This is one reason why very short-term loans are advantageously bought by discount rather than as interest-bearing.

If a bond runs over 50 years it might even be bought on an interest date and yet have untabulated duration, since the tables ordinarily give prices and bases only at 5-year intervals for terms longer than 50 years. But this lustral variation in net yield admits correction by proportion.

To find the net yield of a 98-year 5 per cent. bond selling at 220.

$$
\begin{array}{ccc}
\text{Duration} & & \text{Net Yield} \\
100 \text{ years} & = & 2.11 \\
98 \text{ years} & = & \text{x} \\
95 \text{ years} & = & 2.09
\end{array}
$$

$\frac{2}{5} \times .02 = .01$ (to 2 decimals)

$2.11 - .01 = 2.10$

To Find the Price at an Untabulated Duration. Since only two of the 365 days in the year are interest dates (for most bonds), and the price at a given yield always changes radically from one semiannual period to the next, it is almost always necessary, in finding the price of a bond at a given net yield, to adjust it to the day of purchase. This is done by proportion. At what price will a bond running 20 years, 4 months, and 10 days, net 4 per cent.?

Difference	Duration	Price	Difference
4 1–3 mos.	20 yrs. $=$	113.68	
	20 yrs. 4 1–3 mos. =	x	.22
1 2–3 mos.	20 1–2 yrs. $=$	113.90	
6 months			

$\dfrac{4\ 1\text{–}3 \times .22}{6} = .16$ (approx.)

$113.68 + .16 = 113.84$

Since the price of this bond varies .22 in 180 days, or .01 in about 8 days, or 10 cents in 8 days, there is an approximate variation of about a cent a day. At the given net and cash bases the *rate* of difference in price over a number of years is so constant (not varying over .01 per annum) that no correction of the method of proportion is necessary, within an interest interval.

Bond Values Between Coupon Maturities. Bond value tables for the handling of bonds payable semiannually show the value of bonds longer than 6 months on coupon date only—once in 180 days. At all other times the values in the tables need some adjustment. This does not apply to short term bond value tables which show values and yields every day 1 to 180 days. There is no implication of inaccuracy or incompleteness of the tables; they show exactly what their authors maintain: accuracy at the coupon maturity. It takes 740 large pages for a complete bond value table, and it would be utterly impracticable to multiply this by 180.

Bond value tables (except for short bonds) are based on compounding of interest semiannually, and the mathematically correct value for bonds at a date other than the coupon maturity must be computed in such way as to give due consideration to the compounding of interest during the broken period as well as for all the complete coupon periods during the life of the bond.

The United States Treasury Department, the Federal Reserve banks, dealers in government bonds, certificates of indebtedness and short term equipment notes compute these broken periods accurately, and require them to be so computed on the part of others trading with them. To accomplish this their accounting departments are required to compute their problems according to the formula for bond values.

With the exception of the instances just noted, values of bonds and notes at broken periods longer than 6 months are generally figured by ordinary interpolation, so-called. This method, in spite of its mathematical inaccuracy, became the practice more or less of necessity on account of the large amount of labor and time necessary to figure out ordinary transactions by a mathematical formula. It is common knowledge that the value of a bond for 9 months is not one half the sum of the values for 6 months and 1 year, yet the agreement to treat it as such is the basis of ordinary interpolation.

The error resulting from the use of ordinary interpolation—direct proportioning—always favors the seller, if the exact days are taken into the calculations. This, however, is of no advantage to the dealer since he buys as much as he sells; however, the investor, insurance company, savings bank, or trustee who buys to hold to maturity, makes a positive and permanent loss through this inaccuracy.

Ordinary interpolation itself is not applied according to a definite and fixed method. Some dealers, usually by agreement within a given group or territory, disregard odd days over the even months. This plan not only increases the error but it aggravates the lack of uniformity. If an institution purchases $1,000,000 of 5 per cent. bonds having a maturity of 15 years, 8 months and 15 days on a 6 per cent. basis, it will pay $258 more than the true basis if the invoice is figured by ordinary interpolation and the time treated as exactly 8 months. It will pay $70 less than a true basis in the same transaction assuming that the maturity be treated as 15 years and 9 months.

When a trade is made at a price, say 99 or 101 and interest, the price and accrued interest alone are concerned. When, however, securities are sold upon a basis, which is very common in the case of municipal bonds and equipment notes, the yield rate is the prime consideration. Where several propositions to loan money to a municipality or corporation differ either in coupon rates or maturities, or both, the basis is the only true measure of the cost of the loan; the basis alone determines which of several propositions is the better for the borrower.

VARIATION FROM ACCURACY RESULTING FROM PROPORTIONING THE DIFFERENCES, OR ORDINARY INTERPOLATION

(Seven per Cent. Bond—Six per Cent. Basis)

Time to Run (Years, Months and Days)	Result by Ordinary Plan	Correct	Error per $1,000,000
8–11–29	106.875125	106.874865	$ 2.60
8–11–0	106.827807	106.821247	65.60
8–10–0	106.778858	106.768344	105.14
8– 9–0	106.729908	106.718062	118.46
8– 8–0	106.680958	106.670411	105.47
8– 7–0	106.632009	106.625406	66.03
8– 6–1	106.584691	106.584429	2.62

The minimum error is for dates close to either coupon maturity, and the maximum error is at the mid-point, or three months between coupon dates, which is the average time for all transactions.

The discrepancy for an 8 years, 9 months 4 per cent. bond on an 8 per cent. basis would be: $146.45 on $1,000,000. A high yield produces a relatively higher discrepancy.

Practically every commodity which sells upon the market has its standard of weight and measure; every city and town employs an official whose duty it is to see that the weights and measures comply with the standard. Therefore it seems highly important that there should be a true measure for bonds and notes, applicable at all times and in all places, giving both buyer and seller the same effective rate when a transaction is made on a basis. The agreement to accept ordinary interpolation which gives to the seller something more than the true basis and to the buyer something less than the true basis, does not give to financial transactions a true standard of measure such as is demanded in all mercantile transactions.

Incorrect interpolation is no longer necessary. A table of Factors [1] has recently been published which, coördinated with ordinary bond tables, gives the value of bonds and notes at any day during their life with mathematical accuracy. The results can be obtained not only correctly, but more quickly than by the old method of incorrect interpolation.

To Find the Net Yield at an Untabulated Interest Interval. The bond tables in ordinary use are, of course, based on an interest interval of 6 months. It is sometimes desirable to compare semiannual interest-bearing bonds with quarterly and annual interest-bearing bonds to see what would be gained in net yield or price, in the former case, or lost, in the latter.

In order to compare such bonds it must be remembered that by net yield is meant, as before, net yield per annum, figured *semiannually;* for if net yield meant one thing in a semiannual bond, and another thing in a quarterly or annual bond, there would be no common basis of comparison.

What would be the gain in the semiannual net yield if a 20-year 6 per cent. semiannual bond, selling at 125, were payable quarterly?

Find the cash rate of the quarterly bond.

First quarter's coupon....................$15.00
Interest on coupon at 4 per cent. for 91 days.. .15
Second quarter's coupon................... 15.00
Semiannual cash rate of quarterly bond......30.15 = 6.03 per cent.
                                                                       coupon rate
Semiannual cash rate of semiannual bond....30.00 = 6.00 per cent.
                                                                       coupon rate

The problem now resolves itself into finding the net yield of a 20-year 6 per cent. semiannual bond at 125, and a 20-year 6.03 per cent. semiannual bond at 125. The difference in net yield will be the figure sought.

Coupon Rate		Net Yield
6.00	=	4.149
6.03	=	x
7.00	=	5.007

x = 5.174
4.175 − 4.149 = .026 = .03

[1] Devised by Arthur S. Little. Published by Financial Publishing Co., Boston.

Approximately, then, the gain would be .03 per cent. in net yield if this semiannual bond were payable quarterly. Quite generally, as in this case, the gain in net rate and in cash rate will be the same.

To Find the Price at an Untabulated Interest Interval. Suppose the two 20-year semiannual 6 per cent. bonds just mentioned were not selling at 125, but on a 4 per cent. semiannual basis. To find the value of the quarterly bond. The process again is based on the coupon or cash rates.

$$
\begin{array}{ccc}
\text{Coupon Rate} & & \text{Price} \\
6.00 & = & 127.36 \\
6.03 & = & \text{x} \\
7.00 & = & 127.03
\end{array}
$$

$$\frac{3}{100} \times 13.67 = .41$$

$$127.36 + .41 = 127.77$$

To Find the Price of Bonds Issued or Maturing at Other than the Regular Interest Dates. There are issues of bonds, the prices of which cannot under any conditions be determined by the bond value tables. There has been reference, for illustration, to an issue which is called at a premium, and thus not conformable to the conditions of the tables. There are other issues which, for price, are not referable to the tables (although the error of the tables might be slight) because the date of issuance, or maturity, or both, does not coincide with the regular interest dates; and the bond tables presuppose coincidence.

There are two ways by which the issuing company can meet the resulting irregular interest obligations: by establishing long or short initial or terminal periods. If the overlap is only a month or two, the adjacent periods will probably be lengthened; otherwise there will be short periods. In either case the value of the interest coupons will naturally bear the same relation to the semiannual coupons as the duration of the irregular period bears to the six months' period.

Now we have seen that, in accordance with the principle of interest-compounding, the bond value for each successive period is found by multiplying the value of the preceding period by the ratio of increase, and subtracting the coupon value. Conversely, therefore, the value of any period can be found by adding the coupon to the next succeeding value, and dividing by the ratio of increase.

If, for instance, then, we are seeking to ascertain the value of a bond with an irregular initial period, but a regular terminal, we have only to find the value for the regular periods by the bond interest tables, add to this the long or short coupon value, and divide by the long or short interest ratio. The result is the initial value of the bond.

Since the principle is applicable at any point in the life of the bond, the same process may be applied to short or long terminal periods. First find the value for the regular periods, add the irregular terminal coupon value, and divide by the irregular ratio of increase. This rule gives us the basis price of a bond having less than six months to run.

So, also, if we are seeking the price at issuance, of a bond with irregular initial and terminal periods, the process must be applied to both irregular periods.

The Pennsylvania Railroad Company had outstanding an issue of Convertible $3\frac{1}{2}$s, due Oct. 1, 1915. Interest was payable June 1, and Dec. 1. There was a short coupon of $11.67. Suppose a bond of this issue was bought Nov. 1, 1910, to net 4 per cent. To find the cost it will be necessary to use the extended tables.

Price as of June 1, 1915, maturity.......................$979.2526
Terminal Coupon..   11.67
                                                        ─────────
                                                        $990.9226

Terminal ratio of increase $=1.01333$, etc.

Price for the full life of the bond $\dfrac{990.9226}{1.01333,\text{ etc.}}$ $977.88

The natural impulse would be to figure the price from the tables as if the interest dates were April and October. This price is 977.89. The difference in this case is, and it ordinarily would be, 1 cent per bond. Therefore the correct method of price ascertainment is necessary only for schedules of amortization and accumulation.

Bond Issues of Serial Duration. One of the characteristics of industrial corporations is that they consume their own assets, very generally, in the production of wealth. Now that many of the larger industrial companies have reached a financial stability that warrants bonding, many of their conservative issues are planned to be retired in serial instalments in such way that the depreciation of the plant or commodity, or stock, which is behind the bonds, will be less, annually, than the decrease in amount of bonds outstanding. In this way the equity, or margin of safety, increases during the life of the loan.

To Find the Price of a Serial Issue. If the loan is not paid off in equal amounts at equal intervals, there will probably be no way of computing the price at which the loan, as a whole, should be bought to return a given ratio on the investment for the length of time each bond is held. All that can be done in such a case is to price each maturity on its basis of net return and add the various costs.

But, perhaps, more often than not there is uniformity in the amounts and intervals. The commonest funded instalment loans are the 10-year serial equipment, steamship, and timber issues, which are usually retired in equal annual amounts, beginning one year after date of issuance. The price of an issue of this sort, *en bloc*, at a given net yield, will be found by adding the prices of the several members of the series, at the given net rate, and dividing by the number of maturities to get the average. The price of a 10-year serial equipment issue of 5s on a 4 per cent. basis, to be retired in equal annual amounts, is 104.76.

It is still a common but wholly wrongful custom to find the price of a serial issue at the " average maturity," but the result is materially in error, because the price of the several maturities is governed not only by *duration* (to which the arithmetical mean would apply), but also by the semiannual compounding of the difference between the net and the cash rates, to build the sinking fund, and there is no arithmetical mean to compound interest.

The average price of this serial loan is 104.76, and the price at the average maturity is 104.89. Therefore the error in averaging the maturity is .13, which, in premium bonds, results in so much loss to the dealer who buys the entire issue on "basis" at the average maturity, and sells on basis, figuring each maturity. Conversely, in discount bonds the dealer would have gained by the error.

To Find the Net Yield of a Serial Issue. If this loan were brought to a dealer in its entirety, and offered at the price of 104.76, he would have no mathematical means of finding by the tables that the net rates of the several maturities *taken separately* were all 4 per cent. The average price was not found directly from the tables but by averaging the several prices, and to find the net yield he must have the several prices. But although the average price can be found from the several prices, the process does not admit of reversal within the reasonable limits of simple arithmetic or algebra.

If the dealer knows or believes that the price was based on a uniform net yield for the several maturities, his rule of thumb method of ascertaining it is to take the average maturity, and if the average price is a premium, to find what net yield in the tables corresponds in the 5 per cent. column to the next lower price. If the price is a discount—to the next higher price.

Bonds of Optional Duration. Many issues of bonds that have a definite date of maturity may be redeemed by the issuing company before maturity. These are sometimes called redeemable issues, although, unfortunately, the same term is also applied, generally, to all bonds that do not represent perpetual loans. For this reason the writer advocates (and has followed in this book) the use of the phrases " terminable bonds " in antithesis to " perpetual bonds," and " redeemable bonds " in antithesis to bonds not callable before maturity. The terms of redemption for bonds of fixed maturity are various. They may be callable any time after issuance; or at a certain date; or before a certain date; [1] or between certain dates; or on and after a certain date. They may be callable at par; or at a premium. All these phases of optional redemption affect the mathematics of investment, particularly of bond values.

Since *duration* is the variable, the problem is to find whether the earliest or latest maturity should be the basis for computations of price and net return. The principle involved is that the interests of borrower and lender are antagonistic, and since the option of redemption (or repayment) lies with the borrower, the lender should be on the safe side, and figure the value (return) of his investment on the least favorable possibility.

Duration Computed for Bonds Redeemable at Par.

(a) When the cost is par and the redemption at par, duration is negligible, for the cash and net return are always the same.

(b) When the cost is a discount and the redemption at par, the longer the duration the less it will yield, or be worth; therefore assume ultimate maturity.

---

[1] An unusual restriction; but the Chicago City Railway Company First 5s are optional at 110 and interest if called for payment before February 1, 1912, but not thereafter.

(c) When the cost is a premium and the redemption at par, the longer the duration the greater the yield; therefore assume proximate maturity.

Duration Computed for Bonds Redeemable at a Premium.

(a) When the cost of the bond is par, or

(b) When the cost of the bond is a discount, and the redemption at a premium, the yield will be least if held to maturity, therefore assume ultimate maturity.

(c) When cost and redemption are at a premium, it will be necessary to find the net return to the ultimate maturity; and then, if the price which corresponds to this net return or value, at the proximate maturity, is less than the callable price, it is correct to assume the bond will not be called (since if it were called, more would be paid, mathematically, than it is worth), and consequently to figure the bond to the ultimate maturity. But if the basis price is more than the callable price, we must assume proximate maturity.

In the two cases in which it is fair to assume the bonds will be called at the earliest possible time, it is customary to indicate the possibilities of duration and net return, for instance as follows:

"20–40 year 6s, to net 4.40–6.00 per cent."

That is, the bonds are 40-year 6s, redeemable in 20 years, and selling at a price to net 4.40 per cent., if called as soon as redeemable, and it is right to expect they will be. For any length of time they may be allowed to run after 20 years they will return the investor the full cash rate.

Other Bond Tables. Besides the ordinary commercial tables and the extended tables, there are others of service to people who deal extensively in bonds, notably those for serial issues and for convertible bonds, and the tables used in Canada in connection with municipal bond issues, to figure the cost and net return of bonds which must be repaid, periodically, in sums to cover the interest and such proportionate part of the principal as will retire the issue by equal instalments after a certain number of years. This scholarly treatment of debt reduction is on the decline in Canada, and it has never been of much interest to United States investors. Our bond houses do not encourage it because investors prefer to have their principal returned to them in round amounts.

CHAPTER XLI

THE KEEPING OF INVESTMENT ACCOUNTS

The Basis of Investment Value. It is the main premise on which rests this entire treatment of bond principles, that the fundamental difference between speculation and investment lies in the source of anticipated revenue and the methods employed to achieve that revenue. Profit is the aim of speculation: income, that of investment. One of the leading periodicals devoted to the subject of speculation, on the first page of text regularly prints the distinction for its motto:

"Speculation: Operations wherein intelligent foresight is employed for the purpose of deriving a profit from price changes.

"Investment: The placing of capital in a more or less permanent way, mainly for the income to be derived therefrom." [1]

Although security of principal is of first investment importance, it is not the *distinguishing* characteristic of investment, but rather of hoarding. Hoarding does not come within the category of finance. Security of principal may be as strong an influence in real estate speculation,—particularly speculation in improved business property,—as it is in bond investment.

Again, in the opening paragraphs of the first of these chapters on bond mathematics, income, the investment essential, was seized upon as the value-determining factor on which all else depended. " Value is most significantly expressed in terms of income yield. Indeed income yield is the only common denominator of security values."

By the statement that the net return is the only common denominator of values is meant that there is no value significance to an isolated fact of price or cash return, or duration.

For example, a $1,000, 5 per cent. bond, selling at 99.07 and interest, may be cheaper than another selling at 98.07 and interest, because it may " run off " in two years and thus net $5\frac{1}{2}$ per cent., whereas the other may run for 10 years and net only $5\frac{1}{4}$ per cent.

[1] *The Ticker and Investment Digest*, New York.

Or the second bond, running 10 years, might be bought at 98.07 and 8 years later be sold at 99.07, yet result in a loss, because it was bought at such a high price that it netted only $5\frac{1}{4}$ per cent., and to avoid loss should have been sold at not less than 99.53, a $5\frac{1}{4}$ per cent. basis.   Or again, a 6 per cent. bond, with 4 years to run, which is purchased at 105.44, is cheaper, mathematically, than a 3 per cent. bond of like duration purchased at 95, because the premium bond makes a net return of $4\frac{1}{2}$ per cent. and the 3 per cent. bond, of only $4\frac{3}{8}$ per cent.

It is, therefore, only in the interrelation of all three facts: the price, the periodic cash interest, and the life of the loan,—that valid investment value is derived for purposes of appraisal and comparison.   There is only one universal expression of this value: in percentage of net income to invested capital.   Any $1,000 bond that nets 5 per cent., semiannual, is always more valuable, mathematically, than any $1,000 semiannual bond that nets 4.99 per cent., irrespective of cost, coupons, or maturity.

Book Value.   If the contention is correct that investment, as distinguished from speculation, seeks revenue from income rather than from profit, and that investment value is expressed by, and determined by the rate of net income, then a proper keeping of investment accounts has, as its basis, the net income return on the capital.   Since the investment assumption ordinarily is that the bond will be held to maturity, it is entered on the books at cost, and carried from interest date to interest date on the basis of investment value corresponding to the cost. Or, to reverse the statement,—more in line with the facts,—since the cost of the bond is determined *solely* by the rate of income yielded by bonds of its particular grade and characteristics, the cost is entered as the first investment value, and all subsequent investment values to the last, which is par, are entered at the same net rate.

True book value, therefore, may be defined as the price at which the bond must be sold, at any given time, to bring the new purchaser the same basis of yield as the bond brought the former purchaser at the former cost.

Then how absurd it is for any one who pretends to keep books, to carry at the purchase price until maturity any bond not bought at par, and then, as by magic, to wipe out the premium cost or to create the discount gain. Equally fictitious is the labor-saving device of charging to profit and loss the premium or discount of a bond, at the time it is bought. In either case, if the bond should be sold, there would be no record, on the books, of the gain or loss by the sale. Such a system of bookkeeping for trust accounts is illegal in some states and inequitable everywhere; for the integrity of either capital or income will be impaired, with hardship to the beneficiaries under one or the other. More illogical, although more safe, are regulations such as those under which the savings banks of Massachusetts keep their books, by which discount bonds must be carried at cost, but premium bonds may be charged down to par, or not, within the discretion of the bank.

Market Value. Although income is the sole revenue consideration of *pure* investment, and net income return the sole basis of book value, yet, perhaps, as often as not there is the twofold purpose to seek revenue and profit; or even if profit does not enter in, at some future time it may be desirable to convert the investment into cash. The latter is often the situation when a mercantile concern puts its surplus into bonds, or is to be dissolved. Liquidation value, or market value, therefore, may often be written to advantage with book value; but the two should not be confused. Market value, in bonds, is not the definite, predicable amount that book value is. The market value of all issues, except the very active, is very generally overestimated in the annual report. Just as book value is the investment value, market value is the speculative value; and is to be associated with the speculative possibilities indicated in the quotations of the following chapters.

When an investment is liquidated by sale, the profit or loss, which should be the difference between the book value and the true market value, will, in the case of trust funds, be credited to, or debited from the capital, and should not be accounted to affect the income; but the income thereafter is based on the new principal, and thus is affected in its proper ratio.

SCHEDULES OF AMORTIZATION AND ACCUMULATION

Mr. Charles E. Sprague has published various schedules of amortization and accumulation, showing how bond accounts should be carried. To these the reader is referred for a series of models more complete than the following, which are based on Mr. Sprague's. [1]

The constructive principle is from the second formula: that " the cost of the bonds equals the principal or par value plus the premium, or minus the discount; " and that " the premium or discount of a bond . . . bought above or below par, is the present worth of an annuity of the difference of rates." [2]

Schedules for Bonds Bought on Basis. To cover in a brief account the entire mathematical history of a loan, suppose a 6 per cent. 4-year semiannual bond, issued Feb. 1, 1920, and bought at a price to net $4\frac{1}{2}$ per cent.

Date	Cash Interest 6%	Net Income $4\frac{1}{2}$%	Amortization	Book Value	Par
1920 Feb. 1				(cost) 1054.40	1000.00
Aug. 1	30.00	23.70	6.30	1048.10	
1921 Feb. 1	30.00	23.60	6.40	1041.70	
Aug. 1	30.00	23.40	6.60	1035.10	
1922 Feb. 1	30.00	23.30	6.70	1028.40	
Aug. 1	30.00	23.10	6.90	1021.50	
1923 Feb. 1	30.00	23.00	7.00	1014.50	
Aug. 1	30.00	22.80	7.20	1007.30	
1924 Feb. 1	30.00	22.70	7.30	1000.00	
	240.00	185.60	54.40		

The derivation of the tables is explained on page 530 et seq. An interpretation might be as follows: On Aug. 1, 1912, the value of this investment will be $1,021.50. To realize without loss, this sum at least must be obtained if the bond should then be sold. Of the $30.00 received on cashing the coupon, $23.10 goes to the person entitled to receive the income from the investment; and the remaining $6.90 must be laid aside in the sinking fund with the previous sums, so that at maturity the fund will wipe out the premium which was paid at purchase, but which will not be returned at maturity. As it is, the sinking fund now amounts to $32.90; and this, added to the premium of $21.50 which the bond is still worth, would not take care of the total premium of $54.40.

The person entitled at maturity to the capital invested in this bond is protected therefore by the amortization fund; for

[1] *The Accountancy of Investment*, Chas. E. Sprague, New York, 1906, pp. 38 et seq.

[2] *The Accountancy of Investment*, p. 37.

at any interest date the book value, which is the investment value, will, with the accumulated sums laid aside, equal the original capital. This principle, put in terms of the schedule, is: The amortization fund, with the book value, is always a constant, and equal to the capital or corpus of the investment.

If more than one bond of this issue were bought, the several items of cash interest, net income, amortization, and value, would simply be multiplied by the number of bonds bought. The greater the number of bonds in the account, the greater the cash error in using the two place tables.

A schedule of accumulation would treat a discount bond account in exactly the same way. Suppose a 3 per cent. 4-year-semiannual bond, issued Feb. 1, 1920, as before, at a price to net $4\frac{1}{2}$ per cent. This is worth 94.56, or exactly as much less than par as the other was worth more.

Date	Cash Interest 3%	Net Income $4\frac{1}{2}$%	Accumulation	Book Value	Par
1920 Feb. 1				(cost) 945.60	1000.00
Aug. 1	15.00	21.30	6.30	951.90	
1921 Feb. 1	15.00	21.40	6.40	958.30	
Aug. 1	15.00	21.60	6.60	964.90	
1922 Feb. 1	15.00	21.70	6.70	971.60	
Aug. 1	15.00	21.90	6.90	978.50	
1923 Feb. 1	15.00	22.00	7.00	985.50	
Aug. 1	15.00	22.20	7.20	992.70	
1924 Feb. 1	15.00	22.30	7.30	1000.00	
	120.00	174.40	54.40		

The investor, or bank, or insurance officer may easily carry along such a schedule by ascertaining from the tables the approximate book values each six-months' period. Or if the cost at the given basis has been correctly found to the cent (from the extended tables), he may find the net income directly from the book value of the preceding interest date, and put aside in the sinking fund the difference between the net income and the cash interest. The new book value will be the difference between the old book value and the sinking fund; whether less or more depending on whether the process is amortization or accumulation. This is because the book value must decline or advance, as the case may be, from cost to par, or the extent of the premium or discount, to wipe out the difference in four years.

The principal relationships of figures in these two schedules of amortization and accumulation may be understood at a glance by a plot of the two symmetrical isorropic curves of investment value. The reason these curves are not straight lines is because of the compounding interest, which accelerates, to the extent of $2\frac{1}{4}$ per cent. each interest date, the fall in cash value of bonds bought above par, or rise in bonds bought below.

CHART II

The Curves of Investment Value

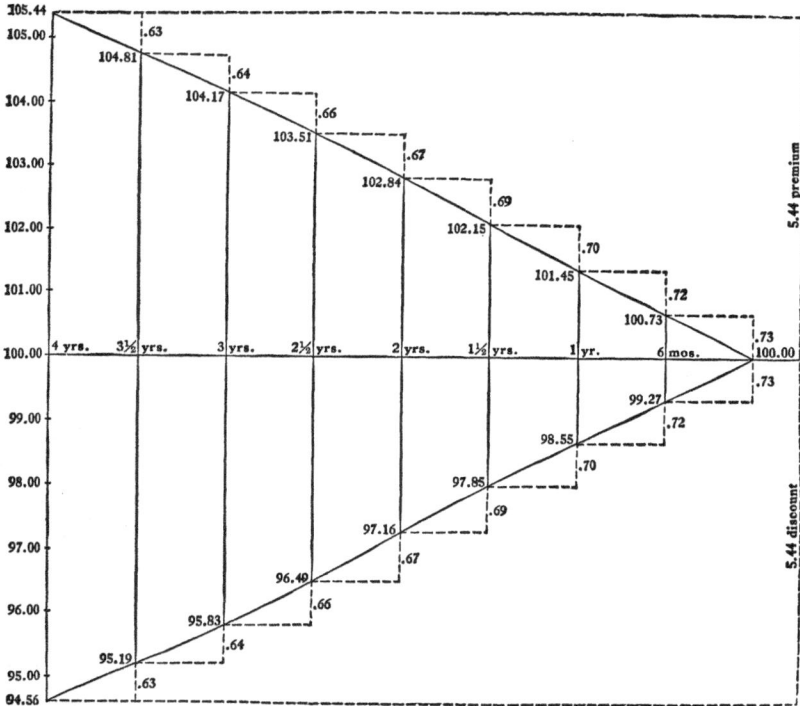

Since bonds are so seldom bought on interest dates, it will be necessary to revise the schedule for ordinary use. Suppose the premium bond of the illustration had been bought on May 1, 1920. Adjustment of price by payment to the seller of three months' accrued interest works a slight injustice to the buyer, but since this injustice is not corrected in business practice, the schedule is not altered except in the returns of the next interest period, and in the totals.

Date	Cash Interest 6%	Net Income 4½%	Amortization	Book Value	Par
1920 May 1				(cost) 1051.25	1000.00
Aug. 1	15.00 net	11.85	3.15	1048.10	
1921 Feb. 1	30.00	23.60	6.40	1041.70	
Aug. 1	30.00	23.40	6.60	1035.10	
1922 Feb. 1	30.00	23.30	6.70	1028.40	
Aug. 1	30.00	23.10	6.90	1021.50	
1923 Feb. 1	30.00	23.00	7.00	1014.50	
Aug. 1	30.00	22.80	7.20	1007.30	
1924 Feb. 1	30.00	22.70	7.30	1000.00	
	225.00	173.75	51.25		

Although the cost of the bond is \$1,051.25 on May 1, the bond is bought " and interest," and therefore the cash outlay May 1, is \$1,051.25+15.00 = \$1,066.25; but by carrying the cash interest on July 1, as 15.00 *net*, rather than at 30.00, which is actually received, the item of accrued interest need not be entered into the account.

The interest dates of different bond issues fall at different times, but generally on the first day of the month. Whether on the first or any other day, or whatever the month, it will be necessary to value all holdings as of the dates the account books are closed. These dates are customarily June 30, and Dec. 31.

To achieve this result in the 4-year bond before us it should be entered as of May 1, 1920, and the book values for June 30, and Dec. 31, 1920, by the rough commercial method of proportion with the known bond table values of Aug. 1, 1920, and Feb. 1, 1921,—as follows:

Interest Date	Book Values	Interest Date	New Book Values by Proportion
1920 May 1 (cost)	1051.25	May 1 (cost)	1051.25
		June 30	1049–15
Aug. 1	1048.10		
		Dec. 31	1042.77
1921 Feb. 1	1041.70		
		June 30	1036.20
Aug. 1	1035.10		
		Dec. 31	1029.52

Interest Date 1922 Feb. 1	Book Values 1028.40	Interest Due	New Book Values by Proportion
		June 30	1022.65
Aug. 1	1021.50		
		Dec. 31	1015.67
1923 Feb. 1	1014.50		
		June 30	1008.50
Aug. 1	1007.30		
		Dec. 31	1001.22
1924 Feb. 1	1000.00	Feb. 1	1000.00

Having obtained June 30 and Dec. 31 book values, the schedule may be constructed as before:

Date	Cash Interest 6%	Net Income $4\frac{1}{2}\%$	Amortization	Book Value	Par
1920 May 1			(cost)	1051.25	1000.00
June 30	10.00	7.90	2.10	1049.15	
Dec. 31	30.00	23.62	6.38	1042.77	
1921 June 30	30.00	23.43	6.57	1036.20	
Dec. 31	30.00	23.32	6.68	1029.52	
1922 June 30	30.00	23.13	6.87	1022.65	
Dec. 31	30.00	23.02	6.98	1015.67	
1923 June 30	30.00	22.83	7.17	1008.50	
Dec. 31	30.00	22.72	7.28	1001.22	
1924 Feb. 1	5.00	3.78	1.22	1000.00	
	225.00	173.75	51.25		

The schedules have been based on the two-place tables because these are the tables in common use. The consequent inaccuracy is not great, but worth avoiding by the use of the extended tables. As previously stated, if extended tables had been used the book values would have been correct to the nearest cent, and the semiannual income could have been correctly figured for six months at $4\frac{1}{2}$ per cent. on the investment (or book) value. By comparing the multiplicand of $2\frac{1}{4}$ per cent. of any book value with the net income of the succeeding six months' interest period, an idea may be had of the amount of inaccuracy in this schedule. If it were not for this inaccuracy it would not be necessary to obtain book values by proportion after Dec. 31, 1920 for the semiannual instalment of amortization, which is the difference between the cash and the net interest, is also the difference between the investment value of the present and the preceding period.

Schedules for Bonds Bought at Price and Interest. Since the whole scheme of investment accounts depends on the rate of net income as its basis, when bonds are bought at " price and interest " it is necessary to convert the price into terms of equivalent net income. For illustration take a 30-year 6 per cent. bond, bought on the interest date, Feb. 1, 1910, at 124.65. The nearest net yield at this price is 4.50 per cent. To approximate more closely would require a third decimal place for the percentage of return; and this is not only contrary to custom, but also would make the work of accounting altogether too laborious. But the true price to the customary two decimals, at a $4\frac{1}{2}$ per cent. basis of return, is 124.56. Consequently there is .09 per cent., or 90 cents, overcharge, which must be amortized during the life of the loan. If considerations of accuracy are less important than those of convenience, or when the loan is short and therefore the error is small, this 90 cents may be cared for in the first item of amortization, thus:

Date	Cash Interest 6%	Net Income $4\frac{1}{2}\%$	Amortization	Book Value	Par
			(cost)	1246.50	1000.00
1920 Feb. 1			.90		
Aug. 1	30.00	27.10	2.00	1243.60	
1921 Feb. 1	30.00	28.00	2.00	1241.60	
Aug. 1	30.00	28.00	2.00	1239.60	etc.

But if the number of bonds of this issue bought is large, or the loan long, or greater accuracy desired, the overcharge may be distributed as evenly as may be, by apportionment among all the instalments. In this issue there are 60 interest dates. A charge of 2 cents to each Aug. 1,—and 1 cent to each Feb. 1 amortization will distribute the 90 cents properly.

Date	Cash Interest	Net Income	Amortization	Book Value	Par
1920 Feb. 1	6%	$4\frac{1}{2}\%$		(cost) 1246.50	1000.00
Aug. 1	30.00	27.98	2.02	1244.48	
1921 Feb. 1	30.00	27.99	2.01	1242.47	
Aug. 1	30.00	27.98	2.02	1240.45	etc.

If the bond had been bought at 124.47, the nearest net yield would still have been 4.50 per cent., but the investment would have lacked just as much in price to make it yield $4\frac{1}{2}$ per cent. as it exceeded before. And so .09 per cent., or 90 cents, must be accumulated by maturity to meet the price deficit. This is done by withholding 90 cents from the first item of amortization, or by withholding an alternate 2 cents and 1 cent, as in the next preceding schedule.

Date	Cash Interest 6%	Net Income 4½%	Amortization	Book Value	Par
1920 Feb. 1				(cost) 1244.70	1000.00
Aug. 1	30.00	28.02	1.98	1243.72	
1921 Feb. 1	30.00	28.01	1.99	1241.73	
Aug. 1	30.00	29.02	1.98	1240.75	etc.

Schedules for Bonds Maturing at Other Than Regular Interest Dates. Bonds which have a date of issuance or maturity different from the regular interest dates cannot be carried on the books by a schedule derived from the bond tables. The price must first be ascertained by the six place tables, conformably to the irregular initial or terminal period, and the schedule must then be constructed by multiplication. At the irregular periods the investment value must be multiplied by the irregular net rate to find the net income for the period, and this subtracted from the irregular coupon interest will yield the amortization account for the period. The amortization sum, subtracted from the investment value, will give the succeeding value—whether that value be the first regular interest date value (for irregular initial periods) or par (for irregular terminals).

Schedules for Serial Bonds. Bond issues maturing serially, or otherwise partially, are easily scheduled. The cost of the series will be the sum of the costs of each bond, or set of bonds, reckoned according to maturities. That is, the total cost will be a bill of costs on which there will be as many items as there are separate maturities. The schedule can then be carried down by multiplication, as before, until the maturity of the shortest issue. The par value plus the semiannual coupon value of the bonds maturing will then be subtracted from the investment value and the process of interest compounding continued.

Schedules for Redeemable Bonds. Schedules for redeemable bonds involve no principles not already outlined in the paragraphs devoted to Bonds of Optional Duration. Amortization or accumulation should be carried on from half-year to half-year on the basis of that duration which was chosen to determine the cost of the given bond; for it will be remembered that cost and par are only two of the series of investment values, and duration is the only problem in optional bonds.

In case, however, that a bond is not called, when according to the computation it is likely to be, it should thereafter be carried at par, as aforesaid. On the other hand, if it is called before the allotted time, the difference between the investment value, at the time, and the redemption value, should be considered profit, and credited to the capital. Any other accounting would vitiate the previously recorded investment values and be at variance with sound bookkeeping.

CHAPTER XLII

BOND PRICES IN RELATION TO THE BUSINESS CYCLES

In presenting the principles of bond investment, consideration has thus far been given to internal factors which determine the credit position of the issuers of securities and of the securities themselves, and which determine the forms of investment contracts. Analysis also must be made of the external forces inherent in the business cycle which exercise a direct influence on the value of securities. Most of the early discussions on American investment were confined almost exclusively to a study of these internal factors. In the first edition of this book attention was given to external forces such as changes in the purchasing power of money and a chapter was devoted to "Bond Prices in Relation to the Trade Cycles." However, since that time scientific research has made considerable progress in this field, and the results require a restatement of the facts, a reconsideration of the nature of the business cycle, the forces affecting the purchasing power of money, the influence of changes on investment values with particular reference to the present widespread discussion of the relative merits of common stocks and bonds, and finally the various industrial and financial indices that are used in forecasting the external influences affecting security values.

Business Cycles. The business or trade or economic cycle, as it is variously known, has been defined as " the series of changes in business conditions which are characterized by an upward movement toward a boom, followed by a downward movement into depression." [1]

Business cycles are essentially modern economic movements, for they made their appearance only in the eighteenth century when the industrial revolution and the credit system were beginning to transform the economic and financial organization of

[1] *Business Cycles and Unemployment*, p. xii (Report of Committee of President's Conference on Unemployment).

England and Western Europe. Financial disturbances occurred in 1720 when the South Sea Bubble and John Law's Mississippi Bubble collapsed, and again in 1763 when the international conflict between England and France came to an end; but the first true crisis took place in 1817. Succeeding crises happened in 1825, 1837, 1847, 1857, 1873, 1884, 1890, 1893, 1903, 1907, 1910, 1913, and 1920. All these movements directly affected the value of investments, which were growing in importance throughout the nineteenth and twentieth centuries.

Because of the serious consequences of these crises they attracted the interest of economists. Ricardo in England studied closely the financial disturbances of their day, as did Sismondi in France and Engels in Germany. In recent years the recurring business cycles have been carefully analyzed by economists in this country and abroad. Although they have not arrived at an agreement as to the economic value, the cause, or the method of controlling business cycles, a better understanding of these subjects has nevertheless been attained.

Value of Business Cycles. The fluctuations expressing the business cycle are generally regarded in an unfavorable light. It is held that in periods of depression, the value of production is on the average 10 per cent. less than in a normal period and from 15 to 20 per cent. less than in an active period.[1] In terms of money, these fluctuations are said to have cost the American people $9,000,000,000 within the years 1909–1919 an average bill of about $1,000,000,000.[2] Some economists however, see certain offsetting benefits from the movements of the business cycle. It is maintained that business reactions tend to stimulate more efficient methods of production, prevent extreme fluctuations and check unwise speculation. Thus stated, a defensible argument in favor of cyclical movements requires elucidation, for there is no intrinsic logic in the thought that minor periodic fluctuations mitigate extreme casual fluctuations.

Theories of the Business Cycle. The various theories concerning the cause of business cycles may be classified according as the explanation is based on non-economic or on economic forces. The first group includes the theories of Stanley Jevons and Henry L. Moore. Jevons, who was both an astronomer and an economist

---

[1] Ibid., p. 30.

[2] Persons, Foster and Hettinger, *The Problem of Business Forecasting*, p. 85.

of note, in his *Investigations in Currency and Finance* expounded the principle that industrial activity is determined by weather conditions, which in turn are governed by sun spots. The so-called " sun spot " theory of the business cycle is thus based on the connection between weather conditions and economic movements. This relationship has been formulated more scientifically by Henry L. Moore in his *Economic Cycles*. Dr. Moore contends that the conjunctions of Venus cause temperature and rainfall changes, which in turn bring about business variations. He maintains that weather conditions in the United States " pass through cycles of approximately 33 years and 8 years in duration, causing like cycles in the yield per acre of the crops. These cycles of crops constitute the natural material current which drags upon its surface the lagging rhythmically changing values and prices with which the economist is more immediately concerned."[1]

Most of the theories explaining business cycles rest on purely economic factors. These in turn may be classed as either industrial or financial in character. The former group may be further subdivided according to the emphasis placed on production and consumption. Robertson in his *Study of Industrial Fluctuations* (London, 1915) ascribes the movement of the business cycle to the varying length of life of the instruments used in production. In other words, the longer the time it takes to create new instruments of production, such as machines and plant equipment, the greater is the consequent overproduction of capital goods.

On the other hand, J. A. Hobson, in his *Industrial System*, expresses the socialistic interpretation of business disturbances which are regarded as arising from a state of underconsumption. Hobson claims that crises are caused by the existence of surplus incomes in possession of the rich and an insufficient return in the hands of the masses. The time is reached when the wealthy classes obtain incomes which they cannot entirely apply to consumption, and so the surplus is invested in consumers' goods. These, however, cannot all be purchased by the masses with their limited buying power. In consequence, there follows a congested market which forces down prices, lowers profits and in the end reduces the income of the wealthy. After their con-

[1] Henry L. Moore, *Economic Cycle*, p. 49.

sumptive needs are met, they have proportionately less to invest in capital goods than heretofore and so, as industrial equipment does not increase apace, total consumption gradually catches up to plant capacity with a resulting rise in prices, in profits and finally in income. Then again production tends to outrun consumption, and a new crisis is in the making.

In recent years economists, explaining the gyrations of the business cycle, have emphasized the financial rather than the industrial factors in the movement. While Hobson's theory of crises is based on the so-called " lag " of wages, Professor Irving Fisher, in his *Purchasing Power of Money*, contends that the main factor is the " lag " of interest rates. These he claims fail to rise as fast as prices. Thus the cost of business operations in the form of wages, rents and interest charges all tend to rise more slowly than prices, with a resulting increased margin of profits for business men. They are therefore encouraged further to expand their operations, and for these purposes seek more accommodation from their banks. Thus bank loans outstanding are increased and the resultant expansion in deposit currency causes a further rise in prices. Costs in the form of interest rates and wages begin their belated rise and tend to overtake prices. Profits are reduced, business operations are curtailed, bank loans are contracted, prices eventually fall, and a crisis is on until an adjustment has been made between the interest rate and the price level.

Mitchell's Theory of the Business Cycles. A rather complete explanation of the business cycle has been formulated by Dr. Wesley C. Mitchell in his *Business Cycles*. The cycle is divided into four stages or periods, namely, depression, revival, prosperity and crisis. Their course is described by Dr. Mitchell as follows:

"A period of depression produces after a time certain conditions which favor an increase of business activity. Among these conditions are a level of prices low in comparison with the prices of prosperous times, drastic reductions in the cost of doing business, narrow margins of profit, ample bank reserves, and a conservative policy in capitalizing business enterprises and in granting credit. . . .

"While the processes cumulative for a time seem to enhance prosperity, they also cause a slow accumulation of stresses within the balanced system of business—stresses which ultimately undermine the conditions upon which prosperity rests. . . .

"Once begun, the process of liquidation extends very rapidly, partly because most enterprises which are called upon to settle their maturing obligations in turn put similar pressure upon their own debtors, and partly because, despite all efforts to keep secret what is going forward, news presently leaks out and other creditors take alarm. . . .

"The period of severe financial pressure is often followed by the reopening of numerous enterprises which had been shut for a time. But this prompt revival of activity is partial and short lived. It is based chiefly upon the finishing of orders received but not completely executed in the preceding period of prosperity, or upon the effort to work up and market large stocks of material already on hand or contracted for. It comes to an end as this work is gradually finished, because new orders are not forthcoming in sufficient volumes to keep the mills and factories busy. There follows a period during which depression spreads over the whole field of business and grows more severe. . . .

"Old debts have been paid, accumulated stocks of commodities have been absorbed, weak enterprises have been reorganized, the banks are strong—all the clouds upon the financial horizon have disappeared. Everything is ready for a revival of activity, which will begin whenever some fortunate circumstance gives a sudden fillip to demand, or, in the absence of such an event, when the slow growth of the volume of business has filled order books and paved the way for a new rise of prices.

"Such is the stage of the business cycle with which the analysis began, and, having accounted for its own beginning, the analysis ends."

The Value of Money. Since modern economic thought explains the business cycle primarily on the basis of monetary fluctuations, it is well next to inquire into the causes of these changes in the value of money. This expression is interpreted variously by the business man to mean the current rate of interest, but to economists it signifies rather the value of money in exchange or the amount of goods which it can command. This buying power of money is expressed in the price level which moves up or down inversely as the buying power declines or rises. The generally accepted explanation of the changes in the value of money or its buying power is the so-called " quantity theory of money." It was recognized by John Locke, more fully stated by John Stuart Mill and Alfred Marshall, and finally expressed in mathematical form by Irving Fisher. His so-called " equation of exchange " includes the following factors:

$$M = \text{amount of money in circulation}$$
$$V = \text{velocity of circulation.}$$
$$MV = \text{money payments.}$$
$$M' = \text{rights to demand money (bank deposits)}$$
$$V' = \text{deposit turnover.}$$
$$P = \text{average price per unit.}$$
$$T = \text{things purchased.}$$

Taking these symbols as a basis, Professor Fisher has developed the following formula.

$$M V + M' V' = P T$$

This formula may be read as follows: The amount of money in circulation times the rate of turnover plus the amount of bank deposits times the average turnover equals the average unit price times the number of things exchanged for money and deposits.

Again the formula may be restated thus:

$$P \propto \frac{MV}{T}$$

This may now be simply interpreted to mean that prices vary directly with the volume and velocity of the circulating medium, and indirectly with the volume of trade. In its simplest form, the quantity theory of money is merely an application of the law of demand and supply, for the circulating medium may be regarded as the demand factor, and the volume of trade as the supply force. In this form, the quantity theory is merely a truism and must necessarily find general acceptance. The practical application of the theory is, however, limited, and it is in this respect that the more enthusiastic supporters of the quantity theory lay themselves open to criticism. The price level does not always respond immediately to changes in the quantity of money. Thus in recent years, the heavy import of gold into this country has not been followed by a rise in prices but on the contrary a fall has actually occurred. However in the long run prices are bound to respond to the influence of the monetary factor, and so the quantity theory may be considered as a guiding principle in determining fluctuations in the price level and therefore the variations in the business cycle.

Inflation and the Value of Money. In considering the business cycle it has been assumed so far that the movement has developed during a period of comparatively stable monetary conditions. This state was attained before the war in those countries which had maintained the gold standard by a readiness to redeem on demand all their paper money in gold, and by permitting a free movement of the precious metals to and from the country. At the outbreak of the war these conditions were abandoned by the belligerents which prohibited the export of gold and also suspended specie payment. By the latter act the paper money, formerly redeemable, then became irredeemable. Moreover, the volume of this irredeemable or " fiat " money was increased to pay for the conduct of the war. The policy of augmenting the volume of the means of payment without a similar increase in the supply of goods and services is known as " inflation."

Acts of inflation may be retraced in history as far back as 600 B. C. Sallust tells us that on one occasion the Roman state had contracted debts in silver money but discharged these obligations in copper. In the Middle Ages it was common practice for rulers to clip the coins of the realm. Extreme inflation developed with the use of credit. The colony of Massachusetts possesses the rather dubious honor of initiating the practice of emitting irredeemable paper money. The Continental money of the American Colonies, the assignats of the French Revolution and the greenbacks of the Federal Government during the Civil War are brands of fiat money. But these were only local instances of inflation and were dwarfed into insignificance by the almost universal money and credit inflation that developed during and following the Great War. As a result prices everywhere rose to unprecedented levels. In Russia, Austria, and Germany the purchasing power of the ruble, the kronen, and the mark diminished daily, and in the end almost vanished. Even in the United States the buying power of the dollar declined sharply.

Value of Money and Investment. The movements of the business cycle have been outlined with special reference to the fluctuations in the value of money. The effect of these variations upon investment will now be studied. Investment in the broad sense may take the form of either a loan or a proprietary interest. In the former case the investor is acting in the capacity of capitalist, or " rentier," as known on the Continent, since he is contributing only capital as his share in production. On the other hand, he who invests in the form of a proprietary interest is really an enterpriser or rather a part owner. A further distinction lies in the fact that a loan represents part of the debt owed by the concern which has received the loan, while the proprietary interest implies part ownership. The loan may be expressed in such credit instruments as a note, a mortgage, a bond, or a bank deposit, while proprietary interest is conveyed in stock, either preferred or common. The former instruments represent debts, and call for the payment of a fixed sum in the form of interest. The latter instruments involve no promise of reimbursement, for dividends on stock are paid only if the earnings of the corporation justify.

With these distinctions in mind an analysis may now be made of the effects of the changes in the business cycle on the two forms of investment.

The Business Cycle and Bond Prices. As mentioned in previous chapters, the interest return on a bond contains two elements: first, pure interest or the price of riskless capital, and, second, a residual premium for risk. The return on high-grade bonds is largely composed of the former element, and the latter is of greater proportionate significance in the more speculative issues. Therefore it can be concluded that the safer the bond the more responsive is it to changes in the current rate of interest.

The question arises what is the effect of changes in interest rate on the market value of high-grade bonds? This relationship may be seen from an example. Suppose that the prevailing rate of pure interest is 4 per cent., and that there were a borrower with such a high standing that its obligations were regarded as riskless investments and that this borrower issue bonds of $1,000 denomination. The owner of the bond is therefore entitled to an annual return of $40. Assume that, due to abnormal economic conditions, the pure rate of interest rises to 8 per cent. The return on this bond still remains $40, and as it is now possible to obtain $80 interest from bonds of the same riskless class the former issue will tend to decline in market value until it brings the same yield to an owner—namely, to $500. On the other hand, if the pure rate of interest should fall from 4 per cent. to 2 per cent., the market price of the bond in question will then rise to $2,000.

In a period of rising interest rates which occurs during an upswing of the business cycle, the market price of bonds will tend to decline in direct proportion to the element of pure interest involved in the return on the securities. Moreover, such tendencies in the market prices of the bonds will take place irrespective of their credit position.

Commodity Prices and British Consols. This conclusion is supported by the following chart showing the annual movements

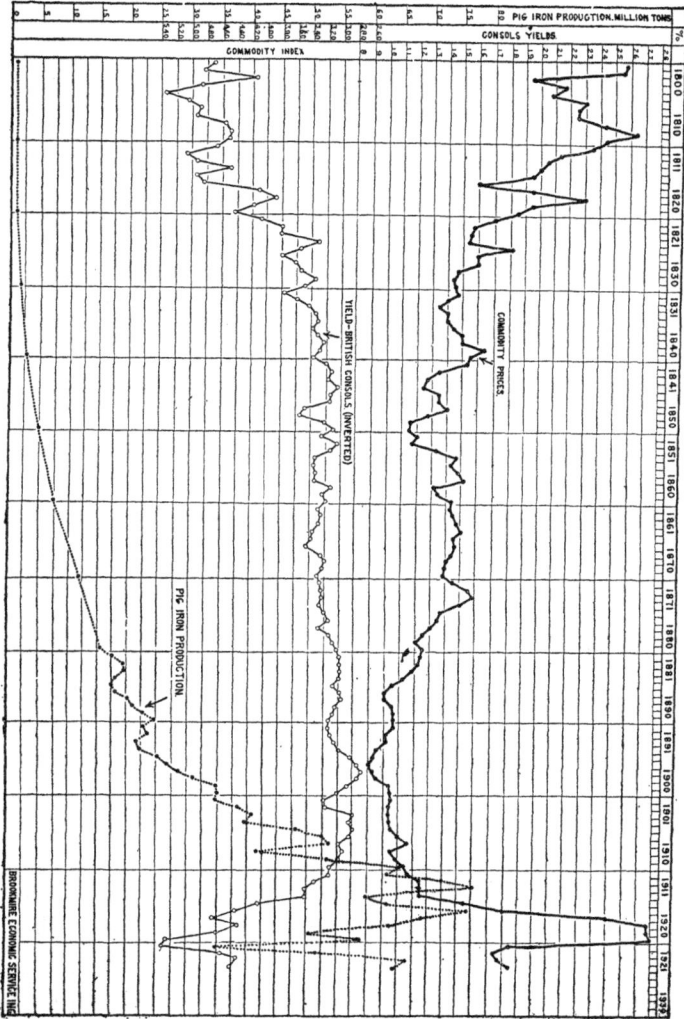

Chart showing PIG IRON PRODUCTION, MILLION TONS; CONSOLS YIELDS; COMMODITY INDEX; with curves labeled YIELD—BRITISH CONSOLS (INVERTED), COMMODITY PRICES, PIG IRON PRODUCTION. Years from 1800 to 1922. BROOKMIRE ECONOMIC SERVICE INC.

of British commodity prices and the trend of British Consols representing an approach toward pure interest, during the period from 1800 until 1924.[1]

This chart shows clearly the rhythmic movement of commodity prices in the various business cycles during the nineteenth and twentieth centuries and also indicates the secular or long-time swing which was generally downward throughout the nineteenth century until about 1896 when the trend turned upward and continued at an accelerated pace after 1914.

These changes are shown in a different manner in the following table on the money price and the purchasing power of the capital value of Consols from 1815 to 1922, with the year 1914 taken as the base, as compiled by John Maynard Keynes in his *Monetary Reform*, p. 18:

Year	Money Price of Capital Value of Consols	Purchasing Power of Capital Value of Consols
1815	92	56
1826	108	92
1841	122	104
1869	127	111
1883	138	144
1896	150	208
1914	100	100
1922	64	22
1921	56	34
1922	76	47

Losses on Fixed Investments. The chart on page 581 and the above table, when studied together, show clearly the effect of the instability of the money medium upon investments with fixed returns. Money is said to perform various functions, such as that of a measure of value, a medium of exchange, a store of value and a standard of deferred payments. It is in this last

[1] This table has been adapted from the chart prepared by the Brookmire Statistical Service and reproduced from Ray Vance, *Business and Investment Forecasting*, p. 40. Commodity prices are based on the Jevons-Sauerbeck-Statist index numbers and the prices of British Consols have been adjusted to take cognizance of changes in the nominal interest rate that they carry from time to time, so that the price changes shown would represent the actual market increases or decreases in the value of an investment in Consols made in 1800 and held over the entire period.

capacity that money determines the relationship between debtors and creditors. Changes in the value of money, as expressed in its purchasing power, therefore impair an equitable adjustment of the claims existing among these parties. Throughout the greater part of the nineteenth century the secular (or long-range) upward swing of commodity prices benefited the creditor class which, as shown in the case of British Consols, gained an increased buying power on the capital value of its holdings of almost four times in the period from 1816 to 1896. Since then the buying power of these fixed investments has declined. The proportion of loss in buying power has varied in different countries. In Germany, Austria, and Russia the buying power disappeared almost entirely; in France, Belgium, and Italy it has fallen to a fraction of its former value; and in England, as shown in the table above, it was reduced in 1920 to little more than one-tenth of its highest value attained in 1896. Even in the United States prices have fluctuated widely, and this decline in the value of the dollar brought serious loss to holders of American fixed investments. Particularly savings, insurance and other institutions that are compelled by law to confine their investments to high-grade securities suffered severe losses. As one writer has pointed out: " In 1921 many highly regarded banking institutions and more than a few life insurance companies in this country were virtually insolvent. . . . On December 31, 1921, one domestic life insurance company reported a loss in market value below cost of over $64,000,000 on its bond holdings, over 10 per cent. of their original cost. In purchasing power at that time they were probably not worth one-half their original value." [1]

Business Cycle and Stock Prices. The losses thus incurred in bonds in recent years have led to a closer scrutiny of the principles of investment, and have given rise to a considerable literature strongly opposing investment in bonds and recommending instead the purchase of stocks. The proponents of this new policy have been particularly active in pressing their claims during the past few years, but the general theory is by no means novel since it was definitely enunciated in 1912 by several eminent economists in a publication entitled *How to Invest When Prices are Rising*. The first edition of the *Principles of Bond Investment*, published in 1911, emphasized the relation of purchasing power

[1] A. Vere Shaw in the *Harvard Business Review*, Vol. 111, p 447.

and bond prices, and on page 456 called attention to the fact that
" no thorough study of the security for bonds can fail to consider
the future of gold prices."

The world-wide inflation movement with its adverse affects
on bond prices, as described above, developed a more voluminous
and an even more critical literature on the subject.[1] The most
careful analysis of the relative value of bonds and common
stocks as long-term investments has been made by Edgar Smith.
He shows, on the one hand, that certain groups of bonds over a
period of years by certain " tests " have proven unprofitable
to the holders because of the depreciation in the value of the
dollar. At the same time, Smith selects a number of leading
common stocks, and after tracing their history over a period of
years formulates the following so-called " law of increasing
stock values and income return ":

" (1) Over a period of years the principal value of a well-diversified
holding of the common stocks of representative corporations in essential
industries tends to increase in accordance with the operation of compound
interest.

" (2) Such stock holdings may be relied upon over a term of years to
pay an average income return on such increasing values of something
more than the average current rate on commercial paper."

Bonds vs. Stocks as Long-Term Investments. Unqualified
acceptance of these views on bonds and stocks would mean a
complete revolution in the traditional investment policy in all
capital-accumulating countries. It would involve a radical
revision of the entire system of legal investment for savings and
trust funds, since in most countries the funds of fiduciaries may
be placed only in high-grade bonds, which have hitherto been
regarded as the safest form of investment.

In seeking now to formulate an investment policy, it is necessary to base it on all the facts thus far presented in this chapter
and in previous parts of this book. Even the severest critics of
bonds will concede that they possess greater technical safety as
provided in the loan contract than stocks, in that the former represent prior claim on the assets of the issuer. (See Chapter V.)

[1] See Smith, E. L., *Common Stocks as Long Term Investments;* Van Strum,
K. S., *Investing in Purchasing Power;* Shaw, A. V., *Investment Counsel;* "Ele-
ments of Investment Safety," *Harvard Business Review,* Vol. No. 4; Pomeroy,
R. W., *Stock Investments.*

Hence from the standpoint of legal safety bonds are the superior form of investment. It is also true that bonds as a class possess greater market resistance to losses in time of depression. Holders of securities are more likely to be compelled to liquidate them during a business depression, and at that time stocks are liable to bring lower prices at forced sales than bonds which tend rather to rise as the interest rate falls.

The important question, however, is the extent to which high-grade bonds possess economic safety in relation to the general trend of business as described above. This trend may, on the one hand, move through minor changes, lasting for a few days or even weeks, but such short-time variations are inconsequential in themselves and may be ignored in this study which is concerned rather with long-time movements. These have been stated to consist of business cycles and secular trends. The supporters of what may be called the "common-stock" theory base their criticism of bonds as long-term investments mainly on the secular trend during the past half century. Within this period the general swing of prices has been upward, and sequentially the rate of interest. As a result the market price bonds have declined in proportion to the extent of pure interest contained in their yield.

But if the entire nineteenth century is taken into consideration, as in the chart and table on pages 581, 582, it is seen that the secular trend was first downward and then upward, and for this entire period from 1806 until 1920 the market price and the purchasing power of British Consols, have remained practically unchanged. This is a fair test of the value of high-grade bonds as long-term investments, for in the first place their value is traced over a period of a rising as well as of a falling secular trend, and also a bond is taken that is representative of pure interest, and that contains no speculative element which may influence the market price either adversely or favorably. In this way a sufficiently long base is used and at the same time a possible element of error is eliminated.

From these figures it therefore appears that the traditional policy of relying at all times and exclusively on high-grade bonds may prove inexpedient in certain stages of the business cycle and during an upward swing of the secular trend. At the same time the recent contention that common stocks as a class are better long-term investments than bonds seems unjustifiable, since it is based on the assumption that the secular trend in the future will continue upward. Some of the stricter construction-ists of the quantity theory of money have sought to show that the future trend of prices is upward, but perhaps equally cogent arguments might be assembled to prove the contrary. In fact, the trend in recent years has been downward, rather than up-ward. At any rate the plea for stocks is based on speculative considerations and is under suspicion from the very nature of investment.

There is a further weakness in the stock-investment theory. Its proponents, such as Smith and Van Strum, make their com-parisons on the one hand by grouping bonds, as *one class* but at the same time by picking out combinations of " selected," " well-chosen," " listed," stocks of " large corporations." How-ever, Scudder's compilation of obsolete American corporations made in 1925 contains a list of approximately 100,000 companies, the stock of which generally may be presumed to be worthless. The compilers of this book are now (1927) at work on additional lists, and they have " blocked out " as it were between 200,000 and 300,000 additional companies, virtually defunct, the shares of which are of equally little value. A list of all the bonds in the United States that had ever defaulted, in any real sense, would be insignificant as compared with this glaring evidence of the frailty of average business endeavor. Very few of these units of business were of a character or of a size to permit a bond issue. But all the shares had owners, and to the extent that the shares represented expenditure of labor or capital, they now represent total losses compared to which the analogous losses from bond investment are negligible.

In establishing an investment policy the above two ex-tremes should be avoided and instead the following principles should be adopted. First there should be a full realization of the uncertainty of the business trend and the unstable value of money. Regardless of its intrinsic worth " an investment which is good to-day may not be good to-morrow." The investor may adopt a policy of " switching " items in his security list in order to accommodate it to changing economic conditions that may in no way impair the internal credit position of his holdings but that may affect the market for them. Under certain conditions it may be a wiser policy to increase his holdings of common stock in proportion to bonds, but the reverse position may be better under different economic movements.

Without reference to the secular trend and the minor fluctuations, but only to the business cycle it may be concluded that:

a. At the bottom of the business cycle, high-grade bonds may be sold and speculative bonds or common stocks may be bought.
b. At the top of the business cycle speculative bonds and common stocks may be sold and high-grade bonds bought.

Indices of the Business Cycle. In applying this policy, the investor does well to obtain the advice of his investment banker. Many investment houses throughout the United States have appreciated the desirability of giving this kind of advisory service to their customers. Investors may, in addition, form their own judgment on the course of the business cycle, the trend of interest rates, and the movement of security prices by analysis of certain industrial and financial indices. The more important are the following: [1]

    Industrial
        Production
            Agricultural output—Crop reports of the Government
            Manufacture—Unfilled orders of the U. S. Steel Corporation
                Output of automobiles
                Pig iron
            Mining—Output of bituminous coal
                Crude oil
            Building—Contracts awarded
            General—Federal Reserve Production Index
        Transportation
            Railroads—Gross earnings
                Net earnings
                Freight car loadings
            Shipping—Tonnage entered and cleared
        Consumption
            Retail trade—Report of department stores
            Foreign trade—Merchandise exports and imports
    Financial
        Money and credit
            Federal Reserve System
                Total bills and securities held by the Reserve Banks
                Total amount of Federal Reserve circulation
                Ratio of reserves to deposits and circulation
            Member banks
                Total bank debits
                Total loans of member banks

[1] See accompanying chart of indices of business conditions as compiled monthly by the Statistical Department of The Bank of America, p. 590.

Rate of interest on call loans
Foreign exchange rates—sterling and francs
Price levels
        Bradstreet wholesale price index
        Fisher's commodity price index
Security markets
        New securities issued
        Stock exchange sales
        Bond and stock prices

Business Forecasting. Indices, such as these, may be used in the preparation of business forecasts. A business forecast is based on the economic cycle theory that has been described. With the aid of economic science it is an attempt at a systematic statement of what should be the normal sequence of future business events in the light of the past.

In recent years a number of industrial concerns and financial institutions have developed barometers intended to forecast the trend of business. Some of these are based on specific business factors and their relation to past business conditions. In the thought that this same relationship will continue, Colonel Leonard Ayres, in the bulletins of the Cleveland Trust Company, has a barometer that seeks to forecast the trend of security prices from an analysis of the volume of pig iron production. It is contended that stock and bond prices will fall whenever more than 60 per cent. of the pig iron furnaces in the United States are active at any one time.[1]

The so-called composite barometers are based not on one but on a number of indices. These are reduced to a common base which is usually graphically represented.[2] The more important of these composite barometers are issued by the following organizations: the Babson Statistical Organization, Brookmire Economic Service, Alexander Hamilton Institute, Harvard Bureau of Business Research, and the Standard Statistics Co. Inc.

This chapter has explained the nature of the business cycle, and the factors influencing the course of interest rates, with particular emphasis on their relation to security prices. Comment has been made on the development of an investment policy based on the movements of the business cycle and the changes of

[1] See Cleveland Trust Company Bulletin, Vol. 5, No. 7. Also Vance, *Business and Investment Forecasting*, p. 85.

[2] For survey of barometers, see C. O. Hardy, "Business Forecasting, its Present Status," *Journal of Business*, May, 1923.

the interest rate. Finally, the various business indices and the forecasting services have been mentioned. In using these forecasting systems, it must be remembered that they are based on a study of business cycles which are rhythmic but not necessarily periodic movements. Business cycles are continually recurring phenomena but they do not move with the regularity of a pendulum. Professor Mitchell has well said: " These cycles differ widely in duration and intensity, in the relative prominence of their various phenomena, and in the sequence of their phases."[1] He adds a true word of caution on the limitations of business forecasts in stating that " the uncertainty attending present forecasts of business conditions arises chiefly from the imperfections of our knowledge concerning these conditions in the immediate past and in the present. For since business cycles result from processes of cumulative change, the main factors in shaping to-morrow are the factors at work yesterday and to-day."[2] The ever-growing study undertaken by government bureaus, business houses, and financial institutions is increasing the knowledge of business conditions in the past and in the present, and therefore changes in the business cycle are being better understood, and the possibility of their control is thereby advanced.

[1] *Business Cycles*, p. 581.
[2] Ibid., 157.

Monthly Chart of Business Barometers
April, 1921—April, 1926
Compiled by the Statistical Department of The Bank of America

	MONEY AND BANKING					Interest Rates	Foreign Exchange	
	Federal Reserve System			Member Banks				
MONTH	Total Bills and Securities (Average) Mil. Dollars	Total Circula-tion (Average) Mil. Dollars	Ratio Reserves to Dep. and Cir. %	Total Bank Debits 141 Cities Mil. Dollars	Total Loans of Member Banks Mil. Dollars	Call Loans %	(1) Sterling Dollars Per £	(1) Francs ¢ Per Frc.
Apr., 1921	2,536	3,047	53.4	29,360	12,341	6.250	3.96	7.33
Apr., 1922	922	2,263	77.8	36,383	10,851	4.094	4.41	9.17
Apr., 1923	1,148	2,231	75.9	39,294	11,841	5.000	4.66	6.65
Apr., 1924	936	1,961	80.5	39,519	12,279	4.313	4.35	6.15
Apr., 1925	1,057	1,699	76.6	44,537	13,149	4.000	4.79	5.18
Sept., 1925	1,195	1,678	73.1	45,242	13,587	4.375	4.85	4.71
Oct., 1925	1,255	1,702	72.2	52,930	13,866	4.650	4.84	4.41
Nov., 1925	1,291	1,716	71.8	48,343	14,006	4.656	4.85	3.97
Dec., 1925	1,450	1,821	67.9	54,370	14,118	5.186	4.85	3.77
Jan., 1926	1,197	1,718	73.1	54,118	14,052	4.375	4.85	3.81
Feb., 1926	1,174	1,668	74.1	44,892	13,973	4.875	4.87	3.69
Mar., 1926	1,164	1,666	74.2	......	13,974	4.500	4.86	3.60
Apr., 1926	1,150	1,665	74.8	......	13,920	4.200	4.86	3.38

PRODUCTION

MONTH	F. R. B. Production Index (1919 = 100)	Unfilled Orders U. S. Steel Corporation Mil. Tons	Pig Iron (Daily Avge.) Thousand Tons	Bituminous Coal (Weekly Avge.) Mil. Tons	Crude Oil (Daily Avge.) Thous. Bbls.	F. W. Dodge's Building Contracts Awarded Million Dollars	Auto-mobiles Thousand Cars
Apr., 1921	78.8	5.85	38.47	6.12	1,293	221.3	194 5
Apr., 1922	85.5	5.10	69.07	5.38	1,422	353.0	219.6
Apr., 1923	124	7.29	118.25	10.09	1,947	362.9	380.5
Apr., 1924	114	4.21	107.78	6.83	1,935	480.1	373.1
Apr., 1925	119	4.45	108.72	7.73	2,041	547.0	422.0
Sept., 1925	112	3.72	90.87	10.72	2,128	548.2	319.9
Oct., 1925	116	4.11	97.53	11.61	2,085	519.5	436.8
Nov., 1925	115	4.58	100.52	12.14	2,048	464.7	365.4
Dec., 1925	121	5.03	104.85	11.72	2,002	510.9	310.2
Jan., 1926	120	4.88	106.97	12.28	1,953	457.2	333.7
Feb., 1926	120	4.61	104.41	11.65	1,910	389.9	364.6
Mar., 1926	123	4.38	111.03	10.47	1,930	597.9	447.2
Apr., 1926	....	3.87	115.00	9.25	1,947	570.6	449.2

RAILROADS   FOREIGN TRADE   COMMODITY PRICES

MONTH	Gross Earnings Million Dollars	Net Earnings Million Dollars	Freight Car Loadings (Weekly Average) Thous. Cars	Mer-chandise Exports Mil. Dollars	Mer-chandise Imports Mil. Dollars	Excess of Gold Imports Over Exports Mil. Dollars	Irving Fisher's Commodity Price Index % 1913 = 100%	Bradstreet Wholesale Price Index No.
Apr., 1921	433.40	57.70	691.2	340.3	254.6	81.28	.....	11.37
Apr., 1922	416.87	80.69	740.5	318.1	217.0	10.66	.....	11.53
Apr., 1923	521.39	118.63	941.0	325.4	364.2	8.53	167.0	13.93
Apr., 1924	474.09	101.68	874.7	347.0	324.3	44.03	145.9	12.66
Apr., 1925	472.59	102.86	931.1	398.2	346.1	*12.73	151.4	13.32
Sept., 1925	564.44	177.24	1,075.0	420.4	350.0	* 2.66	158.2	14.15
Oct., 1925	591.31	137.70	1,107.5	490.6	374.1	22.70	156.7	14.32
Nov., 1925	532.75	148.29	1,025.0	448.0	378.0	*13.91	159.1	14.41
Dec., 1925	524.01	134.45	924.7	468.0	394.0	* 3.97	159.3	14.01
Jan., 1926	480.06	102.27	922.9	399.0	414.0	16.26	159.2	13.72
Feb., 1926	459.23	99.48	919.1	352.9	388.5	21.57	157.6	13.40
Mar., 1926	528.90	133.64	969.3	375.0	445.0	39.19	152.9	13.11
Apr., 1926	......	......	949.0	388.0	398.0	* 4.76	150.9	12.86

SECURITIES MARKETS

MONTH	New Security Issues Mil. Dol.	N. Y. Stock Exchange Avge. Weekly Stock Sales Mil. Shares	Bond Prices (Average)	Stock Prices † Mean Average		Number	Liabilities Mil. Dollars
				Railroads	Industrials		
Apr., 1921	518	3.39	....	69.66	76.96	1,487	38.6
Apr., 1922	656	6.77	....	82.89	91.27	2,167	73.0
Apr., 1923	*458*	*4.75*	71.90	86.71	100.54	*1,520*	*52.5*
Apr., 1924	490	*4.15*	73.15	*81.99*	*91.94*	1,707	48.9
Apr., 1925	607	*5.99*	77.39	95.24	119.71	1,939	*37.2*
Sept., 1925	*490*	8.19	78.24	101.86	142.48	*1,465*	*30.3*
Oct., 1925	503	12.12	*78.17*	103.23	150.65	1,581	*29.5*
Nov., 1925	587	*12.03*	78.52	105.67	153.79	1,672	35.9
Dec., 1925	728	*10.52*	78.96	110.12	154.56	1,878	36.5
Jan., 1926	732	*8.69*	79.73	110.69	156.10	2,296	43.7
Feb., 1926	*608*	8.91	80.55	*109.57*	158.38	*1,801*	*34.2*
Mar., 1926	651	10.91	*80.21*	*105.61*	*144.25*	1,984	*30.6*
Apr., 1926	...	*8.16*	80.62	108.29	*143.71*	*1,957*	38.5

Falling prices or indices are indicated by italics.
Rising or stationary prices or indices are indicated by Arabic figures.
* Excess of gold exports over imports. † From the Dow Jones & Co. Average Price Index.
(1) Average noon buying rate of cable transfers at New York. *Indices of Business Conditions.*

PART V
INVESTMENT ORGANIZATION

CHAPTER XLIII

CLASSES OF INVESTORS

The investment market, like any other, exists by virtue of buyers and sellers. This chapter is concerned with the buyers, the investors. The next chapter is concerned with the professional sellers, the bond houses, and the conduct of the business and profession that they have set up.

Distinction Between Direct and Indirect Investment. In general there are two ways of buying securities, and therefore two systems of investment. One may make a forthright purchase of a group of bonds. That is a direct investment. Or he may invest indirectly by entrusting his funds to an intermediary which in turn purchases securities. In this second event the original investor does not own the securities but holds a claim on the intermediary which owns them. Under the system of direct investment, as found in England and the United States, the stock exchange performs a leading function in the money markets, but its function is not so great in countries like Germany and Sweden where indirect investment prevails.

Direct Investment in the United States. The volume of bonds sold directly to individual investors in the United States is enormous. A large bond issue is placed among thousands of separate buyers all over the country. The Japanese loan in 1923 was distributed among 44,000 investors. It was estimated that the average holding of this issue was $3,660, and that in the case of the Austrian loan of the same year the average holding was $2,980. These individual investors constitute classes, in the sense of persons of means such as capitalists who are seeking an income conservatively derived, professional people who also desire safety but do not ally safety so closely with moderate return, business men and speculators who are concerned rather with the element of profit in the appreciation of the principal of bonds, and finally business houses which wish to place idle funds profitably until the time when they can be better employed in commercial transactions.

Undoubtedly the greater part of American investment is made directly, but there is every reason to believe that the indirect method is increasing at a rapid rate. It has been estimated that the volume of institutional holdings has risen from about $14,000,000,000 in 1919 to approximately $20,000,000,000 in 1924, a gain of 40 per cent.[1]

Legal Investments. In the United States most institutions making investments must observe certain governmental regulations, and funds may be placed only in what are known as "legal" investments. Similar limitations also apply to individuals who, in the capacity of trustees, are making investments of the money of other persons. Violation often renders the trustee personally liable if loss should arise from the purchase of securities not recognized by the law. Such a statutory investment system obtains in New York and in the New England states, where a government officer, such as the superintendent of banking or of insurance, issues annually a list of securities that have met certain tests, and that therefore are eligible. This system presents certain advantages and disadvantages. On the one hand it seeks to reduce the risks which may arise from the fraudulent or unskilful handling of trust funds, by prescribing the limits within which they may be placed. However, in recent years, the system has been severely criticised, mainly on the ground that it fixes stipulations which are too inflexible, particularly in the light of the changing economic and financial conditions of recent years. As Professor Dewing writes, these investments are "determined by arbitrary state laws, representing for the most part, the vague and uncritical investment sentiment of the preceding generation."[2]

In proof, reference is made to the fact that the defaulted 4 per cent. debenture bonds of the Chicago, Milwaukee and St. Paul Railroad were legal investments in several states merely because the dividend record of the road was good, although its obligations had no real security back of them. Notwithstanding this criticism, the system of legal investment still remains unchanged in many states, and determines in large measure the purchasing program of the various financial institutions.

Insurance Companies. Insurance companies, particularly those

[1] *Harvard Economic Review*, Vol. 111, p. 414.
[2] Ibid., Vol. 111, p. 454.

writing life and fire risks, are exceedingly important factors in the security markets. A considerable part of their funds are placed in real estate mortgages, but nevertheless they are large holders of bonds.[1]

Savings Banks. Savings banks in the United States are either of the stock or of the mutual type. The former is the same in constitution as the incorporated bank. The mutual savings bank, of greater importance in the investment market, deserves special analysis. Its organization presents certain peculiar features. It is a non-stock institution, for its funds come not from shareholders but from depositors, who are therefore virtually owners of the bank. The returns they receive on their deposits are not interest payments but really dividends. Mutual savings banks predominate in the New England and in the middle states where institutional investment is more generally regulated by law.

Certain principles may be discerned in these laws. They aim first at safety of the investment, and seek to attain this end by diversification. Therefore, a savings bank may not place more than a certain per cent. of its funds in any one kind of investment. Also, the laws try to maintain liquidity by insisting upon the purchase of a goodly proportion of marketable securities. Not so much consideration is given to the matter of yield, since the fundamental aim is safety. The laws usually encourage local investment by favoring municipalities within the state or in adjacent states.

The savings bank laws of New York state are the most developed, and are analyzed in the following quotation:[2]

" *1. Real-estate Mortgages.*

" In that state the mutual savings banks have invested about one-half of their funds in real-estate mortgages. When a prospective borrower wants a savings bank to advance him a loan on the pledge of his real estate, he first fills out a formal application describing his property. It is then evaluated or appraised by a committee of the trustees, for the loan must not exceed 60 per cent. of the value of the property if improved, and not over 40 per cent. if unimproved. In estimating the worth of the property, such factors are considered as the cost of construction, the further

---

[1] The trend in the investments of life insurance companies is well shown in the charts accompanying an article by Richter and Standish in the *Harvard Economic Review*, Vol. 111, p. 414.

[2] Willis and Edwards, *Banking and Business*, pp. 317–321.

upkeep, and the income derived from rentals. In examining city property, due consideration is also given to desirability of the neighborhood and extent of transportation facilities. In appraising a farm, quality of the soil, kind of crops, condition of buildings, and nearness to markets are carefully studied. If the report is favorable, the title to property is searched by an attorney or a title company. An abstract is made of the title, from which the bank learns whether the owner has a clear or undisputed right to the property and whether it is free from prior taxes or other claims. The property is then insured against fire, so that payment, in case of loss, is made in favor of the bank as mortgagee. The bank closes the transaction by recording the mortgage in the office of the local government and by sending the borrower a check to cover the loan. While a savings bank in a city rarely extends mortgage loans on distant property, country banks lend quite freely in New York and other large cities because of the scarcity of local loans. Economic conditions and likewise real-estate values are more stable in the country, where the character of the neighborhood changes but slowly and where improvement in transportation seldom alters a community for better or for worse. Although rural property possesses stability, it usually has restricted salability. In this respect, an urban lot and building possesses an advantage, since a buyer can be found more readily. In general, limited marketability is the fundamental weakness of all real estate as collateral, especially when contrasted with government or railroad bonds. These are issued in series of large numbers, of which each bears the same value as any of the others and so possesses a relatively uniform market price to all buyers. However, each building or plot of ground possesses features peculiar to itself and stands as a separate unit. Such property has, therefore, no definite market, but is sold according as it appeals to the particular wishes of the individual buyer.

" Under these conditions real estate at times becomes a collateral from which a bank finds difficulty in realizing its money. It sometimes happens that a borrower who has given a piece of property as security for a loan is unable to repay the money. Through the legal process of foreclosure the property is placed at auction, and if no buyer appears the bank must retake it in order to escape loss. This situation is unsatisfactory to the bank, especially if it is unable to dispose of the property at a time when funds are needed to meet the demands of depositors for cash. To avoid this embarrassment the bank may have a mortgage guaranteed by a realty company, which for a small charge assumes entire care during the life of the loan and assures the payment of the yearly interest and final principal. This practice is especially favored by country banks investing in mortgages on city property. A bank may lessen the number of foreclosures on property held as security by insisting upon the amortization of the loan. Under this plan the borrower pays off a certain portion of the loan at the end of every year or a shorter interval. Thus at maturity the loan is entirely liquidated or at least the principal is considerably reduced.

" 2. Investment in Bonds.

" Because of the difficulty encountered in disposing of their mortgage holdings in time of need, savings banks invest heavily in bonds, which possess greater liquidity. The savings banks are usually permitted by law to hold the obligations of such governments as (1) the United States, (2) the state in which the bank is located, (3) any local subdivision thereof, (4) any outside state or city meeting certain tests of safety, such as adequate population, limit of indebtedness, and a satisfactory record in honoring its obligations in the past. A few states permit savings banks to purchase bonds issued by the more stable European governments.

The investments of savings banks in non-government securities are usually limited. The purchase of stock is generally prohibited, and in some states even bonds of industrial and public-service corporations are forbidden. Savings banks in New York State must confine their non-government investments exclusively to first-mortgage bonds of a selected list of railroads. These bonds, especially if listed on the Stock Exchange, can readily be sold by the bank if it is in need of cash, but under certain economic conditions this advantage is offset by the weakness of bond values. Such declines are caused not by any doubt as to payment of interest or principal, but by the low yield as compared with the high rate prevailing in the money market. Nor is there any opportunity to adjust the yield, for these securities usually have a long maturity.

" 3. Short-term Investments.

" It is therefore necessary for a savings bank to place some of its funds in a form which possesses both stability of value and marketability. A checking account may be maintained with a commercial bank, which must repay part or even the full amount on demand, but such funds yield only a small rate of interest. In order to secure a satisfactory yield and at the same time retain the necessary liquidity for their holdings, savings banks are usually permitted to invest in obligations with short maturities. In New York State, loans may be made on a demand promissory note signed by a borrower, who hypothecates such securities as the savings bank itself is permitted to purchase, but the loan in any case must not exceed 90 per cent. of the market value of this collateral. Savings banks are thus able indirectly to lend in the call-money market at a satisfactory rate through a commercial bank which directly places the funds and in return gives its demand note secured by say, Liberty Bonds. A savings bank may also lend on a ninety-day promissory note of a borrower who pledges as collateral either a pass book of another savings bank or a class of mortgage in which the bank itself may invest. The loan must not exceed 90 per cent. of the amount entered on the pass book, or 75 per cent. of the value of the mortgage.

" A greater liquidity has been added to the assets of savings banks by the passing of state laws which permit the purchase of bankers' acceptances. These must be of a kind eligible for purchase in the open market by a Federal Reserve bank, and thus a savings bank may count such holdings as a secondary reserve which can be readily converted into cash."

An application of these laws may be seen from the statement of the Seamen's Bank for Savings, a typical mutual bank located in New York City.

STATEMENT OF THE SEAMEN'S BANK FOR SAVINGS
January 1st, 1926

ASSETS

United States Government Bonds...............	$ 5,954,400.00
State of New York Bonds.....................	1,879,000.00
State of Illinois Bonds......................	288,000.00
Bonds of Cities in New York..................	5,770,300.00
Bonds of Cities in other States................	2,780,000.00
Railroad Bonds, First Mortgage...............	18,174,000.00
Par Value...........................	$34,845,700.00
Loans on Bond and Mortgage.................	$55,208,950.00
Banking House.............................	941,707.04
Cash......................................	2,483,211.02
Demand Loans, with Collateral.................	2,841,964.39
Accrued Interest...........................	823,229.10
	$97,144,761.55

LIABILITIES

Due Depositors..............................	$82,218,349.21
Surplus and Undivided Profits, at Par Value......	14,926,412.34
	$97,144,761.55

Investments of Commercial Banks. In recent years the function of the so-called commercial bank has changed considerably. According to the traditional view, " the test of a commercial bank is that it creates demand liabilities; consequently, it should hold only assets (chiefly the result of loans at short time based on actual transactions in goods) that are liquid and can be quickly converted into cash. The creation of demand liabilities (chiefly in the form of demand deposits) requires as a condition of sound banking a special kind of assets readily adapted to meet an instant demand for cash from customers.[1] However, since the war, the conditions implied in this conception of banking have changed. Banks now hold not only demand deposits but also time accounts. Thus national banks in 1908 held only $331,500,000 of time deposits representing but 7 per cent. of

[1] J. Lawrence Laughlin, *Banking Progress*, p. 158.

their total deposits, while in 1922 time deposits had increased to $3,046,000,000, or 23 per cent. of the total.[1]

The movement in recent years is seen from the fact that member banks in the Federal Reserve System increased their time deposits from $4,300,000,000 in 1920 to $10,870,000,000 in 1925.[2] Because of this change in the nature of their liabilities, the commercial banks have been able to lengthen the maturity of their assets. Whereas formerly they had to maintain their earning assets almost entirely in the form of commercial paper as stated in the above excerpt from Professor Laughlin, they now carry a large volume of securities. These, by law, must consist of bonds, for with minor exceptions, a bank incorporated under state or national law, may not hold the stock of another corporation. National banks increased their investment portfolio from $4,022,116,000 in 1921 to $5,725,622,000 in 1925.[3] As of June 30, 1925, the member banks of the Federal Reserve System held investments amounting to $8,888,345,000, or 29.9 per cent. of their total loans and investments. The distribution of these securities is seen in the table on page 602.[4]

Investment Trusts. A type of financial institution for facilitating indirect investment, is the investment trust. Although new to United States, it has been well developed in Great Britain and to a certain extent in some of the continental countries. It is the belief of many students of the New York money market that the investment trust is destined to become of increasing importance in the United States. A well-managed investment trust is an ideal medium for the indirect investment of individual funds, but it is already apparent that abuses have crept into the American system that will have to come to a head, at the expenses of investors, before the sound fundamental principles will emerge as matters of public knowledge, for investment guidance. The investment trust obtains its funds by selling its own bonds or stocks and then investing the proceeds in the securities of other enterprises. The investment trust is thus a collateral trust enterprise in which the securities are held in joint ownership.[5]

[1] *Federal Reserve Bulletin*, 1925, p. 24.
[2] Ibid., 1926, p. 31.   [3] Ibid., 1926, p. 31.
[4] Ibid., Nov., 1925, p. 831.
[5] See *Investment Trust Organization and Management*, Robinson, L. P., New York, 1926.

CLASSIFICATION OF STOCKS, BONDS, AND OTHER SECURITIES OF MEMBER BANKS AS OF JUNE 30, 1925

(In thousands of dollars)

Class of Banks	Domestic Securities						Foreign Securities		Total Securities
	U. S. Government Securities	State, County, and Municipal Bonds	All Other Bonds	Stock of Federal Reserve Bank	Stock of Other Corporations	Other Domestic Securities	Bonds of Foreign Governments	Other Foreign Bonds and Securities, including those of Municipalities	
Central reserve city banks:									
New York City	911,604	191,537	409,460	22,883	65,859	31,706	40,428	32,924	1,706,401
Chicago	155,834	40,888	66,893	5,228	8,013	4,655	22,486	3,460	307,457
Other reserve city banks	1,341,016	342,996	702,863	38,998	134,077	165,992	92,663	47,781	2,866,386
Country banks	1,393,916	453,485	1,605,546	47,858	67,385	179,146	171,726	89,039	4,008,101
Total	3,802,370	1,028,906	2,784,762	114,967	275,334	381,499	327,303	173,204	8,888,345

CHAPTER XLIV

THE BOND HOUSES

The Bond Business. That part of the public which does not buy bonds has little idea of the importance and value to the community of the bond business. It is not necessary to resort to many figures. It is necessary only to realize that bonds are the chief resource of our government in times of war, of our states and municipalities in furtherance of public works and buildings, of our railroads, of almost all public service corporations and many industrial corporations. The market value of the bonds listed in the New York Stock Exchange on January 1, 1926, amounted to $35,509,211,458. In volume and number the transactions on the exchange are only a fraction of those in direct security merchandising by the bond houses.

In view of the vast importance of the bond business in the economic life of the country, it is surprising that so little is known about bonds and the bond business. No one who has had experience in selling bonds will deny that the " average man " who has accumulated a surplus is far more conversant with stocks and the basic principles of stock speculation than with bonds and the principles of bond investment. The reason, however, is not far to seek. While human nature remains what it is, the element of chance, with its exhilarating risk, will be more attractive to men than the element of approximate certainty that is arrived at by painstaking, uninspired care. Since the stock market is more interesting and problematical than the bond market to the majority of readers, journalism, in the course of its duty to purvey to the majority, perennially fills its financial pages with time-honored summaries of yesterday's exchange doings, to-day's gossip, and circumspect conjectures as to the morrow.

The leading banking houses were not always primarily bond houses. Two generations ago financial business was transacted by " bankers and brokers." Bond selling was an incident to the general banking, exchange, and brokerage routine. It was all done " over the counter." There was comparatively little implied responsibility on the part of the vendor. In the age of Commodore Vanderbilt, the elder Gould, Fisk, and Drew the " caveat emptor " principle of exchange was accepted and the devil took many beside the hindmost. But now the speculative business in New York, so far as it is reputable and consequential, is done by " Members of the New York Stock Exchange " and the investment business is done by " Bankers, Dealers in Investment Bonds." Of course, a house marketing investment securities may have a seat on one of the exchanges, but it is accepted and understood that the firm specializes in one or the other of these two forms of business. The financial atmosphere, the financial temper, and the training necessary to superior service in either occupation have accomplished the severance of stock dealing and bond selling.

The Functions of the Bond Houses. The primary function of the bond house is to obtain capital for the creation of new enterprises or the enlargement of old. So far as concerns these houses in their proper capacity the capital obtained is in the form of loans. The houses purchase the loans outright for their own account and resell to their clients. As in any sort of merchandising, there are few wholesalers and many retailers. The prominent " wholesale " bond dealers, numbering less than two dozen, are responsible for the distribution of the major part (in dollar amount) of American flotations. Some have few, if any, travelling representatives. Their sales, in this country, are effected by public subscription, stimulated through extensive advertising, and by distribution to large institutions, such as the insurance companies, and to the smaller bond houses.[1]

" Retail " is not a term properly descriptive of the firms in mind, although it suggests the relative size of the issues handled and the relative volume of business. It misleads if it suggests that the *main* business of such houses is to distribute among small investors issues that originally were investigated and purchased by " wholesale " houses. This is not the case. For the most part each of the American bond houses buys its issues independently, in accordance with its policy regarding investments, or it buys them in " joint account " with other houses

---

[1] For a detailed description of the principles and practices of security wholesaling see Security Syndicate Operations by Arthur Galston.

having similar policies. These houses are autonomous; their prosperity is built on their ability to find and obtain, on the one hand, funded obligations that merit investment, and on the other, a clientèle that has faith in them and their business judgment and probity. A distinction must be drawn between the large and the small retail houses. The former may originate, that is, assist in creating, securities, as well as sell bonds; the very small retailer, however, must necessarily confine his activities to the function of distribution.

Not only may bond houses be thus classified according to their size and function, but they may also be grouped according to their legal organization. Most houses are unincorporated, since the American public has had greater confidence in this type of organization for the investment field. However, in recent years there has been a tendency to incorporate, and several of the large metropolitan banks have formed security companies. These are chartered under state law and their stock is duly held by the parent company. As a rule the management is practically identical, for the same board of directors and in some cases the same set of officers control both institutions. Besides, many banks throughout the country now operate bond departments.

The success of the bond houses in weathering financial storms while stock exchange houses have gone down by the score, is strong support of the contention that bond investment rests on a basis of principles reducible to a science. There is no business in all the country that has placed itself on more enduring foundations of business wisdom, or that is conducted on a higher plane of business ethics.

Enough has been said of the great services of the American bond houses. Without their help it would be impossible to finance American enterprises on the present scale. By their ultraconservatism they are establishing themselves in public confidence in a way to bring together with the greatest expedition and least middleman's cost the promoters of our national resources and the creditor class from whom must come the capital necessary to municipal and industrial development. They extend the boundaries of credit and exercise a directive and steadying influence upon enterprise. By preaching the principles of bond buying in advertisements, pamphlets, correspondence, and in personal interviews by bond salesmen they are slowly but surely converting the American people into a nation of investors. It will be worth while to examine in greater detail the several functions they perform.

The Purchasing Function. If a municipal loan is offered, the purchase is a comparatively simple matter, provided the municipality is well known to the fraternity. Then no preliminary investigation is required; a bid is made for the loan at the current market rates and acceptance on award is subject to the approval of the bidder's attorney in all respects affecting the validity of the obligation.

If the municipality is not well known to the bidder, a qualified representative will, or should be, sent to learn at first hand the physical and financial condition of the municipality and to form an estimate of its probable future willingness and ability to meet its present and future obligations.

If a corporation loan is offered, it will probably be submitted at the offices of the bankers by a representative of the company or by a promoter. If the applicant is of a social turn of mind he will probably not lack the company of his kind in the anteroom. Competition, fortunately, is keen.

The first step in the process of elimination (there is more elimination than acceptance) is to discard the propositions of companies that conduct a kind of business unfamiliar to the bankers. Except under unusually favorable· circumstances the highest grade of bond houses will not purchase bonds of industrial corporations, mining or irrigation companies, etc.

The next step is to discard loans that have not a claim on property worth, under the most unfavorable conditions, more than the amount of the obligation secured. Most corporations will bond themselves in as large a sum as their bankers will permit. Loans are continually being rejected because of insufficient equity in property values.

The third step is to discard those propositions which do not give reasonable assurance of earning at all times at least 50 per cent. more than all fixed charges, after making extremely liberal estimates for future increased operating expenses.

The fourth step is to decline loans to companies conducted by men or with methods that do not meet with approval.

If the house is satisfied by interview and correspondence in matters of the above nature, and if a suitable price can be agreed upon, then engineers and accountants may be sent to the plant and offices to make a thorough investigation, and the statistical department will assemble all possible data on the prospective borrower. Finally the members of the firm, with counsel, meet officers of the company and their attorneys to settle the matters of form. On acceptance of an issue a careful banking house may demand representation on the directorate of the company until such time as the company shall have discharged its bonded obligation.

Syndicates. It has so far been assumed that a single bond house is undertaking the financial operation. In practice, operations are assumed not singly but in syndicates. A syndicate has been described by Dewing as a " mode of mutual insurance against the risks incident to the final distribution of a large body of investment securities." [1] From the legal viewpoint a syndicate is a form of joint venture which in turn is a kind of partnership. A syndicate differs, however, from a partnership in being limited as to time and purpose since it is formed to continue only during the period of distribution and to accomplish the object of selling an issue of securities.

A distinction must be drawn between buying and selling syndicates. The function of the former is to insure or guarantee the sale of the issue under consideration. This group may be said to purchase these securities not actually but on a contingent basis, so that it takes them over if not finally placed with the investing public. The buying syndicate, in the expression of the street, is then said to " hold the bag." The function of the selling syndicate is that of distribution. Because of this difference in purpose, the members of each syndicate must possess qualifications of a special nature. A member of a buying syndicate must necessarily have strong financial resources so as to be able to take over its share of unsold securities. A member of a selling syndicate should possess an adequate sales force in order to place the securities allotted to it. In general the number in a buying syndicate is small, but membership in a selling syndicate may be nation-wide and include several hundred houses.

Although there are many variations of selling syndicates, two forms, the unlimited and limited forms, may be noted here. The former is really a true syndicate, since the members share a joint responsibility for the placement of the securities. This type of

[1] *Financial Policy of Corporations*, p. 378.

undivided liability is often known as the " Eastern " syndicate since it has long flourished in that section of the United States. The limited type is commonly called the " Western " syndicate from the section in which it finds greater favor.

This illustration may clarify the difference: Let us assume that houses A, B, and C formed a " three-three " syndicate arrangement or account to float an issue of $1,200,000,—that is, each firm assumes one-third of the liabilities of the operation. Firm A sells $500,000, B $275,000, and C disposes of only $125,000. Since total sales amount to only $900,000, there is an unsold amount of $300,000. If the members of the syndicate have entered into an unlimited account then each must take over an equal share of the unsold securities or $100,000 apiece. Therefore, although A has oversold its allotment, it must carry a burden equal to C which has been unsuccessful in placing its share. The account may be summarized as follows:

Firms	A	B	C	Total
Original participation	$400,000	$400,000	$400,000	$1,200,000
Sales	500,000	275,000	125,000	900,000
Liability	100,000	100,000	100,000	300,000

Under a limited account, A would have no further liability, and B and C would have to carry the unsold securities according to the following schedule:

Firms	A	B	C	Total
Original participation	$400,000	$400,000	$400,000	$1,200,000
Sales	500,000	275,000	125,000	900,000
Undischarged liability	−100,000	−125,000	−275,000	−300,000
Net liability		−75,000	−225,000	

The economic value of the syndicate arrangement is unquestioned. As the definition indicates, it is an insurance mechanism that brings about a wider distribution of the risk inherent in the flotation of any issue. Moreover, the syndicate brings together a large aggregation of capital and so assures the borrower of receiving the funds that he is seeking. Finally the syndicate method, by assembling the combined selling forces of a number of houses, results in more rapid and more widespread distribution and thereby reduces the element of risk of a possible unsuccessful placement, and increases the probability of a satis- factory after-market for the securities.

The Advisory Function. The advisory and directive function has its source in the statistical departments which every house of quality must maintain. It finds its chief expression, as already stated, in tabloid investment lessons, printed in the advertising columns of newspapers and periodicals, or with somewhat greater fulness in pamphlets and monographs. If a prospective client has an investment policy that is apparently not suited to his particular needs, the home office may tactfully direct his attention by letter or through their representative in his territory to a means by which he may better his position. Some bond houses maintain a daily news sheet for the benefit of their salesmen in which are printed not only pertinent items of current interest, but timely discussions of different problems.

Activities of this nature, developed to their logical conclusion, have lead to the establishment of the American bond houses in the confidence of the public as their chief advisers in financial matters. The better houses can count upon the absorption by their friends among institutions and investors of a certain amount of any issue they recommend and offer.

This advisory function can become general and economically sound only as the bond houses as a class recognize the *scientific* and *professional* nature of their calling and guide their movements and policies, alive to the power of their position and their responsibility as repositories of a nation's investment confidence.

The Banking Function. Illustrative of the relation between house and client, there has arisen the demand that banking departments be established for the safe-keeping of funds destined, upon enlargement, to go into investment, and also to accommodate those who wish to purchase securities before they have sufficient funds to pay in full for them. From the necessities of these two situations it is only a short step to the conduct on a small scale of a bank of deposit subject to check. But properly and ordinarily, the banking department of a bond house is conducted as a matter of accommodation to its customers and not primarily to do a general banking business. From these beginnings it sometimes has happened that a full-fledged bank has been evolved, in which the savings, deposit, and trust functions of the bank have balanced, nominally at least, the sales function of the bond house, but an exception of this sort would only prove the rule. Although some bond houses are banks, technically, and are entitled to their common designation, " bankers," nevertheless, on the principle that security selling is not best undertaken by obligor companies but is properly left to the bond houses which make it a profession, so the general banking business is best left to banks proper.

The Bond Houses as Fiscal Agents. Because of purchasing, advisory, and banking functions bond houses are called upon to act as fiscal agents for corporations, municipalities, and even states. The long standing, friendly banking relations of the older firms with the Western cities recall the fact that interest, and sometimes the principal, of the loans of these cities is payable at the offices of the bond house. Here and there an Eastern institution is met that will not buy Western municipals which are not payable in the East. This is not so much to save the cost of conversion into New York funds, for that might be arranged in the price, as because of the inconvenience and possible loss of interest in shipping the bonds west for collection. Some of the older bond houses act as depositories for Western cities. In general, the conduct of the bond houses as fiscal agents has merited the trust placed in them.

It is natural that private corporations will look to the bond houses as their financial agents. The disposition of a company's funded loans is not merely a matter of merchandising; it is natural that the relationship begun by the purchase of bonds and banking representation on the directorate shall be continued indefinitely in the thought of future financial needs. Just as the great railroad systems have their long established financial connections with certain large houses, so the public service and other private corporations form alliances with the bond houses. The continuance of such relations implies conformity on the part of the obligor corporations with the policy of the bond houses. This also tends toward a betterment of financial conditions throughout the country.

The Selling Function. American banking houses are not eleemosynary. Whatever may be their usefulness in the community, it is the result of that enlightened self-interest which used to be expressed in the phrase " Honesty is the best policy." Their reason for being is to make money by selling bonds, and the competition is getting keener every day. Many of the ordinary effects of competition are noticeable in the bond business. There is standardization of wares and policies, there is diminution in ratio of profits. But two ordinary effects of competition are conspicuously absent. There is no deterioration of the product and as yet very little tendency toward consolidation among the vendors.

The Protective Function. There is a radical difference in the attitude of bond houses in this matter of repurchasing securities of clients to whom they have sold them. Some take the stand that a sale is a sale, and the responsibility of a house that has acted in good faith ceases upon delivery of the bond and the receipt of payment. This position is logical and just, but again competition steps into benefit the customer. Other houses say: " We shall put out our issues as nearly as possible on a plane of marketability with active listed securities. We make no promises, but, except in times of panic when it may be impossible to raise money to satisfy everybody, we hope and expect to be so situated as to buy back at the fair market price the securities we have sold." Few investors realize the full significance of this protective market policy. They are inclined to remember that they may buy most of the active listed bonds on the exchange and sell them the same day at an average total loss, due to the " higgling of the market," of perhaps only 2 points or so. They do not realize that on a declining bond market they may have to take an additional loss, in listed bonds, of say 8 points, or 10 points in all, whereas in the same circumstance a bond house would think twice before quoting a client a price 10 points below the previous selling price. And, to say nothing of investment guidance, nine times out of ten the issue of the bond house is yielding at least $\frac{1}{2}$ per cent. more per annum than an equally sound listed issue.

Another protective operation is to maintain a market for a new issue until its position is assured. Such a policy is followed by a reputable investment house long after the syndicate has been dissolved and the support of the members withdrawn.

But the protective function of the bond house is most important in respect to the moral responsibility of " seeing clients through " default, reorganization, and rehabilitation in the extremely rare cases in which trouble arises. In some instances losses amounting to hundreds of thousands of dollars have been made good; in many instances firms have volunteered to pay interest which has been suspended; in every case a reputable bond house will feel called upon to take the active leadership, in part at least at its own expense, in upholding the mortgage rights or other legal claims of the bondholders. To this end the investment house will form and direct protective committees.

With the enlightened aid of bond houses the creditor class will do well to take as much pains in the investment of its wealth as in the acquisition of it. Buyers of corporation bonds should exercise almost as much care in the selection of a financial adviser as in the choice of a security. They will do well to seek a bond house with a strong personality, strong convictions on investment matters, and the capital and equipment to back them up.

PART VI

TAXATION OF BONDS

CHAPTER XLV

THE CLASSIFICATION AND DESCRIPTION OF TAXES

Each of the several excellent treatises on investment that have appeared since the earlier editions of this book has laid considerable emphasis on the relation of taxation to investment securities. The relationship becomes more vital as time goes on and the functions of government are multiplied and intensified, and as they coördinate more closely with the daily coming and going of men. The costs of government increase correspondingly, and the taxes also. The taxes not only increase proportionately, and therefore require that new ways and means be devised to levy on.individuals and corporations, but they tend to express the social will that all bear some part of the tax burden to share in the responsibilities of government, even though the cost of collection exceed the avails.

Elements of Taxation. A tax has been well defined by Professor Seligman in his *Essays in Taxation*, page 432, as a " compulsory contribution from the person to the government to defray the expenses incurred in the common interest of all without reference to special benefits derived." Writers on public finance have pointed out certain requisites of a sound taxation system such as the following:

Adequacy—The tax should be sufficient in its productivity to meet the needs of the state.

Economy—The tax should be collected as cheaply as possible.

Simplicity—The tax should be administered with all avoidance of complexity.

Elasticity—The tax should possess the capacity of responding to changes in the demand for revenue.

Flexibility—The tax should be of such nature that it can be modified to meet changing conditions.

Equity—The tax should be levied without favoritism for any special group and with full justice for all classes.

Students of public finance do not agree on the application of these principles, particularly the last. There are various theories as to what is a just tax distribution. There is the theory of the ability to pay, first enunciated by Adam Smith. There is the individualist theory that taxes should be apportioned according to the benefits derived. As these underlying problems are in the field of public finance, this discussion will be confined mainly to a presentation of the various classes of taxes with particular reference to investment.

Previous Investment Writers on Taxation. The approach to this complicated and controversial subject of taxation naturally is somewhat different in each of the leading texts on investment and each approach has its advantages. Jordan (1919) is concerned with the modern tax-phenomena as affecting the net yield of investments. Lagerquist (1921) seeks the fundamental principles involved in the taxation of securities as such, with heavier dependence on law than on economics, and with less regard for the relation of general property taxes to security taxes. Kirshman (1924) entitles his discussion *Taxation and Security Prices*, which is not dissimilar to Jordan's approach through net yield, but Kirshman recognizes, by brief reference, that "the security holder is directly or indirectly concerned with every kind of taxes." Kirshman deals very lightly with the legal subtleties. Lyon (1926), a practicing attorney, member of the *Committee on Double Taxation and Situs for the Purposes of Taxation*, of the National Tax Association (1915), and author of *Principles of Taxation*, gets at the very heart of the subject in his scholarly book on *Investment*, and therefore his main emphasis is on the economics of taxation, although he does not neglect the law. Moreover, the mutual dependence of general property and of security taxation is adequately recognized. Trained in the Harvard Law School, Lyon uses the case method with the poignancy of illustration but misproportioned emphasis and incoördination encouraged by that method. Montgomery's *Financial Handbook* (1925) is not a text on investments, but among its myriad other accomplishments it stops many of the gaps in the array of facts that yawn in all the other treatments. The combination of Lyon who is a sound, constructive thinker, and Montgomery, who is compendious, will give a student of investment taxation most of the parts there are to the jig-saw puzzle, but they do not furnish him with the key picture.

Approaching Taxation via Classification. Therefore the authors of this discussion are not under the embarrassing necessity of merely restating previous adequate expressions; they have the opportunity, to set up the first articulated working model of American tax practice for investment use. If it is to serve its purpose it must comprehend not only the taxation of securities, and of investments and investors, but of all property and all people.

Six Classifications of Taxation. The subjoined classification tables were constructed prior to the explanatory text. Once constructed the text was a mere detail, and almost wrote itself. It is hardly more than the flesh on the skeleton. If students will approach investment taxation in the same light, it is hoped they may get a working acquaintance with tax problems at first reading.

The broadest questions on this subject that occur to an orderly mind, are the following:

1. Who can tax?
2. Who can be taxed?
3. What things are or can be taxed?
4. In what ways and to what extent can men or things be taxed?
5. Where can people be taxed?
6. Where can things be taxed?

From this reasoning comes the division into these six classes:
1. The jurisdiction of tax authority.
2. The direct incidence of taxation.
3. The kinds of taxable property.
4. The method or degree of imposition and collection.
5. The situs or domicile of the corporation or individual taxed.
6. The situs or domicile of the taxable.

Further subdivision of the general field is as follows:

GENERAL CLASSIFICATION OF TAXES

I. By Jurisdiction
- Foreign
- Federal
- State
- Local
  - County
  - Municipal
  - Minor Civil Divisions

II. By the Direct Incidence
- Corporation
  - Foreign to the United States
  - Domestic
    - Foreign, i.e., not incorporated in the State of Jurisdiction
    - Domestic, i.e., incorporated in the State of Jurisdiction
- Individual
  - Alien
    - Non-resident U. S.
    - Resident U. S.
      - Non-resident of the State of Jurisdiction
      - Resident of the State of Jurisdiction
  - Citizen
    - Non-resident U. S.
    - Resident U. S.
      - Non-resident in the State of Jurisdiction
      - Resident in the State of Jurisdiction

III. By the Kinds of Taxables
- Income
  - Corporate
    - Net corporate income is conceived as substantially the same as individual income except that charitable and educational contributions are not deductible
    - Under state jurisdictions the taxable income may or may not be limited to that produced or earned within the state
  - Individual
    - Wages, commissions
    - Profits from own business, or from sale of real estate, securities, etc.
    - Income from partnerships, fiduciaries, and any other income not specifically deductible
    - Interest on bank deposits, corporate bonds, etc.

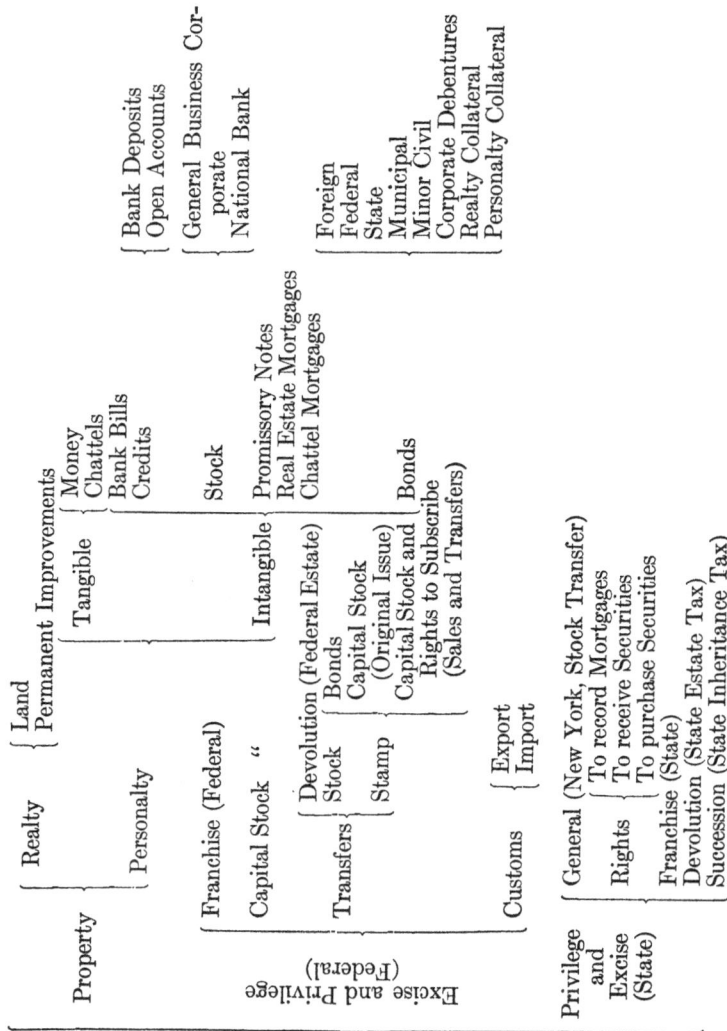

III. By the Kinds of Taxables

- Property
  - Realty
    - Land
    - Permanent Improvements
  - Personalty
    - Tangible
      - Money
      - Chattels
      - Bank Bills
    - Intangible
      - Credits
        - Bank Deposits
        - Open Accounts
      - Stock
        - General Business Corporate
        - National Bank
      - Promissory Notes
      - Real Estate Mortgages
      - Chattel Mortgages
      - Bonds
        - Foreign
        - Federal
        - State
        - Municipal
        - Minor Civil
        - Corporate Debentures
        - Realty Collateral
        - Personalty Collateral

- Excise and Privilege (Federal)
  - Franchise (Federal)
  - Capital Stock "
  - Transfers
    - Stock
      - Devolution (Federal Estate)
      - Bonds
      - Capital Stock (Original Issue)
      - Capital Stock and Rights to Subscribe (Sales and Transfers)
    - Stamp
  - Customs
    - Export
    - Import

- Privilege and Excise (State)
  - General (New York, Stock Transfer)
  - Rights
    - To record Mortgages
    - To receive Securities
    - To purchase Securities
  - Franchise (State)
  - Devolution (State Estate Tax)
  - Succession (State Inheritance Tax)

IV. By the Method or Degree of Imposition or Collection
- Direct and Indirect
- External and Internal
- Normal Tax and Surtax { Progressive, Regressive
- Uniform and Graduated
- Single and Multiple { Double, Triple, etc.
- Exemptions, Credits and Deductions

V. By the Situs of the Corporation or Individual Taxed
- Foreign Country { Alien, American Citizen
- United States
  - Alien { Non-resident, Resident
  - Citizen { Non-resident, Resident
- State or States of Jurisdiction { Non-resident, Resident
- Minor Civil Divisions { Non-resident, Resident

VI. By the Situs of the Taxable
- Income
  - Domestic Corporations and Citizens
  - Foreign Corporations and Non-resident Aliens
  - Companies Incorporated in the State, and Citizens
  - Companies not Incorporated in the State, and Non-residents
- Property
  - Tangible { Realty, Personalty
  - Intangible Personalty
- Inheritance
  - Tangible { Realty, Personalty
  - Intangible Property
- Miscellaneous { Excises, Privileges

I. Classification of Taxes According to Jurisdiction

For reasons of space it is necessary to subdivide by separate table on the opposite page the *classification according to the jurisdiction*. Since all taxes are imposed by governments, and since almost all general governments impose taxes, this first division in its main heads is merely a broad classification of forms of government, from the American standpoint, that we have made in previous chapters.

Foreign Jurisdiction

The only property of American investors resident in America that can be taxed by a foreign government is property (and the income therefrom) that is situated in the jurisdiction of that government. The kinds and rates of taxes are at the discretion of that government. But all kinds of property and income of American citizens resident abroad may be taxed *ad libidum* by the foreign jurisdictions in which they are resident or their properties situated.

However, citizens paying income and profits taxes to foreign countries or to possessions of the United States, residents paying such taxes to possessions of the United States, also residents paying such taxes to a foreign country (if their country of origin allows a similar credit to the United States citizens resident therein), may obtain a deduction from their Federal Income Tax as otherwise computed, known as " the credit on foreign taxes." The amount of the credit is the proportion of the United States tax which the taxpayer's net income from sources without the United States bears to his total net income.

The taxes imposed on European securities, which represent most of our foreign investments that are other than proprietary interests, may be summarized as follows: [1]

In most of the countries treated there are stamp taxes on both the issue and sale of stocks and bonds. The tax on the issue is usually based on the par value, while the one on the transfer or sale, which is commonly called a "sales tax" or "turnover tax," is calculated on the amount of the purchase price. Such is unqualifiedly the case in Belgium, Germany, Netherlands, and Spain. While frequently the tax is the same

[1] Carroll, Mitchell B., *Taxation of Securities in Europe,* U. S. Dept. of Commerce.

I. CLASSIFICATION OF TAXES ACCORDING TO JURISDICTION

Foreign

Income — Federal (1926)

Corporate—$13\frac{1}{2}$% of net income

Individual

Normal Tax
- $1,000 of income of single persons is exempt
- $2,500 of income of married persons is exempt, and $400 additional for each dependent
- $1\frac{1}{2}$% on first $4,000 of *taxable* income
- 3% on second $4,000
- 5% on additional income

Surtax
- 1% on amt. of taxable income between

Taxable income between		Rate	Total Surtax
$ 10,000 and	$14,000.....	2%	$ 40
14,000 and	16,000.....	3%	80
16,000 and	18,000.....	4%	140
18,000 and	20,000.....	5%	220
20,000 and	22,000.....	6%	320
22,000 and	24,000.....	7%	440
24,000 and	28,000.....	8%	720
28,000 and	32,000.....	9%	1,040
32,000 and	36,000.....	10%	1,400
36,000 and	40,000.....	11%	1,800
40,000 and	44,000.....	12%	2,240
44,000 and	48,000.....	13%	2,720
48,000 and	52,000.....	14%	3,240
52,000 and	56,000.....	15%	3,800
56,000 and	60,000.....	16%	4,400
60,000 and	64,000.....	17%	5,040
64,000 and	70,000.....	18%	6,060
70,000 and	80,000.....	19%	7,860
80,000 and	100,000.....	20%	11,660
100,000 and upward.....			

Federal (1926)

- Estate
  - $100,000 of estate of resident decedent is exempt
  - 1% on first $ 50,000 of taxable property
  - 2% on second 50,000
  - 3% on next 100,000
  - 4% on next 200,000
  - 5% on next 200,000
  - 6% on next 200,000
  - 7% on next 200,000
  - 8% on next 500,000
  - 9% on next 500,000
  - 10% on next 500,000
  - 11% on next 500,000
  - 12% on next 500,000
  - 13% on next 500,000
  - 14% on next 1,000,000, and thus progressively to
  - 20% on over 10,000,000
- Excise
  - Stamp
    - Bonds
    - Capital Stock—Original Issue
    - Capital Stock }
    - Rights to Subscribe } Sales and Transfers
    - Miscellaneous
  - Customs
    - Export
    - Import
  - Miscellaneous

State

- Income { General, Classified
- Property { General
- Privilege { Inheritance

Local

- Property { General, Classified
- Privilege

for stocks and bonds, in some instances distinctions are made between them, and between nominative,[1] bearer, and other kinds of securities.

Certain countries have methods peculiar to themselves. For example, in the United Kingdom issues of stock are reached indirectly by means of a stamp duty levied on the statement of the amount which is to form the nominal share capital of registered limited companies, and on the statement of the amount of any increase of registered capital. A similar tax is levied in Austria. In the former country there is also a stamp duty on contract notes.

In most of the countries the sales tax is collected when the transfer is made. France collects a stamp tax on the face value of securities, a transfer tax on bearer securities, which is based on the average quoted price for the preceding year, and a tax on coupon payments is collected on an annual basis. A tax similar to the annual tax on the transfer of securities is found in Italy. Switzerland is unique in that its taxation of securities is effected through levying a stamp duty on the coupons of all kinds of securities.

Special provisions for foreign securities appear only in few instances. In France, while the tax rate is virtually the same as for French securities, nevertheless before the securities of foreign companies can be issued in France or quoted on the bourse, a responsible agent must be named. Belgium levies a special stamp tax on securities issued in that country by foreign companies. In Italy the capital of foreign companies which is employed in operations in Italian territory is subject to a special tax.

No-par-value stock is so rarely found in European bourses that mention of it is rarely made in tax legislation or literature. However, specific provisions are found in the laws of Belgium, Spain, and Switzerland. In the first-mentioned country, the Government may compel the company to make a declaration of the real value of such stock, which is then taxed according to the ordinary rate. A fixed rate is levied in Spain. In Switzerland the coupons of such securities are taxable at a fixed percentage. The issue of no-par-value stock is discouraged in France.

FEDERAL REVENUE SYSTEM

The vicissitudes of foreign tax jurisdictions are of little concern to most American investors. But not so, the direct or indirect taxation of their own national government. In its proper place in these classifications we shall have more to do with direct and indirect taxes, but for immediate purposes we mean by direct taxes those from which the incidence, the " ictus," or the blow, falls directly on property or income of the generality of persons and corporations; by indirect, those from which the blow falls indirectly, and less openly, as in the case of

[1] Equivalent to registered.

customs duties.   Indirect taxes are usually paid in the guise of increased prices.

Indirect federal taxes are mostly the export tariffs and the internal revenue taxes on commodities and services.   By virtue of historical priority they should have priority of treatment in this classified scheme of federal taxation.   But since 1913, and notably since our entrance into the World War, the increasing proportion of the entire national revenue that has been derived from the income tax, and the fact that this tax is the most important of all federal taxes of this generation to the American investor, give it the right of priority in classification.

Federal Corporate Income Tax.   From the standpoint of the individual the direct federal income tax on corporations (now $13\frac{1}{2}$ per cent.) is an indirect tax and not a direct deduction from his taxable income.   It is an indirect tax on the individual who is an owner of any of the securities of the corporation—bonds or stock—in that it reduces the net income of the corporation. It reduces the surplus which represents the equity that determines in part the degree of safety resident in the company's bonds, and it reduces the volume of income, which is the ultimate source of both surplus and dividends.

To the stockholder (who for the purposes of tax-classification may be considered an investor) only a part of this $13\frac{1}{2}$ per cent. is a tax, for the amount of corporate dividends he receives is deductible in ascertaining his net income subject to the normal tax.   For the stockholder of moderate means, whose taxable income does not overstep the normal rates running to 6 per cent. maximum, the main issue is that he does not directly pay any federal income tax on his dividends.

However, if the stockholder is truly an investor, and not really a speculator, if he buys stock for the primary purpose of obtaining the dividends, he buys for long-term ownership, and must bear in mind the mutations in the rate of the corporate income tax and in the individual normal and surtaxes.

These mutations are greater than many realize.   Few remember that four years before the inauguration of the so-called Federal Income Tax,—as early as 1909,—American corporations were subject to an excise tax of 1 per cent. of their net incomes. This rate was maintained in the income law of 1913, but the rate in those days was a higher ratio to the present than is indicated by the figures, for no specific exemptions were then allowed. Under the pressure of war the 1916 law raised the rate to 2 per cent., and the 1917 law created an additional 4 per cent., but excluded from the computation dividends received by the corporation. For 1917 the general run of corporations and partnerships paid also excess profits taxes of from 20 to 60 per cent. In 1918 the normal tax was raised to 12 per cent. and an excess and war profits tax with brackets of 30, 60, and 80 per cent. These abnormal rates lose part of their sinister significance in the duress that occasioned them. Nevertheless, for 1922 the income tax was increased to $12\frac{1}{2}$ per cent., although the excess profits tax was removed, and in 1925 it was raised to $13\frac{1}{2}$ per cent.

The corporate income tax, then, is a permanent (if variable) impressive reality that must be reckoned with directly and indirectly in any appraisal of investment values.

Federal Individual Income Tax. Due to the excessive costs of the World War, governments have fallen back on the ability-to-pay principle of taxation rather than on the taxation-of-property-benefited principle. This has meant a main dependence for revenue on national income taxes, for these tap with precision theoretically all whose ability is based on earnings from personal services rather than the relatively few who are property owners of record. The United States was not one of the earliest to espouse income taxation, though this form of financing is now thoroughly rooted in our national fiscal policies and is spreading among the state governments. There are reported to be about sixty foreign governments and political divisions that employ the income tax and the authors recall no instance of an abandonment.

In this country, as the war debt continues to be amortized, the importance of state income taxation relative to national is likely to increase, and the mutations in rates to which we observed that corporations have been subject, will obtain in the taxation of individuals also, as they have since 1913. The history of corporate income tax changes will suffice to impress the fact of change, without relating the similar changes in the individual income taxes. Nevertheless, it may serve as a base for various comparisons if a schedule is given of the various rates to which individuals are subject for the calendar year 1926. Therefore, they are submitted in the classification. At this writing (in the early part of 1927) there is considerable agitation for reduction in income tax rates, both federal and state, and recessions for a period of years are likely; but with the increase in scope and cost of all government, we are not disposed to join the majority who are hopeful of permanent lessening of tax burdens.

In presenting in this place current schedules of tax rates we have already transgressed the limits of " jurisdiction " or " sovereignty," for rates are properly discussed under the fourth general classification as to the extent that people and things can be taxed. The effect of these taxes on the net income from securities is more properly treated there also.

Federal Income Tax on Estates and Trusts. The net income of estates and trusts is filed in the same manner, and taxed on the same basis, with certain exceptions, as the net income of individuals. If the income is distributed by the fiduciary, the fiduciary renders an information return, the individual beneficiary includes the amount distributed in his income return, and, claiming whatever exemption he may be entitled to, pays his tax. If the fiduciary does not distribute all the income he renders a tax return, claims an exemption of $1,500, and pays a tax just as if the undistributed income represented income to a single individual.

Federal Estate Tax. Our national government first utilized a legacy tax from 1798 to 1802 in the form of a stamp tax, and again, without the stamp feature, in the Civil and Spanish Wars. In 1916, as a war measure, it imposed the first form of our present evolving estate tax, which, as modified from time to time, seems to be with us indefinitely, although demand for its abolition increases.

Second only to income, the most important source of national revenue that is derived from the individual directly, and therefore directly affects investments, on the transfer of property on account of death, is this federal estate tax. In law, this is not a tax on property and the possessions. Therefore it is one of the many forms of federal excise taxes. It is called also the federal inheritance tax, but rather loosely, since the tax is on the privilege to transfer, and not on the privilege to inherit. In considering state inheritance taxes in the next subdivision of jurisdiction we shall find not only that they are more correctly named but that both the privilege to transfer, and the privilege to inherit may be taxed, and in at least one state the privileges to do both.

As a practical business matter the federal estate tax is a direct tax on property in that it is an ad valorem levy (at progressive rates) on the entire amount of the estate. Therefore among other things it is a tax on the value of securities. Since legally it is a tax on a right to transfer (a tax on devolution) and not a tax on securities as such, government and other civil loans that ordinarily may be free from tax are not exempted under this act. (The present schedule of the tax rates will be found in the table "According to Jurisdiction.") In contrast, the usual state inheritance tax is a progressive ad valorem tax based on the amount of the individual inheritance.

It is of great importance, at present, that there is no federal tax on estates of resident testators unless the net worth of the property exceeds $100,000; and the federal tax on non-residents is limited to the property situated in the United States. The tax accrues within a year from death. For the purposes of the law, decedents are classed either as residents or non-residents without respect to citizenship.

The same mutability we have found in federal income taxes extends to federal estate taxes, for these latter, also, are the outgrowth of revenue measures seeking to meet a part of the extraordinary expenses of the world's costliest war. How they may be modified in the future under more stable requirements of national expenditure, and under the criticism of the inequities particularly inherent in estate taxation, is in the lap of the gods. (The rates in effect at the time of the decedent's death are those which apply.) In general, we intend not to dilate on inequities of taxation, for they permeate the entire tax mechanism and they are so disputable as to give whatever justification exists for the propaganda of the single tax. Not specifically relating to investment they belong to a treatise on taxation.

Federal Estate Tax: Residents and Non-residents. The gross estate in the case of residents is considered to be " the value at the time of death of all property (except real property situated outside of the United States) which is subject to the payment of charges against the estate,—and subject to distribution. . . . In the case of non-residents the value of all property situated within the United States should be included. Real estate and stocks and bonds, physically located in the United States at the time of death, moneys due on open accounts, by domestic debtors and stocks of corporations or associations of the United States, constitute property having a situs within the United States. The value of so-called tax-exempt bonds must be included in the gross estate."[1]

Federal Capital Stock Tax. The federal capital stock tax, first operative on January 1, 1917, was another excise tax growing out of the exigencies of the war. It was a tax on the privilege of doing business for profit in a corporate capacity. As an emergency measure it has been repealed. It is referred to because that fact is apparently not common knowledge.

Ordinarily, when we spoke of capital stock taxes we referred to this federal impost on corporations for the right to do business. More loosely we sometimes speak of the taxes imposed by the several states on the capital stock of companies incorporated in the state imposing the tax and payable by the resident (and sometimes the non-resident) owners thereof. Of such taxes we shall see more in the other classification brackets. This should not be confused with the stamp taxes on the issue and the transfer of stock, referred to presently.

Miscellaneous Excise Taxes. We now descend, for disposal with passing reference, to those other kinds of federal taxes that are largely minutiæ, from the investor's standpoint, and with the exception of certain stamp taxes, concern him only as they affect the prices of commodities and services, which in turn affect the earnings of corporations and therefore the security of his investments. These items are mentioned merely to make the tax treatment comprehensive. Nothing perhaps illustrates the illogic—perhaps the necessary illogic—of tax-practice better than the *potpourri* of objects specifically subject to tax, listed under Title VI of the Revenue Act of 1924. For our purposes it is not necessary to give the rates. Automatic slot-machines, automobile truck chassis, automobiles and motorcycles, cameras, cigar or cigarette holders, and amber and meerschaum pipes, films and photographic plates, firearms and their ammunition, humidors, jewelry, mah-jong, pung-chow and similar tile sets, statuary and other works of art, tires and accessories.

Cigars, cigarettes, and tobacco are singled out for a special tax,

[1] Montgomery, *Financial Handbook*, p. 1626.

and the manufacturers of these particular commodities are separately taxed (under Title VII) with persons operating or renting passenger automobiles for hire, bowling alleys and billiard rooms, brewers, distillers, wholesale and retail liquor dealers, various kinds of brokers, opium. Then there are taxes on admissions and dues.

Federal Stamp Taxes. Transfers and conveyances subject to tax by affixation of stamps, are misdemeanors if unaccompanied by stamps. Stamp taxes present an elaborate list of objects for impost including conveyances of real estate, memoranda of sale, passage tickets, playing cards, insurance policies, powers of attorney, sales of produce futures, etc., etc. But those with which we are most directly concerned, with the rates, follow:

Bonds: The original issuance is taxed at the rate of 5c. per $100; but no tax is imposed on subsequent transfers.

Capital Stock: The original issue is taxed 5c. per $100, par value, or if there is no par value, then 1c. for each $20 of actual value if actual value is less than $100, and 5c. if the actual value is $100 or over.

Capital Stock and rights to subscribe: sales and transfers are taxed 2c. each $100 of par value, and 2c. each share if without par value. This is known as the Federal Stock Transfer Tax.

Federal Customs. Import and Export Duties. The Federal Government has a third general source of revenue besides income and excise taxes, namely, import and export duties. These latter are external sources of revenue; the two former, internal sources. Since tariffs only remotely and indirectly concern the investor as such they are merely referred to, although they are important from the standpoint of productivity, and in the early days of the Republic were the chief sources of federal revenue.

STATE JURISDICTION

State Revenue Systems. The revenue receipts of the forty-eight states in 1919 are classified by the Bureau of the Census as follows:

From taxes		Per cent.
General property	$237,234,778	35.1
Special property	104,222,552	15.5
Other special taxes	13,554,063	2.0
Poll	2,114,708	.3
Business	122,667,336	19.4
Non-business license	48,025,730	5.9
Total tax income	527,819,167	87.2

From taxes		Per cent.
From special assessments and from special charges for outlays	4,408,216	.7
From fines, forfeits and escheats	2,873,400	.4
From subventions and grants	11,709,458	1.7
From donations	3,434,935	.5
From pension assessments	1,949,256	.28
From earnings of general departments	83,203,459	12.3
From highway privileges	68,452	.001
From rents	7,643,943	1.1
From interest	28,800,769	4.2
From earnings of public service enterprises	3,306,147	.5
	147,398,035	21.681

The principal items of "special property taxes" were taxes on inheritances and the stock of corporations; of "business taxes," from insurance and other companies; of "non-business license," from motor vehicle licenses. The principal thought of most of those who read this table will be "tempora mutantur."[1] Even only eight years ago how small as factors of state revenues, were income and automobile taxes. We shall meet these latter presently.

Although the present income tax system of Wisconsin, which had its beginnings in 1911, antedates our present federal income tax system, which began in 1913, we had previously employed federal income taxes with somewhat qualified success in the Civil and other wars as emergency measures, and in 1894 had passed an income tax law that was declared unconstitutional. There had been state income taxes, also,—from Colonial times,—but these like the federal war taxes had seen limited usefulness for want of administrative technique.

Kirshman[2] remarks that "the real significance of costs of state governments can be seen only in connection with national government costs. The expenditures of these two political units must be regarded in a cumulative way. National expenditures, in any real test, would prove of greater necessity than State expenditures, for the sovereignty of the nation is surely paramount to that of the state. National government costs, therefore, should be regarded as a prior charge against national incomes; the people of each state respectively must bear their portion."

[1] Dodd, State Government, 1922, p. 421.

[2] The Principles of Investment, p. 386.

Homer nods on occasion. The use of the word "sovereignty" here seems not the happiest. Its connotations are too inherently legal. Under the Constitution the Federal Government has only those powers that are expressly delegated to it. All other powers are expressly delegated to the states. Each sovereignty, federal and state, has complete power of taxation to support its own government functions. The Constitution in some respects defines the methods under which this power may be exercised, but up to the present time there has been no delegation of tax-supremacy to the Federal Government.

But we have seen a tendency toward federal ascendancy in American commercial banking. Perhaps history is to repeat in matters of taxation. With the successful application of the 1913 law to the ultimate test of a great war, with the subsequent actual reduction in rates, and with amendments and modifications to improve the scope and equity of its application, and to demonstrate its flexibility, we may expect the states generally to adopt similar income tax laws.

Income taxes are likely to be more popular and more productive in states that are given to manufacturing and other corporate activity rather than to agriculture, and in states containing metropolitan centres of finance that are clearing houses and repositories for the representative forms of wealth, although no such distinction is observable as yet in the lists of states availing themselves of the income mode.

State Corporate Income Taxes. Since corporate taxes of any sort bear rather indirectly on the investor and his ownership of securities, and since the relationship is particularly remote with respect to his bonds and other creditor securities, only passing reference is made to the states that hitherto have utilized the general corporate income tax. These are Mississippi, Missouri, North Carolina, North Dakota, Oregon, South Carolina, Virginia, and Wisconsin. Those taxing corporate incomes under special laws are Massachusetts and New York.

State Individual Income Tax. The following states have individual income taxes: Arkansas, North Dakota, Delaware, Massachusetts, Mississippi, Missouri, New York, North Carolina, Oklahoma, Oregon, South Carolina, Virginia, and Wisconsin.

It is manifestly inexpedient to set forth the various rates of the several states with exemptions, deductions, etc., either in this place or elsewhere.   Obsolescence as well as complexity deprecate that.   But in general it may be said that the state systems are patterned after the national system but that they impose a lighter levy, thus far, and are much less thorough in reaching sources of uniform productivity, or in maintaining the equities of the situation.   They are face to face with the problem of equitable treatment of the income and property of non-residents in a much more serious way than is the Federal Government, for not only is the proportion of non-residents to residents with income and property in any one state usually much greater than the proportion of aliens and non-residents of the United States to citizens and residents, but the factor of interstate reciprocity in tax legislation also enters in.

General Property Tax.   In the development of corporate society the cost of such organization as exists in the primitive stages is borne by special taxes.   This is true of ancient society and of the early days in America.   As costs increased and wealth assumed a greater variety of form it was natural that the list of specific objects taxed should increase, until finally the number of material things of common knowledge not taxed was smaller than of things taxed.   The second stage, then, was to tax things or property in general, and the list thereafter was the list of things specifically exempted from tax.   In this way arose the general property tax with its exemptions.

The general property tax is based on the correct philosophy that all citizens of means should contribute to the cost of maintaining the social structure, and on the fallacious assumption that " property in general, or viewed as a homogeneous mass is a universally adequate measure of ability to pay taxes." [1]   It is based also on the " unconscious assumption that wealth in its technical economic sense is the same thing as wealth in popular meaning," [2]—that no distinction is to be drawn between wealth resident in material things, such as land, buildings, cattle and goods, and the representatives of wealth, such as interests in ownership: stocks, bonds, etc.   It is double taxation in its worst, or discriminatory, form as we shall find illustrated under " Single and Multiple Taxation " in Class III.   Nevertheless, those states that are strongly maintaining the general

[1] Lutz's *Public Finance*, p. 322.
[2] Lyon's *Investment*, p. 553.

property taxation at flat rates are repudiating the heart of the principle in commonly exempting from taxation the stock of companies incorporated in the state, of which most or all the property is located within the state.

It is of the essence of the general property tax that personal property, including intangibles, be carried on the same footing of assessed value and of tax rate as land and improvements. But notoriously in practice realty has been assessed on the average far below its real worth, as detailed in the chapters on State and Municipal Bonds, whereas, such intangibles as find their way to the law rolls (see the divisions of Class III of "the kinds or taxables") have been assessed on the average at close to their true value because that value has been so easily ascertainable. An unjust law becomes progressively unenforceable. The sequestration of personalty, particularly that most important part of personalty, intangibles, has left the assessor, at least in those states in which the responsibility of making a return is not on the taxpayer, virtually helpless until the death of the owner, to whom post-mortem penalties are hardly deterrents. Hence the decay and perhaps ultimate downfall of the general property tax as it affects personalty.

Classified Property Tax. Some states, notably California, Kentucky, Minnesota, Pennsylvania, and Virginia have resorted to classifications of property with graduated rates. The purpose has been to mitigate the inequity to personal property, and particularly to intangibles, to obviate the resort to " tax colonies" (created to foster citizenship or residence in states or communities that are in position to offer low rates or complete exemptions to personal property and notably to intangibles), also to minimize the sequestration of mobile personal property.

It is recognized by the states using the classified property tax that experience and theory look to land as the broad base of any tax structure not built on income and income-levies. Rate discrimination has been practiced in favor even of those land-improvements, like buildings, that are not commercially mobile. But these aside, it has been found that rates (usually uniform throughout the state) which are more favorable to tangible personalty, and most favorable to intangibles, yield an aggregate return so much in excess of the aggregate return when a uniform rate is applied to all kinds of taxed property that the residue of funds in support of the government necessary to be raised from land are less than under the general property tax. Expediency then as well as justice urge a wider use of the classified rather than the flat-rate tax on property. Therefore investors subject to direct tax on securities may hope for relief from this movement in those states that do not resort to the income tax.

Lyon makes the point that "taxation consists of taking a certain part of the privately owned wealth and transferring it to public ownership in order that it may be used in the public undertakings. Since this is a continuous process, taxes must come out of the economic income of the community. There can be a continuous transference of wealth only as there is a continuous creation of wealth. But a debt is not wealth and does not create wealth—land, labor and capital together produce all the 'ability to pay' there is. When a community taxes credits it does not tax wealth at all. It is taxing the method of conducting business on credits." [1]

Lyon does not contend that the representative forms of property (of which stocks and bonds are the most familiar), should not be taxed at all, since the community undergoes some cost in regulating all methods of doing business, but that the tax burden should bear some relation to the relative productivity of wealth directly owned and productivity which has been somewhat increased by the use of credits or other representative forms. To tax credits at the same rate as tangible property is to assume that the use of credits and other forms increases productivity 100 per cent.

If the question is raised, why does this follow? the answer is because the debtor (who owns the wealth) almost always pays the tax. But this brings us into the fourth classification where the "incidence of taxation" is discussed.

Until the vogue of income taxes in this country the general and the classified property taxes sharply differentiated federal money-raising from state, for by the provisions of the Constitution, just as the states were prohibited from levying import and export duties, so the Federal Government was prohibited from levying direct taxes on property in the several states, except in proportion to population,—of course an impossibility. It is highly improbable that a turn of events will constrain the states to part with this particular right of impost in favor of the Federal Govern-

[1] *Investment*, pp. 556–557.

ment, or to share it, as they now share the right of impost on incomes by virtue of the XVI Amendment consequent from the Supreme Court decision (Pollock vs. Farmers Loan and Trust Co.) that an income tax is a direct tax.

Investors are gravely concerned with the relative, theoretical and actual deductions from their gross income occasioned by these two major forms of taxation. That matter is part of the discussion of the fourth method of classification: "By the Method or Degree of Imposition or Collection."

State Inheritance Tax. Estate and inheritance taxes have come to be considered in the eyes of the law, not taxes on property but on the devolution, succession or transfer of property at death. We sometimes journey a long way to gather excuses for our acts. Since, like taxes on income, they are not direct charges on property (which has a situs), they do not violate the segregation of the rights to tax as set up in the Federal Constitution. That is why we have found them a resource of the national government as well as of the states.

The American history of these taxes is not dissimilar to that of the income taxes. The Federal Government has been seen to have flirted with the tax since colonial days, and for war purposes. The first state inheritance tax was that of the New York law of 1885. It was followed by laws in twenty other states during the next six years, and at present only Florida, Alabama, Nevada and the District of Columbia are without laws.

There are four states that tax the net estate, two (Mississippi and Rhode Island) that tax both the estate or bequest and the inheritance or distributive shares, one (Utah) that does not tax the inheritance, and the remainder, that tax at all, tax the inheritance solely.

All the outstanding phases of the state inheritance laws: the incidence on direct and collateral heirs, on net estates and on distributive shares, the discrimination between real and personal property, the amount and tendency of exemptions, the degree of progression in rates, retaliatory legislation leading to multiple taxation, divergencies in rates of taxation,—all will receive the classified treatment we have set for ourselves. In general it may be said that the state burden is very much heavier than the national (which is not now operative with respect to estates of net value under $100,000).

However, at present, there is no possibility of much double taxation as between the federal and a state jurisdiction, for the federal tax is credited with any estate, inheritance, legacy or succession taxes in respect of any property included in the gross estate to an amount not exceeding 80 per cent. of the federal tax.

State Privilege Taxes. Perhaps a comprehensive and descriptive term under which to embrace the great body of exactions by states that are not included under the income, general property or inheritance taxes, is State Privilege Taxes. This will cover the poll or capitation tax (the privilege of being alive shall we say?), the million and one fines, fees, registrations, licenses that defray the right to do special things or business, from running a billiard hall to running an automobile, and give the state its administrative revenues. It will cover franchise, incorporation, gross receipts, and business taxes, and the like, designed to levy special charges on corporations and other forms of group industry. These, like the federal excise taxes in general, we pass by with mere recitation, as being indirect taxes from the viewpoint of the investor.

LOCAL JURISDICTION

County, Municipal, and Minor Divisional Taxes. The sovereign states have seen fit to delegate, by constitutional and statutory enactment, the power to levy taxes under certain conditions and for certain purposes. There have been restrictions on this power—some of them sinister, such as the limitation of the tax rate—but throughout the country the power has been freely used in conjunction with the power to create debts. This aspect of the subject has been touched on in the chapters on civil loans. The assessments, equalizations, levies, and collections sometimes are administered by the authorities of the division that is taxed, and sometimes by the granting authorities. Experience seems to prove that outside the more settled East the county is the best agency of the state in tax administration, and usually the most practical tax district. But town jealousy of prerogatives and the conflict of urban and rural interests has retarded county centralization.

In actual practice the state tax, which is at a relatively low uniform rate, is superimposed on the bases of the assessments for local taxes, which may vary in number and purposes and therefore as to gross amount. The securities of the investor are affected by the total tax to the same degree as the land and the tangible property.

II. CLASSIFICATION OF TAXES ACCORDING TO THE DIRECT INCIDENCE

These, then, are the several divisions of tax sovereignty. They answer the first question: Who can tax? The second question: Who can be taxed? relates to the direct "incidence" of taxation. All paying has to be done by " persons " and the law knows two kinds, " corporate " and " private " persons. With respect to federal jurisdictions all corporate persons are either foreign or domestic corporations, and all private persons either aliens or citizens. However, to the federal jurisdiction, both aliens and citizens may be residents or non-residents of the United States.

In the state jurisdiction every corporation is one incorporated either in that state or not. A further possibility is recognized: it may be incorporated in that state and also in another state. Turning to the private person,—just as the federal jurisdiction recognizes aliens and citizens the state jurisdiction recognizes that residents of the federal jurisdiction are either residents or non-residents of that state.

These are all the possible permutations and combinations of taxpayers. It is now for us to see how the various taxes are adjusted to the conditions.

Foreign Corporations. An infelicity in nomenclature is the ambiguity of the word "foreign." A corporation may be "foreign to the United States " and its securities foreign corporation securities. From the standpoint within a state a foreign corporation may be either the above or a domestic corporation incorporated in another state. From the same standpoint that domestic corporation is not domestic, but foreign, and only those corporations that are incorporated in the state of jurisdiction in question are domestic. Strange to say, the latter or state viewpoint is the commoner. But to make confusion worse confounded, observe the New York Central Railroad. This company is a corporation which has its principal place of business in New York state. It also does business and is incorporated in Ohio. We take it that in either state this company is domestic even if it is incorporated in another state. But in cases of multiple incorporation it is necessary for legal purposes that there be a principal state of incorporation.

Corporations foreign to the United States are taxed by the federal jurisdiction only on gross income from sources within the United States determined (except in the case of insurance companies) in the same manner and at the same rate as we shall find the gross income of non-resident aliens. As such they can be taxed also by any state in which they do business; as a matter of actual practice they are taxed at the same rate as other foreign corporations, i.e., those incorporated in some other than the taxing state.

Domestic Corporations. From the domestic standpoint corporations can be taxed by foreign jurisdictions in any way and to any extent. But to incur foreign jurisdiction domestic corporations must have property in, or be doing business in, the foreign jurisdiction. To avoid the inherent possibilities, most domestic corporations do their foreign business through foreign corporations, which in many cases they control. The principal tax of domestic corporations under federal jurisdiction is (at present) the $13\frac{1}{2}$ per cent. tax on corporate net income already mentioned, but they are also liable to one form or another of all the excise taxes except the estate tax; that is, to the special taxes, and the security issue stamp taxes. They are also liable, of course, to external revenue duties on their foreign shipping.

A state may obtain tax-jurisdiction over a corporation by reason of the latter's incorporation under the laws of the state, or because the corporation owns real or personal property in the state, or because the corporation does business in the state. All corporations, domestic and foreign, are subject with few exceptions to taxation on the ownership of real property in the United States in the state or states in which the property is located, at the rate or rates that obtain for that kind of property in the jurisdiction.

Aliens Non-resident in the United States more accurately defines the persons we commonly mean when we speak of " non-resident aliens." Aliens non-resident in the United States come within the purview of federal jurisdiction only if they derive income from, or own property within, the United States. As to income, they are taxed only on that received by them from sources within the United States, which may be lessened by the properly apportioned losses and deductions. Their exemptions, deductions, and rates are less favorable than those for residents. Persons resident in Canada and Mexico are given preference over other non-resident aliens in these matters.[1] As to their property they are taxed as any other non-residents. The justification for the tax is that the subject has received the protection and other benefits of the government of jurisdiction. As to estates at death, we have found that decedents are classed either as residents or non-residents without respect to citizenship. Therefore we have already covered the treatment accorded their estates under the caption " Federal Estate Tax: Residents and Non-residents."

Aliens Resident in the United States. Aliens resident in the United States from the standpoint of a state may be either (a) non-resident in the state of jurisdiction or (b) resident. We have found that the federal jurisdiction has no occasion to discriminate between citizens and resident aliens. Every resident alien individual is liable to the federal income tax even though his income is wholly from sources without the United States. The federal income and estate taxes do not discriminate and the various excise taxes have no occasion to. The state and its subdivisions also are not concerned with foreign citizenship in their exactions. Under both main methods of state taxation the principal issues are the " situs " or location of individuals and of property.

Citizens and Citizenship. Pursuing the logic of our classification, citizens are either non-resident or resident of the United States; if resident, they are either resident or non-resident of any state of jurisdiction. Citizenship may be the result of a condition of mind as well as of a matter of location. With respect to the country one has to be either a citizen or an alien. The comity of civilized nations gives him, if a desirable person, a choice of allegiance irrespective of family, birthplace, or citizenship at birth or sometimes of race. His choice, if he elects to change, may be determined by sentiment or by business considerations. If business considerations are paramount and he is a person of large means subject to foreign jurisdictions he may make his choice to mitigate multiple taxation. This holds whether the

---

[1] For a more detailed discussion of this class see Class V, "Non-resident Alien Individuals."

jurisdictions are foreign to the United States, or within the United States but foreign to a given state.

The situation is complicated by the fact that one may be a citizen of the United States and also a citizen of a single state. But one cannot be a citizen of two states. He may elect residence in only one. And there must be a certain *bona fides* to that residence: usually the possession of a home or a certain duration of physical presence in the elected locality of residence.

Citizens Non-resident in the United States. However, one can be a citizen of the United States and (by being a non-resident citizen of the country) not be a citizen of any state. That may seem far-fetched but it is not. An American citizen may wish for reasons of sentiment to retain lifelong allegiance to the land of his birth; but, as an artist, elect to live the remainder of his life in Florence, or as an importer, in Paris. He will be taxed, probably on the income from his activities in the land of his actual residence, and on any property he may own therein. He may not feel sentimental attachment to any state, or have a legal residence or any interest in any business or property in any state. And no state may demand his citizenship. " Citizens of the United States " (except to the extent that they are affected by income derived from sources in the possessions in the United States) are liable to the federal income tax. It makes no difference that they may own no assets within the United States and may receive no income from sources within the United States.

Put in another form to achieve perfect clarity, one may be a citizen of the United States without being a resident, and one may be a resident without being a citizen. One cannot be a citizen of a state without being a legal resident of that state, and one cannot be a resident of a state without being a citizen of that state, unless an alien.

The principal phase of the taxation of non-residents is the injustice done them by reason of community prejudice. We have inherited through the ages a spirit of invidiousness against the stranger that is within our gates. In this matter it takes the forms of multiple taxation and discrimination in rates and exemptions.

One of the advantages of a classification of intricate phenomena is the gradual emergence of the underlying principles as cross references become more frequent. We begin to notice them now.

Resident Citizens of the United States.   Resident citizens of the United States must be residents and therefore citizens of some one state, but they cannot (after the manner of corporations) be residents or citizens of two or more states.   Residence and citizenship under state jurisdiction go together.   But for tax purposes residence, not citizenship, is the important thing. As residents in a state of jurisdiction they may be subject to a greater number and variety of taxes, and the rates may be higher, than they may be taxed on income, business or services of a jurisdiction (state or minor civil) in which they are not resident. We should keep in mind the *general* rule that realty is taxed at location, and personalty at residence.

III. CLASSIFICATION OF TAXES ACCORDING TO THE KINDS OF TAXABLES

To arrive at this point in our studies it has been necessary to give some thought to the relation of the " kinds of things that are or may be taxed " (1) to the jurisdiction, (2) to the kinds of corporations and of individuals who must pay the tax, (3) to the methods and degrees of taxation, (4) to the situs or location of those who pay the tax, and to the situs or location of the property taxed.   A discussion then of the whole subject of taxation from this angle of the kinds of taxables serves principally to ground us more deeply in the fundamentals of the subject.

There are in truth only three broad divisions of taxables: income, property, and privilege.   But privileges are so commonly called excises when taxed by governments that we consider here the more important federal forms as excises and the state forms as privileges.

Income.   Corporate and individual incomes are taxed by the national government and one or both may be taxed by states. They are not taxed by the lesser divisions.   The table (Class III) outlines the principal constituents of corporate and of individual incomes.

Property.   The main divisions of property are realty and personalty.   The Federal Government cannot, as a practical matter, tax property as such.   The state general property tax levies on both divisions at a uniform rate unless in some particulars prohibited by the state constitution.   The classified property tax may be imposed at one rate for the realty and at another (a lower) for the personalty. Or it may have one rate for the land, and a lower (Ohio) for the permanently attached improvements, and a still lower rate for the personalty. The civil tax payments, except fees and licenses, come mostly from property and especially realty. From earlier chapters devoted to " Civil Loans " we are already familiar with the other forms of property that are reached by state and local jurisdictions.

Excises. It has been remarked that the word " excise " means nothing. It is broader than charity and about as distressing to translate as the Latin " res." Except in being more inclusive it differs hardly at all from the correspondent "privileges." The term excises covers federal tax miscellany and the term privileges, state tax miscellany. The chart is sufficiently descriptive. It will be observed that a considerable proportion of even the minor tax modes are direct investment taxes. Some state taxes are called excises, but possibly a sound nomenclature would not recognize that usage.

Privilege Taxes. With what has gone before little further comment seems necessary except, perhaps, to refer to " rights." Language is a feeble medium in tax matters. One prefers to speak of privileges than of rights. There is no inherent right. By common consent we entitle a long or generally uncontested privilege a right. We give preference in this text where possible to the former word.

Until recently state and local revenues have been derived mostly from taxes on real estate. But the times change. Among the many kinds of income common to the federal, state, and municipal governments are fees, fines, licenses, and sales taxes. A striking illustration of the evolution of tax modes is given us by the motor vehicle. The driver in most states requires a license. That means a fee. The car requires at least one license and one set of license plates. That may mean one or two fees more. Recently some genius arose and invented the very just gasolene sales tax (a benefit tax) of which the proceeds are commonly applied to road construction and repair. About the same time municipal authorities discovered a pleasing source of revenue in fines for motor traffic violations, which in some cities defrays the cost of traffic regulation. The motor industry estimates that the present " toll taken from motor car drivers through American courts must be in the neighborhood of $40,000,000 a year. But it is not in this aspect that the motor car is making its greatest contribution to the upkeep of state and nation. It has been figured that automobiles are furnishing fully 20 per cent. of all the revenues now derived by the states, with the chances that 1927 will see still further levies made on the motorist. In the year 1925 the states of the Union levied in license and motor fuel taxes a total of $285,063,000 on automobilists. In the year 1926 the United States Government collected from motorists in taxes on cars, tires and other accessories a total of $138,-155,094. The state figures for 1926 have not yet been compiled, but as they heavily increased over 1925 it is easy to figure that altogether the motorist paid out last year more than $500,000,000. Not so many years ago the entire United States Government was run on such a budget."

Summary. Whether or not these estimates are authentic they serve to show that the complication of the present American tax structure, federal and state, as contrasted with a generation or two ago, may be a nuisance, but not a delusion. The development of classified property taxes, the increase in the number and kinds of taxables have broadened the revenue base and have increased the number of persons who pay tribute, and the number of capacities in which persons and corporations pay tribute to their governments for benefits derived.

IV. CLASSIFICATION OF TAXES BY THE METHOD OR DEGREE OF IMPOSITION AND COLLECTION

The fourth question was: In what ways and to what extent can men or things be taxed? The physical mechanism of taxation: the appraisal, assessment, equalization, levy, and collection are without our province; but certain phases of the mechanism are worth notice.

Direct and Indirect Taxes. We have referred to the direct incidence of taxation. However, when economists foregather to hear a paper on the incidence of taxation they expect something entirely different. They expect an essay on the shifting of the burden, or "who ultimately pays the tax." We have the ultimate payer in economics as well as the ultimate consumer.

It is a virtue in any tax if it cannot be shifted (although many, such as the motor fuel sales tax, are designed to be shifted), for the process of shifting obscures the economic results and retards or prevents subsequent adjustment to conditions. It is an outstanding virtue of individual income taxes that the payer ordinarily has no means of shifting the burden. There are numerous exceptions of course. If the individual is a seller of merchandise he may shift it to the buyer in the merchandise price. Those who purchase securities subsequent to the imposition of taxes on them they have bought may offer a sufficiently lower price for the securities to offset tax, and thus shift the burden to the sellers. The same holds true of other forms of property. But personal incomes are not bought and sold. No legal evasion is possible. The commonest modern definition of a direct tax is that it is one which is intended to be borne by the corporation or individual on whom it is levied, and of an indirect tax that it is one suitable or intended to be shifted from the corporation or person on whom it is directly levied.

Applying this division to the kinds of taxes we have encountered as expressed in the kinds of taxables (Class IV), we have the following loose subclasses, bearing in mind that the payment of the tax on occasional and unstandardized transactions such as are accompanied by stamps and promissory notes, e.g., between mortgagee and mortgagor, may be a subject for negotiation between the contracting principals.

Direct Taxes on	*Indirect Taxes on*
Real estate	Devolution (bequest)
Individual income	Succession (inheritance)
Tangible personal property	Franchises
Bank bills	Rights
Bank deposits	General privileges
Corporate stock	Stock transfers
Bonds	
Real estate mortgages	
Promissory notes	
Open accounts	
Chattel mortgages	
Stamped documents	

Strictly speaking, things cannot be taxed, but only persons (corporate and individuals). Individuals are taxed in their private capacities and as fiduciaries. The assumption is that people will always shift burdens if the object burdened permits. We have seen that generally, there is no way of shifting the levy based on one's income. A clearer case is a tax based on the privilege of inheriting property. There is no way for the legatee to cause any one else to pay a tax imposed upon him.

But, on the other hand, if a state imposes a tax on a corporation or individual based on the amount or value of his open accounts then that corporation or individual is going to charge sufficiently more for products or services to cover the tax and thereby to shift it. The tax on theatre tickets is a tax on the privilege of being amused. As a war measure it had its own amusement in an unnecessary government motion to insure that the tax be paid by the consumer of the amusement. It is never necessary to stipulate that a privilege tax be shifted.

It is significant that no classes of property representing debts in a true sense come under direct taxes. Bank bills and bank deposits to be sure represent technical obligations on the part of the banks. That is, the bank owes the depositor his deposit. But that is quite a different thing from the kind of obligation or debtorship represented by bonds and mortgages. He who borrows has to pay all the costs of borrowing. " The incidence of taxation of credits falls on the debtor and stays on him. Through the shifting of the incidence of taxation, any tax which is evenly levied on the capital employed in a given line of production comes out of the ultimate consumer of the product. If all producers of a given product have to pay the same amount of tax on the capital employed in their business, they will simply add the tax to the price charged for the product."[1]

It is obvious that *as a class* investors (creditors) do not pay the taxes on their bonds (loans). The tax is paid *indirectly* by the consumers of capital (borrowers) *as a class* in the higher price they pay for their capital. That higher price is represented by a higher interest rate on loans or by the receipt of lower percentage of the par value of the loan. In either case the higher price is represented by a higher net yield on the investment.

External and Internal Taxes may be dismissed with a word. The Federal Constitution specifically gives the National Government jurisdiction over external national taxes (called custom duties) and prohibits the states from levying external taxes.

[1] Lyon's *Investment*, p. 558.

Degrees of Taxation. We are concerned with phases not only of the method but also of the degree of taxation. The principal factors of degree are the rate or rates (with the types of taxes that spring from them), and the exemptions and credits. Yet valuation is more important than rate in direct ad valorem taxes. In respect to the income tax particularly, exemptions and credits,—unfortunately irrespective of which word is used to describe them,—are deductions from gross income to arrive at net taxable income, or deductions from one form or another of gross tax to arrive at a net tax. To illustrate the two principal factors of degree, surtaxes, estate, and inheritance taxes are vitally affected by progressive rates; general property, other excise and inheritance taxes are not. Federal normal income taxes and federal estate taxes are vitally affected by exemptions; general property and other federal excise taxes are not, etc. Exemptions, credits, and deductions are analyzed further in later paragraphs under that heading.

Normal Tax and Surtax. Coming now to the varying rates and degrees of taxation we find in our earlier federal income tax laws the imposition of a " flat rate " or " proportional " tax on the amount of all net incomes in excess of a certain minimum. The minimum net income was derived from the gross by subtraction of stipulated credits, deductions, and allowances. It was not until the Federal Revenue Act of 1913 that Congress introduced the strange bipartite division of levy into " normal " taxes and " surtaxes. " The 1913 normal was a flat rate levy on incomes between a certain minimum and maximum.

The surtax was a tax at increasing rates on the increments of income. As the income mounted by steps, as it were, from the normal base, a higher rate of tax was imposed on each increment or step. It is progressive taxation with a vengeance. It was occasioned by the undistributed income of corporations carried to surplus. We do not consider this an adequate defense of the normal-surtax complication of the income tax-structure, already rendered intricate enough by the additions, deductions, credits, exemptions, all necessary to compute in arriving at the taxable income in the first instance.

But this was not enough. The Revenue Act of 1918 changed the earlier normal flat rate into a double, progressive rate, the higher rate applying on net incomes in excess of $4,000; and, in the shadow of the War, the progression of the surtax rates was steepened.

The present Revenue Act (1926) is the latest refinement of intricacy. A reference to Class I in the General Classification Table will show three progressions in the normal tax as applied to citizens and residents. Non-resident alien individuals pay the maximum (5 per cent.) normal rate on net income from sources within the United States. The surtaxes and rates as diminished by 1926 are also given. Although the printer's ink may hardly be dry before these are changed they will illustrate the way this particular progressive tax operates. " The surtax for any amount of net income not shown in the table is computed by adding to the surtax for the largest amount shown which is less than the income the surtax on the excess over that amount at the rate indicated in the table."

Uniform and Graduated Taxes. We have spoken of uniform (flat-rate, one-rate, proportional, etc.) and graduated taxes. The former is almost self-elucidating. It is the one-rate tax that is often called proportional in that the amount paid is proportional to the value of the taxable. We find it in the normal division of the older income taxes, in the general property tax, and in most of the minor taxes. Graduated taxes are either progressive or regressive, as the rate increases or decreases with increase in the amount of the taxable. With our present tax schemes resting heavily on the ability to pay theory, regressive tax rates are rare for they favor the well-to-do, but covert regressive taxation is practiced under the general property tax in under-appraising large properties. Most present income, estate and inheritance taxes are progressive. (See the General Classification.) Therefore the effect of their tax rate on the prices of stocks and bonds is not susceptible of accurate determination. However, all inheritance taxes are not progressive. The representative of the decedent is under the burden of carrying through inheritance tax proceedings in most jurisdictions that can find property of the decedent which has a situs within it. This in ordinary course means a prorating of allowed deductions so as to arrive at the net taxable in the jurisdiction. Literally, this involves higher mathematics for accurate establishment, and an enormous amount of other routine labor on the part of the fiduciary or his attorneys out of all proportion to the value of taxes ordinarily resulting to any one jurisdiction. Therefore some states now permit the representative to assent to non-resident taxation at a low flat-rate, say 2 per cent., on the gross property having a situs in the jurisdiction.

Single and Multiple Taxation. Another classing of the degree of tax burden is with respect to the number of taxes imposed on the same taxable. The commonest expression for this phase is " double taxation," although we shall find " triple," " quadruple taxation," etc., not uncommon. There is no necessary demerit in multiple taxation as such, for we have no quarrel with the necessary diversity of tax media in the complicated structure of modern society. We have just seen how the little rivulets of fees, fines, sales-taxes and the like from one industry go to form a large part of the stream of tax and administrative revenues of the state. Yet the economist tells us that all these multifarious sources of state income must be paid out of rent, wages, interest, profits or property as such. Multiple taxation is involved in the very fact.

Rather, the demerit is with the single tax. Where an approach toward the raising of all tax revenues from one single source, land, has been tried, as in Western Canada, it has been found that simplicity, even, has its grave weaknesses.

It follows inevitably in this day of prevalent income taxes that multiple taxation exists on every hand and that one who thinks about it at all is bound to be a " single taxer " or a " multiple taxer." There is no middle ground. Again we have recourse to the classification to exhaust the possibilities of the subject.

Multiple Taxation as Affected (I) by the Jurisdiction. Corporate and individual income are taxable by both federal and state governments. On the whole the tax powers over income of these two jurisdictions are approximately equal although not coextensive. We have seen under Civil Loans (Part II) that although never finally adjudicated it is the best opinion that the federal jurisdiction may not tax income from municipal bonds, and conversely that state jurisdictions may not tax income from United States bonds.

Real and personal property, whether corporately or individually owned may be a source of revenue to state, county, municipal, and other jurisdictions.

Excises and privileges, which, speaking broadly, we have found to be the same thing, are more nearly universal objects of taxation than either property or income, for in one form or another they are amenable to all jurisdictions, since most forms of government are dispensers and regulators of privileges.

Multiple Taxation as Affected (II) by the Direct Incidence, or the Persons Taxed. (Persons, be it remembered, in the vocabulary of taxation may be either corporate or individual.) Since all taxes ultimately are imposed on persons and not on things, for only persons can pay taxes, only loose thinking permits us to consider multiple taxation with respect to two or more payers. Yet it is convenient to call "double taxation" the phenomenon that exists when a corporation is directly taxed on the real estate that it owns, and its stockholders taxed for their ownership in the corporation that owns the real estate.

Multiple Taxation in Relation to (III) the Kinds of Taxables. But if we assume that this land was owned by a corporation all the stock of which was owned by one taxpayer who (for the sake of illustration) had lent money to the corporation secured by mortgage on the land, then under present customary tax laws he might be subject to direct tax on his income from any dividends on that stock, plus interest from that mortgage, and to direct tax on his ownership of the stock and of the mortgage, and to indirect tax through his ownership of the corporation which was taxed directly on its ownership of the land. His only corresponding offset would probably be a deduction allowed the corporation on computing its taxable income, of the amount of the interest paid on the mortgage. Technically he might be considered an investor, although practically no one but a half-wit would put his neck through such a tax-noose; but the relation of it all to investment is plain enough. Under less punitive conditions individuals do of course incorporate in order to limit their personal liabilities.

Multiple Taxation with Respect to the Situs of (V) the Corporation or Person Taxed, and (VI) the Things Taxed. Now consider, if you will, that the taxpayer goes stark mad and elects to reside in State A, incorporate his company in State B, although the land and buildings and the stock and the mortgage of his company are in State C. Assume that all three states have general property taxes and income taxes,—a condition contrary to fact, but possible.

The state of his domicile (A) might tax him on his dividends and interest as a resident, also on his ownership of the same securities; the state of incorporation (B) might levy on the company an original incorporation tax, an annual franchise or business tax, one or more of the numerous privilege taxes, and a tax on the entire income of the corporation, or at least on any part of that income derived from sources within the state. The individual owner of all the stock of this company is the ultimate payer of these taxes, which are direct as respects the company and indirect as respects himself. The state (C) in which are located the tangible and intangible property might tax the company for its ownership of the land and improvements, and might tax the owner for his ownership of the mortgage on a recording tax—on the basis that the mortgage represents an interest in the real estate. In this state then he would be taxed both indirectly and directly.

If, although residing in perhaps an adjoining state, he served as an executive officer of the corporation he owned, he might be taxed on his salary. In addition to these imposts he would suffer taxation by the federal corporate income tax, and (if his company exported or imported) customs duties besides, and possibly other excise taxes if his company dealt in certain commodities or did certain kinds of business (a few of this kind have been mentioned under "Miscellaneous Excise Taxes" and "Stamp Taxes").

Furthermore, to be sure that he did his share the federal jurisdiction would impose the direct income tax under the administrative provisions of which any questions of proper interpretation and imposition would in fact be decided in favor of the government and against the taxpayer, in spite of the legal theory that tax statutes are to be interpreted strictly and in favor of the taxpayer.

This is of course an egregious example cited for disciplinary purposes, but let persons of substance apply the laws as they actually exist to their own incomes and property. The results will show surprising discrimination against capital as contrasted with rent and wages, not only with respect to multiple taxation, but also to rates, deductions, and entire exemptions.

A glance at the appalling possibilities of multiple taxation in the detailed classificate table accompanying the text to Class VI with respect to inheritance taxes will be more effective than further dilation on this subject in this place.

The solutions seem to be, superficially, the enactment and enforcement through state tax commissions, after recommendation by a national tax commission or its equivalent, of relatively uniform acts of state legislation and fundamentally by continuance of the present process of converting manual (and particularly agricultural) labor into corporate and other capital groups, which process first fosters and then dissipates class consciousness.

Exemptions, Credits, and Deductions. There is one other noteworthy factor in the degree one is taxed, i.e., the kind and amount of exemptions, credits, and deductions that lessen the amount of the total tax. It is natural that the most modern, most flexible and most just tax—that on incomes (or really on corporations and persons through incomes) should qualify its burden with some subtlety to mete out what is crudely considered as justice. Again we look to the federal rather than to the several state laws, for convenience and because of its growing leadership.

Federal Individual Income Exemptions. The following are among the items of interest to investors generally that are not now subject to the federal individual income tax:

Alimony.

Allowances received under the federal war beneficence acts.

Bequests, inheritances, and gifts.

Damages received in personal actions at law.

Dividends on stock of federal reserve banks, federal land banks, federal intermediate credit banks, and national farm loan associations.

Dividends (or interest) from building and loan associations to the amount of $300 per year.

Earned income from sources without the United States by an individual citizen of the United States who is a bona fide non-resident for more than six months during the taxable year.

Insurance proceeds (accident, health, workman's compensation, and life proceeds received by reason of the death of the insured).

Interest on United States bonds issued before Sept. 1, 1917, on liberty bonds, not in excess of certain exemptions, on federal farm loan bonds, on bonds of the states and their civil divisions.

Pensions received from the states, and also from the United States for services in war.

Soldiers' Bonus (state and federal).

Of the last item Kirshman writes:[1] "Stock dividends, however, are counted in the taxable income for levying surtaxes. The Supreme Court of the United States has recently decided that stock dividends are not taxable. Corporations have, in large numbers, taken advantage of this by declaring large stock dividends and thus distributing profits in tax-free form. The influence of this decision of the court is pernicious because it leads to overcapitalization and reduction of tax-receipts to the government."

We regret to take issue again with such an excellent writer, but the importance of the subject demands it. We pass over the fact that by " stock dividends " in the first sentence he means dividends from stock and confine ourselves to the use of the phrase thereafter. We contend that the decision of the court is not pernicious because stock dividends are not profits and are not income. The capital stock of a corporation is represented by shares. If the corporation issues additional shares to an amount equal to 10 per cent. of the former shares outstanding without acquiring any additional wealth for these shares to represent it has diluted the value of the previously outstanding stock by 10 per cent. and the total value of the new amount of outstanding stock remains the same as the total value of the previous amount of outstanding shares. There is no escape from it. What a stock dividend really does is to lock surplus into capital stock. And any references to stock-watering or overcapitalization or what not, are beside the mark and beg the question. The owners of the stock are no better off as to true stock value than before.

The fact that the new stock may have a cash market value had nothing to do with the case. It has a true value exactly equal to the total value of the equity in the corporation applicable to the stock divided by the number of shares. This value *always* is lessened by the issuance of new stock *exactly* in proportion to the percentage of dilution caused by the issuance.

[1] *Principles of Investment*, p. 124.

A boy has a red apple and two slips of paper each representing half of the apple. He gives one slip to each of two friends promising to deliver to the holder of each his share of the apple on demand. Can the donor by any necromancy hand out two more slips against the same apple to the same two boys and thereby deliver more apple? Suppose all this happened in the George Junior Republic and the Government of the Republic imposed an income tax on the receipt of gifts of part apples. Suppose the tax was not imposed on the transfer of the parts of the apple, but on the two pieces of paper that represented the right to parts,— one cent a paper. Suppose the Government proceeded to impose a tax of one cent a paper when the right to each half of the apple was represented by two papers. Every George Junior schoolboy would see through it!

But the opposition may contend that this is fine theory but poor practice; that as a matter of fact a stock dividend means increased cash returns and that the financial public knows it and proclaims the " melon-cutting."

When you cut into your melon you are about to consume it. You are eating your capital.

No, the answer is that the financial public, which has often been suspected of buying at the top and selling at the bottom, is wrong. The average result of stock dividends and the issuance of rights is a decline in market value of the individual old shares to (or toward, or through) the total value of the old shares divided by the new total number of shares,—and this despite the fact that stock dividends and rights are usually issued when companies are on the up-grade and the potential value of the stock increasing. Some years ago, the *Magazine of Wall Street* made a study of this principle in an essay entitled " Why Stocks Decline when Rights are Issued."

Such temporary market inflation as may occur is usually the response of the Street to the increase in future aggregate cash dividends that the stock dividend may occasion. If they occur the federal internal revenue is augmented thereby. The same result on the market value of the stock is attained by raising the dividend rate, without paying a stock dividend.

Returning to Kirshman's criticism we refrain from discussing " what is overcapitalization? " and " why is it pernicious if a company pays less taxes to the government? " for the point of the controversy is to contribute our mite toward quelling one of the most apparent, most prevalent, and yet most " pernicious " of current financial fallacies.

Federal Personal Exemptions and Credits.   In addition to the items of income exemptions, the law permits the deduction of fixed amounts in accordance with the family status of the individual before computing the normal tax.   For a single person or a fiduciary the present amount is $1,500, for a married person or head of family $3,500.   Credits of $400 for each dependent person are allowed.   These credits are in no way different from the exemptions.   The amount can be defended as logical provided the dependents of the head of the house paying the normal income tax after exemptions can be maintained in the manner the head of the house and his or her spouse are accustomed to live, on $400 a year each.   Otherwise not.   The questions at issue respecting the gross amount of exemptions are, how much weight should we give to the social importance of having as many residents of the country as possible understand the nature of, and in a measure, contribute to, governmental revenues? and on the other hand, how much weight should be given to the excess of cost over receipts in taxing low incomes at a trifling rate?   Or put more broadly, to what extent should the tax power be used for educative purposes?

Perhaps a tax on incomes is the best suited for such purposes. We disagree with those writers who see in the general property tax such an educative medium.   It requires business ability to convert tangibles, particularly small bits of land, into current funds with which to pay " educative taxes," and business ability is not presupposed in persons with incomes of perhaps $1,000 a year.   In Massachusetts, a dear old lady in some retreat for the aged is taxed each year on an amethyst brooch that has come down to her from forebears in the misty years of long ago. That is not right.   But there might be some reasonableness if under the Massachusetts income tax law she were obliged to pay one-half of 1 per cent. of a taxable income of $1,000, not in behalf of state revenues, but to relate her to the social order as a beneficiary from the financial organization of society.   For it costs something to maintain that organization.

Other Normal Tax Credits.   A credit is also allowed (a) of the amount received as dividends from a domestic corporation, or (b) from a foreign corporation which derives from sources within the United States more than 50 per cent. of its gross income for the three taxable years preceding. And a citizen of the United States is entitled to a credit of the amount of any income paid during the taxable year to any foreign country.

Federal Estate Exemptions. Perhaps owing to pressure of public opinion, both informed and uninformed, the Revenue Act of 1926 has reduced the maximum tax rate from 40 to 20 per cent., and has raised the amount of taxable property that is exempt from $50,000 to $100,000. This particular form of impost is especially worthy of abolishment or should be held in reserve for war measures and the like because it is a tax on the right of transfer which can be granted only by the states, and therefore it belongs to the state and not to the federal fields of taxation. As a stretch of the excise tax power of the Federal Government some consider that it is now being continued only as a federal club to control state inheritance tax policies through the 80 per cent. credit. The proper form for a tax reserve to take, it appears to us, is a lower rate than the traffic will bear and we endorse with enthusiasm the dictum of the great Mill that "no tax ought to be kept so high as to furnish a motive to its evasion too strong to be counteracted by ordinary means of prevention."

" The rates are applied to the gross estate, less, in the case of residents, funeral expenses, debts and the like items, property previously taxed under estate or old gift tax within a period of five years " (the gift tax was abolished as of January 1, 1926) " property left to the United States, or to any state or municipality or to eleemosynary incorporated institutions, and the specific exemption of $100,000. . . . Insurance paid to the Estate and the aggregate of insurance paid to beneficiaries in excess of $40,000 are included in the gross taxable estate." [1]

Credits for Inheritance Taxes. Credits on the federal estate tax are given for inheritance taxes paid to the various states, to a maximum of not in excess of 80 per cent. of the federal tax.

We have already proceeded far enough in this subclass " Exemptions, Credits, and Deductions " to observe that Congress does not, and therefore makes it difficult for others to discriminate in use of these terms. In the income computations we have found that income taxable at the lowest normal rate (whatever that

[1] Revenue Act of 1926 with explanatory Digest, Prentice-Hall., Inc, p. 42.

may signify except as to dollar amount) is earned net income (not over $10,000) " less personal exemption and credit for dependents." In other words, these normal tax exemptions and credits are deductions from earned income to arrive at taxable income. But for the estate tax, exemptions are deductions from the gross estate to arrive at the net taxable estate and credits are something vastly more significant: they are the part of the actual estate tax that does not have to be paid. But in both tax forms exemptions and credits are deductions. Any attempt at differentiation through terminology is therefore futile until our legislation becomes more scientific—as it certainly will.

Credits on Earned Income. But we return to the income tax to find that " credit on earned income " is of this same more significant kind. The normal tax on earned net income is credited with 25 per cent. of the amount of tax which would be payable if the earned net income constituted the entire net income. But this credit in no case may exceed 25 per cent. of the normal tax computed in the ordinary manner plus 25 per cent. of the surtax which would be payable if the earned income constituted entire net income.

Exemptions Allowed Beneficiaries. To return to inheritance taxes, exemptions are customarily allowed beneficiaries as to estates under the Federal Estate Law. Most states impose what may be called a progressive tax on the several bequests of the estate depending first on the existence of blood relationship, and nearness of kinship, and second on the amount of the individual inheritance above exemptions that seem to run, for direct heirs, from $500 to $75,000.

Property Tax-exemptions. Tax-exemption may be of kinds of taxables as well as amounts of income or value. Owners of realty have never been favored with ingenious reasoning that might lead to tax-exemption although there is usually a flat exemption of a certain amount of personal property from tax. In certain states the classified property tax with its lower rates is giving relief that is equivalent to partial exemption.

Tax-exempt Securities. But real exemption for intangibles lies in the ownership of tax-exempt securities. Bonds of the United States and of the federal farm loan system are and always have been tax-exempt. Many state jurisdictions exempt their own bonds, and many exempt the bonds of their tax-divisions.

Almost every state exempts the stock of companies incorporated in the state.   The other common forms of securities are usually taxable; mortgages at the domicile of the mortgagor unless the mortgagor is of the same jurisdiction and has agreed to pay the tax; all bonds (mortgage and debenture) that are not civil loans, etc.

Table of Net Yields of Taxable and Tax-exempt Bonds. Exemption from tax is of the utmost importance to investors. Put in its boldest form a general property tax of $2\frac{1}{2}$ per cent. of full value on a taxable 5 per cent. bond is equivalent to a 50 per cent. income tax.   The table based on the Federal Revenue Act of 1926 gives the relative yield of tax-free versus taxable securities in the ownership of persons of varying incomes.   This will be found opposite p. 262.

Tax-covenant Bonds.   Partial exemption from tax, equivalent to a reduction in rate or amount—not as respects the taxable but the owner—is to be found in the case of tax-covenant bonds. In reviewing the incidence of taxation and direct and indirect taxes we recalled that in the matter of loans the question as to whether lender or borrower should pay the tax was a matter of negotiation and therefore of the investment contract.   As the result of Civil War taxation it became customary to insert in the railroad indentures of the seventies and eighties an agreement on the part of the borrower to pay to the bondholder the entire amount of the interest payments without deduction for any taxes on this interest that the borrower might be required to retain and pay under any existing or future laws.   In that form the investment contract was called a "tax-free covenant." The bond buyer came to look upon it as a matter of course like the covenant that interest and principal were to be payable in gold dollars of the present standard of weight and fineness. (Parenthetically, we make the prediction that the time will come when this latter phase of the investment contract will no longer be taken for granted.)

The inception of the federal income tax in 1913 with provision for a normal tax of 1 per cent. that could be paid at its source of income immediately gave vitality to the dormant tax-free covenant, and corporations faced an unexpected but tolerable item of expense.   Under the Revenue Act of 1918 the rate was raised to 2 per cent., and on presentation of coupons for collection or payment, certificates were required certifying that the payment at the source had been made by the obligor corporation. As the normal rate rose and the labor and cost of collection at the source exceeded any possible revenue therefrom and had no educational value—merely informative—the tax-procedure was changed from " collection at the source " to " information at the source," except that to give some deference to the spirit of the tax covenant of investment contracts an arbitrary 2 per cent. of the total normal tax was withheld at the source and eventually certificates of ownership were not required for the collection of interest on bonds, the indentures of which contained no tax-covenant.

As these indentures are now commonly drawn the obligor no longer agrees to pay any taxes required to be withheld under any other than federal revenue laws and under these only to the extent of 2 per cent.   But many of the indentures agree to *refund* certain specific taxes in certain jurisdictions of large investing capacity, such as the long-established Pennsylvania mill tax, the Connecticut tax, and the relatively new Massachusetts securities income tax.   Except in the case of Pennsylvania (which provides for collection at the source of the mill tax in the case of Pennsylvania corporations) investors will benefit from the special covenant only by reimbursement on submission of evidence of payment.

V. Classification of Taxes According to the Situs or Domicile of the Corporation or Individual Taxed

For a rounded survey of all the phases of American taxation there yet remains the consideration of the situs or domicile of those who are taxed and of the things taxed. We should be greatly assisted in these final reviews by the previous four approaches from the four other angles, and from this point we can afford to touch the phases with lightness and despatch,—with such emphasis as may be on the individual who is considered the investor, rather than on the corporation, for the latter is presumed to be relatively qualified to handle such of its assets as are used for real investment.

Corporations Foreign to the United States. Corporations foreign to the United States have been described as subject to tax only on gross income from sources within the United States, determined (except in the case of insurance companies) in the same manner as the gross income of non-resident alien individuals, which see immediately below under that caption. Their subjection to excise, property, and privilege taxes is not materially affected by their situs.

Non-resident Alien Individuals. Non-resident alien individuals, as described in Class II, are taxed only on income from sources within the United States. By reason of their foreign situs the constituents of their income are somewhat different from those of residents. They include:

(1) Interest on obligations of resident corporations and individuals, but not including interest on deposits with bankers paid to persons not engaged in business in the United States, and not having an office or place of business therein. And not including interest received from a resident alien individual, a resident foreign corporation, or a domestic corporation, less than 20 per cent. of the gross income of which is not received from sources within the United States.

(2) Dividends from domestic corporations other than those of which the interest is exempted in (1); and dividends from a foreign corporation unless less than 50 per cent. of its income is derived from sources within the United States.

(3) Compensation for labor and personal services within the United States.

(4) Rentals or royalties from property or interest in property within the United States.

(5) Profits from the sale of real property located in the United States.

The foreign situs presupposes income from sources without the United States and therefore it is natural to find the personal exemption a flat amount of only $1,500.

The relation of a foreign situs to the federal estate tax has been taken up in Class II: " Aliens non-resident in the United States." We know of no essential difference of treatment accorded non-resident aliens as compared with citizens non-resident in any jurisdiction of the United States in respect to the ownership of property tangible or intangible. The same holds true of the excises and privilege taxes.

Aliens Resident in the United States. In Class II we have noted under this same caption that " situs " is the main issue with respect to tax treatment in all jurisdictions as it concerns individuals, rather than citizenship except as citizenship in state jurisdictions implies residence and therefore situs.

Domestic Corporations and Citizens. There remain as the only other possible "persons" to pay taxes, domestic corporations and citizens, i.e., payers resident in their respective jurisdictions against whom as majors the tax laws are directed and who, therefore, present no variations due to situs for discriminative treatment.

VI. Classification of Taxes According to the Situs or Domicile of the Taxable

The reflex of American taxes on the taxable, the thing or object taxed, can best be comprehended in its entirety by a continuance of our seriatim method of approach, which will throw us back to Class III in which virtually all taxables were described and classified. But the classification of the taxables from the standpoint of situs is somewhat different from the classification of taxables (Class III) for other more general purposes. Therefore, we submit on the opposite page a more detailed division of Class VI than was given at the beginning of this chapter under the head " General Classification of Taxes." The principal differences between Class III and Class VI are the somewhat altered division of property which previously was between realty and personalty and now is between tangible property and intangible personalty and the emphasis on inheritance rather than on excises and privileges.

Furthermore, on the right-hand side of each division of taxables is given (mostly in brackets) the class of jurisdiction which in turn is determined by the situs of the taxable.

1. The Situs of Income

The only effect of situs we have in mind in connection with federal income taxation is that all domestic corporations and all citizens are taxed on income, whencesoever derived; but foreign corporations and non-resident aliens are taxed only on income from sources within the United States. Similarly, for purposes of the state income tax, corporations incorporated in a state and citizens or residents of a state are taxed on all income whencesoever derived, but foreign (extra state-incorporated) corporations and non-residents are taxed only on income from sources within the state.

VI.
By the
Situs
of the
Taxable

Income
- Domestic Corporations and Citizens
- Foreign Corporations and Non-resident Aliens } Federal Jurisdiction
- Companies Incorporated in the State, and Citizens
- Companies not Incorporated in the State, and Non-residents } State Jurisdiction

Property
- Tangible
  - Realty
    - Land
    - Improvements
  - Personalty
    - Coin
    - Chattels
    - Bank Bills
  } State and Minor Jurisdictions
- Intangible—Personalty
  - Credits
    - Bank Deposits
    - Open Accounts
    - General Business
    - National Bank
  - Stock
  - Promissory Notes
  - Real Estate Mortgages
  - Real Estate Collateral Bonds
  - Chattel Mortgages
  - Bonds
    - Federal
    - State
    - Municipal
    - Minor Civil
    - Corporate Debentures
    - Personalty Collateral
    - Foreign

  Credits { Federal Jurisdiction

  Stock, Promissory Notes, Real Estate Mortgages, Real Estate Collateral Bonds, Chattel Mortgages, Bonds } State and Minor Jurisdictions

Inheritance
- Tangible
  - Realty
    - Land
    - Improvements
  - Personalty
  } Jurisdiction of State in which Located
- Intangible—Personalty
  - Simple Contract Debt
  - Joint Obligation
  - Promissory Note
  - Debenture Bond
  - Note with { Tangible
  - Bond with { Collateral
  } For Jurisdiction See Text
  - Stock—Situs each State in which Co. is incorporated

Miscellaneous
- Excises } Federal Jurisdiction
- Privileges } State Jurisdiction
  or
  Minor Jurisdictions

2. The Situs of Property

Situs of Real Estate. Real estate we have seen is taxed in and by the state in which it is located, and cannot be taxed by any other state government.

Situs of Tangible Personal Property. For the United States the situs of tangible personal property has been definitely decided by the Supreme Court of the United States in the case of Frick vs. Commonwealth of Pennsylvania, (270 U. S. 230–46 S. Ct. 260. Am. Fed. Tax Rep.). That case held that the transfer of such property is subject to inheritance tax in the state where it is "permanently located and employed, irrespective of the domicile of the owner," and is not subject to such tax in the state of domicile, when not located there. The court proceeded to say that "the jurisdiction possessed by the States of the situs was not partial but plenary, and included power to regulate the transfer both *inter vivos* and on the death of the owner, and power to tax both the property and the transfer." Since the latter sentence, though in strict analysis a dictum as to taxes other than death duties, occurs in an opinion in which the entire court concurred, and is in line with its previous utterances when dealing with property taxation, it may be regarded as a final pronouncement as to all manner of taxation of tangible personalty in the United States. Such property has its tax situs in the state where it is permanently "kept and used," and nowhere else.

Situs of Intangible Personal Property. The whole subject of the taxation of intangibles, and particularly of the tax situs of intangibles, is in a state of chaos, and not only the statutes, but the decisions and rulings are almost hopelessly at variance. To such an extent is this true that it is impossible to present a worthwhile summary within the limitations of this study. Therefore the reader should not seek to determine his own situations from the necessarily loose generalizations of the following paragraphs, but should consult one of the tax services (such as that published by Prentice-Hall, Inc.) whose profession it is to follow and interpret the kaleidoscopic succession of laws and rulings that govern these matters.

As for the future there is more than a ray of hope in the legislative reciprocity movement now well under way. To simplify inheritance taxation already there is a group of twelve "reciprocal states." By reciprocity movement we mean the development of the principle that any state which has a reciprocity act exempts from death taxes intangible personal property (including the securities of its domestic corporations) belonging to the estates of decedents who were residents of any other state within the group.

The uncertainty attending the subject of the tax situs of intangibles arises from the very nature of intangible property. Although property right in a tangible—a jackknife, a table, or a Ghirlandajo—is a right to possess and enjoy as against *all the world*, property in an intangible is a claim or right directed against a *definite person or group of persons or a legal entity* that will be recognized and enforced by courts. Such rights may or may not be evidenced by paper writings, and if they are so evidenced such documents may be of various degrees of dignity. If the right is without paper evidence—a mechanic's claim for labor performed, for example—two "loci" are obviously involved: the place where the mechanic lives and the place where his debtor lives; and if the right is evidenced by a writing, a third locus, the place where the document is kept, may enter the situation. If each is in a different jurisdiction or state, the problem manifestly is not simple, for each state may try to extract a tax from the unfortunate individual, who may need to invoke the power of the state to realize his right.

The mechanic without a writing may nevertheless sue his debtor and recover the value of his work. He may go into another state where his debtor lives and sue him. His right is personal to himself and travels with him wherever he may go. It is a property right; if he dies after performing but before collecting, his executors may sue the debtor. But if the debtor lives in another state, which of the two states can impose a death tax with respect to that right to collect, which the executor seeks to exercise?

A man living in a Wisconsin suburb of Chicago writes to a contractor whose office is in Chicago, but who lives in Indiana, "I will pay you $1,000 if you will, before June 1, build a garage on my place here, like the sketch below." The contractor builds the garage; the letter is in his safe in Chicago; he dies. Has Illinois a claim to death duties because the letter is there? Under the Statute of Frauds the letter might be necessary to enable the executor to collect the full contract price. If the contractor has received from his customer a promissory note, payable a year from date, which he keeps in Chicago, can Illinois collect a tax? If he has done a job for a Wisconsin railroad which has paid him by an issue of bonds that are in Illinois at his death, will Illinois impose a tax? Would it make a difference if the railroad were an Illinois corporation? Would it make a difference if he had been paid in stock of the railroad instead of bonds? Would correct answers to these questions hold true in case another state were substituted for Illinois?

No set of principles has been evolved by the aid of which any man can sit in his chair and answer any one of those questions for any state. Only two principles hold true for all; (1) the state of domicile will surely tax the transfer of the intangible personalty of its deceased resident if it has an inheritance tax law at all because the situs of "choses in action," (stock or bonds) is with the owner. (2) The state in which a corporation is organized may provide for the taxation of all its shares, whether owned by residents or non-residents. These principles are specifically recognized by the United States Supreme Court in the case of Rhode Island Hospital Trust Company vs. Doughton. Beyond that firm ground lies a morass of vague statutes, decisions which decide only specific cases, departmental regulations and special rulings.

It has been pointed out that an intangible is a right against some person, real or corporate. Conversely, it is an obligation of some person, real or corporate. The obligation has a taxable situs in the state of the owner, and also may have a taxable situs in the state where the evidence—a stock certificate, for example—is kept. Taxation of the mere paper writing physically present in the jurisdiction depends to some extent on the grade or degree of dignity of that writing. The mere evidentiary letter mentioned above would nowhere be taxable. Promissory notes and bills of exchange are taxable in some jurisdictions when physically present there, though they are the property of a non-resident's estate. Bonds more frequently are taxable. Stock certificates of foreign corporations belonging to non-resident's estates when physically present are taxed by some states.

The debt is regarded as having a situs in the state of residence of the debtor in some states, particularly if evidenced by notes. Mortgages on land are regarded in Massachusetts and many other states as interests in land and so have a situs for taxation there; but the rule is otherwise in New York, Pennsylvania, and some other states.

3. THE SITUS OF EXCISES AND PRIVILEGES

Excises,—a term, which, with the exception of estate taxes, is largely synonymous with miscellaneous federal internal taxes,— are not affected as to the fact of taxation or as to the rate by any particular location within the United States. Some state privileges are sometimes called excises.

Privileges,—a term which, with the exception of devolution and succession taxes (taxes on estates of decedents and taxes on inheritance) is synonymous with miscellaneous state and local taxes,—are largely the product of local autonomy. The importance of the situs of a privilege, if it has any, lies in the application of the proceeds of the tax, or the allocation of the proceeds to some tax jurisdiction within the state.

In presenting the subject of state and municipal loans elsewhere, we felt obliged to emphasize the historical aspects of civil credit in order that those who have not the advantage of historical perspective on this subject might not take municipal credit for granted, but we concluded by according to municipal loans the highest present credit of any type of investment security commonly purchased in America.

By the same token, we have laid emphasis on matters like multiple taxation and the difficulty arising from the conflict of situs, because they create very real difficulties in preserving the beneficial income of investors, and because the elimination of tax conflict and of obscurity is in the interest of all. We wish, however, to leave the impression that American taxation as a whole tends to become fairer and more satisfactory from the standpoint of the federal and state governments and of the taxpayers as the years go by and legislation improves.

BIBLIOGRAPHY

Current Periodicals, Services, Manuals, and Newspapers.
Alexander Hamilton Institute, Reports. New York.
Academy of Political Science, Quarterly. New York.
American Academy Political and Social Science, Annals. Philadelphia.
American Economic Association, Review. Chicago.
Babson Service. Wellesley Hills.
Barron's Weekly. New York.
Brookmire Investment Service. New York.
Commercial and Financial Chronicle, with Supplements. New York.
Federal Reserve Bulletin. Washington.
Financial World. New York.
Fitch Bond Book. New York.
Harvard Economic Review. Cambridge.
Investment Bankers' Association, Proceedings. Chicago.
Journal of Commerce. New York.
Magazine of Wall Street. New York.
Moody's Analysis of Investments (Railroads—Industrials—Public Utilities—Government and Municipal Securities). New York.
Moody's Investors Service. New York.
Manual of Statistics. New York.
New York Times. New York.
New York Times Annalist. New York.
Poor's Manual. New York.
Standard Bond Card Service. New York.
Standard Daily Trade Service. New York.
United States Department of Commerce, Survey of Current Business. Washington.
Wall Street Journal. New York.

General Works on Investments.
American Institute of Banking, Loans and Investments. New York.
Annals, American Academy Political & Social Science, "Bonds and the Bond Market," Vol. LXXXVIII, Part II, March, 1920.
Gibson, Thomas, Simple Principles of Investment. New York, 1919.
Halsey, Stuart & Co., Essentials of a Sound Investment Policy. New York, 1925.
Herschel, A. H., Selection and Care of Sound Investments. New York, 1925.
Hobson, J. A., An Economic Interpretation of Investments. London, 1911.
Jordan, David Francis, Jordan on Investments. New York, 1924.

Kirschman, John E., Principles of Investments. Chicago, 1924.
Lagerquist, Walter Edwards, Investment Analysis. Macmillan, 1921.
Lowenhaupt, Frederick, Investment Bonds. New York, 1908.
Lyon, Walter Hastings, Investments. New York, 1926.
Rice, S., Fundamental Principles of Investment. New York, 1926.
Rollins, Montgomery, Money and Investments. Boston, 1910.
Sakolski, Aaron M., Principles of Investment. New York, 1925.

PART I

Channels of Investment.
Hardy, Charles Oscar, Risk and Risk Bearing. University of Chicago, 1923.
Lilly, William, Individual and Corporate Mortgages. Investment Bankers' Association, 1918.

PART II

Public Finance.
Bastable, C. F., Public Finance. London, 1922.
Cohn, G., Science of Finance (English Translation by T. Veblen). University of Chicago, 1895.
Daniels, W. M., Public Finance. New York, 1899.
Hunter, Merlin Harold, Outlines of Public Finance. New York, 1921.
Lutz, Harley L., Public Finance. New York, 1924.
Seligman, E. R. A., Essays in Taxation. 9th ed., New York, 1921
Stamp, Sir Josiah Charles, Fundamental Principles of Taxation. London, 1921.

Foreign Securities.
Council of Foreign Bondholders. Annual Reports. London.
Edwards, George W., Investing in Foreign Securities. New York, 1926.
Hobson, C. K., Export of Capital. London, 1914.
Friedman, E. M., International Finance and its Reorganization. New York, 1922.
Kimber, A. W., Foreign Government Securities. New York, 1919.
Kimber, A. W., Record of Government Debts and Other Foreign Securities. New York.
Raymond, W. L., National Government Loans. Boston, 1925.

State and Local Bonds.
Brown, Fraser, Municipal Bonds. New York, 1922.
Dillon, John Forrest, The Law of Municipal Corporations, 1873.
Financial Statistics of Cities. U. S. Census Bureau, 1919.
National Industrial Conference Board, Cost of Government in the United States. New York, 1926.
Scott, W. A., The Repudiation of State Debts. New York, 1893.

PART III

Railroads.

Annual Reports of Interstate Commerce Commission. Washington.

Bureau of Railway Economics, Comparative Statement of Physical Valuation and Capitalization (Bureau of Railway Economics, Series No. 4, Washington, D. C., 1911, p. 11); Comparative Railway Statistics of Foreign Countries, 1913 (Bureau of Railway Economics, Wash. Misc. Series No. 25, 1916, p. 78).

Cleveland, Frederick A. and Powell, F. W., Railroad Finance. New York, 1912.

Duncan, Kenneth, Equipment Obligations. New York, 1924.

Haney, Lewis H., The Business of Railway Transportation. New York, 1922.

Heft, Louis, Holders of Railroad Bonds and Notes; Their Rights and Remedies. New York, 1916.

Mitchell, T. W., Collateral Trust Mortgage in Railway Finance. Quarterly Journal of Economics, 1906, p. 443.

Railway Age. Chicago.

Ripley, William Zebina, Railroads: Finance and Organization. New York, 1915.

Sakolski, Aaron Morton, American Railroad Economics. New York, 1913.

Van Deusen, Edgar, Electric Interurban Railway Bonds as Investments, in "Bonds as Investment Securities," American Academy of Political and Social Science. Philadelphia, 1907.

White and Kemble's Atlas and Digest of Railroad Mortgages.

Public Utilities.

American Gas Journal.

Bauer, John, Effective Regulation of Public Utilities.

Cooke, M. L., Public Utility Regulation.

Ignatius, Milton B., Financing of Public Service Corporations.

Lyndon, Lamar, Rate Making for Public Utilities.

Maltbie, W. H., Theory and Practice of Public Utilities Valuation.

Mitchell, S. Z., To-day's Problems in Public Utility Finance.

Morgan, Charles S., Regulation and Management of Public Utilities.

Nash, L. R., Economics of Public Utilities.

Proceedings of the National Gas Association.

Watkins, G. P., Electric Rates.

Whitten, Robert H., Valuation of Public Service Corporations.

Real Estate Bonds.

Babcock, F. M., Appraising Real Estate. New York, 1924.

Benson, P. A. & North, N. L., Real Estate, Principles & Practices. New York, 1922.

Bingham, R. F. & Andrews, E. L., Financing Real Estate. Cleveland, 1924.

Hecht, R. S., Louisiana Municipal Drainage Bonds (Proceedings of the First Annual Convention of the Investment Bankers' Association, 1912, pp. 172–180).

Hurd, George A., Real Estate Bonds as an Investment Security (Annals Amer. Acad. of Pol. and Soc. Sci., Vol. lxxxviii, Mar. 1920, pp. 79–95).

Moffett, C. T., Real Estate Investments. New York, 1924.

National Association of Real Estate Boards, Proceedings of the General Sessions, 1925. Real Estate Finance.

Proceedings of Mortgage and Finance Division of National Association of Real Estate Boards. Seventh Annual Convention. Washington, D. C., June 3–6, 1924.

Smith, John, Drainage Bonds. (Proc. of the Fourth Annual Convention of the Investment Bankers' Association, 1915, pp. 120–130). Reclamation of Swamp Lands and the Modern Drainage Bond. (Annals of Amer. Acad. of Pol. & Soc. Sci., Vol. lxxxviii, No. 177. March, 1920, pp. 102–113.)

Stabler, W., Real Estate Bonds Issues. American Bankers' Association, Journal, Vol. 18:537–9.

Farm Loan System.

Federal Farm Loan Board, Annual Report. Washington.

Holt, W. S., Federal Farm Loan Bureau. Institute for Government Research. New York, 1924.

Lagerquist, W. E., Joint Stock Bank, System 48:666–D25.

Robins, K. N., Farm Mortgage Handbook. Garden City, N. Y., 1916.

Industrials.

Badger, Ralph Eastman, Valuation of Industrial Securities. New York, 1925.

Dewing, A. S., Financial Policy of Corporations. New York, 1926.

Reports, Federal Trade Commission. Washington.

Iron Age. New York.

Stetson, F. L., Some Legal Phases of Corporate Financing, Reorganization and Regulation. 1917.

PART IV

Mathematics of Investment.

Reitz, Crathorne and Reitz, Mathematics of Finance. New York, 1921.

Skinner, E. B., The Mathematical Theory of Investment. Boston, 1924

Sprague, C. E., The Accountancy of Investments. New York, 1914.

Business Cycle.

Aftalion, A., Les Crises Périodiques de Surproduction. Paris, 1913.

Hansen, A. H., Cycle of Prosperity and Depression in the United States, Great Britain, and Germany. University of Wisconsin. Studies in Social Sciences and History, 1921.

Fisher, Irving, Purchasing Power of Money. New York, 1911.

Hobson, J. A., Industrial System. London, 1909.
Hull, George H., Industrial Depression. New York, 1911.
Macaulay, F. R., Construction of an Index Number of Bond Yields. American Statistical Association Journal, 21:27 Mr. 26.
Mitchell, W. C., Business Cycles. 1913.
Moore, Henry Ludwell, Economic Cycles: Their Law and Cause. New York, 1914, p. 149.
Robertson, D. H., A Study of Industrial Fluctuations. London, 1915.
Veblen, Thorstein B., Theory of Business Enterprise. New York, 1904.

Business Cycles and Investments.
Anderson, B. M., State and Municipal Borrowing in Relation to the Business Cycle. Chase Econ. Bul. 5:2–18 Je. 10 '25.
Dewing, A. S., Investment and the Individual Cycle. Harvard Business Review, Oct. 23, p. 2.
Fisher, Irving, How to Invest when Prices Are Rising. Scranton, 1912.
Fisher, Irving, Stabilized Bond. Annalist. 26:669:603. N. 13 '25.
Herschel, A. H., The Investment Risk of Common Stocks. Commercial Chronicle, Nov. 14, 1925, p. 2337.
Smith, Edgar Lawrence, Common Stocks as Long Term Investments. New York, 1924.

PART V

Classes of Investors.
Zartman, L. W., The Investments of Life Insurance Companies. New York, 1906.
Motelle, A., Bond Holdings of Insurance Cos. Annalist. 26:701 D. 4 '25.
Richter, E. E. & Standish, Alexander, Investment of Banks and Insurance Companies. Harvard Business Review, 1924–5.
Institutional Holdings of Securities, Institutional Holdings Co. (Contains investment holdings of insurance company savings banks, classified under names of securities. Look up foreign.)
Rollins, Montgomery, Laws Regulating the Investment of Bank Funds.
Insurance Year Book, Spectator Company. Figures on Investments. See Ackerman.
Maine, G. E., How heavily should a bank invest in bonds? Am. Bankers' Assn., J. 17:72; Ag. '2.

Blue Sky Laws.
Angell, L. W., Blue Sky Laws. Jour. Pol. Econ., April, 1919, pp. 307–21.
O'Brien, A. H., Report on Blue Sky Legislation. Toronto, 1922.
Reed, R. R. & Washburn, L. H., Blue Sky Laws. 1924.
Smythe, R. M., Obsolete American Securities and Corporations. New York, 1904–1911. 2 vols. published by R. M. Smythe.

Bond Houses.
Harley, H. K., Organization of the Investment Business. (Unpublished lectures given by Mr. Harley of Halsey, 1925.)

Chamberlain, Lawrence, Work of the Bond House.	New York.	Moody's
	Magazine Book Dept., 1912. (Out of print).
Galston, Arthur, Security Syndicate Operations.	New York, 1921.
Franklin, L. B., Syndicates (pamphlet issued by Guaranty Trust
	Company of New York).
Pratt, Sereno, The Work of Wall Street.	New York, 1921 (30 ed.).
Methods in the distribution of securities to investors.	Harvard Bus
	R. 3:104–12 O. '24.

INDEX